Nep

a Lonely Planet travel survival kit

Hugh Finlay
Richard Everist
Tony Wheeler

Nepal

3rd edition

Published by
Lonely Planet Publications
Head Office: PO Box 617, Hawthorn, Vic 3122, Australia
Branches: 155 Filbert St, Suite 251, Oakland, CA 94607, USA
            10 Barley Mow Passage, Chiswick, London W4 4PH, UK
            71 bis rue du Cardinal Lemoine, 75005 Paris, France

Printed by
Colorcraft Ltd, Hong Kong

Photographs by

David Allardice	Stan Armington	Glenn Beanland
Paul Beinssen	Sonia Berto	Sara-Jane Cleland
Greg Elms	Richard Everist	Hugh Finlay
Richard I'Anson	James Lyon	Adam McCrow
Peter Morris	Simon Rowe	Paul Steel
Valerie Tellini	Tony Wheeler	Jeff Williams

Front cover: Nagarjun Stupa, Kathmandu Valley (Richard I'Anson)

First Published
1990

This Edition
November 1996

Although the authors and publisher have tried to make the information as accurate as possible, they accept no responsibility for any loss, injury or inconvenience sustained by any person using this book.

National Library of Australia Cataloguing-in-Publication Data

Finlay, Hugh.
Nepal.

3rd ed.
Includes index.
ISBN 0 86442 397 7.

1. Nepal - Guidebooks. I. Wheeler, Tony, 1946- , Nepal.
II Title. III. Title: Nepal. (Series : Lonely Planet
travel survival kit).

915.49604

text & maps © Lonely Planet 1996
photos © photographers as indicated 1996
Pokhara climate chart compiled from information supplied by Patrick J Tyson, © Patrick J Tyson, 1996

Hugh Finlay

After deciding there must be more to life than civil engineering, Hugh took off around Australia in the mid-70s, working at everything from spray painting to diamond prospecting, before hitting the overland trail. He joined Lonely Planet in 1985 and has written *Jordan & Syria*, co-authored *Morocco, Algeria & Tunisia* and *Kenya*, and has contributed to other LP guides including *Africa, India* and *Australia*. Hugh updated this edition of *Nepal*. He lives in central Victoria, Australia, with his wife Linda and his daughters Ella and Vera.

Richard Everist

Richard grew up in Geelong, Australia, has travelled a bit and had a wide variety of jobs. He worked full time in Lonely Planet's Melbourne office before jumping the fence to become a freelance writer. In late 1994 he was lured back into the home paddock to be Publishing General Manager.

He has co-written LP's *Nepal, South Africa* and *Britain* guides, updated *Papua New Guinea*, and contributed to the shoe-string guides for *West Asia, Africa, Western Europe* and *Mediterranean Europe*.

Tony Wheeler

Tony was born in England but spent most of his youth overseas. He returned to England to do a university degree in engineering, worked as an automative engineer, returned to university to complete an MBA then dropped out on the overland trail with his wife Maureen. They've been travelling, writing and publishing guidebooks ever since, having set up Lonely Planet Publications in the mid-70s. Travel for the Wheelers is now considerably enlivened by their daughter Tashi and their son Kieran.

From Hugh

This was my first research trip to Nepal, and I was knocked out by the tremendous support and assistance I was given by many, many people during my stay. Thanks above all to Chris Beall, a long-time resident of Nepal who put me in touch with many people whom I may otherwise have missed.

Stan Armington and Sushil Upadhyay, both of Malla Treks, helped with pinning down a lot of last-minute detail which, thanks to e-mail, reached me in no time. Badri Adhikari, of Lucky Traveller Service, went out of his way to ensure my trip to the Terai went smoothly. John Edwards of Tiger Mountain lent great logistical support with a slippery lift in pissing rain on the 'road' from Nepalganj to Mahendranagar. Thanks also to Richard Everist for supplying me with a list of contacts before I set off.

Many others also helped and to all of them, many thanks. In particular, Carolyn Syangbo (Tiger Mountain); Dave Allardice & Ravi Fry (Ultimate Descents); Tejendra Shrestha (Thamel Tourism Development Committee, Third Eye Restaurant); Subarna Chhetri (*The Independent*); Basant Mishra (Temple Tiger); Bimal Bista (Necon Air); Yogendra Sakya (Hotel Association Nepal, Kathmandu Guest House); Bharat Basnet (Explore Nepal); Hikmat Bisht (Silent Safari); and the staff at the Utse Hotel in Kathmandu.

This Book
The first five editions of Lonely Planet's *Nepal* guide were the work of the Nepali writer Prakash A Raj. In 1989, Tony Wheeler and Richard Everist completely rewrote the book to bring it into line with other LP guidebooks.

In 1992 Richard Everist researched the 2nd edition, and in 1996 Hugh Finlay returned to Nepal to research the 3rd edition. The Geography, Flora & Fauna and Ecology sections were written by Lewis Underwood. John Prosser contributed the Mountain Biking chapter. Dave Allardice, operations manager for Ultimate Descents and co-

author of *White Water Nepal*, who originally wrote the Rafting & Kayaking chapter for the 2nd edition, updated the chapter for this edition, with the able assistance of Ravi Fry, also of Ultimate Descents.

From the Publisher
The 3rd edition of *Nepal* was edited and proofed by Anne Mulvaney and Tom Smallman, with assistance from Helen Castle, Jane Rawson and David Andrew. Mapping was done by Louise Klep, Sally Gerdan and Paul Piaia. Design and layout were by Valerie Tellini. Illustrations were by Bishnu Shrestha, Margaret Jung, Paul Clifton, Louise and Trudi Canavan. The cover was designed by David Kemp and Adam McCrow, and the index was compiled by Sharon Wertheim.

Warning & Request
Things change – prices go up, schedules change, good places go bad and bad places go bankrupt – nothing stays the same. So if you find things better or worse, recently opened or long since closed, please write and tell us and help make the next edition better.

Your letters will be used to help update future editions and, where possible, important changes will also be included in an Update section in reprints.

We greatly appreciate all information that is sent to us by travellers. Back at Lonely Planet we employ a hard-working readers' letters team to sort through the many letters we receive. The best ones will be rewarded with a free copy of the next edition or another Lonely Planet guide if you prefer. We give away lots of books, but, unfortunately, not every letter/postcard receives one.

Contents

THE HIMALAYA & MOUNTAINEERING 345

TREKKING 351

MOUNTAIN BIKING.. 383

RAFTING & KAYAKING 389

GLOSSARY 398

INDEX 404

Map Legend

BOUNDARIES

.... International Boundary
.... Local/Suburban Boundary

ROUTES

.... Freeway
.... Major Road
.... Secondary Road
.... Unsealed Road or Track
.... City Road
.... City Street
.... Railway
.... Underground Railway
.... Tram
.... Walking Track
.... Walking Tour
.... Ferry Route
.... Cable Car or Chairlift

AREA FEATURES

.... Parks
.... Built-Up Area
.... Pedestrian Mall
.... Market
.... Cemetery
.... Reef
.... Beach or Desert
.... Rocks

HYDROGRAPHIC FEATURES

.... Coastline
.... River, Creek
.... Intermittent River or Creek
.... Rapids, Waterfalls
.... Lake, Intermittent Lake
.... Canal
.... Swamp

SYMBOLS

✪	CAPITAL	National Capital	◐	◓	Embassy, Petrol Station
◉	Capital	Regional Capital	✈	✝	Airport, Airfield
◍	CITY	Major City	⬛	✿	Swimming Pool, Gardens
●	City	City	❖	🐘	Shopping Centre, Zoo
●	Town	Town	⚲	▦	Winery or Vineyard, Picnic Site
●	Village	Village	←	A25	One Way Street, Route Number
■	▼	Place to Stay, Place to Eat	🏛	🗼	Stately Home, Monument
☕	♟	Cafe, Pub or Bar	⛏	▣	Castle, Tomb
✉	☎	Post Office, Telephone	⌒	⌂	Cave, Hut or Chalet
❶	$	Tourist Information, Bank	▲	✳	Mountain or Hill, Lookout
⊖	⚲	Transport, Bicycle Rental	苯	◺	Lighthouse, Shipwreck
🏛	⛺	Museum, Youth Hostel	)(	◎	Pass, Spring
⚏	⛏	Caravan Park, Camping Ground	🦅	⚘	Beach, Surf Beach
✝	✚	Church, Cathedral		∴	Archaeological Site or Ruins
☾	✡	Mosque, Synagogue			Ancient or City Wall
⚏	⟁	Temple, Stupa			Cliff or Escarpment, Tunnel
✛	★	Hospital, Police Station			Railway Station

Note: not all symbols displayed above appear in this book

Introduction

Draped along the greatest heights of the Himalaya, the kingdom of Nepal is a land of eternal fascination, a place where one visit is rarely enough. It's a land of ancient history, colourful cultures and people, superb scenery and some of the best walking on earth.

Nepal's history is closely related to its geographical location, separating the fertile plains of India from the desert-like plateau of Tibet. Its position between India and China meant the country was able at times to play the role of intermediary – a canny trader between two great powers – while at other times it faced the threat of invasion. Internally, its history was just as dynamic, with city-states in the hills vying with each other for power until one powerful king, Prithvi Narayan Shah, overran them all. That history is very visible today with the three great

towns of the Kathmandu Valley – Kathmandu, Patan and Bhaktapur – still bearing witness to their days as fiercely competitive mediaeval mini-kingdoms. Indeed, in Nepal it's often possible to suspend belief and mentally roll the clock right back to the mediaeval era.

Behind the time-worn temples and palaces of the Kathmandu Valley, above and beyond the hills that ring the valley, another 'kingdom' rises skyward. The 'abode of snows', which is what *Himalaya* means in Sanskrit, is a natural 'kingdom' and a magnet to mountaineers from all over the world. Fortunately you don't have to be a Sherpa and your surname doesn't have to be Messner or Hillary in order for you to get in amongst these great mountains. With a dash of enterprise and a modicum of fitness most

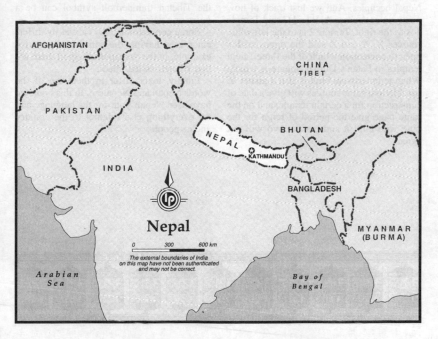

AFGHANISTAN

CHINA
TIBET

PAKISTAN

NEPAL

BHUTAN

KATHMANDU

INDIA

BANGLADESH

Nepal

MYANMAR
(BURMA)

0   300   600 km

The external boundaries of India
on this map have not been authenticated
and may not be correct.

*Arabian
Sea*

*Bay of
Bengal*

travellers can walk the trails that lead into the roadless heights of the Himalaya. One trek is rarely enough, and many visitors soon find themselves planning to return.

Fascinating old towns, magnificent temples and great walking are not all Nepal has to offer. Many visitors come to Nepal expecting to find these things but also discover how outstandingly friendly the Nepalis are.

Nor is trekking the only activity which draws visitors – Nepal also has some superb white-water rafting opportunities, mountain biking is becoming more and more popular, and down in the jungle lowland in the south of the country, safaris on elephant-back into the Royal Chitwan National Park are another not-to-be-missed part of the Nepal experience.

Warning about Figures, Dates & Names

There doesn't seem to be any 100% correct reference for anything in Nepal. As an example we've seen half a dozen different figures for the number of square km that Nepal occupies. And we lost track of how many times sources A, B and C said Temple 1 is to the right, Temple 2 is to the left while sources X, Y and Z said the opposite. It's open to contention which of the three Taleju temples in Patan's Durbar Square is which. When temples were built is also a matter of speculation: some sources will give a date of construction for a certain temple, and on the same page give the period of reign for the king who built it and yet the two will not agree.

Many temples in Nepal have alternative names. For example, the Vishnu Temple in Patan's Durbar Square is referred to as the Jagannarayan or Charnarayan Temple; the great Shiva Temple in Kathmandu's Durbar Square is sometimes called the Maju Deval, at other times simply the Shiva Temple. Where possible, alternative names that are commonly used have been given.

Mandir simply means 'temple' and generally we have used the English word except in cases where mandir is always used, as with the Krishna Mandir in Patan.

Further confusion can be caused by different systems of transliteration from Sanskrit – the letter 'h' appears in some systems, but doesn't appear in others, so you may see Manjushri and Manjusri, Machhendranath and Machendranath. The letters 'b' and 'v' are also used interchangeably in different systems – Shiva's fearsome manifestation can be Bhairab or Bhairav, Vishnu is often written as Bishnu and the Nepali word for the Tibetan thunderbolt symbol can be a *bajra* or a *vajra*.

Some confusion is also caused by different places having the same name; so for example, in the Annapurna region there are two villages called Phedi.

Finally, texts differ in their use of the words Nepali and Nepalese. In this book we have used Nepali both for the language and for everything else relating to the country and its people.

Facts about the Country

HISTORY

Historically, culturally and linguistically Nepal has been the meeting point between the Mongoloid peoples of Asia (Tibeto-Burmese languages) and the Caucasoid people of the Indian plains (Indo-European languages). In earlier times, Nepal exploited its position as an intermediary in the trade between India and China. Today, the country continues to take advantage of its strategic position between these uneasy giants.

Over the centuries, the boundaries of Nepal have extended to include huge tracts of neighbouring India, or contracted to little more than the Kathmandu Valley and a handful of surrounding city-states.

Legends recount that the Kathmandu Valley was once a great lake and that Manjushri broached the valley wall with a magical sword, draining the water and creating the Kathmandu Valley we know. Or perhaps it wasn't Manjushri; he was, after all, a Buddhist from China. Hindus claim it was Krishna who performed the mighty deed, hurling a thunderbolt to create the Chobar Gorge. Choose whichever legend you prefer, but scientists agree that the valley was submerged at one time and the rivers of the valley do indeed flow southward through the narrow Chobar Gorge.

The Kiratis

Recorded history begins with the Kiratis, Mongoloid people who arrived in Nepal from the east around the 7th or 8th century BCE (before the common era). Although they are the first known rulers of the Kathmandu Valley, and Yalambar (the first of their kings) is mentioned in the Hindu epic the *Mahabharata*, little more is known about them.

It was during the Kirati period that Buddhism first arrived in the country; indeed it is claimed that during the reign of the seventh of the 28 Kirati kings, Buddha, together with his disciple Ananda, visited the valley and stayed for a time in Patan.

Other accounts of the Kirati period include a 4th century BCE description of their sheep breeding and agricultural activities. Around the 2nd century BCE the great Buddhist Indian emperor, Ashoka, visited Nepal and erected a pillar at the Buddha's birthplace at Lumbini, south of Pokhara near the present-day Indian border. Ashoka also visited the Kathmandu Valley and evidence of four stupas he erected around Patan can still be clearly seen. Ashoka may have also enlarged the stupas at Bodhnath and Swayambhunath. His daughter Charumati was said to have founded Chabahil, a village on the road between Kathmandu and Bodhnath, which has now been swallowed up by the capital. There is a stupa, which is a smaller version of Bodhnath, and a monastery here that are claimed to date back to her time in Nepal.

Kirati domination ended around 300 CE (common era) but the Rai and Limbu people of eastern Nepal are said to be modern descendants.

The Licchavis

Buddhism faded and Hinduism reasserted itself with the Licchavis, Indo-Aryan people who invaded from northern India about 300 CE and overthrew the last Kirati king. They brought with them the caste divisions which continue in Nepal to this day but also ushered in a golden age of Nepali art and architecture.

Manadeva I established the Licchavis' political and military might; a valley inscription dated to 476 CE tells of his prowess and can be seen at the beautiful Changu Narayan Temple in the eastern part of the Kathmandu Valley. His successor, Manadeva II, left numerous stone inscriptions around his kingdom, most of them commenting on what a wonderful mother he had and how he wouldn't have got anywhere without her!

The Thakuris

Amsuvarman, the first Thakuri king, came to

power in 602 CE, succeeding his Licchavi father-in-law. Amsuvarman consolidated his power with strategic family connections to the north and south. His daughter Bhrikuti married a Tibetan prince and collected the Buddha's begging bowl in her wedding dowry. She was said to be a reincarnation of Tibetan Buddhism's Green Tara, seen on many *thangkas* (Tibetan paintings on cotton). Meanwhile in Nepal, Amsuvarman constructed a marvellous seven storey palace at Deopatan near Pashupatinath and contemporary accounts speak with wonder of his luxurious life.

Amsuvarman's was the first of three Thakuri dynasties and although the centuries that followed were a time of invasion and turmoil, the Kathmandu Valley's strategic location ensured the kingdom's survival and growth. It is believed that the city of Kantipur, today's Kathmandu, was founded around the 10th century by Gunakamadeva. His Kasthamandap (House of Wood) gave the city its name and can be seen in Kathmandu's Durbar Square.

The Golden Age of the Mallas
In 1200, so another legend goes, King Arideva was wrestling when news came of the birth of his son. He instantly awarded his son the title *malla* or 'wrestler' and thus founded the illustrious Malla dynasty. This golden age saw great wealth flow to the valley and the kingdom's architects constructed many of the wonderful buildings we see in Nepal today, but the early Malla years actually saw a series of terrible disasters. A huge earthquake shook the valley and killed thousands, an invasion from the north-west followed and the town of Patan was destroyed in 1311.

The Hindu Mallas were followers of Shiva but were considered to be incarnations of the god Vishnu, and their tolerance of Buddhism allowed the Himalayan Tantric form of the religion to continue to flourish. An aristocracy grew up under the Malla rulers and the Hindu caste rule were strengthened and became more rigid. Hari Singh, who arrived in the valley sometime between 1325 and 1330,

was one of the best known early Malla rulers and through him Taleju Bhawani became the royal goddess of Nepal. Hari Singh's southern Indian followers may have been the Newars whose name the people of the Kathmandu Valley take to this day.

During this period Nepal began to divide into numerous independent city-states with frequently feuding kings and princes. The hill country began to be more densely settled as agricultural techniques improved, but a Muslim invasion from Bengal swept through the valley and damaged Hindu and Buddhist shrines. The wave of Muslim destruction soon passed Nepal, but in India the damage was more widespread and many Hindus were driven from the plains, establishing more small Rajput principalities in the hills and mountains of Nepal. The country we know today was divided at that time into 46 separate small states. These kingdoms minted their own coins and maintained standing armies.

In the Kathmandu Valley the three great towns which remain to this day – Kathmandu, Patan and Bhaktapur – were independent kingdoms with powerful kings who encouraged the construction of many temples and the creation of many enduring works of art. Each city centred around the king's palace, with the nobility and high castes concentrated close to the centre. High walls were built to fend off the city's neighbours.

In 1372, however, Jayasthiti Malla founded the third Malla dynasty and took first Patan and, 10 years later, Bhaktapur, to unify the whole valley. In the 15th century Malla art and culture reached their peak and during the reign of Yaksha Malla (1428-82) the kingdom extended south to the Ganges River, north to the edge of Tibet, west to the Kali Gandaki River and east to Sikkim. With his death, however, the kingdom again split into small warring states and another two centuries of conflict were to follow. Trade was booming, agriculture continued to improve and the valley towns enjoyed an orgy of temple and palace construction, but the constant squabbling of the Malla kingdoms opened the door to a new dynasty.

The Shah Dynasty Unifies Nepal

From the tiny kingdom of Gorkha, halfway between Kathmandu and Pokhara, the Shah kings gradually strengthened and extended their power and dreamed of conquering the rich Kathmandu Valley. In 1768 Prithvi Narayan Shah, ninth of the Shah kings, conquered the valley and moved his capital to Kathmandu. The Shah dynasty, which continues to this day, was established.

From this new base the kingdom's power continued to expand until a clash with the Chinese in Tibet led to an ignominious defeat. The Nepalis had first fought the Chinese in 1790, but by 1792 the Chinese army had struck back and in the ensuing treaty the Nepalis had to stop their attacks on Tibet and pay tribute to the Chinese emperor in Beijing; the payments continued until 1912.

British power on the subcontinent was growing at this time and a British envoy arrived in Kathmandu in 1792, too late to aid the Nepalis against the Chinese invasion. Despite treaties with the British the expanding Nepali boundaries, stretching all the way from Kashmir to Sikkim by the early 19th century, were bound to cause problems with the Raj, and disputes over the Terai (the lowlands south of the Himalayan foothills) led to war with the British. In 1810 Nepal was approximately twice its current size but the 1816 Sugauli Treaty with the British ended its growth. Britain took Sikkim and most of the Terai, and Nepal's present-day eastern and western borders were established. Some of the land was restored to Nepal in 1858 as a reward for Nepali support for the British during the Indian Mutiny (or War of Independence as it is referred to in modern India).

The Sugauli treaty opened the door for Indian business influence in Nepal and when, a century later, new direct trade routes were established between India and Tibet, the Nepalis also began to lose their influence as an intermediary in trade between the two countries. A British resident was sent to Kathmandu to keep an eye on things. The Nepalis, less than entranced with the British, allotted him a piece of land which they considered to be disease-prone and a haven for evil spirits but the British stiff upper lip prevailed. In fact the defeat so rankled with the Nepalis that they decided to shut off all foreign contact and from 1816 right through to 1951 the country's borders were firmly closed to outsiders. The British residents in Kathmandu were the only westerners to set eyes on Nepal for over 100 years.

Many Nepali eyes were, however, viewing the outside world. The British were so impressed by the fighting qualities of the Nepalis that they brought mercenaries, known as 'Gurkhas', into the British army. Gurkha mercenaries have fought in the British army ever since, even spreading fear amongst the Argentinians during the Falklands War in 1982. Gurkha earnings are an important element of Nepal's income today and although the importance of Gurkha troops to Britain is diminishing, various other nations are only too happy to pay for their soldiering abilities. The Sultan of Brunei, for example, has a contingent of Gurkha troops.

The Ranas

Although the Shah dynasty continued in power a curious palace revolt occurred in 1846 when Jung Bahadur Rana engineered the Kot Massacre.

Jung Bahadur was an ambitious and ruthless young Chhetri noble from western Nepal. Taking advantage of the complex, often bloody, power struggles within the ruling family, he developed his own power base. On 15 September 1846, he initiated a decisive coup. His soldiers massacred several hundred of the most important men in the kingdom – noblemen, soldiers and courtiers – while they were assembled in the Kot courtyard adjoining Kathmandu's Durbar Square. Jung Bahadur took the title of prime minister and changed his family name to the more prestigious Rana. Later, he extended his title to maharajah and then made the title hereditary. The Ranas became a second 'royal family' within the kingdom and held the real power, keeping the Shah kings as pampered figureheads.

For over a century, the hereditary family of Rana prime ministers held power and although development in Nepal stagnated, the country did manage to preserve its independence during the period when European colonial powers were snatching up virtually every country unable to defend itself. Nepal was never ruled by a colonial power, but it was almost completely isolated from the outside world right through the Rana period. Only on rare occasions were visitors allowed into Nepal and even then they were only allowed to visit a very limited part of the country.

Jung Bahadur Rana travelled to Europe in 1850 and brought back a taste for neoclassical architecture (examples of it can be seen in Kathmandu today). To the Ranas' credit, *suttee* (the Hindu practice of casting widows on their husband's funeral pyre) was abolished, forced labour was ended and a school and a college were established in Kathmandu. While the Ranas and their relations lived luxurious lives in huge Kathmandu palaces the peasants in the hills were locked in a mediaeval existence.

Elsewhere in the region dramatic changes were taking place. After WWII India gained its independence and a revolution took place in China. Tibetan refugees fled into Nepal when the new People's Republic of China annexed Tibet, and Nepal became a buffer zone between the two Asian giants. The turmoil naturally spread over Nepal's closed borders and while one Rana made moves towards liberalising the country's moribund political system another attempted to move towards stronger central control. Under the charismatic BP Koirala the Nepali Congress party, supported by the ruling Indian Congress party, was established by many Nepalis and even by some Rana family members. At the same time King Tribhuvan, forgotten in his palace, was being primed to overthrow the Ranas.

The Shah's Restoration

In late 1950 the king escaped from his palace to the Indian Embassy and from there to India. Meanwhile BP Koirala's forces managed to take most of the Terai from the Ranas and established a provisional government which ruled from the border town of Birganj. Nepal was in turmoil, but there was no clear victor. Finally, India exerted its influence and negotiated a solution. King Tribhuvan returned to Nepal in 1951 and set up a new government comprised of Ranas and commoners from BP Koirala's Nepali Congress.

Although Nepal gradually reopened its long-closed doors and established relations with many other nations, dreams of a new democratic system were not permanently realised. King Tribhuvan died in 1955 and was followed by his son Mahendra. A new constitution provided for a parliamentary system of government and in 1959 Nepal held its first general election. The Nepali Congress won a clear victory, somewhat to the king's surprise, and BP Koirala became the new prime minister. In late 1960, however, the king decided the government wasn't working to his taste and had the cabinet arrested. Political parties were banned and the king swapped his ceremonial role for real control.

In 1962 King Mahendra decided that a partyless, indirect *panchayat* system of government was more appropriate to Nepal. Local panchayats (councils) chose representatives to district panchayats which in turn were represented in the National Panchayat. The real power, however, remained with the king who retained executive power, directly chose 16 members of the 35 member National Panchayat, and appointed the prime minister and his cabinet. Political parties continued to be banned.

In 1972 Mahendra died and was followed by his son Birendra, who had been educated at Eton and Harvard. Birendra's view that Nepal now had the correct political system was not supported by everybody, however. Popular discontent with slow development, corrupt officials and rising costs simmered in the 70s. Finally, in 1979 the smouldering anger exploded into violent riots in Kathmandu, and King Birendra announced that a referendum would be held to choose between the panchayat system and one that would permit political parties to operate.

BP Koirala, who had been in jail or in self-imposed exile since 1960, was allowed to campaign but the 1980 referendum result was 55% to 45% in favour of the panchayat system.

Nevertheless, the king had already declared that whichever way the vote went, the people would elect the country's legislature on a five year term and it, in turn, would elect the prime minister. The king, however, would continue to directly appoint 20% of the legislature, and all candidates would have to be members of one of six government approved organisations and stand under their own name, not as a representative of any party. The first elections under this system were held in 1981.

On the surface, the panchayat system, which allowed a secret vote and universal suffrage, did not appear to be dictatorial: the constitution theoretically guaranteed freedom of speech and peaceful assembly, and the right to form unions and associations (so long as they were not motivated by party politics).

The reality was somewhat different. Nepal's military/police apparatus was one of the least publicly accountable in the world and there was strict censorship. Mass arrests, torture and beatings of suspected activists are well documented, and the leaders of the main opposition, the Nepali Congress, spent the years between 1960 and 1990 in and out of prison. (BP Koirala died in 1983.)

Until early 1990, the king wielded considerable power. It is difficult to know quite how much – the inner workings of the palace and the king's relationships with members of the cabinet were not made public – but the constitution guaranteed his supremacy and the National Panchayat basically acted as a rubber stamp.

The aristocracy, in general, managed to retain its influence and wealth (the king and his brothers are all married to Ranas) and the panchayat system did not seem to cramp its style. Firm figures are impossible to find, but it is generally accepted that a huge portion of foreign aid (perhaps up to 50%) was routinely creamed off into royal and ministerial accounts.

People Power

In 1989 the opposition parties formed a coalition to fight for a multi-party democracy with the king as constitutional head; the upsurge of protest was called the Jana Andolan or People's Movement. Popular support was motivated in part by economic problems caused by an Indian government blockade, and by widespread discontent with blatant corruption.

In February 1990 the government responded to non-violent protest meetings with bullets, tear gas, thousands of arrests and torture. However, after several months of intermittent rioting, curfews, a successful strike, and pressure from various foreign aid donors, the government was forced to back down. The people's victory did not come cheaply. Estimates of the number who died range to more than 300.

On 9 April the king announced on national radio that he was lifting the ban on political parties and on 16 April he asked the opposition to lead an interim government. He also announced his readiness to accept a role as a constitutional monarch.

Democracy

In May 1991, 20 parties contested a general election for a 205 seat parliament. The Nepali Congress and a communist party were the two major players. The Nepali Congress won power with 37.75% of the vote, which secured it 110 seats. The Communist Party of Nepal-Unified Marxist-Leninist (CPN-UML) won 27.98% of the vote, giving it 69 seats. The next largest party, the United People's Front, received only 4.83% of the vote.

In the years immediately following the 1991 election, the political atmosphere in the country was uneasy. For those on the right of the political spectrum, the king's popularity never waned. Many ordinary people, however, had unrealistically high expectations and they were unsettled by political infighting and hurt by price rises. Economic pressures were intense and in April 1992 a general strike degenerated into street violence between protesters and police, and resulted in a number of deaths.

In late 1994 the Nepali Congress government call a mid-term election. The outcome failed to give any party a clear mandate, and in the end the communist CPN-UML won out, in a coalition with the third major party, the RPP (Rastriya Prajatantra Party, the old panchayats), and with the support of the Nepali Congress. It's one of the very few times in the world that a communist government has come to power by popular vote.

The CPN-UML party presented itself as the champion of the downtrodden masses, but it's hard to see how a communist party could justify its participation in a multi-party democratic system with a constitutional monarch and supporting a free-market economy. Nevertheless, the party was well organised and began consolidating support at the grass-roots level.

Political stability remained elusive, infighting and factionalism was rife, and within nine months the Congress had withdrawn its support for the CPN, fearing the communists were becoming too well entrenched. A new Congress government was formed, with the support of the opportunistic RPP.

The Congress government, led by Sher Bahadur Deuba, has a tenuous hold on power. It narrowly – and, to many, surprisingly – escaped being defeated by a no-confidence vote initiated by the CPN in March 1996.

On the positive side, democracy has brought a renewed sense of national pride and optimism to many, especially the educated middle classes. Many cite examples showing a new flexibility and responsiveness on the part of Kathmandu's bloated and stifling government bureaucracy. In November 1992 the government showed some steel by sacking 8000 civil servants. A degree of economic liberalisation and improved relations with India have helped boost several infant industries, including the carpet and clothing sectors. Freedom of the press and improved human rights are other benefits which have flowed from the democratic change.

Establishing a workable democratic system at a national level, where one has never existed before, is an enormously difficult task. One of the biggest problems lies in the attitude of many of the politicians. Having spent so many years in the political wilderness during the panchayat days, when they finally get a taste of power their first concern has been their own financial security and political survival. The interests of the country and the people seem to come a distant second.

As long as political immaturity exists, it seems unlikely that one party will gain clear majority support. There is no doubt that there exists within the nation's political parties a will to change, but as long as those in power are in such a position of insecurity, little real change is likely. In Nepal this is further complicated by a fragile economy, extreme poverty, illiteracy, and an ethnically and religiously fragmented population that is continuing to grow at a frightening rate.

GEOLOGY

This section, along with the following Geography, Ecology and Flora & Fauna sections, was originally written by Lewis Underwood, an avid naturalist who first visited Nepal in the 1970s and continues to work there as a trek leader for Mountain Travel and Malla Treks.

Imagine the space Nepal occupies as an open expanse of water, once part of the Mediterranean Sea, and the Tibetan Plateau, or 'roof of the world', as a beachfront property. This was the prehistoric setting until 60 million years ago, prior to the Indo-Australian plate's collision with the Eurasian continent. As the former was pushed under Eurasia, the earth's crust buckled and folded and mountain building began.

The upheaval of mountains caused the temporary obstruction of rivers that once flowed unimpeded from Eurasia to the sea. However, on the southern slopes of the young mountains, new rivers formed as

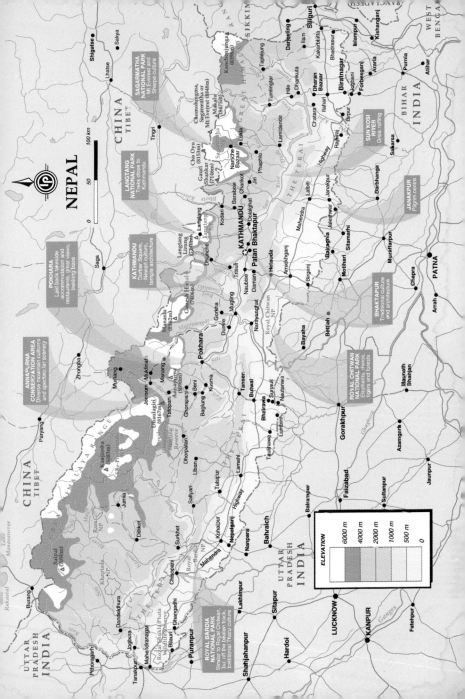

TONY WHEELER

STAN ARMINGTON

Top: A typical scene along trekking routes.
Bottom: Alpine meadow, Danphe Langa near Rana Lake

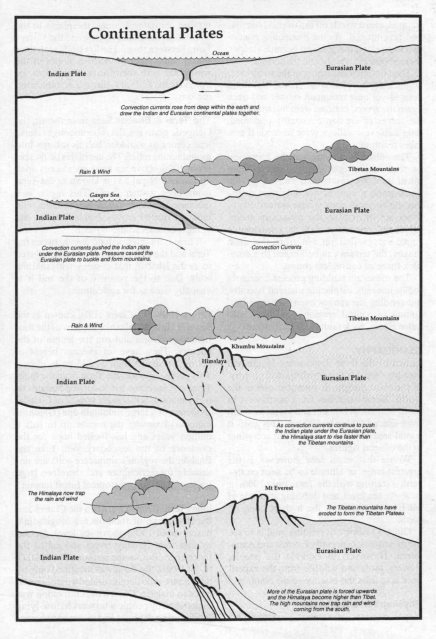

Continental Plates

Ocean

Indian Plate

Eurasian Plate

Convection currents rose from deep within the earth and drew the Indian and Eurasian continental plates together.

Rain & Wind

Tibetan Mountains

Ganges Sea

Indian Plate

Eurasian Plate

Convection Currents

Convection currents pushed the Indian plate under the Eurasian plate. Pressure caused the Eurasian plate to buckle and form mountains.

Rain & Wind

Tibetan Mountains

Khumbu Mountains

Himalaya

Indian Plate

Eurasian Plate

As convection currents continue to push the Indian plate under the Eurasian plate, the Himalaya start to rise faster than the Tibetan mountains.

The Himalaya now trap the rain and wind

Mt Everest

The Tibetan mountains have eroded to form the Tibetan Plateau

Indian Plate

Eurasian Plate

More of the Eurasian plate is forced upwards and the Himalaya become higher than Tibet. The high mountains now trap rain and wind coming from the south.

trapped, moist winds off the tropical sea rose and precipitated. As the mountains continued to rise and the gradient became steeper, these rivers cut deeply into the terrain.

The continual crunching of the two plates, augmented by phases of crustal uplifting, created yet new mountain ranges and once again the rivers' courses were interrupted. If the forces of erosion eventually prevailed, long east-west valleys were formed. If not, lakes resulted.

The colossal outcome was the formation of four major mountain systems running north-west by south-east, incised by the north-south gorges of not only new rivers, but the original ones whose watersheds in Tibet are older than the mountains themselves. In conjunction with the innumerable rogue ridges that jut out from the main ranges, the terrain can be likened to a complex maze of ceilingless rooms.

The mountain building process continues today, not only displacing material laterally, but sending the ranges even higher and resulting in natural erosion, landslides, silt-laden rivers, rock faults and earthquakes.

GEOGRAPHY

In two of the three dimensions, length and breadth, Nepal is just another small country. In the third, height, it's number one in the world. Nepal stretches from north-west to south-east about 800 km and varies in width from around 90 km to 230 km. This gives it a total area of just 147,181 sq km according to the official figures.

Within that small area, however, is the greatest range of altitude to be seen on this earth – starting with the Terai, only 100m or so above sea level, and finishing at the top of Mt Everest (8848m), the highest point on earth.

Often a visitor's overriding goal is to see the mountains, especially Everest and Annapurna. However, to exclude the people, flowers, birds and wildlife from the experience is to miss the essence of the country.

Physiographic Regions

Nepal consists of several physiographic regions, or natural zones: the plains in the south, four mountain ranges, and the valleys lying between them. The lowlands with their fertile soils, and the southern slopes of the mountains with sunny exposures, allow for cultivation and are the main inhabited regions.

The Terai & Bhabar Seen from the air, the Gangetic plain is a flat monotonous expanse that comes to a sudden halt as it turns into mountainous relief. The last of this landscape, about 100m above sea level, encroaches up to 40 km into Nepal and is known as the Terai (sometimes written Tarai). This region is a montage of paddy fields, interspersed with oases of mango groves, bamboo stands and villages beneath scattered palms.

There is an intermediate strip between the Terai and the first range of foothills, referred to as the Bhabar, that is stony with shallow soils. Due to the porosity of the soil it is virtually useless for agriculture.

Chure Hills The Chure Hills, known as the Siwalik Hills in India, are the first of the four mountain ranges and run the length of the country. They have an average height of 900m, but are as high as 1350m in places. This range separates the Terai from the Inner Terai and harbours the fossilised remains of many mammals no longer typical of Eurasia. Evidence of a large mountain ape *(Gigantopithecus)* roaming the region up to half a million years ago has fuelled hope for the existence of the legendary yeti. Like the Bhabar, the region's immature soils are unsuitable for agriculture and therefore large tracts of undisturbed tropical forest remain.

Inner Terai (Duns) Between the Chures and the next range of foothills are longitudinal basins about 150m above sea level, formed by east-west flowing rivers and called the Inner Terai. Before the introduction of DDT in the 1950s, the Terai was inhabited only by the Tharus, who demonstrated a partial resistance to malaria. Otherwise, cultivation was undertaken by people who worked low-lying fields during daylight and returned to homes

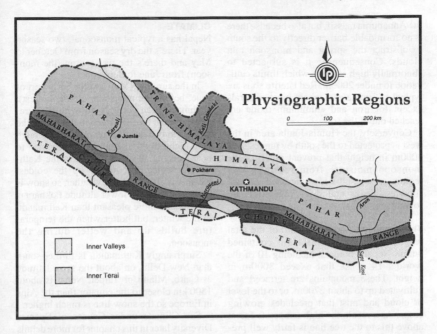

Physiographic Regions

0   100   200 km

Inner Valleys

Inner Terai

above 1200m before sundown. The Rana prime ministers (1846 to 1951) deliberately preserved portions of the tropical jungles to use the malarial zone as a safeguard against possible invasion from the south by the British.

After the eradication of malaria, a large resettlement by hill people looking for fertile land occurred. Over a period of less than a decade, more than 50% of the natural forest was cleared to make way for cultivated land. The establishment of Royal Chitwan National Park in 1973 helped abate this trend and preserved prime habitat for indigenous wildlife, such as the royal Bengal tiger and the one-horned rhinoceros.

Mahabharat Range Still northwards, the next range of foothills, often referred to as the Middle Hills, is the Mahabharat Range. These vary between 1500m and 2700m, and though quite steep, are characterised by water-retentive soils allowing for cultivation

and extensive terracing. On the lower slopes, remnants of subtropical forests can be found, whereas on the upper reaches, above cultivation, temperate elements begin. These mountains are severed by three major river systems: the Karnali, the Narayani and the Sapt Kosi.

Pahar Zone Between the Mahabharat Range and the Himalaya lies a broad belt referred to as the midlands, or Pahar zone. This includes fertile valleys (previously large lakes) such as Kathmandu, Banepa and Pokhara. This area, which has been inhabited for centuries, supports nearly half of Nepal's population. As a result, the central and eastern parts of this zone have been extensively cultivated. Ranging mostly between 1000m and 2000m, subtropical and lower temperate forests are found here, but have been disrupted by fuel and fodder gathering.

The Pokhara area is unique, not only because of its magnificent setting at the foot of the Annapurna massif, but also because there is no formidable barrier directly to the south to obstruct the spring and monsoon rain clouds. Consequently, it is subjected to abnormally high rainfall, which limits cultivation to under 2000m. Red laterite soils are typical of such areas, where most minerals except for iron and aluminium oxide are leached out of the soil.

Conversely, the Humla-Jumla area in the west is protected to the south by ranges over 4000m in height that prevent much of the monsoon moisture from reaching this region. As a result wide, uneroded valleys, snowless peaks and drier vegetation are found here.

The Himalaya About one-third of the total length of the great Himalaya is contained within Nepal's borders, including 10 of the world's 14 peaks that exceed 8000m in height. These mountains are terraced and cultivated up to about 2700m, or to the level of cloud and mist that precludes growing crops. As a result, the high temperate forest above this to the tree line is fairly well preserved.

Inner Valleys The inner valleys are those cradled within the Himalayan ranges. These broad glacier-worn valleys, which are found in the Everest, Langtang and upper Kali Gandaki areas, are not affected by the strong winds that desiccate the valley floors. The partial rain screen of these high valleys creates still different ecologies.

Trans-Himalaya North of the Himalaya is the high desert region, similar to the Tibetan Plateau. This area encompasses the arid valleys of Mustang, Manang and Dolpo, as well as the Tibetan marginals (the fourth range of mountains that sweep from central to north-western Nepal, averaging below 6000m in height). The trans-Himalaya is in the rain-shadow area and receives significantly less precipitation than the southern slopes. Uneroded crags, spires and formations like crumbling fortresses are typical of this stark landscape.

CLIMATE

Nepal has a typical monsoonal, two season year. There's the dry season from October to May and there's the wet season (the monsoon) from June to September.

In the summer (May and the early part of June, before the monsoon, are the hottest), Kathmandu can get very hot with temperatures often in the 30s. Even in the winter the bright sunny days often reach 20°C although with nightfall the mercury may plummet to near freezing. It never snows in the Kathmandu Valley and higher up the coldest weather is also the driest weather, so snow is unusual. Due to its lower altitude Pokhara is warmer and more pleasant than Kathmandu in the winter, but hotter when the temperature builds up and wetter during the monsoon.

Surprisingly Kathmandu is further south than New Delhi, on about the same latitude as Cairo, Miami or Taipei. Nepal is about 1500 km closer to the equator than the Alps in Europe so the snow line is much higher.

See Climate under Causes of Species Diversity later in this chapter for more details about Nepal's monsoonal climate. Also, When to Go under Planning in the Facts for the Visitor chapter has information about the importance of climatic factors in planning a visit to Nepal.

ECOLOGY & ENVIRONMENT

Much of the land between the Himalaya and the Terai has been vigorously modified by human activities and represents the lifeblood of Nepal. This land has been worked and sculpted over the centuries to provide space for crops, animals and houses. Because of this, forests lying within the inhabited zone, especially on the southern slopes, have been lopped, cut and cleared.

Farming Practices

Plant Use The Terai is considered the rice bowl of Nepal, though rice is usually grown up to 2000m, or higher in the west. It is usually planted before the advent of the monsoon, transplanted soon after and harvested in the autumn. The rich vibrant greens during

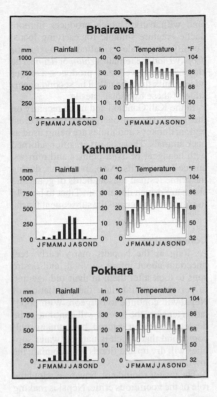

Bhairawa

mm Rainfall in	°C Temperature °F

Kathmandu

mm Rainfall in	°C Temperature °F

Pokhara

mm Rainfall in	°C Temperature °F

the monsoon contrast with the subtle, diffused tones as it ripens.

If possible, wheat is planted in the cleared rice fields and harvested in spring. Fields of yellow-flowering mustard are planted for making cooking oil. Corn is planted in spring, especially on the hillsides, while millet is grown above the rice zone. Barley is sowed in the higher altitudes, as well as buckwheat with its pink and white flower cluster. The Sherpas grow potatoes up to 4000m, and have been doing so since the crop was introduced, probably from Darjeeling in the middle of the last century. Besides providing an important food staple, the prosperity attained from trading potatoes allowed Sherpas to begin building their *gompas* (monasteries) and for their culture to flourish.

In amongst the crops, various other food crops are grown on the berms dividing the plots, including soya beans, lentils, sesame and chilli peppers. The bright red and yellow plants with clustered seed heads seen amidst the shades of green are amaranthus, once an important food and medicinal grain for the Aztecs and Incas.

To keep animals out of crops, Nepalis use assorted spiny or unpalatable exotics as natural barriers. Besides prickly pear cactus and agave, there are several euphorbias used, such as the red-flowering crown of thorns, spurge and physic nut.

There are numerous trees planted around villages and fields, all for some kind of purpose, whether for shade, fruit, fodder or medicine. Bananas, mangoes, papaya, citrus fruits, peaches and apples have all brought new income to the remote hill areas.

Fodder such as rice stalks and corn sheaves is often dried and stored in trees, while seed corn is stored under the eaves of houses. A variety of fig trees provide shade for pilgrims and travellers. The magnificent mushrooming canopies of banyan and pipal trees are unmistakable, usually found together atop a stone dais designed for accommodating porters' loads. The banyan has hanging aerial roots and leathery elliptical leaves, while the pipal has a heart-shaped leaf with a long spur. The Buddha is believed to have attained enlightenment under a pipal tree, and Hindus revere the banyan as an embodiment of Lakshmi, the goddess of wealth, and the pipal as an embodiment of Narayan (Vishnu).

Bamboo grows under a variety of conditions and is found throughout Nepal. Giant bamboo is common in the tropics and dwarf bamboo in the temperate regions. This grass species is used for basketry, and where forests are depleted, particularly in the east, for building. The Rais work bamboo into everything from water vessels to entire houses.

Another common feature in villages are kitchen gardens comprised of greens, beans, turnips, radishes, pumpkins, cucumbers, taro and squash. Bauhinia, with its distinctive camel-hoof leaves and orchid-like flowers, is grown near houses, the former for fodder and the latter cooked or pickled. In the west, tobacco is a commonly seen plot in villages, as are fields of cannabis, grown for hemp. In addition, stinging nettles are picked with thongs, anaesthetised by boiling and eaten as greens.

Eupatorium is a red-stemmed daisy with heart-shaped leaves called *ban mara* (death of forest) by the Nepalis. A native of Latin America introduced into the Himalaya during the last century, it invades subtropical and temperate zones, and is widespread. Covering deforested hillsides, it is unpalatable, even for sheep and goats, and is a prime indicator of environmental degradation.

Animal Husbandry Bovines play an important role in rural and urban Nepal. Cows are sacred and are not slaughtered, nor used as beasts of burden – they bear calves, and provide milk and multipurpose dung. In the Kathmandu Valley, the cows wandering and sleeping in the streets have been let loose by pious Hindus. Because the bull is Shiva's steed, and Pashupatinath is a major Shaivite temple, bulls are also considered holy and generally are not used to pull ploughs in the valley. The beasts of burden on the lowlands are usually castrated bulls, or oxen.

Water buffaloes belong to a different genus, but are still lumped with the bovines. These animals lose their body hair as they mature and must wallow to dissipate heat, and for sun protection. The males are used as beasts of burden and are butchered. The females produce a creamy milk, which is also converted into yoghurt. These animals tend to be skittish, a trait probably inherited from their wild ancestors, and those at the Koshi Tappu Wildlife Reserve in the eastern Terai are considered aggressive and dangerous.

Long-haired yaks, no longer found in the wilds of Nepal, are also very temperamental and are mostly used for stud service. What one generally sees are hybrids, which have confusing names. First of all, the female yak is called a *nak*. The nak or yak can be cross-

bred with cattle, which produces a more docile creature suitable for carrying loads. Locally, the male is called a *zopkiok* or *dzopkyo* and the female a *zhum* or *dzum*. The zhum lactates well and produces a better quality milk than the nak. The second generation of these hybrids is sterile.

In the Kali Gandaki and more recently in the southern approaches to the Everest region, donkeys and mules are being used as pack animals. These beasts are often adorned with headgear of dyed plumes and mirrors, and collars of bells. Also, in autumn, during the prime festival season, herds of goats and sheep are driven down from Tibet to be sold for ritual slaughter and the subsequent feasts.

Conservation

As long as the Nepalis marry early, feel uncertain about infant survival, and desire sons to look after them in their old age and to perform funeral rites, the population of Nepal will continue to burgeon. With population tension, the forests will continue to be depleted, erosion caused by humans will compound that which is natural, water supplies will dry up and floods will inundate the lowlands.

The visitor should not, however, adopt the role of the vociferous critic. Nepal is making positive changes, but traditional societies require long lead times for change. There are various alternative energy schemes underway, probably the most successful being the hydroelectric project of Solu and the unit above Namche Bazaar. The Annapurna Conservation Area Project (ACAP) is also an innovative approach, not only incorporating other alternative energy developments, forest conservation and environmental education, but being an effective strategy for getting the Nepali people directly involved in determining their own destiny.

Conservation is typically a concept of affluent countries with land and resources to spare, a luxury unknown in the Third World. With dwindling space and forests, it is difficult for a farmer to grasp why land should be set aside for tigers and rhino, especially when they ravage crops, take domestic animals and generally make a hard life even harder.

Visitors should ensure that they minimise their impact on the environment. Trekking groups or individuals staying in lodges should insist that kerosene, as opposed to firewood, is used for cooking meals and heating water. One should also minimise the use of nonbiodegradable products (especially plastic and batteries) as there are no facilities for their disposal. One potential nightmare is the trend to sell water in plastic

KEEP Nepal Green

Ecotourism, low-impact trekking, adventure travel and cultural tours are the tourist buzzwords of the 90s. Unfortunately, their meaning has been quickly debased. Package tourists consider any exposure to nature to be adventurous, and independent travellers think that because they are living on a shoestring budget they are ecologically and culturally sound.

The ugly side effects of tourism in Nepal have been widely publicised, but little has been said about what can be done to address the problems. The solution is not to cancel your visit – Nepal's fragile economy needs every dollar it can get – but it is important to be well informed, and to act accordingly. Responsible tourism doesn't take a great deal of effort, but the payoffs are enormous.

Tens of thousands of trekkers visit the Nepal Himalaya each year, so the potential for damage is enormous. In 1994, for example, a total of 76,865 trekking permits were issued by the Department of Tourism.

The average trekker consumes as much fuel wood in a day as an entire Nepali household uses in a week, but for around $2 to $3 a day, camping trekkers and support staff (including porters) can eat food cooked on kerosene stoves.

Independent trekkers can stay in lodges that use kerosene or fuel-efficient stoves, only take hot showers when the water is heated with solar energy, hydroelectricity or back-burner stoves, and choose their meal times to coincide with other trekkers to minimise the amount of cooking time.

An estimated 50,000 kg of garbage is left behind in the mountains by camping trekkers, but just eight cents a day per person covers the cost of having the rubbish carried out of the hills.

Independent trekkers should support lodges and trekking agencies that practice an environmentally sound approach, creating a financial incentive for others to adopt similar methods. They should also carry out nonbiodegradable rubbish, especially plastics and batteries.

On the cultural side, dressing in a way that is consistent with the Nepali norm will not only ease the communication gap, but help regain respect for women, now sadly eroded by the number of female tourists who sport skimpy and skin-tight clothes.

If you want to find out more, or just want to talk to someone about where and how to trek, visit the Kathmandu Environmental Education Project (KEEP). KEEP operates a Travellers' Information Centre in Kathmandu. Located on the edge of Thamel, about 100 metres west of the Department of Immigration, the Information Centre is open from 10 am to 5 pm daily except Saturday and Nepali public holidays.

Visitors can get information on how to minimise their negative impact and maximise their positive impact. Displays and hand-outs illustrate practical do's and don'ts, and there are also professional Nepali staff and western volunteers to deal with specific questions. During trekking seasons a slide show on conservation practices and a talk on prevention of acute mountain sickness is given every afternoon.

Green-Keeper's coffee shop sells freshly brewed cappuccinos, home-made cakes and cookies, KEEP T-shirts, biodegradable soaps, sun screen, lip balm, and other items useful for ecologically sound trekking. Guidebooks, periodicals and maps are available in the library. A journal records trekkers' comments on treks, and an outside notice board carries notices from people selling gear, looking for trekking partners, looking for friends...

Although KEEP information is particularly useful for individual trekkers, it is also helpful for group trekkers, mountaineers and city sightseers – everyone is welcome. Eventually, KEEP hopes to become a clearing house for information on the environment and conservation for the entire Himalayan region.

Visitor contributions are much appreciated. An annual fee of $20 for individuals, $50 for businesses/institutions, $160 for life, and $200 to $500 for 'Friends of Keep' entitles members to the biannual newsletter and a KEEP T-shirt. KEEP has nonprofit, charitable status.

For more information, contact KEEP (☎ 01-410303; fax 411533), PO Box 9178, Thamel, Kathmandu.

Wendy Brewer Lama

bottles, which are expensive and completely unnecessary if you carry your own water bottle and iodine.

See the Trekking chapter for more information on minimising your impact on the environment. Also, see Natural History under the Books section in the Facts for the Visitor chapter for a list of supplementary reading on flora, fauna and national parks.

FLORA & FAUNA
Flora
There are 6500 known species of trees, shrubs and wild flowers in Nepal. In the temperate areas the flowers emerge as winter recedes and the rivers swell with snow melt, while in the subtropics, the bloom is triggered by warmer temperatures and spring showers. Americans and Europeans will recognise many of the species in the temperate areas, and residents of South-East Asia will recognise many of the subtropical species.

The height of floral glory can be witnessed in March and April when rhododendrons burst into colour. The huge magnolias of the east with their showy white flowers borne on bare branches are also spectacular, as are the orchids (there are over 300 species in Nepal). Not far behind is the blossoming of a variety of shrubs, while on the ground, blue irises and lavender primulas appear.

Unless you're able to identify wild flowers by their leaves or dried seed capsules, it is necessary to visit the temperate and alpine areas during the monsoon season. In order to do this, you must be prepared to sacrifice comfort and views. However, this is the time to see the true colours of the Himalaya. The southern slopes and the inner valleys are particularly lush at this time. Mints, scrophs, buttercups, cinquefoils, polygonums and composites abound in these areas, while in the alpine areas, dwarf rhododendrons, junipers, ephedras, cotoneasters, saxifrages and primulas paint the bleak landscape.

Western Nepal, particularly the Dolpo area, is reminiscent of Kashmir in its rich variety of flora. Being in the rain-shadow area, monsoon conditions are more amenable for visitors – the region is dry and free of

leeches. In order to witness the full regalia, the time to visit is July and August. From Jumla east one may recognise ground orchids, edelweiss, corydalis, campanulas, anemones, forget-me-nots, impatiens and roses. Higher up in the alpine areas, larkspurs, geraniums, poppies, sedums and saxifrages proliferate.

In the trans-Himalaya, common vegetation is primarily from the legume family, such as the spiny caragana and astragalus, as well as lonicera from the honeysuckle family.

In the post-monsoon season, when most people choose to visit, the flowers of summer are all but gone, save for some straggler

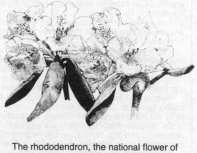

The rhododendron, the national flower of Nepal, is especially spectacular in March and April.

blooms and those not palatable to grazing animals. However, in the subtropical and lower temperate areas, some wild flowers which have survived environmental degradation include pink luculia, mauve osbeckia and yellow St John's wort. Flowering cherry trees also add colour to the autumn village scenes as do, in the temperate areas, blue gentians. Otherwise, one can enjoy the autumn yellows of withering maples and ginger, and the reds of barberry shrubs. When the dark temperate forests are back lit, the moss appears luminescent, and the epiphytic ferns and orchids shine like tiny paper lanterns.

In the Kathmandu Valley, Australians will

Vegetation Zones

In western Nepal, forests usually extend to higher elevations than elsewhere in the country due to drier conditions and a more northerly latitude. Above the temperate cultivation zone and below the tree line, the forests are less disrupted, although they do come under pressure from summer herders and wood gatherers.

Tropical Zone (up to 300m) Sal, a broad-leafed, semideciduous hardwood, dominates here. The leaves are used for 'disposable' plates, and the wood is used for construction. It varies little from east to west and is a fire-climax species.

There is also a deciduous moist forest in this zone, of acacia and rosewood, as well as open areas of tall elephant grass. The grass areas are burned off in winter, which helps preserve them – otherwise they would be succeeded by a moist forest. These two habitats are known as seral communities, because if they are left undisturbed, they would both be replaced by the sal climax forest.

The silky cotton tree *(Ceiba pentandra)* with its thorny trunks when young, and smooth-buttressed trunk bases when older, has leafless limbs that burst into bright red flowers in early spring. It is also a part of the moist forest. The cotton or 'kapok' from these trees is used for stuffing cushions and mattresses.

These forest types are typical of the Chure and Inner Terai, though sal and silky cotton are also found in the subtropical zone.

Subtropical Zone (1000m to 2000m) The dominant species east of the Kali Gandaki are the true chestnuts and a member of the tea family, schima. The spiky flower clusters of the chestnuts appear in the fall, while the fragrant white flowers of the schima bloom in late spring. Due to the popularity of chestnut wood as a source of fuel, it is often depleted.

In the west, the chir pine is found on all aspects. The species has long needles in bundles of three and is also found in the east, but confined to drier southern slopes.

Lower Temperate Zone (1700m to 2700m) Evergreen oaks are indigenous to this zone. In the east, the oaks of the wet forests are festooned with moss and epiphytes and have dense understoreys. In the west, another oak preferring dry conditions is present, as well as on the sunny slopes of the east.

A common wet forest that occurs mostly on north and west faces in western Nepal is comprised of horse chestnut, maple and walnut. Alder and birch are prevalent along water courses.

Homogeneous blue-pine forests occur extensively in the west, mostly on south faces, and range to the tree line. This species is hardy and fire resistant, thriving well in habitats modified by humans. It is also found throughout the east, but to a lesser extent. The blue pine is distinguished from the only other pine in Nepal, the chir pine, by its shorter needles in bundles of five, and long, pendulous cones. Both species are used for carpentry and roofing, while the resin is converted to turpentine.

Upper Temperate Zone (2400m to 4000m) Another evergreen oak that is widespread throughout the dry forests of the west exhibits two types of leaves, the young ones spiny, while the older have leaf margins. In the east, this species is confined to southern slopes, but is heavily cut for fodder and fuel.

The spectacular wet rhododendron forests are interspersed with hemlock and fir. *Rhododendron arboreum*, the national flower, reaches heights of 18m and ranges in colour from red to white. There are over 30 species of rhododendron in Nepal, but these are found more extensively in the east than the west. Unfortunately, this tree is felled for fuel or turned into charcoal.

There is also a high conifer forest where blue pine is again found, occurring in the west with fir and spruce, both of which also form pure stands. In the east, firs, hemlocks and yews associate with blue pine. Firewood and roofing shingles are the common usages for these species. A mixed broad-leafed forest of maple and laurel is also typical of this zone.

Subalpine Zone (3000m to 4000m) Silver fir mixed with oak and birch extend to the tree line in the west. East of the Kali Gandaki, only birch is found to the tree line, though under wetter conditions, dwarf bamboo and shrub rhododendron replace it. In dry areas, juniper species occur to the tree line.

Alpine Zone (4000m to snow line) In this realm above the tree line, vegetation must cope with extremes in ground temperatures, and moisture gradients that range from nothing in winter to profuse in summer. Only the most tenacious of wild flowers thrive here, generally by being hirsute or having thick underground stems (rhizomes). A successful example is stellara, common above 5500m.

In the trans-Himalaya, the vegetation is restricted to the arid-adapted species of the Tibetan Plateau. ∎

Causes of Species Diversity

Not only does Nepal's phenomenal topography range from near sea level to 8848m, but it is contained within a country approximately the size of the US state of Iowa, or that of England and Wales together. The distance between the tropical lowlands and the realm under ice and snow is, in some places, less than 100 km apart. In most parts of the world these zones are separated by thousands of km! In how many places in the world can one see myna birds chattering on banana fronds at 2700m before a snowy mountain backdrop seemingly close enough to reach out and touch?

Geographical Location The 28° latitude line runs just north of Mt Everest, as well as through Morocco and central Florida. This southerly latitude is the reason the permanent snow line is above 5000m. Longitudinally, Nepal straddles two of the world's zoo-geographical zones: the Holarctic to the north and the Oriental to the south. This means that one finds life forms from Europe and northern Asia, typical in the Holarctic and species of India and tropical South-East Asia, in the Oriental.

Climate Nepal is subject to a monsoon-type climate where wet summers and dry winters are characteristic. Without this weather pattern, the country would be a desert with much less extensive speciation.

Every summer between June and July, the sun moves northwards and heats up the mountains, creating a massive convection cell. The subsequent rising air produces a vacuum that draws the moisture-laden air off the Bay of Bengal. This air runs into the Himalayan barriers, cools as it rises and condenses in the form of rain. Thus begins the monsoon season, three to four months of high humidity, overcast skies and gentle rain. Deluges that occur during this time are due to tropical storms or squalls in the Indian Ocean.

The eastern Himalaya receives the brunt of the monsoon which loses its impetus as it moves west along the mountains. Consequently there is a distinct moisture gradient from east to west. Bio-geographically, there are life forms east of the Kali Gandaki Valley associated with wet forests (typically more prolific in species diversity), while west of this line are dissimilar ones preferring drier habitats.

In winter, western Nepal experiences a reverse monsoon caused by a shift in the jet stream. This phenomenon, which drags weather patterns from the west off the Arabian Sea, brings moisture to the region in the form of snow and is essential for agriculture. The oscillation of the jet stream lasts between November and March and is not only responsible for Everest's snow plume and black appearance, but also renders mountaineering difficult.

Altitude & Aspect Altitude and aspect (the direction that a slope faces) play equal roles in determining climate and vegetation. Temperature decreases with elevation, which affects flora as well as fauna. Conversely, rainfall increases with altitude, up to about 2700m. At this level, the clouds have spent their moisture and form a ceiling. This not only establishes the limit for crops, but affects natural vegetation distribution as well.

Aspect, or exposure, is also important in terms of moisture content, fire resistance and defining the height of the tree line. South and east-facing slopes receive more sun and therefore are drier. The shadier northern and western faces are more moist, less prone to fire and thus richer in species. ■

find familiar silky oak with its spring golden inflorescence, and bottlebrush and eucalyptus. Though fast-growing timber species in their native country, in the valley these trees are planted as ornamentals along with cherry, poplar and jacaranda. The latter, with its lavender blossoms, is from South America, as are bougainvillaea and the giant poinsettias. Historically, the Nepalis have been avid gardeners of such exotics as hibiscus, camellia, cosmos, salvia and marigold.

Fauna

Birds More than 800 species are known in Nepal, more birds than in Canada and the USA combined, or nearly 10% of the world's species! Resident bird numbers are augmented by migratory species, as well as winter and summer visitors.

Eight species of stork, some as high as 150 cm, have been identified along the water courses of the Terai. Similar in appearance are the cranes, but not as well represented, save for the demoiselle cranes that fly down the Kali Gandaki and Dudh Kosi for the winter, before returning in spring to their Tibetan nesting grounds. Herons and egrets are quite common in the tropics and subtropics, and distinguished in flight by their curved-neck posture, as opposed to the outstretched necks of storks and cranes.

Most of the waterfowl are migratory. Many can be seen at the Kosi Barrage in the eastern Terai and in the Chitwan and Bardia areas. The bar-headed goose has been observed flying at altitudes near 8000m.

Raptors or birds of prey are found in all sizes in the Himalaya, and are especially prevalent with the onset of winter. One of the first raptors to leave is the small Eurasian kestrel that must flap its wings at regular intervals, or rapidly when hovering, as compared to the Himalayan griffon, a heavy bird that must wait for thermal updrafts to allow its soaring, gliding flight. The griffon, as well as the lammergeier, with a wingspan of nearly three metres, are carrion eaters, though often mistaken for eagles. There are, however, true eagles present, including the resident golden eagle common in the Khumbu, as well as other species that are known to migrate in large numbers in the Kali Gandaki region. Many medium-sized raptors have highly variable plumages and are difficult to identify in the sky.

There are six species of pheasant in Nepal, including the national bird, the impeyan pheasant, the male of which has a plumage of iridescent colours. These birds are known as downhill fliers, as they do not fly, per se, and must walk uphill! When flushed they will cant and swerve downhill to evade enemies such as the golden eagle. The cheer and koklas pheasants are only found west of the Kali Gandaki, while the kalij pheasant is common throughout Nepal, but with different colour phases.

Nepal hosts 17 species of cuckoo which are characterised by their distinctive calls. Arriving in March, they herald the coming of spring. The Indian cuckoo is recognised by its 'kaphal pakyo' call, which is Nepali for announcing that the fruit of the box myrtle is ripe. The common hawk cuckoo has a repetitious call that sounds like 'brain fever', which rises in a crescendo – aptly described by British sahibs as they lay sweating with malarial fevers. Most cuckoos are social parasites, meaning they lay their eggs in the nests of other species.

One of the most colourful, varied and vocal families is the timalids, or babblers and laughing thrushes, common from the tropical Terai to the upper temperate forest. They are from eight to 33 cm in size and live in both terrestrial and arboreal habitats. They are found individually or in large, foraging parties, and can often be identified by their raucous calls. The black-capped sibia with its constant prattle and ringing song is an integral part of the wet temperate forests. The spiny babbler is Nepal's only endemic species.

There are three pairs of species amongst the crow family; their appearance and behaviour are virtually identical, but each species occupies a different altitudinal range. The red-billed blue magpies are residents of the subtropical zone, while the yellow-billed species are found in the temperates. The Indian tree pie prefers the tropics while the Himalayan species lives in the subtropics and temperates. Above the tree line, two species of chough, congregating in large flocks in winter, are prevalent. Though they often overlap in range, the yellow-billed chough is found higher and is known to enter mountaineers' tents high on Everest. Another of the crow family, also bold and conspicuous in the trans-Himalayan region, is the large raven.

Besides such families as kingfishers, bee-eaters, drongos, minivets, parakeets and sunbirds, there are a host of other passerines, or perching birds, present throughout Nepal. These include 30 species of flycatchers and nearly 60 species of thrushes and warblers. Many smaller species congregate in heterogeneous flocks, not only for feeding purposes, but for protection.

In the Kathmandu Valley, sparrows and pigeons demonstrate adaptability to urban centres by their sheer numbers. Dark kites, hawk-like birds with forked tails, are common over the city. At sunset, loose groups of crows, mynas, egrets and kites fly to their respective roosts. After dark, the noisy ruckus of the spotted owlets substitutes for the cacophony of car horns. The robin dayal, with its cocked tail, is the common songster of early mornings. Pulchowki, Nagarjun and Shivapuri are excellent areas for finding birds of subtropical and temperate habitats.

In the Pokhara region, the Indian roller is conspicuous when it takes flight and flashes the iridescent turquoise on its wings. Otherwise, while perched, it appears as a plain brown bird. Local superstition has it that if someone about to embark on a journey sees a roller going their way it is a good omen. If they see a crow, however, it is a bad omen and the trip is aborted. Many trips must be destined for delay thanks to the presence of the common crow!

Mammals As one might expect, due to habitat degeneration from both natural and human causes, opportunities for seeing wildlife are usually restricted to national parks, reserves and western Nepal, where the population is sparse. Wildlife numbers have also been thinned due to poaching for pelts or other animal parts that are considered to be delicacies or medicinally valuable. Animals are also hunted because of the damage they inflict on crops and domestic animals.

At the top of the food chain is the royal Bengal tiger, the most magnificent cat, which is solitary and territorial. Males have territorial ranges that encompass those of two or three females and may span as much as 100 sq km. Royal Chitwan National Park of the Inner Terai and Royal Bardia National Park in the western Terai protect sufficient habitat to sustain viable breeding populations.

The spotted leopard is an avid tree climber and in general more elusive than the tiger. Like tigers, these nocturnal creatures have been known to prefer human flesh when they have grown old or been maimed. Humans are not only easy prey, but once the taste is acquired, human-flesh eaters lose interest in

their natural prey. Local people have likened them to evil spirits because their success at evading hunters suggests they can read minds.

The snow leopard is often protected from hunters, not only by national parks, but also by inhabiting inhospitable domains above the tree line and sensitive border regions. Its territory depends upon the ranges of ungulate (hooved) herds, its prey species, as well as breeding females. Packs of wolves compete directly and when territories overlap, the solitary snow leopard will be displaced.

The beautiful snow leopard lives often in inhospitable regions above the tree line.

The one-horned rhinoceros is the largest of three Asian species and is a totally different genus from the two-horned African varieties. It has poor eyesight and though weighing up to two tonnes, is amazingly quick. Anyone who encounters a mother with its calf is likely to witness a charge, which is disconcertingly swift, even if you are on an elephant. The rhino is a denizen of the grasslands of the Inner Terai, specifically the Chitwan Valley, although it has also been reintroduced to Royal Bardia National Park.

The Indian elephant, like the one-horned rhino, is starkly different to its African relative, belonging to a separate genus. The only wild elephants known to exist in Nepal are in the western part of the Terai and Chure Hills, though individuals often range across the border from India. Elephants are known to maintain matriarchal societies, and females up to 60 years of age bear calves. Though able to reach 80 years of age, elephants' life spans are determined by dentition. Molars are replaced as they wear down, but only up to six times. When the final set is worn, the animal dies of starvation.

Periodically, male and occasionally female elephants, enter a 'musth' condition that makes them excitable and highly aggressive. While in this agitated state they have been known to trample villages. When a herd goes on the rampage, outsiders or non-Hindus are often summoned, as the elephant is considered a holy animal because of the much-loved Ganesh, the elephant-headed god of the Hindu pantheon.

There are several species of deer, but most are confined to the lowlands. The spotted deer is probably the most beautiful, while the sambar is the largest. The muntjac, or barking deer, which usually makes its presence known by its sharp, one note alarm call, is found up to 2400m, while the unusual musk deer, which has antelope-like features and is only 50 cm high at the shoulder, ranges even higher.

There are two primates: the rhesus macaque and the common langur. The rhesus are earth-coloured with short tails and travel on the ground in large, structured troops, unafraid of humans. The langur are arboreal, with black faces, grey fur, long limbs and tails. Because of Hanuman, the monkey god in the Hindu epic the *Ramayana*, both species are considered holy and are well protected. The rhesus ranges from the Terai up to 2400m, while the langur goes up to 3600m.

In the Kathmandu Valley, rhesus macaques at the Swayambhunath and Pashupatinath temples take advantage of their holy status and relieve worshippers of their picnic lunches and consecrated food.

Two even-toed ungulate mammals are found in the alpine regions. They are the Himalayan tahr, a near-true goat, and the blue sheep, which is genetically stranded somewhere between the goat and sheep. The male tahr pose majestically in their flowing manes on the grassy slopes of inner valleys, while the blue sheep turn a bluish-grey in winter and are found in the trans-Himalayan region.

The Himalayan black bear is omnivorous and a bane to corn crops in the temperate forests. Though it rarely attacks humans, its poor eyesight may lead it to interpret a standing person as making a threatening gesture and to attack. If so, the best defence is not to run, but to lie face down on the ground – particularly effective when one is wearing a backpack. Nepal's bears are known to roam in winter instead of hibernating.

There are some prominent canines, though behaviourally they are fairly shy. The jackal, with its eerie howling that sets village dogs barking at night, ranges from the Terai to alpine regions. It is both a hunter and scavenger, and will take chickens and raid crops.

The pika, or mouse-hare, is the common guinea pig-like mammal of the inner valleys, often seen scurrying nervously between rocks. The marmot of western Nepal is a large rodent; it commonly dwells in the trans-Himalaya. The marmot is also found in Sikkim and Bhutan, but not eastern Nepal – such gaps in speciation are not uncommon across the Himalaya.

Noisy colonies of flying foxes or fruit bats have chosen the trees near the old Royal Palace in Kathmandu and the chir pines at the entrance to Bhaktapur as their haunts. They are known to fly great distances at night to raid orchards, before returning at dawn. They have adequate eyesight for their feeding habits and do not require the sonar system of insectivorous bats.

Pulchowki, Nagarjun and Shivapuri are good areas for possible sightings of small mammals.

Reptiles There are two indigenous species of crocodile: the Gharial and marsh mugger. The Gharial inhabits rivers and is a prehistoric-looking fish-eating creature with bulging eyes and a long, narrow snout. The marsh mugger prefers stagnant water and is omnivorous, feeding on anything within reach. Due to the value of its hide and eggs, the Gharial was hunted to the brink of extinction, but has increased in numbers since the establishment of a hatchery and rearing centre in Chitwan. Both crocodiles inhabit the Terai.

Though venomous snakes such as cobras, vipers and kraits are present, the chance of encountering one is small, not only because of their usual evasive tactics, but also because they are indiscriminately slaughtered. The majority of species are found in the Terai, though the mountain pit viper is known higher up, along with a few other nonvenomous species.

NATIONAL PARKS & CONSERVATION AREAS

Nepal has nine national parks and four wildlife reserves that protect every significant ecological system in the country – from the tropical plains of the Terai and the fertile midland valleys, to the highest mountains in the world.

Over 12,000 sq km are protected, or over 8% of the country's area, and you can add another 2600 sq km if you include the Annapurna Conservation Area. Considering the strength of the demand for land, there has been a particularly impressive commitment to conservation.

Travellers are almost certain to visit a protected area – the Sagarmatha National Park includes Mt Everest; the Annapurna Conservation Area includes many of the most popular treks around the Annapurna Himal; and Royal Chitwan National Park is famous for its elephant-back safaris in search of royal Bengal tigers and one-horned rhinoceroses.

All visitors are charged Rs 650 to enter a park or reserve, and this includes the Annapurna Conservation Area. There is no fee for using a camera or video camera within the parks. The Department of National Parks & Wildlife Conservation (☎ 01-220912) can be contacted through PO Box 860, Babar Mahal, Kathmandu.

The problems that Nepal has faced in

setting aside areas for conservation are more acute than those faced in most industrially developed countries, but the Nepalis are responding by developing new management concepts – it is not possible or desirable to set aside areas of land that are totally untouched by humans.

Firstly, very little of Nepal can be accurately described as wilderness. Most of the country is, in some way, used by humans. Virtually every possible sq cm of arable land is used for farming; the remaining forests are utilised for firewood and hunting; the high country is used for hunting and grazing; and the whole country is crisscrossed with trade routes. The only exceptions are several royal hunting reserves, some of the Terai (large parts of which were virtually untouched until the 1950s) and mountain peaks at high altitude.

Secondly, developing national parks and conservation areas by following the western model would have meant totally blocking local people's access to a resource that might literally mean the difference between life and death. In most cases, therefore, the Nepalis have attempted to marry the competing interests between conservation (and tourist attractions?) on the one hand and farming (and food?) on the other.

For instance, the Sagarmatha National Park is the traditional home to several thousand Sherpas whose ancestors settled the area 500 years ago. Banishing them from their homeland would have been unthinkable, so the park management has been responsible for encouraging sustainable economic development, as well as controlling the impact of a growing number of tourists. In another example, although thousands of recent settlers were actually moved outside the park's boundary when it was declared, Royal Chitwan National Park is still used by them as an important source for thatching grass, which is harvested every year.

Despite these essential compromises, there have been some notable successes. The magnificent royal Bengal tiger has been saved in Chitwan and there have been impressive achievements in the Sagarmatha

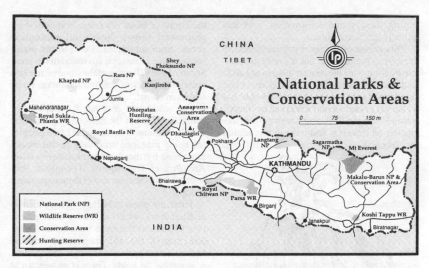

National Parks & Conservation Areas

National Park and the Annapurna Conservation Area – in forestry, agriculture, health and education, as well as in protecting the most spectacular scenery in the world. See those sections later in this book.

Koshi Tappu Wildlife Reserve

The Koshi Tappu Wildlife Reserve is a small (175 sq km) reserve that lies on the beautiful flood plain of the Sapt Kosi (one of the three largest tributaries to the Ganges) in eastern Nepal. It runs north from the massive Kosi Barrage and the Indian border.

The reserve is often flooded during the monsoon, although mostly to shallow depths only. It is, nonetheless, home to the last surviving group of wild buffalo and several species of deer. The vegetation is mainly grassland with some mixed riverine forest. A total of 280 different species of birds – including many migratory birds – have been recorded. Local villagers harvest grasses for thatching, and also fish and collect edible fruits and ferns.

The Mahendra Highway skirts the reserve, and the only accommodation option is one top-end tented camp. See the Terai chapter for more details.

Sagarmatha National Park

North-east of Kathmandu and alongside the Tibetan border, the Sagarmatha National Park covers 1148 sq km, all above 3000m in altitude. Mt Everest (Sagarmatha to the Nepalis) is the single main attraction, but there are a number of other well known peaks, including Lhotse and Ama Dablam. The mountains are broken by deep gorges, glacial valleys and lakes.

Tree species include pine, fir, juniper and birch, and there are numerous species of rhododendron. Amongst the animals, there are musk deer, Himalayan tahr, black bears, wolves and fascinating bird life. The most famous would be the beautiful impeyan pheasant, the national bird of Nepal, but there are choughs, snow pigeons and Himalayan griffons among 130 others.

Over 3500 Sherpas use the park for cropping and grazing (their villages are not included in the park proper) and their unique culture provides yet another reason to visit. There are several important monasteries. For detailed information on this park try to find a copy of *Mt Everest National Park: Sagarmatha, Mother of the Universe* by Margaret Jefferies, an excellent book that gives fascinating background information, and has some magnificent photos.

This is one of the most popular trekking regions in the country, but it's only accessible by foot, with the nearest airstrip at Lukla and the roadhead at Jiri. Many trekkers visit, lured by the highest and most spectacular mountain scenery in the world and by Sherpa culture. See the Trekking chapter for information on trekking, and treks in this region in particular.

The long-haired tahr is found on the grassy slopes of the inner Himalayan valleys.

Makalu-Barun National Park & Conservation Area

The Makalu-Barun National Park & Conservation Area, just to the east of Mt Everest, was inaugurated in November 1992. It covers 2330 sq km and its boundaries are marked by the Arun River to the east and the Sagarmatha National Park to the north-west. Its northern boundary is the 35,000 sq km Qomolangma (Mt Everest) Nature Preserve in Tibet. Together these three parks protect a vast area around the Everest massif.

The park includes Makalu, at 8463m the fifth highest mountain in the world, and each year a small number of trekkers walk in to the base camp. Elevations range from 435m on the Arun River to the 8000m summits of the Himal (a *himal* is a range or massif with permanent snow). Nearly all ecological zones, from subtropical forest to the arctic snows of the Himalaya, are found in the area. Some of the valleys contain some of the last remaining tracts of pristine mountain landscapes in Nepal.

The wilderness area has the status of a national park, but the surrounding regions, which are home to more than 32,000 people, are being managed according to the model pioneered by the Annapurna Conservation Area Project. The majority of people are Rai, followed by Sherpa and Tibetan-speaking groups.

There are plans to build a visitors' centre at Khandbari, which will have road access (via Dhankuta) thanks to the proposed construction of the 402 megawatt Arun III hydroelectric project (although this project is currently on hold). There is an airstrip at Tumlingtar about 10 km south of Khandbari.

Royal Chitwan National Park

South-west of Kathmandu, near the Indian border on the tropical Terai, Royal Chitwan National Park and the contiguous Parsa Wildlife Reserve cover just over 1431 sq km. The park includes a section of the Chure Hills and the Rapti, Narayani and Reu valleys.

Sal forest covers 70% of the park, with the remainder consisting of grasslands and riverine forests. This is home to the only significant number of one-horned rhinoceroses surviving in Nepal, and to other endangered species like the royal Bengal tiger, Gangetic dolphin and Gharial crocodile. Altogether, there are over 50 species of large mammals and over 400 species of birds. There are no human communities living in the park, but the surrounding countryside is intensively cultivated.

For detailed information on this park, try to find a copy of *Royal Chitwan National Park: Wildlife Heritage of Nepal* by Hemanta R Mishra & Margaret Jefferies; some of the photos are magnificent.

The park is easily accessible by road, and accommodation ranges from five star and expensive, to zero star and cheap. Many people visit for two or three days (especially if they are going to or from India) to take advantage of elephant safaris through the forest. See the Terai chapter for more details.

Annapurna Conservation Area

North of Pokhara and extending to the Tibetan border, the Annapurna Conservation Area covers 2600 sq km. It includes the Annapurna peaks, the famous Annapurna Sanctuary and a significant section of the Kali Gandaki Valley.

The conservation area is run by the Annapurna Conservation Area Project, or ACAP, a nongovernmental, nonprofit organisation which is funded by various trusts. ACAP's primary objectives are to improve local standards of living, to protect the environment and to develop more sensitive forms of tourism.

This is the most popular trekking region in Nepal, especially for individual trekkers, and this influx of visitors has added to the pre-existing problems in the mountains. The trekkers' demands for heating and hot water have led to increased deforestation, there are litter and sanitation problems, and wildlife has been driven away from many parts.

In response, ACAP has started work on a number of projects, such as forestry nurseries, introducing wood-saving technologies (eg efficient stoves), banning fires altogether in certain areas, and building rubbish tips and latrines. Many problems still remain, and it is vital that trekkers cooperate with these and other initiatives. If you would like more information on ACAP activities, contact the King Mahendra Trust for Nature Conservation (☎ 01-526571; fax 526570), PO Box 3712, Babar Mahal, Kathmandu.

The treks around the Annapurna Himal are undoubtedly some of the best in the world – not only for the grandeur of the mountains, but for the variety of fascinating cultures that you can visit (Bhotiya, Tibetan, Tamang, Magar, Gurung, Thakali and others). The area is easily accessible from Pokhara and there is an airstrip at Jomsom. See the Trekking chapter for more information.

Langtang National Park

This is the nearest national park to Kathmandu, extending from 32 km north of Kathmandu to the Tibetan border, and covering 1710 sq km. The park encloses the catchments for two major rivers – the Trisuli and the Sun Kosi – and several 7000m mountains.

The complex topography and geology of the area together with the varied climatic patterns means there is a wide variety of vegetation types and animals. There are small areas of subtropical forest below 1000m, then temperate oak and pine forests, subalpine juniper, larch and birch, and finally alpine scrub, rocks and snow. The fauna includes pandas, muntjac, musk deer, black bear, ghoral, serows (antelope) and monkeys.

About 45 villages lie within the park boundaries (although they do not come under park jurisdiction). In total, around 18,000 people depend on the park's resources, mainly for wood and pasture land. There are several ethnic groups, but the majority are Tamangs (settlers from Tibet and followers of the pre-Buddhist Bon religion).

There are a number of popular treks in the park, ranging in length and difficulty. There is road access to Dhunche (near the park headquarters) from Kathmandu, or you can walk in from Sundarijal, Panchkhal, or from Chautara or Tatopani on the Kodari road. See the Trekking chapter for more details.

Dhorpatan Hunting Reserve

The Dhorpatan Hunting Reserve lies in the Dhaulagiri Himal in western Nepal. It is characterised by a dry climate in the north and well developed mixed hardwood forests at lower elevations.

The 1325 sq km reserve is one of the prime habitats for the blue sheep, a highly prized trophy animal. Other 'game' animals include ghoral, serow, Himalayan tahr, Himalayan black bear, pheasants and partridges. I imagine trekkers would also make good sport.

The only access, unless you have a helicopter, is by foot from Jelbang.

Shey Phoksundo National Park

The Shey Phoksundo National Park is the largest park in Nepal at 3555 sq km. It encompasses the Kanjiroba Himal in western Nepal and runs north to the Tibetan border.

The park stretches across all possible vegetation zones – from the luxuriant forests of the lower Himalaya to the near desert of the Tibetan Plateau. Typical animals include the Tibetan hare, Himalayan weasel and the beautiful snow leopard. Lake Phoksundo and the Shey monastery are the two main attractions in the park, but the entire region has been little touched by the 20th century.

Very few people visit this region, partly because access has, in the past, been officially restricted and entails a dangerous 14 day trek from Pokhara. Permits can be arranged through trekking companies. See *Trekking in Hidden Land of Dolpa-Tarap & Shey Poksumdo* by Paolo Gondini (available at Tiwari's Pilgrims Book House, Kathmandu) for more detailed information. According to information from the department, it takes two days to walk to the entrance gate for Sumduwa from Dunai, the district headquarters for Dolpo.

Rara National Park

In little-visited western Nepal, the 106 sq km Rara National Park was established to preserve the catchment and surrounds of the beautiful Rara Lake – a clear high-altitude lake ringed with pine, spruce and juniper forests and snow-capped peaks. The lake is the largest in Nepal and is an important water bird habitat.

The only way to get to Rara Lake is a strenuous four day walk from the airstrip at Jumla, or from the roadhead at Surkhet. Trekking in this area is much more difficult than in east or central Nepal: some areas are still closed and there are frequent food shortages. See Lonely Planet's *Trekking in the Nepal Himalaya* by Stan Armington for more details.

Royal Bardia National Park

In the western Terai, bordering the Karnali River, this 968 sq km reserve is reminiscent in many ways of Royal Chitwan National Park. The relative difficulty of access, however, means it is much less popular. And there is a higher likelihood of seeing a royal Bengal tiger.

The reserve is bordered to the north by the Chure Hills, but is predominantly flat and dominated by sal forests and grasslands. Apart from tigers there is a small herd of introduced rhinoceroses, blue bull, a variety of deer and a few wild elephants. If you're lucky you might also see Gangetic dolphin in the river.

The park is 2½ hours by road from Nepalganj and there is accommodation available, ranging from budget to top of the range. See the Terai chapter for more details.

Khaptad National Park

Another rarely visited park, Khaptad covers 225 sq km in far western Nepal. Lying at around 3000m it is largely a rolling plateau with grasslands, and oak and coniferous forests.

Royal Sukla Phanta Wildlife Reserve

This 155 sq km reserve lies in the far south-western corner of Nepal on the Indian border. It covers a riverine flood plain, dominated by sal forest, but like both Chitwan and Bardia national parks, there are also grasslands which make it ideal for wildlife observation.

Sukla Phanta is one of the last strongholds for the endangered swamp deer, but there are also tigers and possibly a wild elephant or two.

Access to the park is by road from Mahendranagar and it is possible to stay in a tented camp. See the Terai chapter for more details.

GOVERNMENT & POLITICS

The Jana Andolan, or People's Movement, of April 1990 forced King Birendra to abandon the panchayat system that had been established by his father and under which the king enjoyed virtually sole power. (See the History section earlier for more information.)

A new constitution was adopted in November 1990. Basically it provided for a constitutional monarchy, universal adult franchise and a multi-party parliamentary system.

Members of the 205 seat House of Representatives (Pratinidhi Sabha) are elected every five years according to the first-past-the-post system. In the May 1991 elections, the Nepali Congress won 110 seats, giving it a simple majority, and formed the government with Girija Prasad Koirala as prime minister. Since May 1996 the government has changed twice. A mid-term poll in late 1994 brought the communist CPN-UML party to power, and this was followed by a Congress-led coalition which defeated the Communists with a no-confidence vote in mid-1995.

Members of the 60 seat National Assembly (Rastriya Sabha) have a six year tenure; one third retire every two years. Thirty-five members are elected by proportional representation, 15 members are elected by local government representatives and 10 members are nominated by the king.

ECONOMY

Judged by western standards, Nepal is one of the poorest countries in the world with an estimated annual Gross Domestic Product (GDP) of only US$156 per person in 1994. To a certain extent, this suggests an overly bleak picture because more than 90% of the population is basically, and will almost certainly remain, subsistence farmers operating outside the cash economy.

Agriculture

At present, most farmers succeed in meeting their basic needs and producing a small surplus for cash sales. Indeed, aid workers on the Terai have been known to bemoan the fact that they can't convince peasant farmers to work harder and produce additional cash crops.

The problem is that the rewards are not believed to be worth the effort. After all, if a family has food, a house, and perhaps access to a radio and bicycle, what more could they want – or realistically aspire to?

In the late 1970s Nepal actually exported large quantities of rice. The development of the Terai opened up new land, temporarily relieving some of the population pressure in the hills, and the so-called green revolution (utilising improved seeds, artificial fertilisers and pesticides) led to increased productivity. The population, however, has again begun to grow more rapidly than production and Nepal will soon be forced to import rice to meet its needs. It is already a net importer of food.

The average size of land-holdings has continued to drop; it now stands at around half a hectare in the hills and a little over 1.5 hectares in the Terai. In a good year, half a hectare in the hills around Kathmandu might produce around 1000 kg of rice and 500 kg of mixed vegetables, but if the farmer does not own the land up to 50% of this production will go to the owner as rent. Although there are theoretical limits on the amount of land an individual may own, tenant farmers are still common and many are in debt to moneylenders.

Where possible, crops are supplemented with livestock (especially in the mountain areas), but the animals are often of poor quality, partly because there is a serious shortage of fodder, especially in winter. One of the important uses for Nepal's remaining forests is as a source for animal fodder; unfortunately this can also lead to unsustainable damage. See the earlier Ecology section for more information on plant use and animal husbandry in Nepal.

Manufacturing & Services

Obviously, for many people there's not much food to spare, especially if the rains fail. Although outright starvation is rare, undernourishment is very common, particularly in the undeveloped west of the country. A growing number of people are forced to seek seasonal work, or rely on money that is repatriated by other family members, to supplement what they can produce from their land.

Unfortunately, Nepal's embryonic manufacturing industries (mainly on the Terai) and service sector are unable to meet the demand for work, so there is significant underemployment.

Perhaps the most extraordinary success story of the last few decades, however, has been that of Tibetan carpets. Although weaving is an indigenous craft, in 1960 the Nepal International Tibetan Refugee Relief Committee, with the particular support of the Swiss government, began encouraging Tibetan refugees in Jawlakhel, Patan, to make and sell carpets. Today, Nepal exports more than 1.5 million sq metres of rugs, valued at over US$100 million. This industry now earns more than half the country's foreign exchange, and is the largest single employer with nearly 300,000 workers.

For many people, however, the only accessible source of income is the tourist trade – either as a market for handicrafts and other small-scale businesses (lodges, shops, travel agencies etc) or as an employee (hotel staff, porters etc). Others work as day labourers for wealthy peasants, or try to pick up menial work in Kathmandu.

Foreign Exchange & Trade

Tourism accounts for 15.5% of foreign-exchange earnings, although there is some controversy over how much of this leaks out of the country again in paying for the goods and services that westerners require. Remittances, primarily from Gurkha soldiers in the Indian, British and Sultan of Brunei's armies, account for another 6.5%.

Some cynics claim that the two mainstays of the Nepali economy are really smuggling and foreign aid – there are no official figures for the smuggling, but foreign aid accounts for 30% of hard currency receipts! Almost half the government's revenue depends on foreign aid and borrowing.

The country has always been an intermediary between India and China. More recently, it has become a transit point for goods from Japan, Singapore and Hong Kong. Additionally, it is claimed that many goods travel in a circuit from India to Nepal and back to India.

Nepal's trade is dominated by India and many activities within the country are Indian-owned or controlled. In the 1990-91 financial year India had a trade surplus with Nepal that amounted to over Rs 6000 million.

Development

It is hard to be optimistic when looking at the prospects for Nepal, despite the ingenuity and decency of the Nepali people. The growing population threatens to overwhelm the developments that have already taken place, and future developments will always be hampered by the impossible terrain.

Whether the country can continue to carry the population it already has – given that soils and forests are already being exploited at unsustainable levels – might even be questioned. For a very large number of peasant families, existence appears set to become increasingly perilous. This is likely to lead to increased migration to the Kathmandu Valley (where resources are already strained), to the Terai and to India.

In Kathmandu, the gulf between rich and poor is extreme. The aristocracy still wields considerable power and influence and many of its members lead lives that are extraordinarily pampered and unrealistic. These feudal survivors have been joined by a new business elite, whose strikingly ugly houses now dot the outskirts of Kathmandu. Corruption is endemic at every level of government.

The challenges facing Nepal are clearly immense. A large and growing proportion of the population lives in poverty and nearly 75% is illiterate. Health services, especially outside the Kathmandu Valley, are minimal – the ratio of doctors to people was one to 15,000 in 1991, and there were only 4700 hospital beds. The average life expectancy is only 54 years.

Since most people are dependent on agriculture, this is the most important area for development. Much can be done to increase and sustain productivity, but here as elsewhere, the topography means there is an amazing diversity of problems, not least of which is reaching the isolated valleys and ridges where so many of the people live.

On the positive side, education is spreading into distant valleys, and trekkers are likely to come across thriving primary schools in the most remote areas. Also highly visible are the improvements in Nepal's communications network. The telephone system links all major towns, and roads continue to extend further and further into distant parts of the country. Often, however, new roads bring undesirable social changes (thanks to an influx of outsiders and trade goods) and some question whether the huge sums of money involved in road construction and maintenance might not be better allocated to expanding and improving the existing network of walking tracks and bridges.

Nepal's physical resources are extremely limited. There are few accessible minerals, and there is little unexploited arable land. There are, however, great hydroelectric power resources, although the market for them is likely to be found in India, and the capital and ecological costs involved in construction are huge. Perhaps one of the most optimistic trade delegations in recent times was one from Bangladesh that suggested a number of ways trade could be expanded between the two countries. Amongst other things, they were interested in importing Nepali boulders!

Foreign Aid

Foreign aid sounds as if it should be a wonderful industry – on the surface, totally nonpolluting and ecologically sound. Nepal has lots of it and the end result is highly questionable. If you're interested in the impact of foreign aid on a country like Nepal the magazine *Himal* regularly has articles which will provide food for thought. Two other books, ostensibly accounts of travels in Nepal, will also prove enlightening.

Peter Somerville-Large's *To the Navel of the World* (Hamish Hamilton, London, 1987) contrasts the successful, heavily touristed and heavily aided Solu Khumbu region of the Sherpas in eastern Nepal with the neglected regions of the far north-west. While critics debate the damage caused by tourism it seems hardly likely that the people living in the areas where trekkers are plentiful and aid projects abound would willingly switch to the areas of Nepal which are still 'off limits'.

Charlie Pye-Smith's *Travels in Nepal* (Aurum Press, London, 1988) was essentially a trek from one aid project to another and what he saw was not always a pretty sight. Too often the projects were pointless, imposed without consulting the people they were aimed at, or without adequately understanding the local physical and cultural environment. Often the only people who benefited were the foreign companies who supplied equipment and expertise and the affluent Nepalis who skimmed off a profit as the project passed by them.

Pye-Smith contends that most aid donors look for big projects (they like to have something visible to show off) and that government officials like the big ones too (there's more likely to be something in it for them). The projects that actually work, however, are much closer to ground level. He describes disastrous Japanese irrigation projects, ill-planned Austrian hydroelectric power projects and well meaning but inept US ecological projects, but also tells of a British agricultural project near Dhankuta in the east which really seemed to work and an Australian forestry project which operated on a shoestring and seemed to work much better because of that.

He concludes, however, by questioning the whole basis of foreign aid in Nepal. Along the way he turns up numerous interesting thoughts. Hydroelectric power, for example, is touted as an enormous energy saver but its main use is for electric lighting. Lighting with hydroelectric power generated electricity is much cheaper than with kerosene and a great deal of expensive kerosene can be saved. But with cheap lighting people stay up later and when they stay up they burn firewood. The end result of providing hydroelectric power can actually be an increase in the consumption of scarce timber!

One aid project disaster he observed was a tree-planting exercise where the trees were not only badly planted but also planted in an area where the first monsoon deluge washed them away. This totally wasted plantation was fenced in by cutting down healthy trees! Even the whole horror story of Himalayan deforestation is brought into question. 'The only number which has any scientific validity at all in the Himalaya is sixty-seven', he writes. This is the factor by which estimates of per capita firewood consumption vary.

POPULATION

Nepal's population currently stands at around 23 million (1995 estimate). The rate of population growth is terrifying. Every year the population increases by nearly 600,000. The largest city is Kathmandu, the capital, with more than 700,000 people.

In the mountains the rate of increase is lower than in the Terai, but this is because many people are migrating in search of land and work. Despite (or because of) extremely high rates of infant mortality and the life expectancy of only a horrifying 54 years, the overall annual rate of population increase is a rapid 2.6%, which is putting enormous pressures on Nepal's fragile ecology.

Family planning is of primary importance, but most people continue to regard children

as a blessing. A child is seen as a vital and fulfilling part of the parents' lives, an extra worker and someone to care for them in old age, not just an extra stomach. Women have an average of more than five children each.

PEOPLE

Like the geography, the population of Nepal is extremely diverse and highly complex. Simplistically, Nepal is the meeting point for the Indo-Aryan people of India with the Tibeto-Burman of the Himalaya, but this gives little hint of the dynamic ethnic mosaic that has developed and continues to change to this day.

In a south-north direction, as you move from the plains to the mountains, the ethnic map can be roughly divided into layers: the Terai, the midlands or Pahar zone, and the Himalaya. Each zone is dominated by characteristic ethnic groups whose agriculture and lifestyles are adapted to suit the physical constraints of their environment. (See earlier in this chapter under Geography for more detail about the physiographic features of each area.) These zones can be further subdivided from east to west, with different

Two-Legged Transport
Most ethnic groups are increasingly influenced by Indian and western fashions, so it is difficult to pick someone's ethnicity by their clothing. The method someone uses to carry a load, however, often provides an interesting clue. Mountain people carry goods in woven baskets (doko) on their backs, but suspended from a jute headband (namlo) worn around the top of the head.

The people from the valleys of the Middle Hills, especially the Newars, often carry loads slung on bamboo poles balanced across their shoulders. People of the plains, more particularly women, balance goods on their heads. And western travellers carry possessions in bags suspended from their shoulders! ■

groups in the east, central and western regions of each zone.

Zone	Western	Central	Eastern
Himalaya	Khas Bhotiya	Bhotiya	Bhotiya
Midlands	Khas	Magar Gurung Newar	Rai Limbu
Terai	Tharu Abadhi	Tharu Danuwar Bhojpuri	Danuwar Mithila

Himalayan Zone

In the Himalayan zone, the people are Mongoloids of Tibetan descent. They are known in Nepali as Bhotiya or Bhote, terms that are now often considered derogatory because the Shah and Rana regimes categorised Bhotiya as untouchables who could legally be enslaved.

Most Bhotiya identify with a particular region, and attach the suffix pa (people) to the name. These include the Sherpa, of the Everest region, the Manangpa of the Manang region north of the Annapurna Himal, and the Lopa, of the Mustang region. This group also includes Thakalis, the well known inn-keepers from the Thak Khola (Kali Gandaki) on the Jomsom Trek, and Tamangs, around the Kathmandu Valley and the Langtang region.

With a few exceptions in the far west, all these people are Buddhist and have a similar culture to Tibetans.

Midlands Zone

In the east of the midlands zone, one finds the Kirati (also known as Kiranti) people, who are divided into the Rai and Limbu groups. These groups are also Mongoloid peoples who speak Tibeto-Burman languages. Their religion is shamanistic – neither Buddhist nor Hindu – although Hinduism is becoming increasingly influential. They entered Nepal from the north and east and founded a kingdom in the Kath-mandu Valley around the 7th century BCE that continued for 1000 years. Independent Kirati kingdoms survived in the east until the end of the 18th century.

In the central midlands zone around the Kathmandu Valley live the Newars. Some believe the Newars are Kirati, others believe they are survivors from a still older group. They have absorbed successive waves of immigrants and created a religious environment that is in many ways a synthesis of Hinduism and Buddhism.

In the central midlands around the Kali Gandaki, the two main groups are the Magar and Gurung. Both groups are Mongoloid and speak Tibeto-Burman languages, which indicates they came from Tibet, although no-one knows when. The Gurungs tend to occupy middle elevations to the southern flanks of the Annapurna massif, while the Magars occupy lower elevations.

The Gurung's shamanistic religion is under pressure from Hinduism in the south and Buddhism in the north. The Magars have long been Hindu, and have developed close ties with the Indo-Aryan Khas, further to the west. In many cases they have taken the high-status Chhetri (Kshatriya) caste. Until the 18th century, Magar kingdoms dominated the region. The most famous was Palpa, with its capital at Tansen, which fought alongside Gorkha at the beginning of Prithvi Narayan Shah's expansionist wars. (See the History section.)

In the western midlands, the situation becomes confusing, partly because there are few written historical records and ethnicity becomes confused with caste. The area is dominated by Khas, an Indo-Aryan people whose language has evolved into present day Nepali. The numbers of Khas have been continually supplemented by the arrival of Parbatiyas (Hindus of varying caste and ethnicity) from the Indian plains. In the 12th century the Khas, who controlled a large empire, were joined by Bahun (Brahman) and Chhetri refugees from the Muslim invasion of India. Although the Khas were technically low caste, many were given the high Chhetri caste by the Bahun, and the children of Bahun men and Khas women were also made Chhetris.

The unusual fluidity of caste allowed ambitious families to adopt higher castes – the most powerful Chhetris from among the Khas and Magar became Thakuris. The Khas empire fragmented into many small kingdoms ruled by powerful families who further embellished their pedigrees by claiming royal antecedents in India. After Prithvi Narayan Shah's triumph, many Bahuns and Chhetris were rewarded with grants of land in central and eastern Nepal, and since then they have spread throughout the country. In the west, however, they are numerically dominant.

Terai Zone

Until the eradication of malaria in the 1950s the only people to live in the valleys of the Inner Terai, and along much of the length of the Terai proper, were Tharus and a few small, associated groups. Most Tharus, though not all, have a Mongoloid appearance. There is considerable speculation, but no hard facts about where they originated. Their religion is animist, with increasingly important Hindu overtones.

Along the Terai proper, a number of numerically significant groups straddle the border between India and Nepal. In the eastern Terai, Mithila people dominate; in the central Terai, Bhojpuri-speaking people dominate, and in the western Terai, Abadhi-speaking people are significant. All these are essentially cultures of the Gangetic plain, and Hindu caste structure is strictly upheld. In various parts, notably around Nepalganj and Lumbini, there are also large numbers of Muslims.

Since the Terai has been opened for development, it has also been settled by large numbers of people from the midlands – every group is represented.

Ethnic & Caste Groups

Sherpas Living high in the mountains of eastern and central Nepal, in particular in the Solu Khumbu region at the foot of Mt Everest, the Sherpas are probably the best

known Nepali ethnic group. Originally from Tibet, they settled in the area about 500 years ago, and were probably nomadic herders until the introduction of the potato in the middle of the 19th century. The relative increase in wealth that this new crop created allowed them to settle in permanent villages and to create a number of monasteries known as *gompas*.

The Sherpas are Buddhists, and this century their name has become synonymous with mountaineering and trekking. Not all sherpas – the small 's' word describes a trek guide or mountaineer – are Sherpas but many of them are and they've won worldwide fame for their skill, hardiness and loyalty.

Thakalis Originating along the Kali Gandaki Valley in central Nepal, the Thakalis are a Tibeto-Burman people who have become the entrepreneurs of Nepal. They honed these skills from the days when they played an important part in the salt trade between the subcontinent and Tibet but now they are found in many areas of modern commercial life. Originally Buddhist, many pragmatic Thakalis have now adopted Hinduism.

Most Thakalis are small farmers, but travellers will regularly meet them in their adopted roles as hoteliers. Many small hotels in Nepal are run by Thakalis; the Pokhara to Jomsom trek along the Kali Gandaki Valley is the best 'village inn' trek in Nepal, because of the numerous Thakali lodges along this route through their homeland. The actual number of Thakalis is very small.

Tamangs Tamangs are the largest Tibeto-Burman ethnic group in Nepal, but unlike many smaller groups, little is known of their history. Tamangs are now sedentary farmers and labourers. Their appearance, language and Buddhist beliefs all bear testimony to their origins. Indeed, many of the 'Tibetan' souvenirs for sale in Kathmandu are actually made by Tamangs.

Around half the Himalayan zone of Nepal is inhabited by Tamangs, and it is likely they have been there longer than any other group. Tamangs dominate the high hills surrounding the Kathmandu Valley and the central Himalayan zone, especially in the Langtang region. Unlike the Newars, their homesteads are often solitary. Houses may be constructed out of brick or stone, but they are often modest in size with a porch and courtyard, a mud finish and a thatched roof.

Many Tamangs have been influenced in their dress by both western and Newari styles. Traditionally, women wear a colourful wraparound skirt, a blouse, jacket and scarf. On important occasions they wear chunky gold or brass ear and nose rings set with semiprecious stones. Men wear loincloths or the traditional Newari pants, short-sleeved jackets and topis. Both men and women wear several metres of cloth wrapped around the waist.

Their religion is closely associated with Tibetan Buddhism (see the Religion section later in this chapter). Some Tamang follow Bon, the pre-Buddhist religion of Tibet. In Tamang areas you are certain to come across *chortens* (Buddhist shrines with a square base, topped with an onion-shaped dome), and *mani* walls. Manis are prayer stones engraved with mantras.

Tamangs are one of the largest groups in Nepal, but they have been seriously exploited, especially since the unification of Nepal under the Shahs. In the 19th century their legally defined status was the lowest of any hill people, and much of their land was distributed to Bahuns and Chhetris.

Tamangs were relegated to bonded labour, and were dependent on menial work, particularly as porters. They were prevented from joining the government or the military (unlike many other hill groups), and they remain, in general, extremely poor, and continue to work as *thela gada* (cart pushers), rickshaw pullers, auto-rickshaw drivers and porters. They produce more than 90% of the thangka paintings sold in Kathmandu, and 70% of Tibetan carpets. Many women have been forced into prostitution, both in Nepal and India.

Tibetans Mongoloid people from Tibet have settled in Nepal for thousands of years, but

the most recent arrivals have been refugees. In 1950 the communist People's Republic of China overpowered the Tibetan army. For the next eight years the Chinese made a heavy-handed attempt to bring the Tibetans into the communist fold, including the imposition of inappropriate agricultural policies that led to mass famine. In March 1959 a Tibetan uprising was brutally crushed, and the Dalai Lama, Tibet's spiritual and political leader fled to India. Thousands of Tibetans followed him across the Himalaya.

There are currently around 120,000 Tibetans in exile, and about 12,000 of them are in Nepal, mostly in Kathmandu and Pokhara. Although their numbers are only small, they have a high profile, partly because of the important role they play in tourism. Many hotels and restaurants in Kathmandu are owned or operated by Tibetans. They have also been responsible for the extraordinary success story of the Tibetan carpet industry, which has grown in 30 years from nothing to being the largest single employer in the country. (See the earlier Economy section.)

Tibetans are devout Buddhists and their arrival in the valley has rejuvenated a number of important religious sites, most notably the stupas at Swayambhunath and Bodhnath. A number of large new monasteries have been established.

Rai & Limbu These two large groups are known as Kirati people, the descendants of the Kiratis who formed the first recorded kingdom in the Kathmandu Valley. They now inhabit the eastern midlands, and many have migrated to the eastern Terai. Large numbers find employment with Gurkha regiments.

They are Tibeto-Burman people, but their traditional religion is distinct from either Buddhism or Hinduism, although Hinduism is exerting a growing influence. The traditional religion is entirely oral and is based on the periodic appeasement of ancestor divinities and nature spirits; there are priests, elders and shamans. Rais and Limbus both bury their dead. The Limbus use a common burial site and erect a whitewashed rectangular grave marker with three tiers for a female, four for men.

The Rais and Limbus cultivate wet and dry fields, and slash-and-burn shifting agriculture is still important in places. In the hills, most villages are scattered and the houses are small one storey edifices built of stone. Along the Arun River and in the Terai, the houses are often timber and bamboo, built on high wooden piles. In the Terai, these houses can be large, and are often surrounded by a verandah.

Newars The Newars of the Kathmandu Valley, who make up 5.6% of the total population, are a good example of the result of this Himalayan melting pot. They number about 600,000 and speak Newari, a language distinct from Tibetan, Nepali or Hindi, and they follow a version of Hinduism with many Buddhist overtones. See the Kathmandu, Patan & Bhaktapur chapter for more details.

Gurungs The Gurungs tend to live in higher country and generally further to the east than the Magars (see below), but otherwise are similar to them in many respects. Their homeland is the central midlands, ranging from Gorkha and Baglung to quite high on the southern slopes of the Annapurnas. They are a Tibeto-Burman people with a unique shamanistic religion that is gradually giving way to Hinduism and Buddhism.

They are farmers, raising rice, wheat, maize and millet. Sheep husbandry is also important, with village families contributing a handful of sheep to a larger village flock. During the summer months they move their sheep to higher pastures, then with the end of the monsoon they bring them down to the villages. Like the Magars, the Gurungs often work as Gurkha soldiers.

Magars A numerically large group (7.6% of the total population), the Magars are a Tibeto-Burman people who are found in many parts of the midlands zone of western and central Nepal. Until the 18th century

they had their own kingdoms, but they also had close contact with the Hindu Indo-Aryans in the west. This led to a gradual increase in Hindu influence and cultural assimilation. Nowadays in terms of religion, farming practices, housing and dress, they are hard to distinguish from Chhetris.

The Magars are farmers, and renowned soldiers; they fought with Prithvi Narayan Shah, and their kingdom of Palpa (based at Tansen) was one of the last to be incorporated into the new unified Nepal. Their martial qualities have been recognised by the British and Indian armies, since Magars are the single largest group in the Gurkha regiments. Gurkha earnings play an enormously important role, both in improving living standards in the villages, and in the Nepali economy as a whole.

The Magars generally live in two storey rectangular or square thatched houses washed in red clay. Historically, these houses were often round or oval in shape. The Magars also include Thakalis (see earlier in this section).

Bahuns & Chhetris In Hindu theory there is no relationship between caste and ethnicity, so Bahuns and Chhetris are simply the two highest castes (respectively the Brahman priests and Kshatriya warriors). In Nepal, however, most are from the Khas kingdoms that flourished in western Nepal for at least a millennia before the unification of Nepal. Today they account for 29% of the total population.

The Khas are Indo-Aryans who migrated to Nepal over the centuries; in the Middle Ages their numbers, and their consciousness of caste, were supplemented by refugees from the Muslim invasions of India. The progeny of Bahun men and hill women were considered Chhetri, and a number of high-status families from other hill groups have also adopted Chhetri status, so some do have Mongoloid tribal ancestry.

Bahuns and Chhetris played an important role in the court and armies of Prithvi Narayan Shah, and after unification they were rewarded with lands throughout the country. The Khas' language, Khas Kura, became the national language Nepali, and the position of Bahuns and Chhetris at the top of the heap was religiously, culturally and legally enforced. Ever since, they have dominated the processes of government in Kathmandu.

Outside the valley, the majority of Bahuns and Chhetris, however, are simple peasant farmers, indistinguishable in most respects from their neighbours. Sometimes their wealth is reflected by relatively large houses (compared to those of neighbouring tribal groups). Most live in two storey stone or mud-brick thatched houses that are washed with lime or red ochre. Many had roles as tax collectors under the Shah and Rana regimes, and to this day many are moneylenders with a great deal of power.

All Bahuns and Chhetris are Hindu, but the Bahuns tend to be more caste-conscious and orthodox than other Nepali Hindus and this sometimes creates difficulties in their relationship with 'untouchable' westerners. Many are vegetarians and do not drink alcohol; marriages are arranged within the caste.

There is no particular dress by which they can be recognised but men in both castes wear a sacred thread – the *janai* (see Janai Purnima under Public Holidays & Special Events in the Facts for the Visitor chapter).

Tharus Tharus are one of the largest ethnic groups in Nepal. The original inhabitants of the Terai, they are now often heavily exploited by newly arrived hill people, or *zamindars* (moneylenders). Many have been forced by debt into a form of bonded labour (the *kamaiya* system) little different to slavery. They are generally Mongoloid in appearance, and have an animist religion that is increasingly influenced by Hinduism. See the Terai chapter for more information.

EDUCATION

While education is gradually spreading to the small villages, it has been a slow process, especially in the mountains. At 74%, the illiteracy rate in the country is uncomfortably high.

In recent years the education system has been thrown open to private enterprise. This has led to a dramatic increase in the number of schools – seemingly every town you pass through has a high number of 'English Medium Boarding Schools'. On the surface this is a good thing, but unfortunately the reality is somewhat less encouraging. With profit being the bottom line of any business, it seems many of these schools are business ventures first and foremost; the education side of things comes a poor second. Parents have to pay anything from Rs 90 to Rs 150 a month for their children to attend such schools.

It is a sad fact that the standard of education offered by the free government schools is also lacking.

ARTS

The whole Kathmandu Valley is really one enormous art gallery and museum, and the arts and architecture in Nepal are inextricably intermingled. The finest woodcarving and the best sculpture are often part of a building – a temple is simply not a temple without its finely carved roof struts. The crafts also reflect the uniquely Nepali melting pot where religious art has Tantric Hindu and Buddhist overtones and the dividing line between one religion and another is hard to discern.

Lydia Aran's *The Art of Nepal* is a handy and interesting introduction to Nepali art and its religious background. There are detailed descriptions of the many Hindu, Buddhist and Hindu-Buddhist deities and their associated religious terminology. This book is particularly interesting because it concentrates on the art still in Nepal, as opposed to objects in overseas museums and private collections.

Architecture & Sculpture

The earliest architecture in the valley has faded with history. The four Ashoka stupas of Patan are simply grassy mounds today and the great stupas of Swayambhunath and Bodhnath have undoubtedly changed many times over the centuries. Nevertheless these simple hemispherical Buddhist structures are essentially unchanged from their earliest appearance – they're simply a solid mound rising from the ground and topped with a spire. You can find similar Buddhist stupas in Sri Lanka, Myanmar (Burma) and Thailand.

The Licchavi period from the 4th to 9th centuries CE was a golden age for Nepal and while the temples may have disappeared the superb stone sculptures can still be found. Many temples around the valley have beautiful pieces of Licchavi craftwork in their courtyards, the temple of Changu Narayan at the eastern end of the valley in particular. The great reclining Vishnu image at Budhanilkantha is another wonderful example of Licchavi stonework. The Licchavis undoubtedly worked in wood as well but no wooden buildings or carvings survive from that era.

It was in the Malla period that Nepali artistry with wood really came into its own. The earliest woodcarving in the valley dates from the 12th and 13th centuries and includes the roof struts of the great Basantapur Tower in the old Royal Palace in Kathmandu's Durbar Square, and the Kasthamandap building, also in the square. The Uku Bahal monastery in Patan also dates from this period but you have to go out of the valley to Panauti, near Banepa, to find one of the oldest and finest survivors in the shape of the Indreshwar Mahadev Temple.

The artistic skills of the Newar people of the valley flourished under the Mallas and not only woodcarving but metalwork, terra-

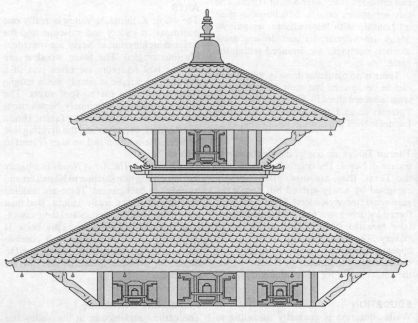

The historic double-roofed temple of Changu Narayan incorporates elements of the Licchavi golden age in its courtyard craftwork.

cotta, brickwork, stone sculptures and other crafts all enjoyed a long golden age. The finest metalwork includes the images of the two Tara goddesses at Swayambhunath and the river goddesses Ganga and Jamuna, standing guard in the palace of Patan.

The spread of the multi-roofed Nepali pagoda design to China and eastern Asia is credited to the architect Arniko, who with 24 assistants visited Tibet in the late 13th century and later also worked for the Ming emperor. The road to the Tibetan border is named the Arniko Highway in his honour. The contact with Tibet also began to make its way back to Nepal and vivid Tibetan colours and fantastic Tibetan creatures also started to appear in Nepali art and architecture.

The last centuries of the Malla period saw temple after temple rise over the Kathmandu Valley skyline. The squabbling city-states of Kathmandu, Patan and Bhaktapur vied with each other to raise yet more glorious temples and palaces. Much of the construction was still in the traditional multi-roofed Nepali pagoda style but there was also a great deal of Indian influence, such as the stone Krishna Mandir of Patan's Durbar Square or the spires of the Mahabouddha Temple in Patan and the two temples at the top of the stairway to Swayambhunath.

With the invasion of the valley by King Prithvi Narayan Shah from Gorkha, the great age of Nepali architecture came to a dramatic end. The great woodcarved temples and palaces you marvel at in the valley today mainly date from that brilliant period prior to 1767. Although the skills used to build them have lain dormant in the centuries since then, there is no doubt that these skills are still present. When the Hanuman Dhoka palace in Kathmandu and the Tachupal Tole buildings in Bhaktapur were restored in the 1970s the work was performed by purely traditional means and with craftwork every bit as good as in the past. More recently the Chyasilin Mandapa in Bhaktapur, completely destroyed in the great earthquake of 1934, was totally rebuilt in 1989-90, again using traditional skills.

Painting

Nepal has a long history of painting and some high-quality traditional work is still being done today. The earliest Newari paintings were illuminated manuscripts dating from the 11th century and these were followed by miniature paintings influenced by the miniature styles of northern India, and then by scrolls and murals. By this time the Tibetan influence was starting to make itself felt on Newari painting, although from the 14th to 16th centuries the Newars also had a great influence on Tibetan art.

Today some of the best examples of old Newari painting are hung in temples where they are rarely seen, but the art gallery in Bhaktapur has a fine collection and is an excellent introduction to the development of art in Nepal. Newari artists have their own special caste of Chitrakar. For more information on painting in Nepal today see Thangkas in the Things to Buy section in the Facts for the Visitor chapter.

Music & Dance

Despite the pervasiveness of western music, Nepali music hangs constantly in the air, whether it is the plaintive notes of a flute or the gentle twang of the four stringed *saringhi*. Although the *gaines*, traditional professional musicians, are a dying breed they can still be heard. The folk music of rural Nepal still has a strong following and the gaines are often as much storytellers as musicians.

The *damais* are modern professional musicians, all drawn from the tailor caste, who form the backbone of wedding bands. This music can definitely be hard on western ears, falling uncomfortably close to the painful standards of Indian video-bus music. The blaring wail of long Tibetan horns at Buddhist religious sites probably also qualifies for the unlistenable category.

Dance also has a long and strong history in Nepal both in cheerfully performed folk dances and in the more formal classical dances. The Newars of the Kathmandu Valley are the chief exponents of classical dancing, but there are also masked dances with a Tantric background, and the colourful masked dances of Bhaktapur which are performed during the Indra Jatra festival each year.

Some of the more important traditional dances include: Bajrayogini, based on Tantric Buddhism; Bhairavkali, a classical dance of Shiva and Kali; Bhojpuri, a popular dance from the Terai; Jhagad, from the eastern Terai; Lakhe, a mask dance of the Newars; and Sangini, which is a prayer dance from the women of the Bahun-Chhetri.

SOCIETY & CONDUCT
Nepal has always been a dividing line between civilisations and cultures, and a crossroads for the flow of commerce and culture. Here the plains of the subcontinent climb up to the high plateau of Tibet, the languages and people of India give way to those of China, and the Hindu religion blends into Buddhism. Nepal, the land at the margin, is often a complex blend of the two influences and this variation is further complicated by the diversity of ethnic groups within the country.

Cultural Considerations
The challenge for you as a visitor to Nepal is to respect the rights and beliefs of the local people, and to minimise your impact – culturally and environmentally. Remember Nepal is not an adventure park or museum established for your convenience, but home to a vital, changing culture. Life for many is extremely hard, but despite the scarcity of material possessions, there are many qualities that shame the so-called 'developed' world.

Your very presence in Nepal will have an effect – an increasing number of people say a negative one. In a totally different culture it is also inevitable that the visitor will make some gaffe at some point. Most Nepalis make allowances, but they do appreciate it when a genuine effort is made to observe local customs. Following is a miscellaneous collection of simple suggestions that will help avoid offence.

Dress
- Always remove your shoes before entering a Nepali home.
- Dress appropriately – shorts or revealing clothes are never suitable for women. Shorts are acceptable for men only when trekking; going without a shirt anywhere is not. Nudity is not acceptable anywhere.

Behaviour
- Public displays of affection are frowned upon. Nepali men often walk around hand in hand, but this does not have the same implications as it does in San Francisco!
- Raising your voice or shouting shows extreme bad manners and will not solve your problem, whatever it might be. Always try to remain cool, calm and collected.
- Bodily contact is rarely made, even for shaking hands, although amongst Nepali men with frequent western connections it is becoming more accepted. Never touch anything or point at anything with your feet, the 'lowest' part of the body. In contrast the head is spiritually the 'highest' part of the body, so don't pat children on the head.
- Don't inquire about a person's caste.
- The Nepalis do not like to give negative answers or no answer at all: if you are given a wrong direction or told a place is much nearer than it turns out to be, it may be through fear of disappointing you!
- Don't encourage begging children. If you want to help there are lots of excellent aid organisations which will make good use of your contribution and local schools will be only too happy with a gift of ballpoint pens. See the following information on Begging in this chapter for more information.

Visiting a Temple
- Always walk clockwise around Buddhist stupas, chortens or mani walls. Always remove your shoes before entering a Buddhist or Hindu temple or sanctuary. You may also have to remove any items made from leather, such as belts and bags. Many Hindu temples do not permit westerners to enter.
- It's the custom to give a white scarf or khata to a Buddhist abbot when you are introduced. The honorific title Rimpoche (which means 'precious one') is usually bestowed on abbots. The scarves can easily be found at Tibetan shops.

Visiting a Nepali Home
- Fire is sacred so do not throw rubbish into it. This particularly applies to a kitchen fire in a Nepali home and theoretically should apply to a camping site fire when trekking as well. In practice, burning the garbage before leaving camp is accepted, but it's probably best to wait until just before leaving

Begging

Begging of various kinds is relatively common in Nepal, partly because both Hinduism and Buddhism encourage the giving of alms. This presents many visitors with a heart-rending moral dilemma. Should you give? Sometimes, especially if you've just spent Rs 500 (around US$10) on drinks, it seems grotesque to ignore someone who is genuinely in need. It is often worth checking to see how the local Nepalis react; if they give, it's a reasonably safe assumption that the beneficiary is genuine.

Around the main religious shrines, especially Pashupatinath, there are long lines of beggars. Pilgrims customarily give a coin to everyone in the line (there are special moneychangers nearby who will change notes for small-denomination coins). This is a culturally sanctioned and traditional form, but most westerners find it difficult to deal with, and are not really expected to give. Sadhus are another special case, and are usually completely dependent on alms. There are plenty of con men amongst their ranks, but equally, plenty of genuine holy men.

The main tourist centres, especially Thamel and Durbar Marg, have also attracted numbers of beggars. Here, westerners are expected to give, although whether they should is another matter.

Thamel attracts many of Kathmandu's estimated 1000 street kids. Giving to them, however, is, at best, a double-edged sword. Firstly, the lure of easy money actually attracts kids onto the streets in the first place, and then gives them a powerful incentive to remain. Secondly, it's a dog-eat-dog world, and if a child is seen receiving money, he may well be beaten up and have it stolen.

If you do want to give in this case, it is immensely preferable to give a donation to Child Workers in Nepal, an excellent organisation known as CWIN. This is a nongovernmental organisation that was established by graduates from Tribhuvan University in 1987. Apart from actively campaigning for children's rights, it has established a common room where street children are given a locker (essential if they are going to accumulate any possessions or money), counselling, medical care, literacy classes, a midday meal and entertainment facilities. CWIN runs a programme called Friends of CWIN (☎ 01-271658, 270336), which encourages various forms of voluntary participation. The common room is off Tripureshwar Marg, and can be contacted through PO Box 4374, Kaumati, Kathmandu.

Also highly visible are women, usually clutching one or two children. Rumours suggest that these women are often part of organised begging rings, and that the money they receive is passed on to a Fagan figure. By giving to them, you are encouraging a further influx of people into Kathmandu where very few facilities exist for them. In this case, your money could be profitably used by a number of craft shops that specialise in marketing handicrafts produced by low-income women. These are nonprofit development organisations, so the money actually goes to the craftspeople in the form of fair wages (as opposed to charity), and also in training, product development, and rehabilitation programmes.

One of the best of these organisations is Mahaguthi (☎ 01-521493), PO Box 396, Kathmandu, which was established with the help of Oxfam. It now has three shops and sells a wide range of crafts produced by thousands of people. Among other things it runs a programme to rehabilitate destitute women and children.

Dhankuta Sisters is an outlet for women from the eastern hills, and Dhukuti also works with low-income women. Mahaguthi and Dhukuti have shops on the way to Patan, in Kopundol, just beyond the bridge over the Bagmati River, and Dhukuti has another outlet at Lakeside in Pokhara.

Actually in Patan, near the well known Kumbeshwar Temple, the Kumbeshwar Technical School (☎ 01-522271), PO Box 2181, Kathmandu, was established to help provide the untouchable community of Patan with skills. They now produce excellent carpets, jumpers and woodwork. See the Kathmandu and Patan Things to Buy sections for more information.

Although the blind and lepers are probably genuinely dependent on begging for their survival, long-term solutions are offered by the Nepal Eye Programme – Australia (NEPA; ☎ 01-474685), PO Box 561, Kathmandu; and the Leprosy Hospital (☎ 01-290545), PO Box 151, Anandban, Kathmandu.

NEPA is an innovative and effective programme well known to most Australians because of the involvement of the late Professor Fred Hollows. Many forms of blindness are dealt with in rural clinics; often, relatively simple treatments and surgical techniques can restore people's sight. NEPA has opened a factory in Nepal which manufactures the plastic lenses used in cataract operations. Excess production will be exported to India and China and any profits will be ploughed back into the programme, hopefully making it self-sustaining. In the meantime, NEPA can do with donations.

In the countryside, visitors will quickly be discovered by small children who chant a mantra that sounds something like: 'bonbonpenonerupeeee?'. Someone, somewhere started giving children sweets (bonbons), pens and money, and it sometimes seems that every child in Nepal now tries their luck. Do not encourage this behaviour. Most Nepalis find it offensive and demeaning (as do most visitors), and it encourages a whole range of unhealthy attitudes.

See the Kathmandu Information section for a list of some nongovernmental organisations to which you can make donations. ■

camp before doing it, certainly not before cooking. In a Nepali home the kitchen is off limits to strangers.

Avoid 'polluting' food by inadvertently touching it or bringing it into contact with a used plate or utensil. Using your own fork or spoon to serve out more food will do this. Putting your used plate on a buffet table risks making the food still on the table *jutho* or polluted. Notice how Nepalis drink from a cup or water vessel without letting it touch their lips.

Photography
Do not intrude with a camera, unless it is clearly OK with the people you are photographing. Ask before entering a temple compound whether it is permissible to enter and take photographs. Do not exchange addresses or offer copies of photos unless you definitely intend to follow it up later.

RELIGION
In Nepal, Hinduism and Buddhism are mingled into a complex blend which is often impossible to separate. The Buddha was actually born in Nepal but the Buddhist religion first arrived in the country around 250 BCE, introduced, so it is said, by the great Indian Buddhist emperor Ashoka himself. Later, Buddhism gave way to Hinduism but from around the 8th century CE the Tantric form of Buddhism practised in Tibet also began to make its way across the Himalaya into Nepal. Today Buddhism is mainly practised by the people of the high Himalaya, like the Sherpas and Tamangs, and by the Tibetan refugees who have settled in Nepal.

Officially Nepal is a Hindu country but in practice the religion is a strange blend of Hindu and Buddhist beliefs with a pantheon of Tantric deities tagged onto the list of Hindu gods or, in many cases, inextricably blended with them. Thus Avalokitesvara, the prime Bodhisattva of this Buddhist era, becomes Lokesvara, a manifestation of the Hindu god Shiva, and then appears as Machhendranath, one of the most popular gods of the Kathmandu Valley. Is he Hindu or Buddhist? Nobody can tell.

Although the vast majority of the population is Hindu or Buddhist (around 95%) there are also small groups of Muslims (3.5%) and Christians (0.2%).

Hinduism
India, Bali, Mauritius and possibly Fiji are the only places apart from Nepal where Hindus predominate, but it is the largest religion in Asia in terms of the number of adherents. Hinduism is one of the oldest extant religions with firm roots extending back to beyond 1000 BCE.

The Indus Valley civilisation developed a religion which shows a close relationship to Hinduism in many ways. Later, it further developed on the subcontinent through the combined religious practices of the Dravidians and the Aryan invaders who arrived in northern India around 1500 BCE. Around 1000 BCE, the Vedic scriptures were introduced and gave the first loose framework to the religion.

Hinduism today has a number of holy books, the most important being the four *Vedas*, or 'Divine Knowledge', which are the foundation of Hindu philosophy. The *Upanishads* are contained within the *Vedas* and delve into the metaphysical nature of the universe and soul. The *Mahabharata* is an epic poem describing in over 220,000 lines the battles between the Kauravas and Pandavas. It contains the story of Rama, and it is probable that the most famous Hindu epic, the *Ramayana*, was based on this. The *Bhagavad Gita* is a famous episode of the *Mahabharata* where Krishna relates his philosophies to Arjuna.

Hinduism postulates that we will all go through a series of rebirths or reincarnations that eventually lead to *moksha*, the spiritual salvation which frees one from the cycle of rebirths. With each rebirth you can move closer to or further from eventual moksha; the deciding factor is your *karma*, which is literally a law of cause and effect. Bad actions during your life result in bad karma, which ends in a lower reincarnation. Conversely, if your deeds and actions have been good you will reincarnate on a higher level and be a step closer to eventual freedom from rebirth.

Dharma is the natural law which defines the total social, ethical and spiritual harmony of your life. There are three categories of

RICHARD I'ANSON

TONY WHEELER   RICHARD EVERIST   TONY WHEELER

RICHARD I'ANSON

Top: Women of Sibaghat
Centre: (left to right) Erotic art, female image, Jal Binayak, Chobar; Colourful offerings at
Pashupatinath; Erotic art, couple, Jal Binayak, Chobar.
Bottom: Painting the town red and yellow and blue...Holi festival, Kathmandu

SONIA BERTO

PAUL STEEL

DAVID ALLARDICE

PAUL STEEL

RICHARD l'ANSON

Top: Men of Patan having a good yak.
Centre: (left to right) Monk at Swayambhunath; Young boy; Braid vendor, Kathmandu
Bottom: Almost medieval village scene in the Kathmandu Valley

dharma, the first being the eternal harmony which involves the whole universe. The second category is the dharma that controls castes and the relations between castes. The third dharma is the moral code which an individual should follow.

The Hindu religion has three basic practices. They are *puja* or worship, the cremation of the dead, and the rules and regulations of the caste system. There are four main castes: the Brahman, or priest caste; the Kshatriya, or soldiers and governors; the Vaisyas, or tradespeople and farmers; and the Sudras or menial workers and craftspeople. These castes are then subdivided, although this is not taken to the same extreme in Nepal as in India. Beneath all the castes are the Harijans, or untouchables, the lowest, casteless class for whom all the most menial and degrading tasks are reserved.

Westerners may have trouble understanding Hinduism principally because of its vast pantheon of gods. In fact you can look upon all these different gods simply as pictorial representations of the many attributes of a god. The one omnipresent god usually has three physical representations: Brahma is the creator, Vishnu is the preserver and Shiva is the destroyer and reproducer. All three gods are usually shown with four arms, but Brahma has the added advantage of four heads.

Each god has an associated animal known as the 'vehicle' on which they ride, as well as a consort with certain attributes and abilities. Generally each god also holds symbols. You can often pick out which god is represented by identifying either the vehicle or the symbols.

Most temples are dedicated to one or other of the gods, but most Hindus profess to be either Vaishnavites (followers of Vishnu) or Shaivites (followers of Shiva). A variety of lesser gods and goddesses also crowd the scene. The cow is, of course, the holy animal of Hinduism.

Hinduism is not a proselytising religion since you cannot be converted. You're either born a Hindu or you are not; you can never become one. Similarly, once you are a Hindu you cannot change your caste – you're born into it and are stuck with it for the rest of that lifetime. Nevertheless Hinduism has a great attraction for many westerners and India's 'export gurus' are numerous and successful.

Hanuman & Medicine

Hanuman the monkey god has an important medicinal connection in Nepal and other Hindu countries. The *Ramayana* recounts how Rama desperately needed a rare herb grown only in the Himalaya and sent Hanuman to procure it for him. Unfortunately by the time he arrived in the mountains Hanuman had forgotten specifically which herb he had been requested to bring back, but got around the problem by simply grabbing a whole mountain, confident that somewhere on the mountain would be the required plant.

On the walls of the Bir Hospital in Kathmandu you can see a large illustration of Hanuman flying through the air, tightly clasping a whole mountain. It's said that he paused for a rest on the banks of the Hanumante River in Bhaktapur and a picture of this event can also be seen there. ■

A guru is not so much a teacher as a spiritual guide, somebody who by example or simply by their presence indicates what path you should follow. In a spiritual search one always needs a guru. A sadhu is an individual on a spiritual search. They're an easily recognised group, usually wandering around half-naked, smeared in dust with their hair and beard matted.

Buddhism

Strictly speaking, Buddhism is not a religion, since it is not centred on a god, but a system of philosophy and a code of morality. Bud-

dhism was founded in northern India about 500 BCE when Siddhartha Gautama, born a prince, achieved enlightenment. According to some, Gautama Buddha was not the first Buddha but the fourth, and neither is he expected to be the last 'enlightened one'. Buddhists believe that the achievement of enlightenment is the goal of every being so eventually we will all reach buddhahood.

The Buddha never wrote down his dharma or teachings, and a schism later developed so that today there are two major Buddhist schools. The Theravada (doctrine of the elders) or Hinayana holds that the path to

Sadhus

Sadhus are often people who have decided that their business and family life have reached their natural conclusions and that it is time to throw everything aside and go out on a spiritual search. They may have been anything from the village postal worker, to a wealthy business person. While many sadhus are, of course, completely genuine in their search, others are simply beggars and con men following a more sophisticated approach to gathering in the *paisa*.

Sadhus perform various feats of self-mortification and wander all over the subcontinent, occasionally coming together in pilgrimages and other religious gatherings *(melas)*. Most sadhus follow Shiva and are known as Shaivas, but there are also those who follow Vishnu and are known as Vaishnavas.

The sadhus you see around Pashupatinath are Shaivas, and can be further recognised by Shiva's symbol, the trident, which they carry. Shaivas apply lines *(tilaka)* to their foreheads in horizontal stripes. Vaishnavas are numerous at Janakpur. They don't carry a symbol but the tilaka on their forehead consists of vertical lines – sometimes three vertical lines that look confusingly like a trident. ∎

nirvana, the eventual aim of all Buddhists, is an individual pursuit. In contrast, the Mahayana school holds that the combined belief of its followers will eventually be great enough to encompass all of humanity and bear it to salvation. To some, the less austere and ascetic Mahayana school is considered a 'soft option'. Today it is chiefly practised in Vietnam, Japan and China, while the Hinayana school is followed in Sri Lanka, Myanmar and Thailand. There are still other, sometimes more esoteric, divisions of Buddhism, including the Hindu-Tantric Buddhism of Tibet, which is the version found in Nepal.

The Buddha renounced his material life to search for enlightenment but, unlike other prophets, found that starvation did not lead to discovery. Therefore he developed his rule of the 'middle way', meaning moderation in all things. The Buddha taught that all life is suffering, but that suffering comes from our sensual desires and the illusion that they are important. By following the 'eightfold path' these desires will be extinguished and a state of nirvana, where they are extinct and we are free from their delusions, will be reached. Following this process requires going through a series of rebirths until the goal is eventually reached and no more rebirths into the world of suffering are necessary. The path that takes you through this cycle of births is karma, but this is not simply fate. Karma is a law of cause and effect; your actions in one life determine the role you will play and what you will have to go through in your next life.

In India, Buddhism developed rapidly when it was embraced by the great emperor Ashoka. As his empire extended over much of the subcontinent, so Buddhism was carried forth. Later, however, Buddhism began to contract in India because it had never really taken a hold on the great mass of people. As Hinduism revived, Buddhism in India was gradually reabsorbed into the older religion.

Tibetan Buddhism There are four major schools of Tibetan Buddhism and all of them

are represented in the Kathmandu Valley: Nyingmapa, Kargyupa, Sakyapa and Gelugpa. The differences are quite esoteric with their roots often in political as well as major theological disputes.

The Indian sage Padmasambhava (also known as Guru Rimpoche) is credited with establishing Buddhism in Tibet in the 8th century, when he helped build a gompa at Samye. The Nyingmapa order, sometimes referred to as the Old One, traces its origins back to Padmasambhava. The Kargyupa (whispered transmission) order was established by Marpa in the 11th century and has a strong Tantric influence. Marpa's most famous disciple was Milarepa, Tibet's most revered poet.

The Sakyapa was also founded in the 11th century and rose to a position where it ruled Tibet (with the support of the Mongols) until it came into conflict with the Gelugpa (virtuous) order, which had been founded in the 14th century by Tsongkhapa.

The Gelugpa were celibate and advocated monastic discipline. The school introduced the system of reincarnated spiritual leaders and ultimately came to power – again with the support of the Mongols – in the late 17th century. It was a Mongol ruler who conferred the title Dalai Lama (ocean of wisdom) on its leader. The Gelugpa completely isolated Tibet and maintained a strict theocratic state.

In some texts, Tibetan Buddhism may be referred to as Lamaism, and the Gelugpa are known (for obvious reasons) as the Yellow Hats, while the other schools are sometimes collectively identified as the Red Hats.

Islam

Nepal's small population of Muslims (around 750,000 people, or 3.5% of the total population) originated from different parts of Asia, and today are mainly found close to the border with India and in a handful of isolated villages.

The first Muslims, who were mostly Kashmiri traders, arrived in the Kathmandu Valley in the 15th century. A second group arrived in the 17th century from northern

The Gods of Nepal
There are so many gods and related auspicious beings in Nepal that being able to identify some of them makes understanding and enjoying Nepali culture much easier. The definitions that follow include the most interesting and most frequently encountered 'big names' plus associated creatures, consorts, vehicles and religious terminology.

Incarnations, Manifestations & Aspects There's a subtle difference between these three possibilities. Vishnu has incarnations, 10 of them in all. They include Narsingha the man-lion, Krishna the cowherd and Buddha the teacher. Shiva, on the other hand, may be the god of 1000 names but these are manifestations – what he shows himself as – not incarnations. When you start to look at the Buddhist 'gods' their various appearances are aspects rather than incarnations or manifestations.

Vehicles Each of the gods is associated with a particular animal which can either be an attendant or a vehicle on which the god may ride. These creatures are a clue to identifying a god. Vishnu's vehicle, for example, is the man-bird Garuda and the winged kneeling figure of Garuda in front of a temple usually indicates that it is a Vishnu temple. Similarly elephant-headed Ganesh's creature is the rat or shrew and a statue of a rat will indicate that you are in a Ganesh shrine.

Other vehicles include an elephant, which is the vehicle of Indra, the king of the Vedic gods. Agni, the Vedic god of fire, has a chariot drawn by parrots while Vasudhara, the wife of Jambhala the god of wealth, has a chariot drawn by a pig! Yama the god of death is accompanied by a crow. Ganesh's brother Kartikkaya, the god of war, has a cock. Brahma's consort Saraswati has a swan.

Shiva

Shiva Shiva is probably the most important god in Nepal – as creator and destroyer – so it's important to keep on his good side! Shiva is often represented by the phallic *lingam*, symbolic of his creative role. His vehicle is the bull Nandi and you'll often see this figure outside Shiva temples; there's a huge Nandi guarding the entrance to Pashupatinath. The symbol most often seen in Shiva's hand is the trident or *trisul*. Sadhus, the wandering pilgrims who are often followers of Shiva, frequently carry a trident.

Shiva is also known as Nataraja, the cosmic dancer whose dance shook the cosmos and created the world. Shiva's home is Mt Kailash in the Himalaya, but across the border in Tibet, and he's also supposed to be keen on smoking hashish. He takes various forms including peaceful Pashupati and destructive Bhairab.

Bhairab In Nepal Shiva appears as Bhairab when he is in his fearful or 'terrific' form. Bhairab can appear in 64 different ways but none of them are pretty. Typically he has multiple arms, each clutching a weapon, he dances on a body and wears a headdress of skulls. More skulls dangle from his belt, and his staring eyes and bared fangs complete the picture. Bhairab is usually black, carries a cup made from a human skull and is attended by a dog. The gruesome figure of Bhairab near the Hanuman Dhoka palace entrance in Kathmandu is a good example of this fearsome god at his worst.

Pashupati In the Kathmandu Valley Shiva is most popularly worshipped as Pashupati, the lord of the beasts. As the keeper of all living things Pashupati is Shiva in a good mood and the temple of Pashupatinath is the most important Hindu temple in the country.

Shakti While Shakti the goddess is Shiva's consort, *shakti* is the creative/reproductive energy of the gods which often manifests in their consorts. A Hindu god's consort is also known as his shakti, as she is far more than just a companion. A shakti often symbolises certain parts of a god's personality, so while Shiva is the god of both creation and destruction it is often his shakti Parvati, manifesting as Kali or Durga, who handles the destructive business and demands the blood sacrifices; these are usually made not to the male but to the female and must be of male animals. She is also the energetic and dominant partner in their sexual relationship, and shakti has come to mean any goddess in her energetic and dynamic mode.

The Kathmandu Valley has numerous shrines and temples dedicated to the great goddesses including four shrines dedicated to the Joginis, the mystical goddesses who are the female counterpart to the Bhairabs. These shrines are found near Sankhu at the eastern end of the valley, at Guhyeshwari near Pashupatinath, at Pharping and at Vijeshwari. Another group of four temples are known as *varahis* and are dedicated to shaktis as ohe-boars. Other shrines to goddesses are dedicated to the Ashta Matrikas, mother goddesses.

Parvati Shiva's shakti is Parvati the beautiful and she is the dynamic element in their relationship. Just as Shiva is also known as Mahadev, the Great God, so she is Mahadevi, the Great Goddess. Just as Shiva is often symbolised by the phallic lingam so his shakti's symbol is the *yoni*, representing the female sex organ. Their relationship is a sexual one and it is often Parvati who is the energetic and dominant partner.

Shiva's shakti has as many forms as the Great God himself. She may be peaceful Parvati but she may also be fearsome Kali, the black goddess, or Durga, the terrible. In these terrific forms she holds a variety of weapons in her 10 hands, struggles with demons and rides a lion. As Kali, the fiercest of the gods and goddesses, she demands sacrifices and wears a garland of skulls. The festival of Dasain, celebrated in her honour, is characterised by the sacrifice of animals.

Machhendranath Machhendranath is a strictly Nepali Hindu god who has power over the rains and the monsoon. It's typical of the intermingling of Hindu and Buddhist beliefs in Nepal that, in the Kathmandu Valley at least, Machhendranath has come to be thought of as an incarnation of Avalokitesvara, the Bodhisattva of our era. In actual fact the connection from Avalokitesvara to Machhendranath is not quite so direct. Purely Buddhist Avalokitesvara is linked with Shiva through Lokesvara, the lord of the world. Machhendranath is then a manifestation of Lokesvara.

Ganesh With his elephant head Ganesh is probably the most easily recognised of the gods and also the most popular. Ganesh is the god of prosperity and wisdom and there are many Ganesh shrines and temples in Nepal. Ganesh's parents are Shiva and Parvati and he obtained his elephant head due to his father's notorious temper. Coming back from a long trip, Shiva discovered Parvati in bed with a young man. Not pausing to think that their son might have grown up a little during his absence, Shiva lopped his head off! He was then forced by Parvati to bring his son back to life but could only do so by giving him the head of the first living thing he saw – which happened to be an elephant.

Shiva and Parvati's other son is Kumar, the god of war. He is also known as Kartikkaya.

Hanuman Hanuman is the monkey god, the important character from the *Ramayana* who came to the aid of Rama and helped to defeat the evil Rawana and release Sita from his grasp. Hanuman's trustworthy and alert nature is commemorated by the many statues of Hanuman seen guarding palace entrances. The best known in Nepal is the image of Hanuman

Parvati

Ganesh

which stands beside the old Royal Palace entrance in Kathmandu, and indeed gives the old palace its name of Hanuman Dhoka.

Vishnu

Krishna

Vishnu Vishnu is the preserver, although in Nepal, where he often appears as Narayan, he also plays a role in the original creation of the universe. Narayan is the reclining Vishnu, sleeping on the cosmic ocean, and from his navel appears Brahma, who creates the universe.

Vishnu has four arms and can often be identified by the symbols he holds – the conch shell or *sankha*, the disc-like weapon known as a *chakra*, the stick-like weapon known as a *gada* and a lotus flower or *padma*. Vishnu's vehicle is the faithful man-bird Garuda and a winged Garuda will often be seen kneeling reverently in front of a Vishnu temple – Garuda has an intense hatred of snakes and is often seen destroying them. Vishnu's shakti is Lakshmi, the goddess of wealth and prosperity.

Vishnu has 10 incarnations starting with Matsya, the fish. Then he appeared as Kurma, the tortoise on which the universe is built. Number three was his boar incarnation as Varaha, who destroyed a demon who would have drowned the world. Vishnu was again in a demon-destroying mood in incarnation four as Narsingha (or Narsimha), half man and half lion. See the Changu Narayan section in the Around the Kathmandu Valley chapter for the legend behind this appearance. Narsingha statues often show a man with a lion's head and four arms holding the traditional Vishnu symbols. On the man-lion's lap will be the demon which Narsingha is about to disembowel.

Still facing difficulties from demons, Vishnu's next incarnation was Vamana, the dwarf who reclaimed the world from the demon-king Bali. The dwarf politely asked the demon for a patch of ground upon which to meditate, saying that the patch need only be big enough that he, the dwarf, could walk across it in three paces. The demon agreed, only to see the dwarf swell into a giant who strode across the universe in three gigantic steps. Vishnu as the 'long strider' is often seen with his left leg raised, just about to take a mighty step.

In his sixth incarnation Vishnu appeared as Parasurama, a warlike Brahman who proceeded to put the warrior caste Chhetris in their place. The noble Rajputs of India's state of Rajasthan claim they are descended from the survivors of this clash with a god.

Incarnation seven was as Rama, the hero of the *Ramayana* who, with help from Hanuman the monkey god, rescued his beautiful wife Sita from the clutches of Rawana, evil king of Lanka. See the Janakpur section in the Terai chapter for more information on the *Ramayana* . Sita is believed to have been born in Janakpur, and this is also where she and Rama married.

Incarnation eight was the gentle and much-loved Krishna, the fun-loving cowherd, who dallied with the *gopis* or milk-maids, danced, played his flute and still managed to remain devoted to his wife Radha. The Bhakti cult follow this passionate and happy incarnation.

For number nine Vishnu appeared as the teacher, the Buddha. Of course the Buddhists don't accept that Buddha was just an incarnation of some other religion's god but perhaps it was just a ploy to bring Hindu converts back into the fold. Incarnation 10? Well we haven't seen that one yet but it will be as Kalki the destroyer, when Vishnu wields the sword which will destroy the world at the end of the Kaliyuga, the age which we are currently in.

Brahma Brahma, despite his supreme position, appears much less often than Shiva or Vishnu. Like those gods he has four arms but Brahma also has four heads, to represent his all-seeing presence. The four *Vedas* are supposed to have emanated from his mouths.

Saraswati The goddess of learning and consort of Brahma. She rides upon a white swan and holds the stringed musical instrument known as a *veena*.

Tara Another deity who appears in both the Hindu and Buddhist pantheons are the Tara goddesses. There are actually 108 different Taras, but the best known are Green Tara and White Tara. They are sometimes believed to be the two wives of King Songtsen Gompo who was the first royal patron of Buddhism in Tibet. The Taras are two of the female consorts to the Dhyani Buddhas. See the Swayambhunath section of the Around the Kathmandu Valley chapter for details of the Dhyani Buddhas and their shaktis.

Brahma

Nagas The *nagas* are the eight snake deities and their king is Anantnag. Snakes make many appearances in Hindu and Buddhist mythology in Nepal. Vishnu images usually have a snake somewhere in the picture and the sleeping Vishnu reclines upon a bed made from the coils of a snake. Vishnu's consort, Lakshmi, often carries a snake, but Garuda, Vishnu's man-bird attendant, has a passionate hatred of snakes and often kills them. Snakes are thought to have power over water so this means they're important for ensuring a good monsoon. They also appear guarding doorways to prevent evil entering, but if you get bitten by one you can turn to Janguli, the goddess who cures snake bites. Amoghasiddhi, the Dhyani Buddha of the north, sits under a canopy of seven hooded snakes and Vishnu's snake bed also has seven heads which form a canopy for him. ■

India, and they primarily manufactured armaments for the small hill states. The descendants of these early immigrants today speak Nepali and are indistinguishable from upper-caste Hindus.

The largest Muslim group are the Terai Muslims, many of whom had arrived before unification. Others gradually drifted north from India, especially following the War of Independence in 1857. Many of them still have strong ties with the Muslim communities in the Indian states of Bihar and Uttar Pradesh.

A number of Tibetan Muslims arrived in the country along with their Buddhist counterparts following the 1959 Chinese overthrow of Tibet.

Unlike in India, where communal tension is a major problem, Nepal's Hindu and Muslim communities seem able to co-exist peacefully.

LANGUAGE

It's quite easy to get by with English in Nepal; most of the people the average visitor will have to deal with in the Kathmandu Valley and in Pokhara will speak some English. Along the main trekking trails, particularly the Annapurna Circuit, English is widely understood.

However, it's interesting to learn at least a little Nepali and it's quite an easy language to pick up. Nepali is closely related to Hindi and, like Hindi, is a member of the Indo-European group of languages. If you want to know a bit more Nepali than the phrases and vocabulary that follow, the Lonely Planet *Nepali phrasebook* is a handy introduction to the language.

Although Nepali is the national language of Nepal and is the linking language between all the country's ethnic groups there are many other languages spoken. The Newars of the Kathmandu Valley, for example, speak Newari and there are other languages spoken by the Tamangs, Sherpas, Rais, Limbus, Magars, Gurungs and other groups. In the Terai, bordering India, Hindi and Maithili, another Indian language of this region, are often spoken.

See the table below for a breakdown of the languages spoken by Nepalis as their first language.

Languages of Nepal	
Language	*% of Total Population*
Nepali	58.4
Maithili	11.1
Bhojpuri	7.6
Tharu	3.6
Tamang	3.5
Newari	3.0
Abadhi	1.5
Rai	1.5
Magar	1.4
Gurung	1.2
Limbu	0.9
Other	6.3

Even if you learn no other Nepali, there is one word every visitor soon picks up – *namaste*. Strictly translated it means 'I salute the god in you', but it is used as an everyday greeting encompassing everything from 'Hello' to 'How are you?' and even 'See you again soon'. Properly used it should be accompanied with the hands held in a prayer-like position, the Nepali gesture which is the equivalent of westerners shaking hands.

Studying Nepali
With a few exceptions, Nepali pronunciation is straightforward. Peace Corps and other aid workers pick up a working knowledge of the language very quickly and there are language courses available which will enable you to get by with just four to eight weeks of intensive study. See the Courses section in the Facts for the Visitor chapter for details.

Pronunciation
Vowels These are pronounced according to the following guide:

a	as the 'u' in 'hut'
aa	as the 'ar' in 'garden'
e	as the 'e' in 'best' but longer
i	as the 'i' in 'sister' but longer
o	as the 'o' in 'sold'
u	as the 'u' in 'put'
ai	as the 'i' in 'mine'
au	as the 'ow' in 'cow'

Consonants Most of the consonants are quite similar to their English equivalents. The exceptions are the so-called retroflex consonants and the aspirated consonants. Retroflex sounds are made by touching the roof of your mouth with the tip of your tongue as you make the consonant; they are indicated by doubling the consonant:

tt	*Katthmanddu*

Aspirated consonants are sounded more forcefully than they would be in English and are made with a short puff of air; they are indicated by an 'h' after the consonant:

bh	*bhatmaas*

Both retroflex and aspirated consonants are best learned by having a Nepali demonstrate them for you. You could start with the word *Katthmanddu*, which contains both retroflex and aspirated consonants.

Greetings & Civilities

Hello/Goodbye.	*namaste*
How are you?	*tapaailai kasto chha?*
Excuse me.	*hajur*
Please (give me).	*dinuhos*
Please (you have).	*khaanuhos*
Thank you.	*dhanyabad*

People are not thanked as often as in the west. Although you may feel a little uncomfortable, saying 'Thank you' is rarely necessary in a simple commercial transaction; foreigners going round saying *dhanyabad* all the time sounds distinctly odd to Nepalis.

Basics

I	*ma*
Yes. (I have)	*chaa*
No. (I don't have)	*chhaina*
OK.	*theekcha*
Where?	*kata?*
here	*yaha*
there	*tyaha*
good/pretty	*ramro*

I only speak a little Nepali.
ma ali nepaali bolchhu
I don't understand.
maile bujhina
Please say it again.
pheri bhannuhos
Please speak more slowly.
tapai bistaarai bolnuhos
I don't need it.
malai chahinna
I don't have it.
ma sanga chhaina
Wait a minute.
ek chhin parkhanos

Getting Around

bus	*bus*
taxi	*taxi*
boat	*naau*
ticket	*tikat*

How can I get to ...?
... kolaagi kati paisaa laagchha?
Is it far from here?
yahaabata ke taadhaa chha?
Where does this bus go?
yo bus kahaa jaanchha?
How much does it cost to go to ... ?
... jaana kati parchha?
I want a one-way/return ticket.
jaane/jaane-aaune tikat dinuhos.
Does your taxi have a meter?
tapaai ko taxi maa meter chha?

Accommodation

Where is a guest house/hotel?
paunaghar/hottel kahaa chha?
Can I get a place to stay here?
yahaa baas paunchha?
May I look at the room?
kothaa herna sakchhu?
Does it include breakfast?
bihaanako khaana samet ho?

room	*kothaa*
clean	*safaa*
dirty	*mailo*
fan	*pankhaa*

Around Town

bank	*baink*
... embassy	*... raajdutaavas*
museum	*samgrahaalaya*
police	*prahari*
post office	*post afis*
stamp	*tikat*
envelope	*kham*
tourist office	*turist afis*

What time does it open/close?
kati baje kholchha/banda gurchha?
I want to change some money.
paisaa saatnu manlaagchha

Trekking

way/trail	*bato*
bridge	*pool*
descent	*oralo*
ascent	*ukao*
left	*baya*
right	*daya*
cold	*jado*
tea house	*bati*

Please give me ...
malai ... dinuhos.
Please give me water.
malai pani dinuhos.
Which is the way to ...?
... jaane bato kata parchha?
Is there a village nearby?
najikai gaun parchha?
Where is the porter?
bhariya kata gayo?

I want to sleep.
   malai sutna man lagyo
I feel cold.
   malai jado lagyo
The food is cold.
   khaana cheeso chha

Food & Drink

I'm a vegetarian.
   ma saakaahari hun
What is this/that?
   yo/tyo ke ho?

food/meal	khaana
bread	pauroti
rice	chamal
(cooked)	bhat
meat	masu
green, leafy vegetable	saag
vegetable (cooked)	tarkari
lentils	dal
egg	phool
fruit	phala
sugar	chini
salt	noon
pepper	marich
curd	dhai
milk	doodh
tea	chiya
water	pani

Shopping

How much?
   kati?
What is it made of?
   kele baneko?
That's enough.
   pugyo
I (like/don't like) this.
   malai yo ramro (lagyo/lagena)
Where is the market?
   bazar kata parchha?

money	paisa
cheap	sasto
expensive	mahango
less	kam
more	badhi
little bit	alikati

Health & Emergencies

Help!
   guhaar!
Where is the nearest hospital?
   yahaa aspataal kahaa chha?
Please call a doctor for me.
   daktar bolaidinus
I don't feel well.
   malai sancho chhaina
I have diarrhoea.
   dishaa laagyo
I have altitude sickness.
   lekh laagyo
I have a fever.
   joro aayo

| medicine | ausadhi |
| pharmacy | ausadhi pasal |

Times & Dates

What time is it?   *kati bajyo?*
It's one o'clock.   *ek bajyo*

minute	minet
hour	ghantaa
day	din
today	aaja
yesterday	hijo
tomorrow	bholi
now	aile
week	haptaa
month	mahinaa

What day is it today?   *aaja ke baar?*

Today is ...   *aaja ... ho*
Monday	sombaar
Tuesday	mangalbaar
Wednesday	budhbaar
Thursday	bihibaar
Friday	sukrabaar
Saturday	sanibaar
Sunday	aitbaar

Numbers

1	ek	40	chaalis
2	dui	50	pachas
3	teen	60	saathi
4	char	70	sattari
5	panch	80	assi
6	chha	90	nabbe
7	saat	100	saya
8	aath	200	dui saya
9	nau	500	panch saya
10	das	1000	hazar
20	bees	100,000	lakh
30	tees	1,000,000	das lakh
		10,000,000	crore

Nepalese numerals

१ २ ३ ४ ५
1   2   3   4   5

६ ७ ८ ९ १०
6   7   8   9   10

Facts for the Visitor

PLANNING
When to Go

Climatic factors are very important in deciding on a visit to Nepal. October-November, the start of the dry season, is in many ways the best time of year in Nepal. With the monsoon only recently finished the countryside is green and lush and Nepal is at its most beautiful. Rice is harvested and there are some important and colourful festivals to enjoy. Bear in mind, however, that these festivals can be disruptive; see the Public Holidays & Special Events section later in this chapter for more details. At this time of year the air is sparkling clean, visibility is unexcelled and the Himalayan views are as near perfect as you can ask. Furthermore the weather is still balmy, neither too hot (as it can be towards the end of the dry season or during the monsoon) nor too cold (as it can be at the height of winter). For obvious reasons, this is also the peak tourist season.

In December-January the climate and visibility are still good, though it can get very cold. Trekkers need to be well prepared, as snow can be encountered on high-altitude treks. Heading for the Everest Base Camp at this time of year can be a real feat of endurance and the Annapurna Circuit trek is often closed by snow on the Thorong La pass. Down in Kathmandu the cheaper hotels, where heating is nonexistent, are often chilly and gloomy in the evenings. There's sometimes a brief 'winter monsoon', lasting just a day or two in January.

February-March-April, the tail end of the dry season, is a good second-best time. The weather gets warmer so high-altitude treks are no longer as arduous, although by the end of the dry season, before the monsoon breaks, it starts to get too hot for comfort. Visibility is not as good as earlier in the dry season since the country is now very dry, and dust in the air reduces that crystal Himalayan clarity. In compensation, Nepal's wonderful rhododendrons and many other flowers are in bloom so there's plenty of colour to be seen along the trekking trails.

May and the early part of June are not the best months as it is extremely hot and dusty and the coming monsoon hangs over you like a threat. Mid-June to September, when the monsoon finally arrives, is the least popular time to visit Nepal. The rains wash the dust out of the air, but the clouds obscure the mountains so you're unlikely to enjoy more than a rare glimpse of the Himalaya. Although it doesn't rain all day it usually does rain every day and the trails (and the roads in most Nepali towns) will be muddy and plagued by leeches.

Despite this, it is possible to trek during the monsoon, although high rivers may further complicate matters and it's certainly not as pleasant as other times of year. Landslides sometimes block roads during the monsoon but many visitors still come to Nepal from India as the weather is even less pleasant down on the plains. The latter part of the monsoon, the months of August-September, are a time of festivals which will certainly enliven a visit to Kathmandu.

How Long to Visit

If you are visiting during the monsoon, and your stay is restricted to the Kathmandu Valley, a week is probably quite enough. During the dry season you really need more like a month to enjoy the country: a week or two for Kathmandu and the surrounding area, a week for a short trek, and a week for Pokhara and a visit to Royal Chitwan National Park. If you want to walk some of the longer trekking routes then you had better extend your visit – it takes three weeks to walk the Annapurna Circuit.

Maps

An interesting account of the history of mapping in Nepal is found in Harka Gurung's *Maps of Nepal* which covers historic maps right up to the trekking maps of the early 80s.

The Research Scheme Nepal Himalaya maps are better known as Schneider Maps, after their cartographer. These are the best trekking maps available although their price is as high as their quality. The series covers the routes into the Everest region in six separate maps, and the Langtang and Annapurna areas.

There are many locally produced maps available in Nepal which are much cheaper and for most trekkers prove quite adequate. Most of these are produced by Mandala Trekking Maps, and although they are generally only in blueprint form they have recently produced coloured versions for the most popular trekking routes.

The problem with all the detailed maps of Nepal is that villages often have widely diverse names and their actual position is often equally open to question. Reality, when you're there on foot, is often very different from what the map says. Even the Schneider maps often have highly original versions of common place names.

What to Bring

Nepal's climatic variations due to altitude mean that at certain times of year you'll have to come prepared for almost anything. If you're in Nepal during the winter you'll find it's T-shirt weather if you're tracking wildlife in the Terai, but up at the Everest Base Camp you'll want the best thermal or duck-down gear money can buy!

In the Kathmandu Valley the daytime weather is pleasant year round, but in winter the temperature drops as soon as the sun sets, or even goes behind a cloud. It never reaches freezing in the valley, however, so it's sweater or warm-jacket weather, nothing worse. Climb higher to the valley edge at Nagarkot and you can find it much colder. If you plan to ride a bike, or have a respiratory problem, Kathmandu's air pollution is sufficiently bad to justify a mask.

During the monsoon you'll need an umbrella or raincoat, particularly in Pokhara where the rainfall is much heavier than in Kathmandu. In the first month after the monsoon it can be pleasantly warm, even on treks, so long as you're sticking to lower altitudes. Sunglasses, a hat and covering for unprotected skin are all necessary on high-altitude treks or for prolonged exposure in the Terai. (See the Trekking chapter for more details on clothing recommendations for trekking.)

Most clothing is easily and cheaply available in Nepal so if there's a question about a particular item, leave it behind – you can always get one if you need it.

These days most toiletries are readily available, including toilet paper. Women should, however, bring tampons if needed. Ear plugs can be more than a luxury if you sleep lightly – cheap hotels and lodges are often very noisy. If you're staying in cheap hotels a padlock can be useful as hotels in this category often lock the doors with a latch and padlock. If you're visiting Royal Chitwan National Park or other places in the Terai a good insect repellent is a near necessity. Bring a torch (flashlight) for trekking and for power cuts.

HIGHLIGHTS

While many people come to Nepal just for trekking in the Himalaya, there is indeed much more to Nepal than just that. The Kathmandu Valley is worth at least a week in itself, although most people seem to fly in and get out as quickly as possible. The temples at Patan, Bhaktapur, Swayambhunath, Pashupatinath and Bodhnath should not be missed.

The Terai, that lowland strip which runs the breadth of the country, is a fascinating area usually completely overlooked by foreign visitors but one which has a great deal to offer. Visiting the Royal Chitwan and Royal Bardia national parks in the Terai offers visitors a chance to see an incredible variety of bird and animal life, including the royal Bengal tiger and the rhinoceros. Other Terai towns, such as Janakpur and Lumbini, are significant religious sites and are also worth a visit.

TOURIST OFFICES

The Ministry of Tourism does not overdo things; there is very little printed information available and the handful of tourist offices around the country are of extremely limited use.

Local Tourist Offices

There are tourist offices in Kathmandu, Pokhara, Bhairawa, Birganj, Janakpur and Kakarbhitta. See the relevant sections for contact details.

VISAS & DOCUMENTS

Visas

Visas are required by most nationalities (Indians are an exception) and they are available from embassies and consulates abroad, at the border with India or on arrival at Kathmandu's Tribhuvan airport.

Single entry tourist visas are available for 15 days ($15) or 30 days ($25), or you can also get multiple entry 60 day visas for $60.

At the airport, and sometimes at border crossings, officials insist on payment in US cash dollars. One passport photo is also required. It is possible to get US dollars at the airport currency exchange counter, but US dollars in cash will almost certainly be unavailable at the land borders (bring your own!).

There are inevitably queues at the immigration counter at Tribhuvan airport, and there can be hassles at the land crossings, so it is preferable to get your visa before arrival. Outside your home country, they are most conveniently obtained in Bangkok (Thailand), and Calcutta and Delhi (India). You must, however, use your visa within three months of the date it is issued.

Visa Extensions Tourist visas can be extended for a total of 150 days, although a further 30 days can be granted 'on reasonable grounds'. Over the course of one calendar year (1 January to 31 December) a tourist may not stay longer than 180 days. The fee levied for any extension beyond 30 days and up to 150 days is US$1 per day. One passport photo is also required.

The Department of Immigration's Kathmandu office (☎ 01-412337) is only a short stroll from Thamel, on Tridevi Marg directly across from the Sanchaya Kosh Bhawan Shopping Centre and the South Asian Association for Regional Cooperation (SAARC). See the Government Offices section in the Kathmandu, Patan & Bhaktapur chapter for details of opening hours. In Pokhara the immigration office is near the lake.

Trekking Permits

A Nepali visa is valid for the Kathmandu and Pokhara valleys and all driveable roads throughout the country. If you intend to strike out for more than a day's walk from the main roads, you must first apply for a trekking permit.

Trekking permits are only issued in Kathmandu and Pokhara, and can only be extended at those cities. The immigration office also issues trekking permits. The Pokhara immigration office can only issue trekking permits to the Annapurna region. Police stations cannot extend visas or trekking permits.

See the Permits section in the Trekking chapter for more details.

Other Documents

If it is possible you might drive a car or ride a motorbike while in Nepal then it is worth having an international driving permit.

When travelling in Asia it's a good idea to keep a number of passport photos with your passport so they are immediately handy for trekking permits, visa applications and other official documents. Passport photos are easily and cheaply obtained in Kathmandu – around Rs 100 for four in B&W or Rs 150 for four in colour.

EMBASSIES

Nepali Diplomatic Offices Overseas

Australia

Level 1, 17 Castlereagh St, Sydney, NSW 2000 (☎ 02-9233-6161; fax 9261-1974)

72 Lincoln Rd, Essendon, Melbourne, Vic 3040 (☎ 03-9379-0666; fax 9331-1378)

Suite 2, 16 Robinson St, Nedlands, WA 6009 (☎ 08-9386-2102; fax 9386-3087)

Level 21, AMP Place, 10 Eagle St, Brisbane, Qld 4000 (☎ 07-3232-0336)

Bangladesh
United Nations Rd, Road 2, Baridhara, Dhaka (☎ 601890)

Belgium
?1 Ave Champel, B-1640 Rhode St, Genese (☎ 02-358-5808; fax 358-3384)

Canada
Royal Bank Plaza, South Tower, Toronto (☎ (416) 2268722; fax (416) 2268878)

China
No 1, Sanlitun Xiliujie-Lu, Beijing (☎ 532-1795; fax 532-3251)
Norbulingka Rd 13, Lhasa, Tibet Autonomous Region (☎ 36890)

Denmark
2 Teglgaardstraede, 1452 Copenhagen K (☎ 3312-4166; fax 3315-1045)

Finland
Kaisaniemenkarul B a, 00100 Helsinki (☎ 1311-6230; fax 680-1024)

France
45 bis Rue des Acacias, 75017 Paris (☎ 1-4622-4867; fax 4227-0865)
7 bis Allee des Soupirs, 31000 Toulouse (☎ 061-329-1222; fax 4737-0474)

Germany
Im Hag 15, D-5300 Bonn 2 (☎ 0228-343097; fax 856747)
Flinschstrasse 63, Frankfurt am Main 6000 (☎ 069-40871; fax 408-7235)
Landsberger Str 191, D-8000 München 21 (☎ 089-570-4406; fax 570-1386)
Uhlandstrasse 171/2, 1000 Berlin 15 (☎ 030-881-4049; fax 882-5917)

India
1 Barakhamba Rd, New Delhi 110001 (☎ 011-332-9969; fax 332-6857)
19 Woodlands, Sterndale Rd, Alipore, Calcutta 700027 (☎ 033-711224)

Italy
Piazzale Medaglie d'Oro 20, Rome 00136 (☎ 348176)

Japan
14-9 Tokoroki 7-chome, Setagaya-ku, Tokyo 158 (☎ 03-3705-5558; fax 3705-8264)
6-6-23-318 Vehonmochi, Tennoji-ki, Osaka 543 (☎ 06-776-0120; fax 779-3325)

Myanmar (Burma)
16 Natmauk Yeiktha (Park Ave), PO Box 84, Yangon (Rangoon) (☎ 550633)

Pakistan
4th Floor, Qamar House, 419 MA Jinnah Rd, Karachi-2 (☎ 200979)

Spain
Mallorca 194 Pral 2A, 08036 Barcelona (☎ 03-323-1323; fax 253-2030)

Switzerland
Asylstrasse 81, 8030 Zurich (☎ 01-475993; fax 251-9152)

Thailand
189 Sukhumvit 71 Rd, Bangkok 10110 (☎ 391-7240; fax 381-2406)

Tibet
Norbulingka Rd 13, Lhasa (☎ 36890)

UK
12A Kensington Palace Gardens, London W8 4QU (☎ 0171-229-6231; fax 792-8861)

USA
1500 Lake Shore Drive, Chicago, Illinois 60610 (☎ 312-787-9199)
Heideberg College, Tiffin, Ohio 44883 (☎ 419-448-2202)
Suite 400, 909 Montgomery St, San Francisco, California 94133 (☎ 415-434-1111)
16250 Dallas Parkway, Suite 110, Dallas, Texas 75248 (☎ 214-931-1212)
212 15th St NE, Atlanta, Georgia 30309 (☎ 404-892-8152)
2131 Leroy Place NW, Washington, DC 20008 (☎ 202-667-4550; fax 667-5534)

Foreign Embassies in Nepal

Travellers continuing beyond Nepal may need visas for Bangladesh, China, India, Myanmar (Burma) or Thailand. The only visas for Tibet/China dished out in Kathmandu are for organised groups; individuals wishing to travel to Tibet should get a visa before arriving in Nepal (Delhi is a good place to get them). Foreign embassies in Kathmandu (area code 01) include:

Australia
Bansbari, just beyond the Ring Rd on Maharajganj (☎ 411578; fax 417533)

Bangladesh
Naxal, Bhagwati Bahal (☎ 414943; fax 414265)
open Sunday to Thursday from 9 am to 1 pm and 1.30 to 5 pm
visa applications up to 11 am only; no charge, two photos, 24 hours.

Canada
Lazimpat (☎ 415193, 415389; fax 410422)

China
Baluwatar (☎ 411740; fax 414045)
open Monday to Friday from 9 am to 1 pm and 3.30 to 5.30 pm
visa applications Monday, Wednesday and Friday from 10 to 11.30 am; passports returned the next working day

France
Lazimpat (☎ 412332; fax 419968)

Germany
> Gyaneshwor (☎ 412786; fax 416899)

India
> Lainchaur (☎ 410900, 414990; fax 413132)
> open Monday to Friday from 9 am to 1 pm and 1.30 to 5.30 pm
> visa applications Monday to Friday from 9.30 am to 12.30 pm, collect from 4.45 to 5.30 pm – allow at least seven days for processing; 15 day to six month (multiple entry possible) visas available, cost varies according to nationality

Israel
> Bishramalaya House, Lazimpat (☎ 411811; fax 413920)

Italy
> Baluwatar (Lalita Niwas Rd) (☎ 412743; fax 413879)

Japan
> Durbar Marg (☎ 231101; fax 228638)

Myanmar (Burma)
> Chakupat, Patan City Gate, Patan (☎ 521788; fax 523402)
> open Monday to Friday from 9.30 am to 1 pm and 2 to 4.30 pm
> visa applications morning only, 14 day visas available, three photos, 24 hours

Pakistan
> Panipokhari (☎ 411421)
> open Sunday to Thursday from 9 am to 1 pm and 2 to 5 pm

Thailand
> Jyoti Kendra, Thapathali (☎ 213910; fax 226599)
> open Monday to Friday from 8.30 am to 12.30 pm and 1.30 to 4.30 pm
> visa applications Monday to Friday from 9.30 am to 12.30 pm, about $10, two photos, 24 hours

UK
> Lainchaur (☎ 410583; fax 411789)

USA
> Panipokhari (☎ 411179; fax 419963)

CUSTOMS

You may be searched very thoroughly when you depart. In addition to drugs, customs is concerned with the illegal export of antiques. Visitors are permitted to import the following articles for their personal use (and we quote):

Cigarettes, 200 sticks; cigars, 50 sticks; alcoholic liquor, one bottle not exceeding 1.15 litre; one binocular; one movie camera with 12 rolls of film; one video camera; one ordinary camera with 15 rolls of film; one tape recorder with 15 tape reels or cassettes; one perambulator; one bicycle; and one stick.

Antiques

Customs' main concern is preventing the export of antique works of art – with good reason since Nepal has a great many treasures, many kept under conditions of very light security. It would be a great shame if international art thieves and 'collectors' forced more of it to be kept under lock and key. Unfortunately a lucrative international market has led to the theft of a staggering amount of irreplaceable art.

It is very unlikely that souvenirs sold to travellers will be antique (despite the claims of the vendors), but if there is any doubt, they should be cleared and a certificate obtained from the Department of Archaeology (☎ 01-215358) in the National Archives building on Ram Shah Path. These controls also apply to the export of precious and semiprecious stones.

Animal Furs & Trophies

Unfortunately, there is still a thriving trade in animal furs and trophies, despite the fact that this is also officially prohibited. Many seriously endangered species, including the beautiful snow leopard, are still being hunted for valuable parts of their corpses.

While there is a market this will no doubt continue – the argument that because the animal is already dead there is no further harm caused by having its skin made into a coat is entirely spurious. If there is any cosmic justice, those that encourage the trade will be reincarnated as rabbits on fur farms in Siberia!

MONEY
Costs

If you stay in rock-bottom accommodation and survive on a predominantly Nepali diet you could live in Nepal for less than $5 a day. On an independent 'village inn' or 'tea house' trek your living costs are likely to be around that level.

On the other hand if you stay in comfortable mid-range hotels (say $10 to $20 a double), eat in popular tourist-oriented restaurants, rent bicycles and take taxis from time to time your living costs could be around $20 to $30 a day.

At the top end it is possible to spend $100 a night for a five-star double room in Kathmandu; a meal for two in one of Nepal's very best restaurants can cost $30 to $40; and a deluxe trek booked from overseas can cost $100 a day.

Residents should bear in mind that most of the major up-market tour and trekking operators offer significant discounts, so make your status clear when you ask for prices and make bookings.

Credit Cards
Major credit cards are widely accepted at mid-range and better hotels, restaurants and fancy shops in the Kathmandu Valley and at Pokhara. Elsewhere it's safer to assume that credit cards won't be accepted, and so you will need to carry enough cash or travellers' cheques to cover your costs.

Branches of Nepal Grindlays bank will make cash advances against Visa and MasterCard in Nepali rupees, and will also sell travellers' cheques against the cards. The bank charges a 2% commission.

American Express has an office off the forecourt of the Hotel Mayalu on Jamal Tol just around the corner from Durbar Marg in Kathmandu. They will accept personal cheques (you can use a standard form so long as you know your account details) and advance travellers' cheques to card holders. There's a standard 1% commission. The office is open from 10 am to 1 pm and 2 to 5 pm.

International Transfers
If you do not follow the right steps money transfers from overseas can be very time-consuming. Make any transfer by fax as transfers by mail can take forever. Pin down every possible detail, ensure that you know which bank the money is going to, make sure they have your name exactly right and if possible ensure that you are notified at the same time as the bank. It's important to choose the right bank as well – check that your bank has links with a bank in Nepal and does not have to operate through an interme-

diary. See the Kathmandu chapter for addresses of international banks with offices in Kathmandu.

Currency
The Nepali rupee (Rs) is divided into 100 paisa (p).

There are coins for five, 10, 25 and 50 paisa, and for one, two, five and 10 rupees, although as the rupee coins are not in wide circulation and prices are generally rounded to the nearest rupee, you often don't come across any coins at all. This is a great contrast to a time not all that long ago, when once outside the Kathmandu Valley, it was rare to see any paper money. Mountaineering books from the 1950s often comment on the porters whose sole duty was to carry the expedition's money – in cold, hard cash!

Bank notes are for one, two, five, 10, 20, 50, 100, 500 and 1000 rupees. Away from major centres changing an Rs 500 or Rs 1000 note can be very difficult, so it is always wise to have at least some of your money in small denomination notes. Even in Kathmandu, many small businesses, especially rickshaw and taxi drivers, simply don't have sufficient spare money to allow them the luxury of carrying a wad of change.

Note that all dollar prices quoted in this book are US dollars.

Currency Exchange
Major international currencies including the US dollar and pounds sterling, are readily accepted, and in Nepal the Indian rupee is also like a hard currency – the Nepali rupee is pegged to the Indian rupee at the rate of IRs 100 = NRs 160. Beware that Indian Rs 500 notes are not accepted anywhere in Nepal, apparently due to the presence of forgeries.

Australia A$1	=	Rs 44
France FFr 1	=	Rs 11
Germany DM1	=	Rs 37
India IRs 100	=	Rs 160
Japan Yen 100	=	Rs 50
United Kingdom UK£1	=	Rs 83
USA US$1	=	Rs 55

Changing Money

Official exchange rates are set by the government's Nepal Rastra Bank. Rates at the private banks vary, but are generally not far from the official rate. The daily *Rising Nepal* and *Kathmandu Post* newspapers list the Nepal Rastra Bank's rate, providing a useful reference point.

There are exchange counters at the international terminal at Kathmandu's airport and banks and/or moneychangers at the various border crossings. Pokhara and the major border towns also have official money-changing facilities, but changing travellers' cheques can be difficult elsewhere in the country, even in some quite large towns. If you're trekking take enough small denomination cash with you to last the whole trek.

The usual banking hours are from 10 am to 2 pm from Sunday to Thursday and from 10 am till noon on Friday.

Legal Exchange When you change money officially, you are required to show your passport, and you are issued with a Foreign Exchange Encashment Receipt showing your identity and the amount of hard currency you have changed. Hang onto the receipts as they have a number of potential uses.

Many up-market hotels and businesses are obliged by the government to demand payment in hard currency; they will also accept rupees, but only if you can show a Foreign Exchange Encashment Receipt that covers the amount you owe them. In practice this regulation seems to be widely disregarded and you are not asked to prove the source of your rupees.

Airlines are also required to charge tourists in hard currency, but most seem unwilling to accept anything other than cash, travellers' cheques or credit cards. Budget hotels, bus companies and most small businesses are only too happy to get rupees and do not muck around with encashment receipts.

If you leave Nepal via Kathmandu's airport the downstairs exchange counter will re-exchange up to 15% of the amount shown on 'unused' exchange certificates. The receipts used for re-exchange are kept by the bank, so make sure you have photocopies if you need them for other purposes. Be warned that official re-exchange is not possible at any bank branches at the border crossings.

The best private banks are the Nepal Bank Ltd, Nepal Grindlays Bank, Rastriya Banijya Bank and the Nepal Indo-Suez Bank. Some hotels and resorts are also licensed to change money, and while their rates are usually OK it's best to check first.

Rates and commissions charged vary from bank to bank, so it pays to shop around.

In addition to the banks there are licensed moneychangers in Kathmandu, Pokhara and Sunauli/Bhairawa. The rates are often marginally better than the banks, but the commissions are higher, so check before changing. The big advantages of the moneychangers over the banks is that they open much longer hours (typically 9 am to 7 pm) and often seven days a week, and they are also much quicker, the whole process often taking no more than a few minutes.

Black Market Exchange Nepal has an active and remarkably open black market although it's principally found around Kathmandu and to a lesser extent in Pokhara. It is by definition illegal, but rip-offs are rare and legal harassment even rarer. Keep your wits about you, however. Don't do a deal in the street, and don't hand over your money until you have counted and checked the rupees and actually have them in your hand.

The black market is principally interested in cash US dollars, but US dollar travellers' cheques are nearly as good. The $50 note is the most popular cash, apparently because of a proliferation of forged $100 notes. You can change European currencies on the black market, but rates are often little different to those offered by private banks. For dollars you can expect to get about 10% more than the bank rates for large bills, slightly less for travellers' cheques.

The young hustlers on the street usually lead you to a shop – often a travel agency or carpet shop – where the transaction is actually completed. Once you know which shop to go to you don't have to deal with the people in the street, and you will also get a slightly better rate if you cut out the intermediary. You're almost certain to be offered below the going rate the first time, so shop around.

Black market dollars are used in a number of ways, sometimes completely unsavoury. A huge demand comes from the carpet industry because the government has set a legally enforced floor price for export carpets. The real price is currently lower, so the carpet buyers pay the official floor price with a bank transfer, but are reimbursed by the seller, under the table, with cash. Smugglers also need hard currency, whether they trade in drugs, or something less destructive. One popular scam is to sell drugs to westerners for rupees; change the rupees to dollars; smuggle the dollars to Hong Kong and buy gold; smuggle the gold back to Nepal; and finally, smuggle the gold to India. Using the black market facilitates and encourages these practices.

Tipping

Tipping is becoming more prevalent in Kathmandu. In expensive establishments you should tip up to 10% whereas in smaller places the loose change or Rs 10 will be appreciated. Don't worry about it in the really cheap restaurants. Taxi drivers don't expect to be tipped.

Bargaining

Before bargaining, try to establish a fair price by talking to locals and other travellers. Paying too much feeds inflation, while paying too little denies the locals a reasonable return for their efforts and investments. Not everything is subject to bargaining: respect standard food, accommodation and entry charges, and follow the going rate for services.

Bargaining should never be treated as a matter of life and death importance – it's usually regarded as an integral part of a transaction and is, ideally, an enjoyable social exchange. Nepalis do not ever appreciate aggressive behaviour. A good deal is when both parties are happy. Try to remember that Rs 10 might make quite a difference to the seller, but in US hard currency it amounts to less than 20 cents.

POST & COMMUNICATIONS

The postal service to and from Nepal is, at best, erratic and can be extremely slow. Most articles do finally arrive, but they can take weeks. Poste restante services are reasonably well organised, but as with any other Asian country you should ask people writing to you to print your family name clearly and to underline it. Misfiled mail often results from confusion between family names and given names.

Postal Rates

In Kathmandu, stamps are sold from 8 am to 7 pm from Sunday to Friday, and from 11 am to 3 pm on Saturday. Most bookshops in Thamel, including Pilgrims, also sell stamps and deliver postcards to the post office, which is much easier than making a special trip to the post office yourself. See the Postal Rates from Nepal table for a list of prices:

Parcel Post

Having stocked up on souvenirs and gifts in Nepal, many people take the opportunity to send them home from Kathmandu. Parcel post is not cheap, but the service is reliable although slow.

The contents of a parcel must be inspected by officials before it is wrapped so do not take it to the post office already wrapped up. There are packers at the Kathmandu Foreign post office who will package it for a small fee. The maximum weight for sea mail is 20 kg; for air mail it's 10 kg. The Parcel Post Rates from Nepal table on the following page has a list of prices.

See also the Things to Buy section at the end of this chapter for details on sending things home by courier, which is even more expensive.

Telephone & Fax

Thankfully the telephone system works

Parcel Post Rates from Nepal

Sea Mail	1 kg	5 kg	10 kg	20 kg
Australia	Rs 864	Rs 1410	Rs 2027	Rs 3388
UK/EU	Rs 1006	Rs 1720	Rs 2364	Rs 3952
USA	Rs 672	Rs 1593	Rs 2664	Rs 5598

Air Mail	First 250 gm	Each Additional 250 gm		
Australia	Rs 1056	Rs 156		
UK/EU	Rs 1075	Rs 185		
USA	Rs 898	Rs 230		

Postal Rates from Nepal

EU & UK	Australia & USA	
Aerogrammes	Rs 14	Rs 17
Postcards	Rs 12	Rs 15
Letters (to 20 gm)	Rs 18	Rs 20

pretty well, and it's easy to make local, STD and international calls. Reverse-charge (collect) calls can only be made to Canada, Japan and the UK.

So-called 'communications centres' (often complete with fax machines) have mushroomed in Nepal and although rates do vary, they're pretty competitive. It's really only worth using the government telegraph offices if you have to make a lengthy international call.

With the private operators, expect to pay around Rs 170 per minute to Australia, France, the UK and USA, and around Rs 185 to New Zealand and Germany. Many of the hotels also have direct-dial facilities, but always check their charges before you phone. International faxes to anywhere cost Rs 185 per page to send, and around Rs 20 per page to receive.

At the government telegraph offices, there is a minimum charge for the first three minutes (whether you use all the time or not), then a per-minute rate. For Australia, Canada, France, Germany, New Zealand, the UK and the USA, the first three minutes is Rs 432 and additional minutes are Rs 144.

For southern Africa, Denmark, Israel and Italy, the first three minutes cost Rs 540, followed by Rs 180 per minute. Faxes are charged at the 'additional minute' rate, and there's no minimum charge.

STD calls usually cost Rs 15 per minute regardless of destination.

E-Mail Services

E-mail services are offered by a couple of places in Kathmandu and there's one in Pokhara. It costs around Rs 70 to send one kb of text (around half a page), and Rs 20 to receive the same amount. See the relevant sections for locations.

BOOKS

There is no shortage of books about Nepal – the Himalaya and heroic mountaineers, the colourful religions and exotic temples, the reclusive history and brave Gurkhas have all inspired writers and photographers, and the results are piled high in numerous bookshops in Nepal, of which there are a surprisingly good selection. Most are in Kathmandu, although there are a number in Pokhara.

Most books are published in different editions by different publishers in different countries. As a result, a book might be a hardcover rarity in one country while it's readily available in paperback in another. Fortunately, bookshops and libraries search by title or author, so your local bookshop or library is best placed to advise you on the availability of the following recommendations. These are only some of the more interesting titles and include books that are long out of print and others which may only be available in Nepal.

Lonely Planet

There are a number of Lonely Planet books that are of interest to visitors to Nepal. *Shopping for Buddhas* by Jeff Greenwald is an acute and funny book about the author's travels in Nepal, motivated by the obsessive pursuit of a perfect Buddha statue. The book is part of Journeys, Lonely Planet's exciting new travel literature series. The *Nepali phrasebook* is a valuable introduction to the language, and travellers who want to take the kids and still get the most out of their trip will find *Travel with Children* by Maureen Wheeler a handy reference.

Trekking in the Nepal Himalaya by Stan Armington covers everything you need to know before setting out on a trek in Nepal, plus day-by-day coverage of all the main trekking routes. Stan's book has an excellent medical section covering the problems likely to be encountered in the mountains.

Travel Guides

Other guidebooks to Nepal include APA's *Nepal*, one of the Insight series of photographic coffee table guides. APA also publishes a useful pocket guide, *Nepal* by Lisa Choegyal, which gives some good day-trip itineraries and plenty of tips. *Nepal Namaste* by Robert Rieffel is an excellent locally produced book with all sorts of odd titbits of information.

The Himalaya Experience by Jonathan Chester is an interesting, colourful appetite-whetter for the entire Himalayan region. It has a great deal of interesting information about trekking and climbing and some wonderful photographs.

An Introduction to the Hanuman Dhoka is no longer readily available, but it gives a good short description of the buildings around the Durbar Square area of Kathmandu.

Kathmandu – The Hidden City by Annick Holle is a small, locally produced book which takes you on a number of walks around Kathmandu, revealing some of the lesser known back streets where tourists rarely get to. It is definitely for the dedicated sightseer.

Trekking, Biking & Rafting Guides

A Guide to Trekking in Nepal by Stephen Bezruchka covers all the main trekking routes with detailed descriptions, and is probably the best all-round reference for the individual trekker.

Other excellent guides are the Trailblazer series, with separate guides to the Annapurna and Everest regions.

If you're interested in treks close to Kathmandu, *Treks on the Kathmandu Valley Rim* by Alton C Byers III details a number of one day and overnight treks near Kathmandu.

A more up-to-date alternative is James Giambrone's *Kathmandu: Bikes & Hikes* which gives details on 10 hikes and 11 mountain-bike rides around the valley; it also has a decent fold-out map.

Anyone who is seriously interested in rafting and kayaking, and especially anyone contemplating a private expedition, should get hold of Peter Knowles & David Allardice's *White Water Nepal*, which is usually available in Kathmandu. It has detailed information on river trips, 60 maps, river profiles and hydrographs, plus advice on equipment and health – in short all the information a prospective river runner could want.

History & Economics

Although browsing through a good Kathmandu bookshop will reveal plenty of histories of Nepal there is no definitive book which tells it all in a readable fashion. In particular there has been little accounting of recent events in Nepal, especially the push for greater democracy and the underlying political unrest.

Fatalism & Development – Nepal's Struggle for Modernization by Dor Bahadur Bista is an often controversial analysis of Nepali society and its dynamics. It has a very good historical introduction, and the author looks especially critically at the role of the caste system.

The Political History of Nepal by Margaret W Fisher is now more than 35 years old and even *Nepal in Crisis* by Blaikie, Cameron & Seddon is rather dated.

Charlie Pye-Smith's *Travels in Nepal* is a travel account on one level, but the author's travels around the country are highly directed: he was there to study the impacts and benefits of foreign aid to Nepal and his conclusions are incisive and interesting. In between the aid projects he chain-smokes his way around quite a few interesting places and appears to finish up as much in love with the country as many less single-minded visitors! See Foreign Aid under Economy in the Facts about the Country chapter for more about this book.

General

Although Toni Hagen's *Nepal – the Kingdom in the Himalaya* (1980) is now rather out of date, it is still one of the most complete studies of Nepal's people, geography and geology. Hagen travelled extensively through Nepal in the 50s and the book reflects his intimate knowledge of the country and also has fine colour plates.

Another now rather dated account of Nepal is Jeremy Bernstein's *The Wildest Dreams of Kew* (1970) which covers the country's history in a very readable style and includes an interesting trek to the Everest Base Camp.

Michel Peissel takes a trip to the fabled region of Mustang, close to the border with Tibet and to the north of Jomsom, in *Mustang – A Lost Tibetan Kingdom*, but again, it's pretty old, having been published in the late 1960s.

A more recent saunter around Nepal and Tibet is recounted in the amusingly written *To the Navel of the World* by Peter Somerville-Large. The author also does some deep-winter trekking, using yaks, in the Solu Khumbu and up to the Everest Base Camp. His encounters with tourism in remote locations are very funny.

Although Pico Iyer's best seller *Video Night in Kathmandu* gallivants all around Asia, the chapter on Nepal has some astute and amusing observations on the collision between Nepali tradition and western culture, particularly video culture.

The Waiting Land: A Spell in Nepal by Dervla Murphy is an interesting account of a visit to Nepal at a time when great changes were at hand. In *Mister Raja's Neighbourhood*, Jeff Greenwald gives an amusing account of his travels in Nepal.

Helping a captured yeti *Escape from Kathmandu* is only one adventure in Kim Stanley Robinson's off-the-wall romp around Nepal. There's also an illegal ascent of Everest with a reincarnate lama, an attempt to kidnap King Birendra, a visit to Shambhala, a very logical explanation for why Prince Charles is the way he is, and the best ever description of what they do to Kathmandu while you're away trekking.

Han Suyin's *The Mountain is Young* is an overly romantic novel set in Nepal in the mid-50s. It is surprising more novelists haven't used Nepal's colourful background in their writing.

Misery Behind the Looms is a sobering account of the plight of the young children who are forced to work in almost slave-like conditions in the carpet factories of the Kathmandu Valley.

Culture, People & Festivals

Festivals of Nepal by Mary Anderson is an excellent rundown on Nepal's many festivals and includes interesting accounts of many of the legends and tales behind them. There is also a great deal of background information about the Hindu religion. Mary Rubel's *The Gods of Nepal* is a detailed description of Hindu and Buddhist deities.

People of Nepal, by the Nepali anthropologist Dor Bahadur Bista, describes the many and diverse ethnic groupings found in the country, as does the recently published *Ethnic Groups of Nepal*, by DB Shrestha & CB Singh.

Sherpas of Nepal by C Von Furer Haimendorf describes the Sherpas of the Everest region in a rather dry and academic manner.

From the same author *Himalayan Traders* is a rather more readable follow-up, concentrating on the changes in trading patterns and cultures among Nepal's Himalayan people.

Michel Peissel's *Tiger for Breakfast* is a biography of the colourful gentleman who was probably the best known resident expatriate in the kingdom – Boris Lissanevitch of the Royal Hotel and Yak & Yeti Restaurant.

The lives of a number of Nepali village women are depicted in *Bending Bamboo Changing Winds* by Eva Kipps. Also giving an interesting insight into Nepali women is *Nepali Aama* by Broughton Coburn, a book which details the life of a remarkable Gurung woman.

Natural History

The Royal Chitwan National Park's wildlife is detailed in KK Gurung's *The Heart of the Jungle. Indian Wildlife* covers all the national parks on the subcontinent, including Chitwan and Bardia in Nepal with APA's usual high standards of photography.

Birds of Nepal by Robert Fleming Sr, Robert Fleming Jr & Lain Singh Bangdel is a field guide to Nepal's many hundreds of birds. *Himalayan Flowers & Trees* by Dorothy Mierow & Tirtha Bahadur Shrestha is the best available field guide to the plants of Nepal.

Other titles recommended by Lewis Underwood (the author of the Geography, Geology, Flora & Fauna and Ecology sections in the Facts about the Country chapter) are:

A Popular Guide to the Birds & Mammals of the Annapurna Conservation Area by Carol Inskipp
Birdwatchers' Guide to Nepal by Carol Inskipp
Flowers of the Himalaya by Oleg Polunin & Adam Stainton
Forests of Nepal by Adam Stainton
Mount Everest National Park: Sagarmatha, Mother of the Universe by Margaret Jefferies
Nepal's Forest Birds: Their Status and Conservation by Carol Inskipp
Royal Chitwan National Park: Wildlife Heritage of Nepal by Hemanta R Mishra & Margaret Jefferies
The Book of Indian Animals by SH Prater

Trees & Shrubs of Nepal & the Himalaya by Adrian & Jimmie Storrs.

Art & Architecture

Lydia Aran's *The Art of Nepal* is readily available in Nepal and concentrates on the art that can actually be seen in the country. See Arts in the Facts about the Country chapter for more on this book.

The Austrian publisher Anton Schroll has published two exhaustive studies of the architecture of the Kathmandu Valley. *Kathmandu Valley I* covers the most important temples and buildings in great detail while *Kathmandu Valley II* has individual plans of a great many temples and buildings. This is strictly for the academics but it's amusing to see how many other guidebooks have used these titles in their research. Often they've even copied the mistakes!

The Traditional Architecture of Kathmandu Valley by Wolfgang Korn has some superb line drawings showing the most important architectural forms, and an interesting text describing their historical development.

Mary Shepherd Sluiser's *Nepal Mandala – A Cultural Study of the Kathmandu Valley* is another two volume academic study of the valley.

Nepal – Art Treasures from the Himalaya by Waldschmidt describes and illustrates many Nepali works of art. The art of the whole Himalayan region is covered in Madanjeet Singh's *Himalayan Art*, again with excellent photographs.

In *Kathmandu Valley Towns*, Fran Hosken writes about the temples, people, history and festivals of the towns of the Kathmandu Valley. The book is illustrated with a great many colour photographs and halftones.

Erotic Themes of Nepal by Trilok Chandra Majupuria & Indra Majupuria is an interesting locally produced book on the erotic art seen on some temples, although it has to work hard to make a book-length study of the subject!

Hallvard Kåre Kuløøy's *Tibetan Rugs* is a fascinating and well illustrated introduction to the subject. If you enjoy the Tibetan rugs made in Nepal you may be disappointed to find that the author summarily dismisses modern rugs as doing 'very little justice to a very splendid tradition'.

Trekking Accounts

John Morris' *A Winter in Nepal* recounts in a very readable fashion a trek from Kathmandu to Pokhara. Like other accounts of the time it's interesting to compare it with the situation today – there was no Kathmandu to Pokhara road in those days. Morris was a retired British army Gurkha officer and his ability to speak Nepali gave him an excellent insight into Nepali life.

Peter Matthiessen's *The Snow Leopard* is, on one level, an account of a trek from Pokhara up to Dolpo in the west of Nepal, keeping an eye open for snow leopards on the way. On other levels, however, it's clear the author is searching for much more than rare wildlife and this widely acclaimed book doggedly pursues the big questions with the Himalaya as a background.

George Schaller, Matthiessen's companion on this trek, includes this same journey in *Stones of Silence*, an account of various journeys in the Himalaya.

Mountains & Mountaineering

There can be few activities that so inspire people to write about them as that of mountaineering. Every first ascent of a Himalayan peak seems to have resulted in a book about it, together with the numerous other books about the mountains written simply because it seemed a good idea. *The Ascent of Rum Doodle* by WE Bowman is a classic spoof of these often all-too-serious tomes.

Some mountaineering books, however, are excellent reads. If you can find HW Tilman's *Nepal Himalaya* in a library it gives an often amusing account of some early trekking expeditions together with the odd mountain assault which had, by today's standards, an amazing lack of advance planning. Although Tilman was a Himalayan mountaineering pioneer he probably contributed even more to the current popularity of trekking. His book has recently been republished together with other Tilman classics in *The*

Seven Mountain-Travel Books. Tilman's dry wit is quite delightful.

Maurice Herzog's *Annapurna* is a mountaineering classic. Herzog led the first group to reach the top of an 8000m peak, but the descent turned into a frostbitten nightmare taking them to the very outer edges of human endurance.

Naturally there have been numerous books about climbing Everest, including *Forerunners to Everest* by Rene Dittert, Gabriel Chevalley & Raymond Lambert. It describes the two Swiss expeditions to Everest in 1952 and includes a good description of the old expedition route march. Sir John Hunt's *The Conquest of Everest* is the official account of the first successful climb of the world's highest mountain. *Everest* by Walt Unsworth is probably the best history of Everest mountaineering.

In the 1970s unconquered peaks were few and far between so attention turned to climbing by more difficult or spectacular routes. This was technical climbing of a high order and Englishman Chris Bonnington's various expeditions were the best known examples of the craft. His book *Annapurna South Face* describes in detail the planning that goes into making a major expedition, the complicated logistics of the actual climb, and makes an authoritative account of a highly technical assault on a difficult face.

Bonnington also wrote *Everest the Hard Way*, describing his expedition's first ascent of the south-western face in 1975. This climb was a perfectly planned and executed race to the top, and the book is illustrated with superb mountain photography. Despite his record of leading some of the most acclaimed mountaineering expeditions of the time, Bonnington did not reach the top of Everest until 1985, when he set a record as the oldest Everest summiteer. He was 50 years old at the time but just nine days later his record fell to 55 year old American climber Dick Bass.

Galen Rowell, the renowned mountain photographer, has written *Many people come, looking, looking*. It is a thought provoking study of the impact of trekking and mountaineering on the Himalayan region.

There's a good description of the Annapurna Circuit trek and a quick sidetrip to knock off a little 6000m peak!

Other mountaineering books include *Annapurna to Dhaulagiri* by Harka Gurung, which covers the period between 1950 and 1960, when most of Nepal's major peaks 'fell' to mountaineering expeditions. Herbert Tichy's *Himalaya* describes the author's journeys in the region from the 1930s, including his ascent of Cho Oyu, the third highest peak climbed at that time.

Finally, for keen do-it-yourself mountaineers Bill O'Connor's *The Trekking Peaks of Nepal* is a complete description of the climbing routes up Nepal's 18 'trekking peaks'.

ONLINE SERVICES

There are a number of interesting sites which carry a great deal of information about Nepal. The following four sites are good places to start looking and have excellent links to other information on Nepal:
http://www.catmando.com/wwwvlnp.htm
http://www.math.grin.edu:80/~pradhan
http://www.cen.uiuc.edu/~rshresth/nepal.html

NEWSPAPERS & MAGAZINES

Nepal's main English-language daily paper, *Rising Nepal*, is basically a government mouthpiece. It covers most important international news while events in Nepal are reported in a very individual style!

For a more balanced view of local issues there's the daily *Kathmandu Post*, which is not too bad.

The only paper that really tackles the main issues in any depth is the weekly *Independent*, which gives some interesting insights into the local political scene.

The *International Herald Tribune* is widely available in Kathmandu – at a price. *Time* and *Newsweek* are readily available and Indian dailies like the *Statesman* or the *Times of India* can also be found.

Traveller's Nepal is a useful free monthly tourist magazine distributed at many hotels, including the Kathmandu Guest House. It often has very interesting articles about sightseeing, festivals, trekking and other activities in Nepal.

Himal is a bimonthly magazine devoted to development and environment issues. Unfortunately its recent shift to focus on south Asia rather than simply Nepal and the Himalaya means that there will no doubt be less coverage of Nepal issues. It's an excellent publication with top-class contributors.

There are also a number of Nepali newspapers and magazines online, including:
Himal:
http://www.south-asia.com/himal.html
Kathmandu Post:
http://www.south-asia.com/news-ktmpost.html
Independent:
http://www.south-asia.com/news-indep.html

RADIO & TV

Radio Nepal has news bulletins in English at 8 am and 8 pm daily. Local television arrived in Nepal in the mid-80s, but the most revolutionary change has been the arrival of satellite TV. Most up-market hotels have dishes, and you can watch everything from the BBC world service to MTV and American wrestling.

PHOTOGRAPHY & VIDEO
Film & Equipment

A few years ago running out of film in Nepal could be a real problem but now there are numerous camera and film shops and good-quality film is readily available. Do check, however, that the packaging has not been tampered with, and that the expiry date has not been exceeded. There have been cases where people have bought exposed film that has been wound back on the spool. If in doubt, open the cardboard packaging and check, but you are extremely unlikely to be ripped off in the larger shops.

Colour-print film can be processed rapidly, competently and economically in Kathmandu and Pokhara, and there are numerous places offering a same-day service for print film. The developing charge is typically Rs 40 plus around Rs 5 for each print. Colour slides can be developed in Kathmandu (although some have complained of scratched negatives). Prepaid Kodachrome and Fujichrome has to go overseas.

Typically, Fujicolor 100 colour-print film costs about Rs 145 (36 exposures), Fujichrome 36 exposure slide film about Rs 345 and Ektachrome 100 36 exposure slide film about Rs 350.

Taking Good Photos

Nepal is an exceptionally scenic country so bring plenty of film. It can also provide you with some challenging photo opportunities. For great shots you need a variety of lenses, from a wide-angle lens if you're shooting inside compact temple compounds to a long telephoto lens if you're after perfect mountain shots or close-ups of wildlife. A polarising filter is useful to increase contrast and bring out the blue of the sky.

Remember to allow for the exceptional intensity of mountain light when setting exposures at high altitude. At the other extreme it's surprising how often in Nepal you find the light is insufficient. Early in the morning, in dense jungle in Royal Chitwan National Park, or in gloomy temples and narrow streets you may often find yourself wishing you had high-speed film. A flash is often necessary for shots inside temples or to fill in shots of sculptures and reliefs.

Video

Bringing a video camera to Nepal poses no real problem, and there are no camera fees to worry about.

Photographing People

Most Nepalis are content to have their photograph taken but you should always get permission first. Sherpa people are an exception and can be very camera shy. Bear in mind that if someone poses for you (especially those saintly sadhus), they may insist on being given some baksheesh for doing so.

Respect people's privacy and bear in mind that most Nepalis are extremely modest. Although people carry out many activities in public (they have no choice), it does not follow that passers-by have the right to watch or take photographs. Riverbanks and

village wells, for example, are often used as bathrooms, but the users expect as much consideration and privacy as you would in your own house.

Religious ceremonies are also often private affairs, so first ask yourself whether it would be acceptable for a tourist to intrude and to take photographs at a corresponding ceremony in your home country, and then get explicit permission from the senior participants. The behaviour of many would-be National Geographic photographers at places like Pashupatinath (the most holy cremation site in Nepal) is horrendous. Imagine the outrage a busload of scantily clad, camera toting tourists would create if they invaded a family funeral in the west.

Airport Security

All luggage (including carry-on cabin baggage) is X-rayed at Kathmandu airport on the way in and the way out of the country, and while the X-ray equipment is supposedly film-safe, there have been instances where exposed film has been damaged. If you are really concerned, get exposed film inspected manually when leaving the country.

TIME

Nepal is five hours 45 minutes ahead of GMT; this curious time differential is intended to make it very clear that Nepal is a separate place to India, where the time is five hours 30 minutes ahead of GMT!

When it's noon in Nepal it's 1.15 pm in Bangkok, 6.15 am in London, 1.15 am in New York, 10.15 pm the previous day in Los Angeles or San Francisco, and 4.15 pm in Sydney or Melbourne, not allowing for daylight saving time or other local variations.

ELECTRICITY

Electricity is only found in major towns and some odd outposts like Namche Bazaar in the Solu Khumbu. When available it is 220 volts/50 cycles and 120 volt appliances from the USA need a transformer. Sockets usually take three round pin plugs, sometimes the small variety, sometimes the large. Some sockets take plugs with two round pins.

Outside Kathmandu blackouts are a fact of life and can be random, or regular. In winter, power shortages are endemic, especially if there has been low rainfall in the previous monsoon (which means water flow is reduced and the hydroelectric resources have to be rationed).

Power surges are also likely. If you are using expensive equipment (computers, TVs, fridges etc) it is worth buying a volt guard with spike suppressor (meaning an automatic cut-off switch). These are widely available from most electronic shops for around Rs 1000. Beltronix (☎ 01-224984) on Kantipath is one reliable supplier.

HEALTH

Travel health depends on your predeparture preparations, your day-to-day health care while travelling and how you handle any medical problem or emergency that does develop. While the list of potential dangers can seem quite frightening with a little luck, some basic precautions and adequate information few travellers experience more than upset stomachs.

Travel Health Guides

There are a number of books on travel health:

Staying Healthy in Asia, Africa & Latin America by Dirk Schroeder. Probably the best all-round guide to carry, as it's compact but very detailed and well organised.

Travellers' Health by Dr Richard Dawood. Comprehensive, easy to read, authoritative and also highly recommended, although it's rather large to lug around.

Where There is No Doctor by David Werner. A very detailed guide intended for someone, like a Peace Corps worker, going to work in a developing country, rather than for the average traveller.

Travel with Children by Maureen Wheeler, Lonely Planet Publications, 1995. Includes basic advice on travel health for younger children.

Predeparture Planning

Health Insurance A travel insurance policy to cover theft, loss and medical problems is a good idea. There is a wide variety of policies available and your travel agent will be able to make recommendations. The policies handled by STA Travel and other student travel organisations are usually good value. Some policies offer lower and higher medical-expense options but the higher ones are chiefly for countries, such as the USA, which have extremely high medical costs. Bear in mind that if you get seriously ill in Nepal you will almost certainly have to be evacuated, at least as far as Bangkok. Check the small print:

- Some policies specifically exclude 'dangerous activities' which can include motorcycling and even trekking. If such activities are on your agenda you don't want that sort of policy.
- You may prefer a policy which pays doctors or hospitals direct rather than you having to pay on the spot and claim later. If you have to claim later make sure you keep all documentation. Some policies ask you to call collect (reverse charges) to a centre in your home country where an immediate assessment of your problem is made (this service was only available to Canada, Japan and the UK at the time of going to print).
- Check that the policy covers ambulances or an emergency flight home. If you have to stretch out you will need two seats and somebody has to pay for them! If you take out trekking insurance make sure it covers a helicopter rescue service as well. Being flown out by helicopter costs $1500 to $2000 and the companies operate on a pay-first, fly-afterwards basis.

Medical Kit It's wise to carry a small, straightforward medical kit. Virtually any legal drug is available over the counter in pharmacies in Nepal, but you need to know the generic name of the drug as well as the brand name. Most drugs are much cheaper than in the west, and are usually made in India or Nepal. A basic medical kit should include:

- Aspirin or paracetamol (acetaminophen in the USA) – for pain or fever.
- Antihistamine (such as Benadryl) – useful as a decongestant for colds and allergies, to ease the itch from insect bites or stings, and to help prevent motion sickness. There are several antihistamines on the market, all with different pros and cons (eg a tendency to cause drowsiness), so it's worth discussing your requirements with a pharmacist or doctor. Antihistamines may cause sedation and interact with alcohol so care should be taken when using them.

- Antibiotics – useful if you're travelling well off the beaten track, but they must be prescribed and you should carry the prescription with you. Some individuals are allergic to commonly prescribed antibiotics such as penicillin or sulpha drugs. It would be sensible to always carry this information when travelling.
- Loperamide (eg Imodium) or Lomotil for diarrhoea; prochlorperazine (eg Stemetil) or metaclopramide (eg Maxalon) for nausea and vomiting. Antidiarrhoea medication should not be given to children under the age of 12.
- Rehydration mixture – for treatment of severe diarrhoea. This is particularly important if travelling with children, but is recommended for everyone.
- Antiseptic such as povidone-iodine (eg Betadine), which comes as a solution, ointment, powder and impregnated swabs – for cuts and grazes.
- Calamine lotion or Stingose spray – to ease irritation from bites or stings.
- Bandages and Band-aids – for minor injuries.
- Scissors, tweezers and a thermometer (note that mercury thermometers are prohibited by airlines).
- Cold and flu tablets and throat lozenges.
- Insect repellent, sunscreen, chap stick and water purification tablets.
- A couple of syringes in case you need injections. Ask your doctor for a note explaining why they have been prescribed.

Ideally antibiotics should be administered only under medical supervision and should never be taken indiscriminately. Take only the recommended dose at the prescribed intervals and continue using the antibiotic for the prescribed period, even if the illness seems to be cured earlier. Antibiotics are quite specific to the infections they can treat. Stop immediately if there are any serious reactions and don't use the antibiotic at all if you are unsure that you have the correct one.

It is a good idea to leave unwanted medicines, syringes etc with a reputable local clinic, rather than carry them home.

Health Preparations Make sure you're healthy before you start travelling. If you are embarking on a long trip make sure your teeth are OK; there are lots of places where a visit to the dentist would be the last thing you'd want.

If you wear glasses take a spare pair and your prescription. Losing your glasses can be a real problem.

If you require a particular medication take an adequate supply, as it may not be available locally. Take the prescription or, better still, part of the packaging showing the generic rather than the brand name (which may not be locally available), as it will make getting replacements easier. It's wise to have a legible prescription or a letter from your doctor with you to show that you legally use the medication.

Immunisations Vaccinations provide protection against diseases you might meet along the way. No specific immunisations are required for Nepal, but a number are certainly advisable, particularly if you plan to visit other Asian countries before or after Nepal.

It is important to understand the distinction between vaccines recommended for travel in certain areas and those required by law. Essentially the number of vaccines subject to international health regulations has been dramatically reduced over the last 10 years. Currently yellow fever is the only vaccine subject to international health regulations. Vaccination as an entry requirement is usually only enforced when coming from an infected area.

All vaccinations should be recorded on an International Health Certificate, which is available from your physician or government health department.

Plan ahead for getting your vaccinations: some of them require an initial shot followed by a booster, while some vaccinations should not be given together. It is recommended you seek medical advice at least six weeks prior to travel.

Most travellers from western countries will have been immunised against various diseases during childhood but your doctor may still recommend booster shots against measles or polio, diseases still prevalent in many developing countries. The period of protection offered by vaccinations differs widely and some are contraindicated if you are pregnant.

In Kathmandu, the two best places to go are the CIWEC and Nepal International clinics (see Medical Facilities in Nepal later in this section). Vaccinations include:

Tetanus & Diphtheria Boosters are necessary every 10 years and protection is highly recommended.

Polio A booster of either the oral or injected vaccine is required every 10 years to maintain your immunity from childhood vaccination. Polio is a very serious, easily transmitted disease which is still prevalent in many developing countries.

Typhoid Available either as an injection or oral capsules. Protection lasts from one to five years depending on the vaccine and is useful if you are travelling for long in rural, tropical areas. You may get some side effects such as pain at the injection site, fever, headache and a general unwell feeling. A new single-dose injectable vaccine, which appears to have few side effects, is now available but is more expensive. Side effects are unusual with the oral form but occasionally an individual will have stomach cramps.

Hepatitis A The most common travel-acquired illness which can be prevented by vaccination. Protection can be provided in two ways – either with the antibody gamma globulin or with a new vaccine called Havrix.

Havrix provides long term immunity (possibly more than 10 years) after an initial course of two injections and a booster at one year. It may be more expensive than gamma globulin but certainly has many advantages, including length of protection and ease of administration. It is important to know that being a vaccine it will take about three weeks to provide satisfactory protection – hence the need for careful planning prior to travel.

Gamma globulin is not a vaccination but a ready-made antibody which has proven very successful in reducing the chances of hepatitis infection. It should be given as close as possible to departure because it is at its most effective in the first few weeks after administration and the effectiveness tapers off gradually between three and six months.

Hepatitis B Travellers at risk of contact (see Infectious Diseases section) are strongly advised to be vaccinated, especially if they are children or will have close contact with children. The vaccination course comprises three injections given over a six month period followed by boosters every three to five years. The initial course of injections can be given over as short a period as 28 days then boosted after 12 months if more rapid protection is required.

Meningococcal Meningitis Immunisation is important as there have been recent outbreaks in Nepal. A single injection will give good protection against the A, C, W and Y groups of the bacteria for at least a year. The vaccine is not, however, recommended for children under two years because they do not develop satisfactory immunity from it.

Japanese B Encephalitis Vaccination is usually considered for those intending to spend more than a month or longer in a risk area, for those making repeated trips into a risk area or those visiting during an epidemic. The vaccination course consists of three injections given over 30 days. The vaccine has been associated with serious allergic reactions so the decision to have it should be balanced against the risk of contracting the illness.

Tuberculosis TB risk should be considered for people travelling more than three months to high risk areas such as Asia. As most healthy adults do not develop symptoms, a skin test before and after travel to determine whether exposure has occurred is recommended. Vaccination for children who will be travelling for more than three months is recommended.

Rabies Pretravel rabies vaccination involves having three injections over 21 to 28 days and should be considered by those who will spend a month or longer in a country where rabies is common, especially if they are cycling, handling animals, caving or travelling to remote areas, and for children (who may not report a bite). If someone who has been vaccinated is bitten or scratched by an animal they will require two booster injections of vaccine.

Smallpox Smallpox has been wiped out worldwide, so immunisation is no longer necessary.

Basic Rules

Care in what you eat and drink is the most important health rule; stomach upsets are the most likely travel health problem (between 30% and 50% of travellers in a two week stay experience this) but the majority of these upsets will be relatively minor. Don't become paranoid; trying the local food is part of the experience of travel, after all.

Water The number one rule is *don't drink the water* and that includes ice. If you don't know for certain that the water is safe always assume the worst.

Water Purification The simplest way of purifying water is to boil it thoroughly. Vigorous boiling for five minutes should be satisfactory; however, at high altitude water boils at a lower temperature, so germs are less likely to be killed.

Simple filtering will not remove all dangerous organisms, so if you cannot boil water it should be treated chemically. Chlorine tablets (Puritabs, Steritabs or other brand names) will kill many but not all pathogens. They will not kill giardia and amoebic cysts. Iodine is very effective in purifying water and is available in tablet form (such as Potable Aqua), but follow the directions carefully and remember that too much iodine can be harmful.

If you can't find tablets, tincture of iodine (2%) can be used. Four drops of tincture of iodine per litre or quart of clear water is the recommended dosage; the treated water should be left to stand for 20 to 30 minutes before drinking. Iodine crystals can also be used to purify water but this is a more complicated process, as you have to first prepare a saturated iodine solution. Iodine loses its effectiveness if exposed to air or damp so keep it in a tightly sealed container. Flavoured powder will disguise the taste of treated water and is a good idea if you are travelling with children.

Micropur water filters are useful for long trips. They filter out parasites, bacteria and viruses, and although expensive they are more cost effective than buying water.

Purchased Drinks Reputable brands of bottled water or soft drinks are generally fine, although in some places bottles refilled with tap water are not unknown. Only use water from containers with a serrated seal – not tops or corks. Take care with fruit juice, particularly if water may have been added. Milk should be treated with suspicion, as it is often unpasteurised. Boiled milk is fine if it is kept hygienically. Tea or coffee should also be OK, since the water should have been boiled.

Food There is an old colonial adage which says: 'If you can cook it, boil it or peel it you can eat it...otherwise forget it'. Salads and fruit should be washed with purified water or peeled where possible. Ice cream is usually OK if it is a reputable brand name, but beware of street vendors and of ice cream that has melted and been refrozen. Thoroughly cooked food is safest but not if it has been left to cool or if it has been reheated.

If a place looks clean and well run and if the vendor also looks clean and healthy, then the food is probably safe. In general, places that are packed with travellers or locals will be fine, while empty restaurants are questionable. The food in busy restaurants is cooked and eaten quite quickly with little standing around and is probably not reheated.

Nutrition

If your food is poor or limited in availability, if you're travelling hard and fast and therefore missing meals, or if you simply lose your appetite, you can soon start to lose weight and place your health at risk.

Make sure your diet is well balanced. Eggs, beans, lentils (dal in Nepal) and nuts are all safe ways to get protein. Fruit you can peel (bananas, oranges or mandarins for example) is usually safe (melons can harbour bacteria in their flesh and are best avoided) and a good source of vitamins. Try to eat plenty of grains (rice) and bread. Remember that although food is generally safer if it is cooked well, overcooked food loses much of its nutritional value. If your diet isn't well balanced or if your food intake is insufficient, it's a good idea to take vitamin and iron pills.

In hot climates make sure you drink enough – don't rely on feeling thirsty to indicate when you should drink. Not needing to urinate or very dark yellow urine is a danger sign. Always carry a water bottle with you on long trips. Excessive sweating can lead to loss of salt and therefore muscle cramping. Salt tablets are not a good idea as a preventative, but in places where salt is not used much, adding salt to food can help.

Everyday Health Normal body temperature is 98.6°F or 37°C; more than 2°C (4°F) higher indicates a high fever. The normal adult pulse rate is 60 to 100 per minute (children 80 to 100, babies 100 to 140). You should know how to take a temperature and a pulse rate. As a general rule the pulse increases about 20 beats per minute for each °C (2°F) rise in fever.

Respiration (breathing) rate is also an indicator of illness. Count the number of breaths per minute: between 12 and 20 is normal for adults and older children (up to 30 for younger children, 40 for babies). People with a high fever or serious respiratory illness (like pneumonia) breathe more quickly than normal. More than 40 shallow breaths a minute may indicate pneumonia.

In western countries with safe water and excellent human waste disposal systems we often take good health for granted. In years gone by, when public health facilities were not as good as they are today, certain rules attached to eating and drinking were observed, eg washing your hands before a meal. It is important for people travelling in areas of poor sanitation to be aware of this and adjust their own personal hygiene habits. Clean your teeth with purified water rather than straight from the tap.

Avoid climatic extremes: keep out of the sun when it's hot, dress warmly when it's cold. Avoid potential diseases by dressing sensibly. You can get worm infections through walking barefoot. You can avoid insect bites by covering bare skin when insects are around, by screening windows or beds and by using insect repellents. Seek local advice, and in situations where there is no information, discretion is the better part of valour.

Medical Facilities in Nepal

Medical facilities in Nepal are distinctly limited. The entire country of around 19 million has a meagre 4600 hospital beds, and in most cases you wouldn't want to be seen dead in them. Anyone requiring serious surgery or critical care – and who has the necessary insurance or money – flies out to Bangkok or the west.

See the Kathmandu Information section for details of the facilities available in the capital.

Medical Problems & Treatment

Potential medical problems can be broken down into several areas. Firstly there are the problems caused by extremes of temperature, altitude or motion. Then there are diseases and illnesses caused through poor environmental sanitation, insect bites or stings, and animal or human contact. Simple cuts, bites and scratches can also cause problems.

Self-diagnosis and treatment can be risky, so wherever possible seek qualified help. Although we do give drug dosages in this section, they are for emergency use only. Medical advice should be sought where possible before administering any drugs.

An embassy or consulate can usually recommend a good place to go for such advice. So can five star hotels, although they often recommend doctors with five star prices. (This is when that medical insurance really comes in useful!) For serious illnesses the best advice is to get on a plane and go somewhere else, such as Bangkok.

Environmental Hazards

Sunburn At high altitude you can get sunburnt surprisingly quickly, even through cloud. A hat provides added protection, and you should also use zinc cream or some other barrier cream for your nose and lips. Calamine lotion is good for mild sunburn.

Fungal Infections Fungal infections, which occur with greater frequency in hot weather, are most likely to occur on the scalp, between the toes or fingers (athlete's foot), in the groin (jock itch or crotch rot) and on the body (ringworm). You get ringworm (which is a fungal infection, not a worm) from infected animals or by walking on damp areas, like shower floors.

To prevent fungal infections wear loose, comfortable clothes, avoid artificial fibres, wash frequently and dry carefully. If you do get an infection, wash the infected area daily with a disinfectant or medicated soap and water, and rinse and dry well. Apply an antifungal cream or powder like the widely available Tinaderm. Try to expose the infected area to air or sunlight as much as possible and wash all towels and underwear in hot water as well as changing them often.

Hypothermia Too much cold is just as dangerous as too much heat, particularly if it leads to hypothermia. If you are trekking at high altitudes you should always be prepared for cold, wet or windy conditions.

Hypothermia occurs when the body loses heat faster than it can produce it and the core temperature of the body falls. It is surprisingly easy to progress from very cold to dangerously cold due to a combination of wind, wet clothing, fatigue and hunger, even if the air temperature is above freezing. It is best to dress in layers; silk, wool and some of the new artificial fibres are all good insulating materials. A hat is important, as a lot of heat is lost through the head. A strong, waterproof outer layer is essential, as keeping dry is vital. Carry basic supplies, including food containing simple sugars to generate heat quickly and lots of fluid to drink. A space blanket is something all travellers in cold environments should carry.

Symptoms of hypothermia are exhaustion, numb skin (particularly toes and fingers), shivering, slurred speech, irrational or violent behaviour, lethargy, stumbling, dizzy spells, muscle cramps and violent bursts of energy. Irrationality may take the form of sufferers claiming they are warm and trying to take off their clothes.

To treat mild hypothermia, first get the person out of the wind and/or rain, remove their clothing if it's wet and replace it with dry, warm clothing. Give them hot liquids – not alcohol – and some high-kilojoule, easily digestible food. Do not rub victims, instead allow them to slowly warm themselves. This should be enough to treat the early stages of hypothermia. The early recognition and treatment of mild hypothermia is the only way to prevent severe hypothermia, which is a critical condition.

Altitude Sickness Acute Mountain Sickness, or AMS, occurs at high altitude and can

be fatal. The lack of oxygen at high altitudes (over 2500m) affects most people to some extent. It may be mild (benign AMS) or severe (malignant AMS) and occurs because less oxygen reaches the muscles and the brain at high altitude, requiring the heart and lungs to compensate by working harder.

AMS symptoms usually develop during the first 24 hours at altitude but may be delayed up to three weeks. Symptoms of benign AMS include headache, lethargy, dizziness, difficulty with sleeping and loss of appetite. Malignant AMS may develop from benign AMS or without warning and can be fatal. These symptoms include breathlessness, dry cough (which may progress to the production of pink, frothy sputum), severe headache, lack of coordination and balance, confusion, irrational behaviour, vomiting, drowsiness and unconsciousness. There is no hard-and-fast rule as to how high is too high: AMS has been fatal at altitudes of 3000m, although 3500m to 4500m is the usual range.

For benign AMS the treatment is to remain resting at the same altitude until recovery, usually a day or two. Paracetamol or aspirin can be taken for headaches. If symptoms persist or become worse, however, descent is necessary; even 500m can help. The treatment of malignant AMS is immediate descent to a lower altitude. There are various drug treatments available but they should never be used to avoid descent or enable further ascent by a person with AMS.

The voluntary Himalayan Rescue Association publishes a pamphlet on AMS which is available from the immigration office and from all trekking agencies. They have an office in the Tilicho Hotel in Thamel or have a look at their web site:
http://ws.gorge.net/hra

A number of measures can be adopted to prevent acute mountain sickness:

- Ascend slowly – have frequent rest days, spending two to three nights at each rise of 1000m. If you reach a high altitude by trekking, acclimatisation takes place gradually and you are less likely to be affected than if you fly direct.

- The altitude at which a person sleeps is an important factor. It is always wise to sleep at a lower altitude than the greatest height reached during the day. Also, once above 3000m, care should be taken not to increase the sleeping altitude by more than 300m per day.
- Drink extra fluids. The mountain air is dry and cold, and moisture is lost as you breathe.
- Eat light, high-carbohydrate meals for more energy.
- Avoid alcohol as it may increase the risk of dehydration.
- Avoid sedatives.
- The drugs acetazolamide (Diamox) and dexamethasone have been recommended for prevention of AMS. They can reduce the symptoms, but they also mask warning signs; severe and fatal AMS has occurred in people taking these drugs. In general they are not recommended for travellers.

Motion Sickness Eating lightly before and during a trip will reduce the chances of motion sickness. If you are prone to motion sickness try to find a place that minimises disturbance – near the wing on aircraft, near the centre on buses. Fresh air usually helps; reading and cigarette smoke don't. Commercial motion-sickness preparations, which can cause drowsiness, have to be taken before the trip commences; when you're feeling sick it's too late. Ginger (available in capsule form) and peppermint (including mint-flavoured sweets) are natural preventatives.

Infectious Diseases
Diarrhoea A change of water, food or climate can all cause the runs; diarrhoea caused by contaminated food or water is more serious. Despite all your precautions you may still get a mild bout of travellers' diarrhoea but a few rushed toilet trips with no other symptoms is not indicative of a serious problem. Moderate diarrhoea, involving half a dozen loose movements in a day, is more of a nuisance.

Dehydration is the main danger with any diarrhoea, particularly for children where dehydration can occur quite quickly. Fluid replacement remains the mainstay of management. Weak black tea with a little sugar, soda water, or soft drinks allowed to go flat and diluted 50% with water are all good.

With severe diarrhoea a rehydrating solution is necessary to replace minerals and salts. Commercially available ORS (oral rehydration salts) are very useful; add the contents of one sachet to a litre of boiled or bottled water. In an emergency you can make up a solution of eight teaspoons of sugar to a litre of boiled water and provide salted cracker biscuits at the same time. You should stick to a bland diet as you recover.

Lomotil or Imodium can be used to bring relief from symptoms, although they do not actually cure the problem. Only use these drugs if absolutely necessary – eg if you *must* travel. For children under 12 years Lomotil and Imodium are not recommended. Under all circumstances fluid replacement is the most important thing to remember. Do not use these drugs if the person has a high fever or is severely dehydrated.

In certain situations antibiotics may be indicated:

- Watery diarrhoea with blood and mucus. (Gut-paralysing drugs like Imodium or Lomotil should be avoided in this situation.)
- Watery diarrhoea with fever and lethargy.
- Persistent diarrhoea not improving after 48 hours.
- Severe diarrhoea, if it is logistically difficult to stay in one place.

The recommended drugs (adults only) would be either norfloxacin 400 mg twice daily for three days or ciprofloxacin 500 mg twice daily for three days.

The drug bismuth subsalicylate has also been used successfully. It is not available in some countries. The dosage for adults is two tablets or 30 ml and for children it is one tablet or 10 ml. This dose can be repeated every 30 minutes to one hour, with no more than eight doses in a 24 hour period.

The drug of choice for children would be co-trimoxazole (Bactrim, Septrin, Resprim) with dosage dependent on weight. A five day course is given.

Ampicillin has been recommended in the past and may still be an alternative.

Giardiasis The parasite causing this intestinal disorder is present in contaminated water.

The symptoms are stomach cramps, nausea, a bloated stomach, watery, foul-smelling diarrhoea and frequent gas. Giardiasis can appear several weeks after you have been exposed to the parasite. The symptoms may disappear for a few days and then return; this can go on for several weeks. Tinidazole, known as Fasigyn, or metronidazole (Flagyl) are the recommended drugs for treatment. Either can be used in a single treatment dose. Other antibiotics are of no use.

Dysentery This serious illness is caused by contaminated food or water and is characterised by severe diarrhoea, often with blood or mucus in the stool. There are two kinds of dysentery. Bacillary dysentery is characterised by a high fever and rapid onset; headache, vomiting and stomach pains are also symptoms. It generally does not last longer than a week, but it is highly contagious.

Amoebic dysentery is often more gradual in the onset of symptoms, with cramping abdominal pain and vomiting less likely; fever may not be present. This disease is not self-limiting: it will persist until treated and can recur and cause long-term health problems.

A stool test is necessary to diagnose which kind of dysentery you have, so you should seek medical help urgently. In case of an emergency the drugs norfloxacin or ciprofloxacin can be used as presumptive treatment for bacillary dysentery, and metronidazole (Flagyl) for amoebic dysentery.

For bacillary dysentery, norfloxacin 400 mg twice daily for seven days or ciprofloxacin 500 mg twice daily for seven days are the recommended dosages.

If you're unable to find either of these drugs then a useful alternative is co-trimoxazole 160/800 mg (Bactrim, Septrin, Resprim) twice daily for seven days. This is a sulpha drug and must not be used by people with a known sulpha allergy. For children the drug co-trimoxazole is a reasonable first-line treatment.

For amoebic dysentery, the recommended adult dosage of metronidazole (Flagyl) is one 750 mg to 800 mg capsule three times daily for five days. Children aged between eight and 12 years should have half the adult dose; the dosage for younger children is one third the adult dose.

An alternative to Flagyl is Fasigyn, taken as a two gram daily dose for three days. Alcohol must be avoided during treatment and for 48 hours afterwards.

Cholera Cholera vaccination is not very effective. The bacteria responsible for this disease are waterborne, so attention to the rules of eating and drinking should protect the traveller.

Outbreaks of cholera are generally widely reported, so you can avoid such problem areas. The disease is characterised by a sudden onset of acute diarrhoea with 'rice water' stools, vomiting, muscular cramps and extreme weakness. You need medical help – but treat for dehydration, which can be extreme, and if there is an appreciable delay in getting to hospital then begin taking tetracycline. The adult dose is 250 mg four times daily. It is not recommended for children aged eight years or under nor for pregnant women. An alternative drug is Ampicillin. People allergic to penicillin should not take Ampicillin. Remember that while antibiotics might kill the bacteria, it is a toxin produced by the bacteria which causes the massive fluid loss. Fluid replacement is by far the most important aspect of treatment.

Viral Gastroenteritis This is caused not by bacteria but, as the name suggests, by a virus. It is characterised by stomach cramps, diarrhoea, and sometimes by vomiting and/or a slight fever. All you can do is rest and drink lots of fluids.

Hepatitis Hepatitis is a general term for inflammation of the liver. There are many causes of this condition: drugs, alcohol and infections are but a few.

The discovery of new strains has led to a virtual alphabet soup, with hepatitis A, B, C, D, E, G and others. These letters identify specific agents that cause viral hepatitis. Viral hepatitis is an infection of the liver, which can lead to jaundice (yellow skin), fever, lethargy and digestive problems. It can have no symptoms at all, with the infected person not knowing that they have the disease. Travellers shouldn't be too paranoid about this apparent proliferation of hepatitis strains; hep C, D, E and G are fairly rare (so far) and following the same precautions as for A and B should be all that's necessary to avoid them.

Viral hepatitis can be divided into two groups on the basis of how it is spread. The first route of transmission is via contaminated food and water (leading to hepatitis A and E) and the second route is via blood and bodily fluids (resulting in hepatitis B, C and D).

Hepatitis A This is a very common disease in most countries, especially those with poor standards of sanitation. Most people in developing countries are infected as children; they often don't develop symptoms, but do develop life-long immunity. The disease poses a real threat to the traveller, as people are unlikely to have been exposed to hepatitis A in developed countries.

The symptoms are fever, chills, headache, fatigue, feelings of weakness and aches and pains, followed by loss of appetite, nausea, vomiting, abdominal pain, dark urine, light-coloured faeces, jaundiced skin and the whites of the eyes may turn yellow. In some cases you may feel unwell, tired, have no appetite, experience aches and pains and be jaundiced. You should seek medical advice, but in general there is not much you can do apart from resting, drinking lots of fluids, eating lightly and avoiding fatty foods. People who have had hepatitis must forego alcohol for six months after the illness, as hepatitis attacks the liver and it needs that amount of time to recover.

The routes of transmission are via contaminated water, shellfish contaminated by sewerage, or foodstuffs handled by people with poor standards of hygiene.

Taking care with what you eat and drink can go a long way towards preventing this disease. But this is a very infectious virus, so if there is any risk of exposure, additional cover is highly recommended. This cover comes in two forms: Gammaglobulin and Havrix. Gammaglobulin is an injection where you are given the antibodies for hepatitis A, which provide immunity for a limited time. Havrix is a vaccine, where you develop your own antibodies, which gives lasting immunity.

Hepatitis E This is a very recently discovered virus, of which little is yet known. It appears to be rather common in developing countries, generally causing mild hepatitis, although it can be very serious in pregnant women.

Care with water supplies is the only current prevention, as there are no specific vaccines for this type of hepatitis. At present it doesn't appear to be too great a risk for travellers.

The following strains are spread by contact with blood and bodily fluids:

Hepatitis B This is also a very common disease, with almost 300 million chronic carriers in the world. Hepatitis B, which used to be called serum hepatitis, is spread through contact with infected blood, blood products or bodily fluids, for example through sexual contact, unsterilised needles and blood transfusions, or via small breaks in the skin. Other risk situations include having a shave or tattoo in a local shop, or having your body pierced.

The symptoms of type B are much the same as type A except that they are more severe and may lead to irreparable liver damage or even liver cancer. Although there is no treatment for hepatitis B, a cheap and effective vaccine is available; the only problem is that for long-lasting cover you need a six-month course.

Persons who should receive a hepatitis B vaccination include anyone who anticipates contact with blood or other bodily secretions, either as a health-care worker or through sexual contact with the local population, particularly those who intend to stay in the country for a long period of time.

Hepatitis C This is another recently defined virus. It is a concern because it seems to lead to liver disease more rapidly than hepatitis B.

The virus is spread by contact with blood – usually via contaminated transfusions or shared needles. Avoiding these is the only means of prevention, as there is no available vaccine.

Hepatitis D Often referred to as the 'Delta' virus, this infection only occurs in chronic carriers of hepatitis B. It is transmitted by blood and bodily fluids. Again there is no vaccine for this virus, so avoidance is the best prevention. The risk to travellers is certainly limited.

Typhoid Typhoid fever is another gut infection that travels the faecal-oral route – ie contaminated water and food are responsible. Vaccination against typhoid is not totally effective and it is one of the most dangerous infections, so medical help must be sought.

In its early stages typhoid resembles many other illnesses: sufferers may feel like they have a bad cold or flu on the way, as early symptoms are a headache, a sore throat, and a fever which rises a little each day until it is around 40°C or more. The victim's pulse is often slow relative to the degree of fever present and gets slower as the fever rises – unlike a normal fever where the pulse increases. There may also be vomiting, diarrhoea or constipation.

In the second week the high fever and slow pulse continue and a few pink spots may appear on the body; trembling, delirium, weakness, weight loss and dehydration are other symptoms. If there are no further complications, the fever and other symptoms will slowly diminish during the third week. However you must get medical help before this because pneumonia (acute infection of the lungs) or peritonitis (perforated bowel) are common complications, and because typhoid is very infectious.

The fever should be treated by keeping the victim cool and dehydration should also be watched for.

The drug of choice is ciprofloxacin at a dose of one gram daily for 14 days. It is quite expensive and may not be available. The alternative, chloramphenicol, has been the mainstay of treatment for many years. In many countries it is still the recommended antibiotic but there are fewer side affects with Ampicillin. The adult dosage is two 250 mg capsules four times a day. Children aged between eight and 12 years should have half the adult dose; younger children should have one third the adult dose.

People who are allergic to penicillin should not be given Ampicillin.

Worms These parasites are most common in rural, tropical areas and a stool test when you return home is not a bad idea. They can be present on unwashed vegetables or in undercooked meat and you can pick them up through your skin by walking in bare feet. Infestations may not show up for some time, and although they are generally not serious, if left untreated they can cause severe health problems. A stool test is necessary to pinpoint the problem and medication is often available over the counter.

Tetanus This potentially fatal disease is found worldwide, occurring more commonly in undeveloped tropical areas. It is difficult to treat but is preventable with immunisation. Tetanus occurs when a wound becomes infected by a germ which lives in soil and in the faeces of horses and other animals, so clean all cuts, punctures or animal bites. Tetanus is also known as lockjaw, and the first symptom may be discomfort in swallowing, or stiffening of the jaw and neck; this is followed by painful convulsions of the jaw and whole body.

Rabies Rabies is a fatal viral infection found in many countries and is caused by a bite or scratch by an infected animal. Dogs are noted carriers as are monkeys and cats. Any bite, scratch or even lick from a warm-blooded, furry animal should be cleaned immediately and thoroughly. Scrub with soap and running water, and then clean with an alcohol or iodine solution. If there is any possibility that the animal is infected medical help should be sought immediately to prevent the onset of symptoms and death. In a person who has not been immunised against rabies this involves having five injections of vaccine and one of immunoglobulin over 28 days starting as soon as possible after the exposure. Even if the animal is not rabid, all bites should be treated seriously as they can become infected or can result in tetanus.

A rabies vaccination is available and should be considered if you are in a high-risk category – eg if you intend to explore caves (bat bites can be dangerous), work with animals, or travel so far off the beaten track that medical help is more than two days away.

Meningococcal Meningitis There have been outbreaks of meningitis in Nepal. An epidemic occurred in the Kathmandu Valley in 1983 and in the ensuing two years, six foreigners contracted meningococcal meningitis and two died. In 1985 the US Centres for Disease Control advised travellers to be vaccinated against the disease, and since then there have still been sporadic cases in travellers. Vaccination is still sound advice, especially for trekkers, as the disease is spread by close contact with people who carry it in their throats and noses, spread it through coughs and sneezes and may not be aware that they are carriers. Lodges in the hills where travellers spend the night are prime spots for the spread of infection.

This very serious disease attacks the brain and can be fatal. A scattered, blotchy rash, fever, severe headache, sensitivity to light and neck stiffness which prevents forward bending of the head are the first symptoms. Death can occur within a few hours, so immediate treatment is important.

Treatment is large doses of penicillin given intravenously, or, if that is not possible, intramuscularly (ie in the buttocks). Vaccination offers good protection for over a year,

but you should also check for reports of current epidemics.

Tuberculosis (TB) There is a worldwide resurgence of tuberculosis, a bacterial infection which is widespread in many developing countries. It is usually transmitted from person to person by coughing but may be transmitted through consumption of unpasteurised milk. Milk that has been boiled is safe to drink, and the souring of milk to make yoghurt or cheese also kills the bacilli. Typically many months of contact with the infected person are required before the disease is passed on. The usual site of the disease is the lungs, although other organs may be involved.

Most infected people never develop symptoms. In those who do, especially infants, symptoms may arise within weeks of the infection occurring and may be severe. In most, however, the disease lies dormant for many years until, for some reason, the infected person becomes physically run down. Symptoms include fever, weight loss, night sweats and coughing.

Diphtheria Diphtheria can be a skin infection or a more dangerous throat infection. It is spread by contaminated dust contacting the skin or by the inhalation of infected cough or sneeze droplets. Frequent washing and keeping the skin dry will help prevent skin infection. The mainstay of treatment of the diphtheria throat infection is an intravenous infusion of diphtheria antitoxin. The antitoxin is produced in horses so may be associated with allergic reactions in some people. Because of this it must be administered under close medical supervision. Antibiotics such as erythromycin or penicillin are then given to eradicate the diphtheria bacteria from the patient so that it is not transmitted to others. A vaccination is available to prevent the throat infection.

Sexually Transmitted Diseases Sexual contact with an infected sexual partner spreads these diseases. While abstinence is the only 100% preventative, using condoms is also effective. Gonorrhoea, herpes and syphilis are the most common STDs; sores, blisters or rashes around the genitals, discharges or pain when urinating are common symptoms. Symptoms may be less marked or not observed at all in women. Syphilis symptoms eventually disappear completely but the disease continues and can cause severe problems in later years. The treatment of gonorrhoea and syphilis is with antibiotics.

There are numerous other sexually transmitted diseases, for most of which effective treatment is available. However, there is no cure for herpes and there is also currently no cure for AIDS.

HIV/AIDS HIV, the Human Immunodeficiency Virus, may develop into AIDS, Acquired Immune Deficiency Syndrome. HIV is a major problem in many countries. Any exposure to blood, blood products or bodily fluids may put the individual at risk. In many developing countries transmission is predominantly through heterosexual sexual activity. This is quite different from industrialised countries where transmission is mostly through contact between homosexual or bisexual males, or via contaminated needles shared by IV drug users. Apart from abstinence, the most effective preventative is always to practise safe sex using condoms. It is impossible to detect the HIV-positive status of an otherwise healthy-looking person without a blood test.

HIV/AIDS can also be spread through infected blood transfusions; some developing countries cannot afford to screen blood for transfusions. It can also be spread by dirty needles – vaccinations, acupuncture, tattooing and ear or nose piercing can be potentially as dangerous as intravenous drug use if the equipment is not clean. If you do need an injection, ask to see the syringe unwrapped in front of you, or better still, take a needle and syringe pack with you overseas – it is a cheap insurance package against infection with HIV.

Fear of HIV infection should never preclude treatment for serious medical conditions.

Although there may be a risk of infection, it is very small indeed.

Insect-Borne Diseases
Malaria This serious disease is spread by mosquito bites. Malaria has been virtually eradicated from the Terai but malarial phrophylactics are still advisable, especially if you are travelling during the wet season. If your visit to Nepal is restricted to the high country – Kathmandu, Pokhara and the trekking routes – malaria protection is not necessary.

Symptoms include headaches, fever, chills and sweating which may subside and recur. Without treatment malaria can develop more serious, potentially fatal effects.

Antimalarial drugs do not prevent you from being infected but kill the parasites during a stage in their development.

There are a number of different types of malaria. The one of most concern is falciparum malaria. This is responsible for the very serious cerebral malaria.

The problem in recent years has been the emergence of increasing resistance to commonly used antimalarials like chloroquine, maloprim and proguanil. Chloroquine resistant malaria is not a problem in Nepal. Newer drugs such as mefloquine (Lariam) and doxycycline (Vibramycin, Doryx) are often recommended for chloroquine and multidrug resistant areas.

Expert advice should be sought, as there are many factors to consider when deciding on the type of antimalarial medication, including the area to be visited, the risk of exposure to malaria-carrying mosquitoes, your medical history, and your age and pregnancy status. It is also important to discuss the side effects of the medication, so you can work out some level of risk versus benefit ratio. It is also very important to be sure of the correct dosage of the medication prescribed to you. Some people have inadvertently taken weekly medication (chloroquine) on a daily basis, with disastrous effects. While discussing dosages for prevention of malaria, it is often advisable to include the dosages required for treatment, especially if your trip is through a high-risk area that would isolate you from medical care.

The main messages are:

1. Primary prevention must always be in the form of mosquito-avoidance measures. The mosquitoes that transmit malaria bite from dusk to dawn and during this period travellers are advised to:

   - wear light coloured clothing
   - wear long pants and long sleeved shirts
   - use mosquito repellents containing the compound DEET on exposed areas (overuse of DEET may be harmful, especially to children, but its use is considered preferable to being bitten by disease- transmitting mosquitoes)
   - avoid highly scented perfumes or aftershave
   - use a mosquito net – it may be worth taking your own

2. While no antimalarial is 100% effective, taking the most appropriate drug significantly reduces the risk of contracting the disease.

3. No-one should ever die from malaria. It can be diagnosed by a simple blood test. Symptoms range from fever, chills and sweating, headache and abdominal pains to a vague feeling of ill-health, so seek examination immediately if there is any suggestion of malaria.

Contrary to popular belief, once a person contracts malaria they do not have it for life. Two species of the parasite may lie dormant in the liver but they can also be eradicated using a specific medication. Malaria is curable, as long as the traveller seeks medical help when symptoms occur.

Dengue Fever Dengue fever is not present in Nepal, though it does exist in India. There is no prophylactic available for this mosquito-spread disease; the main preventative measure is to avoid mosquito bites. A sudden onset of fever, headaches and severe joint and muscle pains are the first signs before a rash starts on the trunk of the body and spreads to the limbs and face. After a further few days, the fever will subside and recovery will begin. Serious complications are not common but full recovery can take up to a month or more.

Japanese B Encephalitis This viral infection of the brain is transmitted by mosquitoes. It is usually a severe illness with a high mortality rate. Most cases occur in rural areas because part of the life cycle of the virus takes place in pigs or wading birds. Symptoms include fever, headache, vomiting, neck stiffness, pain in the eyes when looking at light, alteration in consciousness, seizures and paralysis or muscle weakness. Correct diagnosis and treatment require hospitalisation. There are annual outbreaks of this disease in the lowlands of Nepal.

Filariasis This is a mosquito-transmitted parasitic infection which is found in Nepal in urban and rural areas up to 1900m. There

---

AIDS in Nepal

Prostitution does exist in Nepal, particularly in the border towns and along the main truck routes, but it is virtually invisible to western visitors. In addition, it is believed that over 100,000 Nepali women work in Indian brothels, often in conditions little different to slavery, and over 30,000 of these are estimated to be HIV positive. When obvious AIDS symptoms force these women to retire, some do manage to return to Nepal. Sadly, they are shunned by their families and there is virtually no assistance available to them or their children.

Up to half a million Nepali men seek seasonal work in Indian cities, and in common with migrant workers elsewhere it is likely that many patronise brothels while they are away. Finally, there are estimated to be 10,000 intravenous drug users in Nepal who are at risk. No official figures are available, but it is clear that AIDS has the potential to become a major problem. ■

is a range of possible manifestations of the infection, depending on which filarial parasite species has caused the infection. These include fever, pain and swelling of the lymph glands; inflammation of lymph drainage areas; swelling of a limb or the scrotum; skin rashes and blindness. Treatment is available to eliminate the parasites from the body, but some of the damage may be irreversible. Medical advice should be obtained promptly if the infection is suspected.

Typhus Typhus is spread by ticks, mites or lice. It begins with fever, chills, headache and muscle pains followed a few days later by a body rash. There is often a large painful sore at the site of the bite and nearby lymph nodes are swollen and painful. Treatment is with tetracycline, or chloramphenicol under medical supervision.

Lyme Disease Lyme disease is an infection transmitted by ticks which may be acquired throughout Europe, in Asia and in Australia. The illness usually begins with a spreading rash at the site of the tick bite and is accompanied by fever, headache, extreme fatigue, aching joints and muscles and mild neck stiffness. If untreated, these symptoms usually resolve over several weeks but over subsequent weeks or months disorders of the nervous system, heart and joints may develop. The response to treatment is best early in the illness. The longer the delay, the longer the recovery period. Treatment involves the use of antibiotics – often tetracycline, 250 mg four times a day for at least 10 days. Alternative or additional treatment would depend upon the patient and the severity of the symptoms.

Cuts, Bites & Stings

Skin punctures can easily become infected in hot climates and may be difficult to heal. Treat any cut with an antiseptic such as povidone-iodine. Where possible avoid bandages and Band-aids, which can keep wounds wet.

Bee and wasp stings are usually painful rather than dangerous. Calamine lotion or Stingose spray will give relief and ice packs will reduce the pain and swelling. There are some spiders with dangerous bites but anti-venenes are usually available.

Snakes The chances of being bitten by a snake in Nepal are remote. To minimise your chances always wear boots, socks and long trousers when walking through undergrowth where snakes may be present. Don't put your hands into holes and crevices, and be careful when collecting firewood.

Snake bites do not cause instantaneous death and antivenenes are usually available. Keep the victim calm and still, wrap the bitten limb tightly, as you would for a sprained ankle, and then attach a splint to immobilise it. Then seek medical help, if possible with the dead snake for identification. Don't attempt to catch the snake if there is even a remote possibility of being bitten again. Tourniquets and sucking out the poison are now comprehensively discredited.

Bedbugs & Lice Bedbugs live in various places, but particularly in dirty mattresses and bedding. Spots of blood on bedclothes or on the wall around the bed can be read as a suggestion to find another hotel. Bedbugs leave itchy bites in neat rows. Calamine lotion or Stingose spray may help.

All lice cause itching and discomfort. They make themselves at home in your hair (head lice), your clothing (body lice) or in your pubic hair (crabs). You catch lice through direct contact with infected people or by sharing combs, clothing and the like. Powder or shampoo treatment will kill the lice and infected clothing should then be washed in very hot water.

Leeches & Ticks Leeches (*jukha*) are common along trekking trails or in the Royal Chitwan National Park during the monsoon. Trekkers often get them on their legs or in their boots. Salt or a lighted cigarette end will make them fall off. Do not pull them off, as the bite is then more likely to become infected. An insect repellent may keep them away.

You should always check your body if you have been walking through a potentially tick-infested area as ticks can cause skin infections and other more serious diseases. If a tick is found attached, press down around the tick's head with tweezers, grab the head and gently pull upwards. Avoid pulling the rear of the body as this may squeeze the tick's gut contents through the attached mouth parts into the skin, increasing the risk of infection and disease. Smearing chemicals on the tick will not make it let go and is not recommended.

Women's Health

Gynaecological Problems Poor diet, lowered resistance due to using antibiotics for stomach upsets, and even contraceptive pills can lead to vaginal infections when travelling in hot climates. Maintaining good personal hygiene, and wearing skirts or loose-fitting trousers and cotton underwear will help to prevent infections.

Yeast infections, characterised by a rash, itch and discharge, can be treated with a vinegar or lemon-juice douche, or with yoghurt. Nystatin, miconazole or clotrimazole suppositories are the usual medical prescription. Trichomoniasis and gardnerella are more serious infections; symptoms are a smelly discharge and sometimes a burning sensation when urinating. Male sexual partners must also be treated, and if a vinegar-water douche is not effective medical attention should be sought. Metronidazole (Flagyl) is the prescribed drug.

Pregnancy Most miscarriages occur during the first three months of pregnancy, so this is the most risky time to travel as far as your own health is concerned. Miscarriage is not uncommon, and can occasionally lead to severe bleeding. The last three months should also be spent within reasonable distance of good medical care. A baby born as early as 24 weeks stands a chance of survival, but only in a good modern hospital. Pregnant women should avoid all unneces-

sary medication, but vaccinations and malarial prophylactics should still be taken where possible. Additional care should be taken to prevent illness and particular attention should be paid to diet and nutrition. Alcohol and nicotine, for example, should be avoided.

WOMEN TRAVELLERS

Nepal is perhaps among the safest countries in the world for women travellers; theft is rare and prostitution is non-existent from a westerner's point of view. However, as is the case in most countries, women should still be cautious, especially when trekking. Never trek alone, and only trek with companies that have been recommended by trustworthy friends. Also, bear in mind that some Nepali men have peculiar ideas about the morality of western women, given their exposure to western films, 'immodest' clothing, and inter-racial holiday flings. Dress modestly, and avoid situations where you cannot call for help should a situation get out of hand.

TRAVEL WITH CHILDREN

Surprisingly few people travel with children in Nepal, yet with a bit of planning it is remarkably hassle free. Certainly it's hard work, but then staying home with kids is hard work too, so why not get out and enjoy it? As always, children are great ice-breakers, and the local hospitality and friendliness shines through even more.

In the main tourist centres (Kathmandu and Pokhara), most hotels will have triple rooms, and quite often rooms with four beds, which are ideal for families with young children. Finding a room with a bath tub can be a problem, however, especially at the bottom end of the market. Garden space is at a premium in Kathmandu hotels, but many places have a roof garden, and some of these can be good play areas for kids. Check thoroughly, however, as some are definitely not safe.

One of the hardest parts about life on the road with kids in Nepal is eating out at restaurants. While the food is excellent and there's always something on the menu which will appeal to kids – even if it's only chips or banana porridge – service is usually quite slow and things take quite a while to arrive. By the time the food arrives your kids (especially if they are really young) will be bored stiff and ready to leave. You can minimise the hassles by eating breakfast at your hotel, having lunch at a place with a garden (there's plenty of these) where the children can let off steam, and in the evening going to the restaurant armed with pencils, colouring books, stories and other distractions to keep them busy for half an hour. High chairs are virtually non-existent.

Walking the crowded and narrow streets of Kathmandu can be a hassle with young kids unless you can get them up off the ground – a backpack is ideal, but a pusher (not of drugs, but of children) or stroller would be more trouble than it's worth.

One of the most rewarding things to do with kids is to take them trekking in the mountains. Once again, very few people seem to do this yet the experience for everyone is well worth the effort. The main consideration is that to have an easy trip you need to hire enough porters to carry not only your gear but also any young children. This is not as expensive as it sounds, with porters costing around $5 per day. See the Trekking chapter for more details.

If your child needs disposable nappies, these are available in Kathmandu and Pokhara – for a price. Better to bring them with you if possible. Even better would be to use cloth ones, but this can be a headache and you may well decide the convenience of disposable ones worth it. Bear in mind, however, that disposable nappies are far from disposable – they are in fact almost indestructible – and waste disposal in Nepal is already a major problem.

DANGERS & ANNOYANCES
Trekking
Surrounded by western comforts in Kathmandu, it is easy to forget that Nepal is, in terms of many physical resources, an undeveloped country. This means that people are extremely poor, hygiene is often bad,

transport (particularly of the road variety) is dangerous, rescue facilities are limited, and medical facilities are often primitive or nonexistent.

Fired up by the gung-ho stories of adventurous travellers, it is also easy to forget that mountainous terrain is always potentially dangerous. Nepal, of course, is a continuous series of the most spectacular mountains in the world. And the risks are correspondingly real.

Only a tiny minority of people do finally end up in trouble, but the tragedy is that accidents and their consequences can often be avoided or minimised if people have a realistic understanding of where they are and what they are doing, and if they observe common sense rules and take a few basic precautions. See the Trekking chapter for more details.

The Kathmandu Environment Education Project (KEEP) and the Himalayan Rescue Association (HRA) offices, in the Potala Hotel and Hotel Tilicho respectively (both near the immigration office on Tridevi Marg, Kathmandu) can give up-to-date information on trekking conditions and health risks. A visit to either or both is strongly recommended. Several embassies and consulates have registration forms at the centres; if they don't, you can register at the actual embassy or consulate. The forms record your name, rough itinerary, insurance details and next of kin, and can obviously speed up a search or medical evacuation.

Theft
Things do get stolen in Nepal, just like anywhere else in the world, but theft is still extremely rare. There are pickpockets in crowded areas of old Kathmandu; backpacks can disappear from bus roofs and from hotel storage rooms; possessions get stolen from camp sites; and on rare occasions lone trekkers have even been mugged and robbed.

There's little chance of ever retrieving your gear if it is stolen, and even getting a police report for an insurance claim, can be difficult. Try the local police station, but if you aren't getting anywhere, go straight to

Interpol (☎ 01-411210, 410088) at the Police Headquarters in Naxal, Kathmandu; the postal address is PO Box 407. There is a local Interpol office just off Durbar Square but it will only handle your case if the theft actually took place in Kathmandu. The documentation requires a passport photo, and photocopies of your passport and visa; the process takes two days.

BUSINESS HOURS

Most government offices in Kathmandu are open from 10 am to 5 pm from Sunday to Thursday during summer and from 9 am to 4 pm during the winter months (roughly mid-November to mid-February since the winter starting date for the change of hours varies with the Nepali calendar). Offices close at 3 pm on Friday. Saturday is the weekly holiday and most shops and all offices and banks will be closed, but Sunday is a regular working day.

PUBLIC HOLIDAYS & SPECIAL EVENTS

Many holidays and festivals affect the working hours of government offices and banks. These will be closed for, amongst others, Shivaratri, the Nepali New Year, Teej, Indra Jatra, Dasain, Tihar, the queen's birthday on 7 November and the king's birthday on 29 December.

Nepal's colourful holidays and festivals occur virtually year round and a visit to Nepal is almost certain to coincide with at least one, particularly in the Kathmandu Valley. Certain times of year, particularly August and September towards the end of the monsoon, are packed with festivals. They go a long way towards compensating for the less-than-ideal weather at this time of year.

Dasain is the most important of all Nepali celebrations, perhaps most closely approximated by Christmas and New Year in the west. Tens of thousands of Nepalis hit the road to return home to celebrate with their families. This means the villages are full of life if you are trekking, but it also means that all the buses are fully booked and overflowing, that porters may be hard to find (or more expensive than usual), and that cars are hard to hire. Doing business

in Kathmandu, outside of Thamel, becomes almost impossible.

The most important days, when everything comes to a total halt, are the ninth day when thousands of animals are sacrificed, and the tenth day when blessings are received from elder relatives and superiors. Banks and government offices are generally closed from the eighth day to the twelfth. The final day of Dasain is on the full moon in September or October.

For interesting accounts of many of the festivals and the legends behind them read Mary M Anderson's *The Festivals of Nepal*.

Nepali holidays and festivals are principally dated by the lunar calendar, falling on days relating to new or full moons. The Nepali new year starts on 13 April with the month of Baisakh and is 57 years ahead of the Gregorian calendar used in the west. The year 1997 in the west is 2054 in Nepal. The Newars, on the other hand, start their new year from the day after Deepavali, which falls on the night of the new moon in late October or early November. Their calendar is 880 years behind the Gregorian calendar so 1997 in the west is 1117 to the Newars of the Kathmandu Valley.

Predicting the exact dates for Nepali holidays and festivals is not always easy. In Nepal the lunar calendar is divided into bright and dark fortnights. The bright fortnight is the two weeks of the waxing moon, as it grows to become the full moon (*purnima*). The dark fortnight is the two weeks of the waning moon, as the full moon shrinks to become the new moon (*aunsi*). Therefore a festival might fall 'on the 11th day of the bright fortnight of Falgun'.

What sometimes seems like a cavalier attitude towards numbering days actually has a logical explanation. The sun rises every 24 hours but the period between successive moonrises can vary from 22 to 27 hours. Thus several times each year there can be a 'moon day' (the period from one moonrise to the next) which has no sunrise within it, and several others that have two sunrises. Thus the lunar calendar will sometimes jump a day, and on other occasions it will hiccup and repeat a day. Predicting a date far in advance is additionally complicated by the periodic adjustments which have to be made to bring the shorter lunar year back into line with the solar year which the Gregorian calendar follows. See the Nepali Calender for the corresponding Gregorian months in the Nepali year.

The Festival Calendar covers dates through to mid-January 1999, hopefully with reasonable accuracy. Check the dates when you're in Kathmandu.

Nepali Calendar	
January-February	*Magh*
February-March	*Falgun*
March-April	*Chaitra*
April-May	*Baisakh*
May-June	*Jeth*
June-July	*Asaar*
July-August	*Saaun*
August-September	*Bhadra*
September-October	*Ashwin*
October-November	*Kartik*
November-December	*Mangsir*
December-January	*Pus*

January-February

Magh Sankranti The end of the coldest winter months is marked by this festival with ritual bathing, despite the cold, during the Nepali month of Magh. The festival is dated by the movement north of the winter sun and is one of the few festivals not timed by the lunar calendar. Soon after, on the new-moon day, the Tribeni Mela (a *mela* is a fair) is held at various places including Devghat, on the banks of the Narayani River near the town of Narayanghat in the Terai.

Basant Panchami The beginning of spring is celebrated by honouring Saraswati and since she is the goddess of learning this festival has special importance for students and scholars. The shrine to Saraswati just below the platform at the top of Sway-

ambhunath is the most popular locale for the festivities. This is also a particularly auspicious occasion for weddings.

February

Losar The Tibetan new year commences with the new moon in February and is welcomed with particular fervour at the great Bodhnath stupa. Colourfully dressed lamas parade around the stupa carrying banners and portraits of the Dalai Lama. Ceremonies are also performed at Swayambhunath and in the Tibetan community at Jawlakhel near Patan. Crowds of Tibetans dressed in their most traditional costumes and furiously twirling their prayer wheels, watch the proceedings.

February-March

Maha Shivaratri Shiva's birthday falls on the new-moon day of the month of Falgun. Festivities take place at all Shiva temples but most particularly at the great Pashupatinath Temple, and devotees flock there not only from all over Nepal but also from all over India.

Many sadhus make the long trek to Nepal for this festival and the King of Nepal will also appear late in the day since Shiva, as Lord Pashupati, is asked to protect Nepal at the conclusion of any official message. The crowds bathing in the Bagmati's holy waters at this time are a colourful and wonderful sight. The sadhus, meanwhile, will be up to all their usual fun and games whether it's rolling in the ashes, performing impossible feats of yoga or sticking thorns through their tongues. Overall, however, Maha Shivaratri is a serene and peaceful festival, reflecting the deep devotion which Hindus hold for their religion.

Holi/Fagu This exciting festival is closely related to the water festivals of Thailand and Myanmar and takes place on the full-moon day in the month of Falgun. By this time, late in the dry season, it is beginning to get rather hot and the water which is sprayed around so liberally during the festival is a reminder of the cooling monsoon days to come. Holi is also known as the Festival of Colours and as well as spraying water on everything and everyone, coloured powder (particularly red) and coloured water are also dispensed. Foreigners get special attention, so if you venture out on Holi leave your camera behind (or keep it well protected) and wear old clothes which you won't mind getting colour-stained.

At one time Holi used to take place on the eight days leading up to the full moon; these days (perhaps fortunately) the full onslaught of activities is usually restricted to one day.

The festival is said to be inspired by the exploits of Krishna, particularly an incident when he caught his favourite milkmaids sporting in the Jamuna River. A pole supporting a three tiered umbrella is set up in front of the Basantapur Tower in the centre of Kathmandu and on the final day the umbrella is taken down and burnt.

Other activities also take place during Holi. Guru Mapa, the demon of the Yitum Bahal in Kathmandu (see Walking Tour 1 in the Kathmandu section), has his annual feed on Holi night. The inhabitants of Yitum Bahal sacrifice a buffalo on the banks of the Vishnumati River, cook it in the afternoon in their great courtyard and in the middle of the night carry it in huge cauldrons to the Tundikhel where the demon is said to live to this day.

More peacefully, singing and dancing continues until late at night during another cheerful festival in the village of Tarke Gyang on the Helambu trek.

March-April

Chaitra Dasain Also known as Small Dasain, in contrast with the Big Dasain in the month of Kartik, this festival takes place exactly six months prior to the more important one. Like the other Dasain it's dedicated to Durga and once again it's a bad day for

Festival Calendar
As the actual holidays aren't declared more than a year in advance, many of the following dates are estimates only, but should be correct to within a day or so. Check in Nepal for exact dates.

Name of Festival	Place	1997	1998	1999
Magh Sankranti	Narayanghat	mid-Jan	mid-Jan	mid-Jan
Basant Panchami Losar	Swayambhunath	12 Feb	1 Feb	22 Jan
Maha Shivaratri	Pashupatinath	7 Feb	26 Feb	15 Feb
Holi	all over Nepal	21 Feb	12 Mar	1 Mar
Chaitra Dasain	all over Nepal	15 April	3 May	24 April
Bisket Jatara	Bhaktapur	13 April	13 April	13 April
Buddha Jayanti	Swayambhunath	22 April	10 May	29 April
Naga Panchami	all over Nepal	5 Aug	27 July	15 Aug
Gai Jatra	Kathmandu	17 Aug	5 Sep	27 Aug
Krishna Jayanti	Patan	24 Aug	12 Sep	2 Sep
Teej	Pashupatinath	3 Sep	23 Aug	10 Sep
Dasain				
Fulpati	all over Nepal	7 Oct	26 Oct	16 Oct
Vijaya Dashami	all over Nepal	10 Oct	29 Oct	19 Oct
Kartika Purnima	all over Nepal	15 Oct	3 Nov	24 Oct
Tihar				
Deepavali	all over Nepal	30 Oct	19 Oct	7 Nov
Bhai Tika	all over Nepal	1 Nov	21 Oct	9 Nov
Haribodhini Ekadashi	Kathmandu	10 Nov	30 Oct	18 Nov
Bala Chaturdashi	Pashupatinath	29 Nov	18 Nov	7 Dec
Sita Bibaha Panchami	Janakpur	4 Dec	23 Nov	12 Dec
Mani Rimdu	Solu Khumbu	Nov	Nov	Nov

goats and buffaloes who do their unwilling bit for the goddess early in the morning in Kot Square.

Sweta Machhendranath The Chaitra Dasain sacrifices also signal the start of the Sweta (White) Machhendranath festival, a month prior to the much larger and more important Rato (Red) Machhendranath festival in Patan. The festival starts with removing the image of Sweta Machhendranath from the temple at Kel Tole and placing it on a towering and creaky wooden temple chariot or *rath*. For the next four evenings the chariot proceeds from one historic location to another eventually arriving at Lagankhel in the south of Kathmandu. There the image is taken down from the chariot and carried back to its starting point in a palanquin while the chariot is disassembled and put away until next year.

April

Bisket Jatra The Nepali new year starts in mid-April, at the beginning of the month of Baisakh, and the Bisket festival in Bhaktapur is the most spectacular welcome for the new year and one of the most exciting annual events in the valley. Magh Sankranti is the only other important religious festival set by the solar rather than the lunar calendar.

Bisket is Bhaktapur's great chariot festival but whereas in Kathmandu and Patan it is Machhendranath who gets taken for a ride, here it is Bhairab, accompanied by Betal and, in a second chariot, the goddess Bhadrakali. The ponderous chariots of the gods always appear shaky and unsafe and moving them requires enormous amounts of energy.

From Taumadhi Tole, outside Bhairab's temple, the huge temple chariot proceeds around the town, pausing for a huge tug of war between the eastern and western sides of town. The winning side is charged with looking after the images of the gods during their week-long riverside sojourn. After the battle the chariots slither down the steep road leading to the river, where a huge 25m high lingam is erected. In the evening of the following day, new year's day, the pole is pulled down, again in an often violent tug of war. As the pole crashes to the ground the new year officially commences.

As is usual in Nepal, legend is piled upon legend, and far in the past there's a tale of a beautiful princess and a valiant prince behind the Bisket festival:

The king of Bhaktapur had an insatiable daughter who not only required a new lover each night but left them dead each morning! Finally a brave prince showed up and despite an exhausting session with the princess forced himself to stay awake afterwards. Late that night two thread-like wisps emerged from the beautiful princess's nostrils, and grew into venomous snakes in the night air. Before they could strike and consign the prince to the scrap heap of discarded lovers he drew his sword and killed them both. Of course the prince and princess married and lived happily ever after and from the top of the towering Bisket lingam stream two banners, symbolic of those two deadly snakes.

Other festivals and events also take place around Bhaktapur for a week preceding the new year and for some days thereafter. Members of the potters' caste put up and haul down their own lingam, and processions also carry images of Ganesh, Lakshmi and Mahakali around the town. The new year is also an important time in the valley for ritual bathing, and crowds of hill people come down to visit the Buddhist stupas of Swayambhunath and Bodhnath.

Balkumari Jatra Thimi, the smaller town near Bhaktapur, also welcomes the new year with an exciting festival. This event was instituted by King Jagat Jyoti Malla in the early 1600s but here it is Balkumari, another of Bhairab's consorts, who is honoured. All through new year's day devotees crowd around her temple in Thimi and as dusk falls hundreds of ceremonial oil lamps *(chirags)* are lit. Some devotees lie motionless around the temple all night with burning oil lamps balanced on their legs, arms, chests and foreheads.

The next morning men come from the various *toles* or quarters of Thimi and from surrounding villages, each team carrying a palanquin known as a *khat* with images of different gods. As the 32 khats whirl around the temple red powder is hurled at them and the ceremony reaches fever pitch as the khat bearing Ganesh arrives from the village of Nagadish. The crowds parade up and down the main street until late in the morning when Ganesh, borne by hundreds of men, makes a break for home, pursued by the other khats. If they can catch Ganesh the activities are prolonged but eventually Ganesh departs and the festival moves on to the Taleju Temple.

Sacrifices are now made to Balkumari and in the small village of Bode another khat festival, with just seven khats rather than 32, takes place. Here a volunteer spends the whole day with an iron spike piercing his tongue. Successful completion of this painful rite brings merit to the whole village as well as the devotee.

April-May
Rato Machhendranath Although Sweta and Rato Machhendranath may well be the same deity, the Rato or Red Machhendranath festival of Patan is a much more important occasion than the Kathmandu event. Machhendranath is considered to have great powers over rain and, since the monsoon is approaching at this time, this festival is a plea for good rain.

As in Kathmandu the festival consists of a day-by-day temple chariot procession through the streets of the town, but here it takes a full month to move from the Pulchowk area, where the image is installed in the chariot, to Jawlakhel where the chariot is dismantled.

Along the way the main chariot is accompanied for most of its journey by a second smaller chariot containing the image of Rato Machhendranath's Bodhisattva companion from the Minanath Temple, near the Rato Machhendranath Temple south of Patan's Durbar Square.

From Jawlakhel, Rato Machhendranath does not return to his Patan temple, however. He has a second home in the village of Bungamati and he spends six months of each year at this temple, to where he is now con-

veyed on a khat. Every 12 years, however, the Rato Machhendranath festival becomes an even more important and time-consuming event when the chariot continues all the way to Bungamati. The next enactment of the complete Patan to Bungamati procession will be in 2003.

The temple chariots *(raths)* used in these processions are immense wooden affairs with wheels metres in diameter and a towering but often rather ramshackle edifice constructed on top. It takes hundreds of devotees to tow the main chariot and the Nepali army is often called in to help in the Patan Rato Machhendranath festival, despite the intense local enthusiasm to take part in pulling the chariot. The long procession is often halted to await an auspicious occasion for the next leg, or to make important roadside repairs to the chariot.

Similar temple chariot processions take place in India including the largest of them all, the great Jagannath procession at Puri in the state of Orissa.

Buddha Jayanti (Buddha's Birthday)
Siddhartha Gautama (Buddha) was born at Lumbini, so it is fitting that his birthday should be celebrated in Nepal. Swayambhunath is the centre for the celebrations although events also take place at Bodhnath and in Patan.

A constant procession of pilgrims makes its way around the stupa at Swayambhunath. The stupa's collection of rare thangkas and mandalas is shown on the southern wall of the stupa courtyard on this single day each year. The stupa's lamas dress in colourful silk robes and dance around the stupa with accompaniment provided by musicians.

Mata Tirtha Puja The last day of the dark fortnight of Baisakh is Mata Tirtha Puja. It's the Nepali equivalent of Mother's Day and every Nepali should go to 'look upon their mother's face'. Those whose mothers have died in the past year are supposed to bathe at the Mata Tirtha pond, about 10 km southwest of Kathmandu near the Thankot road.

May-June

Kumar Sasthi The birthday of Kumar or Kartikkaya, the god of war and brother of Ganesh, is also known as Sithinakha. The festival also marks the start of the rice planting season and is an annual occasion for cleaning wells. Once upon a time the god of war's birthday was commemorated by stone-throwing contests. Since these often turned into strictly local, but often decidedly real, 'wars' they're now mainly confined to young boys.

July-August

Naga Panchami On the fifth day after the new moon in the month of Saaun, snakes *(nagas)* are honoured in this festival. Numerous legends are told about snakes and they are said to have all sorts of magical powers including special powers over the monsoon rains. Pictures of the nagas are hung over the doorways of houses and this not only propitiates the snakes but also keeps harm from the household. Various foods are put out for the snakes and there are interesting legends behind the offerings of milk and boiled rice:

A farmer inadvertently killed three baby snakes with his plough and the enraged mother snake chased the farmer back to his house and killed the farmer, his wife and his two sons. The daughter was about to get the same treatment when she offered the serpent a bowl of milk. The snake was so taken by this act of kindness that it spared the daughter and offered her any wish. 'Bring my parents and brothers back to life', replied the daughter and the snake duly did so. Ever since then snakes are offered a bowl of milk on Naga Panchami.

The bowl of rice is offered because of an incident at the Siddha Pokhari pond just outside Bhaktapur which, the legend relates, was once inhabited by an evil naga. A holy man determined to kill the naga himself by taking the form of a snake, and told his companion to be ready with a bowl of magic rice. If, after he entered the pond, the water turned white then the naga had won and it was all over. If, on the other hand, the water turned red then he had defeated the naga and although he would emerge from the pond in the form of a snake, the magical rice would restore his original form.

Sure enough the water turned red but when the holy man in the form of a hideous serpent emerged from the water his horrified companion simply turned tail and ran, taking the rice with him. The holy man

tried to catch him but failed and eventually decided to return to the pond and remain there. To this day the inhabitants of Bhaktapur keep well clear of the Siddha Pokhari pond and on the day of Naga Panchami a bowl of rice is put out – just in case the holy man/snake turns up.

Janai Purnima On the day prior to and on the day of the full moon in the month of Saaun all high-caste men (Chhetri and Brahman) must change the *janai* (sacred thread) which they wear looped over their left shoulder and tied under their right arm. The three cords of the sacred thread symbolise body, speech and mind, and young men first put on the thread in an important ritual that officially welcomes them into their religion. From that date they wear the sacred thread for the rest of their lives, changing it on this one occasion each year as well as any time it has been damaged or defiled. One way of defiling the sacred thread is to come into contact with a woman while she is menstruating.

Although only men wear the thread, anybody, including curious foreigners, can wear a yellow thread or *raksha bandhan* around their wrist – right for men, left for women. Wearing this thread on your wrist is said to bring good fortune and on this day priests tie the threads on all comers. You are supposed to wear it for at least a week, but preferably for three months until the Festival of Lights (during Tihar) in October-November.

Janai Purnima also brings crowds of pilgrims to the sacred Gosainkund Lake, across the mountains to the north of Kathmandu. There they garland a statue of Shiva and throw coins at the sacred lingam which rises up from the lake. A direct channel is said to lead from the lake to the pond in the Kumbeshwar Temple in Patan and a silver lingam is installed in the pond for the occasion. The rituals at the temple attract *jhankris*, faith healers who perform in a trance while beating drums.

Gai Jatra The Gai Jatra (Cow Festival) takes place immediately after Janai Purnima on the day after the Saaun full moon, and is dedicated to those who died during the preceding year. Hindus believe that after death cows will guide them to Yama, the god of the underworld, and finding your way on this important journey will be much easier if by chance you should be holding on to a cow's tail at the moment of death! Therefore on this day cows are lead through the streets of the valley's towns or, if a cow is not available, small boys dress up as cows.

The festival also celebrates an event during the reign of King Pratap Malla (1641-74). The king's youngest son died and the queen was utterly grief-stricken. Nothing could cheer her up and eventually the king offered rewards to anybody who could bring a smile to her face. The next day crowds of people appeared before the royal palace and danced and clowned, dressed in outlandish costumes. The queen could not help laughing at this mass outbreak of merry madness and the king proclaimed that henceforward Gai Jatra would be a day for costumes and games. So it is that many other peculiar outfits appear on the streets, apart from boys dressed up as cows, and the festival is celebrated with maximum energy on the streets of Bhaktapur.

Ghanta Karna Ghanta Karna ('night of the devil'), falls on the 14th day of the dark fortnight of Saaun. Ghanta Karna, which means 'bell ears', was a horrible demon who was so named because he wore bell earrings to drown out the name of Vishnu, his sworn enemy. The festival celebrates his destruction when a god, disguised as a frog, lured him into a deep well where the people stoned and clubbed him to death. Ghanta Karna is burnt in effigy on this night and evil is cleansed from the land for another year.

August-September
Krishna Jayanti (Krishna's Birthday) The

seventh day after the full moon in the month of Bhadra is celebrated as Krishna's birthday, sometimes known as Krishnasthami. Krishna is an incarnation of Vishnu and his daring exploits, good nature and general love of a good time endear him to many people.

The Krishna Mandir in Patan is the centre for the celebrations and an all-night vigil is kept at the temple on the night before his birthday. Oil lamps light the temple and singing continues through the night.

Teej The Festival of Women lasts for three days, from the second to the fifth day following the new moon in the month of Bhadra. It is centred on Pashupatinath and women celebrate the festival in honour of their husbands and in hope of a long and happy married life.

The festival starts with a sumptuous meal and the women gather together and spend the rest of the day feasting and talking, right through until midnight when they must commence 24 hours of fasting. During the day of the fast women from all over the valley converge on Pashupatinath, traditionally dressed in red and gold saris, usually the ones in which they were married. At Pashupatinath the women take ritual dips in the river and call on the gods to protect their husbands.

The following morning the women must offer their husbands small items of food which have previously been offered to the gods. The day-long fast can then be broken although in some years the festival continues for an extra day in which case this is a day of partial fasting. Another ritual bathing ceremony takes place on this day, preferably at a river confluence, such as where the Bagmati and Vishnumati rivers meet, just south of Kathmandu. Completion of these ceremonies washes away all female sin, including the sin of a woman touching her husband during her period!

Gunla The 15 days before and after the full moon in August or early September is celebrated as a full month of Buddhist ceremonies, penance and fasting. Activities are centred on Swayambhunath. Pancha Dan, the Festival of Five Offerings, is held in Patan during Gunla but there are various other festivals and ceremonies during the month.

Gokarna Aunsi The Nepali equivalent of Father's Day is celebrated at Gokarna by visiting living fathers at their homes and honouring deceased fathers.

September

Indra Jatra This important festival runs from the end of the month of Bhadra into the beginning of Ashwin. Indra Jatra is a colourful and exciting festival which manages to combine homage to Indra with an important annual appearance by Kumari (the living goddess), respects to Bhairab and commemoration of the conquest of the valley by Prithvi Narayan Shah. The festival also marks the end of the monsoon and the start of the fine months which follow.

Indra is the ancient Aryan god of rain and he once paid a visit to the Kathmandu Valley to pick a certain flower which his mother Dagini needed for the festival of Teej. Unfortunately for Indra he was captured in the act of stealing the flowers and imprisoned until his mother came down to rescue him. When she revealed whom they had imprisoned, his captors gladly released him but the festival continues to celebrate this remarkable achievement – villagers don't capture a real god every day of the week! In return for his release Dagini promised to spread morning moisture and dew over the crops for the coming months and to take back with her to heaven all those who had died in the past year.

The festival therefore honours the recently deceased and pays homage to Indra and Dagini for the coming harvests. It starts with the erection of a huge pole outside the Hanuman Dhoka palace. The carefully selected pole has first been brought to the Tundikhel and then carried to the square. The pole is set up while images and representations of Indra, usually as a captive, are displayed and sacrifices of goats and roosters are made. At the same time the screened doors obscuring the horrific face of White Bhairab are opened and for the next three days his gruesome visage will stare out at the proceedings.

The day before all this activity, three golden temple chariots have been assembled in Basantapur Square, outside the home of the Kumari, the living goddess. In the afternoon, with the Durbar Square packed with colourful and cheerful crowds, two boys emerge from the Kumari's house. They play the roles of Ganesh and Bhairab and will each ride in a chariot as an attendant to the goddess. Finally, the Kumari herself appears either walking on a rolled-out carpet or carried by attendants so that her feet do not touch the ground.

The chariots move off and the Kumari is greeted from the balcony of the old palace by the king. The procession then continues out of Durbar Square towards Hanuman Dhoka where it stops in front of the huge White Bhairab mask. The Kumari greets the image of Bhairab and then, with loud musical accompaniment, beer starts to pour from Bhairab's mouth! Grabbing a sip of this beer is guaranteed to bring good fortune, but one lucky individual will also get the small fish which has been put to swim in the beer – this brings especially good luck!

The procession moves off again and for the remaining days of the festival it moves from place to place around the town, to the accompaniment of ceremonies, dances and other activities. Numerous other processions also take place around the town until the final day when the great pole is lowered and carried down to the river. It was during the Indra Jatra festival back in 1768 that Prithvi Narayan Shah conquered the valley and unified Nepal so this important event is also commemorated in this most spectacular of Kathmandu occasions.

Ganesh Chata On Ganesh Chata, the fourth day of the bright fortnight in September, offerings are made to Ganesh. The festival celebrates a bitter dispute between Ganesh and the moon goddess, and the Nepalis try to stay indoors on this night and shut out all signs of moonlight.

September-October

Pachali Bhairab Jatra The fearsome form of Bhairab, as Pachali Bhairab, is honoured on the fourth day of the bright fortnight in September or early October. The festivities are in line with Bhairab's bloodthirsty nature as there are numerous sacrifices.

October-November

Dasain The pleasant post-monsoon period when the sky is clearest, the air is cleanest and the rice is ready for harvesting is also the time for Nepal's biggest annual festival. Dasain lasts for 15 days, finishing on the full-moon day of late September or early October, and there are a number of important days right through the festival. Although much of Dasain is a quiet family affair there are colourful events for visitors to see both in Kathmandu and in the country. Dasain is also known as Durga Puja since the festival celebrates the victory of the goddess Durga over the forces of evil in the guise of the buffalo demon Mahisasura. Since Durga is a bloodthirsty goddess, the festival is marked by wholesale bloodletting and features the biggest animal sacrifice of the year.

Even before Dasain commences the Nepalis spring-clean their houses, while in the country, swings and primitive hand-powered Ferris wheels are erected at the entrance to villages or in their main square. For trekkers, Dasain is very much 'the festival of swings'! On the first day of the festival, a sacred jar of water is prepared in each house and barley seeds are planted in carefully prepared soil. Getting the seeds to sprout a few cm during Dasain ensures a good harvest.

Fulpati is the first really important day of Dasain and is called 'the seventh day' although it may not actually fall on the seventh day. Fulpati means 'day of flowers' and a jar containing flowers is carried from Gorkha to Kathmandu and presented to the king at the Tundikhel parade ground. The flowers symbolise Taleju, the goddess of the royal family, whose most important image is in the Gorkha palace. From the parade ground the flowers are transported on a palanquin to the old Royal Palace on Durbar Square where they are inspected again by the king and his entourage.

Maha Astami or the 'great eighth day' and Kala Ratri the 'black night' follow Fulpati and this is the start of the sacrifices and offerings to Durga. The hundreds of goats you may see contentedly grazing in the Tundikhel parkland on the days prior to Maha Astami are destined to die for the goddess. At midnight, in a temple courtyard near Durbar Square, eight buffaloes and 108 goats are beheaded and their executioners must perform the deed with a single stroke of the sword or knife.

The next day is Navami and the Kot Square near Durbar Square, scene of the great massacre of noblemen which led to the Rana period of Nepali history, is the scene for another great massacre. Visitors can witness the bloodshed but you need to arrive early to secure a place on the foreigners' balcony. Sacrifices continue through the day and blood is sprinkled on the wheels of cars and other vehicles to ensure a safe year on the road. At the airport each Royal Nepal Airlines aircraft will have a goat sacrificed to it! The average Nepali does not eat much meat, but on this day almost everybody in the country will find that goat is on the menu for dinner.

The 10th day of the festival, Vijaya Dashami, is again a family affair as cards and greetings are exchanged, family visits are made and parents place a red *tika* mark on their children's foreheads. In the evening, the conclusion of Dasain is marked by processions and masked dances in the towns of the Kathmandu Valley. The Kharga Jatra or sword processions feature priests dressed up as the various gods and carrying wooden swords, symbolic of the weapon with which Durga slew the buffalo demon. This day also celebrates the victory of Lord Rama over the evil King Rawana in the *Ramayana*. The barley sprouts which were planted on the first day are picked and worn as small bouquets in the hair.

Kartika Purnima, the full-moon day which marks the end of the festival, is celebrated with gambling in many households and you will see even small children avidly putting a few coins down on various local games of chance. Women fast and many of them make a pilgrimage to Pashupatinath near Kathmandu. Although Dasain is principally a Hindu festival it has also been adopted by Buddhists, and special activities also take place at Buddhist shrines in Patan and Bhaktapur. In the country the swings and Ferris wheels will be busier than ever, before finally being dismantled for another year.

Tihar With its colourful Festival of Lights (Deepavali), Tihar is the most important Hindu festival in India, and in Nepal it ranks second only to Dasain. The five days of activities take place in late October or early November.

The festival honours certain animals on successive days, starting with offerings of rice to the crows which are sent by Yama, the god of death, as his 'messengers of death'. On the second day, dogs are honoured with garlands of flowers and tikas. This must be a considerable surprise to most Nepali dogs, who are usually honoured with no more than the occasional kick, but the fact that, in the afterworld, it is dogs who guide departed souls across the river of the dead must not be forgotten. Bhairab's vehicle also happens to be a dog. On the third day it is cows who are remembered and on this day you will often see cows with one horn painted silver, one gold. On the fourth day bullocks are honoured.

The third day, Deepavali, is the most important day of the festival when Lakshmi (Vishnu's consort and the goddess of wealth) comes to visit every home which has been suitably lit for her presence. Since one can hardly turn down a surprise visit from the goddess of wealth, homes throughout the country will be brightly lit with candles and lamps for the Festival of Lights. The effect is highlighted because Deepavali falls on the new-moon day.

The fourth day is also the start of the new year for the Newar people of the Kathmandu Valley. The fifth day is known as Bhai Tika and on this day brothers and sisters are supposed to meet and place tikas on each others' foreheads. Sisters offer small gifts of fruit and sweets to their brothers while the brothers give their sisters money in return. The markets and bazaars of Kathmandu will be busy supplying the appropriate gifts.

Haribodhini Ekadashi Ekadashi falls twice in each lunar month, on the 11th day after each new and full moon. Each Ekadashi is celebrated with ceremonies and activities but the Haribodhini Ekadashi, falling in late October or early November on the 11th day after the new moon, is the most important of them. On this day Vishnu awakens from his four month monsoonal slumbers and the best place to see the associated festivities is at Budhanilkantha, the temple of the sleeping Vishnu. Activities also take place at other Vishnu temples and many Vishnu devotees make a circuit of the important ones from Ichangu Narayan to Changu Narayan, Bishanku Narayan and Sekh Narayan.

Mahalakshmi Puja Lakshmi is the goddess of wealth, but to farmers wealth is rice so this harvest festival, following immediately after Haribodhini Ekadashi, honours the goddess with sacrifices and colourful dances.

November-December
Bala Chaturdashi Like Ekadashi there are two Chaturdashis each month and Bala Chaturdashi falls on the new-moon day in late November or early December. Pilgrims flock to Pashupatinath for this festival, burning oil lamps at night and bathing in the holy river on the following morning. A pilgrimage is then made along a traditional route through the woods overlooking Pashupatinath, and as they walk the devotees scatter sweets and seeds for their deceased relatives to enjoy in the afterlife. The festival is at its most colourful during the first evening and is best observed from the other side of the Bagmati River, looking down towards the temple with its singing and dancing lamplit pilgrims.

Bala, incidentally, once worked at Pashupatinath where he cremated corpses until an unfortunate incident transformed him into a demon. He then haunted the area around the temple until a means was found to dispose of him. Various legends relate how the demon was killed by one of poor Bala's former friends and the festival of Bala Chaturdashi was then instituted.

Sita Bibaha Panchami On the fifth day of the bright fortnight in late November or early December, pilgrims from all over Nepal and India flock to Janakpur to celebrate the marriage of Sita to Rama. It was in Janakpur that Sita was born and she and Rama both have temples in the town. The wedding is re-enacted with a procession carrying Rama's image to Sita's temple by elephant. Rama's birthday is celebrated in March in Janakpur and Kathmandu.

Mani Rimdu The Sherpa festival of Mani Rimdu takes place at the monastery of Thyangboche in the Solu Khumbu region. The three day festival features masked dances and dramas performed by the monastery's monks and celebrates the victory of Buddhism over the older Bon religion. Another Mani Rimdu takes place six months later in May-June at the Thami monastery, a day's walk west of Namche Bazaar.

Other Festivals & Ceremonies
Ekadashi Ekadashi falls twice in each lunar month, 11 days after the full moon and the new moon. The annual Haribodhini Ekadashi is a major festival but the other Ekadashis are also celebrated, often with music and singing.

Marriage Ceremonies It is important that weddings take place on an auspicious date and some months of the year (Pus in particular) are extremely ill-starred for marriages. Only five months of the year – Magh,

Falgun, Baisakh, Jeth and Mangsir – are ideal, although if pressed, a talented astrologer can find an auspicious date at even the most inconvenient time. Spring is the favourite time of year and on ideal days in Baisakh there will be numerous wedding bands marching around town at the same time.

A traditional Newari wedding is a complicated affair lasting up to a week. The various stages of the ceremony move back and forth between the bride and groom's homes and include a procession led by a band. The religious ceremony, where a fire 'witnesses' the marriage, is held at the bride's house and the festivities conclude with a wedding banquet. Although more couples are making their own choice of partners many marriages are still arranged.

Very different forms of marriage take place in the hills, and in parts of the Sherpa country polyandry, where a woman takes more than one husband, is still practised.

In Nepal, as in a number of other Asian countries, the bride never wears white. White is the colour of death and funerals, red is a much happier and more auspicious colour. Married women wear vermilion in the parting of their hair.

COURSES
Yoga & Meditation
Nepal is a popular place for people to take up spiritual pursuits. Activity is centred around the Kathmandu Valley, and there are a number of places and options. See the

---

The Ages of Brahma
Each universe has a Brahma who lives for 100 years, Brahma years, that is, which are much longer than our earth years. Each day in a Brahma year is a Kalpa, and each Kalpa or Brahma day is in turn divided into 1000 Mahayugas or Great Ages.

In a single Great Age there are four Yugas which follow a prescribed pattern. In the first Yuga everything is fine, but in the second Yuga evil makes its appearance and the eternal struggle between good and evil commences. In the third Yuga good is in serious trouble and in the fourth Yuga, the Kaliyuga, evil comes out on top and it's time for Vishnu to take on his 10th incarnation as Kalki the destroyer and bring the whole mess to a quick end. And where are we currently in this cycle of existence? About halfway through the fourth Yuga. ∎

Kathmandu, Patan & Bhaktapur chapter for further details.

Language

Nepali is not a difficult language to learn, and there are a number of courses available. You will often see signs and notices around Kathmandu advertising language courses, many of them conducted by ex-Peace Corps workers. Embassies should be able to recommend somewhere that they themselves use.

Most schools offer courses (often around two weeks long) or individual tuition. Places to try in Kathmandu include the Speed Language Institute (☎ 01-220999) in Bagh Bazaar; Insight Nepal (☎ 01-418963); the Bud Language Institute (☎ 01-226713); or the School of International Languages (☎ 01-211713) at the university. Expect to pay about US$50 for a two week course, around US$3 for private hourly tuition.

WORK

For a western visitor, working in Nepal is very difficult, although it is not impossible. The easiest work to find is teaching English as there are many private schools and a great demand for English-language lessons. At less than $100 a month the pay is very low. Other possibilities include work with airline offices, travel and trekking agencies, consultants or aid groups but the prospects are remote.

Officially you need a work permit if you intend to find employment in Nepal and you are supposed to have this before you arrive in the country. Changing from a tourist visa once you are in the country is rarely permissible. The work permit has to be applied for by your employer and you are supposed to leave the country while the paperwork is negotiated. The process can take months.

ACCOMMODATION

In Kathmandu there is a very wide variety of accommodation from rock-bottom flea pits to five star international hotels. The intense competition between the many cheaper places keeps prices down and standards up – Kathmandu has many fine places with pleas-

ant gardens and rooms for less than $10 a night including private bathroom and hot water. At peak times, on the other hand, rooms in the four and five star places can be in short supply.

Pokhara also has a variety of accommodation. The choice is concentrated more at the bottom end of the market, although there are a couple of luxury hotels.

The main towns of the Terai all have accommodation ranging from hotels of reasonable standard, where rooms with fans and mosquito nets are around Rs 250, to grimy, basic places catering to local demand for around Rs 30. Some of the cheap places will only have tattered mosquito nets, if any at all, so if you're on a tight budget and want to sleep at night, bring one with you.

Elsewhere in the country the choice of hotels can be very limited but there are places to stay along most of the major trekking trails. These days it's quite possible to trek from lodge to lodge rather than camp site to camp site. On some trails the standards may be spartan – the accommodation may be dormitory-style or simply an open room to unroll your sleeping bag. Smoke can be a real problem in places where the chimney has yet to make an appearance. At the other extreme some trails, like the popular Pokhara to Jomsom route, have excellent lodges and guest houses at every stopping place.

FOOD & DRINK

Real Nepali food is distinctly dull. Most of the time it consists of a dish called *dal bhat tarkari* which is made up of lentil soup, rice and curried vegetables. The occasional dal bhat tarkari, prepared to tourist tastes in Kathmandu restaurants, can be just fine. Strictly local versions, eaten day in and day out while trekking, can get very boring indeed. Of course Indian cuisine has had a major influence on Nepal and many Tibetan dishes have come over the border, along with the many Tibetan refugees. Other popular local food and drink includes:

beer – the locally produced beer is quite
    good, especially after a hard day's walking

or bicycling around the valley. Beer is usually found in the hills as well, carried there by porters especially for thirsty trekkers, but is unlikely to be very cold. There are a number of locally produced brands that theoretically replicate the original recipes – Tuborg (Danish), Star (German), Iceberg (Indian), San Miguel (Filipino), Star and Iceberg are generally less expensive.

buff – water buffalo, casually abbreviated to buff, is the usual substitute for beef since cows are sacred and (officially at least) cannot be eaten. You may come across anything from buff burgers to buff steaks. Increasingly, 'real' beef is imported from India.

chang – the home brew of the Himalaya, a mildly alcoholic concoction made from barley.

curd – yoghurt is known throughout the sub-continent as curd and the buffalo milk curd of Nepal can be very good.

gundruk – dried vegetables are used in this traditional Nepali soup

gurr – potatoes are the staple food of the Sherpas and although they are a relatively recent introduction, have come to assume the same importance in the Solu Khumbu as they do in Ireland. Gurr is made from raw potatoes ground and mixed with spices and then grilled like a large pancake and eaten with cheese.

lassi – refreshing drink of curd mixed with water; make sure the water is safe.

momo or *kothe* – typical Tibetan dish made by steaming or frying meat or vegetables wrapped in dough; similar to dim sum or ravioli.

sikarni – a sweet curd dessert that may include nuts and dried fruit.

tama – traditional Nepali soup made from dried bamboo shoots.

thupka – traditional Tibetan meat soup.

tsampa – ground grain, usually barley, mixed with tea, water or milk and eaten dry either instead of rice or mixed with it; the staple dish in the hill country.

Although the real local food is often limited in its scope and is heavily influenced by Indian cuisine, Kathmandu's restaurants offer an amazing variety of dishes. In the days of 'Asia overlanding', when many travellers arrived in Kathmandu having made a long and often wearisome trip through Asia from Europe, Kathmandu's restaurants had a near mythical appeal. Ecstatic reports filtered back along the trail of superb restaurants and fine cuisine.

These days, when most travellers jet straight in from abroad, the food doesn't seem quite so amazing, but Kathmandu's many restaurants still do give international cuisine a damn good try and they will attempt almost anything. There's a special appeal to being high in the Himalaya and being able to choose between not just European and Asian dishes but also almost anything else from Mexican tacos to Japanese sukiyaki. Of course Nepali interpretations of foreign dishes often arrive a little off target but Nepal is a great place to try Tibetan dishes and the Indian food can also be very good.

Such a variety of restaurants is particularly amazing when you consider that in 1955 Kathmandu had just one restaurant. Leave Kathmandu (and Pokhara) behind, however, and you're soon back to dal bhat tarkari.

Many of the 'international' restaurants use large quantities of imported food. Cows, for instance, are theoretically not killed in Hindu Nepal, so beef is imported frozen from Calcutta or Delhi. By ordering with a little care, and especially avoiding beef steaks, it is possible to eat local ingredients and prevent the vital foreign currency you are contributing to the economy heading straight out of the country to pay for your luxuries.

Eating & Drinking Customs

There are a number of 'rules' and customs relating to eating and drinking in Nepal and a number of ways in which you can make life much easier for yourself. For a start the Nepali eating schedule is quite different from that in the west. The morning usually begins with little more than a cup of tea. Not until late morning is a substantial 'brunch' taken.

In areas where western visitors are not often seen and even more rarely catered for, finding food will be much simpler if you go along with this schedule.

You can also save yourself a lot of time and frustration if you pay attention to what you order as well as when you order it. In small local restaurants the cooking equipment and facilities are often very primitive.

Places with some experience of catering to western tastes will often offer amazingly varied menus, but just because they offer 20 different dishes doesn't mean they can fix two of them at the same time. If you and your five friends turn up at some small and remote cafe and order six different dishes you can expect to be waiting for dinner when breakfast time rolls around next day. In that situation it makes a lot of sense to order the same dish six times! Not only will you save time, but you will also save firewood.

If you are eating dal bhat, most local restaurants and roadside stalls will be able to find a spoon with a dubious past if you insist, but the custom is to eat with your right hand. The number one eating rule in Nepal, as in much of Asia, is always use your right hand. The left hand, used for washing yourself after defecating, is never used to eat food and certainly should not be used to pass food (or, strictly speaking, anything at all) to someone else. See also Society & Conduct in the Facts about the Country chapter for information about religious restrictions.

Caste rules also play a part in Nepali eating habits. A high-caste Brahman simply cannot eat food prepared by a lower caste individual, which effectively bans practising Brahmans from restaurants since they cannot know what is going on behind the kitchen door. And of course some foods are strictly taboo in Nepal. High-caste Hindus and all Brahmans are, ostensibly at least, vegetarian, but carnivore or not, beef is strictly banned from the menu since the cow is a holy animal.

If you are invited to a meal at a Nepali home you may find the women of the household remain totally in the background and do not eat with the men or with guests. As in India, even at quite westernised homes, socialising goes on before the meal rather than afterwards. As the last mouthful is consumed the guests head out the door – nobody hangs around for conversation over the coffee!

Care in Eating & Drinking

Don't drink the water is the prime health rule on the subcontinent and it certainly applies to Nepal. Diarrhoea, dysentery or even hepatitis can all result from indulging in contaminated drinking water.

In actual fact the relative safety of the water varies with the season. Drinking tap water is never a good idea, but during the dry season from around November to April you would probably get away with it, in

---

Chang Recipe

If you develop a taste for chang and would like to brew some at home here's the recipe. Get a 25 or 50 litre fermenting vessel from a brewery supply shop. For the smaller vessel boil about two kg of millet for several hours. Millet swells considerably so make sure there is plenty of water and it doesn't stick. When it cools, stick it in the fermenting vessel and fill it with water. (You can pass the millet through a blender to smooth it out first, if desired.) Then add burgundy yeast and the juice of a lemon and leave to ferment. This can take several weeks or a couple of months depending on taste. If you like a little extra kick to your chang add sugar, a kg or two, to the fermenting brew – this is really cheating since in Nepal sugar would be too expensive to be used in this way.

The final product will have to be strained through a cloth and racked to remove the yeasty taste. This should not be taken as the only way to produce chang – experiment with it; in Bhutan for example they drink a chang made from half millet and half rice.

Karel Tiller

Kathmandu at least. During the monsoon, however, when the heavy rains wash all sorts of stuff into the water supply, don't even consider it. Drinking boiled and filtered water is a better idea at any time of year and absolutely imperative in the wet season.

Most good restaurants do boil and filter their water, and although there's no way of telling if it has been boiled or not, tea will be safe, because boiling water is essential for its preparation. Plastic bottles of mineral water are ubiquitous. Although these seem to be safe (mostly anyway), the empty bottles are creating a major litter problem. The best alternative is to have your own water bottle and to treat the water with iodine. This is 100% safe and has the added benefit of not requiring a fire. See the Health section earlier in this chapter for information on iodine treatment.

At higher altitudes the water is generally safer than it is lower down and in more densely populated areas. Nevertheless, trekkers should never drink water from springs or streams unless they are absolutely positive they are at a higher level than any villages or cattle. In Nepal that is a very hard thing to guarantee and it is always wiser to prepare your drinking water carefully. Chang, the popular Tibetan beer, is generally safe and is found along many trekking routes.

Food stalls on the street should be approached with extreme caution and ice cream from street vendors should be completely avoided. In good restaurants the ice cream is usually fine. Meat is more likely to be unhealthy than vegetable or egg dishes; a glance at most Nepali butchers will soon show you why! If you're in doubt about the quality of meat dishes stick to vegetarian.

Beware of salads except in places you know take special care with their food preparation. Salads rinsed in untreated water are notorious for causing stomach problems. Sandwiches can also be risky.

Many travellers do develop some sort of stomach upset while in Nepal although fortunately it's usually just travellers' diarrhoea. In that case a little fasting, hot tea and fighting it off naturally are the best cure. That way you develop some resistance against further attacks. See the Health section for more details.

THINGS TO BUY

Nepal is a shopper's paradise whether you are looking for a cheap souvenir or a real work of art. Although you can find almost anything in the tourist areas of Kathmandu there are specific specialities in different parts of the valley. Wherever you shop remember to bargain, although with the increasing number of totally tourist-oriented shops more fixed-price establishments are beginning to appear.

One place you could start is the Amrita Craft Collection, south of the Kathmandu Guest House in Thamel. They have quite a broad collection of crafts and clothing, all priced. (Subtract 20% and you get a good bench mark for what you should pay on the street if you are an excellent bargainer.)

Antiquities cannot be taken out of the country, and baggage is inspected by Nepali customs with greater thoroughness on departure than on arrival. If you've bought something which is possibly antique, you should get a receipt and a description of the object from the shop where you bought it. Art theft is a real problem in Nepal and it would be a great shame if some of the superb museum pieces which currently stand in the open, where they may have been for over 1000 years, have to be moved into protected museums.

A permit is required from the Department of Archaeology (☎ 01-215358) in order to take out of the country any object which looks as if it could be more than 100 years old. The office is in the National Archives building on Ram Shah Path and if you visit between 10 am and 1 pm you should be able to pick up a permit by 5 pm the same day. The customs office (☎ 01-215525) at Tripureshwar can also provide information.

Thangkas

Thangkas are the traditional Tibetan paintings of religious and ceremonial subjects. They illustrate gods, associated deities,

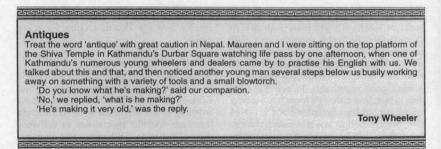

Antiques
Treat the word 'antique' with great caution in Nepal. Maureen and I were sitting on the top platform of the Shiva Temple in Kathmandu's Durbar Square watching life pass by one afternoon, when one of Kathmandu's numerous young wheelers and dealers came by to practise his English with us. We talked about this and that, and then noticed another young man several steps below us busily working away on something with a variety of tools and a small blowtorch.
   'Do you know what he's making?' said our companion.
   'No,' we replied, 'what is he making?'
   'He's making it very old,' was the reply.

Tony Wheeler

mandalas, the wheel of life and other such subjects. The figures may be of the various Buddhas, Bodhisattvas or Taras although often they are of the fierce and angry aspects of gods. Thangkas are usually colourful and packed with detail to every corner of the painting.

Although there are genuine antique thangkas to be found it's highly unlikely that anything offered to the average visitor will date from much beyond last week. Judicious use of a smoky fire can add the odd century in no time at all. Thangkas do vary considerably in quality but buy one because you like it, not as a valuable investment.

Thangkas are available in many locations including the Tibetan shops around Bodhnath. There are some good thangka shops in Thamel in Kathmandu and in the Durbar Square shops in Bhaktapur. There is also an outlet near the Pujari Math monastery. Thangkas can cost anything from Rs 200 to Rs 2000 and beyond, and like many other crafts the more you see the more you will appreciate the difference between those of average and those of superior quality. Size also plays a part in the final price of course. Traditionally thangkas are framed in silk brocade.

Block Prints

Locally produced rice paper is used for the block prints of Nepali, Tibetan and Chinese deities. They are sold as pictures or are used for calendars, cards, lanterns and many other uses. A print typically costs from Rs 50 to Rs 100. In Thamel near the Kathmandu Guest House there is a particularly good selection in The Print Shop.

Tibetan Carpets

Carpet-weaving is a major trade in Nepal, brought from Tibet by the refugees who now carry on the craft with great success in their new homes. There are carpet-weavers around the Kathmandu Valley and also in Pokhara. Some of their output is now exported to Tibet, where the Chinese have unfortunately managed to totally stamp out the archaic craft. A genuine Tibetan carpet purchased in Tibet is probably indeed made by genuine Tibetans, but in Nepal. The Tamang people also make carpets.

Jawlakhel, on the southern outskirts of Patan, is the carpet-weaving centre in the valley and there are numerous carpet shops as you enter the area. You can see carpets being woven here and also in other places around the valley, including around the Bodhnath Stupa. There are larger and smaller sizes available, but the traditional size for a Tibetan carpet is 1.8m by 90 cm. They're sturdily woven with colourful designs featuring Tibetan Buddhist symbols and dragons. These days it is more difficult to find the brilliant reds and blues produced by chemical dyes: more often carpets will be in the pale pastel shades which come from vegetable dyes. Small square carpets are often used to make seat cushions.

Clothing & Embroidery

Tibetan and Nepali clothes have always been a popular buy but recently western fashions made strictly for the tourist market have also become an important industry. You can buy handmade shirts at outlets in Thamel and there are also shops in Kathmandu (see the Kathmandu Things to Buy section) selling superb hand-painted silk dresses at a fraction of what they would cost in the west.

There is still a demand for traditional styles such as the Tibetan wool jackets which are popularly known as *yakets*. Nepali coats, crossing over at the front, closed with four ties and traditionally made in purple velvet material, are a popular buy.

Embroidery has always been popular in Nepal and there are lots of little tailor shops around Kathmandu where the sewing machines rattle on until late at night adding colourful dragons and Tibetan symbols to customers jackets and jeans. Mountaineers like to return from Nepal with jackets carrying the message that this was the Country X, Year Y expedition to Peak Z. You can take your own clothes to be embroidered or buy T-shirts and other items already embroidered. Badges embroidered with suitable messages are another good buy – you can add a badge to your backpack saying that you walked to the Everest Base Camp or completed the Annapurna Circuit.

A Nepali cap or *topi* is part of Nepali formal wear for a man and they are traditionally made in Bhaktapur. There's a cap shop right beside the Bhairabnath Temple in Bhaktapur as well as a group of cap specialists between Indra Chowk and Asan Tole in the old part of Kathmandu. Caps typically cost from Rs 50 to Rs 300.

Pottery

Terracotta pottery is made in a number of sites but particularly in Thimi and Bhaktapur. The Potters' Square, just south of Durbar Square in Bhaktapur, is a wonderful sight. Thousands of pots are neatly lined up across the square while in the shelters around the sides of the square, potters busily turn out more and more.

In Thimi they specialise in making attractive little flowerpots, often in the shape of dragons, elephants or mythical beasts. You can buy them in Thimi or from stalls near Indra Chowk in Kathmandu or Taumadhi Tole in Bhaktapur.

Jewellery

Kathmandu's many small jewellery manufacturers turn out a wide variety of designs with an equally wide range of standards. You can buy jewellery ready-made; ask them to create a design for you or bring in something you would like copied. There are several good shops around Thamel, particularly down towards Chhetrapati.

These outlets mainly cater to western tastes but there are also many shops for the local market as Nepali women, like Indian women, traditionally wear their wealth in jewellery. Cheap ornaments can also be fun; you can buy an armful of glass bangles for a few rupees or colourful beads by the handful.

Masks & Puppets

Papier-mâché masks and colourful puppets are sold at shops in Kathmandu, Patan and Bhaktapur. Thimi is the centre for manufacturing the masks which are used in the traditional masked dances in September and it's interesting to see them being made and painted there. Ganesh, Bhairab and the Kumari are the most popular subjects for the mask and they make good wall decorations.

Masks, used for traditional dances in September, can be easily bought.

Prices typically range from around Rs 50 to Rs 200.

Puppets make good buys as gifts for children and are made in Bhaktapur as well as other centres. They're often of multi-armed deities clutching little wooden weapons in each hand. The puppet heads may be made of easily broken clay or more durable papier-mâché. Smaller puppets cost from around Rs 100 to Rs 300 but you can also pay Rs 500 to Rs 700 for a larger figure. As usual, quality does vary and the more puppets you inspect the more you will begin to appreciate the differences.

Metalwork
Patan is the valley centre for bronze casting and the best variety of metalwork is found in the shops around Patan's Durbar Square. (See the Patan Things to Buy section for more details.) Often, beautifully made figures featuring the full range of Tantric Buddhist deities can be bought at costs ranging from Rs 2000 to Rs 5000 for good-quality smaller figures. Of course cheaper and simpler work can be found much more cheaply. The metal game boards and pieces for the traditional Nepali game *bagh chal* make a good buy.

Other Nepali Crafts
A khukuri, the traditional knife of the Gurkhas, can cost from Rs 300 to Rs 1000. Khukuri House, next to the Rum Doodle Bar in Thamel is a good place to start looking.

Bhaktapur is the centre for woodcarving and you can find good objects in and around Tachupal Tole. Cassettes of Nepali, Indian and general Himalayan music are a fine souvenir of a visit to Nepal. There are lots of music shops in Kathmandu selling local music as well as bootlegged western tapes.

For all sorts of small souvenirs the huge market area in Basantapur Square in Kathmandu is a good place to browse. Wandering the crowded and bustling market street from Indra Chowk to Asan Tole is always likely to turn up some interesting bargain.

Other Tibetan Crafts
Tibetan crafts include a variety of religious items such as the *dorje* (thunderbolt symbol) and the popular prayer wheels. Tibetans are keen traders and prices at Bodhnath and Swayambhunath are often very high.

Tea
Tea is grown in the east of Nepal, close to the border with India near Darjeeling where the finest Indian tea is grown. Ilam and Mai Valley are the best Nepali brands, but they are not cheap. Expect to pay around Rs 500 per kg for good Ilam tea, which is not much cheaper than Darjeeling tea.

Sending Purchases Home
By far the best way of getting something back home is to take it with you. Shipping or mailing objects can be fraught with dangers and hidden expenses. For a start there's no guarantee that it will be sent at all. If you leave your purchase for a shop to mail to you and it never turns up what can you prove? They will say they mailed it and the post office has lost it somewhere along the line, and you have no idea whether they have or not.

If an object is shipped to you, you may find that customs charges for clearance and collection at your end add up to more than the initial cost of sending it. Often it would have been worth paying extra to bring it with you in the first place.

Unless you are very sure about the reliability of the shop, do not ask the shop where you made the purchase to send it for you. There are a number of packing companies in Kathmandu but some of them are no more reliable than a shop might be. Diki Continental Exports (☎ 01-417681; fax 414997), opposite the Hotel Mandap in Thamel, and Sharmasons Movers (☎ 01-222709; fax 222026) are two that have been recommended. The international courier company DHL (☎ 01-222358) has an office on Durbar Marg and in Thamel.

Air freight costs are punitive – around $40

per kg to Europe or Australia, $50 to the USA. Sea freight is much cheaper than air, but it is also much slower and less reliable –

packages are sent overland to Calcutta or Bombay, and then wait until a full container has been consolidated.

Getting There & Away

AIR

Kathmandu is the site for Nepal's only international airport, Tribhuvan airport. Flying from Europe, North America or Australia usually requires a change of aircraft and/or airline en route.

Airlines

Lufthansa has a Frankfurt to Kathmandu service, and Royal Nepal Airlines Corporation (RNAC) has a London, Frankfurt, Kathmandu service. Aeroflot also connects Nepal with Europe. These are the only three airlines with direct connections with Europe. Travellers arriving from Europe or from the east coast of North America with other airlines transfer to RNAC or Indian Airlines in New Delhi for the final short flight from New Delhi to Kathmandu.

From the west coast of North America or from Australasia, Bangkok is the usual transfer point, although there are also flights to Kathmandu from Hong Kong and Singapore. Thai International and RNAC share the Bangkok to Kathmandu route.

The UK & Europe

Trailfinders in west London produces a lavishly illustrated brochure which includes airfare details. STA also has branches in the UK. Look for ads in the listings magazine *Time Out* plus the Sunday papers and *Exchange & Mart*. Also look for the free magazines widely available in London – start by looking outside the main railway stations.

Most British travel agents are registered with ABTA (Association of British Travel Agents). If you have paid for your flight with an ABTA-registered agent who then goes out of business, ABTA will guarantee a refund or an alternative. Unregistered bucket shops are riskier but also sometimes cheaper.

The Globetrotters Club (BCM Roving, London WC1N 3XX) publishes a newsletter called *Globe* which covers obscure destinations and can help in finding travelling companions.

Reliable specialists for cheap tickets in London include Trailfinders at 46 Earls Court Rd, London W8, and STA (Student Travel Australia) at 74 Old Brompton Rd, London SW7, or 117 Euston Rd, London NW1. Count on around UK£563 to UK£729 for a London to Kathmandu return ticket.

Kathmandu to Frankfurt on Lufthansa's direct flight is US$895 return, US$580 one way. Aeroflot has Kathmandu-Moscow-Europe flights for US$450 (one way). Pakistan International Airlines (PIA) has connections to Kathmandu via Karachi; Kathmandu to Karachi one way is US$189. You won't save money by flying via Delhi, but seat availability is usually much better than on the direct flights. The flight from Delhi to Kathmandu is US$142.

The USA & Canada

The *New York Times*, the *LA Times*, the *Chicago Tribune* and the *San Francisco Examiner* produce weekly travel sections in which you'll find any number of travel agents' ads. Council Travel and STA Travel have offices in major cities nationwide. The magazine *Travel Unlimited* (PO Box 1058, Allston, Mass 02134) publishes details of the cheapest airfares and courier possibilities for destinations all over the world from the USA.

Fares to Kathmandu will often be about the same from the east or west coast – it's about as far away as you can get in either direction! Typical return fares are from around US$1575.

Fares from Canada are similar to the USA, either westbound from Vancouver or eastbound from Toronto or Montreal.

Australia & New Zealand

STA and Flight Centres International are major dealers in cheap airfares. Check the travel agents' ads in the Yellow Pages and phone around.

Fares from Australia depend on the season and typically cost around A$1500 return. Bangkok is the most popular transit point although you can also fly via Singapore or Hong Kong.

From Kathmandu to east coast Australia, a one-way ticket with Singapore Airlines costs US$650.

India

Royal Nepal Airlines Corporation (RNAC) and Indian Airlines share routes between India and Kathmandu. Both airlines give a 25% discount to those under 30 years of age on flights between Kathmandu and India; no student card is needed.

New Delhi is the main departure point for flights between India and Kathmandu. The daily one hour New Delhi to Kathmandu flight costs US$142.

Other cities in India with direct air connections with Kathmandu are Bombay (US$257), Calcutta (US$96) and Varanasi (US$71). The flight from Varanasi is the last leg of the popular New Delhi, Agra, Khajuraho, Varanasi, Kathmandu tourist flight.

Elsewhere in Asia

Other departure points for Kathmandu and approximate one-way fares include:

Bangkok, Thailand	US$220
Dhaka, Bangladesh	US$86
Dubai, UAE	US$200
Hong Kong	US$310
Karachi, Pakistan	US$189
Lhasa, Tibet	US$190
Singapore	US$315

In most cases return advance-purchase excursion (APEX) fares are available. There are also some interesting through fares; one to consider is Bangladesh Biman's Kathmandu, Dhaka, Rangoon, Bangkok ticket which sells for around US$400. A direct Kathmandu to Bangkok ticket costs US$220.

Where to Sit

If you want to see the mountains as you fly into Kathmandu you must sit on the correct side. Flying in from the east – Bangkok, Calcutta, Hong Kong, Rangoon or Singapore – you want the right side. Flying in from the west – New Delhi or Varanasi – you want the left side.

Arriving in Nepal by Air

The international terminal is a modern building and everything operates reasonably smoothly. The most gruelling part is the thorough baggage search. Touts are excluded from the building, so everything is fairly calm until you hit the outside world.

There's a branch of the Nabil Bank prior to clearing immigration on the 1st floor. There's another branch on the ground floor of the departure section; both are open for flights, which normally means till around 8 pm.

There's a duty-free shop with a limited range of liquor and cigarettes available for sale in US dollars to arriving and departing passengers.

Leaving Nepal by Air

The departure tax for international flights is Rs 700, payable in rupees at the check-in counters.

Check in at least two hours early; for some airlines in the high season (those that have a reputation for overbooking) it is worth getting there even earlier. Also, don't forget to confirm and reconfirm your flight at least 72 hours before departure. At the airport, it is possible to re-exchange up to 15% of the Nepali rupees you have officially changed, but you must be able to show unused Foreign Exchange Encashment Receipts. If you are leaving for India, you can get between Indian Rs 500 and Rs 2000 on presentation of your ticket.

Make sure you have clearance for anything that might be construed as an antique – metal statues show up on the baggage x-ray and are often checked. The x-ray machines that screen cargo baggage are definitely not film safe. Those that screen hand luggage are

Air Travel Glossary

Apex Apex, or 'advance purchase excursion', is a discounted ticket which must be paid for in advance. There are penalties if you wish to change it.

Baggage Allowance This will be written on your ticket: usually one 20 kg item to go in the hold, plus one item of hand luggage.

Bucket Shop An unbonded travel agency specialising in discounted airline tickets.

Bumped Just because you have a confirmed seat doesn't mean you're going to get on the plane – see Overbooking.

Cancellation Penalties If you have to cancel or change an Apex ticket there are often heavy penalties involved, although insurance can sometimes be taken out against these penalties. Some airlines impose penalties on regular tickets as well, particularly against 'no show' passengers.

Check-In Airlines ask you to check in a certain time ahead of the flight departure (usually 1½ hours on international flights). If you fail to check in on time and the flight is overbooked, the airline can cancel your booking and give your seat to somebody else.

Confirmation Having a ticket written out with the flight and date you want doesn't mean you have a seat until the agent has checked with the airline that your status is 'OK', or confirmed. Meanwhile you could just be 'on request'.

Discounted Tickets There are two types of discounted fares – officially discounted (see Promotional Fares) and unofficially discounted. The lowest prices often impose drawbacks like flying with unpopular airlines, inconvenient schedules, or unpleasant routes and connections. A discounted ticket can save you things other than money – you may be able to pay Apex prices without the associated Apex advance booking and other requirements. Discounted tickets only exist where there is fierce competition.

Full Fares Airlines traditionally offer first class (coded F), business class (coded J) and economy class (coded Y) tickets. These days there are so many promotional and discounted fares available from the regular economy class that few passengers pay full economy fare.

Lost Tickets If you lose your ticket an airline will usually treat it like a travellers' cheque and, after inquiries, issue you with another. Legally, however, an airline is entitled to treat it like cash and if you lose it then it's gone forever. Take good care of your tickets.

No Shows No shows are passengers who fail to show up for their flight, sometimes due to unexpected delays or disasters, sometimes due to simply forgetting, sometimes because they made more than one booking and didn't bother to cancel the one they didn't want. Full fare passengers who fail to turn up are sometimes entitled to travel on a later flight. The rest of us are penalised (see Cancellation Penalties).

On Request An unconfirmed booking for a flight – see Confirmation.

---

meant to be film safe, but on one trip, my film was fogged in either Nepal or Bangkok. Insist that the security officers physically inspect your precious film.

There is a pleasant restaurant on the top (2nd) floor, which is open to all, or go through immigration on the 1st floor, where there is a restaurant, open to passengers only. On the ground floor is a post office.

The small duty-free shop has a limited range of liquor and cigarettes available for purchase with US dollars. Shoestring travellers often take their duty-free allowances

with the intention of selling them at their next halt. Myanmar (Burma) is a particularly popular country for selling duty-free items.

LAND

Political and weather conditions permitting there are four main entry points into Nepal by land: three from India, one from Tibet.

A steady trickle of people drive their own motorbikes or vehicles overland from Europe – there are some interesting, though difficult, new routes to the subcontinent through Eastern Europe and the republics that were

Open Jaws A return ticket where you fly out to one place but return from another. If available this can save you backtracking to your arrival point.

Overbooking Airlines hate to fly empty seats and since every flight has some passengers who fail to show up (see No Shows) airlines often book more passengers than they have seats. Usually the excess passengers balance those who fail to show up but occasionally somebody gets bumped. If this happens guess who it is most likely to be? The passengers who check in late.

Promotional Fares Officially discounted fares like Apex fares which are available from travel agents or direct from the airline.

Reconfirmation At least 72 hours prior to departure time of an onward or return flight you must contact the airline and 'reconfirm' that you intend to be on the flight. If you don't do this the airline can delete your name from the passenger list and you could lose your seat. You don't have to reconfirm the first flight on your itinerary or if your stopover is less than 72 hours. It doesn't hurt to reconfirm more than once.

Restrictions Discounted tickets often have various restrictions on them – advance purchase is the most usual one (see Apex). Others are restrictions on the minimum and maximum period you must be away, such as a minimum of 14 days or a maximum of one year – see Cancellation Penalties.

Standby A discounted ticket where you only fly if there is a seat free at the last moment. Standby fares are usually only available on domestic routes.

Tickets Out An entry requirement for many countries is that you have an onward or return ticket, in other words, a ticket out of the country. If you're not sure what you intend to do next, the easiest solution is to buy the cheapest onward ticket to a neighbouring country or a ticket from a reliable airline which can later be refunded if you do not use it.

Transferred Tickets Airline tickets cannot be transferred from one person to another. Travellers sometimes try to sell the return half of their ticket, but officials can ask you to prove that you are the person named on the ticket. This is unlikely to happen on domestic flights, but on an international flight tickets may be compared with passports.

Travel Agencies Travel agencies vary widely so use one that suits your needs. Some simply handle tours while full-service agencies handle everything from tours and tickets to car rental and hotel bookings. A good agency will do all these things and can save you a lot of money but if all you want is a ticket at the lowest possible price, then you really need an agency specialising in discounted tickets.

Travel Periods Some officially discounted fares, Apex fares in particular, vary with the time of year. There is often a low (off-peak) season and a high (peak) season. Sometimes there's an intermediate or shoulder season as well. At peak times, when everyone wants to fly, not only will the officially discounted fares be higher but so will unofficially discounted fares, or there may simply be no discounted tickets available. Usually the fare depends on your outward flight – if you depart in the high season and return in the low season, you pay the high-season fare. ∎

once a part of the USSR. An international carnet is required. If you want to abandon your transport in Nepal, you must either pay a prohibitive import duty or surrender it to customs. It is not possible to import cars more than five years old.

India

The most popular crossing points from India are Sunauli/Bhairawa (south of Pokhara), Raxaul Bazaar/Birganj (south of Kathmandu) and Kakarbhitta (near Siliguri and Darjeeling in the far east). There are other less popular, but still viable, options.

Through Tickets Many travellers have complained about scams involving ticket packages to India. The package usually involves coordination between at least three different companies so the potential for an honest cock-up is at least as high as the potential for a deliberate rip-off. (See the Ticket Scams to India aside in this chapter.)

Two long-standing and reliable Nepali companies handling through tickets are

Student Travels & Tours (☎ 01-225452; fax 226348) in Thamel, Kathmandu; and Yeti Travels (☎ 221234; fax 226152) in Durbar Marg, Kathmandu. Bear in mind, however, that everyone has to change buses at the border whether they book a through ticket or not, and that despite claims to the contrary, there are no 'tourist' buses on either side of the border. Buses through to Varanasi cost from Rs 500, and to Darjeeling Rs 650. Bus/train packages to Agra cost Rs 2250 including an air-con sleeper on the train, or Rs 950 in 2nd class. Bus/train to Delhi costs Rs 2550 with air-con, Rs 950 in 2nd class.

It is worth considering making advance bookings if you are in a major hurry, or plan to use the Indian railway system. Some trains, and especially sleeping compartments, can be heavily booked (this is apparently the case for Gorakhpur to Delhi trains). A Nepali agent will need a week to organise a booking. Beware – there's always a chance that what you pay for and what you get will be two different things. Make sure you get a receipt clearly specifying what you think you have paid for, and hang on to it.

To/From Delhi If you are travelling to or from New Delhi or elsewhere in western India the route through Sunauli/Bhairawa is the most convenient, but you can also enter at Mahendranagar in the far west of Nepal, although this is a much more difficult route.

Via Sunauli Delhi to Gorakhpur involves an overnight rail journey, from where frequent buses make the three hour run to the border.

Buses to Kathmandu from Sunauli travel north along the beautiful Siddhartha Highway to Mugling before joining the Kathmandu-Pokhara (Prithvi) Highway. The journey takes around nine hours, but unfortunately direct buses only run at night. To do the journey in the daytime, take a day bus heading for Pokhara as far as Mugling. The government-owned, blue Sajha Yatayat buses are faster and less crowded than most of the privately run buses.

Buses to Pokhara also travel via Mugling, and the trip also takes nine hours.

See the Sunauli/Bhairawa section in the Terai chapter for more details.

Via Mahendranagar The border crossing at Mahendranagar is the most interesting option. It will take a while for things to start operating smoothly, but when they do, this will present an interesting alternative route from Delhi or some of the hill stations in northern Uttar Pradesh. When the Mahendra Highway is finally completed (some time this century would be nothing short of a

---

Ticket Scams to India

Many people have written complaining about scams involving through tickets to India, especially out of Pokhara. Mind you, there's always plenty of scope for disaster when travelling on the subcontinent. That's why it's such good fun! The following extract is a classic example:

I paid Rs 2000 ($40) for a bus to the Indian border, a bus from there to Gorakhpur and an air-con sleeper on a train to Delhi. The bus to the border ran out of fuel three times and was four hours late. The bus to Gorakhpur broke down five km into the 100 km trip and was abandoned, forcing me to catch a taxi for the remainder of the journey.

Once in Gorakhpur, I was to take a receipt to a travel agency to have my air-con sleeper ticket to Delhi issued. The receipt was issued by the travel agent in Pokhara, but the travel agent in Gorakhpur denied any knowledge of air-con on this particular train and refused to issue me with anything other than a 2nd-class ticket. I spoke to the station master about my problem and he was extremely unhelpful, arousing my suspicion that he may have been in with the travel agent.

While I was in the middle of a heated argument with the Gorakhpur travel agent, two English guys stormed into the shop screaming 'Liar, I'll kill you!' The three of us bombarded the agent with facts, asking for our money back, but he just laughed, closed up his shop for the night and walked off. ■

miracle) the route will be open all year, but until then it is a dry season-only proposition, and strictly for the hardy.

There are daily buses from New Delhi to Banbassa, the nearest Indian village to the border (11 hours). Banbassa is also connected by rail to Bareilly, and by bus with the hill station Almora in India.

There are direct buses from Mahendranagar to Kathmandu (at 2 pm), but they take a gruelling 25 hours. The countryside is beautiful and fascinating, so it's much better to do the whole trip during daylight and to break the journey at Nepalganj. There are plenty of night and day buses from Nepalganj to Kathmandu (16 hours) and night buses to Pokhara (15 hours).

See the Mahendranagar section in the Terai chapter for details of the border crossing.

To/From Varanasi Once again, the Sunauli/ Bhairawa crossing is the most convenient. There are direct buses from Varanasi for Indian Rs 81 to Rs 100, depending on the degree of luxury, and the journey takes about nine hours.

From Sunauli it's another nine hours to Kathmandu (night buses only) or Pokhara (day and night buses).

Some private companies make bookings all the way through to Kathmandu and Pokhara for around Indian Rs 250, including spartan accommodation at Sunauli. However, if you organise things yourself as you go, it will be cheaper, plus you will have more flexibility, including a choice of bus within Nepal and also of accommodation in Sunauli. Catch a bus to Sunauli, stay overnight on the Nepal side of the border (there are several reasonable hotels in Sunauli and Bhairawa), then catch a Nepali bus the next morning.

To/From Calcutta & Patna The Raxaul Bazaar/Birganj entry point is the most convenient option in the east of India. Since the completion of the Narayanghat to Mugling road, all buses from Birganj to Kathmandu or Pokhara travel via Mugling rather than the slower, though more scenic, Tribhuvan Highway via Daman. This does mean however, that all buses go through Tadi Bazaar, the jumping-off point for Sauraha and Royal Chitwan National Park.

Calcutta to Patna takes about 10 hours, and you can do this by overnight train. It's then a five hour journey from Patna to Raxaul Bazaar (the Indian border town).

Raxaul Bazaar is virtually a twin town with Birganj in Nepal. Both towns are dirty, unattractive transit points strung along the highway and are full of heavy traffic. The border is open from 7 am to 7 pm every day.

All direct buses between Birganj and Kathmandu or Pokhara turn west at Hetauda, then at Narayanghat turn north to Mugling which is on the Kathmandu-Pokhara (Prithvi) Highway. Although it is not as spectacular as the Tribhuvan Highway, this is nonetheless an interesting route with some beautiful views.

Between Birganj and Kathmandu direct buses take around 11 hours; between Birganj and Pokhara they are marginally quicker. There are numerous night and day buses. The best buses are the blue, government-owned Sajha Yatayat buses which are faster and less crowded than most of the privately run buses.

See the Birganj section in the Terai chapter for border crossing details.

To/From Darjeeling Kakarbhitta is the obvious entry point, but the Mahendra Highway can be blocked by floods during the monsoon, in which case it would be necessary to travel by train from Siliguri to Patna before entering Nepal at Birganj.

There are a number of companies that handle bookings between Darjeeling and Kathmandu, although with all of them you have to change buses at the border and Siliguri.

It's almost as easy to get from Darjeeling to Kathmandu on your own though this involves four changes – a bus from Darjeeling to Siliguri, then a minibus from Siliguri to Raniganj at the border, a rickshaw across the border to Kakarbhitta and a bus from Kakarbhitta to Kathmandu. This is cheaper than the package deal, you have a choice of buses from the border, plus you have the option of travelling during the day and overnighting along the way.

Buses to Kathmandu travel west along the Mahendra Highway to the Tribhuvan Highway between Birganj and Hetauda, then head briefly north to Hetauda. They then travel west again until Narayanghat where they turn north to Mugling, on the Kathmandu-Pokhara (Prithvi) Highway.

It's more than 600 km between Kakarbhitta and Kathmandu, which means direct buses can take an exhausting 17 hours to complete the trip, and the direct buses all travel at night.

If you have time it is worth considering breaking your journey at Janakpur, which is roughly halfway, and an interesting place in its own right. This will enable you to travel during the day and get a feel for the Terai; the flood plain of the Sapt Kosi is particularly interesting. There are day buses from Kakarbhitta that go to a number of towns on the Terai including Janakpur, and night buses direct to Pokhara. See the Kakarbhitta section in the Terai chapter for details.

WARNING
Carbon-Monoxide Poisoning
A number of people have died in Darjeeling of carbon-monoxide poisoning from burning charcoal in poorly ventilated hotel rooms. Avoid lighting charcoal-fuelled fires; ask the proprietor for more blankets if you need to get warm. If lighting a fire, make sure the room is well ventilated and that the fuel does not give off toxic fumes. ∎

Tibet
Currently the route to Tibet from Nepal (via Kodari) is closed to individual travellers, but independent travellers are entering Tibet through China and continuing, without problems, to Nepal. Only organised groups are allowed to cross from Nepal into Tibet, but this option is expensive.

On the face of it, it doesn't make much sense to allow individuals into Tibet from China, but not from Nepal. However, the package business is so lucrative and Nepal is so full of seditious Tibetans, that the Chinese must see little incentive to change. Bear in mind the road is of poor quality and is regularly closed by landslides during the monsoon.

Political disasters are even more likely than natural ones. Tibet is a volatile region with regular violent protests against Chinese rule and these upheavals are often followed by restrictions on visitors to the region. Usually these restrictions are applied more stringently to independent visitors than to people on organised tours. The baseline is that if you intend to enter or leave Nepal via Tibet you should come prepared with alternative plans in case travel along this route proves impossible.

Organised Tours A number of agencies in Kathmandu organise fully inclusive return trips to Lhasa, with prices around US$100 per day for eight to 12 day trips.

Most tours from Kathmandu take eight days and involve a flight to Lhasa and an overland return trip (or vice versa). The flights stop from the end of November to the end of March because of the weather. China International Travel Service (CITS), the state travel agency, operates the tours within China.

Travel agencies in Nepal specialising in trips to Tibet include:

Green Hill Tours
    PO Box 5072, Thamel
    (☎ 01-414803; fax 416697)
Kathmandu Travels & Tours
    PO Box 459, Ganga Path, Kathmandu
    (☎ 01-224536; fax 225131)
Natraj Tours & Travels
    PO Box 495, Durbar Marg, Kathmandu
    (☎ 01-222014; fax 227372)
Nepal Travel Agency
    PO Box 1501, Ram Shah Path, Kathmandu
    (☎ 01-413188; fax 420861)
Tibet Travels & Tours
    PO Box 1397, Tridevi Marg, Thamel, Kathmandu (☎ 01-231130; fax 228986)

Yeti Travels
  PO Box 76, Durbar Marg, Kathmandu
  (☎ 01-221234; fax 226152)

Independent Travel If independent travel into Tibet is permitted you must first get a Chinese visa (see the Embassy section in the Facts for the Visitor chapter for more details).

From Khasa (Zhangmu), the Tibetan town just over the border, there are just two buses a week to Lhasa, so you must plan carefully or you may be stranded for several days. Take food and drink on this trip, as there's not much available along the way. It's also possible to get rides on trucks to Shigatse, but the 15 hour trip in the back of a truck is strictly for the hardy. From Shigatse there are local buses to Gyantse and from there to Lhasa.

This is not an easy trip by any means. Altitude sickness is a real danger as the maximum altitude along the road is 5140m and there have been reports of deaths.

It is not possible to catch a bus direct from Kathmandu to Kodari, but eight buses a day do run to Barabise. They take around five agonising hours. From Barabise there are buses that take two hours to get to Kodari. Since there's nothing much to see from Kodari, travelling out here by bus is a little pointless unless you are actually going on to Tibet. See the Around the Kathmandu Valley chapter for more information on the Arniko Highway.

> **WARNING**
> The information in this chapter is particularly vulnerable to change. Prices for international travel are volatile, routes are introduced and cancelled, schedules change, rules are amended and special deals come and go. Airlines and governments seem to take a perverse pleasure in making price structures and regulations as complicated as possible and you should check directly with the airline or a travel agent to make sure you understand how a fare (and any ticket you may buy) works.
>
> The upshot of this is that you should get opinions, quotes and advice from as many airlines and travel agencies as possible before you part with your hard-earned cash. The details given in this chapter should be regarded as pointers and are not a substitute for your own careful, up-to-the-minute research. ■

Getting Around

Getting around Nepal can be a challenging business. The impossible terrain and extreme weather conditions, plus incompetence and disorganisation, mean that trips rarely go exactly according to plan. On the other hand, Nepali ingenuity will usually get you to your destination in the end. Although travel can be frustrating, it also creates memorable moments by the score. Good humour and patience are essential prerequisites. Losing your cool will get you nowhere fast.

The whole gamut of transport options is available, with the possible exception of submarine and monorail. Most of the others can be found together on the average road, simultaneously competing with ducks, dogs, chickens, pigs, children and adults, and none of them has the vaguest traffic sense.

Walking is still the most important, and the most reliable, method of getting from A to B and for moving cargo; more is carried by people and porters than by every other form of transport combined.

Biking is quickly gaining popularity with visitors – local buses are so slow and uncomfortable that bikes are often almost as quick, over short distances at least, and have the added advantage of allowing you to travel at your own speed and to stop whenever you like. There are a number of other human-powered contraptions ranging from barrows to bicycle rickshaws, canoes, kayaks and rafts.

There are numerous forms of animal transport. Bullocks, oxen, buffaloes and ponies are all attached to carts. Elephants, donkeys and yaks are all ridden or used to carry loads.

The 'infernal' combustion engine is making an increasingly obnoxious impact on the environment. There are two-stroke autorickshaws, three wheeled *tempos* and motorbikes, petrol-driven cars and motorbikes, and smoke-belching diesel buses and trucks. The buses range from lumbering dinosaurs held together by bits of wire and

the combined hopes of the passengers, to brand new Tatas from India, the kings of the road.

Then there are planes (of ranging sizes) and huge Russian helicopters. There's even a train at Janakpur and a cableway (a kind of ski lift that carries cargo) at Hetauda.

AIR

There are a number of private companies operating alongside the long-running, government-owned Royal Nepal Airlines Corporation (RNAC). These are Everest Air, Necon Air, Nepal Airways and Himalayan Helicopters. So far at least, these airlines only operate on the more popular (ie economically viable) routes. The prices are the same as RNAC, but the private companies offer better service, and are more reliable. Necon Air is very efficient and highly recommended.

The main air travel hubs are Kathmandu, Pokhara, Nepalganj in the west and Biratnagar in the east.

RNAC operates by far the most comprehensive range of scheduled flights around the country. The aircraft used are Hawker Siddeley 748s on the major routes and short take-off and landing (STOL) Twin Otters and Pilatus Porters to the smaller places. RNAC has flights to Baglung, Baitadi, Bajhang, Bajura, Bhairawa, Bharatpur, Bhojpur, Biratnagar, Chaurjhari, Dang, Darchula, Dhangadhi, Dolpa, Janakpur, Jomsom, Jumla, Kathmandu, Lamdanda, Lukla, Mahendranagar, Manang, Meghauli, Nepalganj, Phaplu, Pokhara, Ramechhap, Rumjatar, Sanfebagar, Silgadhidoti, Simara, Simikot, Surkhet, Taplejung, Tikapur and Tumlingtar.

Necon Air is the next-biggest, with 48 seater Avros and one eight seater Cessna servicing Kathmandu, Pokhara, Bhairawa, Biratnagar, Janakpur, Nepalganj and Mahendranagar.

Everest Air flies two German Dornier 228 planes to Kathmandu, Pokhara, Jomsom,

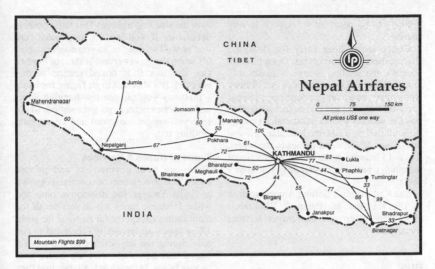

Bharatpur, Biratnagar, Jumla and Nepalganj. It also operates Russian MI-17 helicopters that carry 20 or more passengers from Kathmandu to Lukla.

Nepal Airways has Y12s, which are Chinese-made Twin Otter-type aircraft, and flies to Biratnagar, Nepalganj, Bhairawa and Pokhara.

Himalayan Helicopters is basically a charter operation and has two Bell helicopters.

Some flights, such as Kathmandu to Lukla, are used mainly by trekkers. These flights are frequent during the trekking season, but the schedules can be extremely variable. Kathmandu to Jomsom flights, for example, are plagued by bad weather at both ends. Early-morning departures from Kathmandu are often delayed by fog, but if they don't arrive in Jomsom by around 11 am landing may be impossible due to high winds! The end result is regular cancellations. Flights out of Lukla are equally unreliable – the airport can easily be closed for a week by bad weather – and there are often enormous backlogs of frustrated trekkers waiting for flights, both in Kathmandu and Lukla, although the situation has

improved with regular helicopter flights now available.

It is advisable to book domestic flights a week in advance and, just as for flights out of Nepal, the most important rule is to reconfirm and reconfirm again. Names can easily 'fall off' the passenger list, particularly where there is pressure for seats.

Airfares

Residents and Nepali citizens pay approximately 75% of the tourist price for domestic airfares. Airlines will only accept payment in hard currency from visitors. See the Nepal Airfares chart for details.

All the airlines also have daily mountain flights which costs $99. See the Himalaya & Mountaineering chapter for details.

Domestic Airport

The domestic terminal is the old Kathmandu airport, and its age shows. It can be a nasty and chaotic spot, particularly when flights are cancelled and crowds of stressed tourists generate an atmosphere of fear and loathing. You can escape the worst of the crush in the restaurant on the 1st floor; it's allegedly run by the Hotel de l'Annapurna, so you are unlikely to be poisoned although it is very shabby.

Check in an hour early for domestic flights; there is no airport tax. Once through security, the waiting lounge is reasonably comfortable and you can also get drinks. Remember not to carry pocket knives in your carry-on luggage, and do not feel obliged to pay the security guards baksheesh. It can be difficult finding a taxi into Kathmandu if you arrive late. If the worst comes to the worst, it's a 15 minute walk to the international terminal, where you are certain to find something.

See Kathmandu's Getting Around section in the Kathmandu, Patan & Bhaktapur chapter for information on transport to/from the airport.

BUS

Buses are the main form of public transport in Nepal and in relative terms they're incredibly cheap. Very often, they're also incredibly uncomfortable. It's always best to book a couple of days in advance. Keep an eye on the festival calendar; buses are packed out for days either side of an important festival, as everyone wants to go home and party.

There are numerous services with buses and smaller minibuses around the Kathmandu Valley, out from Kathmandu towards the Tibetan border, down to the Indian border or to Pokhara. Buses also run from Pokhara to the Indian border as well as along the length of the country from near Darjeeling in the east to Mahendranagar in the west. This road runs through the Inner Terai, parallel to the Indian border. As well as the regular public buses between Kathmandu and Pokhara there are a number of services aimed particularly at the western tourist market.

Many people – locals and westerners – prefer to ride on bus roofs. The arguments in favour are that you get an exhilarating ride with great views, the opportunity to watch your bags and, sometimes, room to stretch your legs. Some people argue it is also safer, because you can jump off before the bus goes over the side into a gorge! This latter point is debatable. If you are on top, make sure you're well wedged in, so you don't catapult off when the bus swerves, brakes, or lurches (see the Bus Ride boxed section in this chapter). It's also best to sit facing forwards – that way you can see low-hanging wires and branches before you get swatted. Make sure you've got sunscreen and appropriate clothing too.

Types of Buses & Services

There are both government and private buses. The government bus company, known as Sajha Yatayat, has distinctive blue and white Japanese buses which service all the main routes except the far east and far west. These buses are generally scheduled to run only during the day, except on the longest routes. On the whole they are better than private buses, in theory at least, because they stop less frequently (usually), are cheaper, less crowded (it's all relative!) and are more powerful and therefore faster (not necessarily a good thing). They also don't have roof racks, so they don't carry the mountains of baggage and freight (not to mention passengers) that the private ones do. Each major town has a Sajha office where you can make advance reservations.

There are literally dozens of private bus companies – it seems all you need is one bus and you've got yourself a company. The vehicles are all Indian Tata buses, and range from new and reasonably comfortable to unbelievably shabby, poorly maintained death-traps. As with the Sajha buses, there is a booking office in each town where you can buy tickets in advance on the long-distance routes.

Private buses run on all routes, and on the longer routes there are 'express' buses scheduled both by day and night. Fares are ridiculously cheap, but day buses are marginally cheaper than night buses. Day travel is generally preferable because you get to see the countryside (and there are some spectacular roads) and it's safer. Express bus drivers have mastered the art of maniacal driving, and accidents are not at all uncommon. Daylight travel is slower than at night simply because there are more people getting on and off.

There's nothing very express about the express buses, but they are lightning fast in comparison to local buses which run shorter routes, carry people, their luggage and often animals, and seem to stop more than they go. Travelling by local bus is no fun and should be kept to a minimum, although to get to many of the trekking road-heads there is little alternative.

NEPAL'S HIGHWAYS

There are just two main highways in Nepal, and they vary from new and well-engineered to bone-jarring and potholed – more of the latter than the former, unfortunately.

The main highway is the busy Mahendra Highway, which runs the length of the country from the Indian border at Kakarbhitta in the

east to the Indian border at Mahendranagr in the west.

The busy Prithvi Highway links Kathmandu with Pokhara. Between Kathmandu and Mugling the road parallels the Trisuli River, the most popular rafting river in the country. It then follows the Marsyangdi (which joins the Trisuli at Mugling) as far as Dumre, and from Damauli to Pokhara it follows the Seti Gandaki River. See the Kathmandu to Pokhara section in the Pokhara chapter for a full description of this route.

There are two minor highways, although they're hardly deserving of the title. Both offer spectacular views and are well worth travelling on. The Tribhuvan Highway (or Rajpath) branches off the Prithvi Highway at Naubise, about 30 km from Kathmandu, and heads south over the mountains to Hetauda, and on to the Indian border at Birganj. The other is the Siddhartha Highway, which joins

---

Bus Ride – A traveller's account

Ah! The Kathmandu to Kakarbhitta bus trip. I remember it as if it were yesterday. It was. I'm sitting in Darjeeling eating buffalo curd and reflecting on how nice it is to be alive.

As we climbed out of the Kathmandu Valley at 4.30 pm we were 'shaking down' – trying to contort ourselves into the tight spaces we had rented and attempting to find some semblance of comfort. Then we reached the rim of the valley and began hurtling down that *awesome* series of hairpin bends and switchbacks. As we thundered suicidally down this impossible road I mused whimsically on the average life expectancy of Nepali bus drivers, that is until the rather obvious realisation dawned that, given my present position, a much more pertinent question might be the life expectancy of the average passenger!

I gave up such dark thoughts to think about the love of my life, far off in England, but the moment was rudely interrupted as, lurching into yet another precipice-edged corner, the driver breaked violently to avoid another bus lying on its side diagonally across the road. Not a sight calculated to inspire confidence, but one has to look on the bright side. Firstly, it had toppled *onto* the road rather than *off* into the chasm. Secondly, it wasn't my bus.

The road steadily deteriorated, as roads are wont to do in Nepal. A little over an hour later I found my face pressed against the window, a gravel embankment flying towards me, inches from ruining my complexion. Looking on the bright side seemed rather more difficult. I am convinced it was only my slender 54 kg frame catapulting across the lap of my Nepali travelling companion that tipped the balance – literally – in favour of the bus returning to the point at which any good bus should be: extremely horizontal.

Things returned to normal – or as normal as they could be. Several hellish hours later, the road surface suddenly changed from obscene to impeccable. But the cruel hoax was soon revealed when the road quickly reverted to type. This stretch on the Terai is the worst road I've ever travelled, worse even than one memorable track into the Australian outback.

All in all it was a great trip, but don't forget to pack your stoicism and humour, and get some extra fat on your bum in Kathmandu to absorb the bumps!

Lloyd Donaldson, New Zealand

Pokhara with Butwal on the Mahendra Highway, going via the interesting town of Tansen (Palpa).

Mahendra Highway

East – Kakarbhitta to Narayanghat Fifteen

minutes from Kakarbhitta, past several tea plantations, is the town of Birtamod. A dirt road from here goes to Ilam, a starting point for treks in the Kanchenjunga region. A reasonable dirt road goes from here to Ilam. Buses cost Rs 70 and take seven hours.

The first town of real consequence that you come to is Itahari, 100 km from Kakarbhitta. There's nothing much to be said for it, however, apart from the fact that it is at the intersection of the road that runs south to Biratnagar, Nepal's second largest city, and north to Hile and Basantpur, starting points for Kanchenjunga, Makalu and Arun Valley treks.

After Itahari the road enters the flood plain of the Sapt Kosi, one of the largest tributaries to the Ganges. This mighty river is now partially controlled by the impressive Kosi Barrage and its surrounding earthworks. Even so, the low-lying region seems at times to be more water than land. Metres of silt have obviously made the fields extremely fertile and there is a high population density.

Mud and thatch villages are built on small areas of high ground, and the people are closely related to their Indian neighbours. Emerald green paddies stretch to the horizon and the villages are surrounded by water lilies and hyacinths. Often, the houses are overgrown with pumpkin plants, which are trained onto the roofs. Fish is a vital part of the local diet, and wherever you look you'll see children and women fishing in the canals and ponds. The bird life is prolific, with Brahmani kites, greater and lesser egrets, and cranes and ducks of every description.

On either side of the barrage the road is built on a raised levy, but parts are in extremely poor condition. By the time you get to Mohanpur, you'll be lucky to have your teeth fillings still in place. After Mohanpur you begin a long stretch of the

Terai proper, skirting the Chure Hills, which seem to jump from the plains.

Since the eradication of malaria in the 1950s, much of this land has been settled. Many of the settlers have come from the hills, but have swiftly adapted to their new environment and have prospered. Frequently, houses have been built on stilts to cope with the annual floods.

Nearly 110 km past the Kosi Barrage you reach Lalbiti: the turn-off to Janakpur (25 km from the highway) and one of the most attractive cities in Nepal. The countryside is intensively cultivated and densely populated. As you travel further east, however, there are fewer people, fewer of the bright Indian saris and more trees. Between Dalkebar and Amlekhganj there is an almost unbroken stretch of magnificent sal forest.

At Amlekhganj the Mahendra Highway briefly joins the Tribhuvan Highway to Hetauda. From Hetauda, the road runs along the edge of the Mahabharat Range and the Rapti River. There are some rich, cultivated fields, but a great deal of forest remains. On the other side of the Rapti lies the Royal Chitwan National Park, famous for its tigers and rhinoceroses.

After Belva, the valley begins to broaden and the reason it is called the Inner Terai becomes clear – it's flat, fertile and heavily populated. There are some Tharu villages as well as many Gurung and other hill peoples. Seventy-seven km after Hetauda, you come to the small roadside town of Tadi Bazaar, the departure point for Royal Chitwan National Park.

The road from Tadi to Narayanghat is not particularly interesting; there's a lot of development and Narayanghat and Bharatpur run together and sprawl a long way to the east. All buses travel west to Narayanghat and then turn north, following the Narayani River through the hills to Mugling on the Kathmandu-Pokhara (Prithvi) Highway.

West – Mahendranagar to Narayanghat

The far west is the least developed and most traditional part of the Terai. It's inhabited by Tharus, Bajis (Abadhi speakers from India),

Muslims and more recent migrants from the hills.

The 45 km stretch from Mahendranagar to Ataria is a diabolical mess. It was single lane bitumen at one stage, but these days there are more potholes than black top, and vehicles travel at a crawl.

Between Ataria and Chisopani (on the western bank of the Karnali River) there are a number of bridges still to be completed, and the last 10 km stretch into Chisopani is basically a winding dirt track along the bank of the Karnali. This section from Mahendranagar may be improved with Indian assistance following the signing of the Mahakali Agreement in 1996, one of the aims of which is to improve Nepali-Indian cooperation.

The Karnali is one of the largest rivers in Nepal, draining the western third of the country. Thanks to the World Bank an enormous single-span suspension bridge has been built at Chisopani, at the point where the river flows through its last gorge and spills out onto the plains. The World Bank also plans to build the world's largest hydroelectric dam, a km further up the gorge; fortunately these plans are currently on hold. There is no formal accommodation at Chisopani, but travellers have stayed with families and at chai shops (around Rs 15).

After the Karnali River the road is excellent black-top. It runs through the sal forest of the Royal Bardia National Park; keep your eyes peeled for monkeys, deer and peacocks. After you leave the forest you enter an agricultural zone inhabited by Tharus and a growing number of migrants from the hills. As you approach Kohalpur, 71 km from Chisopani and the turn-off for Nepalganj, there are increasing numbers of Muslims – the white spires of mosques can be seen in the villages.

Nepalganj is 16 km south of Kohalpur, and lies on the flat, hot Gangetic plain at the western end of the Rapti Valley. The Rapti Valley, like the Chitwan Valley, is described as the Inner Terai, and lies along the Rapti River between the Duduwa Hills to the south and the Chure Hills and Mahabharat Range

to the north. The valley is attractive and intensively cultivated and seems to become more fertile the further east you travel. There are endless fields of mustard, interspersed with small Tharu settlements and the much grander Newari-style houses of their landlords *(zamindars)*. There are a number of grubby and depressing roadside villages with the usual chai shops – the largest being Kusum (71 km from Nepalganj) and Lamahi (52 km from Kusum).

Twenty-five km from Lamahi, the road crosses the Rapti River and climbs over the foothills before dropping down to the Terai proper. Butwal, where buses turn north to Pokhara along the Siddhartha Highway, is the next major town, 97 km from the bridge over the Rapti and 245 km from Nepalganj.

The road from Butwal to Narayanghat (93 km) is not particularly interesting. There are a couple of places where there are quite steep climbs over ridges of the Chure Hills, but most of the countryside is flat and monotonous sal forest. The soil is too sandy to be farmed. There are some unattractive strips of roadside development, inhabited mainly by relatively recent migrants from the hills. From Narayanghat there is a link to Mugling on the Kathmandu-Pokhara (Prithvi) Highway; see the Kathmandu to Pokhara section in the Pokhara chapter.

Tribhuvan Highway

The Tribhuvan Highway (or Rajpath) was the first road to link the Kathmandu Valley with the outside world; it was built by the Indian government and completed in 1956. If you have time and feel energetic, consider catching a Sajha Yatayat bus over the mountains from Hetauda to Kathmandu.

If you are travelling in a group or have the funds, consider hiring a car. It won't be cheap, partly because you'll have to pay for the driver's return trip whether or not you return yourself. Think in terms of $150. Alternatively, if you're fit and have a mountain bike, this is regarded as one of the most spectacular cycling routes in the country; see the Mountain Biking chapter.

You begin to climb into the Mahabharat

Range the moment you leave Hetauda. The road is in good condition, but it's very narrow, so it's a case of drivers leaning almost constantly on their horns and hoping they won't meet an out-of-control Tata truck around the next blind corner.

The change from the Terai is remarkably sudden; you're soon amongst forested hills and it is almost impossible to believe the plains are so close. As you gain altitude you enter magnificent rhododendron forests. The highest point on the road is 2400m, just before you reach Daman. Daman is famous as a viewpoint with one of the most complete panoramas of the Himalaya that you can find. The view – from Dhaulagiri to Everest – is simply awe-inspiring.

After Daman you travel through the intensely cultivated Palung Valley. From here to Kathmandu, every possible inch of the hills is farmed. There are more good views of the Himalaya before you reach Naubise on the Kathmandu-Pokhara (Prithvi) Highway. Daman is about three hours from Kathmandu and Hetauda by car, four hours by bus.

Siddhartha Highway
From Butwal, the Siddhartha snakes up through the picturesque Mahabharat Range to the historic town of Tansen (Palpa). It is a narrow, winding road with is generally in pretty poor condition.

Between Tansen and Pokhara there are some superb views as the road winds down to cross the Kali Gandaki River at Ramdighat, a popular take-out for rafting trips coming down from the upper stretches of the river. The hills all through this area are heavily cultivated and the road passes though many small villages. The condition of the road improves as you get closer to Pokhara, the last 30 km or so being good bitumen.

CAR & MOTORBIKE
There are no drive-yourself rental cars available in Nepal but you can easily hire cars with drivers. Expect to pay around $50 a day, plus fuel, which is currently set at Rs 29 per litre across the country.

It is quite popular to hire cars for return trips to both Pokhara and Royal Chitwan National Park. A car from Kathmandu to Pokhara should cost around $40 one way, although this can rise to $60 at peak times, maybe even $80. A car to Chitwan should cost around $70, but could rise to $90 at peak times.

Motorbikes can be rented in Kathmandu. See Kathmandu's Getting Around section in the Kathmandu, Patan & Bhaktapur chapter for more details a out car and motorbike rental.

BICYCLE
In Kathmandu and Pokhara there are many bicycle-rental outlets and this is a cheap and convenient way of getting around. Virtually the entire valley is accessible by bike, though if you are venturing far outside the Kathmandu and Patan area, a mountain bike is definitely worthwhile. A regular bicycle only costs around Rs 30 per day, and a mountain bike costs from Rs 100 to Rs 150. Children's bicycles can also be hired. See the Mountain Biking chapter for more information on cycling in Nepal.

LOCAL TRANSPORT
Taxi
Larger towns like Kathmandu and Pokhara have taxis which, between a group of people, can be a good way to explore the Kathmandu Valley. Metered taxis have black licence plates; private cars often operate as taxis, particularly on long-distance routes or for extended periods, and have red plates.

Fuel prices and therefore taxi rates often rise faster than meters can be recalibrated, so frequently there is a surcharge on top of the meter reading. Tourists will, in any case, be hard pushed to convince drivers to use their meters (with or without a surcharge) and will almost certainly have to negotiate the fare in advance.

Rickshaw
Auto-rickshaws, those curious and noxious three wheeled motorcycle-engined devices, are also found in Kathmandu.

Bicycle rickshaws are common in the old part of Kathmandu and can be a good way of making short trips through the crowded and narrow streets.

Note that auto-rickshaws and bicycle rickshaws operate much like taxis, and that the three wheeled *tempos* are more like minibuses – leaving when full and having fixed fares.

ORGANISED TOURS

Travel agencies in Kathmandu run organised tours (public and private) by car or bus to places of interest around the valley and further afield. If your stay in Nepal is too short to permit exploration on your own, then it is best to join a conducted or private tour. For more information, see Tours in the Kathmandu section of the Kathmandu, Patan & Bhaktapur chapter.

Kathmandu, Patan & Bhaktapur

For most visitors to Nepal, the Kathmandu Valley is their arrival point and the focus of their visit. This small mountain-sheltered valley is the historical centre of Nepal, the place where kingdoms rose and fell, palaces and temples were built and rebuilt, and Nepali art and culture were developed and refined.

The three major towns – Kathmandu, Patan and Bhaktapur – each have an artistic and architectural tradition that rivals anything you'll find in the great cities of Europe. Kathmandu is the capital and the largest city in the country; it also has the international airport and is where most visitors stay. Patan, the second largest, is separated from Kathmandu by a river, but in other respects the two cities are virtually continuous. Bhaktapur, the third largest, is towards the eastern end of the valley and its relative isolation is reflected in its slower pace and more distinctly mediaeval atmosphere.

Scattered around the valley are hundreds of temples and shrines, traditional villages and agricultural scenes of timeless beauty (see the Around the Kathmandu Valley chapter for more details). A great deal is easily accessible by foot, bicycle, bus or taxi, but the more time you have the better. You will be hard-pressed to do any justice to the place in less than a week.

HISTORY

The Newars are regarded as the original inhabitants of the valley, but their origins are shrouded in mystery. They speak a Tibeto-Burmese language, which indicates they originated in the east, but their physical features range from distinctively Mongoloid, again suggesting the east, to Indo-Aryan, which of course points to India.

In balance, it seems most likely that the Kathmandu Valley has long been a cultural and racial melting pot, with people coming from both east and west. This fusion has resulted in the unique Newari culture that is

HIGHLIGHTS

- Strolling around and soaking up the atmosphere of the history-rich capital city and towns

- Spending an hour on the steps of the Maju Deval in Kathmandu, just watching the world go by and following up with an evening meal at one of the city's many varied restaurants

- Visiting the glorious Pulchowki rhododendron forest, in bloom from February to April

- Viewing the stunning Newari architecture of Patan, and visiting the Tibetan carpet-making workshops there

- Visiting the famous Golden Gate and Peacock Windows in Bhaktapur, where many of the oldest buildings have been fully restored

responsible for the valley's superb art and architecture.

The Newari golden age peaked in the 17th century when the valley consisted of small city-states, and Nepal was a vitally important trading link between Tibet and the north Indian plains. The valley's visible history is inextricably entangled with the Malla kings. It was during their reign, particularly in the 1600s and 1700s, that many of the valley's finest temples and palaces were built. Competition between the cities was intense and an architectural innovation in one place, such as the erection of a column bearing a statue of the ruling king, would inevitably be copied in the other cities.

Sorting out who built what and when is considerably complicated by the fact that at any one time there was not just one Malla king. Each of the three city-states in the valley – Kathmandu, Patan and Bhaktapur – had its own. Some of the most important Malla kings are listed in the introduction to the relevant cities.

The unification of Nepal in 1768 by

Gorkha's King Prithvi Narayan Shah signalled the end of the Kathmandu Valley's fragmentation. Nepali, an Indo-European language spoken by the Khas of western Nepal, replaced Newari as the country's language of administration.

GEOGRAPHY

The bowl-like Kathmandu Valley is about 25 km from east to west, perhaps 20 km from north to south. Kathmandu lies at a height of around 1300m, while the surrounding hills range from 1500m to 2800m in height. If you fly in, you clearly see how isolated and unusual the valley is – embedded like a jewel amongst endless rugged mountains.

A large and growing human population is posing numerous problems. Due to the surrounding mountains, Kathmandu is particularly vulnerable to air and water pollution, and both problems are already serious. The mountains also make transport extremely difficult: the valley has only three fragile overland lifelines. There's one two-lane road out of the valley to the south and on to India, and another road north-east to Tibet that washes away every year.

The valley is phenomenally fertile, capable of growing grain (rice, corn, wheat) and a wide range of fruit (from bananas to oranges) and vegetables. However, urban development is rapidly encroaching on valuable agricultural land, so the valley is increasingly dependent on imported food and fossil fuels.

A number of rivers drain towards the centre of the valley and join the holy Bagmati River, which then flows south through the Chobar Gorge to finally reach the Ganges River. Geologists have confirmed ancient myths that claim the valley once lay under water.

CLIMATE

The Kathmandu Valley has a temperate climate that is pleasant most of the year. Snow is almost unheard of, although there are frosts, and the monsoons are nowhere near as severe as they are on the plains.

Between October and March it can become quite cold at night (0°C) and the days become short, although it's sunny and warm between mid-morning and mid-afternoon (say 20°C). Visibility is good from October to early February, although there are two impediments: thick early morning fog which doesn't clear until mid-morning and wreaks havoc with airline schedules; and the temperature inversion which often traps a thick layer of warm smog under a layer of colder air.

By April things start to heat up and there are often storms in the afternoon. The real heat and humidity coincide with the monsoon proper, which usually commences in mid-June. Expect daytime temperatures around the low to mid-30°Cs, and night-time temperatures between 15°C and 20°C. Fortunately, much of the rain falls during the night or on the surrounding hills.

FLORA & FAUNA

Most of the valley has been converted to highly productive farmland, but several pockets of uncleared land remain: Gokarna, just past Bodhnath, Nagarjun just past Balaju, and others on several of the surrounding hills, notably Pulchowki.

The native forests consisted of oak and other broad-leafed trees, pines and rhododendrons *(laliguras)* that grow over 15m high. Pulchowki, the highest point overlooking the valley, has a magnificent rhododendron forest and shouldn't be missed if you're in the valley in spring (February to April). Australians will recognise the eucalyptus, grevillea and bottlebrush that line many of the valley's roads.

Once upon a time the valley probably had populations of leopards, jungle cats, wolves, black bears, sloth bears, otters and jackals. Unfortunately these are long gone.

No visitor to Swayambhunath will avoid the rhesus macaque monkeys that infest the hillside. Nor, if you stay near the old Royal Palace in Kathmandu, will you miss the colonies of fruit bats that spend their days chattering in the trees before they take to the sky each evening.

ECONOMY

Today the valley is the most developed part of Nepal, with a network of roads and electricity linking most of the villages. Despite rapid development, however, much of the valley is still devoted to small-scale farming. The availability of improved seeds, fertilisers and extensive irrigation has increased productivity and made it possible to grow wheat as well as the traditional rice.

Nepal's small industrial base is mainly concentrated in the lowland towns of the Terai, although the factories in the valley (including cement, brick, light engineering, food and beverage) contribute nearly 20% of the country's industrial output.

The Kathmandu Valley is the centre for many traditional crafts. Newari craftspeople have long exported pottery, brassware and bronze religious artefacts. The tradition continues, only these days the buyer is often a tourist. The 'Tibetan' carpet industry is now the valley's largest private employer, and carpets are the country's major export earner.

Kathmandu is the administrative and educational centre for the kingdom. Many of the Rana's grand palaces are now home to bureaucracies that are, arguably, of greater benefit to the general populace. Kathmandu is also the main focus for visiting tourists, so there has been a large investment in the necessary infrastructure and many people are dependent on the tourist dollar.

PEOPLE

Today the Newars still form the largest single group in the valley and there are some smaller towns and villages, such as Thimi, Chapagaon or Sankhu, which remain Newari strongholds. Many of the people living on the surrounding hills are Tamangs, Bahuns and Chhetris, who can generally be distinguished from the Newars by their solitary households.

In recent years many immigrants from throughout the country have come to the valley in search of jobs and education. There are, therefore, significant minorities of almost every Nepali ethnic group. Since the Chinese invasion of Tibet in 1959, thousands of Tibetan refugees have settled in the valley; there is also a large community of Indian traders and business people and significant communities of other foreigners.

The 1991 census found that Kathmandu had a population of 419,000 (235,000 in 1981), Patan had 117,000 (110,000) and Bhaktapur had 61,000 (60,000). The combined population of the valley was 1,099,000 (617,000) meaning the valley is home to nearly 6% of Nepal's people and that the population density is about 1800 per sq km.

Newars

It is not surprising that the Newar people were influenced by Tibet and India. What is surprising is their creative response to this stimulus, which actually led to a genuine exchange with their giant neighbours. Mediaeval Newari society has left a religious, architectural and artistic legacy that is unique, and spectacular by any standard.

Although most Newars have Mongoloid physical characteristics, some don't, so their origins are shrouded in mystery. It is now generally accepted that they are a mixture of many different peoples who were attracted to the valley, possibly originating with the Kiratis, or an even earlier group. See History in the Facts about the Country chapter for more details.

Perhaps the Newars' most striking characteristic is their love of communal life. Newari houses were invariably clustered together, usually around sites of religious significance. Although their economy was centred around agriculture and trade, they created sophisticated urban communities which catered to a breadth of human needs in an integrated way that has rarely been matched.

Today there are around 600,000 Newars, largely centred in the Kathmandu Valley. Always traders and merchants, the Newars continue to fill this role throughout the kingdom. Their proximity to the centre of power has also led to them having a disproportionate influence in the bureaucracies of Kathmandu. Many now live in heartbreakingly ugly bungalows on the outskirts of the city proper, and many of their traditions are on the wane.

Architecture The most important social unit was the family and the family house was the starting point for urban planning. Rich Newars built handsomely proportioned brick houses with tiled roofs that were up to five storeys high. In the country, the ground floor was often used for stabling animals, while in the city it was used for commerce.

A community developed when a series of houses was built in a rectangle around a courtyard/square or *chowk*. The chowk, often with running water and a temple or shrine, was the centre of day-to-day life, and still is today. Here, the markets buzz, children play, women work (weaving, washing, drying grain...) and chat, old people doze in the sun, men talk over the community's business and religious ceremonies take place.

The cities and towns of the valley were made up of a compact network of these interlocking squares, courtyards, twisting alleyways, ponds and temples, often centred around a main square. Fortunately, much of this tradition remains. Decorated with carved windows and doorways, statues and shrines, and humming with gregarious people, a Nepali town is a remarkable synthesis of art and life.

Religion The vast majority of Newars are Hindu and fall under a caste system, although there is still a significant minority of Buddhists. This simplistic description, however, masks an incredibly diverse and complex system of beliefs.

Since the 5th century, kings and aristocrats have been Hindu and their influence gradually led to Buddhists adopting castes and a hereditary priesthood (the Banrhas). The many collapsing *bahals* (monasteries) testify to a long-gone Buddhist golden age.

The end result is that a purist from either religion would not recognise many of the Newari gods or the practices that go into their worship. For not only have aspects of both religions combined, they have been added to

by a Tantric tradition, Tibetan Buddhism and even older local deities and beliefs.

This has led to a confusing proliferation of gods who are often hybrids unashamedly shuffled from one pantheon to another. There are literally hundreds of these divinities, and over 150 days of festivals a year to celebrate them. From a functional point of view, most people are free to follow whatever gods and goddesses particularly appeal to them, so theological consistency (including the distinction between Hinduism and Buddhism) is irrelevant, certainly to the people themselves. See Religion in the Facts about the Country chapter for more details.

Customs The Newars are divided into castes, whether they nominally consider themselves Hindu or Buddhist, and these include untouchables (tinkers, butchers and some others). Caste rules are not quite as rigid as in some parts of India, but intermarriage is still rare and untouchables are still grossly disadvantaged.

The usual dress for a Newari woman is a sari and blouse, often with a shawl. The men wear trousers with a baggy seat that are tighter around the calves (like jodhpurs), a long untucked double-breasted shirt, a vest (waistcoat) or coat and the traditional Nepali cap *(topi)*. The most distinctive caste is the Jyapu (farmers), and many of them still lead highly traditional lives. Jyapu women wear black saris with a red border, while the men often wear the traditional trousers and shirt with a long piece of cotton wrapped around the waist. They prefer to carry goods and vegetables on a shoulder pole.

Newari children are welcomed into their community and caste at the age of seven when boys' heads are shaved leaving only a topknot, and girls are symbolically married to the soul of their future husband. Most Newars have arranged marriages and on auspicious dates wedding processions are a common sight. The procession starts at nightfall and is led by a band, often in ragtag uniforms making a cacophony with clarinets, trumpets and drums.

Traditionally, men were members of a

unique cooperative institution known as a *guthi*. This is a religious and social group based on family and other local links. Guthis may own land and are often responsible for the upkeep of particular temples and financing particular rites, as well as the welfare of their members.

Tamangs

The Tamangs are closely related to Tibetans. Their name apparently means 'horse trader', although most are now sedentary farmers or labourers. Their appearance, language and Lamaist Buddhist beliefs all bear testimony to their origins. Indeed, many of the 'Tibetan' souvenirs for sale in Kathmandu are actually made by Tamangs. Tamangs can be found throughout the central Himalaya, and especially around the Kathmandu Valley. See People in the Facts about the Country chapter for more details.

Bahuns (Brahmans) & Chhetris (Kshatriyas)

In Hindu theory Bahuns and Chhetris are the two highest castes (respectively the priests and warriors). In Nepal, however, most are descended from the Khas kingdoms that flourished in western Nepal and were home to Indo-Aryans who migrated to Nepal over the centuries. The Bahuns and Chhetris played an important role in the court and armies of Prithvi Narayan Shah, and after unification many were rewarded with lands in and around the Kathmandu Valley.

They have dominated the processes of government in Kathmandu, and continue to do so. See People in the Facts about the Country chapter for more details.

Kathmandu

Kathmandu is the capital of Nepal, the largest city in the country and the main centre for hotels and restaurants. This amazing city can seem, in places, to be a huge intricate sculpture unchanged since the Middle Ages. At other times it can be just another Third World

capital rushing carelessly into the modern era.

For many people, arriving in Kathmandu is as shocking as stepping out of a time machine – the sights, sounds and smells can lead to sensory overload. There are narrow streets and lanes with carved wooden balconies above tiny hole-in-the-wall shops, town squares packed with extraordinary temples and monuments, markets bright with fruit and vegetables and a constant throng of humanity. Then there's the choking dust and fumes, stinking gutters, concrete monstrosities, touts, Coca-Cola billboards and maimed beggars.

The gap between rich and poor is a chasm, but despite the pressures of extreme overcrowding and poverty, people retain a good-humoured self-respect and integrity. It is probably safer to walk the streets here than it is in your home town – and certainly much more interesting.

Like Patan and Bhaktapur, the other major towns of the valley, Kathmandu's historic centre is concentrated around Durbar Square (*durbar* is Nepali for palace). There's a distinct difference between the tightly packed old city area and the more spacious newer parts of town.

Malla Kings

Malla kings of particular importance in Kathmandu included:

Ratna Malla	1482-1528
Mahendra Malla	1560-1574
Sadasiva Malla	1574-1583
Shiva Singh Malla	1578-1620
Pratap Malla	1641-1674
Prithvibendra Malla	1680-1687
Bhaskara Malla	1687-1714
Jagat Jaya Malla	1722-1736
Jaya Prakash Malla	1736-1768

ORIENTATION

Most of the interesting things to see in Kathmandu are clustered in the old part of town from Kantipath (the main north-south road) west towards the Vishnumati River. New Rd, constructed after the great earthquake of 1934, starts from the ornamental entrance by Kantipath and goes straight into the heart of old Kathmandu, changing its name to Ganga Path before it comes to Durbar Square.

The office of Royal Nepal Airlines (RNAC) is at the Kantipath end of New Rd and along this road are banks, shops and the modern shopping centre where Indian visitors come to buy consumer goods not readily available back home. Continue further along New Rd to Ganga Path and you reach the large Basantapur Square, then Durbar Square where the old Royal Palace is located. Freak St, Kathmandu's famous street from the hippie/overland era, runs south off Basantapur Square.

Running north-east from Durbar Square is the thoroughfare that was once the main trading artery of the city and is still the busiest street in old Kathmandu. This narrow road, usually thronged with people, cuts through the heart of old Kathmandu from Indra Chowk through Kel Tole to Asan Tole.

Kantipath forms the boundary between the older and newer parts of the city. Just south of the New Rd junction is the main post office, easily located by the nearby Bhimsen Tower (also known as Sundhara). On the eastern side of Kantipath is the large open field known as Tundikhel, and on the eastern edge of this is the City Bus Station, for buses around the Kathmandu Valley.

Continuing north along Kantipath from New Rd takes you past the government-run Bir Hospital on the left – look for Hanuman on the wall carrying a Himalayan mountain complete with medicinal herbs. On the right is Ratna Park and then Rani Pokhari. Kantipath crosses Tridevi Marg at the corner of the new Royal Palace compound and continues into Maharajganj, the embassy sector.

Running parallel to and east of Kantipath is Durbar Marg, a wide street flanked by travel agencies, airline offices and a number of restaurants and expensive hotels. It ends at the main entrance to the new Royal Palace. Turn left from Durbar Marg in front of the palace, cross Kantipath, and Tridevi Marg will take you past the South Asian Association for Regional Cooperation (SAARC) and

after a couple of blocks will bring you into the Thamel area, the popular cheap accommodation centre of the city. Thamel is 15 to 20 minutes walk north from the centre of Kathmandu.

The city is encircled by the Ring Road, and on it in the north of the city is the main Kathmandu Bus Station, and on the eastern edge Tribhuvan international airport.

Addresses
In old Kathmandu streets were not given names, and although some of the major thoroughfares now do have names, most still don't. Smaller streets and laneways never do. Kathmandu grew as a series of interlocking squares that gradually swallowed neighbouring villages. The names of these squares, villages, and other landmarks (perhaps a monastery or temple) came to be used as addresses of sorts.

For example, the address of everyone living within a 100m radius of Thahiti Tole is Thahiti Tole and if you want to find them you go to Thahiti Tole and ask around – simple if you can speak Nepali and can find your way around the warren of laneways and courtyards. Thamel is now used to describe a sprawling area with at least a dozen roads and several hundred hotels and restaurants. They all have the same one-word address – Thamel.

Given this anarchic approach it is amazing that any mail gets delivered – it does, but slowly. Most businesses have post office box numbers. If you're trying to find a particular house, shop or business, make sure you get detailed directions (unless, of course, you have a foolproof Lonely Planet map!).

INFORMATION
Tourist Offices
The government tourist office (☎ 01-220818) is on Ganga Path diagonally opposite Basantapur Square, and it may or may not have some brochures and maps. If it doesn't (and it should have a useful visitors' guide) try the Department of Tourism (☎ 01-214519, Babar Mahal, Kathmandu) near the Hotel Everest. There's a tourist office at the international

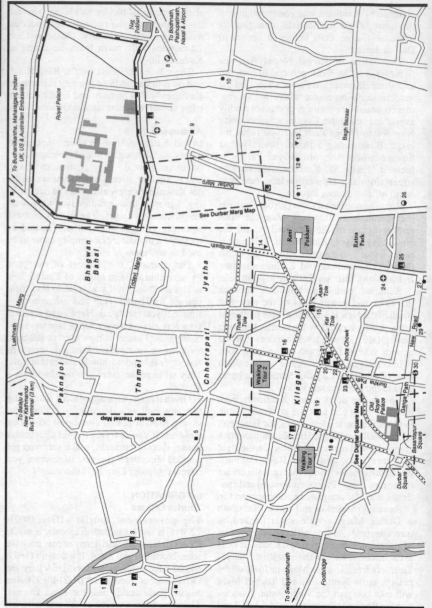

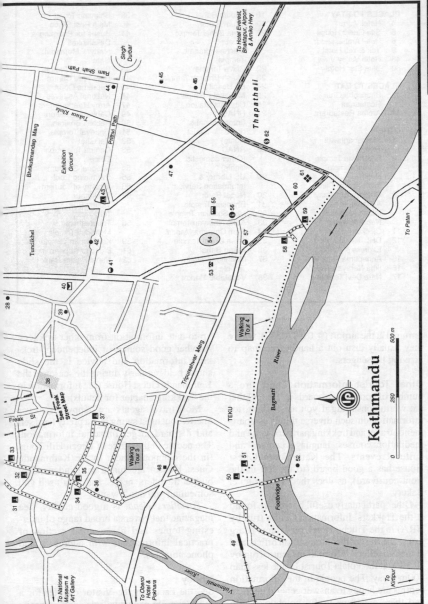

Kathmandu

KATHMANDU

PLACES TO STAY		18	Yatkha Bahal	39	Bhimsen Tower
4	Hotel Vajra	19	Yitum Bahal	40	Main Post Office
5	Sita Guest House	20	Jana Bahal Temple	41	Buses for Pharping &
6	Hotel Ambassador	21	Sweta		Dakshinkali
9	Yak & Yeti Hotel		Machhendranath	42	Martyrs' Memorial
48	Hotel Valley View		Temple		Gate
60	Blue Star Hotel	22	Shiva Temple	43	Bhadrakali Temple
		23	Akash Bhairab Temple	44	Duty Free Centre
PLACES TO EAT		24	Bir Hospital	45	Supreme Court
13	Bhanchha Ghar	25	Mahakala Temple	46	National Archives
	Restaurant	26	City Bus Station	47	Army Headquarters
14	Aroma Restaurant	27	RNAC	49	Cableway Station
			(International &	50	Pachali Bhairab
OTHER			domestic tourist	51	Tindeval Temple
1	Shobabaghwati		flights)	52	Raj Ghat
	Temple	28	RNAC	53	Central Telegraph
2	Bijeshwari Temple		(Other domestic		Office
3	Indrani Temple		flights)	54	National Stadium
7	Nepal	29	US Library &	55	Swimming Pool
	International Clinic		Information Service	56	Ministry of Tourism
8	Chinese Embassy	30	Nepal Bank	57	Bhaktapur
10	Air India,	31	Bhimsen Temple		Trolley-Bus
	Indian Airlines &	32	Hari Shankar Temple		Terminus
	Nepal Airways	33	Adko Narayan Temple	58	Tripureshwar
11	Clocktower	34	Ram Chandra Mandir		Mahadev Temple
12	DHL, Himalayan	35	Jaisa Deval Temple	59	Kalmochan Temple
	Express & Aeroflot	36	Takan Bahal	61	Bluebird Supermarket
15	Annapurna Temple	37	Machhendranath	62	Nepal Rastra Bank
16	Ikha Narayan Temple		Temple		
17	Nara Devi Temple	38	Vegetable Market		

terminal at the airport (☎ 01-470537), where they usually dish out a handy free map to arriving passengers.

Other Tourist Information There are a number of good notice boards in Thamel that are worth consulting if you are looking for information on such diverse things as apartments, travel and trekking partners, yoga and meditation courses, language courses and cultural events. The Kathmandu Guest House has a good board (to the left in the front courtyard), as does the Pumpernickel Bakery.

Other particularly useful boards are found at the Trekkers' Information Centre (run by HRA) in the Tilicho Hotel, on Tridevi Marg just to the west of the immigration office; and at the Travellers' Information Centre (run by KEEP), at the Potala Tourist Home less than 100m away. The people in the information centres are happy to answer general queries, and there are some useful notebooks with

up-to-date information from other trekkers. Another good source of independent trekking information and advice is the slide shows held regularly during the season at the Kathmandu Guest House (see Information in the Trekking chapter for details).

Most travel agents are happy to answer queries, but most swing into a pretty hard sell and it's hard to get impartial information. The people in the office of Green Hill Tours (in the compound next to the Kathmandu Guest House) are tuned into independent budget travellers' needs, and won't sell you something you don't want.

Travellers' Nepal is a good-quality, free magazine that covers a broad range of interesting topics and has a good section of practical information, with addresses and phone numbers.

Money
See the Facts for the Visitor chapter for a discussion on exchange rates and commis-

sions. In brief, it is worth checking the rate that banks and moneychangers offer and the commission they charge – both vary.

The most convenient bank for travellers staying in the Thamel region is the small branch of the Nepal Grindlays Bank (☎ 01-415228) just south of the Kathmandu Guest House. It is open Sunday to Thursday from 9.45 am to 3.30 pm, and on Friday closes at 12.45 pm. There's also a branch of the Rastriya Banijya Bank inside the immigration office building; this can be convenient if you're doing battle with the bureaucrats, but after your first visit to this building you're unlikely to want to return.

The main Nepal Bank (☎ 01-221185; fax 222381) in Dharmapath near New Rd is handy if you're staying in Freak St and has the important advantage of being open from 7.30 am to 7.30 pm seven days a week. There are several banks on Durbar Marg; the Nepal Indo-Suez Bank (☎ 01-228229; fax 226349) is convenient and efficient.

Kathmandu also has a Nepal Grindlays Bank (with superb murals by Mithila women from Janakpur) at the Thamel end of Kantipath (☎ 01-228474; fax 228692); Citibank (☎ 01-228843), GPO Box 2865, with an office in the Yak & Yeti Hotel; and the Nepal Arab Bank (☎ 01-227181; fax 226905), GPO Box 3729, Kantipath.

The American Express agent is Yeti Travels (☎ 01-227635; fax 226153) which has its office off the forecourt of the Hotel Mayalu on Jamal Tole, just around the corner from Durbar Marg. It will make cash advances between 10 am and 1 pm. Grindlays will make advances on Visa and MasterCard in Nepali rupees and travellers' cheques.

Kathmandu also has a great number of 'change money' men and although this black market is officially illegal it is widely accepted. A popular T-shirt worn by many visitors announces that, among other things, they don't want to change money!

Post

The main Kathmandu post office is on the corner of Kantipath and Khichapokhari, close to Bhimsen Tower. The stamp counter

is theoretically open from 8 am to 7 pm, Sunday to Thursday, and from 11 am to 3 pm on Saturdays, but it can provide a classic dose of queueing and frustration. Unless you have a *lot* of mail, you are best off taking advantage of the hotels, bookshops (including Pilgrims) and communications centres who will tackle the bureaucracy for you for a nominal charge. See the Facts for the Visitor chapter for postal charges.

The poste restante section at the main post office is quite efficient: the staff sort letters into alphabetically arranged boxes and you simply sit down and go through them yourself. You are required to show your passport before you take anything away. Make sure your correspondents print and underline your surname; if in doubt check under your first name as well. The section is open from 10.15 am to 4 pm Sunday to Thursday (closing one hour earlier mid-November to mid-February), and from 10.15 am to 2 pm on Fridays; it's closed on Saturdays.

Parcels may be sent from the separate Foreign Post Office just north of the main post office. It's open from 10.15 am to 2 pm Sunday to Thursday and from 10 am to noon on Fridays. Parcels have to be examined and sealed by a customs officer and then packed in an approved manner. It's something of a procedure, so if you're short of time you're best off using one of the many cargo agencies. Diki Continental Exports (☎ 01-417681; fax 414997), opposite the Hotel Mandap in Thamel, and Sharmasons Movers (☎ 01-222709; fax 222026) are two that have been recommended.

American Express has a clients' mail service at its offices off the forecourt of the Hotel Mayalu in Jamal Tol. Address letters to American Express, Yeti Travels Pty Ltd, Hotel Mayalu, Jamal Tole, PO Box 76, Durbar Marg, Kathmandu.

Telephone, Fax & E-Mail

International phone calls can be made and faxes can be sent from the Central Telegraph Office about 500m south of the post office, opposite the National Stadium. The service is open 24 hours and the process is quick and painless.

The dozens of 'communication centres' which have sprung up in Thamel and elsewhere offering fax, telephone and mailing services are more convenient, although somewhat more expensive. Phone calls and faxes cost around $3 per minute to pretty well anywhere. If a phone call is short, the convenience of the private operators outweighs the comparative expense, but if you talk for any length of time you're better off catching a taxi or tempo to the Central Telegraph Office (around Rs 30). See the Facts for the Visitor chapter for more information on rates.

For international call information phone ☎ 186, for domestic information ☎ 197, and for domestic trunk calls ☎ 180.

E-mail service is available from Global Communications (☎ 01-228143; fax 220143; e-mail glocom@globpc.mos.com.np) in the Sanchaya Kosh Bhawan Shopping Centre on Tridevi Marg in Thamel at a cost of Rs 60 to send and Rs 20 to receive one kb of information.

Travel Agencies

Kathmandu has a great number of travel agencies, particularly along Durbar Marg, Kantipath and in Thamel. See the Trekking chapter for details of trekking agencies.

Bookshops

Kathmandu has a large number of very good bookshops. Many have particularly interesting selections of books on Nepal including books that are not usually available outside the country. Prices for British and US books are surprisingly competitive with their home-market prices.

As well as shops with new books there are many shops with second-hand books for sale and trade. Most dealers will buy back books for 50% of what you paid for them.

Tiwari's Pilgrims Book House is a couple of doors north of the Kathmandu Guest House and has an extensive collection of books on Nepal and other Himalayan regions.

There's another even better shop owned by the same company, on the road from Durbar Marg to the Yak & Yeti Hotel. Known as the Kailash Bookshop, it also has an antiquarian section.

There are many other good bookshops around Thamel, including Bookland on Tridevi Marg opposite the immigration office. Mandala Book Point on Kantipath has an excellent selection of books, with a good range in French and German.

Himalayan Book Sellers at Ghantaghar by the clocktower is a long-term survivor in the Kathmandu book business with an excellent selection of books on Nepal and the Himalaya.

Libraries

There are a number of libraries and cultural centres in Kathmandu. The British Council Library (☎ 01-222698) on Kantipath has a good selection of books on Nepal as well as British newspapers and magazines. It's open Sunday to Friday from 11 am to 6 pm.

Unfortunately only Nepalis and foreign residents in Nepal are allowed to use the US Library & Information Service (☎ 01-221078) on New Rd. If you qualify, it's open Monday to Friday from 11 am to 7 pm.

The French Cultural Centre (☎ 01-224326) is in Bagh Bazaar opposite the Bhaktapur bus stand and has French publications and organises French film nights for which there is a small admission charge. The German Goethe Institute (☎ 01-220528) in Ganabahal, near Bhimsen Tower, has film nights and occasional exhibitions as well as library facilities.

Rastriya Pustakalaya, the Nepal National Library (☎ 01-521132), is at Pulchowk in Patan and has books in English and Hindi. The Tribhuvan University Library of Kirtipur has a good collection and is open Sunday to Friday from 9 am to 6 pm.

The Kaiser or Kesar Library (☎ 01-411318) is worth a visit just to see the building. It's on the corner of Kantipath and Tridevi Marg, and has an incredible collection of books on Buddhism, Tibet and Nepal. Kaiser Shamsher Jung Bahadur Rana was a Rana aristocrat, scholar, scientist and gourmet. He built up a superb collection of books all of which, it is said, he read in their original language. Most of his palace is now used for government offices, but his library is kept as he left it and can be visited.

Government Offices

Most government offices in Kathmandu are open from 10 am to 5 pm from Sunday to Thursday, and from 10 am to 4 pm during the three winter months (mid-November to mid-February). Offices close at 3 pm on Friday, and are closed on Saturday.

The immigration office, where trekking permits are also issued, is on Tridevi Marg, close to Thamel. It's open from 10 am to 1 pm Sunday to Thursday and 10 am to noon on Friday for applications, although you have to go back between 3 and 5 pm to retrieve your passport. It's wise to start the process early as renewing a visa or obtaining a trekking permit can be time-consuming. See Visas in the Facts for the Visitor chapter for more details.

Medical Services

The centrally located, government-operated Bir Hospital (☎ 01-221119) cannot be recommended. The best bet in the Kathmandu Valley is the Patan Hospital (☎ 01-521333), which is partially staffed by western missionaries and is in the Lagankhel district of Patan, close to the last stop of the Lagankhel bus. Bear in mind that they have to give reasonable care to as many people as possible. The Teaching Hospital (☎ 01-412404) is reasonably well equipped (they have a ventilator, for instance) and is also OK.

The CIWEC clinic (☎ 01-410983) just off Durbar Marg is used by many foreign residents of Kathmandu. It has operated since 1982 and has developed an international reputation for research into travellers' medical problems. It's open from 9 am to 1 pm and 2 to 4 pm and is staffed by westerners. With a single visit costing around $30, it is hardly surprising the clientele is almost exclusively western as well.

The Nepal International Clinic (☎ 01-412842) is near the Jaya Nepal cinema, close to Thamel. It also has an excellent reputation and is a bit cheaper than the CIWEC clinic. It's open from 9.30 am to 5 pm; a consultation costs around $25.

If you need an optometrist, Mr Kaiser Malla Singh (☎ 01-222504) in Bagh Bazaar next to the French Cultural Centre, has been recommended. For dental work, Dr KK Pradhan (☎ 221142) also has a dental clinic in New Baneshwar with a good reputation.

Emergency

Red Cross Ambulance	☎ 01-228094
Police, Durbar Square	☎ 01-211162
Fire Brigade	☎ 01-221177

Aid Organisations

Kathmandu has several non-government aid organisations pursuing small-scale, community based programmes. These are either run by Nepalis, or in close association with Nepalis, and are recommended. All would gratefully accept donations. (See Begging in the Facts about the Country chapter for background information.) Alternatively, give to reputable organisations in your home country.

Adventist Development & Relief Agency (ADRA)
    PO Box 4481, Kathmandu (☎ 01-417013)
Child Workers in Nepal (CWIN)
    PO Box 4374, Kalimati, Kathmandu
    (☎ 01-270336)
Kumbeshwar Technical School
    PO Box 2182, Patan, Kathmandu
    (☎ 01-522271)
Leprosy Hospital
    PO Box 151, Anandban, Kathmandu
    (☎ 01-290545)
Nepal Eye Programme – Australia (NEPA)
    PO Box 561, Kathmandu (☎ 01-474685)

DURBAR SQUARE

Durbar in Nepali means 'palace' and in Patan and Bhaktapur, as well as Kathmandu, there are durbar squares in front of the old palaces. The king no longer lives in the old Royal Palace in Kathmandu: the palace was moved north to Narayanhiti about a century ago. At that time it was on the edge of the city, now it's close to the popular tourist area of Thamel.

Clustered around the central Durbar Square are the old Royal Palace (Hanuman Dhoka), numerous interesting temples, the Kumari Chowk or Kumari Bahal (House of the Living Goddess) and the Kasthamandap (House of Wood).

It's easy to spend hours wandering around Durbar Square and the adjoining Basantapur Square. This is very much the centre of old Kathmandu and watching the world go by from the terraced platforms of the towering Maju Deval is a wonderful way to get a feel for the city. Although many of the buildings around the square are very old, a great deal of damage was caused by the great earthquake of 1934 and many were rebuilt, not always in their original form.

The Durbar Square area is actually made up of three loosely linked squares. To the south is the open Basantapur Square area, off which runs Freak St. The main Durbar Square area, with its popular watch-the-world-go-by temples, is to the west. Running north-east is a second part of Durbar Square which contains the entrance to the old Royal Palace and an assortment of temples. From this open area Makhan Tole, at one time the main road in Kathmandu and still the most interesting street to walk down, continues north-east.

A good place to start an exploration of the square is with what may well be the oldest building in the valley, the unprepossessing Kasthamandap. Note: the numbers in the following sections correspond to item numbers on the key for the Durbar Square (Kathmandu) map.

Kasthamandap

Kasthamandap (35)

In the south-western corner of the square the Kastha-mandap, or House of Wood, is the building which gave Kathmandu its name. Although its history is uncertain, it was possibly constructed around the 12th century. A legend relates that the whole building was made with the wood from a single sal tree. At first it was a community centre where visitors gathered before major ceremonies, but later it was converted to a temple to Gorakhnath.

A small wooden enclosure in the centre of the building houses the image of the god. Images of Ganesh can be found at each corner of the building and there are also shrines to a number of other gods. Bronze lions guard the entrance, and Hindu epics are illustrated around the 1st-floor cornices of the three storey building.

The squat, mediaeval-looking building is busy in the early-morning hours when porters sit here waiting for customers.

Ashok Binayak (33)

On the northern side of the Kasthamandap, at the top of Maru Tole (the laneway down to the river), stands the tiny Ashok Binayak, or Maru Ganesh Shrine. The small size of this shrine belies its importance, as this is one of the four most important Ganesh shrines in the valley. Ganesh is a much-loved god and there is a constant stream of visitors here. A visit to this shrine is highly recommended by Hindus to ensure safety on a forthcoming journey. It's uncertain how old the temple is, although its gilded roof was added in the 19th century.

Shiva Temple (34)

The Shiva Temple near the Kasthamandap and the Ashok Binayak is used by barbers who can generally be seen squatting on the temple platform, administering 'short back and sides'.

Maru Tole

Maru Tole leads down to the Vishnumati River where a footbridge meets the pathway to Swayambhunath on the other side. This was a busy street in the days of hippies and flower power, but today there's little sign of why it should have been called either Pie or Pig Alley – not only are the pie shops gone but it's also much cleaner. One thing Maru Tole does have is Maru Hiti, one of the finest sunken water conduits in the city.

Maju Deval (31)

A pleasant hour can easily be spent sitting on the platform steps of the Shiva temple known as the Maju Deval. From here you can watch the constant activity of fruit and vegetable hawkers, the comings and goings of taxis and rickshaws, and the flute and other souvenir sellers importuning tourists. The nine stage platform of the Maju Deval is probably the most popular meeting place in the city. The large, triple roofed temple has erotic carvings on its roof struts and offers great views over the square and across the roofs of the city.

The temple dates from 1690 and was built by the mother of Bhaktapur's King Bhupatindra Malla. Although the temple has a well known Shiva lingam inside, the roof is topped by a pinnacle shaped like a Buddhist stupa. At the bottom of the temple stairway is a small temple to Kam Dev, a 'companion' of Shiva. It was built in the Indian *shikhara* style, with a tall corncob-like spire.

Maju Deval

Trailokya Mohan Narayan Temple (40)

The other temple standing in the open area of the square is the smaller five tiered, three roofed Trailokya Mohan Narayan. The temple was built by Prithvibendra Malla in 1680 and is easily identified as a temple to Narayan or Vishnu by the fine Garuda kneeling before it. The Garuda figure was a later addition, erected by the king's widow soon after his death. Look for the Vaishnavite images on the carved roof struts and the window screens with their decoratively carved medallions.

Shiva-Parvati Temple (29)

From the steps of the Maju Deval you can look across the square to the Shiva-Parvati Temple, where images of Shiva and his consort look out from the upstairs window on the comings and goings below them. The temple was built in the late 1700s by Bahadur Shah, son of Prithvi Narayan Shah. Although the temple is not very old by Kathmandu standards, it stands on a two stage platform which may have been an open dancing stage hundreds of years earlier. A Vishnu temple stands to one side of it.

Trailokya Mohan Narayan Temple

Visiting Hindu Temples

Non-Hindus are barred from entering a number of temples in Nepal although Nathalie Nellens, a Belgian visitor, commented that 'non-Hindu is rather meaningless when it is much more your colour than your religious beliefs that count'. She's probably right: a Nepali Christian or Muslim would probably find it easy to gain entrance! ∎

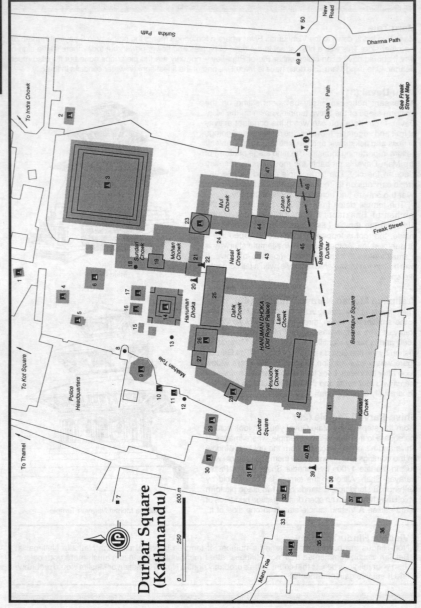

Durbar Square (Kathmandu)

0   250   500 m

PLACES TO STAY
7   Kathmandu Lodge
38 Kumari Guest House
49 Hotel Classic

PLACES TO EAT
50 Ghoomti South Indian
    Restaurant

OTHER
1   Mahendreshwar
    Temple
2   Tana Deval Temple
3   Taleju Temple
4   Mahavishnu Temple
5   Kotilingeshwar
    Mahadev Temple
6   Kakeshwar Temple
8   Great Drums
9   Krishna Temple
10 Saraswati Temple
11 Stone Vishnu Temple
12 Great Bell

13 King Pratap Malla's
    Column
14 Jagannath Temple
15 Kala (Black) Bhairab
16 Indrapur Temple
17 Vishnu Temple
18 Stone Inscription
19 Mohan Tower
20 Hanuman Statue
21 Audience Chamber
22 Narsingha Statue
23 Panch Mukhi
    Hanuman Temple
24 Dancing Shiva Statue
25 Tribhuvan Museum
26 Degutaleju Temple
27 Sweta (White)
    Bhairab
28 Bhagwati Temple
29 Shiva-Parvati Temple
30 Narayan Temple
31 Maju Deval
32 Lakshmi Narayan
    Temple

33 Ashok Binayak (Maru
    Ganesh Shrine)
34 Shiva Temple
35 Kasthamandap
    (House of Wood)
36 Singh Sattal
37 Kabindrapur Temple
39 Garuda Statue
40 Trailokya Mohan
    Narayan Temple
41 Kumari Bahal
42 Gaddhi Baithak
43 Coronation Platform
44 Kirtipur Tower
45 Basantapur Tower
46 Patan Tower
    (Lalitpur Tower)
47 Bhaktapur Tower
    (Lakshmi Bilas)
48 Tourist Office

Kumari Bahal (41)

At the junction of Durbar and Basantapur squares is a white three storey building with intricately carved windows. The Kumari Bahal (House of the Living Goddess) faces Durbar Square, its door guarded by stone lions. The building, in the style of the courtyarded Buddhist *viharas* of the valley, was built in 1757 by Jaya Prakash Malla. Inside lives the young girl (the Kumari) who is selected to be the town's living goddess, until she reaches puberty and reverts to being a normal mortal!

Inside the building the three storey courtyard, or Kumari Chowk, is enclosed by magnificently carved wooden balconies and windows. A little baksheesh to a waiting attendant may well prompt a brief appearance – he calls out 'Hey goddess' in Newari! Photographing the goddess is forbidden, but you are quite free to photograph the courtyard when she is not present. Westerners are not allowed to go beyond this area. The courtyard contains a miniature stupa carrying the symbols of Saraswati, the goddess of learning.

Kumari Bahal

The big gate beside the Kumari Bahal conceals the huge chariot which takes the Kumari around the city of Kathmandu once a year, a festival begun during the rule of Jaya Prakash Malla.

Gaddi Baithak (42)

The eastern side of Durbar Square is closed off by this white neoclassical building. The Gaddi Baithak with its imported European style was built as part of the palace during the Rana period and makes a strange contrast to the traditional Nepali architecture that dominates the square.

Bhagwati Temple

Krishna Temple

Bhagwati Temple (28)

Next to the Gaddi Baithak, this triple storey, triple roofed temple is easily missed since it surmounts the building below it. The best view of the temple with its golden roofs is probably from the Maju Deval across the square. The temple was built by Jagat Jaya Malla and originally had an image of Narayan. This image was stolen in 1766, so when Prithvi Narayan Shah conquered the valley two years later he simply substituted it with an image of the goddess Bhagwati, which he just happened to be toting around with him. In April each year the image of the goddess is conveyed to the village of Nuwakot, 65 km to the north, then returned a few days later.

A succession of interesting buildings and statues stand to the north-east of the Bhagwati Temple.

Great Bell (12)

On your left as you leave the main square along Makhan Tole is the Great Bell erected by Rana Bahadur Shah (son of Prithvi Narayan Shah) in 1797. During the Malla era a novel addition to one of the valley's Durbar squares would almost immediately be imitated in another. Curiously, Patan and Bhaktapur got their bells in 1736, while the Kathmandu version did not follow until long after the fall of the Mallas. The bell's ring will drive off evil spirits, but it is only rung during *puja* (worship) at the Degutaleju Temple (26).

Stone Vishnu Temple (11)

Next to the bell is a small stone Vishnu temple about which very little is known. It was badly damaged by the earthquake of 1934 and has only recently been restored.

Saraswati Temple (10)

Next is the Saraswati Temple which also suffered badly from the great earthquake. Prior to the quake it was over 14m high, but now is only half that height. Like the adjoining Vishnu temple, little is known about its history.

Krishna Temple (9)

The history of the octagonal Krishna Temple is well documented. It was built in 1648 by Pratap Malla, perhaps as a reply to Siddhinarsingh's magnificent Krishna Mandir in Patan. Inside there are images of Krishna and two goddesses which, according to a Sanskrit inscription, are modelled on the king and his two wives! The temple also has a Newari inscription but this neglects to mention the king's little act of vanity. The triple roofed temple has lower roofs of tile topped by a copper roof.

Just beyond the temple are the **Great Drums** (8) to

which a goat and a buffalo must be sacrificed twice a year. Then there is the police headquarters building, beyond which is **Kot Square**. It was here that Jung Bahadur Rana perpetrated the famous 1846 massacre which led to 100 years of Rana rule. *Kot* means 'armoury' or 'fort'. During the Durga Puja festival each year, blood again flows in Kot Square as hundreds of buffaloes and goats are sacrificed. Young soldiers are supposed to lop each head off with a single blow.

King Pratap Malla's Column (13)
Across the road from the Krishna Temple is a host of smaller temples and other structures, all standing on a huge raised platform in front of the old Royal Palace and the towering Taleju Temple (3). The square stone pillar, known as the Pratap Dhvaja, is topped by a statue of the famous King Pratap Malla, seated with folded hands and surrounded by his two wives, his four sons and another, infant, son. He looks towards his private prayer room on the 3rd floor of the Degutaleju Temple (26). The column was erected in 1670 by Pratap Malla and preceded the similar columns in Patan and Bhaktapur.

Sweta Bhairab (27)
Sweta (White) Bhairab's horrible face is hidden away behind a grille opposite the Pratap Malla column. The huge mask dates from 1794 during the reign of Rana Bahadur Shah, the third Shah dynasty king. Each September during the Indra Jatra festival the gates are swung back to reveal the mask for a few days. At that time the face is covered in flowers and rice and at the start of the festivities beer is poured through the horrific mouth. Crowds of men fight to get a drink of this blessed beer! At other times of year you can peek through the lattice to see the mask, which is used as the symbol of Royal Nepal Airlines.

Jagannath Temple (14)
This temple, noted for the erotic carvings on its roof struts, is the oldest structure in this part of the square. Pratap Malla claimed to have constructed the temple during his reign but it may actually be much older, dating back to 1563 during the rule of Mahendra Malla. The temple has a three tiered platform and two storeys. There are three doors on each side of the temple but only the centre door opens.

Jagannath Temple

Kala Bhairab (15)
Behind the Jagannath Temple is the large figure of Kala (Black) Bhairab. Bhairab is Shiva in his most fearsome aspect and this huge stone image of the terrifying Kala Bhairab has six arms, wears a garland of skulls and tramples a corpse, symbolic of mankind's ignorance. The figure was said to have been brought here by Pratap Malla, having been found in a field to the north of the city. The image was originally cut from a single stone although the upper right-hand side has been repaired with another stone, and the sun and moon to the left and the lions at the top are later additions. It is said that telling a lie while standing before Kala Bhairab will bring instant death and it was once used as a form of trial by ordeal!

Indrapur Temple (16)
Immediately to the east of horrific Bhairab stands the mysterious Indrapur Temple. This curious temple may be of great antiquity but little is known of its history. Even the god to which it is dedicated is controversial – inside there is a lingam indicating that it is a Shiva temple. But half-buried on the southern side of the temple is a Garuda image, indicating that the temple is to Vishnu. And to compound the puzzle the temple's name clearly indicates it is dedicated to Indra! The temple's simple design and plain roof struts together

Vishnu Temple

Kakeshwar Temple

with the lack of an identifying *torana* (the space above temple doors indicating the deity to which the temple is dedicated) give no further clues.

Vishnu Temple (17)

Little is known about the adjoining Vishnu Temple either. This triple roofed temple stands on a four-level base. The roof strut carvings and the golden image of Vishnu inside show that it is a Vishnu temple, but it is not known how old it is, although it was in existence during Pratap Malla's reign.

Kakeshwar Temple (6)

North of the Vishnu Temple, this temple was originally built in 1681 but rebuilt after it was badly damaged in the 1934 earthquake. It may have been considerably altered at that time as the temple is a strange combination of styles, starting with a two level base from which rises a lower floor in typical Nepali style. Above the 1st floor, however, the temple is in Indian shikhara style, topped by a spire shaped like a water vase or *kalasa*, indicative of a female deity.

Stone Inscription (18)

On the outside of the palace wall, opposite the Vishnu Temple (17) is a stone inscription to the goddess Kalika written in 15 languages, including English and French. King Pratap Malla, renowned for his scholastic abilities, set up this inscription in 1664 and a Nepali legend relates that milk will flow from the spout in the middle if somebody is able to read all the languages!

Kotilingeshwar Mahadev Temple (5)

This early Malla temple dates from the reign of Mahendra Malla in the 1500s. The three stage plinth is topped by a temple in the *gumbhaj* style, which basically means a square structure topped by a dome. The bull facing the temple indicates that it is a Shiva temple.

Mahavishnu Temple (4)

Built by Jagat Jaya Malla, this double roofed temple on a four level plinth was badly damaged in the 1934 earthquake and was not restored. Only the golden spire on the roof, topped by a golden umbrella, hints at its appearance prior to the tremblor.

Mahendreshwar Temple (1)

At the extreme northern end of the square, this temple dates from 1561, during Mahendra Malla's reign. The temple was restored in 1963 and is dedicated to Shiva. A small image of Shiva's bull Nandi fronts the temple and at the north-eastern corner there is an image of Kam Dev. The temple has a wide, two level plinth and a spire topped by a golden umbrella.

By day or night, Durbar Square is the magical, bustling heart of old Kathmandu.

SARA-JANE CLELAND

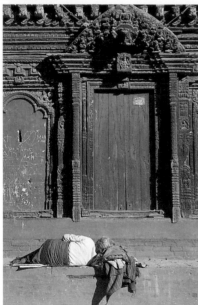

VALERIE TELLINI

HUGH FINLAY

DURBAR SQUARE

Top: Flute vendor's music tree
Left: Knocking on heaven's door?
Right: Sadhus at Durbar Square make a healthy living posing for tourist photos.

Taleju Temple (3)

The square's most magnificent temple stands at its north-eastern extremity but is not open to the public. Even the Nepalis can only visit the temple during the annual Dasain festival.

The Taleju Temple was built in 1564 by Mahendra Malla. Taleju Bhawani was originally a goddess from the south of India, but she became the titular deity or royal goddess of the Malla kings in the 14th century. Taleju temples were erected in her honour in Patan and Bhaktapur as well as in Kathmandu.

The temple stands on a 12 stage plinth and reaches over 35m high, dominating the Durbar Square area. The eighth stage of the plinth has a wall around the temple, in front of which are 12 miniature temples; four more miniature temples stand inside the wall which has four wide and beautifully carved gates. If entry to the temple were permitted it could be reached from within the palace or from the Singh Dhoka (Lion Gate) from the square.

Taleju Temple

HANUMAN DHOKA (OLD ROYAL PALACE)

Hanuman's brave assistance to noble Rama during the exciting events of the *Ramayana* has led to the monkey god's appearance guarding many important entrances. Here, cloaked in red and sheltered by an umbrella, a **Hanuman statue** (20) marks the entrance, or *dhoka*, to Kathmandu's old Royal Palace and has even given the palace its name. The statue dates from 1672, but the face has disappeared under a coating of red paste applied by faithful visitors.

Standards bearing the double-triangle flag of Nepal flank the statue while on each side of the palace gate are stone lions, one ridden by Shiva, the other by his wife Parvati. Above the gate a brightly painted niche is illustrated, with a figure of a ferocious Tantric version of Krishna in the centre. On one side is the gentler Hindu Krishna in his traditional blue colour accompanied by two of his comely gopis (milkmaids). On the other side is King Pratap Malla and his queen.

The palace was originally founded during the Licchavi period, but as it stands today most of it was constructed by King Pratap Malla in the 17th century. The palace was renovated many times in later years. The oldest parts are the smaller Sundari Chowk and Mohan Chowk at the northern part of the palace (both closed). From here construction moved south and in all there are 10 courtyards, or chowks, in the palace.

Entrance to the palace costs Rs 10 and it is open daily from 10.30 am to 4 pm.

Nasal Chowk

From the entrance gate you immediately enter the most famous chowk. *Nasal* means 'dancing one', and the courtyard takes its name from a small figure of the Dancing Shiva (24) inside the whitewashed chamber on the eastern side of the square. Although the courtyard was constructed in the Malla period many of the buildings around the square were Rana constructions. During that time the Nasal Chowk became the square used for coronations, a practice which continues to this day. King Birendra was crowned in the 1975 ceremony on the platform (43) in the centre of the courtyard. The nine storey Basantapur Tower (45) looms over the southern end of the courtyard.

The rectangular courtyard is aligned north-south and the entrance is at the north-western corner. Near the entrance there is a surprisingly small but beautifully carved doorway which once led to the Malla kings' private quarters. The panels have images of four gods.

Beyond the door is a large **statue of Narsingha** (22), Vishnu in his man-lion incarnation in the act of killing a demon. The stone image was erected by Pratap Malla in 1673 and the inscription on the pedestal explains that he placed it here in fear that he had offended Vishnu by dancing in a Narsingha costume. The **Kabindrapur Temple** (37) in Durbar Square was built for the same reason.

Next there is the Audience Chamber (21) of the Malla kings. The open verandah houses the Malla throne and portraits of the Shah kings. A golden image of Mahavishnu is set into an open verandah on the eastern wall. This image was originally in the **Mahavishnu Temple** (4) in the square, but was moved here after the 1934 earthquake.

Panch Mukhi Hanuman Temple (23)

At the north-eastern corner of the Nasal Chowk stands the Panch Mukhi Hanuman with its five circular roofs. Each of the valley towns has one five storey temple, although it is the great Nyatapola Temple of Bhaktapur which is by far the best known. Hanuman is worshipped in the temple in Kathmandu but only the priests of the temple may enter it.

Basantapur Tower (45)

King Prithvi Narayan Shah was involved in the construction of the four red-coloured towers around the Lohan Chowk. The towers represent the four ancient cities of the valley: the Kathmandu or Basantapur Tower, the Kirtipur Tower (44), the Bhaktapur Tower or Lakshmi Bilas (47) and the Patan or Lalitpur Tower (46).

The dominant nine storey Basantapur Tower was extensively restored prior to King Birendra's coronation. A series of steep stairways climbs to the top from where there are superb views over the palace and the city. The struts along the facade of the Basantapur Tower, particularly those facing out to Basantapur Square, are decorated with erotic carvings.

Mul Chowk

This courtyard was completely dedicated to religious functions within the palace and is configured like a vihara (a dwelling place for Buddhist monks), with a two storey building surrounding the courtyard. Mul Chowk is dedicated to Taleju Bhawani, the royal goddess of the Mallas, and sacrifices are made to her in the centre of the courtyard during the Dasain festival. A smaller Taleju temple stands in the southern wing of the square and the image of the goddess is moved here from the main Taleju Temple during the Dasain festival. Images of the river goddesses Ganga and Jamuna guard the golden temple doorway which is topped by a golden torana. Unfortunately, from the Bhaktapur Tower (47), where visitors normally observe the courtyard, the view is less than inspiring and the temple itself cannot be seen at all.

Degutaleju Temple (26)

Degutaleju is another manifestation of the Malla's personal goddess Taleju and this temple was built by Shiva Singh Malla and is integrated into the palace structure itself. The triple roofed temple actually starts from above the common buildings it surmounts.

Mohan Chowk

North of the Nasal Chowk is the residential courtyard of the Malla kings. It dates from 1649 and at one time a Malla king had to be born here to be eligible to wear the crown. The last Malla king, Jaya Prakash Malla, had great difficulties during his reign, even though he was the legitimate heir, because he was born elsewhere. The golden waterspout, known as Sun Dhara, in the centre of the courtyard delivers water from Budhanilkantha in the north of the valley. The richly sculptured spout is actually several metres below the courtyard level. The Malla kings would ritually bathe here each morning.

The courtyard is surrounded by towers at its four corners and north of the Mohan Chowk is the small Sundari Chowk.

Rana Additions & Tribhuvan Museum (25)

The part of the palace west of Nasal Chowk, overlooking the main Durbar Square area, was principally constructed by the Ranas in the mid to late part of the last century. Ironically, it is now home to an interesting museum that celebrates King Tribhuvan's successful revolt against their regime. If you are interested in Nepal's modern history a visit is a must. There are some fascinating re-creations of the king's bedroom and study with genuine personal effects that give quite an eerie insight into his life. There are also lots of photos and newspaper clippings that catch the drama of his escape and triumphant return. And there are several magnificent thrones, some superb stone carvings and, oddly, a coin collection.

Entry is from Nasal Chowk, and cameras have to be deposited in lockers at the door.

FREAK ST

Kathmandu's most famous street from the old hippie overland days of the late 1960s and early 1970s runs south from Basantapur Square. Its real name is still Jochne but since the early 1970s it has been far better known as Freak St. In its hippie prime this was the place for cheap hotels, colourful restaurants, hashish shops, moneychangers and, of course, the weird and wonderful 'freaks' who gave the street its name. In those days Freak St was one of the great gathering places on the road east.

Times change and Freak St today is a pale shadow of its former self and, while there are still cheap hotels and restaurants, it's now the Thamel area in the north of the town which is the main gathering place. However, shoestring travellers still stay here, and as Thamel becomes an increasingly hectic tourist ghetto, it is starting to regain popularity. Its recent historical connections are interesting and you are right in the heart of old Kathmandu where real life continues.

WALKING TOURS

A stroll around Kathmandu will lead the casual wanderer to many intriguing sights, especially in the crowded maze of streets, courtyards and alleys in the market area north of Durbar Square. There are temples, shrines and many individual statues and sculptures hidden away in the most unlikely places. You really appreciate Kathmandu's museum-like quality when you stumble upon a 1000 year old statue, something which would be a prize possession in many western museums, that here is being used as a children's plaything or a washing line. The walks described below can be made any time you have an hour or two to spare. Walking Tour 1 and Walking Tour 2 can be used as routes from the accommodation centre of Thamel to the central Durbar Square area.

All the walks take you to a number of markets, temples and chowks, which are the centre of Nepali life. A number of chowks are surrounded by bahals or bahils, dwellings for monastic Buddhist communities, although none are used for that purpose

Marijuana

In Kathmandu's flower-power era in the 1960s and early 1970s, the easy availability of marijuana and hashish was undoubtedly a major attraction. In its hippie heyday Kathmandu had hash shops and hash calendars, and hash cookies appeared on every hip restaurant menu. Many of the 'freaks' who congregated in Nepal in those days were high in places other than the Himalaya!

The drug had always been easily available, but its users were mainly sadhus, for whom it has religious importance. Then, in the run-up to King Birendra's coronation, hashish was banned and, possibly in protest, the huge Singh Durbar building, a palace from the Rana period, burnt down the next night.

Hashish is still banned, but illegal or not, it's readily available in Nepal, although potential smokers should keep the less than five star condition of Nepali jails firmly in mind. Don't try taking any out of the country either – travellers have been arrested at the airport on departure. ■

today – they have been taken over by families and sometimes schools.

The courtyards may be large and open, dotted with *chaityas* (small stupas) and shrines, or they may be tightly enclosed within a single building. A bahil is distinguished from a bahal because it also includes accommodation for non-monastic visitors, is generally simpler, and the main shrine may

Erotic Art

The most interesting woodcarving on Nepali temples is on the roof struts, and on many temples these carvings include erotic scenes. These scenes are rarely the central carving on the strut, usually they're the smaller carving at the bottom of the strut, like a footnote to the larger image. Nor are they sensuous, finely sculptured erotic figures like those at Khajuraho and Konarak in India. In Nepal the figures are often smaller, cruder, even quite cartoon-like.

The themes have a Tantric element, a clear connection to the intermingling of Tibetan Buddhist and Hindu beliefs in Nepal, but their real purpose is unclear. Are they simply a celebration of an important part of the cycle of life? A more explicit reference to Shiva's creative role than the enigmatic lingams and yonis scattered around so many temples? Or are they supposed to play some sort of protective role for the temple? It's popularly rumoured that the goddess of lightning is a shy virgin who wouldn't dream of striking a temple with such goings-on, although that's probably more a tourist-guide tale than anything else.

Whatever the reason for their existence the Tantric elements can be found on temples in all three of the major towns of the valley. On some temples it may just be the odd depiction here and there while on others something will be happening on every roof strut. The activities range from straightforward exhibitionism to the *mithuna* scenes of couples engaged in often quite athletic acts of intercourse. More exotic carvings include ménages à trois scenes of oral or anal intercourse or couplings with demons or animals. Temples with some of the more interesting erotic carvings include:

Kathmandu In Durbar Square there are carvings on many of the roof struts of the Jagannath Temple just outside the Hanuman Dhoka palace entrance. The lofty Basantapur Tower of the old palace, overlooking Basantapur Square, has some of the finest erotic carvings on its roof struts. The large Shiva Temple in the middle of the square, also known as the Mahadev Temple or the Maju Deval Temple, is a popular place to watch the activity in the square and also has some erotic struts.

North of the centre, near the restaurant and guest house centre of Thamel, the Three Goddesses Temples dedicated to Dakshinkali, Mankamna and Jawalamai have a number of interesting roof struts. The Indrani Temple, on the east bank of the Vishnumati River where you cross it going from Thamel to Swayambhunath, is another temple with interesting scenes. South of Durbar Square the small Ram Chandra Mandir has some tiny carvings on each of its roof struts.

Patan In Patan's Durbar Square the Jagannarayan or Charnarayan Temple is the most interesting temple in the town for erotic carvings.

Bhaktapur Several temples in Bhaktapur have erotic scenes including the Pashupatinath Temple in Durbar Square. There are also some carvings in the Cafe Nyatapola in Taumadhi Tole where the soaring five storey Nyatapola Temple is located. The Dattatraya Temple near the Pujari Math monastery in the eastern part of town also has low-relief figures around its base.

Elsewhere in the Valley There are many other temples with erotic artwork around the valley. The Jar Binayak Temple dedicated to Ganesh at Chobar Gorge, just south of Patan, has many interesting roof struts as does the Mahadev Temple at Gokarna, east of Bodhnath. Other temples worth inspecting include the small Ajima or Shitla Devi Temple in the Balaju park, near the sleeping Vishnu figure, and the Bagh Bhairab Temple in Kirtipur.

Several temples in and around Pashupatinath have erotic scenes but non-Hindus aren't permitted to enter the temple courtyards to see them. En route to Pashupatinath, however, you can visit the Mahadev Gyaneshwar in Deopatan, the village by Pashupatinath. ■

not necessarily be in the centre of the courtyard.

The first three walks can be made as individual strolls or linked together into one longer walk. Walking Tour 1 gives you a taste of the crowded and fascinating shopping streets in the oldest part of Kathmandu and also takes you to some of the city's most important temples. Walking Tour 2 visits some very old bahals, an important Buddhist stupa, passes by a number of ancient and important stoneworks and introduces you to a toothache god. Walking Tour 3 takes you to a lesser known section of Kathmandu, without spectacular attractions but where the normal life of the city goes on and tourists are fairly rare. The final walk, Walking Tour 4, runs along the peaceful banks of the Bagmati River past a number of rarely visited temples.

Walking Tour 1 – North from Durbar Square

The road angling across the city from Durbar Square to the artificial lake of Rani Pokhari is the most interesting street in old Kathmandu. Modern roads like Durbar Marg are no match for this narrow artery's varied and colourful shops, temples and people. The road was at one time the main street in Kathmandu and the start of the route to Tibet. It was not replaced as Kathmandu's most important street until the construction of New Rd, after the great earthquake of 1934, and it was not paved until the 60s.

Makhan Tole The crowded street known as Makhan Tole (*makhan* is Nepali for 'butter') starts from the north-eastern corner of Durbar Square, by the Taleju Temple, and runs towards the busy market place of Indra Chowk. Many shops along this stretch of the street sell thangkas, paintings and clothes.

Directly across from the Taleju Temple, at the start of the street, is a kneeling 10th century **Garuda statue** (1). It probably faced a now long-lost Vishnu temple. To your right, just past the long row of stalls, is the **Tana Deval Temple** (2) with three carved doorways and struts showing the multi-armed Ashta Matrikas (mother goddesses).

Indra Chowk The busy shopping street of Makhan Tole soon spills into Indra Chowk, the courtyard named after the ancient Vedic deity, Indra. On the left of the square is a building covered in brightly coloured modern ceramic tiles. From the balcony four metal lions rear out over the street. This is

the **Akash Bhairab Temple** (3) or Bhairab of the Sky Temple, which is actually upstairs; the ground floor is occupied by shop stalls.

To get to the temple you have to climb a flight of steps at the right-hand end of the building, guarded by two more metal lions. Halfway up a sign announces that non-Hindus may not enter, and in any case there's not much to see. The silver image is visible through the open windows from out in the street, and during important festivals, particularly Indra Jatra, the image is displayed in the square. A large lingam is also erected in the centre of the square at that time.

In a small niche just before the Akash Bhairab Temple is a very small but much visited brass **Ganesh shrine** (4). Indra Chowk is traditionally a centre for the sale of blankets and cloth and there are usually many sellers and buyers on the platforms of the Mahadev Temple. Shawls and woollen rugs are sold from the platform of the **Shiva Temple** (5), which is a smaller and simplified version of Patan's Krishna Mandir.

The many flower sellers around Indra Chowk add a bright touch to the busy square. From the south of the square Shukra Path leads to New Rd; the shops along this road sell consumer goods imported from Hong Kong and Singapore and many of them end up in India. The road heading directly north from Indra Chowk leads to Thamel. Before you leave Indra Chowk look for the narrow alley to the right, crowded with stalls selling the glass bangles and beads which are so popular with Nepali women.

Akash Bhairab Temple

Kel Tole It's only a short stroll from Indra Chowk to the next square, Kel Tole, where you'll find one of the most important and ornate temples in Kathmandu, the **Sweta (White) Machhendranath Temple** (6). The arched entrance to the temple is guarded by a small Buddha figure on a high stone pillar, facing two metal lions. The temple attracts both Buddhists and Hindus as the Buddhists consider Sweta Machhendranath to be a form of Avalokitesvara while to the Hindus he is an incarnation of Shiva who can bring

the rain. Although the temple's age is not known, it was restored during the 17th century.

In the courtyard there are numerous small shrines, chaityas and statues, including a mysteriously European-looking figure facing the temple. It may well have been an import from Europe, which has simply been accepted into the pantheon of gods. Facing the other way, just in front of the temple, are two graceful bronze figures of the Taras seated on top of tall pillars.

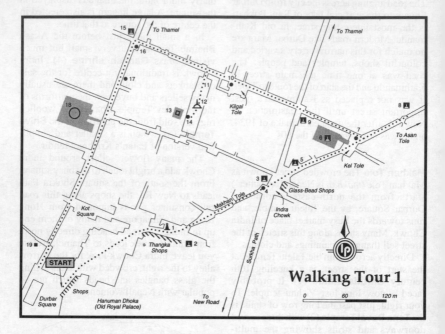

Walking Tour 1

1	Garuda Statue	7	Lunchun Lunbun	13	Kichandra Bahal
2	Tana Deval Temple		Ajima	14	Chaitya
3	Akash Bhairab Temple	8	Krishna Temple	15	Nara Devi Temple
4	Ganesh Shrine	9	Jana Bahal Temple	16	Dance Platform
5	Shiva Temple	10	Pagoda Temple	17	Wooden Window
6	Sweta (White)		Platform	18	Yatkha Bahal
	Machhendranath	11	Yitum Bahal	19	Kathmandu Lodge
	Temple	12	Stupa		

Inside the temple you can see the white-faced image of the god, sitting rather like a seated Buddha image. The image is taken out of the temple during the Sweta Machhendranath festival in March/April each year and paraded around the city in a chariot. The procession finally ends at the Machhendranath Temple in the south of the city (visited on Walking Tour 3).

During the day Kel Tole is busy with worshippers, children playing and the people whose homes surround it, but at night musicians come here to play in the entrance porch. You're quite welcome to drop by; the traditional music usually starts around 9 pm.

As you leave the temple, to the right there are a number of stores which specialise in Nepali caps. The small triple roofed **Lunchun Lunbun Ajima** (7) is a Tantric temple, white-tiled around the lower level and with some erotic carvings on the struts at the back. The diagonal street continues to Asan Tole, the busiest of the junctions along the old street (covered on Walking Tour 2). Walk partway towards Asan Tole to see the three, four and five storey houses, tightly squeezed together on this stretch of the street. On the left, the polygonal **Krishna Temple** (8) is jammed between other buildings with the ground floor occupied by shops. The woodcarvings on this temple are very elaborate.

Return to Kel Tole and turn west. At the next junction the large **Jana Bahal Temple** (9) is on your left. The domed temple is of little interest; it was probably hastily constructed after an earlier temple was destroyed, perhaps by an earthquake.

A Child-Eating Demon Continue across the junction and on your left you pass the small **Kilgal Tole** beside the road. It's a grubby little square with a couple of decaying temples and, in the middle, a fine chaitya with faces on each side. For some reason there is often a calf or two standing on the pagoda-temple platform (10).

An opening on your left leads into the long, rectangular **Yitum Bahal** courtyard (11). A small white-painted stupa (12) stands in the centre of the courtyard. Opposite it, on the western side of the courtyard, is one of the oldest bahals in the city, its entrance flanked by the usual stone lions. This is the **Kichandra Bahal** (13), dating from 1381. A chaitya (14) in front of the entrance is completely shattered by a *bodhi* tree which has grown right up through its centre.

Inside Kichandra Bahal there is a pagoda-like sanctuary in the centre and to the south is a small chaitya decorated with Bodhisattvas in a standing, rather than the usual sitting, position. On the northern side of the courtyard are four brass plaques mounted on the upper storey wall. The one on the extreme left shows a demon known as Guru Mapa taking a child from a woman and stuffing it greedily into his mouth. The demon had an appetite for bad children and the two central plaques show two more children, presumably lining up to be consumed! Eventually the demon was bought off with the promise of an annual feast of buffalo meat, and the plaque to the right shows him sitting down and dipping into a pot of food.

To this day Guru Mapa is said to live in a tree in the Tundikhel field and a buffalo is sacrificed to him every year. With such a clear warning on the end result of juvenile misbehaviour it's probably fitting that the courtyard houses a kindergarten, right under the Guru Mapa plaques!

Nara Devi Temple From Kichandra Bahal go back into the large courtyard, exit at the north and turn left. On your right at the next junction is the Nara Devi Temple (15) which gives the street its name. The temple is dedicated to Kali, Shiva's consort in her destructive incarnation, and is also known as the Sweta Kali (White Kali) Temple.

Although the temple, with its three tiers, glowing golden roof and red and white guardian lions, is quite old, some of the decorations (including the black and white chequerboard paint) are clearly much later additions. Kali's powers protected the temple from the 1934 earthquake which destroyed so many other temples in the valley. A Malla king once stipulated that a dancing ceremony should be held for the goddess every 12 years and dances are still performed on the small platform (16) across the road. Hidden away across the road is a three roofed **Narsingha temple** to Vishnu as the demon-destroying man-lion. You have to find your way to it through a maze of small courtyards.

Postage Stamp Window At the Nara Devi corner turn left (south) and you soon come to a nondescript modern building on your left with an utterly magnificent wooden window (17). It has been called *deshay madu* in Nepali, which means 'there is not another one like it'. An Rs 0.50 postage stamp issued in 1978 showed the window. Next to the building is an unimportant triple roofed pagoda which serves as a locator.

A little further south and on your right is the entrance to the **Yatkha Bahal** (18), a huge open courtyard with an unremarkable stupa in the centre. Directly behind it is an old building which used to have its projecting upper storey supported by four superb carved wooden struts. Dating from the 14th century, they were carved in the form of *yakshis*, or nymphs, one of them gracefully balancing a baby on her hip. Unfortunately they have been removed, hopefully just for refurbishment and replacement.

Back on the road and heading south you soon pass Kot Square, scene of the great massacre that brought the Ranas to power in 1846. The Kathmandu Lodge (19) is on your right and you soon see Durbar Square ahead.

Walking Tour 2 – South of Thamel

The second walk can be started from the southern end of Thamel or can easily be linked to Walking Tour 1 to make a figure eight either from Thamel or Durbar Square. This walk can be started from Thahiti Tole or, if that's hard to find, from the Hotel Gautam on Kantipath. To get to Thahiti Tole walk south from Thamel on the road from the main Thamel chowk. Soon after La Menagerie Restaurant you enter the square.

Thahiti Tole In the stupa (1) in the centre of

the square is a stone inscription indicating it was constructed in the 15th century. Legends relate that it was built over a pond which was plated with gold and the stupa served to keep thieves at bay. Or perhaps the pond was full of dangerous snakes and the stupa kept the snakes in their place – these legends vary!

The **Nateshwar Temple** (2), on the northern side of the square, is dedicated to Shiva and the metal plates on the doors show creatures busily playing a variety of musical instruments. Above the door are somewhat crudely painted pictures of Shiva's *ganas*, or companions, in this case a skeleton-like creature and what looks remarkably like a yeti.

Nateshwar Temple

Two Ancient Bahals Walk to the northeastern corner of the square and take the narrow road running east. You soon come to the entrance of the **Musya Bahal** (3) on your right, guarded by white-painted lions. The road continues east and then takes a right-left bend at the corner of which is a second, and much better preserved, old monastery, the **Chusya Bahal** (4).

This stretch of street is popular with potters and you often see them working in the road outside the bahals, or see their products piled up inside. Often it's just the simple little disposable cups used by *chia* sellers.

Beyond the second bahal there's a string

Chusya Bahal

of upper-level budget hotels, the New Kabab Corner Restaurant (5) and, right at the Kantipath intersection, the Hotel Gautam (6). Turn south and cross the road to the Rani Pokhari.

Rani Pokhari The large fenced lake called Rani Pokhari (Queen's Pond) was built by King Pratap Malla in 1667 to console his queen over the death of their son. Various legends and tales are connected with the tank and it's believed that it may actually have been built by Pratap Malla at an earlier date and only renamed for his queen after their son died; according to records the son was trampled by an elephant.

Unfortunately the gate to the tank is kept locked except on one day each year during the festival of Diwali; you will have to be content with peering through the fence. A causeway leads across the tank to a small and undistinguished **Shiva temple** (7).

Across Kantipath from the tank is the long building originally known as the Durbar School, which was the first school in Nepal. It has been renamed the **Bhanubhakta School** after the Nepali poet of that name. Retrace your steps north to the junction at the north-western corner of the Rani Pokhari and

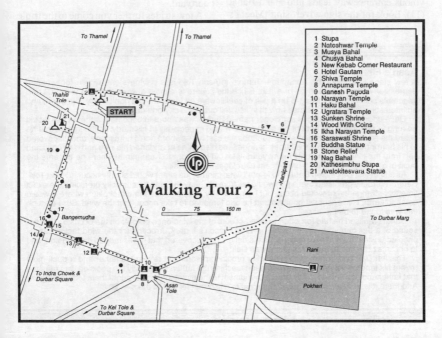

To Thamel   To Thamel

1 Stupa
2 Nateshwar Temple
3 Musya Bahal
4 Chusya Bahal
5 New Kebab Corner Restaurant
6 Hotel Gautam
7 Shiva Temple
8 Annapurna Temple
9 Ganesh Pagoda
10 Narayan Temple
11 Haku Bahal
12 Ugratara Temple
13 Sunken Shrine
14 Wood With Coins
15 Ikha Narayan Temple
16 Saraswati Shrine
17 Buddha Statue
18 Stone Relief
19 Nag Bahal
20 Kathesimbhu Stupa
21 Avalokitesvara Statue

Thahiti Tole

START

Walking Tour 2

0   75   150 m

Bangemudha

To Indra Chowk & Durbar Square

To Kel Tole & Durbar Square

Asan Tole

To Durbar Marg

Rani

Pokhari

cross Kantipath to Bhothahiti, and then walk south-west past the bicycle hire and repair shops to Asan Tole.

Asan Tole From dawn until late at night, Asan Tole is jammed with buyers, sellers and passers-by. The six roads meeting at this crossroads make it the busiest junction in Kathmandu. Every day fresh fruit and vegetables are carried to this popular marketplace from all over the valley so it is fitting that the three storey **Annapurna Temple** (8) is dedicated to the goddess of abundance, Annapurna. The smaller two storey pagoda (9) is dedicated to Ganesh. On the left-hand (western) side of the square are shops which sell dried fruit. Near the centre of the square is a small Narayan or Vishnu temple (10).

Sore Eyes & Toothache Take the road leading directly west out of Asan Tole and after a short distance, on your left, an anonymous entranceway leads into Haku Bahal (11). Look for the sign advertising 'Meeta's

Annapurna Temple

Beauty Parlour'. This tiny bahal has a finely carved wooden window overlooking the courtyard.

A few strides further you come to the triple

Asan's Fish

A few steps in front of the Annapurna Temple in Asan Tole is a paving stone with a foot-shaped depression which is said to be of a fish. Since the square is almost always crowded with fruit and vegetable sellers there's likely to be a pile of cauliflowers on top of it – but don't worry, it is there, and an interesting little legend relates how this 'fish' fell out of the sky one day.

Once upon a time a famous astrologer named Barami was about to become a father. A bell would be rung to announce the birth of his child so he waited expectantly in his study. At the instant that he heard the sound of the bell across the rooftops, he cast his newborn son's horoscope, and discovered to his horror that he was not the father. In anger and disgust he abandoned his wife and new child and fled from the kingdom. Not until many years later did he return to Kathmandu where he became the pupil of a younger but even more brilliant astrologer named Dak.

As a final test Dak asked Barami to foretell what miraculous event would shortly occur in Asan Tole. Barami correctly predicted that a fish would fall from the heavens, and he correctly predicted the exact time this strange event would occur, but he missed by several steps the exact place where it would crash to earth. His teacher suggested that he had forgotten to take account of the wind. Sure enough this was found to be the case.

Barami realised he had forgotten to take account of the wind once before: on the occasion that the sound of a bell carried to his ears the news of his son's birth. Correcting for the wind factor Barami once again cast his son's horoscope. To his delight he discovered that it was indeed his own son, and to his amazement that the boy's name was Dak!

This left Dak and Barami with a peculiar problem: a son must revere his father and a pupil must revere his teacher yet here the son had been teaching the father. Eventually the decision was reached that father and son should jointly erect a monument to the event that had brought them together again. And there it is in Asan Tole, a small memorial to a fish that fell out of the sky. ■

roofed **Ugratara Temple** (12), directly across from a small lane which heads off north. Come here if your eyes are sore: a prayer at the shrine is said to work wonders for the eyes. A few steps further along is a small sunken shrine (13) and you then arrive at a crossroads with a large open square to the north. Turn left (south) and on your left you will see a lump of wood (14) into which thousands coins have been nailed. A coin and nail embedded in the wood is supposed to cure toothache, and the deity who looks after this ailment is represented by a tiny image in the ugly lump of wood. The square at the junction here is known as Bangemudha, which means 'twisted wood'.

Ancient Buddha Turn north again to the open square where the small double roofed **Ikha Narayan Temple** (15) is easily identified by the kneeling Garuda figure in front of it. The temple houses a beautiful 10th or 11th century four armed Vishnu figure. The square also has a fine image of the goddess Saraswati (16) playing her lute.

The northern side of the square is closed off by a modern building with shops shut by roller doors on the ground floor. In the middle of this nondescript frontage, directly beneath an upper storey sign announcing 'Tintin's' is a standing Buddha figure (17), framed by modern blue and white tilework. The image is only about 60 cm high but it dates from the 5th or 6th century. A very similar Buddha figure stands on the riverbank near the temple of Pashupatinath.

If the toothache god hasn't done his duty you now pass a string of dentists' shops, proclaimed by the standard signs showing a smiling mouthful of teeth. On the right there's a small open area surrounded by concrete with a red-coloured Ganesh head and then a small but intricate stone relief (18) dating from the 9th century. It shows Shiva sitting with Parvati on Mt Kailash, her hand resting proprietorially on his knee in the pose known as Uma Maheshwar. Various deities and creatures, including Shiva's bull Nandi, stand around them.

There's a good wooden balcony across the road which is said to have had the first glass windows in Kathmandu. Nearby is a rather worn out, and bricked-in, stone trough. A little further on your left a single broken stone lion (his partner has disappeared) guards a passageway above which hangs a carved wooden torana. Inside is the small enclosed courtyard of the **Nag Bahal** (19), with painted murals above the shrine, which is flanked by banners with double-triangle flags.

Mini Swayambhunath Just a couple of steps beyond the Nag Bahal entranceway is a wider entrance to the **Kathesimbhu Stupa** (20), just south of Thahiti Tole. The entrance is flanked by stone lions which have been beheaded, and more-recent metal lions atop tall pillars.

In the courtyard is a copy, dating from around 1650, of the great Swayambhunath complex just outside Kathmandu. If a devotee is unable to make the ascent to Swayambhunath then a circuit of this miniature replica is said to be a good substitute. Just as at Swayambhunath, there is a small pagoda to Harti, the goddess of smallpox, right behind the main stupa.

Kathesimbhu Stupa

Various statues and smaller chaityas stand around the temple including, off the north-east of the stupa, a fine standing image of Avalokitesvara (21). He carries a lotus flower in his left hand, and the Dhyani Buddha Amitabha is seen in the centre of his crown with downcast eyes.

From Kathesimbhu it's only a short walk north to Thahiti Tole, the starting point of Walking Tour 2.

Walking Tour 3 – South from Durbar Square

Starting from beside the Kasthamandap in Durbar Square another circular walk can be made to the older parts in the south of the city. This area is not as packed with historical interest as the walks north of Durbar Square, but the streets are less crowded and you are far less likely to run into other tourists.

Bhimsen Temple Starting from the Kasthamandap (1) in the south-western corner of Durbar Square, the road out of the square forks almost immediately around the **Singh Sattal** (2), a squat building with small shop stalls around the ground floor and golden-winged lions guarding each corner of the upper floor. Take the road running to the right of this building and you soon come to a square tank-like *hiti* (3), or water conduit, where people will usually be washing clothes.

Immediately beyond this is the brightly painted Bhimsen Temple (4) which is fronted by a brass lion on a pillar and has white-painted lions guarding the two front corners. Bhimsen is supposed to watch over traders and artisans so it's quite appropriate that the ground floor of this well kept temple should be devoted to shop stalls. Immediately beyond the Bhimsen Temple a road branches off down to the river and across to the National Museum and Swayambhunath.

Jaisi Deval Temple Continue south beyond the Bhimsen Temple then turn sharp left (uphill) where the road ends. At the top of the hill you'll come out by the tall, triple roofed, 17th century Jaisi Deval Temple (6). It stands on a seven level base, its tiers

Jaisi Deval Temple

painted a becoming shade of pink. This is a Shiva temple, as shown by the bull on the first few steps and the mildly erotic carvings on some of the temple struts. Right across the road from the temple is a stone lingam (7) rising a good two metres from a yoni. This is definitely a god-sized phallic symbol and a prayer here is said to aid fertility.

In its procession around the town during the Indra Jatra festival, the Kumari Devi's chariot pauses here. During its stop, dances are held on the small platform (8) across the road from the temple.

Ram Chandra Mandir Cross the road from the broken chaitya (9) and enter the courtyard of the Ram Chandra Mandir (10). This small temple is notable for the tiny erotic scenes on its roof struts. This is straightforward sex and no funny business; it looks as if the carver set out to illustrate 16 different positions, starting with the missionary position, and just about made it before running out of ideas.

Bahals & Machhendranath Temple There are a series of bahals on the next stretch of the walk but most of them are of little interest. Cross the road from the Ram Chandra

Kumari Devi

Not only does Nepal have countless gods, goddesses, deities, Bodhisattvas, *avatars* (incarnations of deities living on earth) and manifestations, which are worshipped and revered as statues, images, paintings and symbols, the country also has a real living goddess. The Kumari Devi is a young girl who lives in the building known as the Kumari Bahal, right beside Kathmandu's Durbar Square.

The practice of having a living goddess probably came about during the reign of Jaya Prakash Malla, the last of the Malla kings of Kathmandu, whose reign abruptly ended with the conquest of the valley by Prithvi Narayan Shah in 1768. As usual in Nepal, where there is never one simple answer to any question, there are a number of legends about the Kumari.

One is that the Malla king had intercourse with a pre-pubescent girl, that she died as a result and that he started the practice of venerating a young girl as a living goddess in penance. Another tells of a Malla king who regularly played dice with the goddess Taleju, the protective deity of the valley. When he made an unseemly advance she threatened to withdraw her protection, but relented and promised to return in the form of a young girl. Still another tells of a young girl possessed by the goddess Durga and banished from the kingdom. When the furious queen heard of this she ordered her husband to bring the young girl back and keep her as a real goddess.

Whatever the background, in reality there are a number of living goddesses around the Kathmandu Valley, although the Kumari Devi or Royal Kumari is the most important. The Kumari is selected from a particular caste of Newari gold and silversmiths. She is customarily somewhere between the ages of four and five and puberty and must meet 32 strict physical requirements ranging from the colour of her eyes and the shape of her teeth to the sound of her voice. Her horoscope must also be appropriate, of course.

Once suitable candidates have been found they are gathered together in a darkened room where terrifying noises are made, men dance by in horrific masks and gruesome buffalo heads are on display. Naturally these goings-on are unlikely to frighten a real goddess, particularly one who is an incarnation of Durga, so the young girl who remains calm and collected throughout this ordeal is clearly the new Kumari. In a process similar to the selection of the Dalai Lama, the Kumari then chooses items of clothing and decoration worn by her predecessor as a final test.

Once chosen as the Kumari the young girl moves in to the Kumari Bahal with her family and lives there, apart from a half-dozen ceremonial forays into the outside world each year. The most spectacular of these occasions is the August-September Indra Jatra festival, when she travels through the city on a huge temple chariot over a three day period. During this festival the Kumari customarily blesses the King of Nepal and it is curious that Prithvi Narayan Shah's defeat of the Malla kingdoms took place at this time, just as if the goddess Taleju had indeed withdrawn her protection over the valley. The new king was blessed by the Kumari and the custom continued without skipping a beat!

The Kumari's reign ends with her first period, or any serious accidental loss of blood. Once this first sign of puberty is reached she reverts to being a normal mortal, and the search must start for a new Kumari. During her time as a goddess the Kumari is supported by the temple income and on retirement she is paid a handsome dowry. It is said that marrying an ex-Kumari is unlucky, but it's more likely a natural belief that taking on a spoilt ex-goddess is likely to be hard work! ■

Mandir and enter the small courtyard of the **Takan Bahal** (11). The 14th century stupa in the centre is decidedly dilapidated as a tree has grown straight up through the precise centre of the stupa, lifting the crown a good four metres above the stupa top.

The road continues with a few slight bends then turns sharply back at a junction marked by several temples, including a taller shikhara-style temple (12). If you take the downhill road leading from this junction you merge on to Tripureshwar Marg, just beyond the Vishnumati River bridge. Across this busy road another road continues down to the river and to the starting point of the cableway used to transport goods over the foothills from the Terai. Ignoring this possible diversion, the walk continues to the **Musum Bahal** (13) with four ancient Licchavi chaityas and a caged-in well. Turn sharp left (north) at the next junction and

look into a large, open bahal (14) packed with numerous chaityas.

The road opens into Lagankhel, an open square with a Machhendranath temple (15) standing about 10m high. During the annual Sweta Machhendranath festival the image of the god is transported here from the Sweta Machhendranath Temple in Kel Tole (see Walking Tour 1). The final stage of the procession is to pull the god's chariot three times around the temple, after which the image is taken back to its starting point on a palanquin while the chariot is dismantled here.

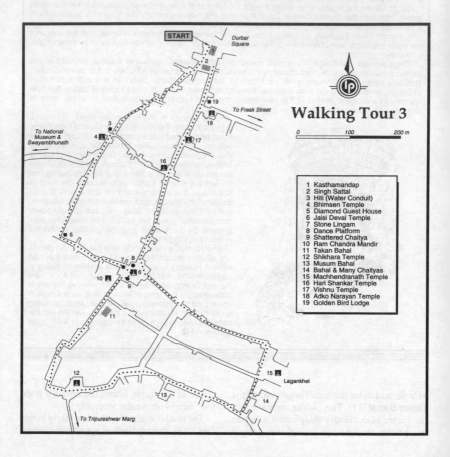

Walking Tour 3

0   100   200 m

1 Kasthamandap
2 Singh Sattal
3 Hiti (Water Conduit)
4 Bhimsen Temple
5 Diamond Guest House
6 Jaisi Deval Temple
7 Stone Lingam
8 Dance Platform
9 Shattered Chaitya
10 Ram Chandra Mandir
11 Takan Bahal
12 Shikhara Temple
13 Musum Bahal
14 Bahal & Many Chaityas
15 Machhendranath Temple
16 Hari Shankar Temple
17 Vishnu Temple
18 Adko Narayan Temple
19 Golden Bird Lodge

START
Durbar Square
To Freak Street
To National Museum & Swayambhunath
Lagankhel
To Tripureshwar Marg

Turn left out of Lagankhel and walk back to the tall Jaisi Deval Temple (6), then turn right (north) back towards Durbar Square.

Shiva & Vishnu Temples At the next crossroads the small, spindly looking **Hari Shankar Temple** (16) stands to the left of the road. The narrow brick-paved laneway beside this combination Shiva and Vishnu temple runs down to the Bhimsen Temple (4) passed earlier on. Continue north past a Vishnu temple (17) to a second Vishnu temple, the **Adko Narayan Temple** (18). Although this may not look impressive, it is said to be one of the four most important Vishnu temples in Kathmandu. A Garuda figure fronts the temple, lions guard each corner, tiny ceramic tiles decorate the ground floor and there are mildly erotic scenes on some of the upper roof struts. It's also the temple of motorbike repairs, and mechanics work away around the back of the building.

Immediately beyond the temple is the long-running Golden Bird Lodge (19) and then you pass the Singh Sattal building once again and arrive back at the starting point of this walk.

Adko Narayan Temple

Walking Tour 4 – Along the Bagmati River

The Bagmati River is a tributary of the Ganges River and is doubly holy to some because of its association with Shiva, who is believed to have lived on its banks at Pashupatinath. Not surprisingly, there are many temples along its length.

Apart from the complex at Pashupatinath there is a string of temples west of Patan Bridge to the Bagmati River's junction with the Vishnumati River. This is a quiet and forgotten corner of Kathmandu; there is no traffic and, although it is only a short walk from Durbar Square, there are few visitors.

Nothing much seems to have happened here in the last 30 years and as a consequence you can see some of the best and worst of Kathmandu. Many of the temples are in a state of picturesque decline and the traffic, crowds and noise of the city seem far away. Their place is taken by water buffaloes, egrets, sadhus and children.

Unfortunately, the riverbanks are littered with rubbish and the impressive ghats are no longer in serious use. There is also a great deal of poverty, with many families living in squalor, in and amongst the decaying buildings or in shanties in the river bed. It is hard to imagine that this was once a thriving, vital part of Kathmandu and difficult not to feel sadness at its decline.

It's possible to walk from Patan Bridge to the confluence of the rivers and back to Tripureshwar Marg in an hour or so, but you may choose to linger. Probably the best way to do the tour is to catch auto-rickshaws, or ride a bike to/from the starting and finishing points. The track is rough in places, too rough to ride, but not so rough that you can't just push a bike along.

Kalmochan Temple (1) On the Kathmandu side of the Bagmati River, 150m to the west of the Patan Bridge, you'll see a huge, square, whitewashed block, topped by a mosque-like onion dome with gilt beasts rearing up at each corner. This is the Kalmochan or Satya Narayan Temple. To get to it and start the walk, descend the steps to the riverbank beside the bridge, turn right and walk downstream past a well kept army building. Enter through a carved doorway.

The Kalmochan Temple may have been commenced as early as 1852, but it was completed in 1873 by Jung Bahadur Rana. It is dedicated to Jagannath and was built to commemorate the Gurkha wars with Tibet and Britain. It is one of the most successful of the buildings in Nepal with Mughal (Muslim north Indian) influences, but the decorations are pure Nepali. The beasts once stood on a Vishnu temple in the Tundikhel field and there is some very high-quality woodcarving.

The temple's name *(kal* means 'death') indicates that it was built in connection with a person's funeral and it is said that the temple is actually built over the mass grave of the noblemen that Jung Bahadur Rana killed in the Kot Massacre. A statue of Mr Rana faces the temple from the courtyard and, whether or not he built it to appease his conscience, the inscription below his statue extols his many achievements, but totally omits the bloody and decisive mass murder which brought him to power.

Tripureshwar Mahadev Temple (2) After leaving the Kalmochan Temple, continue downstream and cross the grubby little Tukucha Khola stream. Veer right from the river towards the huge three roofed temple, Tripureshwar Mahadev. The footpath goes through to Tripureshwar Marg, the main road, past the entry to the temple itself.

The temple was built in the 19th century by the wife of Jung Bahadur Rana but, despite its impressive size, attracts few tourists or worshippers; it doesn't have the same pleasing proportions as the best examples of pagoda architecture. There are some fine gilded figures on columns, including one of Mrs Rana herself sitting under an umbrella.

Tindeval Temple (3) Return to the river and continue to the west on a rough path. After about 10 minutes you'll come to the unusual and beautiful Tindeval Temple. It is easily recognised by its three shikharas (spires reminiscent of a folded umbrella). Enter the chowk from the south. The surrounding bahal is occupied by families and there are bound to be children playing and clothes hanging out to dry.

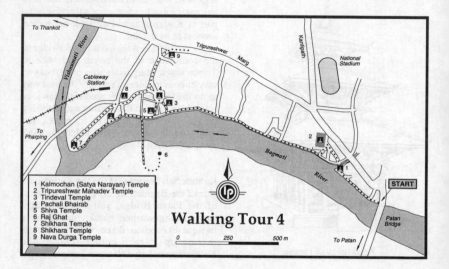

1 Kalmochan (Satya Narayan) Temple
2 Tripureshwar Mahadev Temple
3 Tindeval Temple
4 Pachali Bhairab
5 Shiva Temple
6 Raj Ghat
7 Shikhara Temple
8 Shikhara Temple
9 Nava Durga Temple

Walking Tour 4

0   250   500 m

The shikhara style began to develop under the Guptas in India (during the 5th and 6th centuries) until it became the most distinctive and common temple form in north India (especially from the 9th to 11th centuries). There are a number of examples around the Kathmandu Valley, and the style was also used in Buddhist countries throughout south Asia.

The intriguing aspect of the Tindeval Temple is the way the shikharas have been successfully integrated with a pagoda-style base and 1st floor. Note the beautiful decorative brickwork forming *nagas* (snakes) around the base of the shikharas.

Pachali Bhairab (4) Leave the Tindeval Temple by the western door (to the left as you entered) and veer to the right towards the huge *pipal* tree 25m away. This ancient tree forms a sanctuary over the image of Pachali, which is surrounded by tridents. Nearby lies what some believe to be the brass body of Baital, another of Shiva's manifestations. Others believe it is Surya, the sun god. Worshippers gather here on Tuesdays and Saturdays.

Raj Ghat Return directly to the river past a very dilapidated Shiva temple (5) on the right that nonetheless has some fine erotic carvings. If you're feeling energetic, cross the river on the old pedestrian footbridge to the Raj Ghat (6), where there is another small group of shrines. There's an attractive view looking back to the city.

Teku From the northern end of the footbridge continue along the river towards the confluence of the Vishnumati and Bagmati rivers, which is marked by another shikhara-style temple (7). River junctions are always regarded as significant in Nepal and until recently the riverbank between the bridge and the Vishnumati was a veritable art gallery densely packed with shrines and sculptures. There were Shiva lingams, Buddhist chaityas (most with the Dhyani Buddhas), and statues of Vishnu, elephant-headed Ganesh, Saraswati with her lute and

many more. Sadly, over the last few years, much has disappeared, probably into the hands of western collectors.

Nava Durga Temple From the river junction turn inland (north-east) along a paved road past another dilapidated and unusual shikhara-style temple (8). In five minutes you come to what looks like a bomb site – in actual fact it is a Roads Department depot – adjoining the Pachali Bhairab. When you intersect with the road that runs through to the pedestrian bridge on your right, turn left and keep heading north-east.

After about five minutes you reach a point where the road forks, about 50m before Tripureshwar Marg. Take the right fork and you pass the Nava Durga Temple (9), a small two storey pagoda. From Nava Durga you can turn right along Tripureshwar Marg to complete the loop.

OTHER TEMPLES & BUILDINGS
Three Goddesses Temples
Next to the modern Sanchaya Kosh Bhawan Shopping Centre and across the road from the immigration office in Thamel are the temples of the three goddesses. The street here is named Tridevi Marg – *tri* means 'three' and *devi* means 'goddesses'. The goddesses are Dakshinkali, Mankamna and Jawalamai and the temples are chiefly interesting for the roof struts, some with erotic carvings illustrating rather interesting positions.

Mahakala Temple
This temple, on the Tundikhel (east) side of Kantipath just north of New Rd, was very badly damaged in the 1934 earthquake and is of little architectural merit following its reconstruction. If you can see inside the darkened shrine you may be able to make out the 1.5m high figure of Mahakala, the Great Black One, a particularly ferocious form of Shiva. Kal means 'death' as well as 'black' in Nepali so it can also be described as the Temple of Great Death. The Tantric god has Buddhist as well as Hindu followers. You can climb to the top of one of the buildings

around the courtyard to look over the Tundikhel field.

Bhimsen Tower

This white, minaret-like watchtower, also known as Sundhara, is a useful landmark although it's of no importance. It stands near the main post office and was built by a Rana prime minister and rebuilt after being severely damaged by the 1934 earthquake.

NATIONAL MUSEUM & ART GALLERY

Not far from Swayambhunath, the National Museum is a bit disappointing, but the art gallery (when it is open) has a fine collection of religious art. A visit can easily be combined with a trip to Swayambhunath.

The museum has a rather eccentric collection that includes some moon rock, a number of moth-eaten stuffed animals, a vast number of uniforms and military decorations, swords and guns, and a mind-numbing portrait gallery. The most interesting exhibit is a leather Tibetan cannon.

The gallery displays a number of treasures. There's a superb collection of statues and carvings (stone, wood, bronze, terracotta) – some pieces date to the 1st century BCE. If you have an interest in this area of art a visit is a must.

The museum is closed on Tuesdays and is open from 10.30 am to 2.30 pm on Fridays. The rest of the week it opens from 10.30 am to 4 pm in summer and until 3 pm in winter. Ticket sales stop an hour before the closing time; entry is Rs 5, or Rs 10 with a camera.

COURSES

Check the notice boards in Thamel for up-to-date information about yoga and Buddhism courses, and shop around before you commit yourself. A number of courses are regularly advertised.

The Arogya Ashram (☎ 01-470776) near the Pashupatinath Temple teaches yoga. Arogya also has a branch in Kathmandu.

The Himalayan Yogic Institute & Buddhist Meditation Centre (☎ 01-413094; fax 410992, PO Box 817, Kathmandu) has talks, retreats and courses. To find the centre, head

away from Thamel on Lazimpat until you get to the Hotel Kathmandu; turn right after the hotel and the centre is on the right after about 200m. This centre is affiliated with the monastery at Kopan (☎ 01-226717), north of Bodhnath, which offers very reasonably priced courses which run from seven to 28 days. (See the Around the Kathmandu Valley chapter for details.) For more information on Kopan write to the Nepal Mahayana Centre, PO Box 817, Kathmandu, Nepal.

Yoga Studio (☎ 01-417900, PO Box 5098, Kathmandu) has been highly recommended for Hatha Yoga lessons for all levels. It's at Tangal Pokhari, a 10 minute bicycle ride east of the palace. Buddhist prayer flags are festooned across the roof.

See the Facts for the Visitor chapter for information about language courses.

ACTIVITIES
Swimming Pools & Sauna

Generally, pools in the major hotels can be used by friends of hotel guests or, at some hotels, by outsiders for a $2 to $3 charge. The biggest hotel pool is at the Hotel de l'Annapurna but, reflecting its popularity, it charges a ridiculous Rs 345 for one day membership. Longer membership charges are a bit more reasonable.

There are public pools at Balaju and at the National Stadium although they close during the October to February winter months. The National Stadium pool in the south of Kathmandu costs Rs 15 and is open from 10 am to 5 pm; Monday is reserved for women. The Balaju pool costs Rs 10 but it can get very crowded.

The Kathmandu Physical Fitness Centre (☎ 01-412473) in Lazimpat, has weight-training equipment, a jacuzzi and a sauna. Membership for one week is Rs 350, for one month Rs 900, and for three months Rs 1900. A sauna or jacuzzi for a nonmember costs Rs 200.

There's also an excellent sauna, open to visitors, at the Vajra Hotel on the way to Swayambhunath.

Hot-Air Ballooning

After campaigning for many years, an Australian ballooning outfit was finally given the go-ahead to start commercial flights in early 1996. On a clear day it's a superb way to view the vast expanse of the Himalaya – from over 3000m up – and also to get a couple of hours of clean air!

The flights take place daily during the season and start from Kirtipur, from where you ascend rapidly, then drift basically east – crossing the international airport! – before coming down somewhere near Bhaktapur.

The cost is $195 per person, which includes transport to and from the Hotel Kathmandu, on the Ring Road in Maharajganj north of the city centre, and a *chang* breakfast. For bookings contact Balloon Sunrise Nepal (☎ 01-424131; fax 424157).

PLACES TO STAY

Kathmandu has an excellent range of places to stay, from expensive international-style hotels to cheap and comfortable lodges.

This section is divided by price into bottom, middle and top end, and then by location. A bottom-end hotel or guest house is a place where you can get a double room for less than Rs 550, say $10. There are quite a few where you can get a room for less than Rs 165 ($3) and some where you can pay less than Rs 110 ($2). Middle means from $10 to $50 a night and the top end is from $50 up. A double room in the most expensive hotels in Kathmandu costs more than $125 a night, getting close to the nation's average annual per capita income! Quite a few hotels bridge the bottom-end and middle categories by having a range of room standards and charging accordingly – these places have been grouped according to their lowest price.

All mid-range and top-end hotels charge a government tax which varies from 10% to 15%, depending on the hotel's star rating. Almost all quote their prices in US dollars, but at all but the most expensive places you can pay the equivalent in local currency. Where you are required to pay foreign currency (see Money in the Facts for the Visitor chapter), it means payment by either cash, travellers' cheques, credit cards, or rupees

accompanied by a foreign exchange encashment receipt. Bottom-end places usually quote prices in rupees and rarely bung on a tax.

It is definitely worth looking around if you plan to stay for any length of time. It's difficult to recommend particular hotels, especially in the bottom-end and middle brackets, because particular rooms in each hotel can vary widely. Many of these hotels have additions to additions, and while some rooms may be very gloomy and run-down others might be very pleasant. A friendly crowd of fellow travellers can also make all the difference.

For bottom-end and middle places the Thamel area is the main locale, and it is something of a tourist ghetto. Its development has been rapid and uncontrolled, with ugly multi-storey hotels and signboards taking the place of beautiful Newari houses. The recent introduction of a one-way traffic system and daily garbage collection has gone a long way to halting what seemed like an unstoppable slide into chaos and squalor.

The Thamel area is where the largest number of independent travellers stay, and there are dozens and dozens of lodges, restaurants, travel agencies and shops, and a bustling cosmopolitan atmosphere. It's still a convenient and enjoyable area to stay for a short time, however, especially if you want to meet fellow travellers. It can also be a welcome relief to find western menus, people who speak English and hot showers at budget prices.

The name Thamel is used to describe a sprawling area with at least a dozen roads and several hundred hotels and restaurants. It is so well known and has such cachet that many places now claim Thamel as their address, even though they are in bordering areas that have traditionally had different names. The problem is partly due to the fact that these areas never had strictly defined limits anyway.

Despite what the hotel owners might think, many people prefer to be a bit removed from the crowded centre of Thamel. There are several places on its periphery that are close enough to be reasonably convenient

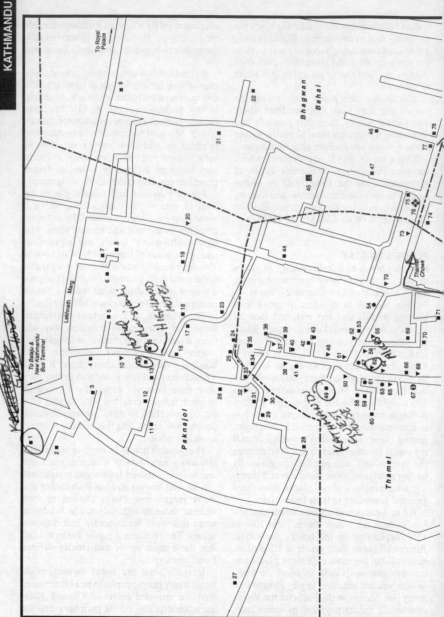

To Royal Palace

9

22

Bhagwan Bahal

46
78
77
47

45

75
76
74

73
72

Thamel Chowk

44

21

Lekhnath Marg

7
8

19
20

6

5

18
23

54
53
52
55
56
64
71
69
70

KATHMANDU GUEST HOUSE

To Balaju &
New Kathmandu
Bus Terminal

4

16
17

24
35
36
39
40
42
43
48
51
50
59
65
67
68

10

15
13
14

34
33
37
38
41
49
61
63
66

25

3

Paknajol

12

26

32
31
30
29

58
60

11

1

2

Hotel Pheasant
HIGHLAND HOTEL

KATHMANDU GUEST HOUSE

Thamel

28

27

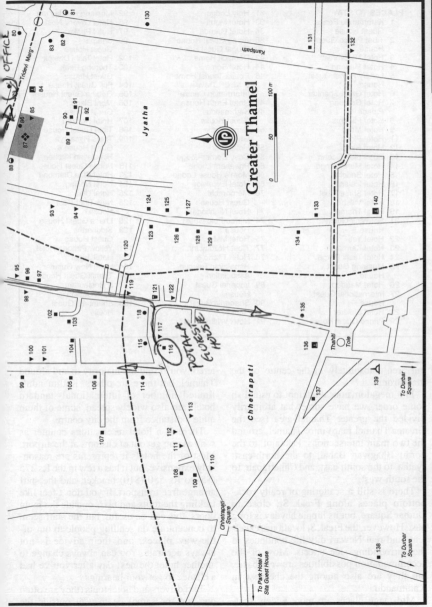

Greater Thamel

RTO OFFICE

Tridevi Marg

Jyatha

Kantipath

Chhetrapati

Chhetrapati Square

Thahiti
Tole

To Durbar
Square

To Durbar
Square

To Park Hotel &
Sita Guest House

POTALA GUESTE
HOUSE

KATHMANDU

PLACES TO STAY

1 Kathmandu Peace Guest House
2 Tibet Peace Guest House
3 Hotel Mt Everest
4 Hotel Manang
5 Lonely Planet Guest House
6 Hotel Gauri Shankar
7 Hotel Greeting Palace
8 Hotel Pilgrims
9 Hotel Malla
11 Hotel Florid
12 Hotel Rimal
13 Hotel Blue Ocean
14 Hotel Marshyangdi
15 Hotel Buddha
16 Hotel Iceland
17 Hotel Shree Tibet
18 Hotel Vaishali
19 Hotel Thamel
21 Souvenir Guest House
22 Hotel Yeti
23 Hotel Karma
24 Hotel Tashi Dargey
25 Mustang Guest House
26 Hotel Mandap
27 International Guest House
28 Hotel Shikhar
29 Prince Guest House

31 Holy Lodge
33 Hotel Mona
34 Hotel Garuda
36 Acme Guest House
39 Frugal Guest House
42 Deutsch Home
44 Hotel Soma
46 Potala Tourist Home & KEEP Travellers' Information Centre
47 Hotel Earth House
49 Kathmandu Guest House
53 Sagarmatha Guest House
58 Hotel Star
59 Cosy Corner Lodge
60 Pheasant Lodge
66 Mom's House Lodge
69 Hotel Excelsior
70 Memorable Guest House
71 Hotel Nightingale
74 Marco Polo Guest House
75 Hotel MM
77 Tibet Holiday Inn
78 Hotel Tilicho & Himalayan Rescue Association
89 Imperial Guest House
90 Shangrila Guest House
91 Hotel White Lotus

92 Mustang Holiday Inn
96 Hotel Lovers' Nest
97 Hotel Puska
99 Sherpa Guest House
102 Hotel Tashi Dhelek
103 Thorong Peak Guest House
104 Fuji Guest House
105 Gorkha Guest House
106 Mont Blanc Guest House
107 Hotel Horizon
108 Tibet Guest House
109 Trans Himalaya Guest House & Himalayan Kitchen
116 Potala Guest House
123 Hotel Blue Diamond
124 Hotel Norling
125 Hotel Utse
126 New Tibet Rest House
128 Lhasa Guest House
129 Siddhartha Guest House
131 Yellow Pagoda Hotel
133 Hotel Jagat
134 Hotel New Gujar
137 Thahiti Guest House & Restaurant de la Cabine
138 Shambala Guest House

but aren't absolutely in the centre of the maelstrom.

In a megalomaniacal attempt to establish some order, we have somewhat arbitrarily divided the greater Thamel area (see the Greater Thamel map) into: Thamel, around the two main intersections; Paknajol, to the north; Bhagwan Bahal, to the north-east; Jyatha, to the south-east; and Chhetrapati, to the south-west.

There is still a scattering of really rock-bottom places along Freak St, close to Durbar Square, but its hippie heyday is long past. However, the Freak St location is excellent, and real Newari city life continues in the surrounding side streets. Most of the accommodation possibilities are *very* basic, but they are also among the cheapest in Kathmandu.

Mid-range places are more widely scat-

tered: you'll find the majority in and around Thamel, but there are others. Kathmandu's limited number of international-standard hotels are also widely spread, some of them quite a distance from the city centre.

There is a hotel reservations counter as soon as you get out of customs at the airport. Most of the hotels it represents are reasonably expensive, but it has a few in the Rs 275 ($5) to Rs 550 ($10) bracket, and the staff arrange free transport. If you don't feel like tackling the touts and taxis outside the main doors, this can be useful, but the staff seem to concentrate on sending people to out-of-the-way places, and their advice is not always accurate. You can always change to another hotel the next day after you've had a chance to get your bearings.

Taxi drivers and hotel touts (they are often one and the same) lie in wait outside the

PLACES TO EAT
10 Hungry Eye Restaurant
20 Thamel House Restaurant
30 Rum Doodle Restaurant & Bar
32 San Francisco Pizza Palace
37 Pizza Hut
38 Northfield Cafe & Ultimate Descents
48 Brezel Bakery
50 Le Bistro Restaurant
51 La Dolce Vita
52 KC's Restaurant
55 Pumpernickel Bakery
56 Helena's Restaurant
62 Alice's Restaurant
64 Third Eye Restaurant
65 Yin Yang Restaurant
68 Khana Ghar Restaurant
72 Ajino Silk Road Japanese Restaurant
73 Old Vienna Inn
85 Fire & Ice and Dechenling Tibetan Restaurants
93 Ngeshyang Restaurant
94 Omei Japanese Restaurant

95 Les Yeux Restaurant
98 Cinderella Restaurant
100 Skala Restaurant
101 Green Leaves Restaurant
110 Everest Steak House
111 Nepalese Kitchen
112 Tibet's Canteena
113 Rimini Pizzeria
117 Narayan's Restaurant
119 Simply Shutters Bistrot
120 Al Pollo Restaurant
122 La Menagerie Bar & Restaurant
127 Dolma Restaurant
132 Delicatessen Center

OTHER
35 Old Spam's Place
40 Tom & Jerry Bar
41 Pilgrims Book House & G's Terrace
43 New Orleans Bar
45 Bhagwan Bahal
54 Postel Fax Business Centre
57 Namche Bazaar Building
61 Tantric Bookshop & Pub Maya

63 Wayfarers Travel Services
67 Nepal Grindlays Bank
76 Best Shopping Centre
79 Immigration Office
80 Kaiser Library
81 Bus Stop for Pokhara Tourist Buses
82 Temple Tiger (not a temple)
83 SAARC Secretariat
84 Three Goddesses Temple
86 Bookland
87 Sanchaya Kosk Bhawan Shopping Centre
88 Taxi & Auto-Rickshaw Stand
114 Amrita Craft Collection
115 Nepal Colour Lab
118 Student Travels & Tours
121 Silk Road Bar
130 British Council
135 Lucky Traveller Service
136 Nateshwar Temple
139 Kathesinbhu Stupa
140 Chusya Bahal

airport terminal and around bus stations. If you ask to be taken to one of the hotels recommended in this book, you may well be told that the place in question has closed or become ridiculously expensive. Though this may be possible, it is considerably more likely that they want you to go to the hotel where they get the best commission – often more than 50% of the room price. The best solution is to take a taxi to Thamel or Freak St (Rs 150, about $3, from the airport) and look for yourself. If you are travelling as a group or couple, leave one person in a restaurant to look after heavy bags while a search is made.

During the peak times (October to November, February to April) rooms in the most popular hotels can be in short supply. Otherwise, there are so many fiercely competitive mid-range and bottom-end places

that only the really popular hotels are likely to be full. The prices given here are the high-season prices shown on hotel tariff cards. At all but the top-end hotels these are pure fiction, shown to you more in the hope that you might be silly enough to pay them, and in reality prices are highly negotiable; 50% discounts are par for the course.

Long-Term Rental
For longer stays you can rent a house for as little as $80 a month. Cheaper places are mainly around Freak St, Swayambhunath or Bodhnath, but there are many other areas where more expensive houses can be found. The Jawlakhel area of Patan is popular with many foreign residents as a number of the aid agencies are based there.

If you're looking for a place to rent, check the notice boards around town or simply inquire in the appropriate areas. If you can take over a house from a departing visitor you will probably save having to find furniture and other essentials. As refrigerators are not readily available try to be near a market.

Real estate agencies which can sometimes find appropriate places include Kantipur Real Estate Services (☎ 01-220566) on Kantipath next to the British Council, or New Kathmandu Real Estate Service (☎ 01-223019) near the clocktower.

Places to Stay – bottom end

Intense competition between Kathmandu's enormous number of low-priced hostelries means that you can find hot showers in even the cheapest places, although it is usually solar-heated and is only hot in the late afternoon.

Hotels in this category do not have heating and Kathmandu in winter is a rather chilly place. In winter you'll appreciate places with a garden as it's always pleasant to sit outside during the cool, but invariably sunny, autumn and winter days. A south-facing room will mean you get some sunlight in your room. In general, the top-floor rooms are the best, as you stand a chance of getting a view and having easy access to the roof (usually a nice place to relax).

Thamel Any mention of Thamel has to start with the *Kathmandu Guest House* (☎ 01-413632; fax 417133) the first hotel to open in the area, and still one of the most popular. It also serves as the central landmark – everything is 'near the Kathmandu Guest House', 'five minutes from the Kathmandu Guest House' or whatever. It's not the best value for money in town, but most people enjoy the atmosphere and it's often booked out. The position is excellent and you definitely feel you're at the nerve centre with various expeditions coming and going, trekkers looking for partners and a constant hum of activity. There's parking space for cars out the front, a very pleasant garden, a money-change desk (guests only), a storage area for luggage and valuables, a phone office where you can conveniently and quickly make overseas calls, a travel desk, a hairdresser and even an art gallery upstairs – this is budget travel in the deluxe category! The cheapest rooms form part of the original 13-room guest house, and cost $6/8 with washbasin. In the newer wing pleasant rooms with bath are $17/20 a single/double. At the top of the scale are very large, modern rooms with air-con at $40/50. Cots are available for $3. There's a 12% tax on top of all these prices, and discounts are available for longer stays.

If this is too luxe for your budget you don't have to go far for something cheaper – there are a dozen or more places within a stone's throw. Turning south from the Kathmandu Guest House there's a cluster of hotels, starting with the *Hotel Star* (☎ 01-414000), right next door. It has long been a popular alternative to the Kathmandu Guest House, although the rooms are shabby and ordinary. They start at $3, and go to $8 with a bathroom. The basic *Cosy Corner Lodge* is adjacent to the Hotel Star, and has OK singles/doubles at Rs 100/150.

The *Pheasant Lodge* (☎ 01-417416) is tucked further around the laneway so it feels quite removed from the Thamel bustle, although it is as central as you can get. There's an atmospheric courtyard and although the rooms are basic, they're good value – which is why it's often full. Singles/doubles are Rs 100/150.

Continue south a bit further along the main street (sometimes known as JP Rd) and you come to *Mom's House Lodge* (☎ 01-417184), which aside from the awful name, is run by very helpful people and has basic but clean singles/doubles from Rs 100/120, or Rs 200/250 with private bath. The only drawback is the noise from the surrounding restaurants and bars, although this does stop around 10 pm.

Further south again is the *Mont Blanc Guest House* (☎ 01-222447), with good cheap rooms at Rs 100 to Rs 200, although it's worth avoiding those at the front.

The *Hotel Horizon* (☎ 01-220904; fax 227919) is off the main street, down near the bank of tapestry shops, and has a range of rooms at reasonable prices. They start at $6 for fairly spartan rooms with bathroom and go to $20 for luxury rooms, which are good if you can deal with the over-the-top decor.

Tucked in behind the Pumpernickel Bakery, the *Memorable Guest House* (☎ 01-243683) is one of the last budget hotels in Thamel to be housed in a traditional Newari building. On the positive side, it's atmospheric, clean and cheap; on the negative side, mutant Europeans keep bumping their heads, and have to shower while sitting on the toilet. Singles/doubles are a bargain at Rs 100/150 with common bath, Rs 150/200 with attached bath.

In this same quiet back lane is the *Hotel Nightingale* (☎ 01-225038), which has good sized rooms at $3/6, or $8/14 with bath, but you can expect to pay a lot less with discount.

Also in this area is the popular *Hotel Potala* (☎ 01-416680), a good, cheap place with double rooms, all with common bath, at Rs 125/180.

The main road from the centre of Kathmandu to Thamel runs into the main Thamel chowk. Cheapies in this area include the *Hotel Puska*, which is not great; and the adjacent *Hotel Lover's Nest* (☎ 01 220541), which is OK at Rs 150/200 with bath.

Closer to the centre of Thamel on the traffic-choked extension of Tridevi Marg, the *Marco Polo Guest House* (☎ 01-227914) is popular. The rooms at the back are particularly good and there are some surprisingly pleasant rooftop patios. Doubles cost Rs 150 or Rs 220 with bath.

Paknajol This area lies to the north of Thamel and can be reached by continuing north from the Kathmandu Guest House, or by approaching on Lekhnath Marg.

There are good-quality hotels along the road, on the right at the next T-intersection. Tucked down an inconspicuous laneway, the *Mustang Guest House* (☎ 01-416596) is good value, with pleasant, quiet rooms. Single/doubles are $5/8 with shared bath, or $9/12 with private bath.

On the main road, the *Hotel Iceland* (☎ 01-416956) is well kept, but characterless – singles/doubles cost $6/8 with shared

bath or from $8/12 to $10/16 with private bath, all plus 10%.

Further north and also down a laneway is the *The Lonely Planet* (☎ 01-412715), but we should point out that it is absolutely no relation! The building is relatively new, and the rooms, though spartan, are quite good. Singles/doubles are from $8/10.

Not far from the steep Paknajol intersection (north-west of Thamel) there are a couple of pleasant guest houses. They're away from traffic, a short walk from Thamel (but it could be a million miles), and they have beautiful views across the valley towards Balaju and Swayambhunath. The small and friendly *Tibet Peace Guest House* (☎ 01-415026; fax 420165) has well equipped rooms with lockers, bathrooms and telephones; singles/doubles cost from $2 to $12, and there's a nice garden. At the end of the road the *Kathmandu Peace Guest House* (☎ 01-415239) offers singles/doubles from $3/6 with shared bath or from $7/12 with private bath.

Turn left at the T-intersection after the Hotel Garuda and you come to several reasonable cheapies. Neat and clean rooms at the *Holy Lodge* (☎ 01-416265) cost from Rs 200/300 without bath to Rs 400/600 with bath. Across the road is the *Prince Guest House* (☎ 01-414150), which is a very decent bottom-end place.

There's a small group of hotels built around a cul de sac off Lekhnath Marg. The *Hotel Pilgrims* (☎ 01-416910; fax 229983) is undistinguished (especially some of the dark singles), but the place is clean, well managed and provides pretty good value for money. Singles/doubles are $8/10 with shared facilities; doubles with bath are $15. As always, the prices are highly negotiable.

In the same group is the popular *Hotel Greeting Palace* (☎ 01-417212; fax 417197), which offers good-sized carpeted rooms at $10/15, or deluxe at $15/25, but nobody pays that much. The *Hotel Gauri Shankar* (☎ 01-417181; fax 411878) is similar.

Bhagwan Bahal This area to the north-east of Thamel takes its name from a Buddhist monastery. It is much quieter than Thamel proper, and has not yet been completely taken over by restaurants, souvenir shops and travel agencies.

The *Hotel Earth House* (☎ 01-418197; fax 418436), just off Tridevi Marg, is a top-class budget hotel, with friendly staff, a nice rooftop garden and a variety of clean and decent rooms. Singles/doubles start at $3/4 but can go as high as $10/16 (although this is a little hard to believe). The rooms at the back are best.

The *Souvenir Guest House* (☎ 01-410277) has a good position beyond Earth House on the way north to the Malla Hotel, and a nice garden. The official rate card says singles/doubles are $5/8 with shared bath, or $8/15 with private bath, but these are highly negotiable – go for 50% less.

Turn right just before the Souvenir (as you head north) and you come to the *Hotel Yeti* (☎ 01-414858) which is a reasonable place with a garden and sunny rooms. Singles/doubles with shared bath are $8/10, or $12/16 with private facilities, but pay much less.

Jyatha The neighbourhood to the south-east of Thamel has traditionally been known as Jyatha, but increasingly the word is used to describe the main north-south road that runs into the western end of Tridevi Marg.

South along Jyatha road you reach the *Hotel Blue Diamond* (☎ 01-226320; fax 226392) which has rooms at $6/8 or $8/10 with bath. There are also more expensive air-con rooms. It's a fairly new place, set well back from the street.

The *New Tibet Rest House* (☎ 01-225319; fax 226945) is run by the same people as the popular Tibet Guest House in Chhetrapati and has singles/doubles at $6/10; $10/15 with bath.

Just a bit further south is the *Siddhartha Guest House* (☎ 01-22719), with a small garden with fruit trees. The rooms are pretty standard for Thamel, and cost $5 for a double with common bath, $7/10 with attached bath. Right next door is the *Lhasa Guest House* (☎ 01-226147; fax 228019), a good place

with rooms at $5/8 with common bath, $8/12 attached bath.

Chhetrapati This neighbourhood is named after the important five-way intersection (with a distinctive bandstand) to the south-east of Thamel. The further you are from Thamel, the more traditional the surroundings become.

South of the Kathmandu Guest House and left at the junction (Narayan's Restaurant is a good landmark here) you'll see the very popular *Potala Guest House* (☎ 01-220467; fax 223256) where singles/doubles are from $8/15, plus 10%. There's hot water and a small, quiet garden.

Just to the west of Thahiti Tole, heading towards Chhetrapati, the *Thahity Guest House* above the Cafe de la Cabine Restaurant, is a surprisingly decent place. It's on a pleasant street and although Thamel is close by you're still in an authentic (untouristed) part of the city. All rooms have hot-water baths, and there's a roof garden. Singles/doubles are $5/8.

Further west, the *Park Hotel* (☎ 01-211753) in Chhetrapati has a few excellent rooms with views across to Swayambhunath; these, however, are often full. Prices are very reasonable with singles/ doubles at Rs 250/300 with private bath, or Rs 150 with shared bath.

The *Sita Guest House* (☎ 01-215927), on the way down to the bridge across to Swayambhunath, has some excellent rooms with good views. Singles/doubles cost $3/4 with shared bath, or $5/8 with private bath.

Freak St & Durbar Square Area

Although Freak St's glory days have passed, a few determined restaurants and lodges have hung on. Staying here offers two big pluses – you won't find anything cheaper, and you're right in the heart of the old city. Thamel is so crowded and hectic that Freak St offers a good alternative, although the choices are much fewer.

Freak St's real name is Jochne (although no-one uses it) and it runs south from Basantapur Square, the open square full of souvenir-sellers adjoining Durbar Square. The *Hotel Sugat* (☎ 01-216656; fax 241576) actually overlooks the square and is one of the best options in the area. Rooms tend to be dark, but they're large and decent. Singles/doubles with shared bath start at Rs 100/250; or Rs 250/325 with private bath.

Just off Freak St proper is the excellent *Annapurna Guest House & Diyalo Restaurant* (☎ 01-213684). The place is well kept and cheerful, in contrast to some of the Freak St dives. A double is Rs 125 with shared bath, or Rs 250 with private bath.

The *Century Lodge* (☎ 01-214341) is one of Freak St's long-term survivors and remains a popular, atmospheric place offering excellent value for money. A single/double room costs just Rs 65/155. The Century is often full, which is the best testimony any place can have. The *Pagoda Lodge* (☎ 01-212029) is reached from the same courtyard in the heart of Freak St. It's about as basic as they get, and rooms cost just Rs 60/120, all with common bath.

Right across the road is the *Monumental Lodge* (☎ 01-214864) with singles/doubles for Rs 45/80, or Rs 150 with private bath. Conditions are as spartan and straightforward as the price would indicate, but if you're travelling on a very tight budget they offer all you can expect!

An excellent place is the *Himalaya's Guest House*, a couple of short blocks west of Freak St. This new place has clean and comfortable rooms, and charges from Rs 100/200 with common bath and Rs 150/250 with attached. There's a good cafe here, too, and the rooftop views are great.

At the south end of Freak St is the *Friendly Home Guest House*, a cheap and cheerful place with rooms with common bath at just Rs 60/120.

The *Kumari Guest House*, run by the friendly Mrs Bhagawati Joshi, is an old-style

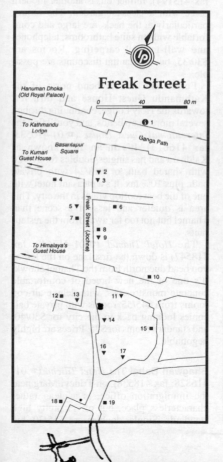

Freak Street

Hanuman Dhoka
(Old Royal Palace)

0   40   80 m

To Kathmandu Lodge

Basantapur Square

Ganga Path

To Kumari Guest House

To Himalaya's Guest House

Freak Street (Jochne)

■ 4
5 ▼
7 ■
■ 6
■ 8
▼ 9
▼ 3
▼ 2
■ 10
12 ■   13 ▼
11 ▼
8
▼ 14
15 ■
16 ▼
17 ▼
18 ■   ● 19

1	Tourist Office
2	Mona Lisa Restaurant
3	Cosmopolitan Restaurant
4	Hotel Sugat
5	Gorman Bakery
6	Kanchan Lodge
7	Monumental Lodge
8	Pagoda Lodge, Century Lodge & Kumari's Restaurant
9	Meggi Restaurant
10	GC's Lodge
11	Snowman Restaurant
12	Annapurna Guest House & Diyalo Restaurant
13	Paradise Restaurant
14	Oasis Garden Restaurant
15	Buddha Guest House
16	New Mandarin Restaurant
17	Jasmine Restaurant
●18	The Friendly Home Guest House
19	Eden Hotel
●	Tibetan Mandarin Res

KATHMANDU

building (mind your head) with great views over Durbar Square. The rooms are basic, but clean. Rooms with shared bathroom are a bargain at Rs 100/120.

Only a few steps north of Durbar Square, then to your left on Pyaphal Tole, the *Kathmandu Lodge* (☎ 01-214893; fax 01-226820) is a popular choice, although it's a bit overpriced these days. Singles/doubles cost Rs 200/250 with shared bath, and Rs 400/500 with private bathroom.

Elsewhere For those who really want to get away from it all, take the road to Swayambhunath via the National Museum; just after you cross the bridge you come to the *Peace Guest House* (☎ 01-271093) where you can still get singles/doubles for as little as Rs 45/50. It's basic, friendly and quite OK.

There are also several interesting possibilities at Bodhnath (see that section).

Places to Stay – middle

Mid-range in Kathmandu means from around $10 to $50 for a double. The borderlines are fuzzy. These days the Kathmandu Guest House is partly a mid-range hotel as many of its rooms are over $10, but it does offer cheaper ones as well.

Thamel The *Thorong Peak Guest House* (☎ 01-224656; fax 229304) has a good location in the centre of things, but off the main street in a small cul de sac. The hotel has a rather garish Tibetan-moderne decor and some of the rooms are a bit dark and expensive for what you get. Singles/doubles are $14/18 with private bath, or $8/12 with shared bath.

Right next door is the *Hotel Tashi Dhelek* (☎ 01-217446), a comfortable, modern hotel with rooms at $18/25, or with TV at $22/30.

Close to the Kathmandu Guest House is the *Hotel The Earth* (☎ 01-228850; fax 228890), another new and rather nondescript place charging $10/12 for rooms with attached bath. Also in the thick of things is the *Hotel Excelsior* (☎ 01-41566; fax 410853), a large place with standard rooms

at $18/23, or deluxe rooms with TV at $22/30.

Paknajol The *Hotel Garuda* (☎ 01-416340; fax 413614), about 100m north of the Kathmandu Guest House, is well run, clean, and excellent value. There's a great view over the Thamel area from the rooftop. Singles/doubles are from $13/17, or $16/20 with balcony, all plus 12% tax.

The *Hotel Mandap* (☎ 01-413321), just around the double bend north of the Kathmandu Guest House, has rooms for $20/25. The *Hotel Buddha* (☎ 01-413366; fax 413194), further on, is another modern place with a pleasant garden. The rooms, particularly at the back, are large and comfortable with en suite bathrooms, telephones and wall-to-wall carpeting. Rooms are $30/35, but substantial discounts are possible.

Follow the double bend north of the Kathmandu Guest House and turn left towards the Holy Lodge, continuing through several more sharp bends, and you'll find the *International Guest House* (☎ 01-410533; fax 416613). It's in an area known as Kaldhara and has singles/doubles for $16/20 with shared bath, or $18/24 with private bath, plus 10% tax. It's a pleasant hotel with one of the best rooftop views in the city. This area is quieter and less of a scene than Thamel but not too far away from the restaurants.

The *Hotel Thamel* (☎ 01-417643; fax 418547) is down the first lane on the left as you head due north from the Thamel chowk. It's one of the new breed of comfortable concrete monstrosities, with deluxe air-con rooms from $45/55, rooms with private balconies looking back to the city for $30/40, and standard rooms for $25. Prices are highly negotiable.

Bhagwan Bahal The *Hotel Tilicho* (☎ 01-416828; fax 418538), on Tridevi Marg near the immigration office, is a clean rather characterless place, but offers pretty high standards. Singles/doubles are $15/20, but it's worth negotiating the price and checking a number of rooms before you pick one.

Almost next door is the *Tibet Holiday Inn* (☎ 01-411453; fax 222223), a similar place but set back from the somewhat noisy street. Large, clean rooms here cost $20/35, or deluxe from $30/45, but discounts are a matter of course.

Jyatha Turn left (east) only a short distance down the Jyatha road and a couple of twists and turns will bring you to a neat little cluster of newer guest houses, directly behind the Sanchaya Kosh Bhawan Shopping Centre on Tridevi Marg. This is a central, but quiet location. The *Mustang Holiday Inn* (☎ 01-226538; fax 228216) has pleasant rooms and is well run. Singles/doubles are $8/10 with shared bath, or $14/18 with private bath, though these are negotiable, even in the high season. Subtract 30% and you're talking good value.

The *New Shangrila Guest House* (☎ 01-227388; fax 213174), the *Imperial Guest House* (☎ 01-229339; fax 225693) and *Hotel White Lotus* (☎ 01-226342) are also in this quiet little enclave. The hotels all seem similar to each other, but the *Imperial* is pleasant and well equipped with singles/doubles at a negotiable $12/15.

The *Hotel Utse* (☎ 01-226946; fax 226945) is a comfortable Tibetan hotel owned by Ugen Tsering, one of the original Thamel pioneers with his long-running and popular Utse Restaurant. The rooms are spotlessly clean and very comfortable – putting some of the more expensive hotels to shame. Singles/doubles cost from $13/20, or there are deluxe rooms with carpet and TV for $17/24. It's a very well run hotel, with a good rooftop area. Right next door, the new *Hotel Norling* (☎ 01-240734; fax 226735), also Tibetan-run, has good-sized rooms at $10/18, or $18/20 with a bit more comfort.

Further south along Jyatha is another new place, the *Hotel Jagat* (☎ 01-227701), which is small, clean and comfortable, and costs $14/20. Very close by and set well back from the street is the large *Hotel New Gujar* (☎ 01-226623; fax 228621), which is popular with

tour groups. It's good value at $12/16, it's just a pity they haven't made better use of the large forecourt, which is currently concrete.

Chhetrapati Two popular mid-range hotels can be found in Chhetrapati. Coming from the Kathmandu Guest House in Thamel turn right at the junction by Narayan's Restaurant and you pass a string of restaurants, bookshops and guest houses on your way to Chhetrapati Square. The *Trans Himalaya Guest House* (☎ 01-214683; fax 226273) and the *Tibet Guest House* (☎ 01-214383, fax 220518) are in adjoining modern buildings, both in the lower-middle bracket. The Tibet Guest House has singles/doubles with bath from $17/18, and others with shared bath for a few dollars less, all plus 10% tax. There's a restaurant, a pleasant garden and good views from the rooftop of this recommended hotel.

Central Kathmandu There are several older mid-range hotels right in the centre of old Kathmandu. The *Hotel Panorama* (☎ 01-221 502) is a larger hotel near New Rd with singles/doubles from $10/15.

On Surkha Path only a minute's walk from Durbar Square is the *Hotel Classic* (☎ 01-222630; fax 224889), which has excellent views over the square from the rooms on the 6th floor. Although the quoted prices are $65/75 for air-con singles/doubles, a discount of 50% seems to be offered as a matter of course. This is not bad value, given the location. The hotel also boasts a 'telescopic tower' for viewing the mountains.

Elsewhere North of Thamel, in the Lazimpat embassy area, the *Hotel Ambassador* (☎ 01-410432; fax 413641) is run by the same people as the Kathmandu Guest House. There's a good restaurant and a small garden. The hotel is within walking distance of Thamel or Durbar Marg. Rooms cost from $24/30 for a single/double.

Further north again, on the Ring Road in Maharajganj, is the *Hotel Melungtse* (☎ 01-418137; fax 227027), a modern place with excellent rooms and facilities for $10/15.

Across the river in the Bijeshwari area, on the way from Thamel to Swayambhunath, the *Hotel Vajra* (☎ 01-222719; fax 271695) is one of Kathmandu's most interesting hotels in any price category. For all the glories of the old Nepali temples, the less said about modern Nepali architecture the better. The Hotel Vajra is a pleasant exception, with a distinct style and a superb location looking across the river to Kathmandu. The hotel has an art gallery, its own theatre where classical Nepali dances are performed as well as its own unusual annual performances, a library with books on Tibet and Buddhism, a rooftop garden and the Explorer's Restaurant. Singles/doubles start at $14/16 with common bath or $33/38 with attached bath, or $53/61 in the much swankier new wing, all plus 12% tax. The one catch to staying at the Hotel Vajra is its location, which makes it terrible for getting a taxi. If you're staying here it's wise to have a bicycle at the ready.

Increasingly, people are looking to escape the pollution and bustle of central Kathmandu, and one of the nicest alternatives, which is not too far removed, is the *Hotel Sunset View* (☎ 01-229172; fax 220049) at New Baneswar – continue along the Arniko Highway and take the first right past the Hotel Everest, opposite the huge conference centre. There's a beautiful garden with great views, 12 comfortable rooms and an excellent restaurant that serves some of the best Nepali cuisine in Kathmandu. Singles/doubles are $48/66, and main meals are around $7.

Places to Stay – top end

Top-end hotels in Kathmandu cost from $50 for a double room; the most expensive hotels are around $200 for a double. Only a handful of these hotels are centrally located although the less conveniently positioned hotels usually offer a free bus service into town. All offer 24 hour room service, 24 hour satellite television and the best available communications. You can also pay by credit card.

Whether the really expensive places are worth the prices they charge is, at least in

some cases, questionable. Most are large, soulless places, and their battle to keep everything in tip-top condition is often only partly successful. Whether it's because of shoddy construction or the climate, things seem to start looking worn very quickly. Some of the mid-range places in Thamel come very close to the same standard, are more convenient, friendlier, and at least half the price.

The rates below are the standard individual rates for the high season; they're certainly negotiable for groups and are also likely to be flexible during the monsoon. A government tax is levied on all hotels and reflects the star rating; 15% for a five-star hotel, 14% for a four-star hotel, 13% for a three-star hotel, and so on.

Thamel The *Hotel Manang* (☎ 01-410993; fax 415821) in Paknajol is a modern three-star hotel with everything you could possibly need. Many of the rooms have magnificent views and all have TV and air-con. Facilities include an in-house restaurant, 24 hour room service and a parking area. Standard singles/doubles are $50/60, and deluxe rooms are $70/80, plus 13% tax.

Next door, the *Hotel Marshyangdi* (☎ 01-414105; fax 410008) has been established longer and offers a similarly high standard. In addition, it has a business centre with secretarial and fax services. Singles/doubles cost $55/65 in standard rooms, $70/80 in deluxe rooms, plus 13% tax.

Central Kathmandu Entered from Durbar Marg, but set well back from the road, the *Yak & Yeti Park Royal Hotel* (☎ 01-413999; fax 227781) boasts probably the best known hotel name in Nepal, due to its connections with the legendary Boris Lissanevitch, its original owner. It is also the hotel that, more than any other in Kathmandu, actually achieves five-star standards without abandoning all references to the country it happens to be in. The oldest part of the hotel is part of a Rana palace, and it houses the hotel's restaurants and casino that retain an overblown but spectacular Rana-baroque decor. The rooms are in two modern wings: the Newari Wing is the older of the two and the rooms incorporate elements of carved wood and local textiles without being kitsch. They're very comfortable and well maintained, and cost $150/160. The newer Durbar Wing has conventional 'international standard' rooms at $160/170. There are also executive rooms in this wing, complete with fax machine, at $190/210. Business people will find a well equipped business centre with secretarial, translation and interpretation facilities.

The *Hotel de l'Annapurna* (☎ 01-221711; fax 225236) is one of Kathmandu's longest established 'new' hotels, and is architecturally an undistinguished example of a 1960s international hotel. Its central location on Durbar Marg is convenient, and apart from the usual five-star facilities, including bars and restaurants, there's a casino, nightly dance shows (see Entertainment), and the largest hotel swimming pool in Kathmandu (about 25m). The rooms are comfortable, and standard singles/doubles are $110/120, or there are much plusher deluxe rooms for $125/135, all plus 15% tax.

The *Hotel Sherpa* (☎ 01-227000; fax 222026), opposite the Hotel de l'Annapurna on Durbar Marg, is cheaper, and rates four stars. It lacks a swimming pool, or even a nice garden (a garden oasis where you can escape can be a much-appreciated luxury in Kathmandu). The rooms are well equipped and quite pleasant. Singles/doubles are $105/115.

Just south of the Hotel de l'Annapurna on Durbar Marg, the *Hotel Woodlands Dynasty Plaza* (☎ 01-222683; fax 225650) is a four-star hotel that has decent facilities, including a swimming pool and the Woodlands vegetarian restaurant. It's much better than its unprepossessing exterior suggests, although these days the better Thamel hotels certainly give it tough competition. Rooms are large and comfortable but overpriced at $105/115 for singles/doubles.

The *Hotel Malla* (☎ 01-418383; fax 418897) is on the northern edge of Thamel, near the new Royal Palace – a five minute walk to all the Thamel restaurants. The rooms are air-con, although the furniture is getting a bit old. There's a restaurant and bar and a superb garden, complete with a mini-stupa topping a mini-hill in the centre. Singles/doubles are $105/125, or there are deluxe rooms for $120/150, all plus 14% tax.

Elsewhere Kathmandu's original luxury hotel, the *Soaltee Holiday Inn Crowne Plaza* (☎ 01-272550), is on the western edge of town but operates a bus service into town for its guests. It's one of the largest hotels in Nepal and apart from restaurants, bars, swimming pool and other facilities it also has a casino. Singles/doubles are $155/165.

The *Hotel Everest* (☎ 01-220567; fax 224421) is on the eastern edge of town, beside the main road to the airport and Bhaktapur. The modern building is eight storeys high, making it one of the tallest buildings in Nepal, and the views, especially on the northern side, are spectacular. The standards are reasonably high and the facilities are good, as well they should be with rooms at $130/140.

North of the city in the Lazimpat embassy area, the *Hotel Shanker* (☎ 01-410151; fax 412691) is an atmospheric place in a converted Rana palace. The exterior of the building is grandly baroque, but the modern decor in the rooms is not the best. The main restaurant has retained its grandeur and has good food and service, and the palace itself has a fine lawn and gardens. Rooms are $90/105.

The *Hotel Shangri-La* (☎ 01-412999; fax 414184), north of Thamel on Kantipath, is one of Kathmandu's best hotels. The rooms are attractive and well maintained, the service is swift and professional, and best of all, there's a beautiful garden with an adjoining restaurant, and a swimming pool. Singles/doubles are not cheap at $110/125, but here the price is fair.

The *Dwarika Village Hotel* (☎ 01-470770; fax 471379), built in traditional style and featuring superb examples of antique woodwork, is an outstanding and unusual hotel. The owners have rescued thousands of carvings from around the valley (from buildings facing demolition or collapse) and many have been incorporated into the complex, which consists of a small cluster of buildings separated by pleasant brick-paved courtyards. A large workshop (funded by the hotel) operates in the hotel grounds, and craftspeople patiently repair and restore lattice windows and carvings that would otherwise almost certainly be lost in Kathmandu's rush to survive and modernise. The end result is a beautiful hybrid – a cross between a museum and a boutique hotel. The hotel is near the airport and Pashupatinath, and its only disadvantage is that it's a bit of a distance to the eating places in Thamel or Durbar Marg; taxis are not a problem, however. The hotel has won a Heritage Award from the Pacific Asia Travel Association (PATA), and has just 31 rooms at $85/100. The rooms are large, atmospheric and very comfortable, but do not have air-con or TV.

PLACES TO EAT

Kathmandu's restaurants attempt an amazing variety of international cuisines with a reasonable degree of success. There are few places in south Asia where your choice of restaurants is so varied. After long months on the road in India or long weeks trekking in Nepal most travellers find Kathmandu a culinary paradise. Recent arrivals from the west may not be quite so impressed, but some places are great value by any standards.

If you are eating in the really rock-bottom restaurants around Kathmandu, be cautious about hygiene. Few travellers spend long in Nepal without coming across something which disagrees with them even if they're very fastidious about where they eat. Eating 'street food' from stalls and pavement kitchens in Kathmandu is likely to wreak havoc on all but the strongest of stomachs. Health standards have definitely improved in Kathmandu over the years, however, and you're very unlikely to have serious problems if you eat in the popular tourist-oriented restaurants. In these places it's even safe to

try a salad, drink a glass of water and eat the ice cream – although some would argue that this is living dangerously.

At the bottom end of the price range Kathmandu has numerous tea stalls and shops. Many may not even have a name but at these stalls dal bhat tarkari – the lentil soup, rice and vegetable everyday meal of most Nepalis – will be the main dish on offer. By up-country standards these places aren't cheap – dal bhat tarkari will probably set you back Rs 30.

In Thamel, if you stay away from beer, you can eat until you burst for less than Rs 200. A bottle of beer can cost anything from Rs 70 to Rs 100 and nearly double your bill.

As you might expect, the top restaurants have prices to match, but they're still reasonable by western standards. More expensive restaurants slap a 10% to 15% government tax on top of their bill, but you'll still probably only pay between $10 and $20 per person.

Tipping is becoming more accepted (and appreciated) in Nepal but your loose change or 5% is fine in cheaper places; a bit more will be expected in the expensive restaurants.

This section is divided geographically, with a final section on expensive places.

Thamel

Thamel restaurants spill into Paknajol, Jyatha and Chhetrapati, just like Thamel hotels. The junction outside the Kathmandu Guest House is the centre of Thamel dining and you can find numerous budget-priced restaurants within a minute's walk in either direction. Many of these restaurants offer a standard try-anything menu with Asian and western dishes. Italian and Mexican food features on many of these menus and you can try some amazing interpretations of pizza, pasta, tacos and the like.

The central Thamel restaurants include the best known of the lot, *KC's Restaurant*. Kaysee himself may no longer preside, but he hit the magic travellers' restaurant formula spot-on. Although the food is still very good, the restaurant has become a bit

PETER MORRIS

RICHARD I'ANSON

KATHMANDU
Top: Gilt statue of Ganga, Mul Chowk, Patan
Bottom: Let a thousand candles bloom - New Year celebrations.

PATAN

Top: The Krishna Mandir illustrates Moghul architectural influences.
Left: Backs for hire – porters awaiting work, Patan
Right: Elaborately carved temple strut, with multi-armed goddess.

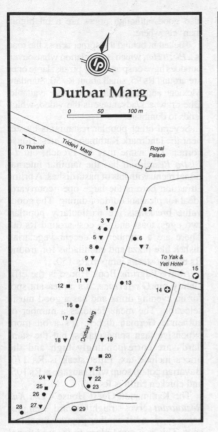

Durbar Marg

0   50   100 m

To Thamel

Tridevi Marg

Royal Palace

To Yak & Yeti Hotel

Durbar Marg

expensive by Thamel standards. A delicious breakfast starts at around Rs 60 (which isn't bad), but a vegetarian lasagne is Rs 150, and one of KC's famous steaks (Kathmandu's sizzle plate mania started right here) is around Rs 175.

On this same stretch of Thamel's restaurant centre you can try the *Pumpernickel Bakery* for freshly baked bread. In the morning, overland travellers crowd in for croissants and filter coffee in the pleasant garden area at the back.

Also across the road from KC's is *Helena's Restaurant* with the standard Kath-

mandu menu ranging from vegetarian dishes and soups through pastas and burgers to steaks, with a great selection of cakes and pies to follow at around Rs 30. Nearby, the *Garden Cafe* is a pleasant spot for al fresco breakfast, without the crowds.

Alice's Restaurant, in the Namche Bazaar building south of the Kathmandu Guest House, is a decent place, a cut above the cheapies, but still very reasonable. Pizza is Rs 90, vegetable moussaka is Rs 85 and pancakes Rs 35.

The *Third Eye* is a long-running favourite that retains something of the old Kathmandu atmosphere. There's a sit-down section at the front, and a more informal section with low tables and cushions at the back. Indian food is the speciality, but there are also a small number of continental offerings, such as excellent chateaubriand using real beef flown in from India. A sensational half tandoori chicken is Rs 190, and is the best you'll find in the city. It's wise to book a table at this popular place in the peak season.

The new *Yin Yang*, across the street from the Third Eye, serves authentic Thai food cooked by an authentic Thai chef. It's not particularly cheap, with starters around Rs 70 and main meals from Rs 120, but the food is a definite cut above the imitation Thai food found elsewhere.

Down the road from the Yin Yang, *Skala* serves good vegetarian food. It has a pleasant garden and is a nice quiet place for breakfast, with newspapers to read and classical music playing in the background. The set breakfast will set you up for the day (Rs 50).

Next door is the *Khana Ghar*, an outdoor place which specialises in Nepali set meals at Rs 65 for vegetarian and Rs 85 non-veg.

Another place on this street worth mentioning is the *Green Leaves Restaurant*, which is mostly outdoor and has Nepali musicians performing each evening. If you sit inside you can watch the kitchen activity through the large window. The pasta dishes are great.

On the next street over (east) is a restaurant popular with local expats. The cosy *Simply Shutters Bistrot* is set in an old Newari building, and has a classy European menu. Main dishes cost Rs 200 to Rs 300.

Nearly every Thamel restaurant has a go at some Italian dishes, but *La Dolce Vita Restaurant*, with the movie motifs, makes the best attempt at true Italian cuisine and, considering the difficulties, it does a very good job. Being on a busy intersection it's a bit noisy, but the food compensates. Prices are a little higher than the rock-bottom Thamel average – pasta Rs 90 to Rs 130, pizzas Rs 80 to Rs 100 – but so is the quality.

Continue a little north, just past the Pilgrims bookshop, and you come to the compound with the Ultimate Descents office and the *Northfield Cafe*, run by the same Mike as the famous Mike's Breakfast in Naxal. This is the place for serious breakfast devotees – omelettes any way you like – and the Mexican lunch dishes are also good, although prices are a bit higher than elsewhere.

Tucked in behind the corner across the road is a *Pizza Hut*, which is no relation whatsoever, but does have crisp and tasty pizzas; large ones are around Rs 95, small about Rs 50. Standard Mexican and Italian dishes are also available. One drawback/advantage is the video, which tends to dominate.

Several other popular restaurants cluster near the landmark Kathmandu Guest House corner. The name may be French, but *Le Bistro Restaurant* has the familiar international menu with lots of pasta dishes. A prime attraction here is the large open courtyard, ideal for pleasant outdoor dining. The good-value breakfasts are particularly popular; two eggs, toast and tea cost around Rs 60. There are a number of decent vegetarian dishes like pizza and enchiladas for around Rs 80, but steaks jump to Rs 150.

Above Pilgrims Book House is the efficiently run *G's Terrace*. It's a pleasant spot for an evening drink and has a good music selection. The menu features a number of authentic German dishes. It's a bit more expensive than some places, but the standards are correspondingly high and the prices include tax. Fillet steak is Rs 170, Bavarian potato soup with sausage is Rs 105, and chicken chilli is Rs 105.

The Kathmandu Guest House's *Las Kus Restaurant* serves straightforward, well prepared food and is another popular breakfast spot. This is a good place to try traditional Tibetan dishes like momo (pasta stuffed with meat and/or vegetables, a bit like large ravioli). Directly across the road and upstairs is the *Brezel Bakery*, a pleasant rooftop spot overlooking the Thamel activity below. This is another good breakfast place, with fresh brown bread.

The *Rum Doodle Restaurant* was named, of course, after the world's highest mountain, the 40,000½-foot Mt Rum Doodle. The heroic conquest of Rum Doodle was dramatically described in that spoof on heroic mountaineering books, *The Ascent of Rum Doodle* (Dark Peak, Sheffield, 1979). The restaurant is in the same side street as the

Holy Lodge, and specialises in steak and pasta. It's a favourite meeting place for mountaineering expeditions, particularly in the upstairs 40,000½ Foot Bar.

In the modern Sanchaya Kosh Bhawan Shopping Centre on Tridevi Marg there are a couple of places worth mentioning. *Fire and Ice* is an excellent open-air Italian place serving some of the best pizzas in Kathmandu (Rs 180 to Rs 270), imported Italian soft-serve ice cream, seriously good coffee and rousing opera – Italian, of course. It's deservedly popular. Next door is the *Dechenling Restaurant*, a good little Tibetan place with very reasonable prices.

The *Utse Restaurant* (☎ 01-412747), in the hotel of the same name in Jyatha, is one of the longest-running restaurants in Thamel and turns out excellent Tibetan dishes, such as momo and kothe (fried pasta stuffed with meat/vegetables). Talumein soup costs around Rs 40, and the traditional Tibetan-style meals are also worth a try: kadug dhayshey or gacok for four are both Rs 860. Gacok (also spelt gyakok) is a meal named after the brass tureen which is heated at the table and from which various meats and vegetables are served.

An excellent spot for momos is the tiny *Dolma Restaurant*, just a few doors along from the Utse. This place is typical of the Tibetan eateries dotted around town – it's just a hole in the wall, and momos are the only thing on the menu, but they are excellent and at Rs 13 for a plate, top value.

In this same street, the *Omei Restaurant* is not a bad Japanese place, and the *Ngeshyang Restaurant* has a nice garden out the back and good bakery items.

On the same side of the road, across from the Marco Polo Guest House, is the *Old Vienna Inn* with excellent service and very good food. If you're after Wiener schnitzel, goulash etc, this is the place. Most mains are around Rs 200 to Rs 250. The *Gourmet Delicatessen* in front of the restaurant is also good, with all sorts of unlikely food – from sausages and salami, to apple strudel and ice cream.

Other good places for deli items are the *Tit Bits* deli in the Hotel Garuda, and the glossy new *Delicatessen Center*, prominently signposted on Kantipath and with a mind-boggling array of imported cheeses.

On the road north from Thamel chowk is an interesting restaurant – the *Thamel House* (☎ 01 410388). It's set in a traditional old Newari building, and so has bags of atmosphere. The food is also traditional Nepali, although they will try to lumber you with the set menu at Rs 450. Ask for the à la carte menu and choose individual dishes; there are a few unusual ones, such as wild boar. It's a good night out if you don't mind the tediously slow service.

Overlooking Thamel chowk itself is the rooftop *Les Yeux*, which has a standard Thamel menu and a good view.

Head south from Thamel into Chhetrapati to find more popular travellers' restaurants including *Narayan's Restaurant*, another of the long-term survivors in this area. It's very popular, competent and low-priced with a wide range of breakfast dishes (fixed menu Rs 60), pasta and pizza from Rs 90. The vegetarian lasagne and the enchiladas are very good (Rs 95). Narayan's also produces delicious ice cream in half a dozen different flavours, and offers a great selection of pies and cakes.

Close by is the *Nepalese Kitchen*, an interesting venture attempting something rather different from the ubiquitous pseudo-western food. Traditional Nepali food is definitely rather unusual in Thamel, and this restaurant does a pretty reasonable job. The *Tibet's Canteena* in the same street is also worth a try.

Across the road, the *Everest Steak House* is very popular, especially with returned trekkers suffering from protein deficiency. The steaks are excellent and range from Rs 150 to Rs 200. There are also some vegetarian alternatives, including pizza and pasta.

Freak St

Freak St still has a number of restaurants where you can find good food at low prices, although the choice is fairly limited. Even if you're staying in other areas of the city it's nice to know there are some good places for lunch if you're sightseeing around Durbar Square.

The *Oasis Garden Restaurant* has a cramped outdoor dining area that is, unfortunately, looking very run-down. It has a standard travellers' menu (with prices from Rs 60 to Rs 80) and does a reasonable job. Across the road, the *Paradise Restaurant* is also good for vegetarian food.

Up at the Basantapur Square end of Freak St, the *Mona Lisa* is a pleasant place with friendly staff. Right next door and also overlooking the square is the *Cosmopolitan Restaurant*.

The *Snowman* is a popular restaurant and has the best range of cakes in this area. It's quite a scene in here in the evenings.

Other consistent Freak St places include *Kumari's Restaurant*, in the same courtyard as the Century Lodge, or there's the *Bluebird*, just south of the Kasthamandap and Singh Sattal, near Durbar Square.

Central Kathmandu

New Rd restaurants are aimed at the local rather than the tourist market, but try *Marwari Sewa Samiti*, near the cinema, or the *Ghoomti Restaurant*, on the corner of Ganga Path and Surkha Path for very economically priced all-you-can-eat south Indian vegetarian thalis, and ghazal music in the evenings.

The restaurants in the glossier Kantipath and Durbar Marg areas are generally more expensive than around Thamel although there are a few lower-priced exceptions. See Expensive Restaurants below for some of Kathmandu's real night-out possibilities.

Several places on Durbar Marg have good food from the subcontinent. The *Mangalore Coffee House* serves good south Indian vegetarian dishes like masala dosa (curried vegetables wrapped in a crisp, lentil-flour pancake) for Rs 24, and is a popular local gathering place.

The *Nanglo Cafe & Pub* has a popular rooftop dining area and an international menu. There's quite a lively atmosphere and the place is a favourite for people in the travel business. A large pizza costs Rs 80, a steak Rs 110, and a fixed Nepali lunch with rice, dal, meat, vegetable curry, pickle and green salad is Rs 85.

Nirula's, near the Hotel de l'Annapurna on Durbar Marg, is an outlet of the well known Indian chain, with a range of pizzas and burgers. However, the air in here is stale and the whole place – staff included – looks thoroughly tired. The only things worth bothering with are the ice creams. Much better is the new *Wimpy* outlet, also on Durbar Marg. Also close by is *Hot Breads*, with good bakery items.

Beside the entrance to the Hotel de l'Annapurna, the *Annapurna Coffee Shop* offers a standard 'big hotel' style menu with burgers from Rs 140, pizza from Rs 150, and milkshakes or lassi (yoghurt with sugar and fruit) at Rs 80. It's popular but the food is only average. Across the road the Hotel Sherpa's *Cafe de la Paix* has a similar coffee-shop menu.

Other Durbar Marg possibilities include the moderately priced *Koto Restaurant*, which many say prepares the best Japanese food in town. A set menu is Rs 300, but there are plenty of dishes for around Rs 150. The *Baan Thai* serves excellent Thai food, and the service is very attentive. Expect to pay around Rs 400, plus service and drinks.

The *Amber Restaurant* serves good-quality Indian food (it also has a continental menu) and attracts a lively crowd of affluent young Nepalis, especially when the music is good. The crowd varies depending on who is playing, but this can be a fun night out. Without beer it's possible to eat well for around Rs 200.

Nearby, the *Moti Mahal* serves, according to some, the best Indian food in Kathmandu. There's occasional live music and most main dishes are around Rs 120.

Elsewhere

You can start the day at one of the best and most popular breakfast places in the city. As the name suggests, *Mike's Breakfast* (☎ 01-424303) specialises in breakfasts and they do them well. The restaurant is in the suburb of

Naxal, opposite the police headquarters about a 15 minute walk from Durbar Marg, and Mike presides over the whole operation. Meals are served in the attractive garden of an old Rana house, and are accompanied by soothing recordings of baroque string quartets. Mike's is open every day for breakfast and lunch (7 am to 4 pm), and does pizza on Tuesday and Friday nights only. It's not cheap, but is certainly a laid-back way to start the day. The breakfast menu includes excellent waffles with yoghurt, fruit and syrup at Rs 140, or a smoked trout omelette at Rs 175. Lunch is also good, with dishes like quiche and salad costing around Rs 130. While you're here take a look at the Indigo Gallery.

Expensive Restaurants

Kathmandu's big hotels have some interesting restaurant possibilities and although the prices are sky-high by Nepali standards, they're remarkably cheap compared to the cost of similar restaurants in the west. One thing you will consistently find in these more expensive places is heating, which is rare in the cheaper places.

One of the most famous possibilities is the Yak & Yeti's *Chimney Room* (☎ 01-413999). It retains a tenuous historical link with Russian-born Boris Lissanevitch, who was the founder of the Royal Hotel, Kathmandu's first hotel for western visitors. The central, open fireplace gives it plenty of atmosphere, but unfortunately apart from the borsch, which is still excellent, there are few reminders of Boris' days. Nevertheless, the food is well prepared, if somewhat bland. The borsch is Rs 110, and chicken stroganoff is Rs 325. Other main dishes are from Rs 550 to Rs 1000.

Also in the Yak & Yeti is the *Naachghar Restaurant* (☎ 01-413999). It's a grand, baroque room with high ceilings, gilt mirrors, marble, and ornate plasterwork. Performances of Nepali music and dance are given, but ring ahead to check what nights they are on. The menu is strong on Indian and Nepali dishes – those from the tandoor are meant to be good – but there are also some continental

options. Vegetarian dishes are around Rs 150 to Rs 300, non-veg from Rs 200 to Rs 250.

The *Ghar-e-Kebab*, on Durbar Marg outside the Hotel de l'Annapurna, has some of the best Indian and tandoori food in the city. Indian miniatures hang on the walls and in the evenings classical Indian music is played and traditional Urdu ghazals (songs) are sung. A complete meal for two including drinks costs about Rs 1200. The *Arniko Room* at the Hotel de l'Annapurna has good Chinese food.

At the Royal Palace end of Kantipath, the *Fuji Restaurant* (☎ 01-225272) serves good-quality Japanese food. It's away from the road in an atmospheric pavilion that was built in 1905 in the grounds of the nearby Bahadur Bhawan Palace (now government offices). It is not cheap (unless you convert from yen). The tempura set menu is Rs 400, and the sukiyaki set menu Rs 450. Alternatively, you can choose from the à la carte menu and probably get away with, say, around Rs 500 per person, including a beer. It's open daily for lunch and dinner.

The trek out to the Soaltee Holiday Crowne Inn Plaza on the western side of town may be worthwhile to try the excellent Indian and Nepali dishes at the *Himalchuli Restaurant*. It features woodcarvings from Bhaktapur and traditional Nepali music plays in the background, but it's only open in the evenings. Local dishes cost around Rs 250, while Indian dishes are Rs 100 to Rs 300. Many say the Oberoi's misnamed *Al Fresco Italian Restaurant* (it's actually indoors) serves the best Italian food in Nepal; soups are around Rs 100, pizzas Rs 200 to Rs 300, pasta Rs 250 to Rs 300 and veal scallopine Rs 460.

Also out of town, the *Far Pavilions Restaurant* at the Hotel Everest offers great views over Kathmandu from its 7th-floor vantage point and serves a popular chicken tandoori. Closer to the centre, the Hotel Shanker's *Kailash Restaurant* does a variety of Indian, Nepali and even Russian dishes.

Bhanchha Ghar (Nepalese Kitchen) is in a traditional three storey Newari house just east of Durbar Marg from the turn-off by the clocktower. It's worth eating here just to see the imaginative redevelopment of this beautiful old building. There's an upstairs loft where you can stretch out on handmade carpets and cushions for a drink, then take advantage of an excellent menu of traditional Nepali dishes and delicacies. Downstairs, musicians stroll between the tables playing traditional Nepali folk songs. It's not cheap (around Rs 1000, for two, with drinks), but the food is delicious.

ENTERTAINMENT

Nepal is an early-to-bed country and even in Kathmandu you find few people on the streets after 10 pm. Few visitors come for nightlife and Kathmandu's discos and other nightspots have had a remarkably low survival rate. Of course the crowded restaurants and bars are great places to meet and talk with people and the big hotels do offer some traditional nightlife for those who positively cannot live without it. Kathmandu also has cultural shows, cinemas and four of west Asia's very few casinos.

Bars

There are half a dozen bars scattered around Thamel, all within a short walk of each other. Each has quite a distinctive atmosphere, so it's worth poking your nose in each to see which has the crowd and the style that appeals to you. Closing time is 10 pm, although every so often one or other of them will get a live band and a midnight late licence, and things really hop.

Tom & Jerry's, upstairs opposite Pilgrims, is a rowdy place with pool tables. Close by is the *New Orleans*, a popular place which often has live music. The *Blue Note* is one of the most civilised offerings, with excellent jazz and blues, and some interesting paintings on the wall (thanks to Bishnu Shrestha who did most of the line illustrations for this book). The nearby *Pub Maya* is rather labyrinthine and poky, but it invariably attracts some hard-core party animals.

One of the most well known places is the *Rum Doodle*, which attracts an interesting crowd of adventurers (see Places to Eat). At the end of the Kathmandu Guest House street, *Old Spam's Place* has a friendly pub-style atmosphere thanks to the inimitable style of the 'guvnar'.

Casinos

Kathmandu has four casinos, all at the up-market hotels – the Soaltee, Everest, de l'Annapurna and the Yak & Yeti.

If you turn up at any of them within a week of arrival with your onward airline ticket and your passport you can get IRs 200 of free coupons. You can play in either Indian rupees (almost a hard currency in Nepali terms) or US dollars, and winnings (in the same currency) can be taken out of the country when you leave. The casinos are open 24 hours a day, and they'll ply you with free beer if you're actually playing at the tables. The main games offered are roulette and blackjack, the main clients are Indian, and Nepalis are forbidden from entering altogether.

Nepali Music & Dance

There are regular performances of Nepali music and dancing in Kathmandu, including at the *National Theatre*, although these are usually in Nepali. All the big hotels have nightly 'cultural shows', usually in their main restaurant around 7 pm, and these typically cost around Rs 200.

The Himalchuli Cultural Group is a dance troupe which performs nightly at the *Cultural Hall* attached to the Hotel Shankar in Lazimpat, north of the Royal Palace. The hour-long shows cost Rs 250 and start at 7 pm in summer, 6.30 pm in winter.

The *Sweta Machhendranath Temple* in Kel Tole has traditional Nepali music around 9.30 pm each evening. 'The warming up of the musicians', reported one visitor, 'is done with a large chillum (clay pipe) and the music begins when the coughing stops.'

Cinemas

Video Night in Kathmandu has certainly had an impact on the city – there are video shops everywhere and cinemas are having a hard time of it. Indian films, usually not subtitled, are the usual cinematic fare, although there are occasional English-language films. Admission charges range from Rs 10 to Rs 15 and catching a Hindi movie is well worthwhile since not understanding the language is not a real obstacle to enjoying these comedy-musical spectaculars. The Indians call them 'masala' movies as they have a little bit of everything in them.

In the small video parlours – and a number of the restaurants in Thamel – popular western movies appear on pirated videos almost as soon as they hit the cinemas in the west. You'll see the movies chalked up on pavement blackboards on the streets.

THINGS TO BUY

Everything turned out in the various centres around the valley can be found in Kathmandu although you may often find a better choice or more unusual items in the real centres – eg head for Jawlakhel, south of Patan, for Tibetan carpets; to Patan for cast metal statues and other craftwork; to Bhaktapur for the finest woodcarvings and pottery; and to Thimi for more pottery and masks. See Things to Buy in the Patan and Bhaktapur sections for more details.

Crafts of various kinds are on sale all around Kathmandu, and the money that tourists spend on craft items makes an important contribution to Nepal's economy, as has been the case for hundreds of years.

The most important rules when buying anything worth a reasonable amount of money are firstly, to put in some legwork and secondly, buy just before you leave, not just after you arrive. Prices vary hugely and until you have done some research, you'll have no idea whether you're being ripped off (to an acceptable degree) or not.

Lastly, all serious shoppers should read Jeff Greenwald's humourous *Shopping for Buddhas* (a title in Lonely Planet's new Journeys series), which gives fair warning of the fate that can befall obsessive types.

Bronze Statues

The best place to start is on Durbar Marg, but there are also some shops worth visiting on New Rd. This is one area where research is vitally important, as quality and prices do not necessarily have any direct correlation. Curio Arts on Durbar Marg is a good place to start.

Curios

An endless supply of curios, stuff, knick knacks, pieces, thingos and plain junk is turned out for tourists. Most does not come from Tibet (but from the local Tamang community) and most are not more than six weeks old, but none of this matters. If you shop around you can find creations that are beautifully made by craftspeople whose time is obviously not worth a lot of money.

Prayer wheels inscribed with a Buddhist mantra are handcrafted in Kathmandu.

Basantapur Square is the headquarters for this trade, but before you match wits with these operators, visit the Amrita Craft Collection in Thamel. This relatively small shop has a wide collection, all with marked prices that are reasonably fair.

Thangkas

The main centre for thangkas is just off Durbar Square, and this is where you'll find the best salespeople (not necessarily the best thangkas). For modern work in Thamel, visit

KATHMANDU

the Tibetan Thangka Treasure, near KC's restaurant. The Indigo Gallery, at Mike's Breakfast in Naxal, has some excellent pieces.

Clothing

Kathmandu is the best place in the valley for clothes and many places have good-quality ready-to-wear western fashions, particularly shirts. Amusing embroidered T-shirts are a popular speciality. There are lots of good tailors around Thamel and, apart from embroidered T-shirts, they'll also embroider just about anything you want on your own jacket or jeans. Tara Boutique, with shops on Tridevi Marg near Thamel and on Durbar Marg, makes wonderful hand-painted pure silk women's fashions. Dresses are certainly not cheap at $50 to $100 and up, but in the west they would be many times that price.

Kathmandu's clothing manufacturing industry seems to be going from strength to strength. Recent trade liberalisation has helped to reduce the traditional problem of maintaining stocks of cloth. The cheapest items have a tendency to shrink and to fall apart, but standards both in terms of durability and design are improving. It's worth trying some of the shops in Freak St; prices tend to be better than in Thamel, partly because rents are more reasonable but also because the usual clients are shoestring travellers.

Gems

Buying gems is always a risky business unless you know what you're doing. Be immediately suspicious of anyone who tells you that you will be able to make an enormous profit – if it was possible and legal they would do it themselves. Noor Gems on Durbar Marg is a long-running and reputable place.

Tibetan Antiques

Kathmandu seems to be the world clearing house for a continual stream of antiques being brought out of Tibet. These include everything from thangkas to carpets, jewellery, storage chests, carvings, religious objects, saddles and

clothing. Since the Chinese have done their utmost to destroy Tibetan culture, removing some of what remains to safety is perhaps more morally acceptable than some other 'collecting' that goes on in Nepal. There are a number of good shops on Durbar Marg, but don't go without a very healthy wallet. The Ritual Art Gallery and Potala Art Gallery are both worth a look.

Kashmiri Goods

Since the war in Kashmir killed the tourist trade there, many Kashmiris have migrated to Nepal to sell traditional crafts such as carpets, tapestry, woollen shawls and papier-mâché. These guys are excellent salespeople, so buy with caution. Prices are pretty good; they would be cheaper in Kashmir of course, but might well come with a bonus bullet. Cottage Crafts on the ground floor of the Sanchaya Kosh Bhawan Shopping Centre (across the road from the immigration office) has a good selection and reliable prices.

A traditional carved knife of the Gurkhas.

Indian Goods

With the resurgence of popularity for Gujarat and Rajasthan's embroidered clothing and manchester, a number of shops have opened in Kathmandu. Prices are, needless to say, considerably higher than if you buy in India, but considerably less than if you buy in the west.

Trekking Supplies

The Bluebird supermarkets have a wide variety of goods. There's a branch near the Blue Star Hotel near the main bridge across the Bagmati to Patan, and another in Lazimpat on the continuation of Kantipath (on the right-hand side about a km from Thamel). In Thamel, for trekking food like noodles, nuts, dried fruit and cheese, there's the Best Shopping Centre, a small 'supermarket' at the end of Tridevi Marg, at the corner where it narrows and enters Thamel proper.

GETTING THERE & AWAY

See the Getting There & Away chapter for details of getting to Kathmandu by air or land.

Air

Kathmandu is the only international arrival point for flights to Nepal and is also the main centre for domestic flights.

International Airlines International airlines with offices in Kathmandu include:

Aeroflot
    Kamaladi (☎ 01-226161)
Air India
    Hattisar (☎ 01-415637)
Bangladesh Biman
    Durbar Marg (☎ 01-416852)
British Airways
    Durbar Marg (☎ 01-222266)
China Southwest Airlines
    Kamaladi (☎ 01-411302)
Cathay Pacific
    Kamaladi (☎ 01-411725)
Dragon Air
    Durbar Marg (☎ 01-223162)
Druk Air
    Durbar Marg (☎ 01-225166)
Indian Airlines
    Hattisar (☎ 01-410906)
Lufthansa
    Durbar Marg (☎ 01-223052)
Myanmar (Burma) Airways
    Durbar Marg (☎ 01-224839)

Pakistan International Airlines
    Durbar Marg (☎ 01-223102)
Royal Nepal Airlines
    Kantipath (☎ 01-220757)
Singapore Airlines
    Durbar Marg (☎ 01-220759)
Thai International
    Durbar Marg (☎ 01-224917)

Numerous other airlines are represented in Kathmandu. There are three important rules with flights out of Kathmandu – reconfirm, reconfirm and reconfirm! This particularly applies to Royal Nepal Airlines, and at peak times when flights are heavily booked you should reconfirm when you first arrive in Nepal and reconfirm again towards the end of your stay. Even this may not guarantee you a seat – make sure you get to the airport very early as people at the end of the queue can still be left behind.

Domestic Airlines The various domestic airlines have offices around the city. These include:

Everest Air
    Durbar Marg, opposite Rani Pokhari
    (☎ 01-228392; fax 226795)
Himalayan Helicopters
    Lalitpur (☎ 01-524664; fax 524944)
Necon Air
    Kamal Pokhari (☎ 01-472542; fax 471679)
    Opposite immigration office, Tridevi Marg,
    Thamel (☎ 01-225388, ext 344)
Nepal Airways
    Hattisar (☎ 01-410134, 410091)
Royal Nepal Airlines Corporation (RNAC)
    Computer reservations for flights to Pokhara,
    Meghauli (for Chitwan), mountain flights, Lukla
    & Bharatpur only: RNAC Building, corner New
    Rd and Kantipath (☎ 01-220757; fax 225348).
    Open daily 9 am to 4 pm.

RNAC has computerised booking only on five routes (see above), and these are booked at the main RNAC office; all other domestic flights are booked in an utterly haphazard manner at a small office just around the corner. Here it seems the booking clerk keeps issuing tickets as long as people keep fronting up with money. There appear to be no reservation charts to speak of, so the potential for overbooking is high. Confirm more than once, and get to the airport early.

The other domestic carriers seem to be well organised.

Bus

The main bus station is on the Ring Rd at Balaju, north-west of the city centre. It is officially called the Gongbu Bus Park, but is generally known as the Kathmandu Bus Terminal. This bus station is basically for all long-distance buses to Pokhara and destinations in the Terai.

Buses for destinations within the Kathmandu Valley, and for those on the Arniko Highway (Jiri, Barabise and the Tibetan border), operate from the City Bus Station, in the centre of the city on the eastern edge of Tundikhel.

The exceptions to this are the more expensive tourist minibuses – heavily promoted in Thamel – which depart from the Thamel end of Kantipath. See the Pokhara and Chitwan sections for more details.

GETTING AROUND

The best way to see Kathmandu and the valley is to walk or ride a bike. Most of the sights in Kathmandu can easily be covered on foot, and this is by far the best way to appreciate the city. When and if you run out of steam, there are plenty of reasonably priced taxis and auto-rickshaws. There are also limitless opportunities for short walks around the valley. A number are described in the Around the Kathmandu Valley chapter.

The valley is the perfect size and shape for bicycling. A single-speed bike is fine around the three main cities, but if you want to get into the countryside consider hiring a multi-geared machine. Since the furthest point in the valley is never more than about 20 km from Kathmandu you can ride out (uphill) and return (downhill) easily within a day. Bike speed allows you to appreciate your surroundings and stop whenever you like.

To/From the Airport

Kathmandu's international airport is named Tribhuvan airport after the late king, though

it used to rejoice in the name Gaucher (literally 'cow pasture'!).

Getting into town is quite straightforward. There is an organised taxi service on the ground-floor foyer immediately after you leave the arrivals baggage collection and customs section. Called Down Town Services, the taxis have a fixed fare of Rs 200 to Thamel or Durbar Marg.

The touts outside the building will often offer a free taxi if you take them up on their suggested hotel. This can be useful at very busy times, as long as you make it clear how much you want to pay. However, the commission they make on your hotel tariff can be outrageous.

Buses are sometimes available from the RNAC Kantipath office for Rs 15. There are public buses which leave from the main road – about 300m from the terminal – but they're only really useable if you have very little luggage.

Bus

While bus travel is very cheap, it is often unbelievably crowded. The primary disadvantage, apart from severe discomfort, is that you cannot see the views or stop when you want. Still, if you're short of cash and want to get from point A to B *reasonably* quickly, they'll do. Over a short distance – say from Thamel to Bodhnath – you'll probably be just as quick on a bicycle. The smaller minibuses and curious little three wheeled tempos are generally quicker than the full-sized buses and are a bit more expensive.

Nearly all buses to points around the valley operate from the City Bus Station. As with anything in Nepal, however, there are exceptions to the rule.

The incredibly dilapidated electric trolley buses to Bhaktapur leave from the southern end of Kantipath near the National Stadium. These cost Rs 2 and drop you off a 10 minute walk from the centre of Bhaktapur.

Tourist buses for Nagarkot leave from Thamel at 1.30 pm. Tickets are available from most tour agencies and tourist information centres.

Buses for a number of destinations leave

from Patan: to Godavari and Chapagaon they leave from Lagankhel, to Bungamati from Jawlakhel, and to Pharping (Dakshinkali) from Martyr's Gate (Tuesday and Saturday only).

Taxi

Taxis are quite reasonably priced, but prices often rise faster than meters can be recalibrated, so there is frequently a surcharge on top of the meter reading. Tourists will, in any case, be hard-pushed to convince drivers to use their meters (with or without a surcharge) and will almost certainly have to negotiate their fare in advance. Shorter rides around town should come to less than Rs 50. Between several people, longer trips around the valley, or even outside it, are also affordable. A half-day sightseeing trip within the valley should cost around Rs 600, and a full-day trip, Rs 1200.

Other approximate taxi fares (from Thamel) include:

Pashupatinath	Rs 50
Bodhnath	Rs 60
Patan	Rs 80
Bhaktapur	Rs 175
Changu Narayan	Rs 300
Dhulikhel/Nagarkot	Rs 500

For longer journeys outside the valley count on about Rs 2500 per day plus fuel, for which prices are set by the government, currently at around Rs 30 per litre.

Note that in Nepal, real taxis have black licence plates while private cars (many of which operate as taxis but don't have meters) have red plates. If you need a taxi at night call ☎ 224374.

Auto & Cycle Rickshaw

Three wheeled metered auto-rickshaws are quite common in Kathmandu and cost as little as half of what you would pay for a cab. They're still a bit of a lottery – most will blankly refuse to use the meter and if this is the case make sure you establish a price. Most rides around town should cost less than Rs 30. If you can get them to use the meter, the adjustment is 40% on top of the reading.

Bicycle rickshaws cost Rs 30 to Rs 50 for most rides around town – they can be more expensive than going by auto-rickshaw or taxi. The tourist rate from Thamel to Durbar Square is Rs 30, from Thamel to the Hotel de l'Annapurna Rs 20. You must be certain to agree on a price before you start.

Car

Although you cannot rent cars on a drive-yourself basis they can readily be rented with a driver from a number of operators. Try Gorkha Travels (☎ 01-224896) or American Express Yeti Travels (☎ 01-221234), or one of the many travel agents in Thamel.

The rental cost is fairly high both in terms of the initial hiring charge and fuel. Full-day charges are as high as Rs 3000 a day, although they can be lower, especially if you are not covering a huge distance. Around the valley expect to pay about Rs 2500 plus fuel.

Motorbike

There are a number of motorbike rental operators around Freak St and Thamel. You need an international drivers' license and are required to leave a substantial deposit. For Rs 400 per day you'll get a 100 cc Indian-made Honda road bike, and will basically be restricted to the Kathmandu Valley (but also including Daman, Kakani, Nagarkot and Dhulikhel). For a 250 cc trail bike the cost is around Rs 1000 per day. Think carefully before you do hire, as you will be encouraging the proliferation of noisy, polluting machines and adding to Nepal's trade imbalance. Most reasonably fit people will find that a mountain bike is a better option, especially as you can get to more places.

Bicycle

Once you get away from the crowded streets of central Kathmandu, cycling is a pleasure, and if you're in reasonable shape this is the ideal way to explore the valley. It costs from Rs 30 to Rs 50 a day for a regular single-speed, sit-up-and-beg Indian or Chinese-made bicycle. Check the brakes before taking it out and be certain to lock it whenever you leave it.

Multi-geared mountain bikes have become the rage in Kathmandu and many places around Thamel rent them out. Count on Rs 150 a day, which, if you are planning to really explore the valley, is money well spent. It's a real pleasure to surge up the long hill into Patan, effortlessly sweeping by all the riders of regular bikes who have to get off and push.

Tours

There are numerous tour operators in Kathmandu with bus and car tours to all the established tourist sights. Typical costs for half-day tours are around Rs 250 and if your time is limited this can be a good way of seeing the valley's scattered attractions.

Grayline (☎ 01-412899) has a wide variety of tours including Bhaktapur to Bodhnath and Pashupatinath on Monday, Wednesday, Friday and Saturday; Patan to Swayambhunath on Sunday, Tuesday and Thursday; Chobar Gorge to Dakshinkali on Tuesday and Saturday; plus dawn trips to Nagarkot, Dhulikhel and Kakani for the Himalayan sunrise.

Kathmandu Travels & Tours (☎ 01-224536), Everest Travel Service (☎ 01-227291) and others also operate tours or will arrange them.

Patan

Patan is separated from Kathmandu only by the Bagmati River and is the second largest town in the valley. It is sometimes referred to as Lalitpur, which means 'city of beauty'. Patan has a long Buddhist history and the four corners of the city are marked by stupas said to have been erected by the great Buddhist emperor Ashoka around 250 BCE. Later inscriptions refer to palaces in the city in the 5th century CE although Patan's great building boom took place under the Mallas in the 16th, 17th and 18th centuries.

Patan's central Durbar Square is absolutely packed with temples: it's an architectural feast with a far greater concentration of temples per sq metre than in Kathmandu or Bhaktapur. Numerous other temples of widely diverse style as well as many bahals (Buddhist monasteries) are scattered around this fascinating town.

Malla Kings

The Malla kings of Patan were responsible for most of the city's great buildings. The Malla kings included:

Jayasthiti Malla	1372-1395
Siddhinarsingh Malla	1620-1661
Srinivasa Malla	1661-1684
Yoganarendra Malla	1684-1705
Vishnu Malla	1729-1745
Rajya Prakash Malla	1745-1758
Visvajita Malla	1758-1760

ORIENTATION & INFORMATION

The Durbar (Palace) Square is the centre of Patan to a greater extent than the equivalent palace squares are of Kathmandu or Bhaktapur. From the square, four main roads lead to the four Ashoka stupas while the city radiates out in concentric circles.

It is possible to stay in Patan, although it's so close to Kathmandu that it scarcely seems worthwhile and the choice of accommodation and restaurants is far more limited than in the capital.

Jawlakhel, to the south of the city, has a major Tibetan population and is the centre for carpet-weaving in the valley.

Buses from Kathmandu drop you at the Patan city gate, about 15 minutes walk from Durbar Square. There's another, larger bus stop directly south of Durbar Square, near the Southern (Lagan) Stupa. Taxis normally drop you at the square. If you come to Patan by bicycle an interesting route is to take the track down to the river from opposite the big convention centre on the Bhaktapur road. A footbridge crosses the river here and you enter Patan by the Northern Stupa near the Kumbeshwar Temple.

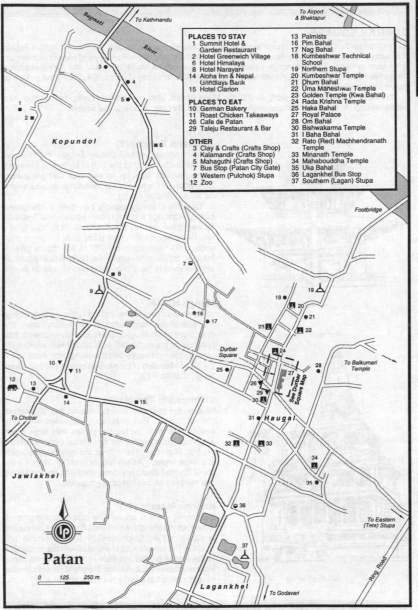

PLACES TO STAY
1 Summit Hotel & Garden Restaurant
2 Hotel Greenwich Village
6 Hotel Himalaya
8 Hotel Narayani
14 Aloha Inn & Nepal Grindlays Bank
15 Hotel Clarion

PLACES TO EAT
10 German Bakery
11 Roast Chicken Takeaways
26 Cafe de Patan
29 Taleju Restaurant & Bar

OTHER
3 Clay & Crafts (Crafts Shop)
4 Kalamandir (Crafts Shop)
5 Mahaguthi (Crafts Shop)
7 Bus Stop (Patan City Gate)
9 Western (Pulchok) Stupa
12 Zoo

13 Palmists
16 Pim Bahal
17 Nag Bahal
18 Kumbeshwar Technical School
19 Northern Stupa
20 Kumbeshwar Temple
21 Dhum Bahal
22 Uma Maheshwar Temple
23 Golden Temple (Kwa Bahal)
24 Rada Krishna Temple
25 Haka Bahal
27 Royal Palace
28 Om Bahal
30 Bishwakarma Temple
31 I Baha Bahal
32 Rato (Red) Machhendranath Temple
33 Minanath Temple
34 Mahabouddha Temple
35 Uka Bahal
36 Lagankhel Bus Stop
37 Southern (Lagan) Stupa

To Kathmandu

To Airport & Bhaktapur

Bagmati River

Kopundol

Footbridge

Durbar Square

See Durbar Square Map

To Balkumari Temple

Haugal

Jawlakhel

To Chobar

Patan

0   125   250 m

Lagankhel

To Godavari

To Eastern (Teta) Stupa

Ring Road

DURBAR SQUARE

As in Kathmandu, the ancient Royal Palace of the city faces on to the square, but Patan's Durbar Square is a concentrated mass of temples, undoubtedly the most visually stunning display of Newari architecture to be seen in Nepal. The rectangular square has its longer axis running north-south and the palace forms the eastern side of the square. A continuous row of temples in widely diverse styles faces the palace on the western side.

The square rose to its full glory during the Malla period, and particularly during the reign of King Siddhinarsingh Malla. Patan's major market, the **Mangal Bazaar,** is beside the square.

Bhimsen Temple

Krishna Mandir

Bhimsen Temple (3)

At the northern end of Durbar Square the Bhimsen Temple is dedicated to the god of trade and business, which possibly explains its well kept and prosperous look. Bhimsen, a hero of the *Mahabharata*, was said to be extraordinarily strong.

The three storey temple has had a chequered history. Although it is not known when it was first built, an inscription records that it was rebuilt in 1682 after a fire. Restorations also took place after the great 1934 earthquake, and again in 1967. A lion tops a pillar in front of the temple, while the brick building has an artificial marble facade and a gilded facade on the 1st floor.

Manga Hiti (8)

Immediately north of the palace is the sunken Manga Hiti, one of the water conduits with which Patan, and even more so Bhaktapur, are so liberally endowed. This one has a lotus-shaped pool and three wonderfully carved stone crocodile-head waterspouts. Next to it is the **Mani Mandap (7),** a pavilion built in 1700 and used for royal crownings.

Vishwanath Temple (9)

Next to the Bhimsen Temple stands the Vishwanath (Shiva) Temple. This elaborately decorated two storey temple was built in 1627 and has two large stone elephants guarding the front entrance. Shiva's vehicle, the bull, is on the other side of the temple while inside is a large lingam. As yet further proof of Shiva's influence, the roof struts are decorated with erotic themes. The temple has been recently restored.

Krishna Mandir (11)

Continuing into the square, the third temple you reach is the Krishna Mandir, which is dedicated to Krishna and was built by King Siddhinarsingh Malla. Records indicate that the temple was completed with the installation of the image on the 1st floor in 1637. With its strong Moghal influences, this stone temple is clearly of Indian design, unlike the nearby brick and timber, multi-roofed

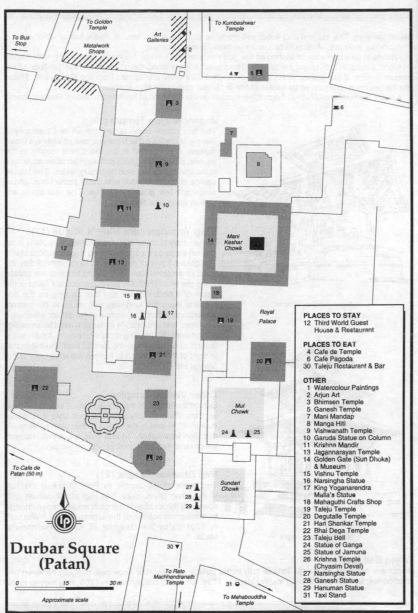

Durbar Square (Patan)

0   15   30 m

Approximate scale

To Bus Stop

To Golden Temple

Metalwork Shops

Art Galleries

To Kumbeshwar Temple

Mani Keshar Chowk

Royal Palace

Mul Chowk

Sundari Chowk

To Cafe de Patan (50 m)

To Rato Machhendranath Temple

To Mahabouddha Temple

PLACES TO STAY
12 Third World Guest House & Restaurant

PLACES TO EAT
4 Cafe de Temple
6 Cafe Pagoda
30 Taleju Restaurant & Bar

OTHER
1 Watercolour Paintings
2 Arjun Art
3 Bhimsen Temple
5 Ganesh Temple
7 Mani Mandap
8 Manga Hiti
9 Vishwanath Temple
10 Garuda Statue on Column
11 Krishna Mandir
12 Jagannarayan Temple
14 Golden Gate (Sun Dhoka) & Museum
15 Vishnu Temple
16 Narsingha Statue
17 King Yoganarendra Malla's Statue
18 Mahaguthi Crafts Shop
19 Taleju Temple
20 Degutalle Temple
21 Hari Shankar Temple
22 Bhai Dega Temple
23 Taleju Bell
24 Statue of Ganga
25 Statue of Jamuna
26 Krishna Temple (Chyasim Deval)
27 Narsingha Statue
28 Ganesh Statue
29 Hanuman Statue
31 Taxi Stand

Nepali temples. The 1st and 2nd floors are made up of a line of pavilions from the top of which rises a corncob-like shikhara. Musicians can often be heard playing upstairs.

Krishna is an incarnation of Vishnu so the god's vehicle, the man-bird Garuda, kneels with folded arms on top of a column (10) facing the temple. The stone carvings along the beam above the 1st-floor pillars recount events of the *Mahabharata* while on the 2nd floor there are scenes from the *Ramayana*. These fine friezes are accompanied by explanations in Newari of the narrative scenes.

A major festival is held here in August/September on the occasion of Krishna's birthday, Krishnasthami.

Jagannarayan Temple

Hari Shankar Temple

Jagannarayan Temple (13)

The two storey brick Jagannarayan or Charnarayan Temple is dedicated to Narayan, one of Vishnu's incarnations. It is reputed to be the oldest temple in the square, dating from 1565, although an alternative date in the late 1600s has also been suggested. The temple stands on a brick plinth with large stone lions, above which are two guardian figures. The roof struts are carved with erotic figures.

King Yoganarendra Malla's Statue (17)

Immediately north of the Hari Shankar Temple is a tall column topped by a figure of King Yoganarendra Malla. The golden figure of the kneeling king, protected by the hood of a cobra, has been facing towards his palace since the year 1700. On top of the cobra's head is the figure of a bird: legends say that as long as the bird remains there the king may still return to his palace. Accordingly a door and window of the palace are always kept open and a hookah (a water pipe used for smoking) is kept ready for the king should he return. A rider to the legend adds that when the bird flies off, the elephants in front of the Vishwanath Temple will stroll over to the Manga Hiti for a drink!

Other Vishnu Temples

Behind the statue of the king are three smaller Vishnu temples. The small plastered shikhara-style temple was built in 1590 and is dedicated to Narsingha, Vishnu's man-lion incarnation. To one side is a small Narayan temple and behind it another Vishnu temple.

Hari Shankar Temple (21)

This three storey temple to Hari Shankar, the half Vishnu, half Shiva deity, has roof struts carved with scenes of the tortures of the damned, a strange change from the erotic scenes on the Jagannarayan. It was built in 1704-05 by the daughter of King Yoganarendra Malla.

Taleju Bell (23)

Diagonally opposite the Taleju Temple (19) in the palace complex, the large bell, hanging between two stout pillars, was erected by King Vishnu Malla in 1736. An earlier bell, erected in 1703, was moved to the

Rato Machhendranath Temple at that time. Petitioners could ring the bell to alert the king to their grievances. Shop stalls are in the building under the bell platform, and behind it is a lotus-shaped pool with a bridge over it.

Krishna Temple (26)
This attractive octagonal stone temple, also known as the Chyasim Deval, completes the 'front line' of temples in the square. The stairway to the temple, which faces the palace's Sundari Chowk, is guarded by two stone lions. The temple was built by King Vishnu Malla in 1723 and, like the square's Krishna Mandir mentioned earlier, makes a clear contrast with the usual Nepali pagoda temple designs.

Bhai Dega Temple (22)
Behind the Krishna Temple stands the squat Bhai Dega, or Biseshvar, dedicated to Shiva. It's a singularly unattractive temple although it is said to contain an impressive lingam. A few steps back from the square is another stone shikhara-style temple, clearly owing inspiration to the important Krishna Mandir of the square. This same design pops up in several other temples around Patan. The popular Cafe de Patan is just behind this temple.

Krishna Temple

ROYAL PALACE
Forming the whole eastern side of the Durbar Square is the Royal Palace of Patan. Parts of the palace were built in the 14th century, but the main construction was during the 17th and 18th centuries by Siddhinarsingh Malla, Srinivasa Malla and Vishnu Malla. The Patan palace predates the palaces of Kathmandu and Bhaktapur. It was severely damaged during the conquest of the valley by Prithvi Narayan Shah in 1768 and also by the great earthquake of 1934, but it remains one of the architectural highlights of the valley with a series of connecting courtyards and three temples dedicated to the valley's main deity, the goddess Taleju.

Bhai Dega Temple

Mul Chowk & the Taleju Temples
The central courtyard is the largest and oldest of the palace's three main chowks. Two stone lions guard the entrance to the courtyard which was built by Siddhinarsingh Malla, destroyed in a fire in 1662 and rebuilt by Srinivasa Malla in 1665-66. At the centre of the courtyard stands the small gilded **Bidya Temple.**

The palace's three Taleju temples stand around the courtyard. The doorway to the Shrine of Taleju or **Taleju Bhawani,** on the southern side of the courtyard, is flanked by the river goddesses Ganga on a tortoise (24) and Jamuna on a mythical crocodile or *makara* (25).

The five storey **Degutalle Temple** (20), topped by its circular triple roofed tower, is on the north-eastern

Taleju Bhawani

corner. The larger, square, triple roofed **Taleju Temple** (19) is directly north, looking out over Durbar Square. It was built by Siddhinarsingh Malla in 1640, rebuilt after a fire and rebuilt after the 1934 earthquake which completely demolished it. The goddess Taleju was the personal deity of the Malla kings from the 14th century, and Tantric rites were performed to her in this temple.

Sundari Chowk & Tusha Hiti

South of the larger Mul Chowk is the Sundari Chowk with its sunken tank known as the Tusha Hiti. The superbly carved stonework in the tank depicts the eight Ashta Matrikas, the eight Bhairabs and the eight Nagas. The tank was originally built in about 1670 and restored in 1960. A toy-size replica of the Krishna Mandir in the main square sits above the tank.

The courtyard is surrounded by a three storey building with finely carved struts and windows. The entrance to the courtyard from the main square is guarded by stone statues of Hanuman (29), Ganesh (28), and Vishnu as Narsingha, the man-lion (27). The gilded metal window over the entrance from the square is flanked by windows of carved ivory. Behind the Sundari Chowk, but unfortunately not open to the public, is the Royal Garden with a water tank known as the Kamal Pokhari.

Mani Keshar Chowk

The northern courtyard is entered from the square by the Golden Gate, or Sun Dhoka (14). This is the newest part of the palace, completed in 1734. The courtyard is entered through a magnificent gilded door topped by a golden torana showing Shiva, Parvati, Ganesh and Kumar. Directly above the golden door is a golden window, at which the king would make public appearances. This part of the palace is now the **Patan Museum,** and there are often exhibitions here.

There is another courtyard reached by a passage between the Mani Keshar Chowk and the Taleju Temple, but this is not open to the public. It was used for dance and drama performances during the Malla period and one wall is decorated with erotic figures.

GOLDEN TEMPLE

Also known as the Kwa Bahal, Hiranya Varna Mahavihar, or the Suwarna Mahavihara (Golden Temple), this unique Buddhist monastery is only a few minutes walk north of Durbar Square. Legends relate that the monastery was founded in the 12th century, although the earliest record of its existence is 1409. From the street a sign points to the monastery, which is entered through a doorway flanked by painted guardian lion figures. The simple entrance gives no hint of the magnificent structure in the courtyard within.

The large rectangular building has three roofs and a copper-gilded facade. Inside the shrine are images of the Buddha and Avalokitesvara and a stairway leads to the 1st floor where monks will show you the various Buddha images and frescoes which illustrate the walls. The life of the Buddha is illustrated in a frieze in front of the main shrine.

The inner courtyard has a railed walk-way around three sides. Leather shoes and other leather articles must be removed if you leave the walkway and enter the inner courtyard itself. In the centre of the courtyard is a small but very richly decorated three storey temple crowned by a golden roof with an extremely ornate *gajur* (a bell-shaped top). Look for the sacred tortoises who potter around in the courtyard; they are temple guardians. The monastery was dedicated by a Patan merchant grown rich from trade with Tibet.

KUMBESHWAR TEMPLE

Directly north of Durbar Square is one of the valley's three five storey temples. The others are the towering Nyatapola Temple of Bhaktapur and the smaller Panch Mukhi Hanuman of the old Royal Palace in Kathmandu.

The Kumbeshwar Temple dominates the streets around it and is said to date from

1392, when it was completed by Jayasthiti Malla, making it the oldest extant temple in Patan. The temple is noted for its fine proportions and elegant woodcarvings and there are numerous statues and sculptures around the courtyard dating from a number of Nepali dynasties, from the Licchavis to the Mallas. They include a particularly fine Ganesh figure. The temple is, however, dedicated to Shiva, as indicated by the large Nandi, or bull, facing the temple inside the main entrance.

The temple platform has two ponds whose water is said to come straight from the holy lake at Gosainkund, a long trek north of the valley (see the Trekking chapter). An annual ritual bath in the Kumbeshwar Temple's tank is claimed to be as meritorious as making the arduous walk to Gosainkund.

South of the courtyard is an important **Bhairab temple** with a life-size wooden image of the god. Also on the southern side of the Kumbeshwar Temple is the single storey **Baglamukhi Temple** where the goddess is represented by the small temple's gilded archway with its canopy of snakes. On the western side of the Kumbeshwar courtyard is the large **Konti Hiti tank**, a popular gathering place for local women.

Also on the western side, the Kumbeshwar Technical School, which was established to train local untouchables, sells very good-value carpets and woollen jumpers and has a small display area on the ground floor (see Things to Buy).

Thousands of pilgrims visit the temple during the Janai Purnima festival in July and August each year to worship the silver and gold lingam which is set up in the tank. It's a colourful occasion with bathers immersing themselves in the tank while members of the Brahman and Chhetri castes replace the sacred thread they wear looped across their left shoulder. *Jhankris* (sorcerers) beating drums and wearing colourful headdresses and skirts dance around the temple to complete the dramatic scene.

UMA MAHESHWAR TEMPLE

There are a number of other interesting temples and bahals in this northern area of Patan. Returning from the Kumbeshwar Temple to Durbar Square the small and inconspicuous double roofed Uma Maheshwar Temple is set back from the road on its eastern side. Peer inside the temple where you can see (a light will help) a very beautiful black-stone relief of Shiva and Parvati in the pose known as Uma Maheshwar – the god sitting cross-legged with his shakti leaning against him rather seductively.

BISHWAKARMA TEMPLE

Walk south from Durbar Square through the Hauga area with its many brassware shops and workshops. There is a small bahal almost immediately on your right (west) and then a laneway also leading west. A short distance down this lane is the brick Bishwakarma Temple, with its entire facade covered in sheets of embossed copper. Directly above the doorway is what looks like a Star of David. The temple is dedicated to carpenters and craftspeople and, as if in proof, you can hear the steady clump and clang of metalworkers' hammers from nearby workshops.

Returning to the main road running south from Durbar Square you soon come to a chaitya shrine of Lakshmi Narayan on the

Bishwakarma Temple

eastern side of the road and the **I Baha Bahil monastery** on the western side. The monastery dates from 1427 but is now rather run-down and decrepit; part of it is being used as a school. A little further south is the old but recently restored **Chakba Lunhiti tank** with three waterspouts.

RATO MACHHENDRANATH TEMPLE

Continue south from Durbar Square for a few more minutes to the Rato (Red) Machhendranath Temple, on the western side of the road. Rato Machhendranath, the god of rain and plenty, comes in a variety of incarnations. To Buddhists he is the Tantric edition of Avalokitesvara while to Hindus he is another version of Shiva.

Standing in a large, spacious courtyard the three storey temple dates from 1673, although an earlier temple may have existed on the site since 1408. The temple's four elaborately carved doorways are each guarded by lion figures and at ground level on the four corners of the temple plinth are reliefs of a curious yeti-like creature. A diverse collection of animals (including peacocks, horses, bulls, lions, elephants and fish) top the pillars facing the northern side of the temple; they are the Tibetan symbols for the months of the year. The metal roof is supported by struts, each showing Avalokitesvara standing above figures being tortured in hell. Prayer wheels are set into the base of the temple.

The Machhendranath image is just a crudely carved piece of red-painted wood, but each year during the Red Machhendranath celebrations it is paraded around the town on a temple chariot. The complex celebration moves the image from place to place over a period of several weeks in the month of Baisakh (April/May), finally ending at Jawlakhel where the chariot is disassembled.

Occurring on a 12 year cycle (the next time will be in 2003) the procession continues out of Patan to the village of Bungamati, five km to the south. Dragging the heavy chariot along this bumpy and often uphill track is no easy feat. In the village the god has another temple where, since 1593, it has been the custom for the image to spend six months of each year. The chariot is returned to Patan (usually on a palanquin) for the other six months.

MINANATH TEMPLE

To the eastern side of the main road from Durbar Square is a two storey temple dedicated to a Buddhist Bodhisattva who is considered to be the brother of Rato Machhendranath. The Minanath image is also towed around town during the Rato

Rato Machhendranath Temple

Minanath Temple

Machhendranath festival, but in a much smaller chariot. The temple originally dates from the Licchavi period but has undergone several recent restorations and 'improvements' and has roof struts carved with figures of multi-armed goddesses, all extraordinarily brightly painted. A large prayer wheel stands in a cage beside the temple.

MAHABOUDDHA TEMPLE

Despite its height, the Temple of the Thousand Buddhas, or Mahabouddha Temple, is not immediately visible because it is tightly surrounded by other buildings. It is a shikhara-style temple, modelled after the original Mahabouddha Temple at Bodhgaya in India, where the Buddha gained enlightenment.

The temple takes its name from the terracotta tiles with which it is covered, each bearing an image of the Buddha. The temple is believed to have originally been built in 1585 although some sources suggest an earlier date. Whatever its first construction, it suffered severe damage in the 1934 earthquake and was completely rebuilt. Unfortunately, without plans to work from, the rebuilders ended up with a different-looking temple and there were enough bricks left over to construct a smaller shikhara-style shrine to Maya Devi, the Buddha's mother. It stands to the southwest of the Mahabouddha.

The Mahabouddha Temple is about 10 minutes walk south-west of Durbar Square. An arrow signpost points down a lane full of curio shops leading to the temple, but if you have trouble finding it simply ask directions. The roof terrace of the shops at the back of the courtyard gives you a good view of the temple.

RUDRA VARNA MAHAVIHARA

Also known as Uku Bahal, this Buddhist monastery near the Mahabouddha Temple is one of the best known in Patan. A large rectangular structure with two storey gilded roofs encloses a courtyard absolutely packed with interesting bits and pieces. There are dorjes, bells, banners, peacocks, elephants, Garudas, rampant goats, kneeling devotees and a regal-looking statue of a Rana general. The lions are particularly curious – apart from regular Nepali ones, seated on pillars with one paw raised in salute, there are also a couple with a decidedly British appearance, looking as if they should be guarding a statue of Queen Victoria in her 'not amused' incarnation rather than a colourful Nepali monastery.

As you enter the courtyard look for the finely carved wooden struts on the right. They are said to be amongst the oldest of this type in the valley and prior to a recent restoration they were actually behind the monastery, but were moved to this safer location inside the courtyard. The monastery in its present form probably dates from the 19th century, but certain features and the actual site are much older.

HAKA BAHAL

Take the road west from the southern end of Durbar Square, past the Cafe de Patan, and you soon come to the Haka Bahal, a typical

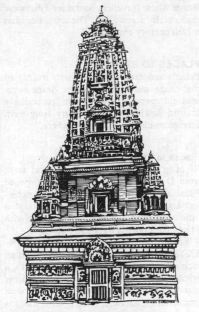
Mahabouddha Temple

rectangular building with an internal court-yard. Traditionally, Patan's Kumari (living goddess) is a daughter of one of the priests of this monastery.

ASHOKAN STUPAS
The four stupas marking the boundaries of Patan are said to have been built when the great Buddhist emperor Ashoka visited the valley 2500 years ago. Although remains of all four can still be seen today they probably bear little similarity to the original stupas. The Northern Stupa is just beyond the Kumbeshwar Temple, not far from Durbar Square. It's well preserved and whitewashed. The other three are all grassed over. The Southern, or Lagan, Stupa is just south of the bus stand and is the largest of the four. The smaller western, or Pulchok, Stupa is beside the main road from Kathmandu through to Jawlakhel and directly opposite the Hotel Narayani. Finally, the small Eastern, or Teta, Stupa is well to the east of centre, across the Ring Road and just beyond a small river.

ZOO
Nepal's only zoo is in the southern part of Patan, just north of Jawlakhel. It includes a reasonably extensive collection of Nepali wildlife, including rhinos, tigers, leopards, monkeys and birds. It is yet another depressing animal prison, although there are plans afoot to give it a major revamp.

Keen naturalists, students of the grotesque and young kids may still enjoy a visit – admission is only Rs 10. Palm readers and their clients gather in the dusty park in front of the zoo entrance and, amongst other things, may well be able to tell you which animal you will be when you are reincarnated.

JAWLAKHEL
The 'Tibetan Refugee Camp' is no longer really a camp at all, but a large centre for carpet production. It was established in 1960 with help from the International Red Cross and the Swiss government and employs 1000 refugees in the production of Tibetan carpets. This is where the enormous carpet industry

of today got its start, and it is still the best place to begin if you want to buy a carpet.

You may well be able to buy cheaper carpets outside the camp, but those in the shops by the entrance have marked prices so you can get a good idea of values (other Tibetan crafts are also on sale). You can go inside to the workshop area and see the carpets being made (see also Things to Buy).

KOTESHWAR MAHADEV TEMPLE
Actually outside the Patan city limits, the important temple of Koteshwar Mahadev is just north of the confluence of the Manohara and Hanumante rivers, which in turn joins the Bagmati River. Mahadev means 'great god', the usual term for Shiva, but Koteshwar can also be translated as 'millions of gods' so this is a temple of Shiva with many faces, a particularly powerful form of Lord Shiva. The shrine's Shiva lingam is said to date from the 8th century.

A little south of the temple is the **Kuti Bahal** where travellers bound for Tibet were customarily farewelled. The monastery has a 15th century chaitya.

PLACES TO STAY
Patan's accommodation consists mainly of mid-range and top-end places. Some overseas aid agencies are in Patan, particularly around Jawlakhel, and many long-term foreign residents of Nepal live here.

Places to Stay – bottom end
Right in the centre of Patan, a short walk from Durbar Square, the popular *Cafe de Patan* also has rooms. The position is excellent and the rooms are pleasant, although a little overpriced. Clean singles/doubles with shared bathroom are Rs 250/300.

The *Third World Guest House* (☎ 01-522187) has an even better location, with all rooms having views over the square. It's a privilege you pay for, however, as the rooms cost $15 with common bath, and $20 with attached bath, although there is some room to negotiate.

Places to Stay – middle

Patan has a popular mid-range hotel if you'd like a complete break from Kathmandu. The *Aloha Inn* (☎ 01-522796; fax 524571) is in the Jawlakhel area, not too far from the southern edge of the old city. Singles/ doubles here are $26/36 plus 12% tax. It's a friendly place, clean, well kept and quiet, and is popular with people working at the aid agencies in the area. There's a very pleasant garden.

Close by and a little closer to the old city is the new *Hotel Clarion* (☎ 01-524512; fax 224464), which is set in a pleasant garden but is still uncomfortably close to the noisy road. Rooms here cost $40/45.

Places to Stay – top end

Patan also has a number of top-end hotels although none of them are close enough to the interesting centre of the old city to be really convenient. Two hotels are found very close to the UN office in Kopundol.

The *Summit Hotel* (☎ 01-521894; fax 523737) tops a hillock in the Kopundol area and has great views across the river to Kathmandu and the distant mountains. There's a very beautiful garden with a swimming pool – a real pleasure in hot weather. The Summit Hotel's inconvenient location is its only drawback; finding taxis can sometimes be difficult and taxi drivers can be reluctant to take you there without extra payment. Standard singles/doubles cost $65/80, or $10 more with mountain views, all plus 12%. There are some budget rooms with common bath and no views for $25/30. There's a pleasant bar and the Garden Restaurant turns out superb food.

Also topping the Kopundol hill is the nearby *Hotel Greenwich Village* (☎ 01-521780, 526683) with singles/doubles at $60/70. There's a top-floor restaurant to take advantage of the view.

Two other Patan hotels are more distinctly in the top-end price bracket. The *Hotel Narayani* (☎ 01-525015; fax 521291) has a garden, a swimming pool and singles/doubles at $70/85, plus 14% tax. The modern *Hotel Himalaya* (☎ 01-523900; fax 523909) has terrific views, a swimming pool, tennis and badminton courts and is at the top of the Kathmandu price range with rooms from $105/115 plus 14%.

PLACES TO EAT

Just a few steps from the south-western corner of Durbar Square the small *Cafe de Patan* is a long-running favourite with two pleasant open-air dining areas – a small courtyard and a rooftop garden. It's a good place for a drink, snack or even a meal. It turns out a superb lassi and a number of good-value dishes from Rs 25 to Rs 50. See the Things to Buy section below about the music you hear with your meal. A little shop just across the alley sells delicious yoghurt in little clay cups for Rs 6.

Overlooking the square, the pleasant, nicely decorated *Third World Restaurant* has a brilliant rooftop area with views over Patan and on a clear day, pagodas with a Himalayan backdrop. Snacks are around Rs 60, burgers, pastas and sandwiches around Rs 80.

The *Cafe de Temple* on the northern edge of the square has excellent views from the roof, and mediocre food, such as garlic chicken and chips for Rs 90. The *Cafe Pagoda* also looks directly onto this northern part of the square, but is tucked off the least interesting corner.

At the opposite end of the square is the *Taleju Restaurant & Bar*. Head for the 5th-floor terrace, as the views from here are outstanding, especially on a clear day when you have the snow-capped Ganesh Himal as a backdrop. The food comes a distant second.

Near the zoo roundabout at Jawlakhel the *German Bakery* does cakes, pastries, cold drinks and sandwiches. At the city gate, by the Patan bus stop, there are a few budget possibilities.

THINGS TO BUY

Patan has many small handicraft shops and for certain crafts it is the best place in the valley. The Tibetan Jawlakhel area in the south of Patan is the place for Tibetan crafts and carpets. There is a string of carpet shops as you enter Jawlakhel, and a shop front, Khukuri House, is the official supplier of khukuri knives to the British Gurkha regiments.

Those interested in crafts should definitely visit the string of interesting shops at Kopundol, just to the south of the main Patan bridge. A number are run as part of nonprofit development organisations, so their prices are fair, and the money actually goes to the craftspeople, sometimes as training and product development.

One of the best of these organisations is Mahaguthi, which was established with the help of Oxfam. It now has three shops and it sells a wide range of crafts produced by thousands of people. Amongst other things they sell beautiful handwoven cotton cloth (dhaka), rice paper, pottery, block prints, woven bamboo, woodcrafts, jewellery, knitwear, embroidery and Mithila paintings. The Kopundol shop is on the right as you go up the hill, but there are also shops on Durbar Square, Patan, and on Durbar Marg, Kathmandu, towards the Royal Palace from the Hotel de l'Annapurna.

Near the Kumbeshwar Temple, the Kumbeshwar Technical School provides the untouchable community of Patan with skills and they produce excellent carpets, jumpers and woodwork. You can buy direct, although they do not have a formal outlet.

Metalwork

Patan is the centre for bronze-casting and other metalwork. The statues you see on sale in Kathmandu will most probably have been made in Patan and there are a number of excellent metalwork shops just north of Durbar Square. They have fine images of Buddha, the Green and White Taras and other figures from the Tantric Buddhist pantheon. Good-quality gold-plated and painted bronze figures will cost Rs 2000 to Rs 5000 for smaller ones, up to more than Rs 10,000 for large images.

Woodcarving

Lee Berch (☎ 01-522627), PO Box 2633, Kathmandu, operates a woodcarving atelier in Jawlakhel, Patan, which could be of interest to serious aficionados.

Paintings

Immediately north of Durbar Square, just beyond the Bhimsen Temple, are a number of interesting shops selling paintings. The Arjun Art Gallery has Sherpa-style paintings rather like the naive art of the Balinese 'young artist'. It's clearly something developed for the tourist trade but never mind, they're nicely done and you can have all of the Kathmandu Valley, or even all of Nepal, in one painting. Prices range from around Rs 2000 to Rs 4000.

A couple of doors down is the Madhu Chandra Art Gallery which has excellent paintings of Nepali birds by CB Singh. The prices range from Rs 300 or Rs 400 and up. The BB Thapa Gallery (☎ 01-524332) in Jawlakhel also has interesting artwork.

Carpets

Those interested in carpets must visit Jawlakhel and Bodhnath. The Tibetan 'Refugee Camp' at Jawlakhel has numerous shops on the approach road. The carpets at the Kumbeshwar Technical School (☎ 01-522271) are fairly priced, and this is possibly the only place where you can buy carpets made from 100% pure Tibetan wool.

Toys

Just south of Durbar Square is Nepalese Wooden Kits, which sells wonderful wooden toys including authentic Nepali trucks from Rs 500 to Rs 650, with auto-rickshaws for Rs 450 and rickshaws for Rs 450. You can find these toys on sale in Kathmandu (including at some of the craft shops), but they're cheaper here where they're made. The factory is only a stone's throw from the shop and it's fascinating to see the parts being cut out with pedal operated jigsaws.

Music

A pleasant attraction at the popular Cafe de Patan near Durbar Square is the selection of Indian, Nepali and Himalayan music played on cassette tapes while you eat. The tapes are sold by the adjoining shop and typically cost around Rs 200. The Cafe de Temple at the northern end of the square has a similar system.

Tigers & Goats

Nepal's national board game is *bagh chal*, which literally means 'move (chal) the tigers' (bagh). The game is played on a lined board with 25 intersecting points. One player has four tigers, the other has 20 goats and the aim is for the tiger player to 'eat' five goats by jumping over them before the goat player can encircle a single tiger and prevent it moving.

The game starts with the four tigers at the four corners of the board. Play alternates between the goats and the tigers and the goat player brings his goats on to the board one at a time. No goat can be moved from its initial position until every goat has been brought on to the board. By backing up one goat with another so that the tiger cannot jump them the goats can soon clutter up the board so effectively that the tigers cannot move. That is if the tigers haven't done a good job of eating the goats!

All you need to play is a board scratched out on the dirt and 24 bottle caps or stones as markers, but you can also buy attractive brass bagh chal sets in Kathmandu, or in Patan where they are made. ■

GETTING THERE & AWAY

You can easily get to Patan from Kathmandu whether by bicycle, taxi, bus or tempo. It's an easy five km ride from Thamel to Patan's Durbar Square. The same trip costs around Rs 80 by taxi, much less by the meter.

Buses leave regularly from the City Bus Station and drop you at the Patan city gate, a short walk from Durbar Square (Rs 2). Tempos also operate from the Kathmandu main post office as soon as they have six passengers.

Bhaktapur

Bhaktapur, also known as Bhadgaon (pronounced 'bud-gown') or the City of Devotees, is the third major town of the valley and in many ways the most mediaeval. Since the major West German-funded Bhaktapur Development Project in the 1970s, it has been a much cleaner and tidier town, but there's still a distinctly timeless air to the place. The project restored buildings, paved dirt streets and brought sewerage facilities.

The oldest part of the town is around Tachupal Tole (Dattatraya Square), to the east. Bhaktapur was the capital of the whole valley during the 14th to 16th centuries and during that time the focus of the town shifted west, to the Durbar Square area. Much of the town's great architecture dates from the end of the 17th century during the rule of King Bhupatindra Malla.

Malla Kings

As in Kathmandu and Patan, the town's important buildings date from the Malla period. Notable Malla kings of Bhaktapur include:

Yaksha Malla	1428-1482
Raya Malla	1482-1505
Eksha Mal Malla	1505-1568
Jagat Jyoti Malla	1613-1637
Jagat Prakash Malla	1644-1673
Jitamitra Malla	1673-1696
Bhupatindra Malla	1696-1722
Jaya Ranjit Malla	1722-1769

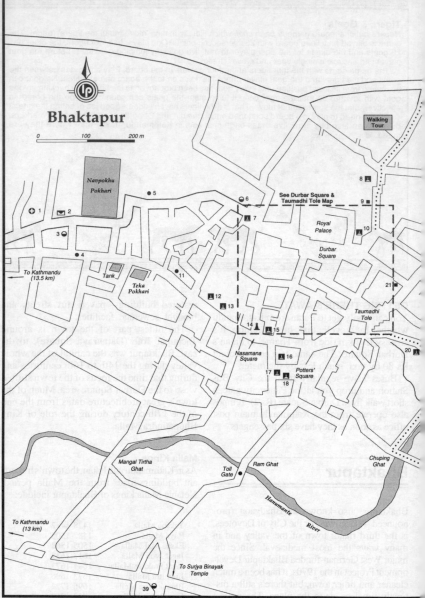

Bhaktapur

0   100   200 m

Navpokhu
Pokhari

● 5

✚ 1   ✉ 2   ● 6

◻ 7

● 3

Walking
Tour

8 ⌂

9 ▣

See Durbar Square &
Taumadhi Tole Map

Royal
Palace

10 ⌂

Durbar
Square

● 4

To Kathmandu
(13.5 km)

Tank

Teka
Pokhari

● 11

21 ⌂

◻ 12

◻ 13

Taumadhi
Tole

14 ◻ ◻ 15

20 ⌂

Nasamana
Square

◻ 16

17 ◻ ◻
18

Potters'
Square

Mangal Tirtha
Ghat

Toll
Gate ●

Ram Ghat

Chuping
Ghat

Hanumante River

To Kathmandu
(13 km)

To Suriya Binayak
Temple

39 ●

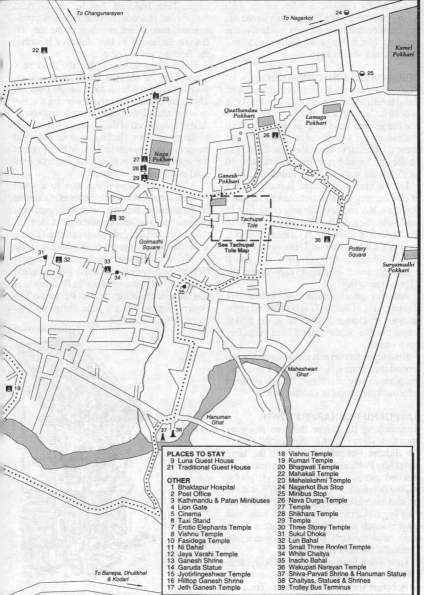

PLACES TO STAY
9 Luna Guest House
21 Traditional Guest House

OTHER
1 Bhaktapur Hospital
2 Post Office
3 Kathmandu & Patan Minibuses
4 Lion Gate
5 Cinema
6 Taxi Stand
7 Erotic Elephants Temple
8 Vishnu Temple
10 Fasidega Temple
11 Ni Bahal
12 Jaya Varahi Temple
13 Ganesh Shrine
14 Garuda Statue
15 Jyotirlingeshwar Temple
16 Hilltop Ganesh Shrine
17 Jeth Ganesh Temple
18 Vishnu Temple
19 Kumari Temple
20 Bhagwati Temple
22 Mahakali Temple
23 Mahalakshmi Temple
24 Nagarkot Bus Stop
25 Minibus Stop
26 Nava Durga Temple
27 Temple
28 Shikhara Temple
29 Temple
30 Three Storey Temple
31 Sukul Dhoka
32 Lun Bahal
33 Small Three Roofed Temple
34 White Chaitya
35 Inacho Bahal
36 Wakupati Narayan Temple
37 Shiva-Parvati Shrine & Hanuman Statue
38 Chaityas, Statues & Shrines
39 Trolley Bus Terminus

Ranjit Malla enjoyed a relationship with King Prithvi Narayan Shah which saved his city from destruction and also resulted in the deposed Malla kings of Kathmandu and Patan taking shelter here.

ORIENTATION & INFORMATION

Bhaktapur rises up on the northern bank of the Hanumante River. It's basically a pedestrian's city and much better for it. Minibuses and taxis stop at the Navpokhu Pokhari on the western edge of town. If you come to Bhaktapur by trolley bus the stop is on the main road bypassing Bhaktapur, a 10 to 15 minute walk south of Taumadhi Tole.

For the visitor Bhaktapur is really a town of one curving road, punctuated by squares. From the bus and taxi halt you come first to the Durbar Square, then Taumadhi Tole with the famous five storey Nyatapola Temple, then to Tachupal Tole, or Dattatraya Square. Keep walking in that direction and you'll eventually reach Nagarkot, high up on the edge of the valley.

All foreigners visiting Bhaktapur are charged a fee of Rs 50. This is collected at the entrance to Durbar Square, or at the bridge across the river when coming from the trolley bus terminus.

Bhaktapur has several cheap guest houses around the centre of town and it's a fascinating place to stay overnight. There's a tourist information counter in Durbar Square.

NAVPOKHU POKHARI TO TOWN

Approaching Bhaktapur the road skirts an open field (also known as the Tundikhel) and the **Siddha Pokhari tank**. From the large Navpokhu Pokhari tank, follow the road a few hundred metres to Durbar Square. If you're staying overnight in Bhaktapur you'll want to get into town as quickly as possible to drop off your bags, otherwise, the southern route into town is much more interesting since it is the main road through Bhaktapur connecting Taumadhi Tole and Tachupal Tole.

Turn south from the corner of Navpokhu Pokhari and then left on the road, immediately before the town's Lion Gate. You pass a small tank on your right and then the much

larger **Teka Pokhari**. Just before the next major road junction, to your left, is the constricted, tunnel-like entrance to the tiny **Ni Bahal**, dedicated to the Maitraya Buddha, the Buddha yet to come.

Cross the junction, where the road runs downhill to the **Mangal Tirtha Ghat**, and on your left is the red-brick **Jaya Varahi Temple**. There are elaborately carved wooden toranas over the central door and the window above it. At the western end of the temple is the entrance to the upper floor, flanked by stone lions and banners. Two ornate windows, on either side of the upper torana, were at one time coloured gold and some traces remain.

A few more steps brings you to a small Ganesh shrine jutting into the street. Continue to **Nasamana Square**, which is somewhat decrepit but has a Garuda statue without a temple. Almost immediately after this is a second square with the Jyotirlingeshwar, a shikhara-style temple which houses an important lingam. Behind the shrine is an attractive hiti, one of the many sunken water conduits in Bhaktapur. A few more steps brings you to the turn-off to Potters' Square while a little further on you come to Taumadhi Tole.

Jaya Varahi Temple

DURBAR SQUARE

Bhaktapur's Durbar Square is much larger and more spacious than Kathmandu's and much less crowded with temples than Patan's. It wasn't planned that way: Victorian illustrations show the square packed with temples and buildings, but the disastrous earthquake of 1934 destroyed many of them and today empty plinths show where some once stood.

Erotic Elephants Temple (2)

Just before you enter the square, coming from the bus stop, pause for a little bit of Newari humour. On your left just before the entranceway to the square is a hiti. A few steps before that, on the south side of the road, perhaps 100m before the entranceway, is a tiny double roofed Shiva-Parvati temple with some erotic carvings on its temple struts. One of these shows a pair of copulating elephants, in the missionary position! It's a hathi (elephant) Kama Sutra.

Ugrachandi & Bhairab Statues

The square is entered from the western end, passing by an entry gate with two large stone lions built by King Bhupatindra Malla. On the northern wall are statues (6) of the terrible Bhairab and the equally terrible Ugrachandi, or Durga, the fearsome manifestation of Shiva's consort Parvati. The statues date from 1701 and it's said that the unfortunate sculptor had his hands cut off afterwards, to prevent him from duplicating his masterpieces.

Ugrachandi has 18 arms holding various weapons and symbols and she is in the act of very casually killing a demon with a trident. Bhairab has to make do with just 12 arms but the god and goddess are both garlanded with necklaces of human heads! The gates and courtyard which these powerful figures guard are of no particular importance.

Western End Temples

A number of less significant temples crowd the western end of Durbar Square. They include the **Rameshwar Temple** (7) to Shiva and the **Bhadri Temple** (8) to Vishnu as Narayan. In front of them is an impressive larger **Krishna temple** (9) and just beyond that is a shikhara-style **Shiva temple** (10) erected by King Jitamitra Malla in 1674.

King Bhupatindra Malla's Column (21)

King Bhupatindra Malla was the best known of the Malla kings of Bhaktapur and had a great influence on the art and architecture of the town. Like the similar column in Patan's Durbar Square this one was a copy of the original in Kathmandu. The king sits with folded arms, studying the magnificent entrance gate to his palace.

Vatsala Durga Temple (22) & Taleju Bell (20)

Beside the king's statue and directly in front of the palace is the stone Vatsala Durga Temple, built by King Jagat Prakash Malla in 1672. The shikhara-style temple has some similarities to the Krishna Mandir in Patan. In front of the temple is the large Taleju Bell which was erected by King Jaya Ranjit Malla in 1737 to call the faithful to prayer at the Taleju Temple.

A second, smaller bell stands on the temple's plinth

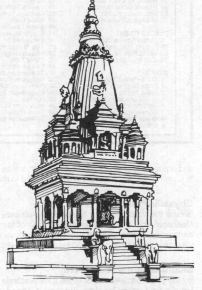

Vatsala Durga Temple

BHAKTAPUR

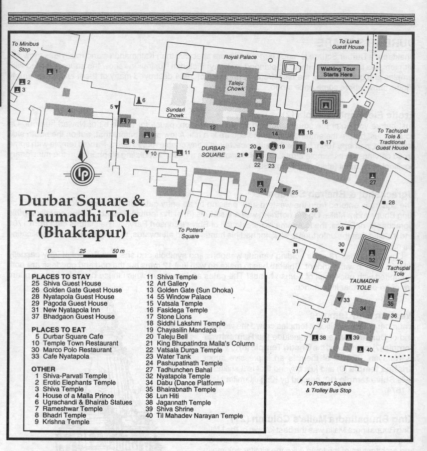

Durbar Square & Taumadhi Tole (Bhaktapur)

0   25   50 m

PLACES TO STAY
25 Shiva Guest House
26 Golden Gate Guest House
28 Nyatapola Guest House
29 Pagoda Guest House
31 New Nyatapola Inn
37 Bhadgaon Guest House

PLACES TO EAT
5 Durbar Square Cafe
10 Temple Town Restaurant
30 Marco Polo Restaurant
33 Cafe Nyatapola

OTHER
1 Shiva-Parvati Temple
2 Erotic Elephants Temple
3 Shiva Temple
4 House of a Malla Prince
6 Ugrachandi & Bhairab Statues
7 Rameshwar Temple
8 Bhadri Temple
9 Krishna Temple

11 Shiva Temple
12 Art Gallery
13 Golden Gate (Sun Dhoka)
14 55 Window Palace
15 Vatsala Temple
16 Fasidega Temple
17 Stone Lions
18 Siddhi Lakshmi Temple
19 Chyasilin Mandapa
20 Taleju Bell
21 King Bhupatindra Malla's Column
22 Vatsala Durga Temple
23 Water Tank
24 Pashupatinath Temple
27 Tadhunchen Bahal
32 Nyatapola Temple
34 Dabu (Dance Platform)
35 Bhairabnath Temple
36 Lun Hiti
38 Jagannath Temple
39 Shiva Shrine
40 Til Mahadev Narayan Temple

and is popularly known as the 'barking bell'. It was erected by King Bhupatindra Malla in 1721, supposedly to counteract a vision he had in a dream, and to this day dogs are said to bark and whine if the bell is rung.

Chyasilin Mandapa (19)
Beside the Vatsala Durga Temple is an attractive water tank (23) and in front of that is the Chyasilin Mandapa. This octagonal temple was one of the finest in the square until it was destroyed by the 1934 earthquake. Using some of the temple's original components it has been totally rebuilt. There's a good view over the square from inside – note the metal construction inside this outwardly authentic building.

Siddhi Lakshmi Temple (18)
By the south-eastern corner of the palace stands the stone Siddhi Lakshmi Temple. The steps up to the temple are flanked by male and female attendants each leading a rather reluctant child and a rather

eager-looking dog. On successive levels the stairs are flanked by horses, rhinos, man-lions and camels. The 17th century temple marks the dividing line between the main Durbar Square and its secondary part, at the eastern end of the Royal Palace. Behind the temple is another **Vatsala temple** (15) while to one side of it are two rather lost-looking large stone lions (17), standing by themselves out in the middle of the square.

Pashupatinath Temple (24)

Behind the Vatsala Durga Temple is the Pashupatinath Temple, dedicated to Shiva as Pashupati. The temple dates from the 17th century and is a replica of the main shrine at Pashupatinath. It's notable for the erotic carvings on the roof struts which show some exhausting looking positions.

Fasidega Temple (16)

The large, white, rather ugly Fasidega Temple is dedicated to Shiva and stands in the centre of the secondary part of Durbar Square. There are various viewpoints around the valley – the Changu Narayan Temple is one of them – from where you can study Bhaktapur at a distance. In each case the white bulk of the Fasidega is always an easy landmark to pick out. The temple sits on a six level plinth with elephant guardians at the bottom of the steps, lions and cows above them.

Tadhunchen Bahal (27)

The southern and eastern side of the secondary part of the square is made up of double storey *dharamsalas* (rest houses for pilgrims), now used as shops. As you enter the street leading east from the square, the Tadhunchen Bahal or Chatur Varna Mahavihara is an ancient-looking monastery on the southern side. In the inner courtyard the roof struts on the eastern side have some highly unusual carvings showing the tortures of the damned. In one a snake is wrapped around a man, another shows two rams butting an unfortunate's head from opposite sides, while a third strut shows a nasty tooth extraction being performed with a large pair of pliers! The monastery dates from the 15th century.

ROYAL PALACE

Bhaktapur's Royal Palace was founded by Yaksha Malla and added to by successive kings, particularly Bhupatindra Malla. As with the old palaces of Kathmandu and Patan, visitors are restricted to certain areas, but only seven courtyards remain of the 99 the palace was once claimed to have. Unfortunately the palace suffered great damage in the 1934 earthquake and its subsequent reconstruction did not match its original artistry.

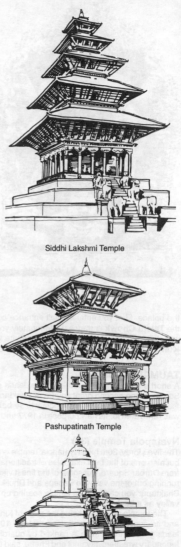

Siddhi Lakshmi Temple

Pashupatinath Temple

Fasidega Temple

Hanuman-Bhairab

Art Gallery (12)

The western end of the palace has been made into an art gallery. The entrance to the gallery is flanked by figures of Hanuman the monkey god and Vishnu as Narsingha, his man-lion incarnation. These guardian figures date from 1698 and Hanuman appears in Tantric form as the four armed Hanuman-Bhairab. The gallery has a fine collection of Hindu and Buddhist paintings, palm-leaf manuscripts, thangkas and metal, stone and woodcrafts. This part of the palace was once known as the Malati Chowk. Admission to the gallery is Rs 5 and it is open daily, except Tuesday, from 10.30 am to 4 pm.

Golden Gate (13) & 55 Window Palace (14)

Adjoining the gallery the magnificent Golden Gate, or Sun Dhoka, is the entrance to the 55 Window Palace. The Golden Gate is generally agreed to be the single most important piece of art in the whole valley. The gate and palace were built by King Bhupatindra Malla but not completed until 1754 during the reign of Jaya Ranjit Malla.

A Garuda, the vehicle of Vishnu, tops the gate and is shown disposing of a number of serpents, the Garuda's sworn enemies. The four headed and 16 armed figure of the goddess Taleju Bhawani is below the Garuda and directly over the door. She is the family deity of the Malla dynasty and there are temples to her in the royal palaces in Kathmandu, Patan and Bhaktapur.

The Golden Gate opens to the inner courtyards of the palace. First you enter a small entrance courtyard then the larger **Mul Chowk** which leads round to the **Taleju Chowk** entrance. Unfortunately you cannot enter Taleju Chowk and a military guard ensures you don't try. The guard will, however, invite you to peer in from the doorway. Beyond Taleju Chowk is **Kumari Chowk** and **Sundari Chowk** with its bathing tank, the Kamal Pokhari.

TAUMADHI TOLE

A short street, lined with tourist shops, leads downhill from behind the Pashupatinath Temple in Durbar Square to the second great square of Bhaktapur, the Taumadhi Tole. Here you find the highest temple in the valley and also Cafe Nyatapola whose balconies provide a great view over the square. The building was renovated for its new purpose in 1977 and even has some finely carved roof struts with erotic themes.

Nyatapola Temple (32)

The five storey, 30m high Nyatapola Temple is not only the highest temple in the whole Kathmandu Valley, but also one of the best examples of traditional Nepali temple architecture. The towering temple is visible from Durbar Square, but some of the finest views of the temple are from further away. If you take the road running out of the valley to Banepa and Dhulikhel or walk up towards the Surjya Binayak Temple south of Bhaktapur you can see the temple soaring up above the other buildings, with the hills at the edge of the valley as a background.

The temple was built during the reign of King Bhupatindra Malla in 1702 and its design was so elegant and its construction so well done that the 1934 earthquake caused only minor damage. The stairway leading up to the temple is flanked by guardian figures at each plinth level. The bottom plinth has the legendary wrestlers Jayamel and Phattu, said to have the strength of 10 normal men. On the plinths above are two elephants, then two lions, two griffins and finally two goddesses, Baghini in the form of a tiger and

HUGH FINLAY

GLENN BEANLAND

BHAKTAPUR

Top: The staggered roof of the Nyatapola Temple dominates the Bhaktapur skyline at Taumadhi Tole.

Bottom: Stone guardians, Nyatapola Temple.

ADAM MCCROW

SONIA BERTO

BHAKTAPUR

Top: The top of the Golden Gate, or Sun Dhoka, depicts Garuda disposing of a number of serpents, and the four-headed, sixteen armed-goddess Taleju Bhawan.

Bottom: Durbar Square, Bhaktapur

Singhini in the form of a lion. Each figure is said to be 10 times as strong as the figure on the level below and presiding over all of them, but hidden away inside the temple, is the mysterious Tantric goddess Siddhi Lakshmi to whom the temple is dedicated.

Only the temple's priests can see the image of the goddess, but the temple's 108 carved and painted roof struts depict her in her various forms. Various legends and tales relate to the temple and its enigmatic inhabitant. One is that she maintains a balance with the powers of the terrifying Bhairab, comfortably ensconced in his own temple just across the square.

Bhairabnath Temple (35)

The triple roofed Bhairabnath Temple (also known as the Kasi Vishwanath or Akash Bhairab) has an unusual rectangular plan and has had a somewhat chequered history. It was originally built as a one storey temple in the early 17th century but was rebuilt with two storeys by King Bhupatindra Malla in 1717. The 1934 earthquake caused great damage to the temple and it was completely rebuilt and the 3rd floor added. A recent restoration should have been completed by now.

Casually stacked beside the temple you can see the enormous wheels and other parts of the temple chariot on which the image of Bhairab is conveyed around town during the Bisket festival. Curiously, despite Bhairab's fearsome powers and his massive temple, his image is only about 30 cm high! A small hole in the central door is used to push offerings into the temple's interior, but the actual entrance to the Bhairabnath Temple is through the small **Betal Temple,** behind the main temple. The temple is guarded by two brass lions and there's a host of interesting details on the front.

Bhairabnath Temple

Til Mahadev Narayan Temple (40)

It's easy to miss the square's third interesting temple, the Til Mahadev Narayan, as it is hidden away behind the buildings on the southern side of the square. You can enter the temple's courtyard through a narrow entrance through those buildings, or through an arched entrance facing west, just to the south of the square.

This double roofed Vishnu temple has a Garuda kneeling on a high pillar in front, flanked by pillars bearing Vishnu's conch and chakra symbols. Some of the temple's struts also have Garudas. A lingam in a yoni stands in a wooden cage in front and to one side of the temple. Despite the temple's neglected setting it is actually an important place of pilgrimage and one of the oldest temple sites in the town: an inscription indicates that the site has been in use since 1080. Another inscription states that the image of Til Mahadev installed inside the temple dates from 1170.

Til Mahadev Narayan Temple

POTTERS' SQUARE

Potters' Square can be approached from Durbar Square, Taumadhi Tole or along the southern road into town from Siddha Pokhari and Navpokhu Pokhari. You also pass right by the square when walking into town from the trolley bus stop.

On the northern side of the square a small hillock is topped by a Ganesh shrine and a shady pipal tree. There are fine views from here over the river to the hills south of Bhaktapur. The square itself has two small temples, a solid-brick **Vishnu temple** and the double roofed **Jeth Ganesh Temple**. The latter is an indicator of how long the activity all around the square has been going on – the temple was donated by a wealthy potter in 1646 and to this day its priest is a potter. Pottery is very clearly what this square is all about. Under the shady open verandahs or tin-roofed sheds all around the square, the potters' wheels spin and clay is thrown. In the square itself, literally thousands of finished pots sit out in the sun to dry, and are sold in the stalls around the square and between the square and Taumadhi Tole.

TAUMADHI TOLE TO TACHUPAL TOLE

The curving main road through Bhaktapur runs from beside the Bhairabnath Temple in Taumadhi Tole to Tachupal Tole, the old centre of town. The first stretch of the street is a busy shopping thoroughfare with a constant hum of activity and everything is on sale, from brass pots to video cassettes, from porters' tumplines (the leather or cloth strips across the forehead or chest used to support a load carried on the back) to tourists' mineral water.

As the road makes its first bend there are two interesting old buildings on the right-hand (southern) side. The **Sukul Dhoka** is a *math* (priest's house), and has superb woodcarving both on its facade and inside in the courtyard. Almost next door is the **Lun Bahal**, originally a 16th century Buddhist monastery, but which was converted into a Hindu shrine with the addition of a stone statue of Bhimsen. If you look into the sanctum, in the inner courtyard, you can see the statue, dating from 1592, complete with a ferocious-looking brass mask.

A little further along, the road opens into the **Golmadhi Square** with a deep hiti, the small, triple roofed Golmadhi Ganesh Temple and adjacent to it a white chaitya. Another short stretch of road brings you to another small open area with a *path* or pilgrim's shelter on your right. Behind it is a tank and the Inacho Bahal, described in the later Walking Tour section. A few more steps brings you to Tachupal Tole.

TACHUPAL TOLE

It's only about 10 minutes walk from the Nyatapola Temple to the square containing the Dattatraya Temple and the Pujari Math monastery. Today you stroll down a well paved street, a result of the major 'renovation' Bhaktapur underwent in the late 70s. These new-looking brick-paved streets are a real contrast to some of the muddy, potholed alleys which you can still find in the back blocks of town. South from this square a maze of narrow laneways, passageways and courtyards runs down to the ghats on the river. Tachupal Tole, also called Dattatraya Square, was probably the original central square of Bhaktapur so this is the oldest part of the town.

Dattatraya Temple

This tall, square temple was originally built in 1427 but alterations were made in 1458. Like some other important structures in the valley it was said to have been built using the timber from a single tree. The temple is dedicated to Dattatraya although the Garuda-topped pillar and the traditional weapons of Vishnu indicate that Dattatraya is actually another of Vishnu's many incarnations. He is also said to have been Shiva's teacher and is even claimed to have been a cousin of the Buddha so the temple is important to Shaivites, Vishnaivites and Buddhists.

The three storey temple is raised well above the ground on its base, around which are carved some erotic scenes. The front section, which was a later addition to the temple, stands almost separate and the

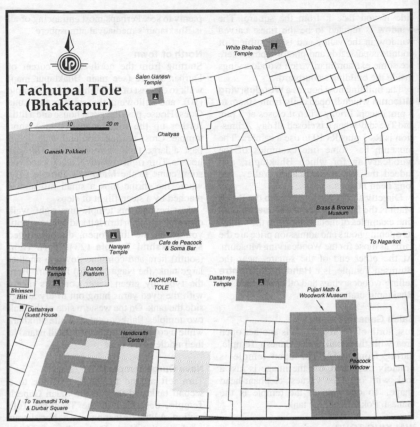

Tachupal Tole (Bhaktapur)

0   10   20 m

White Bhairab Temple

Salen Ganesh Temple

Chaityas

Ganesh Pokhari

Brass & Bronze Museum

To Nagarkot

Narayan Temple

Cafe de Peacock & Soma Bar

Bhimsen Temple

Dance Platform

TACHUPAL TOLE

Dattatraya Temple

Bhimsen Hiti

Dattatraya Guest House

Handicrafts Centre

Pujari Math & Woodwork Museum

Peacock Window

To Taumadhi Tole & Durbar Square

temple entrance is guarded by the same two Malla wrestlers who watch over the first plinth of the Nyatapola Temple.

Bhimsen Temple

At the other end of the square is the two storey Bhimsen Temple, variously dated to 1605, 1645 or 1655. The temple is squat, rectangular and open on the ground floor. It's fronted by a platform with a small double roofed Vishnu temple and a pillar topped by a brass lion. Behind it is the deeply sunken and rather pretty Bhimsen Pokhari.

Pujari Math & Museums

There are 10 buildings around the square which were originally used as maths. The best known was the Pujari Math, which has been restored by the same West German aid project which has done so much work in Bhaktapur. The Pujari Math was originally constructed in the 15th century during the reign of King Yaksha Malla, but restored in 1763. Until this century an annual caravan brought tributes to the monastery from Tibet.

The Pujari Math is principally famed for the superb peacock window, in the small alley beside the monastery, on its left-hand side if you face it from the square. The window is reputed to be the finest carved window in the valley and is the subject of countless postcards and photographs. There are some extraordinarily rich woodcarvings inside the building's courtyard.

The building now houses a **Woodcarving Museum** which is open daily from 10 am to 5 pm, except Friday when it closes at 3 pm, and Tuesday when it is closed all day. Admission is Rs 5 plus Rs 10 to use a camera. The museum has some fine examples of the woodcarving for which Bhaktapur, and indeed the whole Kathmandu Valley, has long been famous.

Directly across the square from the Pujari Math is the **Brass & Bronze Museum** with fine examples of metalwork from the valley. Its opening hours and admission price are the same as those for the Woodcarving Museum. At the other end of the square, near the Bhimsen Temple, is a **Handicrafts Centre** selling woodcarvings and other examples of Bhaktapur crafts.

Salan Ganesh Temple

Just north of Tachupal Tole is another open area with the small Salan Ganesh Temple, dating from 1654. The open temple is ornately decorated, but the image is just a rock with only the vaguest elephant-head shape. To one side of the temple is the Ganesh Pokhari, a large tank.

WALKING TOUR

Bhaktapur is a fascinating town to wander in, and the lack of traffic makes walking a real pleasure, particularly in comparison to Kathmandu where walking would be so much more enjoyable without motor vehicles to dodge. This circular walk takes you by a number of interesting temples and shrines, but in Bhaktapur it's simply observing the timeless and seemingly unchanging rituals of life which is most interesting. Look for grain laid out to dry in the sun, people collecting water or washing under the communal taps, dyed yarns hung out to dry, children's games, fascinating shops, potters at work or women pounding grain: there's

plenty to see. Perhaps most entrancing of all is Bhaktapur's mediaeval atmosphere.

North of Town

Starting from the north-eastern corner of Durbar Square (see main Bhaktapur map) walk to the east of the high Fasidega Temple (10), and following the sign to the Luna Guest House, pass the guest house and a little further up the road, a walled-in Vishnu temple. Cross the junction and walk uphill past a large tank surrounded by fine old houses. Turn right towards Nagarkot and you soon come to the **Mahakali Temple** (22), where the shrine tops a small hill and is reached by a steep flight of steps.

Just beyond this temple turn right, walk downhill and then turn left and continue until you reach the tiny, open, double roofed **Mahalakshmi Temple** (23). Turn right (south) here and continue down to another large tank, the Naga (Snake) Pokhari. Here the typically green water contrasts nicely with the dyed yarns hung out to dry alongside the tank. On the western side of the tank two temples flank a central white shikhara while a cobra rears up from a small island in the middle of the tank.

Nava Durga Temple (26)

Turn left around the tank, continue to a second tank and then to the Salan Ganesh Temple, described in the Tachupal Tole section. A little further on take a short detour north to the Nava Durga Temple. This Tantric temple is said to be the site for strange sacrificial rites. The golden door is surmounted by a golden window and is guarded by metal lions. It all contrasts nicely with the red-painted brick frontage. There's another large tank, the **Quathandau Pokhari**, just north of the temple.

Wakupati Narayan Temple (36)

Back on the route you soon come back to the main east-west road which runs through Taumadhi Tole and Tachupal Tole. Around this area there are more potters at work. Turn right and immediately on your left is the entrance to the Wakupati Narayan Temple.

The ornate, golden temple is double roofed and is fronted by a line-up of no less than four Garudas.

South of Town

Continue on to Tachupal Tole and turn left down the side of the Pujari Math; directions to its famous peacock window are well signposted. Jog right, left, right and left again then immediately on your left is the ornate little **Inacho Bahal** (35) with prayer wheels, Buddha figures and a strange miniature pagoda roof rising up on a pillar above the courtyard.

Riverside Ghats

From here the road drops down to the Hanumante River, leaving urban surroundings for rural ones and passing by a curious collection of shrines, chaityas, statues and lingams (38), including a bas-relief of a well endowed nude Shiva. Just to the left of the bridge on the **Hanuman Ghat** is a shrine with a bas-relief of Rama and Sita, guarded by a statue of their faithful ally Hanuman (37). On the nearby building are four paintings including one showing Hanuman returning to Rama from his Himalayan medicinal herb foray, clutching a whole mountain in his hand. It's said that he paused here for a rest.

Cross the bridge and then take a hairpin turn back from the road onto a pleasant paved footpath. This rural stroll ends by another temple complex where you cross the river by the **Chuping Ghat**. Here, as at the Hanuman Ghat or the Ram Ghat by the bridge to the trolley bus stop, there are areas for ritual bathing and cremations.

Khalna Tole

Above the river is the open area of Khalna Tole, the centre for the spectacular activities during the annual mid-April Bisket Jatra. Bhairab's huge triple roofed chariot is assembled from the parts scattered beside the Bhairabnath Temple and behind the Nyatapola Temple in Taumadhi Tole. The chariot is hauled here with Betal, his sidekick from the tiny temple behind the Bhairabnath

Temple, riding out front like a ship's figure-head while Bhadrakali, his consort, accompanies them in her own chariot. The images of the gods shelter in the octagonal *path* during the festival and a towering 25m high lingam is erected in the stone yoni base. Bisket ends and the Nepali New Year starts when the lingam is taken down. Bhairab and Betal return to Taumadhi Tole while Bhadrakali goes back to her shrine by the river.

The circular walk ends with a gentle climb back into the town, emerging at the southern side of Taumadhi·Tole.

SURJYA BINAYAK TEMPLE

About a km out of town this 17th century Ganesh temple is said to be a good place to visit if you're worried about your children being late speakers! It's also popular with Nepali marriage parties. To get there take the road down past the Potters' Square to Ram Ghat, cross the river and continue to the main road by the trolley bus stop. The road continues across the other side and rises gently uphill with some fine views back over the rice paddies to Bhaktapur.

Where the road turns sharp right, a steep stairway climbs up to the temple on a forested hilltop. As you step inside the temple enclosure the very realistic-looking long-tailed rat, sitting on top of a tall pillar, immediately indicates that this temple belongs to Ganesh. The image of the god sits in an enclosure in the bottom of a shikhara and there's a second golden image on the shikhara spire. Statues of kneeling devotees face the image and the shikhara is flanked by large bells.

PLACES TO STAY

A growing number of visitors to Bhaktapur stay overnight. There's plenty to see and one of the pleasures is that once evening falls all the day-trippers from Kathmandu disappear, and don't return until after breakfast the next day. There are a number of small guest houses, all but one close to Durbar Square.

The *Golden Gate Guest House* (☎ 01-610534) is entered by a passageway from

Durbar Square or from the laneway between Durbar Square and Taumadhi Tole. The owners are friendly, there are fine views from the roof and rooms cost Rs 150/250 for singles/doubles, all with common bath. Some of the rooms have balconies and there's also a restaurant downstairs.

Entered from behind the Pashupatinath Temple on Durbar Square, the *Shiva Guest House* (☎ 01-610740) has singles/doubles at Rs 150/250 with common bath, or there's one double with attached bath at Rs 300. This is again simple and spartan with a restaurant on the top floor and rooftop.

Off the same laneway is the *New Nyatapola Inn*, which is probably overpriced at Rs 400 for a double, especially as there are no views.

Just off Durbar Square, the *Traditional Guest House* (☎ 01-611057) has plain, but adequate rooms. The position is excellent and the views from the rooftop are simply stupendous. A dal bhat dinner for guests only costs Rs 50, and singles/doubles are a reasonable Rs 150/250.

There are a couple of new places just off Taumadhi Tole which have increased the options quite a bit. The *Bhadgaon Guest House* (☎ 01-610488; fax 610481) is just off the south-western corner of the square, and again, has excellent rooftop views. The rooms are large, clean and comfortable, and cost Rs 350/500 with attached bath.

On the lane which heads off from the north-western edge of the square is the squeaky clean *Pagoda Guest House*. This new place has very comfortable rooms and pleasant management. The cost is Rs 800 in double rooms with attached bath, although bargaining may be possible.

For real shoestring accommodation there's the *Nyatapola Guest House* close by, which has basic rooms with common bath at Rs 75/100, and a nice terrace restaurant.

A few minutes walk north of Durbar Square brings you to the basic but friendly *Luna Guest House* with rock-bottom accommodation for Rs 80/120.

Finally there's another choice right on the edge of Tachupal Tole. The *Dattatraya Guest House* is a bit of a modern monstrosity, but

fortunately it doesn't impinge on the square, despite being so close. All the rooms have common bath, and are good value at Rs 150/250. The rooftop views are again excellent.

PLACES TO EAT

Bhaktapur is certainly no competition for Kathmandu when it comes to restaurants, but you won't starve. Right in Taumadhi Tole the *Cafe Nyatapola* is in a building which was once a traditional pagoda temple – it even has erotic carvings on some of the roof struts. From upstairs there are good views over the square but it is often dominated by large groups of tourists. Soft drinks are Rs 20, chips Rs 40, fried rice Rs 75.

On the corner of the square, beside the Nyatapola Temple, the *Marco Polo Restaurant* is a better bet than Cafe Nyatapola if you want a substantial meal. Pizzas are Rs 80, and there's a range of Chinese and Indian dishes for around Rs 75.

On Tachupal Tole, opposite the Dattatraya Temple, the *Cafe de Peacock & Soma Bar* is one of the best spots in the valley to while away an afternoon. The food is good and the views of the beautiful square mesmerising. The full international menu includes pizza and lasagne for around Rs 120, and there is also dal bhat for Rs 120. The curd (dahi) is excellent. The cafe is open from 9 am to 9 pm.

Don't forget to try Bhaktapur's famous speciality – jujudhau, the 'king of curds' – while you are here. You can have it at the three main restaurants, and there are several places selling curd near the Navpokhu Pokhari bus stop.

THINGS TO BUY

As in Patan there are a number of crafts for which Bhaktapur is the centre. You'll find all the Kathmandu Valley crafts on sale in Kathmandu itself, but it's often fun to shop for them close to their point of origin and you may well find better examples or unusual pieces. There are plenty of shops and stalls catering to visitors around Durbar Square and Taumadhi Tole.

Pottery

Bhaktapur is the pottery centre of the valley and a visit to Potters' Square is a must. There are many stalls around the square or just below Taumadhi Tole selling pottery. Much of the work is traditional pots for use in Nepali households (nice but not very transportable), but there are also items catering to tourist tastes, such as attractive elephant or dragon planters.

Woodcarving & Puppets

Bhaktapur is renowned for its woodcarving and you'll see good examples in the Handicrafts Centre on Tachupal Tole. There are other shops around the squares and you will find unusual pieces in the alley beside the Pujari Math, right under the Peacock Window in fact. If you buy anything which looks like it might be old, make sure you get a descriptive receipt for it as it's likely to be checked on departure from Kathmandu. If it really is very old you will not be allowed to take it out of the country.

Some of the best puppets, on sale in their thousands in all the valley towns, come from Bhaktapur.

Thangkas & Caps

Bhaktapur is reputed to be a centre for thangka paintings although these days you find them everywhere. Nepali caps are another Bhaktapur speciality. There's a cap shop right beside the Bhairabnath Temple.

GETTING THERE & AWAY
Bus

Travelling by bus or minibus to Bhaktapur you disembark near the walled water tank called Navpokhu Pokhari, just beyond the even larger Siddha Pokhari and a short walk from Durbar Square. The minibuses from Kathmandu's City Bus Station are strictly for masochists and the poverty-stricken – they are nearly always crowded and can take over an hour, although they only cost Rs 2. If possible, try to get an express bus.

The Chinese-built trolley buses are preferable, even though they are in an advanced state of decay and also get crowded (usually only around peak hour, though). At the Bhaktapur end, you have to walk 10 minutes to get to the town centre (by Ram Ghat and up into the town by Potters' Square).

The trolley buses leave Kathmandu from Tripureshwar Marg, cost Rs 2, and take around 35 minutes, unless you get caught in a traffic jam. The last minibus back to Kathmandu leaves about 6 pm; the trolley buses run until about 9 pm.

Bicycle

The main road to Bhaktapur runs through to Dhulikhel, Barabise and finally to Tibet, so it carries a lot of bellowing, belching buses and trucks. Avoid peak hours. A better alternative for cyclists is to ride via Thimi. Take the Thimi turn-off – left at a T-intersection after the Bhaktapur road crosses the Manohara River. The Herbs Production & Processing Co Ltd is signposted at the corner.

Taxi

Taxis cost around Rs 200, one way. If you were to get the driver to wait for three or four hours and to return, the total bill would be around Rs 500.

Around the Kathmandu Valley

Apart from the three major cities of the valley – Kathmandu, Patan and Bhaktapur – there are countless villages, temples and stupas around the valley and on the surrounding hills. The crowds, traffic and modern trappings of Kathmandu can quickly be left behind for quiet villages and lush, terraced hills.

The valley beyond the cities has certainly changed over the years, and not always for the good, especially along the roads. Fortunately, however, aspects of traditional life are maintained as the people of the valley coax their livelihood from the land, and temples continue to provide a focal point for their lives. The seasons roll on, and the timeless demands of the fields, the family and the gods are still major priorities.

You can even find good treks in the valley, ranging from day walks to more ambitious hikes. Some of the possibilities are described in this chapter.

The ancient Buddhist stupa of Swayambhunath, a dramatic spot within walking distance of central Kathmandu, is probably the best known site in Nepal and attracts a constant stream of worshippers. The hilltop site offers a fine view over the valley that is helpful for orienting yourself if you've just arrived.

The most important Hindu temple is Pashupatinath, on the eastern side of Kathmandu near the airport. It's a centre for pilgrims from all over the Indian subcontinent. A visit here can be combined with Bodhnath, another Buddhist stupa and the centre for a thriving Tibetan community.

If you will not have the opportunity to trek elsewhere, it is especially worth visiting one of the famous viewpoints on the rim of the valley, from where you can see the snow peaks of the Himalaya. There are numerous lodges and hotels at Nagarkot, Dhulikhel and Kakani.

If you have more time, there are less well known, although important, temples such as:

> ## HIGHLIGHTS
>
> * Visiting the ancient Buddhist stupa of Swayambhunath, and Nepal's most important Hindu temple, Pashupatinath
>
> * Taking one of the many short treks around the valley, with the opportunity to visit temples and to view the snow peaks of the Himalaya
>
> * Enjoying the traditional Newari lifestyle of many of the smaller towns and villages
>
> * Heading to the centuries-old Bodhnath stupa, north of Kathmandu, with its strong and lively Tibetan population

Changu Narayan, north of Bhaktapur and a treasure house of Nepali art; Dakshinkali, in the south-western corner of the valley and the site for animal sacrifices to Kali; or Budhanilkantha north of Kathmandu, with a massive 1400 year old statue of Vishnu. There are many more.

The smaller towns and villages have tended to retain a more traditional Newari lifestyle, and if you find Bhaktapur interesting consider visiting Kirtipur (south-west of Kathmandu), Sankhu (north-east of Bhaktapur) or Panauti (outside the valley near Banepa). There are many more alternatives.

Daman, a viewpoint that overlooks the entire Himalaya from Dhaulagiri to Mt Everest, is a day trip from Kathmandu which is worth considering (see the Terai chapter).

CULTURAL CONSIDERATIONS

You do not have to go far to escape the hordes of camera-clutching tourists, but you will nonetheless be unable to escape their legacy: suspicious people and the cries of 'One rupee, one rupee?' from the children. If you do venture off the beaten track, your responsibility as a visitor is greater than ever.

Whatever the temptation, do not give gifts to begging children. Do not intrude with a

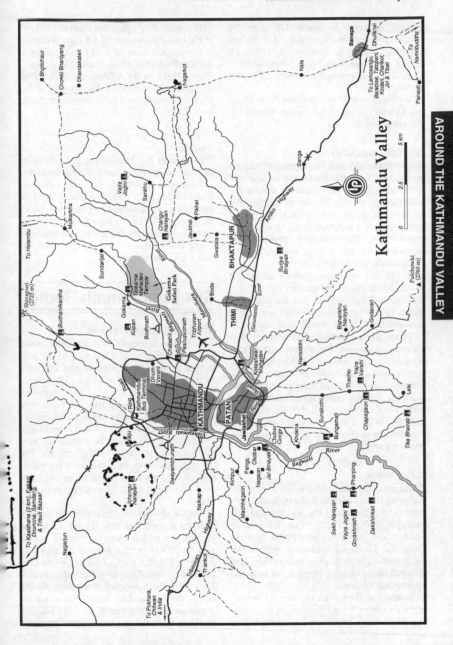

Kathmandu Valley

0   2.5   5 km

camera, unless it is clearly OK with the people you are photographing. Ask before entering a temple compound, although unless otherwise noted it is permissible to enter and photograph the temples described in this chapter.

See Society & Conduct in the Facts about the Country chapter for further details on cultural considerations.

GETTING AROUND

Swayambhunath and Pashupatinath can be reached on foot, but by far the easiest and most economical way of getting around the valley is by bicycle. If you are aiming for somewhere on the rim of the valley, make sure you have a mountain bike, on which it's possible for a reasonably fit person to go anywhere in the valley and return to Kathmandu within daylight.

Buses and minibuses service all of the roads, but although cheap, they are uncomfortable and limiting. If you are part of a group or if the budget allows, you could consider hiring a car or taxi for the day.

There are a number of companies that offer tours around the valley with prices ranging from Rs 200 to Rs 300 for half a day. If you have limited time or want a speedy introduction to the area, they're worth considering. On the other hand, taxis can be hired for Rs 600 per half day, Rs 1200 per full day. With a taxi you aren't stuck to a schedule, and if you have this book who needs a guide?

Valley Walks

There are many interesting walks around the valley and many of them make pleasant alternatives to vehicles or bicycles. You can, for example, follow a trail from Kirtipur to Chobar and from there into Patan, or walk from the Gokarna Mahadev Temple to Bodhnath. These walks, and others, are detailed under Getting There & Away in the appropriate sections.

In addition, there are a number of interesting walks down from Nagarkot on the valley rim to various points in and outside the valley, including a pleasant short stroll down to the beautiful temple of Changu Narayan.

For more details on walks on the edge of the Kathmandu Valley, look for Alton C Byers' *Treks on the Kathmandu Valley Rim*, or James Giamborone's *Kathmandu: Bikes & Hikes*, which are available in Kathmandu bookshops.

Routes

This chapter has been organised following the roads that radiate out from Kathmandu.

Distances quoted are from the centre of Kathmandu. Each route has been named for the most important sites along the route, which are given clockwise from the Swayambhunath route. In most cases there is no alternative to going and returning on the same route unless you walk cross-country.

Swayambhunath Route

SWAYAMBHUNATH (2 km)

The Buddhist temple of Swayambhunath, situated on the top of a hill west of the city, is one of the most popular and instantly recognisable symbols of Nepal. The temple is colloquially known as the 'monkey temple' after the large tribe of handsome monkeys which guards the hill and amuses visitors and devotees with tricks, including sliding gracefully down the double banisters of the main stairway to the temple. The roving monkeys quickly snatch up any offerings of food made by devotees and will just as quickly grab anything you may be carrying.

Geologists believe that the Kathmandu Valley was once a lake and legends relate that the hill on which Swayambhunath stands was an island in that lake. It is said that Emperor Ashoka paid a visit to the site over 2000 years ago. An inscription indicates that King Manadeva ordered work done on the site in 460 CE and by the 1200s it was an important Buddhist centre. In 1346 Mughal invaders from Bengal broke open the stupa to search for gold. Under the Mallas various improvements were made and the great stairway to the stupa was constructed by King Pratap Malla in the 17th century.

Eastern Stairway

Although you can get to the temple by vehicle, and save yourself the long climb up the stairs, the eastern stairway is by far the best way of approaching Swayambhunath. Look for the yellow and red stone seated Buddha figures at the base of the hill. The bottom end of the steps is guarded by figures of Ganesh and Kumar on their animals. Near the start of the steps is a huge 'footprint' on a stone, said to be either that of the Buddha or of Manjushri. Halfway up the steps there's another small collection of stonework including a scene showing the birth of the Buddha, his mother holding a tree branch and the Buddha taking seven miraculous steps immediately after his birth.

As you climb the final stretch look for the pairs of animals – Garudas, lions, elephants, horses and peacocks – the 'vehicles' of the Dhyani Buddhas. If you tire on the ascent, pause to watch the monkeys' antics and when you reach the top remember that you should always walk around a stupa in a clockwise direction.

Great Thunderbolt

As well as building the great stairway, Pratap Malla also added a pair of *shikharas* (Indian-style temples) and the stone lions and *dorje* which visitors see immediately upon reaching the top of the stairs. Dorje is the Tibetan word for this thunderbolt symbol, in Sanskrit it is called a *vajra*. Dorjes are often accompanied by a bell; the thunderbolt symbolises male force and the bell symbolises female wisdom. Around the pedestal supporting Swayambhunath's mighty dorje are the animals of the Tibetan calendar.

Stupa

From the flattened top of the hill, the soaring central stupa is topped by a gold-coloured square block from which the watchful eyes of the Buddha gaze out across the valley in

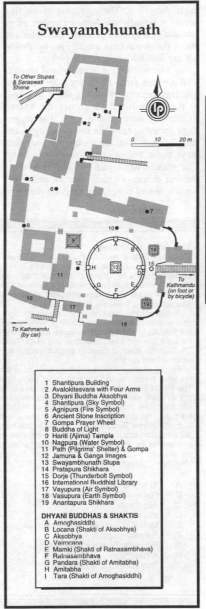

Swayambhunath

To Other Stupas & Saraswati Shrine

0   10   20 m

To Kathmandu (on foot or by bicycle)

To Kathmandu (by car)

1 Shantipura Building
2 Avalokitesvara with Four Arms
3 Dhyani Buddha Aksobhya
4 Shantipura (Sky Symbol)
5 Agnipura (Fire Symbol)
6 Ancient Stone Inscription
7 Gompa Prayer Wheel
8 Buddha of Light
9 Hariti (Ajima) Temple
10 Nagpura (Water Symbol)
11 Path (Pilgrims' Shelter) & Gompa
12 Jamuna & Ganga Images
13 Swayambhunath Stupa
14 Pratapura Shikhara
15 Dorje (Thunderbolt Symbol)
16 International Buddhist Library
17 Vayupura (Air Symbol)
18 Vasupura (Earth Symbol)
19 Anantapura Shikhara

DHYANI BUDDHAS & SHAKTIS
A Amoghasiddhi
B Locana (Shakti of Aksobhya)
C Aksobhya
D Vairocana
E Mamki (Shakti of Ratnasambhava)
F Ratnasambhava
G Pandara (Shakti of Amitabha)
H Amitabha
I Tara (Shakti of Amoghasiddhi)

each direction. The question mark-like 'nose' is actually the Nepali number *ek* or one and is a symbol of unity. Between and above the two eyes is a third eye, symbolising the Buddha's clairvoyant powers.

Set around the base of the central stupa is a continuous series of prayer wheels which pilgrims, circumambulating the stupa, spin as they pass by. Each carries the sacred mantra *om mani padme hum*. The prayer flags fluttering from the lines leading to the stupa's spire also carry mantras and each wave in the breeze carries the words away. The stupa's white-painted base represents the four elements – earth, fire, air and water – while the 13 concentric rings on the spire

symbolise the 13 degrees of knowledge and the 13 steps that must be taken towards nirvana, which in turn is represented by the umbrella at the top.

Stupa Platform
The great stupa is only one of many points of interest at Swayambhunath. Starting from the massive dorje at the top of the stairs turn right to the monastery or *gompa* where, with a great deal of crashing, chanting and trumpeting, a service takes place every day at around 4 pm. Inside the gompa there's a huge prayer wheel and a six metre high figure of Avalokitesvara. Behind the stupa, adjacent to the International Buddhist Library, is a

---

The Dhyani Buddhas

There are five Dhyani Buddhas or 'Buddhas in Meditation' who represent various aspects of Buddhahood, unlike the mortal flesh-and-blood Buddhas like Gautama Buddha. Around many stupas the figures of the five Dhyani Buddhas in different meditative postures face out from the stupa in niches, four of them facing the four cardinal directions. Once you know the hand positions you can use a stupa like a compass! The Swayambhunath stupa is a good place to study the Dhyani Buddhas, and the description that follows is from that stupa.

Amoghasiddhi faces north and raises his right hand, palm out to shoulder height in what is known as a protective position. His animal or 'vehicle' is the Garuda. You can see the animals in niches below the Buddhas' shrines. As you move round the stupa clockwise you'll come to Aksobhya, the lord of the east; one of his hands touches the earth. This is known as the position of subduing the devil, Mara. The Buddha reaches down to touch the earth in order that it witness his resistance to temptation. His vehicle is the elephant.

Facing south is Ratnasambhava who rides a horse and turns his palm outwards. Amitabha faces the west and his hands rest on his lap, palm up in a meditative position. His vehicle is the peacock. The fifth of the Buddhas is Vairocana who usually appears in the centre of the stupa and therefore is not so easily seen. If he is shown he normally faces the south-east, and at Swayambhunath you can see his figure standing beside Aksobhya in the eastern niche. His animal is the lion; his hands are held up to his chest and he makes two circles with his fingers, rather like a scuba diver's 'OK' sign!

Each Dhyani Buddha is identifiable by his colour, his hand positions, his direction and his vehicle but each also has a shakti or female companion and a Bodhisattva or spiritual follower. Their shaktis or consorts are shown at the subcardinal points around the stupa. Amitabha is the Dhyani Buddha of our era and his Bodhisattva is none other than Avalokitesvara or, as he is often known in the valley, Manjushri or Machhendranath. ∎

A	Amoghasiddhi
B	Locana (Shakti of Aksobhya)
C	Aksobhya
D	Vairocana
E	Mamki (Shakti of Ratnasambhava)
F	Ratnasambhava
G	Pandara (Shakti of Amitabha)
H	Amitabha
I	Tara (Shakti of Amoghasiddhi)

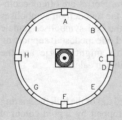

path or rest house for pilgrims with an open ground floor and a gompa above it.

The dorje at the top of the stairs is flanked by two white temples in the Indian shikhara style, both dating from 1646. The one to the right, in front of the gompa, is the Pratapura shikhara while to the left is the identical Anantapura shikhara. Behind the stupa is the pagoda-style Hariti Temple with a beautiful image of Hariti, the goddess of smallpox. This Hindu goddess (to the Newars she is Ajima), who is also responsible for fertility, indicates again the constant interweaving of Hinduism and Buddhism in Nepal.

Near the Hariti Temple there are pillars on which figures of various gods and goddesses are seated. Look for the figure of Tara making the gesture of charity. Actually, there are two Taras, Green Tara and White Tara, who are sometimes believed to be the two wives of King Songtsen Gompo, the first royal patron of Buddhism in Tibet. The Taras are two of the female consorts to the Dhyani Buddhas.

Behind the stupa, bronze images of the river goddesses Jamuna and Ganga guard an eternal flame in a cage.

The symbols for the four elements – earth, air, water and fire – can be found around the hilltop. Behind the Anantapura shikhara are Vasupura, the earth symbol, and Vayupura, the symbol for air. Nagpura, the symbol for water, is just north of the stupa while Agnipura, the symbol for fire, is at the north-western corner of the platform. Shantipura, the symbol for the sky, is at the extreme north of the platform, in front of the Shantipura building.

In this same northern area of the platform you will find an ancient stone inscription, dating from 1372, and a large image of the Buddha, next to the Agnipura symbol. There are numerous little shops and stalls around the stupa that sell jewellery and curios.

From its hilltop setting, Swayambhunath offers fine views over Kathmandu and the valley. It's particularly striking in the early evening when the city is illuminated, and the site is also very attractive under the soft glow of moonlight.

Around Swayambhunath

There are many small buildings and shrines down the hillside behind Swayambhunath. A smaller stupa stands on a hillock, with an adjacent gompa and an important shrine to Saraswati, the goddess of learning. At exam time, many scholars come here to improve their chances and schoolchildren come here during Basant Panchami, the Festival of Knowledge.

There are various Tibetan settlements and gompas around the base of the Swayambhunath hill. Just to the north of the long eastern stairway, on the road round the hill, is a **gompa** with an immense **prayer wheel** standing a good six metres high. The two or three km walk north-west of Swayambhunath will take you to Ichangu Narayan, an interesting Hindu temple (see the section below). The National Museum & Art Gallery (see the Kathmandu, Patan & Bhaktapur chapter) is on the road from Kathmandu to the stupa.

The **Natural History Museum**, west of Swayambhunath, has a large collection of butterflies, fish, reptiles, birds and animals. It's open daily from 10 am to 5 pm except Saturdays and government holidays, and admission is free.

There are several routes to Swayambhunath from Kathmandu and if you take the route from Thamel, via the Chhetrapati Square and down to the Vishnumati River, there are three interesting temples to look at. The **Indrani Temple** is just beside the river on the Kathmandu side and is chiefly notable for the brightly coloured erotic scenes on its roof struts. There are cremation ghats beside the river; in 1989 the bridge here collapsed during a heavy monsoon. Across the river and just upstream is the **Shobabaghwati Temple**. A footpath runs from here up the steep hill to the **Bijeshwari Temple**, from where the road continues to the Swayambhunath hill.

Getting There & Away

You can approach Swayambhunath by taxi or under your own power – either on foot or by bicycle. The taxi will take you on the road

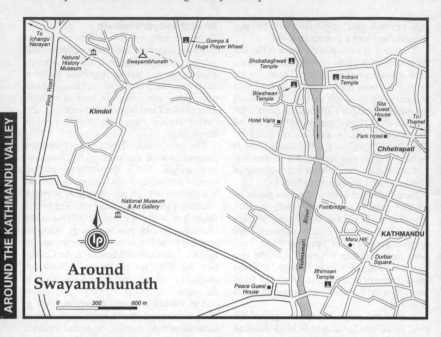

Around Swayambhunath

0   300   600 m

via the National Museum & Art Gallery and deposit you at the southern entrance, from where it's an easy climb to the top of the hill. Share-taxis also operate from Bangemudha, the junction a block south of Thahiti Tole going from Thamel towards New Rd. The other routes end with the long steep climb up the eastern stairway to the stupa, but this is a far more interesting way to approach Swayambhunath and the easy stroll from Kathmandu is a pleasure in itself.

There are two popular foot or bicycle routes to Swayambhunath and using both makes the trip into a pleasant circuit. Starting from Durbar Square take Maru Tole (Pie Alley) down to the river where a footbridge crosses to the western side. Flat, stone cremation ghats can be seen by the riverside. From there the path leads through houses and shops to the open green at the base of the hill. Along the way you'll see people working in vegetable gardens and preparing wool for Tibetan carpets. There's quite a Tibetan community in this area and also a small

group of long-term western visitors near the base of the hill.

If you go there by bicycle you are likely to find a number of small boys offering to 'look after' your bicycle. It's probably wise to pay a rupee or two of 'protection money', otherwise you may find your tyres have gone mysteriously flat and a pump will then have to be rented from one of the nearby shops!

The alternative route starts from Chhetrapati, near Thamel. From the Chhetrapati Tole junction the road descends to the river, with the Swayambhunath stupa clearly visible in the distance, and passes the three riverside temples mentioned.

CHANGU NARAYAN TEMPLE (5 km)

At the edge of the valley floor, two or three km north-west of Swayambhunath, the shrine of Ichangu Narayan (not to be confused with Changu Narayan east of Kathmandu) is one of the Kathmandu Valley's important Vishnu shrines. The two storey, 18th century temple is fronted by two square stone pillars bearing Vishnu's conch shell and chakra symbols. Various statuary can be found around the courtyard. The site of the temple was actually consecrated in 1200 and an earlier temple was built here after a famine in 1512. There's a small temple to Bhagwati on a hill overlooking Ichangu Narayan.

Getting There & Away

The road to Ichangu Narayan starts beyond the Ring Rd, on the western side of the Swayambhunath hill. It quickly changes from a road to a track and as it climbs a steep hill (look back for the views over the valley), the track soon becomes a footpath. From the top of the hill, marked by a small temple, the trail descends slightly and then continues to climb gradually, leaving the valley proper. Finally, at the end of a little village is the temple compound. Going back to Kathmandu by bicycle is one long downhill breeze but you'll certainly work up a sweat getting to the temple.

An alternative route to Ichangu Narayan is a day walk from Balaju, to the north of Kathmandu. The trail climbs from Balaju to the top of Nagarjun hill and skirts around the valley edge through the Jamacho forest reserve and the Nagarjun forest, descending to the Ichangu Narayan trail to the west of the village and temple.

Kakani & Trisuli Bazaar Route

Kakani is a viewpoint with spectacular views of the Ganesh Himal. A narrow, winding tarmac road, in reasonable though not great condition, continues to Trisuli Bazaar. From Trisuli Bazaar to Dhunche the road deteriorates to very rough gravel, but the views are spectacular. Dhunche is the starting point for a number of treks in the Langtang region. From Dhunche, a military road continues along the Langtang Valley before crossing

the Trisuli River and heading westwards to Samdang (at 3600m!) – 4WD is essential.

Just before Malekhu, on the Kathmandu-Pokhara (Prithvi) Highway, a bridge has recently been built over the Trisuli River. This is the new road to Trisuli Bazaar, superseding the road that leaves the valley at Kakani. This makes an interesting circular bike ride a possibility, taking in Kakani, Trisuli, Dhading and Malekhu.

BALAJU (3 km)

The industrial centre of Balaju is less than two km north of Thamel, just beyond the Ring Rd, and the expansion of the capital has virtually swallowed up this nearby suburb. Despite this, the Balaju park is still a peaceful retreat and its image of the sleeping Vishnu makes an interesting contrast with the larger Vishnu image at Budhanilkantha.

The gardens at Balaju were originally constructed in the 18th century and are now known as **Mahendra Park**. They are something of a disappointment – there's a lot of concrete and litter, and numerous ineffectual gardeners. Apart from the Vishnu image, there are a couple of small temples, an interesting group of *chortens* (shrines) and lingams (for the aficionado) and the 22 waterspouts from which the park takes its name, 'Bais Dhara Balaju'.

Officially, the Balaju Vishnu image is said to be a copy of the older image at Budhanilkantha but there is no positive proof of which one is actually older. Certainly the Balaju image is in more pleasant surroundings than its better known relation. Although the king of Nepal cannot visit Budhanilkantha (since he is an incarnation of Vishnu and to gaze on his own image could be disastrous) no such injunction applies to Balaju, where the Vishnu image is just a copy of the real thing!

Admission costs Rs 1, plus another Rs 1 if you take in a camera. The pool, which can often be very crowded, is open between March and September, and the admission fee is Rs 10.

Shitala Mai Temple

The double roofed 19th century Shitala Mai

Temple stands in front of the Vishnu image and around it is a curious assembly of gods. They include a 16th century image of Hari Shankar – the half-Shiva, half-Vishnu deity – and a 14th century figure of the multi-armed goddess of smallpox, Shitala Mai. Others include Bhagwati, Ganesh and, in the usual clash of Hindu and Buddhist imagery, a statue of the Buddha protected by the hood of a snake.

Getting There & Away

You can get to Balaju by tempo from the National Theatre corner of the Rani Pokhari or walk there from Thamel. It's an interesting day walk from Balaju to Ichangu Narayan, west of Swayambhunath, skirting the edge of the valley.

NAGARJUN

On the hill behind Balaju is the walled Nagarjun forest reserve with pheasants, deer and other animals. This, along with the former Gokarna Safari Park and Pulchowki, is one of the last significant areas of untouched forest in the valley. You can continue up the hill to Jamacho, a popular Buddhist pilgrimage site. There are excellent views to the north stretching, on a clear day, all the way from the Annapurnas to Langtang Lirung, while the whole of the Kathmandu Valley is laid at your feet to the south.

There's a steep, 37 km unpaved road to the top, or you can walk up a wide, easy-to-follow trail in about two hours. There are a number of picnic shelters around a stupa and a viewing tower.

Getting There & Away

The main entrance to the reserve is about a 20 minute bike ride from Thamel; entry is Rs 0.25. The walking trail to the top begins just past the gate on the right. It's steep for the first hour, and there is no water along the way or at the top. There are several routes you can take on the way down. Don't take the road – it's 37 km long.

KAKANI (23 km)

Standing at 2073m on a ridge north-west of

Kathmandu, Kakani is nowhere near as popular as Nagarkot, but does offer magnificent views of Ganesh Himal and the central and western Himalaya.

Apart from looking at the view (one could argue this is enough) there's not much to do. There is a century-old summer villa used by the UK Embassy and a large army camp, although this does not seriously impinge on the tranquillity of the surroundings.

The road to Kakani also offers beautiful views. Once you're through the pass and out of the valley, Kathmandu seems light years away. Although the valley is terraced 1000m from top to bottom, many trees have been left behind and prosperous-looking houses dot the hillsides.

Place to Stay & Eat

The only accommodation in Kakani is the *Tara Gaon Kakani Hotel* (☎ 01-290812), an old-fashioned place with wonderful views. Although small, it's also quite comfortable. Singles/doubles cost $16/22 and the hotel serves reasonably priced meals.

Although it's easy to get to Kakani on a day trip, it's worth staying overnight if you want to see the view (you stand a much better chance if you are there early in the morning before the clouds roll in).

Getting There & Away

Kakani is an hour by car from Kathmandu, so it would be a long, though rewarding, bike trip. The road is sealed almost all the way and it is a fairly gentle climb – although consistent. It is downhill all the way home! See the Mountain Biking chapter for details of a route that takes in Kakani.

Kakani is three km from the main Dhunche road. The dirt road is just before the Kaulithana police checkpoint (the first outside Kathmandu) and there is a signpost for a telecommunications tower.

Buses for Kakani, Trisuli and Dhunche leave from the Kathmandu Bus Terminal on the Ring Rd. Kakani is about three km off the main road, so you can catch a Trisuli or Dhunche bus, and get off at Kaulithana (about Rs 14).

TRISULI BAZAAR (68 km)

Trisuli Bazaar is a classically unattractive roadside town that owes its development to a large hydroelectric project on the Trisuli River, and the fact that it was once a trail head for treks into the Langtang region. These days trekkers head straight through to Dhunche, and there are very few persuasive reasons to stop. There's nothing to see, and the only oddity is the proliferation of hairdressers.

Nawakot, a small village a few km southeast of Trisuli, has the ruins of a fortress that was built by Prithvi Narayan Shah when he was planning his campaign to take the Kathmandu Valley. It can be reached by bike or foot and is an interesting spot.

Places to Stay

There are several thoroughly unimpressive places on the eastern side of the bridge, which you reach when you enter town, before the turn-off to Dhunche. If you continue over the bridge, there are a few dal bhat restaurants and a couple of reasonable options. The *Trishuli Rest House* is the best of a bad lot, although the *Ranjit Hotel* is also OK. Doubles are overpriced at Rs 120.

Getting There & Away

It is a spectacular drive from Kakani along a narrow, twisting road with great views, and would be an excellent long descent by bike. Buses to/from Kathmandu take five hours and cost Rs 35. Buses leave from the Kathmandu bus terminal between 6.30 am and 2.30 pm.

DHUNCHE (119 km)

By the time you reach Dhunche you have been inspected by countless redundant police and army checkposts, plus paid Rs 650 to enter the Langtang National Park. Irritation evaporates quickly, however, because there are great views of the Langtang Valley, and although the modern section of Dhunche is pretty tacky, it's definitely a Tamang town, and the old section is virtually unchanged. Many people start trekking from

Dhunche, although these days there is a bus to Syabru as well. (See the Trekking chapter.)

Places to Stay & Eat

There are a number of decent trekking-style hotel restaurants, although several of them are definitely at the up-market end of the spectrum. Prices are competitive. The *Hotel Namaste* is clean and decent, serves good food, and costs Rs 30 a double, or Rs 10 for a dorm bed. The *Hotel Langtang View* has similar prices and is also OK.

Getting There & Away

The road to Dhunche is bad, but it deteriorates further if you continue to Syabru. The views on both stretches are spectacular. A bus leaves from the Kathmandu Bus Terminal at 7 am, and arrives in Dhunche at about 3.30 pm.

SAMDANG (153 km)

The road becomes increasingly steep and spectacular after Dhunche. It drops down to cross the Trisuli River, then climbs steeply up the other side, continuing to Samdang, at 3600m, where there is the pleasant *Ganesh Himal Resort* (☎ 01-227929), run by the same people who run the Gorkha Hill Resort at Gorkha. Rooms cost $30, and advance bookings are essential. This would be a great base for day walks, and the views are stupendous.

Budhanilkantha Route

DHUM VARAHI (5 km)

Lying in an unprepossessing schoolyard just inside the Ring Rd to the north-east of the city proper, a huge pipal tree encloses a small shrine and a dramatic 5th century sculpture of Vishnu. Vishnu is shown reincarnated as a wild boar with a stocky human body, holding Prithvi, the earth goddess, on his left elbow.

From a historical point of view, the statue is interesting because it is an original depiction of an animal-human, created before iconographic rules were established, which perhaps contributes to the unusual sense of movement and vitality that the statue possesses. The statue shows Vishnu rescuing Prithvi from the clutches of a demon.

Getting There & Away

A visit to Dhum Varahi could easily be combined with a visit to Budhanilkantha, especially if you are approaching the Budhanilkantha intersection on the Ring Rd from Pashupatinath. If you are coming from Pashupatinath take the third dirt road on your left after crossing the Dhobi River. The statue lies under a huge pipal tree in the grounds of the Shridhumrabarah Primary School.

If you are coming from the intersection of the Budhanilkantha road with the Ring Rd take the second dirt road on the right after the Panchayat Silver Jubilee Garden, which features a square, black-marble column topped with a conch shell. Continue until you see the pipal tree after about a km.

BUDHANILKANTHA (9 km)

Vishnu has many incarnations and in Nepal he often appears as Narayan, the creator of all life, the god who reclines on the cosmic sea. From his navel grew a lotus and from the lotus came Brahma, who in turn created the world. So in the end everything comes from Vishnu and at Budhanilkantha the legend is made real. Here, a stone image of Vishnu lies serenely in a pond – the most impressive, if not the most important, Vishnu shrine in the kingdom.

The five metre long image of Vishnu as Narayan is believed to have been created in the 7th or 8th century. It was sculpted during the Licchavi period, probably somewhere outside the valley and laboriously dragged here. Two other similar figures of the reclining Vishnu were also carved out of stone and all three were subsequently lost for many centuries. The image here at Budhanilkantha was the first found and is also the largest, but

whether it was also the original (from which the others were copied) remains unresolved.

Narayan lies back peacefully on a most unusual bed – the coils of the multi-headed snake, Ananta. The snake's 11 hooded heads rise protectively around Narayan's head. Narayan's four hands hold the four symbols of Vishnu – a chakra (representing the mind), a mace (primeval knowledge), a conch shell (the four elements) and a lotus seed (the moving universe). A legend relates that the lost image was discovered when a horrified farmer saw blood coming from the ground when his plough struck the huge buried image.

During the early Malla period, Vishnuism had gone into decline as Shiva became more popular. King Jayasthiti Malla is credited with reviving the popularity of Vishnu, in part by claiming to be an incarnation of the multi-incarnated god.

To this day, the kings of Nepal make the same claim and because of this they are forbidden, on pain of death, from seeing the image at Budhanilkantha. They are allowed to look at the valley's other two reclining Vishnu images, which are said to be simply copies of the Budhanilkantha figure. One of these 'replicas' is at Balaju, the other, not on view to tourists, is in the old Royal Palace in Kathmandu.

The sleeping Vishnu image attracts a constant stream of pilgrims, and prayers take place every morning at 9 am. Vishnu is supposed to sleep through the four monsoon months, waking at the end of the monsoon. A great festival takes place at Budhanilkantha each November, on the day Vishnu is supposed to awaken from his long annual slumber.

Getting There & Away

Buses and tempos leave from the Kathmandu City Bus Station (1½ hours, Rs 6). A taxi should cost around Rs 150. By bicycle it's a long uphill haul – hard, sweaty work rewarded with a very pleasant return trip. You could pause at Dhum Varahi on one leg of your trip.

Pashupatinath & Bodhnath Route

PASHUPATINATH (5 km)

Nepal's most important Hindu temple stands on the banks of the Bagmati River, between Kathmandu and the airport and slightly south-west of Bodhnath. You can visit Pashupatinath en route to Bodhnath, as the two sites are an interesting short walk apart.

Pashupatinath Temple

Not only is Pashupatinath the most important Hindu temple in Nepal, it's one of the most important Shiva temples on the subcontinent and draws numerous devotees from all over India, including many colourful sadhus, those wandering ascetic Hindu holy men.

Shiva is the destroyer and creator of the Hindu pantheon and appears in many forms. His 'terrible' forms are probably best known, particularly his appearances in Nepal as the cruel and destructive Bhairabs, but he also has peaceful incarnations including those of Mahadev and Pashupati, the lord of the beasts. As the shepherd of both animals and humans, Shiva as Pashupati shows his most pleasant and creative side.

Pashupati is considered to have a special concern for the kingdom of Nepal and accordingly he features in any message from the king. Before commencing an important journey the king will always pay a visit to Pashupatinath to seek the god's blessing. Although Shiva is often a bloodthirsty god he is not so in his incarnation as Pashupati so no animal sacrifices are made here, although they are made at the nearby Guhyeshwari Temple. Nor is leather (since it comes from cows) allowed inside the temple and you will see Hindus removing their shoes before entering.

Near the entrance to the temple there are people selling flowers, incense and other offerings. Although non-Hindus are not allowed inside the temple you may catch a glimpse inside of the mighty figure of Nandi, Shiva's bull. It dates from the last century but the small bull in front of the temple is about 300 years old. The black, four headed image of Pashupati inside the temple is said to be even older and an even earlier image was destroyed by Mughal invaders in the 14th century.

There is plenty to be seen along the riverbanks and you can look down into the temple from the terraced hillside on the opposite bank.

Nandi, the bull, is the vehicle of Shiva and can be glimpsed inside Pashupatinath Temple.

The Riverbanks

The Bagmati is a holy river and, as at Varanasi on the Ganges, Pashupatinath is a popular place to be cremated. The burning ghats immediately in front of the temple, north of the footbridges, are reserved for the cremation of royalty although you will often see ritual bathing taking place in the river here.

The four square, burning ghats just south of the bridges are for the common people and there is almost always a cremation going on. The log fires are laid, the shrouded body lifted on top and the fire lit with remarkably little ceremony.

There's often a crowd of tourists – cameras and video cameras at the ready – watching like vultures from the opposite bank. Photography is currently permitted, but may not be for much longer if tourists continue to behave with such insensitive disregard for the funeral parties. However extraordinary the sights might seem, this is a religious ceremony, often marking a family tragedy, and the participants should be accorded respect. Please be discreet, and behave as you would wish people to behave at a funeral in your home town.

Further south of these cremation ghats, but still on the western bank of the river, is the ancient 6th century **Bachhareshwari Temple** with Tantric figures and erotic scenes. It is said that at one time Shivaratri festival activities included human sacrifices at this temple. Just outside the temple entrance, right at the end of the western embankment, is a half-buried, but quite

beautiful, 7th century standing Buddha image.

Two footbridges cross the Bagmati River, and facing the temple from across the river are 11 stone *chaityas* (small stupas), each containing a lingam. From this bank you can watch the activities on the other bank, in front of the temple. Offerings and flowers are on sale, devotees dip in the river and there's a constant coming and going. From the northern end of the embankment you can see the cave-like shelters which were used at one time by hermits and sadhus. These days the yogis and sadhus head for the **Ram Temple**,

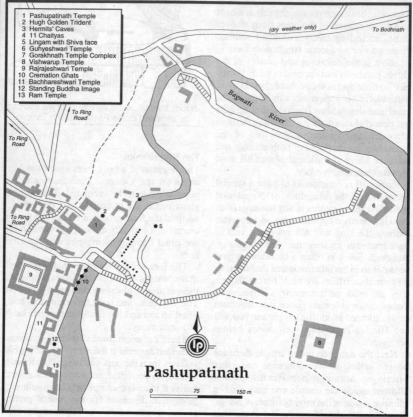

1 Pashupatinath Temple
2 Hugh Golden Trident
3 Hermits' Caves
4 11 Chaityas
5 Lingam with Shiva face
6 Guhyeshwari Temple
7 Gorakhnath Temple Complex
8 Vishwarup Temple
9 Rajrajeshwari Temple
10 Cremation Ghats
11 Bachhareshwari Temple
12 Standing Buddha Image
13 Ram Temple

To Bodhnath

(dry weather only)

Bagmati River

To Ring Road

To Ring Road

To Ring Road

Pashupatinath

0   75   150 m

further down the river, especially during the great festival of Shivaratri.

The Terraces

Climb up the steps from the western riverbank to the terrace where you can look down into the Pashupatinath Temple. It's not a very inspiring sight: the golden roof of the central two tiered pagoda, which dates from 1696, is surrounded by ugly corrugated-iron roofs, just like some worn-out, inner-city Australian suburb. Look for the enormous golden trident rising up on the right (northern) side of the temple and the golden figure of the king kneeling in prayer on the left side. Behind the temple, you can see a brightly coloured illustration of Shiva and his *shakti* (consort) looking out over the temple.

At the northern end of this terrace is a Shiva lingam on a circular pedestal. A finely featured face of the god has been sculptured on one side of the lingam. It's an indication of the richness of Nepal's artistic heritage that this piece of sculpture, so casually standing on the grassy terrace, is a masterpiece dating from the 5th or 6th century!

Gorakhnath & Vishwarup Temples

The steps continue up the hill and, as with the steps to Swayambhunath, are a popular playground for monkeys. The Gorakhnath complex is at the top of the hill. A shikhara fronted by a towering Shiva trident is the main structure, but there's a positive jungle of temples, images, sculptures and chaityas with Shiva imagery everywhere. Images of the bull Nandi stand guard, tridents are dotted around and lingams rise up on every side.

You can turn right from the path and head to the Vishwarup Temple but there's no point since, again, westerners are denied entry to the temple precinct and from outside there's nothing to see. Instead, continue beyond the Gorakhnath Temple where the pathway turns steeply downhill to the river.

Guhyeshwari Temple

The Guhyeshwari Temple is dedicated to Shiva's shakti in her terrible manifestation as Kali. Like the Pashupatinath Temple, entry is banned to all but Hindus, and the high wall around the temple prevents you from seeing inside. Guhyeshwari was built by King Pratap Malla in the 17th century and the temple, standing in a paved courtyard surrounded by *dharamsalas* (pilgrims' rest houses), is topped by an open roof with four gilded snakes arching up to support the roof finial. You can see the snakes from outside. The temple's main entrance gate by the river is an imposing and colourful affair. To the west of the main temple building is a series of white, stupa-like temples.

The temple's curious name comes from *guhya* (vagina) and *ishwari* (goddess) – it's the temple of the goddess' vagina!

When Shiva was insulted by his father-in-law, Parvati was so incensed that she burst into flames and it was this act of self-immolation which gave rise to the practice of *sati* or suttee, where a widow was consigned to the same funeral pyre as her deceased husband. The grieving Shiva carried off his shakti's corpse but as he wandered aimlessly, the body disintegrated and this is where her yoni fell.

Special Events

Activities take place at Pashupatinath almost all the time, but it is generally busiest (with genuine pilgrims, not tourists) from 6 to 10 am and again from 6 to 7.30 pm. The best time to visit the temple is on Ekadashi – 11 days after the full and new moon each month. On those days there will be many pilgrims and in the evening the ringing of bells will indicate that the *arati* (light) ceremony is to take place.

In February-March each year, the festival of Shivaratri celebrates Shiva's birthday with a great fair at the temple. Pilgrims come from all over Nepal and India for this festival, and if you're in Kathmandu at the time don't miss it. Another fair takes place in November.

Getting There & Away

Buses to Bodhnath go via Pashupatinath from the City Bus Station, and the stop for Pashupatinath is called Gosala. Pashupatinath

AROUND THE KATHMANDU VALLEY

is an easy bicycle ride from Kathmandu: simply ride east from Thamel along Tridevi Marg, passing in front of the new Royal Palace. It gets a bit more complicated after that, but you can't really go wrong as long as you keep heading east. The airport is very close to Pashupatinath, so some of the roads carry a lot of traffic.

It's a pleasant, short walk between Pashupatinath and Bodhnath. From the Guhyeshwari Temple, the dome of Bodhnath is clearly visible to the north, but the footbridge shown on some maps right in front of Guhyeshwari does not exist! Walk west along the riverbank

for a couple of hundred metres to the bridge by some ghats, cross the river and a footpath leads off north-east to Bodhnath. You eventually come out on the main road, right across from the main entrance to the stupa enclosure.

CHABAHIL (6 km)

The **Chabahil Stupa** is like a small replica of Bodhnath, about 1.5 km west of Bodhnath, back towards Kathmandu. The small village of Chabahil has been virtually swallowed up by the expansion of Kathmandu

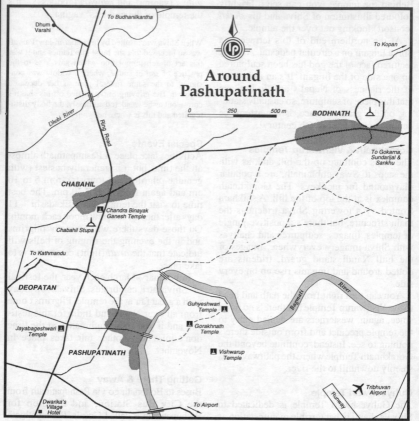

but the site is very old and the original stupa was said to have been built by Ashoka's daughter Charumati. It certainly predates Bodhnath and around the main stupa are a number of small chaityas from the Licchavi period, dating back to between the 5th and 8th centuries. The site includes a one metre high, 9th century statue of a Bodhisattva, which is claimed to be one of the finest pieces of sculpture in the valley.

Nearby is the small **Chandra Binayak Ganesh Temple** with a double roof in brass. Ganesh's shrew stands on a pillar in front of the shrine, waiting for the tiny image of the god inside. A short distance south, but still on the Kathmandu side of the main road, is the well designed **Jayabageshwari Temple** dating from the late 17th century.

BODHNATH (6 km)

On the eastern side of Kathmandu, just north of the airport and an interesting walk from Pashupatinath, is the huge stupa of Bodhnath, the largest stupa in Nepal and one of the largest in the world. It is the religious centre for Nepal's considerable population of Tibetans and there are a number of thriving monasteries and many small shops selling Tibetan artefacts (beware, prices are high and bargaining is essential).

Many of these Tibetans are refugees who fled their country following the unsuccessful uprising against the Chinese invaders in 1959. They have been energetic and successful in the intervening years, as the large houses surrounding Bodhnath testify. While political and religious oppression continues

AROUND THE KATHMANDU VALLEY

Bodhnath Stupa

There does not seem to be any agreement on how old the site is, but it is likely that the first stupa was built some time after 600 CE, after the Tibetan king, Songtsen Gompo, was converted to Buddhism by his two wives – the Nepali princess Bhrikuti (sometimes regarded as an incarnation of the Green Tara) and Wen Cheng Konjo from China (the White Tara). The current stupa was probably built after the depredation of the Mughal invaders in the 14th century.

Stupas were originally built to house holy relics, or to commemorate an event or place, with a structure that symbolises Buddhist beliefs. They are never hollow. It is not certain if there is anything interred at Bodhnath, but some believe that there is a piece of bone that once belonged to Gautama Buddha.

The base of the stupa takes the shape of a mandala (symbolising earth); on this four tiered base sits the dome (symbolising water); then comes the spire (symbolising fire); the umbrella (symbolising air); and the pinnacle (symbolising ether). The Buddha's watchful eyes gaze out in four directions from the square base of the spire. There is a third eye between and above the two normal eyes and the 'nose' is not a nose at all but the Nepali number one, signifying the oneness of all life. The spire is made up of 13 steps, representing the 13 stages on the journey to nirvana.

Around the base of the stupa's circular mound are 108 small images of the Dhyani Buddha Amitabha. A brick wall around the stupa has 147 niches, each with four or five prayer wheels bearing that immortal mantra *om mani padme hum*. On the northern side of the stupa is a small shrine dedicated to Ajima, the goddess of smallpox. ■

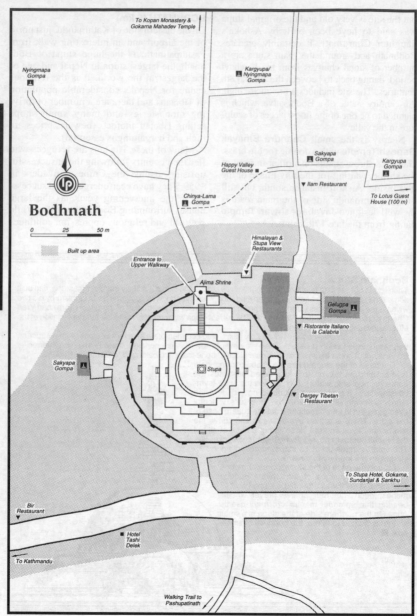

Bodhnath

To Kopan Monastery &
Gokarna Mahadev Temple

Nyingmapa
Gompa

Kargyupa/
Nyingmapa
Gompa

Sakyapa
Gompa

Kargyupa
Gompa

Happy Valley
Guest House

Ilam Restaurant

To Lotus Guest
House (100 m)

Chinya-Lama
Gompa

0   25   50 m

Built up area

Himalayan &
Stupa View
Restaurants

Entrance to
Upper Walkway

Ajima Shrine

Geluppa
Gompa

Ristorante Italiano
la Calabria

Sakyapa
Gompa

Stupa

Dergey Tibetan
Restaurant

To Stupa Hotel, Gokarna,
Sundarijal & Sankhu

Bir
Restaurant

Hotel
Tashi
Delek

To Kathmandu

Walking Trail to
Pashupatinath

AROUND THE KATHMANDU VALLEY

in Tibet, this is one of the few places in the world where Tibetan culture is both accessible and unhindered.

Late afternoon is a good time to visit, when the group tours depart and the place once again becomes a Tibetan town. Prayer services are held in the surrounding gompas and as the sun sets the community turns out to circumambulate the stupa – a ritual that combines religious observance with a social event. Do not forget to walk around the stupa in a clockwise direction.

Bodhnath has always been associated with Lhasa and Tibetan Buddhism. One of the major trade routes from Lhasa came through Sankhu, and Bodhnath therefore lies at the Tibetan traders' entry to Kathmandu. One can easily imagine the traders giving thanks for their successful journey across the Himalaya, or praying for a safe return. People still come here to pray before undertaking a journey in the Himalaya.

Gompas

There are a number of gompas surrounding Bodhnath that can be visited as long as you are respectful and discreet.

Do not forget to remove your shoes and hat before you enter a gompa, and ask before

taking photos. Smoking is not permitted anywhere in the main compounds. Do not step over or sit on the monks' cushions, even if no-one is sitting on them. During ceremonies enter quietly and stand by the wall near the main entrance; do not walk around in front of the altar, or between the monks, or cross the central area of the temple. Do not let loose with your camera flash in the middle of a service.

It is appropriate to make an offering to the lama, especially if you do take photographs. A *khata* (white scarf) is traditional, but these days rupees are also appreciated; monasteries depend for their existence on the donations of the faithful.

Decorations All the gompas are decorated with impressive mural paintings depicting mythological scenes, and sometimes thangkas (painted on cotton, framed in brocade and hung), although there is quite a range in quality. The subjects are usually gods, great lamas, ritual diagrams (mandalas which represent the forces of the universe and aid meditation) and the wheel of life. The wheel of life is represented in the porch of every gompa and represents Buddha's knowledge and the way humans can escape their conditioning and

---

The Tibetan Calendar

Around the base of the great dorje at the top of the stairway to Swayambhunath are the symbols of the 12 animals of the Tibetan calendar. The animals are similar to those of the Chinese calendar and through this century they fall as follows:

Snake	1929	1941	1953	1965	1977	1989
Horse	1930	1942	1954	1966	1978	1990
Sheep	1931	1943	1955	1967	1979	1991
Monkey	1932	1944	1956	1968	1980	1992
Goose	1933	1945	1957	1969	1981	1993
Dog	1934	1946	1958	1970	1982	1994
Pig	1935	1947	1959	1971	1983	1995
Rat	1936	1948	1960	1972	1984	1996
Bull	1937	1949	1961	1973	1985	1997
Tiger	1938	1950	1962	1974	1986	1998
Hare	1939	1951	1963	1975	1987	1999
Dragon	1940	1952	1964	1976	1988	2000

achieve nirvana. Extremely complex rules govern every detail of these traditional arts; all stress spirituality, order and symmetry, not originality.

You will also see huge statues of various Buddhas (the Tibetans believe Buddha has been reincarnated many times), prayer wheels, strategically arranged lamps filled with ghee (clarified butter) and sometimes offerings of rice. To the western eye, the gompas are riots of colour, but awesome nonetheless. Most religious rites involve the recitation of sacred texts and chanting, often punctuated by musical instruments. The instruments dramatise and underline particular passages – usually in a quite unmusical way. Drums and cymbals crash, and trumpets and oboes moan repetitively. The result can be dramatic and moving.

Sakyapa Gompa This is the only gompa that opens directly onto the stupa (on the western side). There are some fine paintings and a magnificent Tara covered in beautiful embroideries. Don't miss the massive prayer wheel on the left of the entrance.

Chinya-Lama Gompa Named after a lama who had trained in China, this gompa is on the right of the path that leaves to the north of the stupa.

Nyingmapa Gompa This is one of the most recently completed (1984) and impressive gompas. It has a large and thriving community – there are lots of young novices. The gompa is a large, reddish-ochre building (designed after a monastery in Tibet) surrounded by lower, white buildings that form a large courtyard. There are some very fine interior decorations that are the work of artists from Bhutan.

Kargyupa/Nyingmapa Gompa Known also as Ka-Nying Sheldrup Ling monastery, this large white gompa is equal to the Nyingmapa Gompa in size. It has a richly decorated interior with some fine paintings and large thangkas. The entrance is to the left of the main metal gates and westerners are welcome;

the lama speaks English. The gompa hosts an annual seminar on Vajrayana training, usually in October for two weeks.

Sakyapa Gompa This gompa, to the north-east of the stupa, does not have the imposing architectural unity of the previous two – it has obviously been built in stages over a number of years – but it is no less interesting. There are some high-quality frescoes (inside the vestibule) and the main room is richly gilded and atmospheric.

Gelugpa Gompa To the right of the lane that runs north-east from the stupa, the Gelugpa Gompa is the least imposing gompa in appearance, but it nonetheless attracts large crowds of worshippers and has many young monks.

Special Events
The Tibetan new year *(losar)* in February is celebrated by large crowds of pilgrims, who come to watch the lamas perform their rites. Long copper horns are blown, a portrait of the Dalai Lama is paraded around, and masked dances are performed.

Places to Stay
There are a number of guest houses in the tangle of lanes north and east of the stupa. The *Lotus Guest House* (☎ 01-472320) provides a very pleasant option if you want to escape the madness of Kathmandu for peace and quiet and if you want to be close to Bodhnath. Rooms are spotlessly clean and there is a nice garden. Singles/doubles with bath cost Rs 220/300, or Rs 190/260 without, plus 10% tax.

Also good, and with excellent rooftop views out over the stupa – and the airport – is the *Happy Valley Guest House* (☎ 01-471241; fax 471876), a modern hotel near the Sakyapa Gompa. This is a very well appointed hotel with very friendly management. Single/double rooms cost $20/25.

The *Hotel Tashi Delek* (☎ 01-471380) is right on the main road not far from the entrance to the stupa. The back rooms are reasonably quiet and look out across the fields to Pashupatinath. The rooms are somewhat gloomy and all have common bath; doubles on the 1st floor cost Rs 165, with views on the 2nd floor they cost Rs 250. There's solar hot water in the afternoons.

Places to Eat
There are a number of small restaurants along the main road outside the stupa enclosure and a couple of restaurants around the stupa itself. On the main road, the best choice is the *Bir Restaurant*, which is a popular meeting place for the local Tibetans and westerners living in the area. Most dishes are under Rs 30.

Near the stupa is the *Stupa View* which really does have a stupendous view, as well as excellent food (if a little overpriced). Main meals including a good range of vegetarian and Italian dishes are around Rs 100. Right next door is the similar *Himalayan Restaurant*.

Also with good rooftop views and worth a try is the *Ristorante Italiano la Calabria*, on the eastern edge of the enclosure. Predictably, pasta features heavily on the menu, and main courses are from Rs 120 to Rs 180.

For those on a shoestring budget, there are plenty of small Tibetan eating houses in the streets behind the stupa – any place with a curtain across an open door is probably one. The *Ilam Restaurant* is typical of these places.

The *Stupa Hotel*, a 10 minute walk from the stupa, has an excellent garden restaurant with good food and reasonable prices.

Getting There & Away
Buses to Bodhnath run regularly from the City Bus Station, take about an hour and cost Rs 3. Bicycles or taxis are better options. It's an interesting short walk between Bodhnath and Pashupatinath (see the Pashupatinath section for details).

Most tour operators include Bodhnath on their itineraries, usually in combination with Pashupatinath, and sometimes with Swayambhunath.

KOPAN (9 km)
The Kopan monastery (☎ 01-226717), a popular centre for courses on Buddhism and other Tibetan-related subjects, stands on a hilltop to the north of Bodhnath. You can visit Kopan on a walk between Bodhnath and the Gokarna Mahadev Temple; locals will point the way.

The centre has short courses on Tibetan medicine, thangka painting and other subjects but the major attraction for westerners is the 10 day residential course introducing Buddhist psychology and philosophy. The cost is about $250 including accommodation and food, but the participants must observe strict disciplinary rules.

In Maharajganj in Kathmandu, the Himalayan Yogic Institute (☎ 01-413094) is associated with the monastery and also operates courses; they can provide information on Kopan. Call the monastery direct or write to the Nepal Mahayana Centre, PO Box 817, Kathmandu, Nepal, for more information.

GOKARNA MAHADEV TEMPLE (10 km)
Only a short distance north-east of Bodhnath the Sundarijal road turns off from the Sankhu road and after a couple of km of twists and turns takes you to the old Newari village of Gokarna. The village is surrounded on three sides by the Gokarna forest reserve and is notable for its fine riverside Shiva temple.

Built in 1582 the triple roofed Mahadev (Great God) or Gokarneshwar (Lord of Gokarna) Temple stands on the banks of the Bagmati River and its inner sanctum enshrines a particularly revered Shiva lingam. Over the temple entrance is a golden *torana* (a space for a deity) with Shiva and Parvati making an appearance in the centre in the Uma Maheshwar position (Parvati's hand resting on Shiva's knee) with a figure of the Garuda above them.

The temple's great interest is the surprisingly varied collection of sculptures and reliefs all around the site. They even line the pathway down from the road to the temple courtyard, starting with a Buddha figure at the top, and feature a varied collection of

AROUND THE KATHMANDU VALLEY

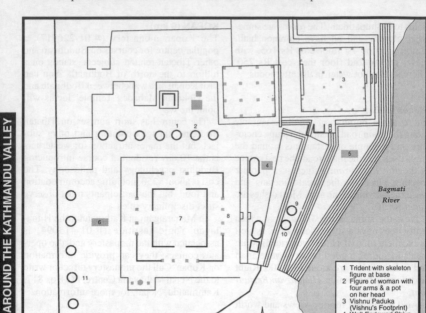

Bagmati River

1 Trident with skeleton figure at base
2 Figure of woman with four arms & a pot on her head
3 Vishnu Paduka (Vishnu's Footprint)
4 Well-Endowed Shiva
5 Shiva Image reclining on a bed of cobras
6 Nandi (Shiva's Bull)
7 Gokarna Mahadev Temple
8 Golden Torana with Uma-Maheshwar in centre
9 Ganesh
10 Hanuman
11 Bearded Brahma
12 Narsingha (Vishnu's man-lion incarnation)
13 Buddha
14 Cow

Gokarna Mahadev

0   3   6 m

gods and goddesses, some dating back over a thousand years.

The sculptures include figures from Hindu mythology including Narad, Surya (sun god), Chandra (moon god) and Kamadeva (god of love). There's a bearded image of Brahma, Ganesh makes his usual cheerful appearance and Vishnu appears as Narsingha, making a particularly thorough job of disembowelling a nasty demon. Shiva's bull, Nandi, stands beside the temple and as well as the inevitable lingams dotted around there's even a nude figure of Shiva, complete with erect lingam. Durga makes three

Durga

appearances, one of them as Ajima. The finest of the Gokarna statuary is in the small shrine house in the north-western corner of the courtyard. This 8th century sculpture of the beautiful goddess Parvati shows her at her radiant best; you can see why Shiva fancied her!

To one side of the main temple, just above the river, is the small, open, single storey **Vishnu Paduka**. This relatively recent addition shelters a metal plate bearing Vishnu's footprint. Outside, and set into the steps above the river, is an image of Shiva reclining on a bed of cobras, just like the reclining Vishnu images at Budhanilkantha and Balaju.

Getting There & Away
You can walk, cycle or take a taxi to Gokarna but there's also an interesting walking route between Gokarna and Bodhnath via the monastery at Kopan. The clear trail starts from just beyond the bridge, on the Kathmandu side of Gokarna. It starts off steeply north-west and runs through fields and bamboo groves past tea houses to Kopan on top of a small hill. From Kopan it's an easy walk south-west to Bodhnath.

SUNDARIJAL (15 km)
At the north-eastern edge of the valley, the streams which eventually join the Bagmati River flow over the waterfalls at Sundarijal into a 100 year old reservoir. This is also the starting point for the popular trek to Helambu, and the main reservoir which supplies drinking water to the valley is about a two hour walk uphill from here. A smaller trail forks off before the reservoir to a small rock cave, where a 13th century image of Mahadevi (great goddess) can be found. See the Nagarkot section for details of the long valley-rim walk to Sundarijal from Nagarkot.

Getting There & Away
Buses leave from the City Bus Station and cost Rs 11. It's a pleasant bicycle ride along the quiet roads past Gokarna.

Sankhu & Vajra Jogini Route

The route to Sankhu follows the old Tibetan trade route past Bodhnath. After Bodhnath the road to Sundarijal turns off to the north-east and the road to Sankhu continues to the east.

GOKARNA SAFARI PARK (10 km)
Continuing east of Bodhnath from Kathmandu, the entrance to the former Royal Game Reserve or King's Forest is off the Sankhu road. A deer park was created here late in the last century and the walled reserve has spotted deer (chital), hog deer (laghuna), monkeys and birds.

This is one of the few woodlands left on the valley floor, and used to be a great spot for picnics and a bit of game-spotting. Unfortunately, it is currently closed and it seems there is little chance of it reopening. Check with the tourist office before making the trip out here.

Getting There & Away
The reserve is about 2.5 km from Bodhnath, so it can be easily reached by bicycle. Buses run quite frequently to Sundarijal from the City Bus Station and you can get off at the entrance.

SANKHU (20 km)
Sankhu was once an important post on the trading route between Kathmandu and Lhasa, and although the town's great days are over, you can still see many signs of its former prosperity. The town was first settled in the Licchavi era and there are many old homes decorated with fine woodcarving. Although many traditional aspects of Newari life continue in the town, the most persuasive reason to visit this place is the beautiful Vajra Jogini Temple complex, about two km north of town.

Getting There & Away
Buses to Sankhu leave from the City Bus Station. They take about two hours and cost Rs 12.

Tantric Goddesses

The name Vajra Jogini suggests a close association with Tantric beliefs. A *vajra (dorje* in Tibetan) is the Buddhist thunderbolt symbol that looks a bit like a hollow dumb-bell and Vajrayana is the name for the Tantric form of Buddhism. Tantric beliefs developed as a synthesis of ancient pre-Hindu religions and new ideas that rejected many orthodox Hindu and Buddhist beliefs. Tantric believers hold that endless rebirths on the journey to nirvana can be avoided by incorporating magical rites with all the energies of existence – both good and bad – under the strict tutelage of a lama. Sex and sexual imagery play a central role.

Hinduism was initially a patriarchal religion introduced by the Aryan invaders of India, and overriding the existing earth goddesses. The development of *shaktis* or the female consorts of the new male gods allowed the resurgence of the female forces. These goddesses have enjoyed tremendous popularity in the Kathmandu Valley, sometimes completely overshadowing their male counterparts, especially in Tantric belief. A parallel development in Buddhism produced the female counterparts to the Dhyani Buddhas.

A Jogini is the female counterpart to a Bhairab, one of the wrathful forms of Shiva. In other words, a Jogini is the wrathful form of Shiva's partner Mahadevi (great goddess) who is Parvati in a more peaceful manifestation. Amongst some of Mahadevi's fearsome manifestations are Kali, Durga, Annapurna and Taleju.

So who is Vajra Jogini you ask? A Tantric goddess is the simple answer – a unique Nepali goddess possibly combining elements from Hinduism, Buddhism and perhaps even earlier religions. ■

It's easy to reach Sankhu by bike. The road is sealed and flat (with a few minor exceptions), and basically follows the Manohara River. It's an attractive and interesting ride taking about 1½ hours beyond Bodhnath. Rather than backtrack all the way, in the dry season at least it is possible to cross the Manohara and climb to the fascinating Changu Narayan Temple (see the Changu Narayan section for details). See the Nagarkot section for details of the interesting walk down to Sankhu.

VAJRA JOGINI (22 km)

Perched high above the valley, in a grove of huge, old trees, this complex of temples is well worth visiting. The main temple was built in 1655 by Pratap Malla of Kathmandu, but it seems likely that the site has been used for much longer than that. The origins of the Tantric goddess who is worshipped in this bewitching spot are hard to determine.

The climb up the stone steps to the temples is steep and hot, but there are a number of waterspouts where you can cool off. About halfway up there's a shelter and some carvings of Kali and Ganesh. A natural stone represents Than Bhairab and sacrifices are made at its foot.

As you enter the main temple compound you will see several fine bells (the Tantric female equivalent to the vajra or thunderbolt) on your right. There are two temples and the one nearest to the entrance is the Vajra Jogini Temple, a pagoda with a three tiered roof of sheet copper. There is some beautiful repoussé work on the southern facade. The struts are carved with protective animals and gods from the Buddhist pantheon. The goddess' image cannot actually be seen through the door.

The two tiered temple furthest from the entrance enshrines a chaitya and commemorates Ugra Tara, or Blue (Nilo) Tara, a Buddhist goddess. The woodcarving around the doors is very fine. There are various chaityas around the platform and a gilt lion on a pillar. In the north-western corner of the courtyard (the far left when you enter) is the entrance to a cave, which is used for Tantric practices, and a Tibetan inscription. Behind the temples and up some stairs are buildings which were once used as pilgrim rest houses and priests' houses.

Getting There & Away

At Sankhu, turn left at the bus stop and walk north through the village (where there is some beautiful woodcarving). Just after the road turns to the right, take the road on the left which runs out of the village (under an ugly concrete archway). There are some fine stone carvings of Vishnu and Ganesh after the arch. The road then forks: the left fork is the traditional approach for pedestrians and follows the small river; the right fork is drivable (though rough) and is OK for bikes.

There's a car park at the foot of the steps to the temple complex. If you get there by bicycle, it will be necessary to pay a few rupees to someone to look after it for you. It's quite a stiff climb to the temples.

Changu Narayan Route

THIMI (10 km)
Thimi is the fourth largest town in the valley, outranked only by Kathmandu, Patan and Bhaktapur. It's a typical Newari town and its 'capable people' (the name of the town is derived from this Newari expression) operate thriving cottage industries producing pottery and papier-mâché masks. They also grow vegetables for the markets of Kathmandu.

The town's main road runs north-south between the old and new Bhaktapur roads which form the northern and southern boundaries of the town. In the centre of the southern square is the 16th century **Balkumari Temple**. Balkumari was one of Bhairab's shaktis and a much less magnificent Bhairab Temple is found nearby (see the aside on Tantric goddesses in the Vajra Jogini section). Thimi also has a 16th century **Narayan temple** and a 15th century **Mahadev temple**.

Just to the north of Thimi is **Nade** and from here a stone pathway leads up through an archway to the **Ganesh Dyochen**. Nearby is a locally popular triple roofed **Ganesh temple**. Further north is Bode, with the interesting 17th century **Mahalakshmi Temple**.

Special Events
In a Nepali new year's day ceremony, 32 deities are carried to the Balkumari Temple

in palanquins. The arrival of the Ganesh image from Nade is the high point of the colourful festivities (a great deal of bright red powder gets chucked around). A similar but smaller ceremony also takes place at the Mahalakshmi Temple in Bode.

CHANGU NARAYAN TEMPLE (22 km)
The beautiful and historic temple of Changu Narayan stands on a hilltop at the eastern end of the valley, about four km north of Bhaktapur. Although the temple dates from 1702, when it was rebuilt after a fire, its origins go right back to the 4th century and there are many important stone images and sculptures dating from the Licchavi period.

Despite the temple's beauty and interest it attracts relatively few visitors because of its comparative inaccessibility, although these days you can drive right to the temple via Bhaktapur. Alternatively, it makes a pleasant walk from that town or an interesting destination on the walk down from Nagarkot.

The double roofed temple is dedicated to Vishnu in his incarnation as Narayan and is exceptionally beautiful with quite amazingly intricate roof struts depicting multi-armed goddesses. The temple is fronted by a figure of Garuda said to date from the 5th century. The man-bird mount of Vishnu has a snake around his neck and kneels with folded hands facing the temple. Stone lions guard the wonderfully gilded door, flanked by equally detailed gilded windows. Two pillars at the front corners carry two of the traditional symbols of Vishnu, the conch shell and the chakra.

Despite the beauty of the temple itself it is, in Nepali terms, relatively recent and the much older images found in the temple courtyard are of equal interest. There are various images of Vishnu, carrying the symbols associated with the god in his four hands. In the north-western corner there is an image of Vishnu astride the Garuda which is illustrated on the Rs 10 banknote. Beside the Garuda figure which faces the front of the temple is one of the oldest Licchavi stone inscriptions in the valley.

Other images include one of Vishnu as

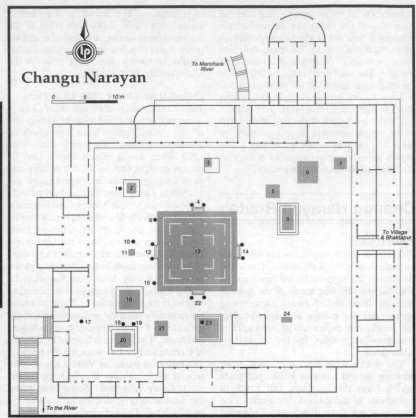

Changu Narayan

0   5   10 m

To Manohara
River

To Village
& Bhaktapur

To the River

AROUND THE KATHMANDU VALLEY

1	Vishnu & Garuda Image (from Rs 10 Note)	10	Garuda Image	19	Relief of Vishnu as Vikrantha
2	Krishna Shrine	11	Statue of King Bhupatindra Malla & His Queen	20	Lakshmi Narayan Temple
3	Nriteshwar Shrine	12	Stone Lions	21	Reliefs of Narayan on the Serpent Ananta & 10 Headed Maheshwar
4	Winged Lions	13	Changu Narayan Temple		
5	Vishnu Image	14	Griffins		
6	Mahavishnu	15	Pillar with Conch Shell Symbol		
7	Mahadev Shiva Lingam	16	Pashupatinath Shrine		
8	Images of Avalokitesvara & Vishnu	17	Bhairab Shrine	22	Elephants
		18	Relief of Vishnu as Narsingha	23	Mahadev Shiva Shrine
9	Pillar with Chakra Symbol			24	Ganesh Shrine

GREG ELMS

PETER MORRIS

PAUL STEEL

HUGH FINLAY

SWAYAMBHUNATH
Top Left & Bottom: The all-seeing eyes of the Buddha are everywhere in Swayambhunath.
Top Right: Bronzed prayer wheels

TONY WHEELER

ADAM MCCROW

BODHNATH

Top: The enormous ancient stupa at Bodhnath, the largest in Nepal.
Bottom: Vibrant mural of Ajima, goddess of smallpox.

BODHNATH

Top: Buddha is watching you!
Bottom: Prayer flags fluttering to heaven.

RICHARD I'ANSON

HUGH FINLAY

TONY WHEELER

KATHMANDU VALLEY
Top: Kathmandu and its fertile valley, from Kirtipur
Centre: Hindu pilgrims throng the Pashupatinath temple for the festival of Shivaratri.
Bottom: Adorning the sleeping Vishnu, Budhanilkantha

Narsingha, his man-lion incarnation, in the act of disembowelling a demon. Another shows him as Vikrantha, the six armed dwarf who transformed into a giant capable of covering the universe in three gigantic steps. Behind these two images is a small black slab showing Narayan reclining on the serpent Ananta at the bottom and Vishnu with 10 heads and 10 arms in the centre. This beautifully carved image dates from the 5th or 6th century.

Other points of interest include the statues of King Bhupatindra Malla and his queen, kneeling in a gilded cage in front of the temple. Look at the brick paving of the courtyard. In the centre, triangular bricks are used while out towards the edge there are older rounded-corner bricks. The village of Changu stands below the temple hill and has some Licchavi remains.

Places to Stay & Eat
The small *Restaurant Champak* is right inside the temple complex. On the road back to Bhaktapur, the *Changu Narayan Hill Resort* offers basic trekking-style accommodation.

Narsingha
The image of Vishnu as Narsingha or Narsimha is a common one in the valley. In his man-lion incarnation the god is traditionally seen with a demon stretched across his legs, in the act of killing the creature by disembowelling it. You can find Narsingha at work at Changu Narayan, in front of the palace in Patan, just inside the Hanuman Dhoka palace entrance in Kathmandu and at the Gokarna Mahadev Temple.

The demon was supposedly undefeatable as it could not be killed by man or beast, by day or night or by any weapon. Vishnu's appearance as Narsingha neatly overcame the first obstacle for a man-lion is neither a man nor a beast. He then waited until evening to attack the demon, for evening is neither day nor night. And instead of a weapon Narsingha used his own nails to tear the demon apart. ■

Getting There & Away
There is no public transport to Changu Narayan. A taxi from Kathmandu costs around Rs 400, and from Bhaktapur around Rs 150.

It takes about two hours on foot or about an hour by mountain bike to get to Changu Narayan from Bhaktapur. It's a wonderful downhill run on the way back but quite a steep climb on the way there. A long spur runs down from the eastern edge of the valley and the temple tops the final bump of this lengthy ridge. There is a sealed road from Bhaktapur right to the village of Changu, which is only a short stroll from the temple, and you can easily get a taxi to Changu Narayan from Bhaktapur. A number of walking trails, clearly signposted, lead to Changu Narayan from Bhaktapur and once you get out of the town the hill is clearly visible.

If you're on foot or bicycle it's possible to continue to Bodhnath, Sankhu, Gokarna or other attractions in the north-east of the valley. From the northern and western entranceways to the temple a short, steep path descends to the Manohara River, which can easily be waded across or crossed by a temporary bridge during the dry season (this won't be possible in the monsoon). This brings you out to the Sankhu road at the village of Bramhakhel about 3.5 km east of Gokarna.

If you approach Changu Narayan from the Sankhu road you'll see a small sign for Changu Narayan on a building wall on the south side at the entry to Bramhakhel. It's a five minute walk across the fields to the river and the temporary bridge. It's quite a steep and difficult scramble up the hill that will take at least 45 minutes (especially if you're carrying a bike). You might like to go slower as there are a couple of small Newari hamlets along the way, and great, views.

There's quite a labyrinth of paths up the hill and it's not a bad idea to have a guide (and bicycle carrier). You will probably find small boys offering their services – establish a price in advance. If not, just keep going up!

From Changu Narayan it's an exhilarating half-hour bike ride to Bhaktapur, which is another 45 minutes from Kathmandu.

A third way of reaching Changu Narayan is by the pleasant downhill stroll from Nagarkot (see the following Nagarkot section). Walking down from Nagarkot to Changu Narayan and then on to Bhaktapur is a much more interesting walk than the straightforward walk down to Bhaktapur.

Nagarkot Route

The route to Nagarkot goes by Thimi and Bhaktapur before climbing steeply up to the village on the valley rim.

NAGARKOT (30 km)

There are various places around the edge of the Kathmandu Valley which offer great mountain views, but the resort village of Nagarkot is generally held to be the best. Mountain watchers make their way up to the village, stay overnight in one of Nagarkot's lodges, then rise at dawn to see the sun appear over the Himalaya.

Nagarkot is on a ridge on the north-eastern rim of the valley and the view extends all the way from Dhaulagiri in the west past Mt Everest (little more than a dot on the horizon) to Kanchenjunga in the east. An easy hour's walk north from the village will give an even better 360° view from a lookout tower on a ridge. You have to cross an army checkpost and they will only let you walk through in the morning.

A pilgrimage to Nagarkot will nearly always be rewarded with a view between October and March, but you will be very lucky to catch more than a glimpse through the clouds of some snow-capped mountains in the June to September monsoon period. It can get very cold at Nagarkot in autumn or winter so if you're staying overnight come prepared with warm clothing.

The main centre of Nagarkot, in reality a small cluster of guest houses, is a 10 minute walk north of the main road that runs through

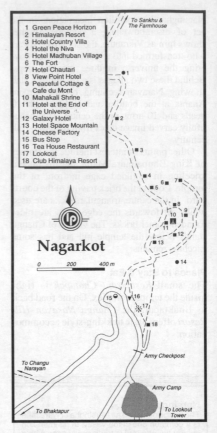

1 Green Peace Horizon
2 Himalayan Resort
3 Hotel Country Villa
4 Hotel the Niva
5 Hotel Madhuban Village
6 The Fort
7 Hotel Chautari
8 View Point Hotel
9 Peaceful Cottage & Cafe du Mont
10 Mahakali Shrine
11 Hotel at the End of the Universe
12 Galaxy Hotel
13 Hotel Space Mountain
14 Cheese Factory
15 Bus Stop
16 Tea House Restaurant
17 Lookout
18 Club Himalaya Resort

To Sankhu & The Farmhouse

Nagarkot

0   200   400 m

To Changu Narayan

To Bhaktapur

Army Checkpost

Army Camp

To Lookout Tower

to the army camp. Nagarkot originally owes its existence to the camp, but more lately to tourism. It was never a traditional village, so while the views can be stunning, and the surrounding countryside is great for walking, the unplanned scatter of lodges is not itself attractive.

Right in the centre of things is a new lookout, between the huge Club Himalaya Resort and the Tea House.

There are a number of walks to and from Nagarkot, including fine walks down to Sundarijal, Sankhu, Changu Narayan or Bhaktapur in the valley or south to Banepa (beyond the valley). There is a cheese factory where you can buy some food to eat on your way down.

Places to Stay & Eat

Nagarkot has a rapidly expanding selection of lodges, guest houses and hotels – most of them far from pretty. They usually offer a range of facilities at a range of prices, and most are expensive for the facilities you get – but what price the view? Most people eat at their lodge, and most are unimpressed with the cuisine.

Nagarkot accommodation is spread out along the dirt track which heads north from the bus stop at the town's one and only intersection. Nagarkot is very much a one-night stand, and few visitors stay longer although you can make some pleasant strolls in the surrounding country.

Late in the afternoon each day there's a mass arrival and after breakfast each morning there's a mass departure. This means that every lodge can simultaneously run out of rooms, so when you reach Nagarkot make sure you find a room first. The best rooms go first, and late arrivals may find the accommodation standards dropping precipitously. In the off season there are fewer visitors and prices are highly negotiable.

Most places have electricity, but hot water and heating are hard to come by, especially at the bottom end of the market. A torch (flashlight) is useful (for an early-morning start to the lookout tower) and warm clothing (even a sleeping bag) can be worthwhile. Most people are in bed pretty early, so bring a book.

The winding road takes a sharp turn at the cluster of shops which mark the Nagarkot bus stop. From here a dirt track veers right and after a couple of hundred metres comes to a hilltop group of hotels which are the most popular and best situated at Nagarkot. They cluster around the Mahakali Shrine, and many have rooms that offer Himalayan views straight from your bed. At the worst you'll just have to take a few steps outside to bring the whole panorama into view.

The first place you come across is the *Hotel Space Mountain* (☎ 01-290871), a modern and unremarkable place with rooms that all face the wrong direction! It's also outrageously overpriced at $34/39.

Next is a group of budget hotels around the Mahakali Shrine. The *Hotel at the End of the Universe* (☎ 01-610874) has some standard rooms from $4/6, including a few pleasant bamboo-walled cottages with attached toilet. There are also some modern brick rooms with hot shower at $15. While none of the rooms has a view, the restaurant does. With a carpeted bench around low tables it's a popular gathering place in the evening. The food is pretty good.

The *Galaxy Hotel*, just below, has singles/doubles with bath for Rs 200, and some new luxury rooms for $15. Most rooms are reasonably pleasant, and have at least partial views, so you may consider the cost worthwhile.

Continue beyond the Mahakali Shrine, skirting the bank official's house, and you reach the *View Point Hotel*, which is a more up-market option, with rooms starting at $14/20 and rising to $24/30 for a combination of comfort and views. All rooms have private bath with hot water. The restaurant has a fireplace.

Just beyond the View Point Hotel is the *Peaceful Cottage* (☎ 01-290877) which has rooms of varying standards. The prices start from $5/8 for hardboard partitioned cells with views, and there are also better rooms with private bath and hot water for $10/20. Topping the rise is the *Cafe du Mont* with magnificent views, and average food (you can't have everything!).

On the downhill side of the Peaceful Cottage is the *The Fort* (☎ 01-290869), a large place built in pseudo-Newari style. The front rooms have excellent views and the whole place is geared towards tour groups. The rooms cost $57/63.

Separated from this group of lodges by a couple of hundred metres is the *Hotel the Niva* with simple, spartan rooms at Rs 250 downstairs and Rs 300 upstairs.

Continuing along the dirt road you get to a couple of modern mid-range places, the

AROUND THE KATHMANDU VALLEY

Hotel Country Villa and the *Himalayan Resort*.

A good place further along still is the relaxed little *Green Peace Horizon*, with small bamboo cottages with stunning views at Rs 300 with attached toilet – also with views. This place is a bit of a walk, but if you're after peace and quiet it could be ideal.

There's another good place about four km away on the Sankhu road, past Green Peace Horizon. *The Farmhouse* is in an old, beautifully renovated Newari house and has been highly recommended. It's run by Kathmandu's Hotel Vajra, and the rates are reasonably high, although meals are included. Singles/doubles are $20/40.

Above the main intersection is the modern *Tea House*, a restaurant with a nice terrace aimed at day-trippers. It is an attractive building with good views, and it's open from 6 am to 8 pm. Main meals are around Rs 100, and a Coke is a steep Rs 30.

A bit further towards the army camp and perched right on the ridge is *Club Himalaya Resort* (☎ 01-290883; fax 417133), which is run by the Kathmandu Guest House. A large construction like this was probably inevitable in Nagarkot, but it really does nothing for the rural ambience. Having said that, the building has been well thought out and each rooms has a private balcony with view, and there are also views from the atrium-type lobby with its restaurant and indoor swimming pool and spa. The rooms are large and well furnished, and cost $80/100 including breakfast.

Further again, on the eastern side of the army camp, is the very rustic *The Pinnacles* (fax 01-411277), tucked away in an old apple orchard. Full board is $60/85.

Getting There & Away

There's a road right to Nagarkot from Bhaktapur so you can take a bus or taxi all the way there. You don't even have to stay overnight as Kathmandu tour operators run dawn trips to Nagarkot to catch the sunrise. Walking to or, preferably, from Nagarkot is, however, an interesting alternative and there are several possible routes, all detailed in the Treks from Nagarkot section in this chapter.

Buses operate to a somewhat unreliable schedule from Bhaktapur, departing every few hours and costing Rs 12. The bus can be very slow (taking up to two hours) and extremely crowded. The roof is not only less crowded but also offers fine views. A taxi from Bhaktapur costs about Rs 500 one way or Rs 800 return.

From Kathmandu, most people catch the tourist bus which leaves from Thamel at 1.30 pm and arrives about 4 pm; on the return journey it leaves Nagarkot at 10 am. Tickets are available from most tour agencies and tourist information centres. A one way fare costs Rs 55, return Rs 115. Pre-dawn tours from Kathmandu cost about Rs 300.

TREKS FROM NAGARKOT

There are a number of trekking routes to or from Nagarkot. If you only want to walk one way it's a good idea to take the bus to Nagarkot and walk back down. The following walks are all written heading downhill from Nagarkot.

Nagarkot to Bhaktapur

Until the road from Nagarkot to Bhaktapur was built, this walking trail was the only way to go. Now with buses running back and forth it's neither necessary nor all that enjoyable. You would be better off taking one of the alternative routes, but if you do want to walk back down it's relatively easy to take the wide, easy trail which short-cuts across the road turns. The trail eventually joins the road on its final gradual ascent to Bhaktapur; you can follow this and turn off at the eastern end of the town or simply catch a bus, should one come by. It takes about two hours to walk down, and perhaps twice that walking up.

Going down you leave the main road to descend steeply through a pine forest, then follow a stream to a cluster of bamboo trees near the city reservoir where you rejoin the main road. From here you enter the town at the eastern end and continue to Tachupal Tole. If you want to walk up from Bhaktapur there are signs to Nagarkot in the town.

Nagarkot to Changu Narayan Temple

Walking down to Changu Narayan is a much more interesting alternative to the walk down to Bhaktapur. From Nagarkot it is very easy to see the long spur which extends into the Kathmandu Valley. At the very end of the spur the ridge line gives one final hiccup and then drops down to the valley floor. The beautiful temple of Changu Narayan is on the top of this final bump on the ridge line.

The walking trail from Nagarkot follows the road to Bhaktapur along a ridge, branching off at a sharp hairpin bend. It's easier to take the bus from Nagarkot down to this bend rather than to walk all the way down to Changu Narayan. The fare is Rs 5 and the ride saves you the tedious part of the walk, where the walking trail runs close to the road.

From the bend, the trail climbs uphill through a pine forest for about 20 minutes until it reaches the top of the ridge and then it simply follows the ridge line undulating gently down to Changu Narayan. The walking trail passes through small Chhetri villages with wonderful views over the valley to the Himalaya beyond. Finally, the shining roof of Changu Narayan appears above the village of **Changu** itself from where a stone-paved street leads to the temple. From the hairpin bend (where you leave the Nagarkot to Bhaktapur road) it takes about one to 1½ hours to walk to the temple. See the earlier Changu Narayan Temple section for information about this temple.

From Changu Narayan you can descend to the Manohara River to the north and take the road back to Bodhnath and Kathmandu. Alternatively you can continue south to Bhaktapur, either by the direct trail or by the road running slightly to the east.

Nagarkot to Sankhu

Fewer walkers follow the trail to Sankhu, just north of the Nagarkot to Changu Narayan ridge line in the north-east of the valley. The picturesque Newari town is surrounded by rich agricultural land and is easily visible from Nagarkot or from the trail down to Changu Narayan. The trail follows a ridge line then drops steeply down the hillside in a north-westerly direction, joining the main Helambu to Sankhu trail and passing a group of tea houses where you can ask directions to the important temple of Vajra Jogini. The temple is to the north of Sankhu and by leaving the main trail you can walk west to this interesting site before completing the descent to Sankhu.

From Sankhu buses run back to Kathmandu via Bodhnath every couple of hours.

Nagarkot to Sundarijal

It takes two easy days or one very long one to reach Sundarijal from Nagarkot on a trail which follows the valley rim. From Sundarijal you can take the road to Gokarna, Bodhnath and Kathmandu or you can continue for another day along the rim to Sheopuri and Budhanilkantha. Some trekking agencies operate treks on this valley-rim walk, but it is also possible to find accommodation in tea houses. There are many confusing trail junctions so ask directions frequently.

The trail starts from the Mahakali Shrine heading north-north-east, and passes the village of Kattike (about one hour) and then turns more northerly to Jorsim Pauwa (about one hour). Walk further down through Bagdhara with its tea houses to Chowki Bhanjyang (about one hour). From Chowki Bhanjyang another hour's walk will take you further north through Nagle to **Bhotechaur**, which makes a good place to stop overnight in a tea house.

The walk continues by returning towards Chowki Bhanjyang for a short distance and then taking the fork by a *chautara* (porters' resting place) uphill and then more steeply uphill to cross a ridge line before dropping down on the middle of three trails to Chule. The trail contours around the edge of the valley, crossing several ridge lines running down into the valley, before dropping down to **Mulkarkha** and the trail past the reservoir and along the pipeline to Sundarijal. The last part of this trail to Sundarijal is the first part of the popular Helambu Trek.

Nagarkot to Banepa

The town of Banepa is outside the valley and is the major junction town on the way to Dhulikhel on the road to the Tibetan border. From Nagarkot, you start this walk near the tower at the southern part of the ridge and follow a steep descent to the east. Following a precise trail is difficult, but that is no problem since they all lead there. A few km north of Banepa the trail passes through the old Newari town of Nala with its interesting temples.

From Banepa, you can take a bus back to Kathmandu or continue to Dhulikhel where many travellers stay in the delightful Dhulikhel Lodge. See Dhulikhel in the next section.

Dhulikhel & Arniko Highway Route

The Arniko Highway to Dhulikhel passes by Thimi, skirts the southern side of Bhaktapur and then climbs out of the valley before dropping down to Banepa, continuing on to Dhulikhel, the Tibetan border and to Lhasa. This route is also covered in the Mountain Biking chapter.

BANEPA (26 km)

Just outside the valley, the small town of Banepa is a busy crossroads with a statue of King Tribhuvan marking the centre of town. The popular village of Dhulikhel is five km beyond Banepa; the temple town of Panauti is about five km south; the interesting village of Nala is just to the north-west; and Chandeshwari, with its legendary old temple, is only a km or so north-east – yet Banepa itself is of very limited interest. Indeed the main road through town, all that most visitors see, is a dusty, noisy affair and waiting for a change of bus at that busy crossroads is often decidedly unpleasant.

Chandeshwari Temple

Only a km or so north-east of Banepa the temple to the goddess Chandeshwari perches on the edge of a gorge. The road out of Banepa runs gently uphill then just as gently downhill through open fields and then a short village street, past an old tank and right to the arched entrance gate to the temple.

The people of this valley were once terrorised by a demon known as Chand and when Parvati, in her demon-slaying mode, got rid of the nuisance she took the name Chandeshwari, 'slayer of Chand', and this temple was built in her honour.

The temple is entered through a doorway topped by a brilliantly coloured relief of Parvati disposing of the demon. The triple roofed temple has roof struts showing the eight Ashta Matrikas and eight Bhairabs, but the temple's most notable feature is on the west wall which is painted with a huge and colourful fresco of Bhairab at his destructive worst.

The temple also has a Shiva shrine complete with lingam, and Nandi and Ganesh also make an appearance. The ghats below the temple, beside the stream, are an auspicious place to die and people come here when their end is nigh.

Other Attractions

Banepa itself has few buildings of interest although there are some pleasant squares and quieter laneways in the older part of town to the north-west. The old town square has two Narayan temples with virtually back-to-back worshipful Garuda statues. Right beside the turn-off to Chandeshwari is an attractive tank with bas reliefs of gods at one end.

Getting There & Away

Regular buses leave from the City Bus Station and the trip to Banepa takes about two hours and costs Rs 12. Buses continue on from Banepa to Dhulikhel and further towards Kodari on the Tibetan border. There are also regular services south from Banepa to Panauti.

NALA

The interesting small town of Nala is about four km north-west of Banepa. Nala's **Bhagwati Temple** dominates the central square of the town and is one of the very few four tiered temples in the valley area. On the edge of the settlement is the Buddhist pagoda temple of **Karunamaya**, dedicated to Avalokitesvara.

PANAUTI

Standing in a valley about six km south of Banepa, the small town of Panauti is at the junction of the rivers Roshi Khola and Pungamati Khola. Like Allahabad in India a third 'invisible' river is said to join the other two at the confluence. The town is relatively untouched and has a number of interesting temples, one of which may be the oldest in Nepal. Panauti once stood at the junction of important trading routes and had a royal palace in its main square. Today it's just a quiet backwater, but all the more interesting for that.

Indreshwar Mahadev Temple

The three storey Indreshwar Mahadev Temple in the village centre is a Shiva temple. It was originally built in 1294 over a Shiva lingam and was subsequently rebuilt in the 15th century. In 1988 an earthquake caused serious damage and there are plans to renovate it. In its original form it may well have been the oldest temple in Nepal – Kathmandu's Kasthamandap may predate it but Kasthamandap was originally built as a dharamsala, not as a temple.

Around the temple are many shrines including one dedicated to Ahilya, the beautiful wife of a Vedic sage.

Legends relate that she was seduced by the god Indra who tricked her by assuming the shape of her husband. When the sage returned and discovered what had happened he took a bizarre revenge upon Indra by causing his body to become covered in yonis, female sexual organs! Naturally Indra was somewhat put out by this and for many years he and his wife Indrayani repented at this auspicious confluence of rivers. Eventually Parvati, Shiva's consort, took pity upon Indrayani and turned her into the invisible river which joins the two visible ones in Panauti. More years passed and eventually Shiva decided to release Indra from his strange problem. Shiva appeared in Panauti as a great lingam and when Indra bathed in the river the yonis disappeared. The lingam is the one which stands in the temple.

The temple, run-down though it may be, is certainly a fine one and the roof struts depicting the various incarnations of Shiva and some discreetly amorous couples are said to be masterpieces of Newari woodcarving. The courtyard has numerous smaller shrines apart from the stone pillar to Ahilya.

To one side of the main temple is a rectangular **Bhairab temple** with faces peering out of the three upstairs windows, rather like the Shiva-Parvati Temple in Kathmandu's Durbar Square. A small double roofed Shiva temple stands by the north-western corner while a Vishnu shrine with a two metre high image of the god faces the temple from the west. Look for the pots and pans hanging under the roof eaves of the main temple. They're donated to the temple by newlyweds to ensure a happy married life.

Other Temples

Across the Pungamati Khola is the 17th century Brahmayani Temple; a suspension bridge crosses the river at this point. Brahmayani is the chief goddess of the village and her image is drawn around the town each year in the chariot festival. This temple was restored with French assistance in 1982-83.

On the town side of the river, actually at the junction where the two rivers meet, is a Krishna Narayan temple with some woodcarvings of similar age and style to the Indreshwar Mahadev Temple. The riverbank stone sculptures are also of interest, but, unfortunately, the late 80s were cruel to Panauti: apart from the earthquake there were also severe floods which swept away the cremation ghats at the river junction.

Special Events

Panauti celebrates a chariot festival at the end of the monsoon each year when images of the gods from the town's various temples are drawn around the streets in temple carts. The festival starts from the town's old Durbar Square.

There are a number of important religious sites across the subcontinent that play host to huge *melas* (religious fairs that attract enormous crowds of pilgrims, worshippers and sadhus). Every 12 years (next in 1998), the Magh Sankranti festival around mid-January (the Nepali month of Magh), is celebrated with a great mela in Panauti.

Getting There & Away

Buses between Dhulikhel and Banepa cost Rs 3. Buses run regularly to Panauti and leave from the *chowk* (marketplace) with the king's statue in the middle of Banepa (Rs 3). See the Dhulikhel section for information on walking to Panauti.

DHULIKHEL (32 km)

Only five km south-east of Banepa is the interesting small town of Dhulikhel. It's popular as a Himalayan viewpoint, in part because the road to Dhulikhel is easier than the steep and winding road to Nagarkot, but also because Dhulikhel is real, not just a tourist resort. It's also a good centre for short day treks – many visitors come here to stretch their legs before setting off on longer treks.

Dhulikhel is a district headquarters and has a number of government offices, a high school and even a small jail. Its population is Newar although there are people of many other groups in the surrounding villages. The prime Himalayan viewpoint is the parade ground, on the ridge just east of the centre. In the late 60s Dhulikhel was a gathering point for hippies who even planned to build their own temple here! An even better view can be found from the hill topped by a Kali temple, about 30 minutes walk along the Namobuddha trail.

Temples

The old part of the town, west of the bus stand and the Dhulikhel Lodge, is an interesting area to wander around with some fine old Newari buildings and several interesting temples. The town's main square has a tank, the small triple roofed **Harisiddhi Temple** and a **Vishnu temple** fronted by two worshipful Garudas in quite different styles. One is a kneeling stone Garuda topping a low pillar while the second Garuda is in bright

metal, flanked by two kneeling devotees, and is more like the bird-faced Garudas of Indonesia than the conventional Nepali Garudas. The triple roofed temple has been decorated with brightly coloured ceramic tiles. Beyond the square, the western end of the town is marked by a hill topped by a modern **Krishna temple** and the **Bhagwati Shiva Temple**.

Walking in the other direction you pass the post office and the mountain viewpoint, and reach the junction where the road turns south to Namobuddha. Continue straight on from the junction and dip down to a picturesque little **Shiva temple** at the bottom of a gorge. Water flows through the site where the main sanctum is a squat, square block decorated with coloured tiles and topped with a metal dome with four *nagas* (snake deities) arching down from the pinnacle. The temple is fronted by figures of Nandi on pillars and kneeling devotees. To one side is a fine image of Ganesh, while in a second small shrine only the feet remain of three images, the result of art thieves' work. Below that is a tank but this is a temple with everything – if you look around you can find images of Hanuman, Saraswati, Shiva and Parvati, lingams, tridents and much more.

Dhulikhel's final temple attraction is the **Kali Temple** high up the hill towards Namobuddha. Climb up here for the excellent view, not for the temple which is of little interest.

Places to Stay & Eat

Dhulikhel has a small number of places to stay, both in and around town.

The *Dhulikhel Lodge* (☎ 011-61152), in Dhulikhel, is a very popular place for shoestring travellers. It's in a fine old building, and has an atmospheric restaurant and a pleasant open courtyard. Singles/doubles cost Rs 150/250 and are very simple but quite comfortable. If you've got a room in the front you don't even need to climb out of bed to enjoy the Himalayan view, although front-room occupants might find the street activity a little disturbing. The lodge is a

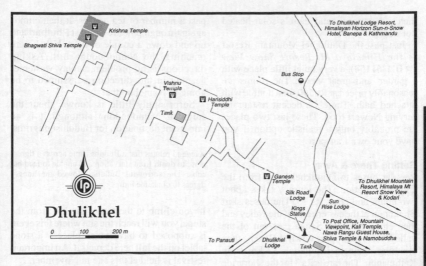

AROUND THE KATHMANDU VALLEY

wonderful place to just laze around and talk to people. The food can be quite good and over the years a veritable library of guest books with lots of interesting information interspersed with the usual dreamy raves have accumulated. The showers and washroom facilities beside the garden have hot water and there is electricity.

The *Nawa Rangu Guest House & Restaurant* (☎ 011-61226), on the way towards the post office and Shiva temple, is a curious place with a restaurant hung with interesting naive-style paintings, and basic trekking lodge-style rooms and bathroom facilities. The food is good, especially the custard pies and wheat porridge! Basic rooms are Rs 150/200.

On the main road there are a couple of possibilities, neither of them very attractive. The *Sun Rise Lodge* (☎ 011-61482) is the better of the two as it has mountain views. Rooms cost Rs 200 for a double, and hot water comes by the bucket. The *Silk Road Lodge* (☎ 011-61269) is cheaper at Rs 100 for a double with common bath.

Just off the main road, near the Dhulikhel bus stand, is the *Dhulikhel Lodge Resort* (☎ 011-61114; fax 01-222926), run by the

same people who have the Dhulikhel Lodge. This is a large, modern place with good rooms and superb views. It is aimed at groups who want to get out of Kathmandu for a day or so, and the cost is $42/48 for single/double rooms. The restaurant here is popular with day-tripping groups.

A km back towards Banepa is the attractive *Himalayan Horizon Sun-n-Snow Hotel* (☎ 011-61296; fax 61476). Singles/doubles in this comfortable hotel are $49/53. The buildings feature traditional woodcarving and all the rooms face straight out on to the Himalayan peaks. There's a restaurant/terrace area in front of the hotel with equally good views plus a beautiful garden running down the hill. The restaurant is relatively expensive, but has excellent food, including a variety of Nepali dishes. It's better value to opt for the room-only accommodation prices, rather than all-inclusive rates.

The *Dhulikhel Mountain Resort* (☎ 011-61466; fax 01-420778 in Kathmandu), is another up-market place, four km beyond the village downhill towards Barabise and the Tibetan border. The Himalayan views from here are equally superb and singles/doubles cost $72/74. Accommodation is in luxurious, thatched cottages, and there's solar-heated hot water.

Just past the Dhulikhel Mountain Resort is the *Himalaya Mt Resort Snow View* (☎ 011-61158), a very quiet little place with a garden and great views. The rooms are reasonably priced at Rs 500 for a double with attached bath. There's a decent restaurant, serving Newari food. These last two places are probably only a realistic option if you have your own transport.

Getting There & Away

Regular buses to Dhulikhel leave from the City Bus Station. The journey takes about two hours and costs Rs 13. The buses skirt Bhaktapur at the eastern end of the valley and then climb over the Sanga pass out of the valley, before dropping down to Banepa then climbing again to Dhulikhel, 32 km from Kathmandu. The fare is Rs 3 for the short ride from Banepa to Dhulikhel. A taxi from Kathmandu costs about Rs 500, or from Bhaktapur about Rs 350.

The walk to Dhulikhel from Nagarkot is an interesting alternative. After watching the sunrise at Nagarkot you can walk down through Nala to Banepa, from where you can take a bus the last few km to Dhulikhel. See the Treks from Nagarkot section earlier in this chapter for more information.

TREKS FROM DHULIKHEL
Namobuddha Trek

The trek from Dhulikhel to Namobuddha or Namura is a fine walk in itself and also a good leg-stretcher for longer treks. It takes about three hours each way, so it makes a good day walk; the Dhulikhel Lodge has a sketch map of the route. The walk can be made either as a return trip or as a loop to avoid backtracking. If you start early enough you can even continue on from Namobuddha to Panauti and return from there via Banepa by bus.

Namobuddha is a relatively easy trek which can even be made during the monsoon. From Dhulikhel the trail first climbs up to the Kali Temple lookout then drops down through the village of **Kavre** and

past a number of tea houses. It then climbs again through pine woods past **Phulbari** and up and down a couple of more hills before reaching the Namobuddha hill. Asking directions is no problem, as any westerner heading in this direction is assumed to be going to Namobuddha!

Surprisingly little is known about the stupa at Namobuddha although it is an important destination for Buddhist pilgrims.

A legend relates that a Buddha came across a tigress close to death from starvation and unable to feed her cubs. The sorrowful Buddha allowed the hungry tigress to consume him.

If you climb to the top of the hill from the stupa, you will reach the site where this event is supposed to have taken place – a stone tablet on the hill here depicts it. An important festival is held at this site in November.

There is basic village-style accommodation in Namobuddha, particularly for use by groups.

From Namobuddha the circuit walk continues downhill through **Sankhu** and past a couple of water mills then climbs for about one hour to **Batase**. Next it passes through another pine wood and drops down to cross a stream before climbing up again to Dhulikhel.

Panauti Trek

Another interesting walk leads from Dhulikhel to the small village of Panauti. The pleasant two hour stroll starts off south from Dhulikhel then turns west, crosses rice fields and runs along the course of a small stream. It eventually meets the Banepa to Panauti road a little north of the town. Panauti is a beautiful little town with numerous temples and magnificent woodcarvings – see the earlier Panauti section.

From Panauti you can take a bus to Banepa, just six km north, and from there back to Dhulikhel or to Kathmandu. Alternatively, you can keep on walking west to Godavari in the south of the Kathmandu Valley. There are several alternative routes to Godavari. One runs west through Bhaleswar and along the Roshi Khola Valley, taking about six hours direct to Godavari.

An alternative to this route runs southwest and climbs up the back of Pulchowki then takes the road down from Pulchowki to Godavari. A third route runs further south through Kalar, but also climbs the back of Pulchowki before taking the road down to Godavari. Either route via Pulchowki entails a long day's walk from Panauti.

ARNIKO HIGHWAY BEYOND DHULIKHEL

The Arniko Highway provides Nepal's overland link with Tibet and China. Many people who make the trek into the Solo Khumbu region and the Everest Base Camp travel out along the highway, taking the turn-off to Jiri, which is the last stop before you have to start walking. Buses to Jiri leave from Kathmandu between 5.30 and 6.30 am (Rs 128, 10 hours).

Past Barabise the road is particularly vulnerable to landslides and during the monsoon large

sections are swept away; it's very unlikely to be open between May and August. Even when the highway is passable it is of limited use in breaking India's stranglehold on Nepal. It is an enormous distance from Lhasa to the industrial centres of China, so it is, in most cases, still cheaper to ship Chinese goods via Calcutta than to truck them over the mountains.

When roadworkers first tackled the Himalaya, they decided to follow the rivers, which had already done the hard work of cutting through the mountains. They have now realised that the zone just above the rivers is particularly vulnerable to erosion from below and landslides from above – which is why Nepali houses and traditional trails are often built along the top of ridges. As a result, many of the roads that were developed by foreign countries' agencies have turned out to be serious liabilities for the Nepali government, who must fund their ongoing maintenance.

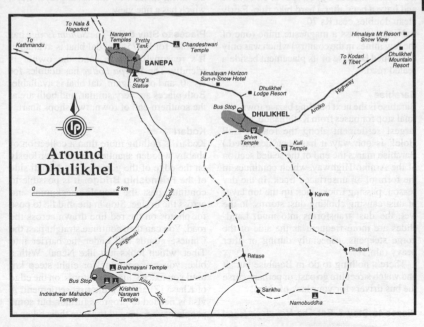

After Dhulikhel the road descends into the beautiful **Panchkhal Valley**, reaching the town of Panchkhal after about 20 minutes drive. About five minutes beyond Panchkhal a dirt road takes off to the left, giving road access to the Helambu region.

Eight km later you arrive at **Dolalghat**, a thriving town at the confluence of the Indrawati River and Sun Kosi (the departure point for many rafting trips). The turn-off to Jiri is another 14 km away, on the right.

Lamosangu

Lamosangu is a few km after the intersection, and is an interesting Sherpa town with some decent trade stores (compared with Barabise, Tatopani and Kodari). There are some standard dal bhat shops, but nothing to do. The *Silu Lodge* is in the middle of town. It's a five storey building with a shop on the ground floor. The first two floors house the owners of the shop and the top two floors are the lodge. Three rooms on the top floor have a terrace which is a good spot to sit outside and have a beer after a hard bike ride. Fairly clean doubles cost Rs 70.

Next you pass a magnesite mine (one of the few mines in the country) which was only developed because of its placement beside a sealed road.

Barabise

Barabise is the next bustling bazaar town, the final stop for buses from Kathmandu, and the largest settlement along the road. ('Hell Hole!' is one way it has been described.) Barabise marks the end of the sealed section of the Arniko Highway, which continues in the form of an unsurfaced track. In the dry season, passing trucks kick up the top layer of dust causing choking dust storms. In the wet, the dust transforms into mud. Landslides are more frequent as the side of the gorge steepens, especially during or after heavy rain.

There's nothing to do in Barabise but sit and watch street life go past, or perhaps curse the bus drivers for your lack of sleep!

Places to Stay & Eat The *Himalaya Hotel*

has doubles for Rs 50 (no toilet) and serves good dal bhat below the rooms. The *Barabise Guest House* has doubles for Rs 70, some of which are at the rear of the building, so take one of these if you want to avoid being woken at the crack of dawn by noisy bus drivers. It has toilets and more than a few bed bugs. Both places are in the middle of town on the left-hand side heading towards Tibet.

Tatopani

The next point of interest is Tatopani, a small village with a string of small guest houses which survive by housing visitors to the hot springs. It is in a more picturesque setting and is much quieter than Barabise.

The thing to do here is go to the hot springs. Five minutes walk north of the bazaar, look for a sign (with a direction arrow) on a building on the right-hand side. You then descend some steps to the springs which come out as a set of showers (great after a hard bike ride from Dhulikhel). There is also a small gompa above the town, marked by the usual prayer flags, which has a fine view.

Places to Stay & Eat The *Sonam Lodge* has doubles for Rs 75, and dal bhat is available. It's reasonably clean, and the owner is friendly. The *Sherpa Lodge* has doubles for Rs 50, and once again, dal bhat is available. Both places are very similar, and both are at the southern end of town, two shops apart.

Kodari

Kodari is nothing more than a collection of shabby wooden shanties perched perilously on the edge of the gorge on the Nepali side of the **Friendship Bridge**. It is possible to continue past the Nepali checkpoint and across the bridge. Stop in the middle to pose for photos on the red line drawn across the road. You can then continue straight past the Chinese guards and under the barrier into Tibet, which looks just like Nepal. With a bike, you can continue for eight steep km until you reach Chinese customs, on the edge of Khasa (Zhangmu), the first settlement. A visa is needed to progress further, but some people have managed to leave their bikes at the barrier and check the town out for a couple of hours. There's not much to see.

Places to Stay & Eat There's one lodge, the *Laxmi Lodge & Bhojanalaya*, which is very basic, serves dal bhat, and has beds for Rs 25 per person.

CHARIKOT

If you take the turn-off to Jiri, the first town you come to is Charikot, a pleasant place situated on a ridge with a stunning view. Located just before the town sign, the *Sagun Guest House* has friendly staff and good food. A double costs Rs 65. Because of its position on the edge of town, it's quiet, but misses the view. The *Laxmi Lodge & Restaurant* is in the main square and offers excellent views. It's a charming traditional building with spiral staircases leading to wooden balconies. Rooms at the front cost Rs 75; back rooms, with no view, are Rs 40.

JIRI

Jiri, also quite a pleasant place, has many lodges to choose from. The bus stops at the far end of town so you walk back up to find somewhere to stay. The *Sagarmatha Lodge & Restaurant* is pretty good with doubles for Rs 30. On the far side of town – furthest from the bus stop – *Sherpa Guide Lodge* has doubles for Rs 20. This is the cheapest and best place in town. The rooms are clean, the staff friendly and the food is good.

Godavari & Pulchowki Route

The road to Godavari is sealed and there's quite a bit of traffic, so this is not one of the best bike rides around the valley. There are quite a number of things to see, however.

If you have access to a car it is worth considering a trip to the top of nearby Pulchowki, especially in spring (March, April and May) when the rhododendrons are in bloom.

HARISIDDHI (10 km)

This is a small Newari village with a four tiered pagoda temple to Harisiddhi Bhawani.

BISHANKHU NARAYAN (15 km)

If you're looking for an excuse to get off the beaten track, the shrine of Bishankhu Narayan will do nicely. The shrine itself is something of a disappointment, despite the fact that it is one of the most important Vishnu shrines in the Kathmandu Valley. A steep stairway leads to a tiny cave – more a fissure in the rock – and there's nothing much to see. On the way, however, you pass through an attractive village, and there are some good views from the shrine itself.

Getting There & Away

The unsealed road to Bishankhu Narayan takes off to the north from the undistinguished village of Bandegaon then veers to the south-east and crosses a small stream. After one km you come to a small village. The road forks at the 'village green'; take the left fork and continue for another km to reach the shrine.

GODAVARI (22 km)

Godavari is not really a proper town, although there are a number of points of interest in the vicinity. This is home to the Royal Botanical Gardens, St Xavier's College, Godavari Kunda, and Pulchowki Mai, as well as a controversial marble quarry. The sealed road from Kathmandu continues to the foot of the hills and to St Xavier's College – the awful scars from the quarry are also clearly visible. At this point an unsealed road continues to the south and the sealed road veers left (north-east) to the botanical gardens.

Royal Botanical Gardens

The main entrance to the gardens is flanked by white-painted walls. Though a quiet and peaceful spot, few of the trees and plants are labelled, so unless you already know what you're looking at you won't end up any the wiser. There really aren't many persuasive reasons for visiting unless you're a keen botanist. The gardens are open from 10 am to 4 pm and entry is Rs 1.

Godavari Kunda

A dirt road continues past the entrance to the botanical gardens and after 100m or so you come to the Godavari Kunda – a sacred spring – on your right. It's a curious spot, and although none of the architecture or sculpture is particularly inspiring it is revered by Hindus. Every 12 years – next in 2003 – thousands of pilgrims come here to bathe and gain merit. Clear mountain water collects in a pool in an inner courtyard, then flows through carved stone spouts into a larger pool in the outer courtyard.

Pulchowki Mai

If you return towards the marble quarry and take the dirt road to the south, Pulchowki Mai is a couple of hundred metres past St Xavier's College and virtually opposite the main gates to the quarry. The site is dilapidated and somewhat overshadowed by the quarry. There's a three tiered pagoda to a Tantric mother goddess flanked by a temple to Ganesh. There are two large pools before the temple compound fed by nine spouts that represent the nine streams that flow off Pulchowki.

Getting There & Away

There are local minibuses and several Sajha Yatayat buses. They leave from Lagankhel in Patan and the one hour journey costs Rs 5. It would be quite feasible to ride a mountain bike – the road is good – but if you're going to make the effort, there are more interesting rides in the valley.

PULCHOWKI

This 2762m mountain is the highest point around the valley and not surprisingly there are absolutely magnificent views from the summit. This is also home to one of the last surviving cloud forests in central Nepal. The mountain is famous for its spring flowers, in particular its magnificent red and white rhododendrons.

Unfortunately, there's a telecommunica-

tions tower on the summit and an army camp. The open shrine to Pulchowki Mai may once have been a pretty spot, but it's now covered in rubbish. The views and the superb forest, however, make the journey worthwhile.

Getting There & Away

The unsealed road is rough in places but quite OK for a normal car if you take it slowly. It takes about 45 minutes from the bottom. You would need to be very keen to undertake the climb on a mountain bike, although it could certainly be done.

Chapagaon & Lele Route

The road to Lele is an ideal mountain-bike trip. It's sealed to Chapagaon and there are great views and some attractive villages along the way. Take the turn-off from the Ring Rd signposted to the Leprosy Mission. By bicycle it's quite a stiff climb in places – which is all the better for the return trip. Allow the best part of a day, although it's only an hour from the Ring Rd to Chapagaon.

SUNAKOTHI & THECHO

The small village of Sunakothi (10 km from Kathmandu) is strung out along the road. There are two temples – one to Jagannath and the other to Bringarshwar Mahadev.

Two km further south, Thecho also has two temples, the brightly coloured Balkumari Temple and a two tiered pagoda to Brahmayani.

CHAPAGAON (13 km)

Chapagaon is a prosperous village with a number of shops and temples and shrines strung along the road. Near the entrance to the village is a Ganesh shrine. There are two dilapidated two tiered temples (one looks as if it has been hit by a truck) dedicated to Narayan and Krishna, and there's also a

Bhairab shrine with erotic carvings on its struts.

Vajra Varahi

A small temple complex – an important Tantric site – lies about 500m east of the main road. When you enter Chapagaon take the path on your left after the two tiered temples. Notice the disused irrigation system, with stone channels and bridges, behind the village. The temple lies in a grove of trees and was built in 1665, but is now surrounded by less-distinguished shelters and an unfortunate amount of litter. Nonetheless, it's an interesting and atmospheric place that has probably been a centre for worship for millennia. Photography is banned.

Getting There & Away

Local minibuses and a Sajha Yatayat bus leave from Lagankhel in Patan and the one to 1½ hour journey costs Rs 6. By mountain bike, Chapagaon is about an hour from the Ring Rd (note the comparison with the bus time!). About 10 minutes after Chapagaon the road starts to climb into the foothills. The

Bhairab

sealed road continues to the Leprosy Mission and Tika Bhairab in the Lele Valley. If you are running out of enthusiasm, an unsealed road takes off to the left – there's a pipal tree and chautara. The road is in poor condition but you are rewarded with fantastic views across the valley to the Ganesh Himal. If you keep going you cross a saddle and enter the tranquil Lele Valley.

LELE (19 km)

The Lele Valley seems a million miles from the hustle and bustle of Kathmandu, and there are few visitors. It's a peaceful, beautiful valley that in many ways seems untouched by the 20th century.

Tika Bhairab

The Tika Bhairab is a huge, multi-coloured painting on a brick wall. The shrine lies at the confluence of two rivers and is marked by a huge sal tree.

Bungamati Route

The road to Bungamati, one of the most picturesque small towns in the valley, provides yet another ideal mountain-biking expedition. The road to Bungamati is the continuation of the main road that runs through Jawlakhel (the Tibetan refugee camp on the outskirts of Patan), on the other side of the Ring Rd.

KHOKNA

Khokna is not as appealing as Bungamati, partly because it was seriously damaged in the 1934 earthquake, but it has retained many traditional aspects of Newari life. It is famous for producing mustard oil. There is no central square, as in Bungamati, but there's plenty of action in the main street, including women spinning wool. The main temple is a two tiered construction of little interest, dedicated to Shekali Mai a mother goddess.

Getting There & Away

From Karya Binayak Temple, Khokna is a 10 minute walk across the paddy fields. Take note of the water tank surrounded by a low brick wall on the outskirts of the village, because if you don't want to retrace your steps to Bungamati, the track that returns to the main road takes off from here.

BUNGAMATI (10 km)

Bungamati is a classic Newari village dating from the 16th century. It is perched on a spur of land overlooking the Bagmati River and is shaded by large trees and stands of bamboo. Fortunately, the village streets are too small and hazardous for cars. Visitors are rare, so tread gently.

Rato Machhendranath Temple

Bungamati is the birthplace of Rato Machhendranath, regarded as the patron of the valley, and the large shikhara-style temple in the centre of the village square is his home for six months of the year. He spends the rest of his time in Patan. The process of moving him around Patan and backwards and forwards to Bungamati is central to one of the most important annual festivals in the valley. See the Rato Machhendranath section in the Kathmandu, Patan & Bhaktapur chapter, and Public Holidays & Special Events in the Facts for the Visitor chapter for details.

The chowk around the temple is one of the most beautiful in the valley – here one can see the heart of a functioning Newari town. There are many chortens, and a huge prayer wheel, clearly pointing to the syncretic nature of the Newari religion.

Karya Binayak Temple

Between Bungamati and Khokna, the Karya Binayak Temple is dedicated to Ganesh. The temple is not particularly interesting and Ganesh is simply represented by a natural stone but the view is spectacular. From this point, surrounded by trees, you can look over the Bagmati Valley to the foothills, or back to Bungamati, tumbling down the opposite hill.

Getting There & Away

Buses to Bungamati leave from Jawlakhel in Patan, take 1½ hours and cost Rs 5.

By bicycle from Patan, continue over the Ring Rd from the main road through Jawlakhel. After you cross the Niche River, veer left. The right fork takes you through to the Chobar Gorge where you can cross the river and return to Kathmandu by a different route. It's a pleasant ride along a gradually climbing ridge to get to Bungamati.

Approximately an hour after leaving the Ring Rd you'll come out at a viewpoint marked by a single, large tree. It's worth pausing here to take in the lie of the land. To the left lies Bungamati, then swinging to the right comes Karya Binayak then about one km away, Khokna. Follow the road down to Bungamati and take the right fork which passes to the left of a large pond. The footpath then veers to the left and climbs up to the distinctive, white shikhara temple and the town square.

To get to Karya Binayak, retrace your steps to the first pond you came to, follow the path around it and take the right fork. It's a five minute walk across the rice paddies to the temple.

Kirtipur, Chobar & Dakshinkali Route

KIRTIPUR (5 km)

Strung out along a ridge south-west of Kathmandu, the small town of Kirtipur is a relatively neglected and timeless backwater despite its proximity to the capital. At one time it was associated with Patan and then became a mini-kingdom in its own right. During the 1768 conquest of the valley by Gorkha's King Prithvi Narayan Shah it was clear that Kirtipur, with its superbly defensible hilltop position, would be the key to defeating the Malla kingdoms so it was here the Gorkha king struck first and hardest.

Kirtipur's resistance was strong but eventually, after a bitter siege, the town was taken and the unfortunate inhabitants paid a terrible price for their courageous resistance. The king, incensed by the long struggle his forces had endured, ordered the nose and lips cut off every male inhabitant in the town. Fortunately, for a small minority, he was practical as well as cruel and those who could play wind instruments were spared. It is said that the news of this barbaric act considerably dampened plans for resistance amongst the inhabitants of the other valley towns, and Patan, Bhaktapur and Kathmandu quickly fell.

At one time there were 12 gates into the city and traces of the old city wall can still be seen. Today the Kirtipur Cottage Industry Centre is a major industry for the town. As you wander through Kirtipur, you can see dyed yarn hanging from upstairs windows and hear the background clatter of the town's handlooms. Many of the town's 9000 inhabitants are weavers or farmers; the lower-caste people generally live outside the old city wall, lower down the hill. Kirtipur's hilltop position offers fine views over Kathmandu with the Himalaya rising behind.

Tribhuvan University

The campus of Nepal's university, named after King Tribhuvan, stands below the Kirtipur hill. The university library has the best facilities to be found in Nepal, but many Kirtipur farmers lost their land to the university site and have had to turn to other employment.

Temples

Kirtipur's ridge is actually two hills, with a lower saddle between them. The **Chilanchu Vihara** tops the southern hill and has a central stupa with four smaller stupas, numerous statues and bells and Buddhist monastery buildings around it.

At the bottom of the saddle where the hills meet is the **Bagh Bhairab Temple**, sacred to both Hindus and Buddhists. This famous triple roofed temple is decorated with swords and shields from the Newari troops defeated by King Prithvi Narayan Shah. They can be seen attached to the walls of the temple,

sheltered by the upper roof. The temple's principal image is of Bhairab in his tiger form. Look for the temple's torana to the left of the entrance door with an image of Vishnu astride the Garuda and, below him, Bhairab between Ganesh and Kumar. Sacrifices are made early on Tuesday and Saturday mornings.

From the saddle, a long stone stairway, flanked by stone elephants, leads to the triple roofed **Uma Maheshwar Temple**, or Hindu Kvat. The elephants wear spiked saddles to keep children from riding them! Curiously, the main image of Shiva and Parvati is a standing one, not in the standard Uma Maheshwar pose. To the left of the central image of the god and his consort is a smaller image in the standard pose. The temple was originally built in 1673 and had four roofs until it was badly damaged by the great earthquake of 1934. Following its restoration the temple itself is not of great interest – the stairway and the fine views from the top are better. From this hilltop you can see the nearby villages of Panga and Nagaon.

Getting There & Away

Numerous buses and minibuses depart from the City Bus Station and take around 45 minutes (Rs 4). They terminate at the university from where you can stroll up the hill to the town itself. Alternatively, and much more comfortably, it's a short trip by taxi (around Rs 150).

It takes around 1½ hours to reach Kirtipur by mountain bike, and it's quite a long steep hill from the Dakshinkali road (first left after the Ring Rd bridge over the Bagmati River). After about a km from the bridge, turn right at the road flanked by two low, brick gatehouses. Continue up the hill for a km or so and take the left fork where the minibuses park (right to the university). You'll notice a modern Thai-designed Buddhist temple to the left of Kirtipur's Naya Bajaar (new bazaar), which has grown up at the foot of the Kirtipur hill.

Instead of simply returning the same way you can continue from Kirtipur to Chobar and the Chobar Gorge then back through

Patan, which is mostly rideable, but also an interesting walk. From the Chilanchu Vihara at the south-eastern end of Kirtipur, go down the hill by the mound known as the Mazadega (built with the intention of being the foundations of a stupa). At the base of the hill follow the Ring Rd around and take the trail leading towards Chobar, just past the Thai temple. You can't go wrong, since Chobar tops the prominent hill to the south-east.

A diversion further south will take you through the small village of Panga which has a number of temples, none of great age or interest. A path continues from Panga to Nagaon, an even smaller village. The trail to Chobar meets a wider road just before the base of the hill, but you can turn off this and follow a narrow footpath straight up the hill until you come into the centre of the interesting small village of Chobar, right on the top of the hill.

After you've visited Chobar's Adinath Lokeshwar Temple continue down the other side of the hill towards the river. Aim for the large cement works, clearly visible beside the river. The Chobar Gorge and the Jal Binayak Temple are immediately to the north

of the cement works. See the Chobar Gorge section for the walk from there to Patan.

CHOBAR (6 km)
The picturesque little village of Chobar tops a hill overlooking the Bagmati River where it flows through the Chobar Gorge. Although the gorge is a regularly visited attraction, far fewer people come to Chobar itself. Perhaps they're put off by the steep hill.

Adinath Lokeshwar Temple
Chobar's main attraction is the Buddhist temple of Adinath Lokeshwar. The temple was originally built in the 15th century and reconstructed in 1640. Inside the main sanctuary the face of Rato Machhendranath can be seen peering out. The temple is dedicated to this popular valley deity and is sacred to both Hindus and Buddhists. Six Buddha faces are lined up beneath the temple's golden torana but the most interesting feature is the many metal pots, pans and water containers which are fixed to boards hanging all around the temple roofs. These kitchen utensils are donated to the temple by newlyweds in order to ensure a happy married life.

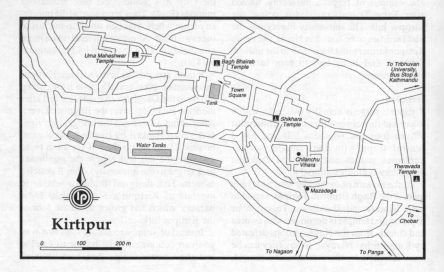

Kirtipur

Uma Maheshwar Temple

Bagh Bhairab Temple

Town Square

Tank

Shikhara Temple

Water Tanks

Chilanchu Vihara

Theravada Temple

Mazadega

To Tribhuvan University, Bus Stop & Kathmandu

To Chobar

To Nagaon

To Panga

0   100   200 m

Getting There & Away

Transport to Pharping and Dakshinkali runs by Chobar, but see the Kirtipur and Chobar Gorge sections for details of walking between Kirtipur and Patan via Chobar and the Chobar Gorge.

CHOBAR GORGE (6 km)

Eons ago the Kathmandu Valley was the Kathmandu Lake. In that long-ago time the hill of Swayambhunath was an island; gradually the lake dried up to leave the valley we see today.

Legends relate that the change from lake to valley was a much more dramatic one, for Manjushri is said to have taken his mighty sword and with one blow cut open the valley edge to release the pent-up waters. The place where his sword struck rock was Chobar on the southern edge of the valley and the result was the Chobar Gorge.

Countless snakes were washed out of the valley with the departing waters but Kartotak, 'king of the snakes', is said to still live near the gorge in the Taudaha pond. Whether or not the great serpent is still there, the pond is certainly a place where ducks pause on their long annual migration from Siberia to India. A hill known as Dinacho (which means 'meditation point') or Champa Devi rises beyond the pond.

The Chobar Gorge is south of Patan and the Bagmati River cuts through the edge of the Chobar hill, the highest hill along this side of the valley. The pretty village of Chobar tops the hill and a stone-paved track runs from the river's edge right to the top of the hill where the Adinath Lokeshwar Temple forms the centre of the settlement. Down by the river, just south of the gorge, is another important temple, the Jal Binayak.

The valley's first cement factory is a more recent and less pleasing addition to the scenery. A neat little suspension bridge spans the river; it was manufactured in Aberdeen in Scotland in 1903. From the bridge there are fine views of the gorge on one side and the Jal Binayak Temple on the other.

Jal Binayak Temple

Just below the gorge on the riverbank stands one of the valley's most important Ganesh shrines. The triple roofed temple dates from 1602 although there was probably a temple here even earlier. On the temple's platform there is an aged and worn image of Shiva and Parvati in the Uma Maheshwar pose which predates the temple itself by 500 years.

The temple's Ganesh image is simply a huge rock, projecting out the back and bearing very little likeness to an elephant-headed god. The temple's roof struts depict eight Bhairabs and the eight mother goddesses or Ashta Matrikas with whom Ganesh always appears. On the lower roof Ganesh himself appears on some of the struts, with beautiful female figures standing beside him and tiny, brightly painted erotic depictions below. A bronze figure of Ganesh's 'vehicle', in this case a shrew rather than a mouse, stands respectfully in the temple courtyard, facing the shrine.

Getting There & Away

The Chobar Gorge is usually visited en route to Pharping and Dakshinkali by road. A more interesting way to reach the gorge is to walk there from Kirtipur via the village of Chobar. See the earlier Kirtipur section for more details.

From the gorge you can cross the bridge and walk up the hill turning north towards Patan. A road suitable for cars ends at a small village at the top of the hill and you can follow this road, past the Nakhu jail and across the Nakhu River, finally crossing the Ring Rd and entering Patan at Jawlakhel.

SEKH NARAYAN TEMPLE (18 km)

The small Sekh Narayan Temple is the centrepiece of an interesting collection of temples, pools and carvings. The pools are beside the road to Pharping, at a point where it makes a sharp left hand turn (coming from Kathmandu) and they are often used by local women for washing clothes. The main temple is above the pools and is sheltered under a multi-coloured, overhanging cliff. It forms an interesting juxtaposition between the work of man and god. In true Nepali style, a Buddhist monastery has been built next door.

The temples and carvings have suitably diverse ages. The Sekh Narayan Temple, one of the most important Vishnu temples in the valley, was built in the 17th century, but it is believed the cave has been a place of pilgrimage for much longer. Beside the shrine is a bas relief of Vishnu Vikrantha, also known as the dwarf Vamana. This possibly dates from the Licchavi period, or the 5th or 6th century.

Half-submerged in one of the crystal-clear ponds is a sculpture of Surya, the sun god, framed by a stone arch and with a lotus flower at each shoulder. This dates from the 12th or 13th century. Finally, the Tibetan gompa is a 20th century addition. Hindus believe that Gautama Buddha was Vishnu's 10th incarnation, but we don't know if this is the connection.

Getting There & Away
Sekh Narayan is close to Pharping and is probably best reached by foot from the village if you haven't got your own transport.

VAJRA JOGINI TEMPLE (18.5 km)
On a hillside overlooking Pharping is the 17th century Vajra Jogini Temple, dedicated to the same goddess as the Vajra Jogini Temple near Sankhu and built at about the same time. See the earlier Vajra Jogini section for a discussion on the goddess' origins. The pagoda-style temple is in a courtyard surrounded by relatively modern two storey, Newari-style living quarters. Vajra Jogini is featured in the temple's toranas.

Getting There & Away
The temple is just a short walk behind Pharping on the hill that overlooks the town. The main gompa at Gorakhnath (see the next section) is only a few hundred metres to the west up a flight of steps. It is possible to walk an interesting circuit from Dakshinkali to Gorakhnath, Vajra Jogini, Pharping and back to Dakshinkali in less than two hours. See

Getting There & Away in the Dakshinkali section later in this chapter.

Coming from Kathmandu and after Sekh Narayan, you approach Pharping past a soccer field. The main road swings left around the field, but if you continue straight ahead you will come first to Vajra Jogini (on the side of the hill) then Gorakhnath.

GORAKHNATH (19 km)
Several gompas and temples have sprung up around the Gorakhnath cave behind Pharping. The white Tibetan gompa – perched high on the hill like an eagle's nest, at the centre of a web of prayer flags – is particularly interesting.

There are magnificent views overlooking Pharping, the Bagmati River and the valley. You can even see the Himalaya on a clear day. Somewhere in the complex is a cave which the Tibetans associate with Padmasambhava, the Bodhisattva sometimes credited with introducing Buddhism to Tibet.

Getting There & Away
Gorakhnath is an easy walk from Pharping and Vajra Jogini, and a bit of a scramble from Dakshinkali. It can be combined with an interesting walk that takes in all these places (see the Dakshinkali section) or reached by road.

PHARPING (19 km)
Pharping is a thriving, traditional Newari town, surprisingly untouched by the swarm of tourists that visit Dakshinkali. The main road skirts the village so there are few vehicles in the village proper. Before King Prithvi Narayan Shah unified Nepal this was another tiny city-state.

Places to Stay & Eat
The *Hattiban Resort* (☎ 01-290623; fax 418561) is a small hotel, popular for weekend lunches. The buildings are pleasant and there are great views. There are 24 rooms as well as workshop and conference facilities. Singles/doubles cost $60/70; the food is fairly pricey at around $10 for a main meal.

Getting There & Away
Buses leave from the City Bus Station, take about two hours and cost Rs 9. On days when buses don't run to Dakshinkali you can catch buses to Pharping, and walk to Dakshinkali, one km away. If you're on a bike, you'll be pleased to know it's all downhill.

DAKSHINKALI

At the southern edge of the valley, in a dark, somewhat spooky location in the cleft between two hills and at the confluence of two rivers, stands the bloody temple of Dakshinkali. The temple is dedicated to the goddess Kali, Shiva's consort in her most bloodthirsty incarnation, and twice a week faithful Nepalis journey here to satisfy her blood lust. The six armed main image of Kali in the temple is of black stone and she tramples upon a male figure.

Sacrifices are always made to goddesses, and the creatures to be sacrificed must be uncastrated male animals. Saturday is the major sacrificial day of the week when a steady parade of buffaloes, chickens, ducks, goats, sheep and pigs come here to have their throats cut or their heads lopped off. Tuesdays is also a sacrificial day, but the blood does not flow quite as freely as on Saturdays. During the festival of Dasain in October the temple is literally awash with blood and the image of Kali is bathed in it.

After their rapid dispatch the animals are butchered in the stream beside the temple and their carcasses will later be brought home for a feast, or a picnic may be held on the hillside. Non-Hindus are not allowed into the compound where Kali's image resides, but it is OK to take photos from outside. The temple itself is not particularly interesting, although there are some fine brass nagas forming a canopy over the compound.

This is one of the most important sites in the valley so on the sacrificial days it is crowded with Nepali families – and tourists. Most of the big hotels and the tour companies cart bus loads of camera-laden visitors along. Tours to the 'exciting animal sacrifices' are big business for Kathmandu travel agencies. As a result, there are a number of tea houses,

and a good number of hustlers selling souvenirs and goodness knows what else. Be prepared to pay picturesque sadhus for the privilege of taking their photograph.

Despite the carnival spirit, witnessing the sacrifices is a strange and, for some, a confronting experience. The slaughter is surprisingly matter-of-fact, but it creates a powerful atmosphere. Unfortunately, many tourists behave poorly, hanging from every available vantage point in order to get the most gory possible photos. They are reminiscent of that most unattractive creature – the vulture. However extraordinary the sights might seem, this is a religious ceremony, and the participants should be treated with respect, not turned into a sideshow.

Getting There & Away
Buses only operate on Tuesdays and Saturdays – the most important days for sacrifice – and though there are plenty of them, they are very crowded. After you pass the police checkpoint on the Ring Rd you can sit on the roof and enjoy the spectacular views. If you have a car, allow 45 minutes for the journey.

It is an enjoyable, but exhausting two hour bike ride from Kathmandu. The views are exhilarating, but it is basically uphill all the way – so mountain bikes are the way to go. Tuesday is probably the better day to pick as the traffic is not too heavy. Make sure you get an early start, as the shrine is busiest early in the morning. You're advised to pay someone a couple of rupees to mind your bike in the car park.

It's possible to make an interesting two hour circuit walk from Dakshinkali to Gorakhnath, Vajra Jogini, Pharping and back to Dakshinkali. Take the path that runs above the left (southern) side of the sacrificial compound. This will bring you out into a cleared part of the gorge where there are several picnic shelters. There's a steep scramble up a goat track that follows a ridge on the right (north-western) side of the gorge. When you get to the top you come out on a plateau and you'll immediately see the white monastery surrounded by prayer flags on the nearby hill. Make your way through the paddy fields, on the narrow paths between the rice. It will take you about 40 minutes to get to Gorakhnath. Vajra Jogini is a few hundred metres down some steps to the east of the gompa, and a short walk to Pharping. From Pharping follow the main road about one km downhill to Dakshinkali.

Pokhara

Pokhara is the most popular destination in Nepal after Kathmandu. Its fame rests on the natural beauty of its lakeside location and its proximity to the mountains, not on a great historical or cultural endowment. It's the starting point for some of the most famous treks in Nepal, and there are also plenty of short walks and day trips that can be made around the valley.

Pokhara has an enormous number of good value hotels and restaurants, and although it is undoubtedly a tourist town, it has a relaxed and peaceful atmosphere, completely removed from the hectic bustle of Kathmandu and even further removed from the outright chaos of many Indian cities. It's an oasis where leisurely meals, good books, and short walks can easily fill several days – ideal if you are recovering from (or gearing up for) a trek, or for travel in India.

The roads linking Pokhara with Kathmandu and the Indian border are comparatively recent innovations and as a result the region is changing rapidly. The road from Naubise to Pokhara, the Kathmandu-Pokhara (Prithvi) Highway, was originally built with Chinese assistance in the early 70s. The Tribhuvan Highway (or Tribhuvan Rajpath, sometimes simply referred to as the Rajpath) was the first road link with Kathmandu and was completed by the Indian government in 1956; it joins the Kathmandu-Pokhara (Prithvi) Highway at Naubise, 29 km from Kathmandu. The most direct route between Pokhara and Sunauli on the Indian border is the attractive Siddhartha Highway, also built by the Indian government.

Most of the heavy traffic from the Terai and India to Kathmandu and Pokhara now uses the road between Narayanghat and Mugling, then either turns east to Kathmandu or west to Pokhara. The sections between Narayanghat and Mugling, and Mugling and Kathmandu, are particularly busy. Mountain biking is a great way to get around Nepal, but it would be worth catching a bus over both these sections.

After travelling elsewhere in Nepal or in India, Pokhara has an almost Disneyland unreality about it. The climate is mild; incredible snow-capped mountains are reflected in a sheltered lake; cool western music drifts from every restaurant; menus offer everything in the world except dal bhat; hotel rooms are clean, and open onto sunny gardens; there's very little traffic; village life persists, but everyone speaks English; and it's very relaxed.

The first tourists to discover Pokhara were the hippie travellers of the early 70s. In Pokhara many discovered the perfect venue for doing the things they were best at – getting stoned, eating, growing their hair, talking, and staring into the middle distance while looking cool. They came for a week and stayed for months. The world has changed since then (and so have the drug laws and visa regulations), but Pokhara retains something of the laid-back, hedonistic style of this time.

Viewed from Pokhara, the Himalaya is indeed a mighty mountain range, looming over the horizon much closer than it does in Kathmandu. Only foothills separate the town from the full height of the mountains, and the magnificent 8000m peaks of the Annapurna Range utterly dominate the view to the north.

POKHARA

POKHARA

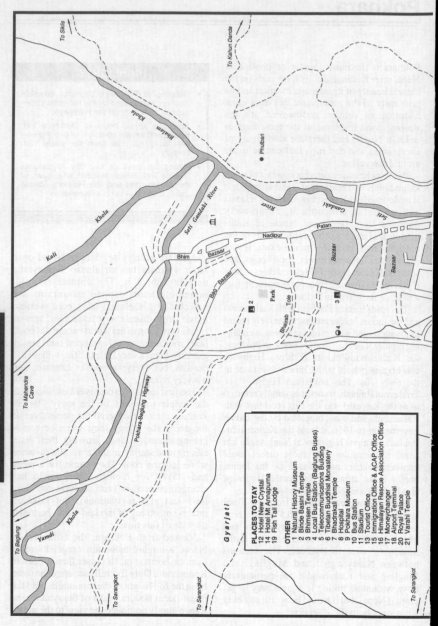

PLACES TO STAY
12 Hotel New Crystal
14 Hotel Mt Annapurna
19 Fish Tail Lodge

OTHER
1 Natural History Museum
2 Binde Basini Temple
3 Bhimsen Temple
4 Local Buses (Baglung Buses)
5 Telecommunications Building
6 Tibetan Buddhist Monastery
7 Bhadrakali Temple
8 Hospital
9 Pokhara Museum
10 Bus Station
11 Stadium
13 Tourist Office
15 Immigration Office & ACAP Office
16 Himalayan Rescue Association Office
17 Moneychanger
18 Airport Terminal
20 Royal Palace
21 Varahi Temple

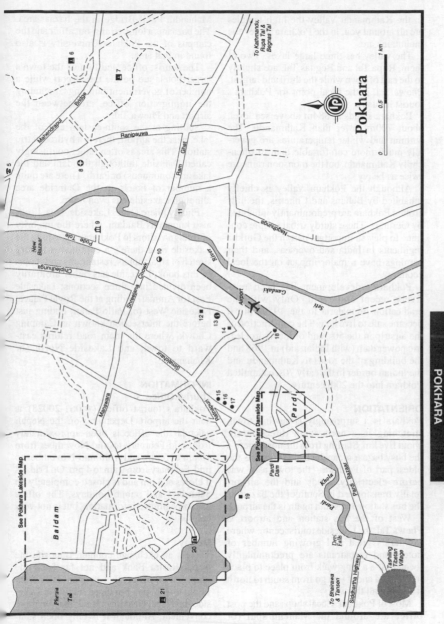

Pokhara

To Kathmandu,
Rupa Tal &
Begnas Tal

0   0.5   1 km

Mahendrapul
Bridge

Ranipauwa

Ram Ghat

New Bazaar

Pode Tole

Chipledhunga

Naghmuna

Srestagua
Chowk

Seti Gandaki

Airport

Manswara

Lindrashwor

Birauthaur

Baidam

See Pokhara Lakeside Map

See Pokhara Damside Map

Pardi

Pardi
Dam

Pardi
Khola

Pardi Bazaar

Pardi

Demi
Falls

Siddhartha Highway

To Bhairawa
& Tansen

Tashiling
Tibetan Village

Phewa Tal

POKHARA

In the Kathmandu Valley the high temples are all around you, in the Pokhara Valley the mountains are.

The valley has three large lakes. Two of them, Rupa Tal and Begnas Tal, are slightly to the east of town while the third and largest, Phewa Tal, is the focal point for Pokhara's tourist industry.

Pokhara stands at 884m above sea level, about 700m lower than Kathmandu. The autumn and winter temperatures are generally much more comfortable than in often-chilly Kathmandu, but the monsoon rains are twice as heavy.

Although the Pokhara Valley is chiefly inhabited by Bahuns and Chhetris, the hills around Pokhara are predominantly inhabited by Gurungs. These sturdy tribal people continue to play an important part in the Gurkha regiments in India and overseas, and their earnings have a major impact on the local economy.

Pokhara's development has been relatively recent and rapid. Only with the eradication of malaria in the 1950s did it become safe to live here. The construction of the airstrip in the 50s, and of the hydroelectric power dam (with Indian aid) in 1968 and the building of the roads to Kathmandu and the Indian border in the early 70s, catapulted Pokhara into the 20th century.

ORIENTATION

Pokhara is a surprisingly sprawling town, stretching in a north-south direction for about five km. Starting from the north there's the busy bazaar area which also contains the oldest part of Pokhara – the town as it was before electricity, roads and the airport totally transformed it. South of the bazaar is the bus station and south again is the airport.

West of the bus station and airport is Phewa Tal, the Lakeside tourist centre where Pokhara's great and growing number of hotels and restaurants are predominantly located. It's a long walk from place to place in Pokhara and if you go from south to north it's uphill all the way.

Most of Pokhara's local shops and the post office are around the Mahendrapul (or Mahendra Pool) Bridge in the bazaar area. The bazaar is a long, strung-out affair and the campus of the Pokhara University is also found in that area.

The tourist office and two of the town's larger hotels are beside the airport while a number of government buildings, including the immigration office, are between the airport and Phewa Tal.

Starting at the south-eastern end of the lake, near the airport, there's a hydroelectric station. This area is often rather confusingly called Damside (although the dam and the lake are continuous) or Pardi. There are quite a number of hotels in the Damside area although Lakeside has even more.

Finally there's the Lakeside area itself, also known as Baidam, where the majority of foreign visitors to Pokhara stay. Along the Lakeside road there's a continuous tawdry stretch of small hotels, restaurants and shops. In this book, Lakeside has rather arbitrarily been divided into three sections: Lakeside East (or Ammat) ending at the Royal Palace; Lakeside West (or Pallo Patan) ending just before the intersection known as Camping Chowk, where the main road returns eastward to town; and Lakeside North (or Khaharey).

INFORMATION
Tourist Office

Pokhara's tourist office (☎ 061-20028) is near the airport. Depending on the Nepali calendar the office is open approximately from mid-February to mid-November from 10 am to 5 pm, and from mid-November to mid-February from 9 am to 4 pm. On Fridays it closes at 3 pm and is closed completely on Saturdays and public holidays. The office has some limited information, but is not very helpful.

Money

There's an exchange counter, opposite the Nepal Rastra Bank and not far from the immigration office, that is open daily from 11 am to 3.30 pm. For those staying at Lakeside the Nepal Grindlays Bank may be more convenient. Although it is only open standard banking hours, you can make cash and travellers' cheque advances against Visa and MasterCard. Alternatively there are a number of private moneychangers strung out the whole length of Lakeside, and these are open seven days a week.

Post & Communications

The post office is a long way from the Lakeside and Damside hotels in the bazaar area near Mahendrapul Bridge. If you want to make overseas phone calls or calls to Kathmandu, there's a telecommunications building east of the post office along the bridge, or any number of private phone centres in Lakeside.

For e-mail users, Ambassador Tours & Travels towards the northern end of Lakeside charges Rs 80 to send, and Rs 20 to receive 1 kb of information.

Immigration Office

The immigration office is convenient to the Lakeside and Damside area hotels. It can extend visas and issue trekking permits (for the Annapurna region only). It's open from 10.30 am to 1 pm for applications and from 3 pm for passport pick-ups.

ACAP Information Office

The Annapurna Conservation Area Project (ACAP) has a small office at Lakeside, just around the corner from the Tea Time Restaurant. This is an excellent place for information on trekking in the Annapurna region, including the latest weather and trail conditions. The office is open Sunday to Friday from 9 am to 4 pm. ACAP also plans to have evening slide shows in Pokhara, so check here to see if these are running.

Bookshops

There are numerous bookshops along the Lakeside road offering both new and secondhand books and maps. Good shops include the Pokhara Bookshop, the As You Like It Bookshop, the Kiwi Bookshop, the Collectors Bookshop and the Holy Bookshop. The Bongsor Valley in Han Suyin's *The Mountain is Young* is based on the Pokhara Valley.

PHEWA TAL

Phewa Tal, or Phewa Lake, is the tourist centre of Pokhara and the second largest lake in Nepal. Only Rara Lake in the far west of the country is larger.

From Phewa Tal you can set off on walks or bicycle rides, or take to the lake in one of the numerous boats *(doongas)* available for rent from the Lakeside canoe operators. The boats cost from Rs 30 or Rs 50 an hour, and are most expensive opposite the Varahi Temple, but get cheaper as you head south to Damside. You can simply paddle yourself lazily around or jump overboard for a swim in the pleasant waters. If rowing yourself is too strenuous, a boat plus boatman will cost from around Rs 100 per hour. Sail boats are hired near the Hotel Fewa for Rs 250 per hour, less for half a day.

If you are boating near Damside, keep well away from the dam wall as currents can be strong especially during and immediately after the monsoon; in the past people have gotten into trouble here.

The Lakeside villages are mainly inhabited by Chhetris although these days there is a great deal of outside influence as well. Although there have been recent efforts to clean out Pokhara's drug pushers, this area still has a bit of the old hippie-scene feel about it.

Along Lakeside are a number of banyan and pipal trees with *chautaras* built around them. These stone platforms were designed to provide a resting place for walkers, and building them was one good way of improving one's karma for future existences.

MOUNTAIN VIEWS

The wonderful Annapurna panorama forms a superb backdrop to Pokhara. You can see the mountains clearly from the lake, while from the other side of Phewa Tal, by the Fish Tail Lodge, you can actually see them twice if you count their reflection in the often placid waters.

Alternatively you can climb to Sarangkot or one of the other viewpoints around the valley and enjoy a closer uninterrupted view.

The incredible Annapurna massif includes

POKHARA

the Lamjung Himal, Hiunchuli, Varahashikhar, Khangsar Kang, Tarke Kang and Gangapurna mountains; but it's the five Annapurna peaks, Annapurna I to IV plus Annapurna South, and the magnificent Machhapuchhare which are best known.

Machhapuchhare means 'fish tail' and if you walk several days west along the Jomsom Trek route you will find that the mountain actually has a second peak, and from that side it does indeed look like a fish tail. From Pokhara, however, it's simply a superb pyramid; a Himalayan Matterhorn, only much higher.

Machhapuchhare stands out not only because of its prominent shape and lonely position, but because it is closer to Pokhara than the other peaks. In actual fact, at 6997m, it is lower than the five Annapurnas.

An attempt to climb it in 1957, led by the legendary Mountain Travel founder Colonel Jimmy Roberts (who, incidentally, settled in Pokhara after his retirement), got to within 50m of the top, but turned back when the Sherpas refused to conquer such a holy summit.

Climbing is now not allowed on this mountain. Robert Rieffel in *Nepal Namaste* questions how Machhapuchhare acquired its holy image: if it's so significant, why on earth is it called 'fish tail' when so many other unholy Nepali peaks are named after gods and goddesses?

The other peak with a mountaineering tale to tell is Annapurna I, which, at 8091m, is the highest in the range. It's also part of a long ridge line and because it's further north appears less conspicuous.

Annapurna I's claim to fame is that when a small French expedition, led by Maurice Herzog, reached the summit in 1950 it was the first time an 8000m peak had been climbed. Herzog's book *Annapurna*, a mountaineering classic, traces the hardships of organising a climb in what was then a remote, inaccessible and little-known area. The harrowing aftermath of the climb, when a severe storm caught the retreating mountaineers, resulted in Herzog losing most of his fingers and toes from frostbite.

To the west of the Annapurnas is Dhaulagiri,

at 8167m. The Kali Gandaki River, which cuts the deepest gorge in the world, flows between Dhaulagiri and the Annapurnas and actually predates the rise of the Himalaya. For a while, before more precise measuring methods were available, it was thought that Dhaulagiri was the world's highest mountain.

TEMPLES
Pokhara, unlike the towns of the Kathmandu Valley, is not noted for its temples. In fact there are very few of even minor note.

In the lake there's a small island with the double roofed **Varahi Temple** dedicated to Varahi, who is Vishnu in his boar incarnation.

In the northern part of the bazaar area, is the small, double-roofed **Bhimsen Temple** with some small and not very notable erotic carvings on the roof struts. The streets of the bazaar area become steadily more attractive and traditional as you move north from the newer area around the bus station to what was the centre of the original settlement of Pokhara. Bhimsen Temple, very much in the Newari style of the Kathmandu Valley, is right on the main road in the oldest part of town.

Slightly further north, atop a small hill with a park at its base, is Pokhara's best known temple, the **Binde Basini Temple**. Its pleasant and shady setting is actually more impressive than the white shikhara-style temple itself. The temple is dedicated to Durga (Parvati) in her Binde Basini Bhagwati manifestation, and interestingly the image of the goddess is a *saligram*. These black ammonite fossils of marine animals date from the Jurassic period over 100 million years ago and are found in the Himalaya, north of Pokhara, and at several points along the Kali Gandaki. Saligrams provide clear proof that this region was once under the sea.

MUSEUMS
Pokhara has two museums. The **Pokhara Museum** is north of the bus station on the main road and has exhibits on local history.

Entry is Rs 5, and it's open daily except Tuesday.

At the northern end of town, on the Pokhara University campus, is the **Natural History Museum**, also known as the Annapurna Regional Museum. ACAP has some interesting exhibits on the environmental problems of the area. The natural history section has cement models of Nepali wildlife (you don't have to feed them) and a large butterfly, moth and insect collection. The museum is open from 9 am to 1 pm and from 2 to 5 pm; there's no entry charge, but make a donation.

SETI GANDAKI RIVER
The Seti Gandaki River flows right through Pokhara but in places it runs completely underground, sometimes dropping to 50m below ground level. *Seti* means 'white' and the water's milky colour comes from limestone in the soil.

There's a good view of this elusive river from the bridge near the old Mission Hospital at the northern end of the bazaar; though an even more dramatic view can be found just beyond the airport runway. From the far side of the airport, follow the trail to the river where a footbridge crosses the canyon. The bridge is only about 10m wide but the river flows past a good 30m below.

Another good view of the river can be found at Mahendrapul Bridge in the main bazaar area.

DEVI FALLS
Also known as Patale Chango, Devin's or David's Falls, this waterfall is about two km south-west of the airport on the main Siddhartha Highway and just before the Tashiling Tibetan village.

The Pardi Khola is the outflow from Phewa Tal and at Devi Falls it suddenly drops down into a hole in the ground and disappears. One of its alternate names comes from a tale that a tourist named David disappeared down the hole as well, taking his girlfriend with him! There's a Rs 3 admission charge to the falls – if there's anyone there to collect it.

The river emerges from its subterranean hideaway 200m further on and then joins the Phusre Khola before flowing into the Seti Gandaki River.

TIBETAN SETTLEMENTS
There are a number of Tibetan settlements around Pokhara and you see many Tibetans around the lake selling their crafts and artefacts. The Tashiling Tibetan village, where they weave Tibetan carpets, is only a couple of km south-west of the airport.

There's a larger settlement known as Tashipalkhel at Hyangja, a short drive or an hour or two's walk north-west of Pokhara on the start of the Jomsom Trek route.

TIBETAN BUDDHIST MONASTERY
Cross Mahendrapul Bridge from the bazaar area and follow the road, at first paved, to this hilltop monastery. It's a comparatively recent construction with a large Buddha statue and colourful wall paintings.

WALKS
The Pokhara area offers some fine walking possibilities ranging from day walks like the climb up to Sarangkot to short three or four day treks. See the Around Pokhara section later in this chapter for full details.

PLACES TO STAY
There are four accommodation areas in Pokhara: around the bus station and bazaar, by the airport, Damside (Pardi) and Lakeside (Baidam).

There's really no reason to stay in the bazaar area; it's crowded, dirty and noisy. Several of Pokhara's larger and more expensive hotels are near the airport, but the advantages of comfortable hotels have to be weighed against the disadvantage of being a long walk from Lakeside.

Damside at the south-eastern end of the lake is more popular, and many of the aggressive touts at the Pokhara bus station will insist that this is the place to go. They will be at pains to point out that the distinction

POKHARA

between Damside and Lakeside is meaningless. In one sense they're right (it is a continuous body of water we're talking about), but in several others they're wrong. Damside has a completely different atmosphere to Lakeside.

Firstly, there is quite a difference between being able to look out across the lake proper, as you can at Lakeside, and looking out on the narrow neck of water by the dam. Damside is a new, rather desolate area, and there are fewer farmhouses, fields and trees interspersed between the hotels. Many of the buildings are of the bleak concrete five storey variety and there is a limited range of restaurants – most people eat in their hotels. Finally, you're a 15 minute walk from the action at Lakeside.

On the other hand, there are a couple of pleasant mid-range hotels, and some people prefer to escape the Lakeside scene. They are further rewarded by the best mountain views – the further south you go, the less the mountains are obscured by the intervening foothills.

The major accommodation site is Lakeside, where you'll find an enormous number of budget to mid-range lodges and guest houses. The Lakeside road is a continuous strip of excellent restaurants that spill out into the open air, and little shops selling everything a traveller could want – tickets, trekking gear, books, fruit juice, clothes, souvenirs. However, if you take any of the eastward-running roads, you quickly escape to land where the buffalo roam. Within two minutes you can be in a cheap and comfortable guest house amongst rice fields, vegetable gardens and Chhetri farmhouses.

Sadly, the traditional village culture is disappearing – for it is the combination of the magnificent location, good-value accommodation and food, and (not least) the proximity of local village life that accounts for much of Pokhara's appeal.

There are so many places to stay and they change so quickly, that making individual recommendations (especially among bottom and mid-range places) is a chancy game. Listen to other travellers' recommendations,

and if you arrive by bus avoid the clutches of the bus station touts. The best thing you can do is grab a taxi to somewhere central on Lakeside, have a drink and a bite to eat at one of the restaurants and then ask to leave your bag somewhere safe (most restaurants will happily do this) while you check out some hotels for yourself.

When looking for somewhere to stay – in any price range – the important variables are the quality of the room, the views and the garden; the availability of hot water; and the position. If you're staying in one of the really rock-bottom Lakeside places take care of your valuables, as theft is not unknown.

As is the case in Kathmandu, most places quote prices in US dollars, but these are highly negotiable and very few people would pay the advertised prices. Bear this in mind with the prices we quote here.

Bazaar Area

There are numerous cheaper hotels around the bus station and near the Mahendrapul Bridge. It's a much less pleasant place to stay than Lakeside and there's no real reason to do so.

By staying in the bazaar area you may be a little closer to the start of the Jomsom and Annapurna trekking trails, but these days you can travel some distance out of Pokhara by road before you start walking, so being a km or two closer will make no difference.

Airport Area

Two of Pokhara's large hotels are directly opposite the airport.

The *Hotel Mt Annapurna* (☎ 061-20037; fax 20027) is decorated in Tibetan style; the murals in the restaurant showing Tibetan traders and other scenes are particularly impressive. There's also a fine view of the Annapurna skyline from the roof, and a pleasant garden area. All rooms have private bathrooms and cost $29/41 for a single/double, plus 12% government tax, which is good value.

The *Hotel New Crystal* (☎ 061-20035; fax 20234) has singles/doubles with air-con for $47/59, but for a room with a view of the mountains it's $58/70. All rooms have private bathrooms and there's a 13% government tax. The facilities are good, but it's a big soulless place that could be pretty much anywhere.

Damside Area (Pardi)

South-west of the airport, at the south-eastern end of Phewa Tal, is the Damside or Pardi area. There are a number of lodges and hotels, many of which are run by Thakalis from the Kali Gandaki Valley.

The *Hotel Tragopan* (☎ 061-21708) is in an intermediate position between Damside and Lakeside, overlooking a busy road. There's a nice garden and the rooms have good views; they're pleasant and well equipped though rather expensive at $40/50.

The *Hotel Holiday* (☎ 061-20189) is a two storey place with clean rooms, some of which have excellent mountain views. Singles/double with shared bath cost from

Rs 300/400, rooms with bath are Rs 500/600. The *Annapurna Hotel* is also very clean, but a bit more expensive at $15 for a double with bath.

There is a group of decent mid-range places right by the dam – there's not much to separate them, and the most crucial variable is probably which direction your room happens to face, because the views can be impressive. The *Ashok Guest House* (☎ 061-20374) is well kept and has singles/doubles with private bath for $10/15, or $15/20 if you want the view. There are a few cheaper rooms for $5. This has a good position right by the lake. The *Mona Lisa Guest House* is similar.

The *Dragon Hotel* (☎ 061-20391) is another reasonable mid-range option. Singles/doubles with air-con and private bath are $30/35, plus 12% government tax. There's a restaurant, bar and roof garden.

The *Tibet Resort* (☎ 061-20853) is a pleasant, modern place with a big garden. Rooms

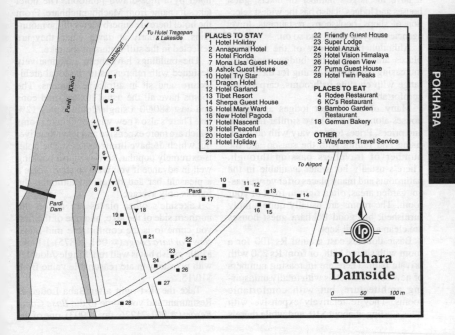

PLACES TO STAY	
1 Hotel Holiday	22 Friendly Guest House
2 Annapurna Hotel	23 Super Lodge
5 Hotel Florida	24 Hotel Anzuk
7 Mona Lisa Guest House	25 Hotel Vision Himalaya
8 Ashok Guest House	26 Hotel Green View
10 Hotel Try Star	27 Puma Guest House
11 Dragon Hotel	28 Hotel Twin Peaks
12 Hotel Garland	
13 Tibet Resort	**PLACES TO EAT**
14 Sherpa Guest House	4 Rodee Restaurant
15 Hotel Mary Ward	6 KC's Restaurant
16 New Hotel Pagoda	9 Bamboo Garden
17 Hotel Nascent	Restaurant
19 Hotel Peaceful	18 German Bakery
20 Hotel Garden	
21 Hotel Holiday	**OTHER**
	3 Wayfarers Travel Service

Tu Hotel Tragopan & Lakeside

Ratnapuri

Pardi Khola

Pardi Dam

Pardi

To Airport

Pokhara Damside

0   50   100 m

POKHARA

here are excellent value at $6/10 with attached bath.

The *New Hotel Pagoda* (☎ 061-21802) is also good value. There are views, and the rooms are very clean. Singles/doubles are $4/6 with shared bath, or $8/12 with private bath.

The *Hotel Green View* is a friendly place with some very basic rooms for $3/5. There's also a comfortable new building which has singles/doubles with good views and private bath for $10/15.

The *Hotel Garden* (☎ 061-20870) and the *Hotel Peaceful* (☎ 061-20861) are both decent places with a range of comfortable rooms. Singles/doubles are $3/5 with shared bath, $7/10 with private bathrooms. The Hotel Garden also has deluxe rooms for $25/35, some with excellent views.

Lakeside Area (Baidam)

The road running alongside Phewa Tal is the real visitors' centre for Pokhara. Not only does it have the largest number of hotels, guest houses and lodges, it also has the widest selection of shops, bookshops, restaurants, travel agencies, bicycle-rental and so on.

Although the majority of the Lakeside places are firmly in the budget range, an increasing number are aiming for the middle range with en suite bathrooms, carpets and comfortable beds.

Many of the budget lodges and guest houses along the lake have similar facilities and prices. Prices tend to vary with demand, rising and falling with the season and the number of travellers passing through. There's usually hot water available in the bathrooms and many places offer very pleasant garden areas, often right in front of your room. The rooms are usually quite simply furnished, but good Pokhara guest houses are clean and well kept.

Basic doubles cost around Rs 100 for a room with shared bath, or from Rs 250 with private bath. There are increasing numbers of new concrete hotels with totally uninspiring architecture, but with comfortable rooms. They're relatively expensive with rates starting at about $10, and while there's

little room for bargaining for the cheapest rooms, there certainly is for the more expensive ones, especially if you plan to stay more than a couple of days.

You can stay close to the centre of things, on or near the main Lakeside road, or opt for a quieter location either back from the main road or way down at the northern end of the lake. The price for peace and quiet is a slightly longer walk to get to the restaurants and other activities by the water. The further north you go (towards the foothills), the more restricted are the views of the mountains.

The following suggestions are just a handful of standard places, plus some of the pricier alternatives.

Lakeside East (Ammat) Pokhara's most expensive hotel is the beautifully positioned *Fish Tail Lodge* (☎ 061-20071; fax 20072). It's across the lake from the lakeside development and guests are shuttled over to the hotel by a rope-drawn pontoon. The hotel takes its name from Machhapuchhare. From the hotel there are superb views of the mountains, particularly at dawn when they are reflected in the still waters of the lake.

The buildings have been imaginatively designed with references to the local architecture, and sit in attractive gardens. The rooms have all the usual luxury mod cons and cost $80/90 a single/double, plus 12% tax. There's also a new wing of deluxe rooms which are more expensive and less attractive, but which do have limited views. The hotel is extremely popular, so it is worth booking well in advance if you want to stay. There's a pleasant bar and restaurant although the food is only average.

Lakeside's other places are all on the northern side of the lake, and one of the first you come to is the comfortable mid-range *New Pokhara Lodge* (☎ 061-20875). It looks a little garish but is well run. Singles/doubles with private bath are reasonable value from $10/15.

Take the first right after Baba Lodge & Restaurant and you come to the *Base Camp Resort* (☎ 061-21226; fax 20903), one of the

RICHARD I'ANSON

SONIA BERTO

Top: Beautiful Machhapuchhare viewed from Dhampus
Bottom: The walls of Annapurna South at sunset.

SARA-JANE CLELAND

RICHARD I'ANSON

Top: Full moon over the Himalayas
Bottom: Sunrise gilds the flanks of Annapurna South.

SARA-JANE CLELAND

GREG ELMS

GREG ELMS

SARA-JANE CLELAND

ANNAPURNA CIRCUIT
Top: Part of the Annapurna massif.
Centre Left: Farm worker at Siklis, in the Annapurna range
Bottom Left: Towards Annapurna
Right: Brightly adorned woman

HUGH FINLAY

TONY WHEELER
POKHARA
Top: During the festival of Dasain, bamboo swings are a part of the fun, here with the backdrop of the Annapurnas, near Pokhara.
Bottom: Blue canoes on Phewa Tal

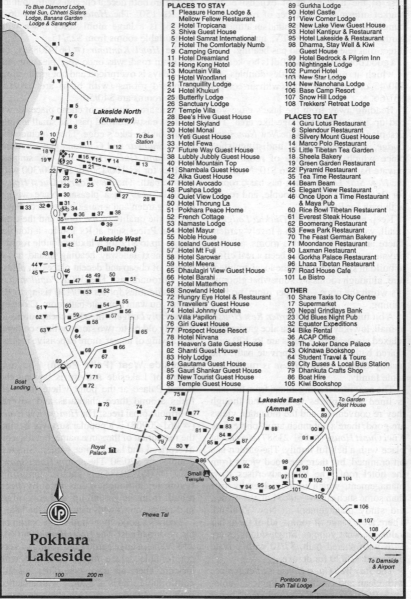

PLACES TO STAY

1 Pleasure Home Lodge &
   Mellow Fellow Restaurant
2 Hotel Tropicana
3 Shiva Guest House
5 Hotel Samrat International
7 Hotel The Comfortably Numb
9 Camping Ground
11 Hotel Dreamland
12 Hong Kong Hotel
13 Mountain Villa
16 Hotel Woodland
21 Tranquillity Lodge
24 Hotel Khukuri
25 Butterfly Lodge
26 Sanctuary Lodge
27 Temple Villa
28 Bee's Hive Guest House
29 Hotel Skyland
30 Hotel Monal
31 Yeti Guest House
33 Hotel Fewa
37 Future Way Guest House
38 Lubbly Jubbly Guest House
40 Hotel Mountain Top
41 Shambala Guest House
42 Alka Guest House
47 Hotel Avocado
48 Pushpa Lodge
49 Quiet View Lodge
50 Hotel Thorung La
51 Pokhara Peace Home
52 French Cottage
53 Namaste Lodge
54 Hotel Mayur
55 Noble House
56 Iceland Guest House
57 Hotel Mt Fuji
58 Hotel Sarowar
59 Hotel Meera
66 Dhaulagiri View Guest House
66 Hotel Barahi
67 Hotel Matterhorn
68 Snowland Hotel
69 Hungry Eye Hotel & Restaurant
73 Travellers' Guest House
74 Hotel Johnny Gurkha
75 Villa Papillon
76 Giri Guest House
77 Prospect House Resort
78 Hotel Nirvana
81 Heaven's Gate Guest House
82 Shanti Guest House
83 Holy Lodge
84 Gautama Guest House
85 Gauri Shankar Guest House
87 New Tourist Guest House
88 Temple Guest House

89 Gurkha Lodge
90 Hotel Castle
91 View Corner Lodge
92 New Lake View Guest House
93 Hotel Kantipur & Restaurant
95 Hotel Lakeside & Restaurant
98 Dharma, Stay Well & Kiwi
    Guest House
99 Hotel Bedrock & Pilgrim Inn
100 Nightingale Lodge
102 Pumori Hotel
103 New Star Lodge
104 New Nanohana Lodge
106 Base Camp Resort
107 Snow Hill Lodge
108 Trekkers' Retreat Lodge

PLACES TO EAT

4 Guru Lotus Restaurant
6 Splendour Restaurant
8 Silvery Mount Guest House
14 Marco Polo Restaurant
15 Little Tibetan Tea Garden
18 Sheela Bakery
19 Green Garden Restaurant
22 Pyramid Restaurant
35 Tea Time Restaurant
44 Beam Beam
45 Elegant View Restaurant
46 Once Upon a Time Restaurant
   & Maya Pub
60 Rice Bowl Tibetan Restaurant
61 Everest Steak House
62 Boomerang Restaurant
63 Fewa Park Restaurant
70 The Feast German Bakery
71 Moondance Restaurant
80 Laxman Restaurant
94 Gorkha Palace Restaurant
96 Lhasa Tibetan Restaurant
97 Road House Cafe
101 Le Bistro

OTHER

10 Share Taxis to City Centre
17 Supermarket
20 Nepal Grindlays Bank
23 Old Blues Night Pub
32 Equator Expeditions
34 Bike Rental
36 ACAP Office
39 The Joker Dance Palace
43 Okinawa Bookshop
64 Student Travel & Tours
79 City Buses & Local Bus Station
79 Dhankuta Crafts Shop
86 Boat Hire
105 Kiwi Bookshop

To Blue Diamond Lodge,
Hotel Sun, Chhetri Sisters
Lodge, Banana Garden
Lodge & Sarangkot

Lakeside North
(Khaharey)

To Bus
Station

Lakeside West
(Pallo Patan)

Boat
Landing

Lakeside East
(Ammat)

To Garden
Rest House

Royal
Palace

Small
Temple

Phewa Tal

POKHARA

Pokhara
Lakeside

0   100   200 m

To Damside
& Airport

Pontoon to
Fish Tail Lodge

best of the new breed of expensive up-market offerings. A number of two storey bungalows are grouped around an attractive garden. There's satellite TV, international direct-dial telephones and gas heating. This is a good option if the Fish Tail is booked out – which it often is. Singles/doubles are $40/45, or for deluxe rooms with air-con it's $61/66.

Heading away from the lake's edge you end up in a pleasant village-like area. The first place you come to is the *New Nanohana Lodge*, a modern, fairly undistinguished place which has a range of rooms with private bath from Rs 250 to $10. Nearby is the *New Star Lodge* which has basic rooms for Rs 100/150 a single/double, and rooms with bath for Rs 350.

Keep going to find the *Gurkha Lodge*, a small, well kept place with a lovely garden. There are only five double rooms, all with private bath, and there has been a real effort to build in sympathy with the local architecture, although rooms are somewhat gloomy. It's worth the price – $11 per room, no bargaining.

A bit further on is the *Garden Rest House*, a small, low-key place with a nice garden and relaxed atmosphere. Rooms are Rs 120 with shared bath, Rs 300 with private bath. The nearby *Garden Guest House* is run by the same family.

The next road leading inland from the lake is lined with places to stay, and though they're convenient, and the mountain views are good, there's not much atmosphere. The *Kiwi Guest House* (☎ 061-21587) is a decent place with a helpful family. The garden is a bit cramped, but there are good views from the hotel roof. The Kiwi advertises Kiwi management, which is more literally true than some such claims, since Lal, the owner, did study management in New Zealand. There are a range of rooms, all of them fair value for what you get. Singles/doubles are $4/6 with shared bath, $7/10 with private bath, and $15/20 for deluxe.

The *Stay Well Guest House* is a small place with clean and comfortable singles/doubles for $10/20. *Dharma House* and *View Corner Lodge* are both decent cheapies with doubles for Rs 150. The *Hotel Bedrock* (☎ 061-21876) is a large multi-storey place with comfortable rooms from $25/45.

The *Hotel Kantipur* (☎ 061-20886), on the main road, was once very pleasant, but these days is overpriced and not great value. Standard rooms (with bath) are $10/15; deluxe rooms are $40/50.

There are a number of cheap places down the first eastward road past the small temple shrine on the lake's edge. These include the *Gauri Shankar* and *Gautama* guest houses. The *Shanti Guest House* has OK singles/doubles for Rs 100/150, or Rs 200/300 with private bath. The *New Tourist Guest House* (☎ 061-21479) is a pleasant place with a decent garden and a range of prices depending on the quality of the room and the time of year. Prices start at Rs 150 for a double, but go up to $12 for a luxury double room.

The next laneway heading inland has a couple of cheap and decent places, in pleasant surroundings. The *Villa Papillon* has singles/doubles for Rs 100/150 rising to Rs 300 if you want a private bathroom. Close by is the *Holy Lodge*, which has cheap rooms in a lovely old rustic two storey village cottage, and a wing of newer, more expensive rooms.

Lakeside West (Pallo Patan) The real centre of Lakeside activity is beyond the Royal Palace at the point where the road forks around three chautaras and several enormous pipal trees. The *Hungry Eye Hotel* (☎ 061-20908) is a popular survivor behind the restaurant of the same name, but it's a bit overpriced and lacks a nice garden. Singles/doubles are $20/30. The nearby *Hotel Snowland* (☎ 061-20384) is another long-time favourite, although it has recently been rebuilt from the ground up, and now offers mid-range rooms with views over the lake.

There's a good upper mid-range option on the next road east. The *Hotel Barahi* (☎ 061-21879) has a huge garden and a wing of very comfortable deluxe rooms at $60/75 with air-con. There are also some older but still comfortable rooms at $20/25 with attached bath.

The road running eastward from the next chautara (beside the incongruous Cape Cod-style Hotel Meera) has a number of options, but the laneway itself is not as pleasant as some. First there is a very simple, very basic, but cheap place – *Noble House*, a small cottage still with a village garden, and quite OK rooms at Rs 50/80. There are also a couple of well run, mid-range places – the *Iceland Guest House*, the *Hotel Mt Fuji* and the *Hotel Sarowar*. They're all pleasant and comfortable with prices starting at around $6/10 for singles/doubles.

We wouldn't stay at the *Hotel Meera* (☎ 061-21031) on principle as it's just totally inappropriate for the setting. Nevertheless, the rooms are good and the front-room views excellent. The cost is $14/23 with common bath, $29/38 with attached.

The next eastward lane (just before the next chautara) is very pleasant and retains some of the old Pokhara atmosphere. There are a number of cheapies (around Rs 150) including the *Namaste Lodge* and the *Quiet View Lodge*. The *French Cottage* is particularly pleasant for the price range. The *Pokhara Peace Home* (☎ 061-23205) along here is also not a bad place. It has a pleasant garden with a village feel, and rooms cost $5/9 with common bath, $8/15 with attached bath. The *Hotel Avocado* (☎ 061-21183) has good rooftop views, but no garden. Rooms range from $5 to $15.

Right on the main road, the *Hotel Mountain Top* (☎ 061-20779) is an unmissable four storey monstrosity, and not an uncommon sight these days. We're loathe to say it, but the comfortable rooms have superb views and they're not bad value. Singles/doubles with private bath are $20/29, and deluxe rooms are $30/40.

Up the side road beside the Mountain Top there are a few more guest houses to choose from, including the *Lubbly Jubbly Guest House*! Despite the absurd name, it's a pleasant little place with a very rural ambience.

The only hotel on the western side of the road is the superbly situated *Hotel Fewa* (☎ 061-20151), right on the edge of the lake. Unfortunately, the rooms are pretty run-down, but the lakeside location is hard to match. The rooms cost RS 200/250 downstairs, or Rs 400/500 upstairs with lake view, all with attached bath.

Back on the eastern side, the *Tranquillity Lodge* (☎ 061-21030) is a pleasant modern hotel set in a sunny garden. Rooms are large and comfortable, but a bit overpriced at $15/25 – there's certainly room for bargaining, especially out of season. The nearby *Butterfly Lodge* is similar, and cheaper. Further along is the *Temple Villa* (☎ 061-21203), a small and pleasant lodge also in a quiet location. The operation, despite the claim of its Nepali-German management, is considerably more Nepali than German. It is clean, however, and the rooms are large and comfortable. They're reasonable value at $5/10, or $10/20 with private bath.

On the same lane is the new *Hotel Khukuri* (☎ 061-21540), a small high-rise place with well appointed rooms at $25/30, but there's no garden and unless you absolutely can't survive without a TV and carpet, there's better value elsewhere.

Lakeside North (Khaharey) There are more places to stay beyond the intersection between the lakeside and main roads, both on the lakeside and on the main road itself. Once you get this far north you are tucked in under the foothills and don't get great views of the mountains.

For those with tents the best bet is to make a deal with one of the lodges to camp in their garden. Alternatively, there's the *camping ground*, by the lake near Camping Chowk. The facilities are very basic and there's not much shade, although it is a nice grassy site and is a good option if you have a large vehicle. It costs Rs 40 to pitch a tent and Rs 80 per vehicle.

The places along the main road don't appeal very much. Not surprisingly, the road lacks the peaceful rural atmosphere that the best parts of Pokhara have, and although the traffic is not particularly heavy, there are regular buses and taxis. Most of the hotels are new and are two or three storey monstrosities with mid-range prices. Some of the

POKHARA

possibilities include the *Hotel Woodland*, *Prince Guest House* and *Hong Kong Hotel*. One of the best is the *Mountain Villa* (☎ 061-21954), which has fairly typical prices at $16/20 for singles/doubles. The garden is pleasant and rooms have private bathrooms.

The *Hotel Tropicana* (☎ 061-22118) is a relatively new place with lake views and rooms from $5/8.

There are some peaceful good-value alternatives along the road that continues around the lake, including the *Blue Diamond Lodge*, the *Hotel Sun* and the *Chhetri Sisters Lodge*. One of the best is the *Banana Garden Lodge*, right on the outskirts, tucked right in at the base of the hill and with good views over the lake. Doubles are a bargain at Rs 100.

Right out on a point, nestled between the road and the lake shore, are two small, cheap lodges which are basic but popular. The *Buddha* and *Green Peace* lodges both have single and double rooms with common bath, but you would need a bicycle as they are a good 20 minutes walk from the nearest restaurants.

PLACES TO EAT

Pokhara may not match the variety of food offered in Kathmandu, but you can certainly eat well although, as usual in Nepal, a little caution is always wise. Upset stomachs are as common in Pokhara as anywhere else in the country.

The bazaar area has local restaurants, and other eating possibilities are found in the big hotels or amongst the numerous cheaper hotels particularly along Lakeside. At most of these travellers' restaurants you'll find the standard 'try anything' menu – which currently means lots of Italian dishes backed up by Indian, Nepali, Mexican, 'Continental' and whatever other possibilities present themselves. The range is certainly an improvement over endless dal bhats or thalis, but despite the apparent variation everything very quickly tastes the same! Most main meals cost from Rs 75 to Rs 150, and a bottle of beer is usually Rs 90.

There is not a great range of restaurants in the Damside area, as most people eat at their hotels. *KC's Restaurant* (no relation to KC's in Thamel) has a pleasant outdoor area and the classic range of Indonesian, Mexican, Indian and Italian dishes. Most are a reasonable Rs 80. In the same area, the *Rodee Restaurant* is also popular.

Most dining possibilities are along the main road skirting Lakeside. Starting at Lakeside East, the first possibility is the *Baba Restaurant* with its fine terrace overlooking the lake. The food is good and the service is snappy.

Continuing on you come to more places, all with the standard Nepali travellers' menu and with open eating areas overlooking the lake. *Le Bistro* has everything from Mexican, Italian, Chinese and Indian to Nepali and they seem to do a pretty good job of all of it. The apple pies are not bad either!

The *Lhasa Tibetan Restaurant* is a big outdoors place with a standard 'try-anything' menu, in addition to a number of Tibetan specialities. The food is very good and the service is fairly fast. Sha bhakley, a Tibetan meat pie, is Rs 80, and momo (meat/vegetable filled pasta) is Rs 40. Chicken tikka kebabs with nan (bread) and salad for Rs 90 are good value, as are the pizzas and vegetable curries.

The *Annapurna Restaurant* has a nice garden and a 4 to 7 pm happy hour when a beer and chips costs Rs 75. A substantial curry costs from Rs 55.

The *Hungry Eye* is a long-standing survivor and one of the biggest restaurants on Lakeside. The food is still good (the cakes are excellent), but the service is chaotic and prices are a bit steep. Pizza ranges from Rs 80 to Rs 120 and a steak is Rs 140.

Next door, the *Moondance Restaurant* has average prices and food, but a good atmosphere. There's a fireplace inside. The *Snowland* has an enormous menu featuring all the standard Indian, Chinese, Mexican and European dishes you can think of. They are all done remarkably well, but the Indian food is excellent.

The *Boomerang Restaurant* is one of a new generation of places that has sprung up right on the edge of the lake. Given that this space should never have been developed, it must also be said that the opportunity has not been wasted. There's a nice garden dotted with chairs, tables and thatched shelters – and great views. It's a great place for breakfast (around Rs 60) or lunch, but dinner is less impressive – for a start you'll be inside, so you're less likely to be tolerant of the friendly but haphazard service. They have the normal eclectic menu and prices.

Beam Beam also fronts onto the lake, and although the garden is much smaller than the Boomerang's, it is still very pleasant – in some ways cosier. The entire restaurant, inside and out, has a pleasant atmosphere, and the decor and layout are considerably more imaginative than most of the clone-like offerings along the lake. The service is excellent, and although the menu is pretty standard, the food is good. The *Elegant View Restaurant* is very similar.

The *Tea Time Restaurant* is a popular place, as is the *Once Upon a Time* one block further along.

For budget breakfasts try one of the small bakeries, such as the *Sheela* up near Camping Chowk. This is a very popular little place, with excellent chocolate croissants (Rs 7) and buns. There's a similar place by the Tea Time Restaurant.

The *Little Tibetan Tea Garden* is a cosy place on the main road into Pokhara from Camping Chowk. Just so no-one feels left out, they do not only excellent Tibetan food (including that traditional favourite, Tibetan pizza!), but also throw in a few Mexican and Italian dishes.

At the top end of the spectrum, the bar and restaurant at the *Fish Tail Lodge* could be a fine place for a more expensive night out but the food is only average, the service once you depart from the fixed meals is appallingly slow, and the is clientele uninspiring. The fixed breakfast costs Rs 375, or a buffet dinner is Rs 560, while an à la carte dinner for two will probably come to at least Rs 1000. The Lakeside restaurants can turn out good food in half the time for a fraction of the cost. On a clear day it's worth coming over here for a drink in the garden, which has stunning views of Machhapuchhare.

ENTERTAINMENT
The *Fish Tail Lodge* puts on an excellent nightly cultural programme featuring Nepali dancing by the Dance Dance Club. It runs from 6 to 7 pm in winter, 6.30 to 7.30 pm in summer and admission is Rs 75.

There are an increasing number of bars in Pokhara, and the music blares out until 10 pm each night. There's nothing very bluesy about the *Old Blues Night Pub*, but the sound system is good (and usually cranked up loud) and the pool tables are popular.

Another good bar is the *Maya Pub*, which has a happy hour in the early evening with two cocktails for the price of one.

There's one disco (well, sort of), which goes by the unlikely name of *The Joker Dance Palace*. It's open from 6 pm and entry is Rs 200 for men, for women it's free.

THINGS TO BUY
Pokhara's large Tibetan population sells many crafts and artefacts. Carpet-weaving is a major local industry for these people.

Saligrams, the fossilised sea creatures found north up the Kali Gandaki Valley, are a popular souvenir, but they are often radically overpriced. You shouldn't pay more than about Rs 100.

Trekking Equipment
There are a number of rental shops in Pokhara, and prices are similar to those in Kathmandu, eg down sleeping bags and jackets are around Rs 10 to Rs 15 per day. The range of equipment is not so large however, so if you want anything out of the ordinary you are best off bringing it from home, or Kathmandu.

GETTING THERE & AWAY
Some travel agencies in Pokhara offer 'through' tickets or package-deal tickets to cities in India. These are dubious value at the best of times and a number of travellers have written to us complaining of various rip-offs perpetrated by unscrupulous Pokhara agents.

POKHARA

These range from promises of tourist buses (there are *no* tourist buses running to/from any of the border crossings), to reserved seats that were definitely not reserved, and air-con train sleepers that turn out to be 2nd class.

See the Getting There & Away chapter for more information, but if you do decide to buy a package, make sure you get everything spelled out in a receipt, and hang on to the receipt.

Air

There are a number of daily services between Kathmandu and Pokhara. As the route is something of a cash cow all the private companies have jumped on the bandwagon; Necon Air (☎ 061-20256) is recommended. The flight takes less than an hour and costs $61. RNAC (☎ 061-21021) has a booking office at the airport; Everest Air (☎ 061-21883) and Nepal Airways (☎ 061-20966) are just across the road. It's probably easiest to get one of the many agents at Lakeside to do the running around for the ticket.

There are great Himalayan views if you sit on the right-hand side of the plane from Kathmandu to Pokhara, and on the left-hand side from Pokhara to Kathmandu.

Bus

To/From Kathmandu The bus trip between Kathmandu and Pokhara takes seven or eight hours and most departures are early in the morning. The first stretch of road from Kathmandu to Naubise is in appalling condition, it's excellent from Naubise to Mugling, appalling from Mugling to Dumre, and fair from Dumre to Pokhara.

Public buses (from the bus station) cost Rs 110, the large tourist buses cost from Rs 140 and tourist minibuses cost Rs 200. It's a bit dubious whether the extra expense of tourist buses is worthwhile. The minibuses are certainly quicker (often considerably scarier as a result), but the full-sized tourist buses aren't significantly different to the public express buses in terms of either time or comfort.

The tourist buses are, however, more convenient when you consider where they pick you up and drop you off. In Kathmandu they pick up and drop off at the Thamel end of Kantipath. In Pokhara, the tourist buses pick up Kathmandu-bound passengers outside their hotels, although all buses coming from Kathmandu terminate at the appalling main Pokhara bus station. Public buses all start and finish at the Pokhara bus station. Whichever bus you take it's wise to book at least a day ahead.

Apparently the tourist-bus operators were forced to unload at the bus station by the Damside-area hotel owners, who observed that most tourists chose to be dropped off at Lakeside. Now everyone is deposited in the squalid bus station where, tired and bewildered, they are fair game for a horde of extremely pushy touts – and the touts representing the Damside hotels are on an equal footing with everyone else.

There is absolutely no reason to get sucked in by these characters who will, apart from anything else, get a 50% commission from the hotel they take you to. The best thing you can do is grab a taxi to somewhere central on Lakeside, have a drink and a bite to eat at one of the restaurants and then ask to leave your bag somewhere safe while you check out some hotels for yourself.

To/From Chitwan Public buses between Pokhara and Tadi Bazaar cost Rs 75, large tourist buses cost Rs 140 and minibuses cost from Rs 200. See the Royal Chitwan National Park section of the Terai chapter for more details.

To/From the Indian Border Buses to Sunauli/Bhairawa near the Indian border depart from the main Pokhara bus station, cost Rs 80 by day (Rs 111 at night) and take nine hours; buses for Birganj cost Rs 90 (Rs 106) and take 10 hours; and buses for Nepalganj leave at 3.30 pm, take 15 hours and cost Rs 190 (via Mugling). We have received a number of letters complaining that Pokhara agents sell overpriced tickets for alleged tourist buses to the border. There are no tourist buses; so while you do get picked up outside your hotel, you go from there to the bus station where everyone else gets on!

The road to India is called the Siddhartha Highway because it ends close to Lumbini where the Buddha, Siddhartha Gautama, was born. See the Getting There & Away chapter for more details on transport to India.

To/From Trekking Routes Pokhara is the base for popular treks such as the Annapurna Sanctuary Trek, Jomsom Trek and the Annapurna Circuit, plus a number of other lesser known alternatives. The road goes all the way to Baglung, so most trekkers take the bus as far as Nayapul (just before Baglung), from where it's just a 20 minute walk to Birethanti. Buses for Baglung leave the local bus station roughly every half hour from early morning until mid-afternoon, and the trip to Nayapul takes about two hours.

To Besisahar, for the start of the Annapurna Sanctuary Trek, there is one bus daily at around 7 am from the main Pokhara bus station, and the journey takes around five hours.

GETTING AROUND

It's a long way between the bazaar and Lakeside; a taxi costs around Rs 100. It's a battle to extract fair prices when catching a taxi from Lakeside to the airport or bus station. Expect to pay at least Rs 50, possibly as much as Rs 100. Buses shuttle between the lake, airport and bazaar with per-person fares at around Rs 5.

Share-taxis operate frequently from Camping Chowk in the northern part of Lakeside into the city centre.

There are lots of bicycle-rental places along the lake, by the dam or by the airport. Ordinary bikes typically cost around Rs 30 per day, mountain bikes around Rs 100. You can also rent children's bicycles. Pokhara looks deceptively flat but actually slopes steadily uphill as you move north. If you ride a bicycle from the lake to the Binde Basini Temple at the northern end of the bazaar area

you'll find it's a wonderfully long freewheel on the way back.

Renting a motorbike costs around Rs 500 per day – a bit more than in Kathmandu. Pokhara and the surrounding roads will not be improved by the growing number of motorbikes.

Around Pokhara

Pokhara is the starting or finishing point for some of Nepal's most popular treks like the Annapurna Circuit, the Jomsom Trek and the Annapurna Sanctuary Trek. See the Trekking chapter for details.

For those with limited time, less enthusiasm for walking or with small children in tow, the Pokhara area also has some fine short treks ranging from half-day and day walks to longer treks lasting from two or three days to a week.

DAY WALKS

The following walks can all be made in a day or less.

Sarangkot

This very pleasant walk up to Sarangkot, at an elevation of 1592m, is probably the most popular short excursion from Pokhara. It can be a good, pre-breakfast stroll to admire the mountain views, a leg-stretcher before you start out on a longer trek or a place you pass through on the first or last hours of one of the longer treks from Pokhara.

Sarangkot has a number of places to stay or eat – like the *Didi Lodge, Restaurant Sarangkot, Trekking Lodge* or *New Tourist Lodge* – so you can climb up to Sarangkot in the evening, stay overnight and catch the view at dawn, or simply walk up for breakfast. The *View Top Restaurant & Lodge* has the prime views over the lake and pretty good food and it's extensively advertised on the steps up from the lake.

There are a number of routes to Sarangkot, but the easiest way is to walk up from the Binde

Basini Temple in Pokhara Bazaar and then head straight down from the top to the lake.

As you approach the temple from the bazaar, ignore the sign to Sarangkot just south of the temple and continue a little further to look at the temple before you start the walk.

From the temple head directly east and follow the vehicle track which runs most of the way up. You can short-cut many of the sharp corners and from where the vehicle track ends there is virtually a stairway to the top. On the way up you pass several places where women work at handlooms. It takes about two hours to walk to Sarangkot from Binde Basini Temple, versus three or four hours from the Lakeside area *if* you don't get seriously lost!

Sarangkot once had a fort or *kot* and its remains can be seen on the very top of the ridge above Sarangkot. There is a lookout point actually inside the old fort walls and the view of the Annapurnas to the north is superb.

The view back down over Phewa Tal is equally fine and from the top it takes about two hours to walk down to the lake. It's easy to get lost on the way up from the lake but coming down from Sarangkot is straightforward: you make a very steep descent, stone-staired all the way, down the hillside and through the forest. If you're exhausted when you reach the lake, there are often boatmen waiting to paddle you back to the Lakeside lodge area.

An alternative to the Binde Basini Temple or Phewa Tal routes to the top is the walk from Bhairab Tole in Pokhara via the village of Gyarjati. Another hour's walk beyond Sarangkot will take you to Kaski or Kaskikot at 1788m. The hill is topped by an unprepossessing Bhagwati temple.

Kahun Danda

To the north-east of the bazaar area of Pokhara is Kahun Danda (*danda* means ridge in Nepali). It takes about three hours to

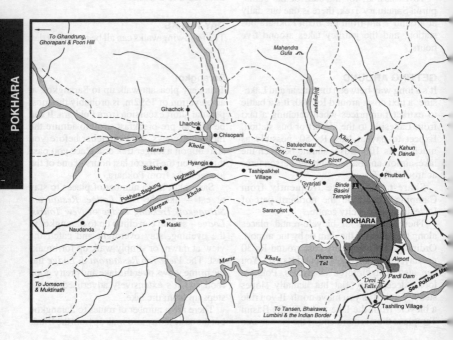

walk to this popular viewpoint at 1560m and there's a lookout tower on top of the ridge. The walk starts from the Mahendrapul Bridge and continues through Phulbari and up the gradual slope to the top. The remains of the 18th century Kanhu Kot stand on the hilltop.

Mahendra Gufa

The limestone caves at Mahendra Gufa have stalactites and stalagmites and make a good destination for a two hour walk north from Pokhara. The trail to the caves crosses the bridge just north of Bagar at the end of the bazaar and heads toward the village of **Batulechaur**. This village was once an important centre for growing citrus fruit until an epidemic killed all the citrus trees in the Pokhara Valley.

Rupa & Begnas Tals

These two lakes are the second and third largest in the valley, but few travellers visit

them even though they're only 15 km east of Pokhara.

Buses run regularly from Pokhara to Begnas Bazaar, the small market centre at the very end of the ridge which divides the two lakes. From there it's a pleasant stroll along the ridge to the other end of either lake.

SHORT TREKS
Annapurna Skyline Trek

The three or four day Annapurna Skyline Trek has also been dubbed the 'Royal Trek' as Britain's Prince Charles walked it some years ago. It's a fine trek to do with children, as it doesn't reach any great altitudes, doesn't entail any particularly long walking days and there's always plenty to see. It's not a heavily trekked area, however, so there is no village inn accommodation along the route.

There are several variations on the route but basically the walk starts from the Kathmandu-Pokhara (Prithvi) Highway, a few km east of Pokhara, climbs up to a ridge

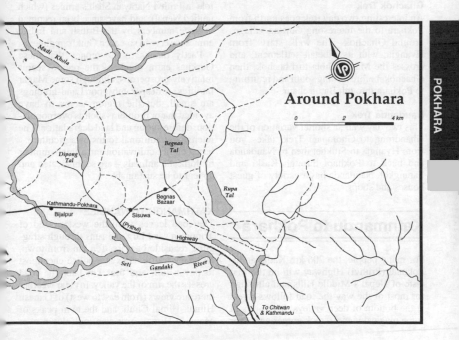

Around Pokhara

0   2   4 km

and then for most of the walk follows ridges with fine views of the Annapurnas and back down into the Pokhara Valley.

The walk passes through small villages like Kalikathan, Shaklung and Chisopani before it drops down to the stream which feeds Rupa Tal. The final stretch is along the ridge separating Rupa Tal and Begnas Tal, emerging on the valley floor at Begnas Bazaar from where buses run to Pokhara.

Ghandrung to Ghorapani Trek

This week-long trek to the west of Pokhara also gives fine views of the Annapurnas. The walk starts and finishes at Birethanti, and essentially links the first few days of the Annapurna Sanctuary Trek as far as Ghandrung with the first few days of the Jomsom Trek as far as Ghorapani, then crosses between those two villages.

Near Ghorapani is Poon Hill, one of the finest lookout points in the region.

Ghachok Trek

An interesting two day trek goes north from Pokhara to the interesting Gurung villages around Ghachok. The walk starts from Hyangja, with its Tibetan settlement, and crosses the Mardi Khola to Lhachok, then Ghachok, before turning south and returning to Pokhara through Batulechaur.

Naudanda Trek

This two day walk, a shorter variation of the Ghandrung to Ghorapani Trek, takes you from Hyangja to Suikhet then to Naudanda and back to Pokhara through Kaski and Sarangkot. Naudanda has a variety of guest houses and shops.

Kathmandu to Pokhara

For many people, the 206 km Kathmandu-Pokhara (Prithvi) Highway will be the first taste of Nepal's Middle Hills and although for most of the way the road follows rivers at the bottom of deep valleys there are still some magical views – rock gorges and river rapids, precipitous hills, tiered rice terraces and glimpses of the Himalaya.

Migrants from around Nepal (especially the Kathmandu Valley) have been attracted by the minimal economic opportunities offered in the roadside towns that have sprung up. Most towns are the usual unattractive collection of shanties and two storey concrete boxes. There are, however, some interesting places (west of Mugling and off the main road) that are worth visiting: Gorkha, which was the original capital for the Shah dynasty; and Bandipur, an old Newari trading settlement.

The countryside is inhabited by Bahuns, Chhetris, Magars and Gurungs. The large multi-storeyed houses, especially before Mugling, are most likely owned by Bahuns and Chhetris, but around Mugling the region is dominated by Magars, and to a lesser extent, Gurungs. Historically, the Magars had their own independent kingdoms in western Nepal, and both Magars and Gurungs played a major role in Prithvi Narayan Shah's armies (which unified Nepal), and have since been recruited in large numbers by the British and Indian armies to serve in so-called Gurkha regiments.

Partly thanks to the money that these Gurkhas earn, much of the region seems relatively prosperous, although some Magar families are desperately poor. Land-holdings are small, but the region seems to have avoided major problems such as overpopulation, deforestation and land degradation. The intensive, traditional forms of agriculture – based on rice cultivation and a small number of domestic animals – are sophisticated and appear to be sustainable.

KATHMANDU TO NAUBISE

The road leaves from the western end of Tripureshwar Marg and runs through straggling roadside bazaars. Ten km from town, all heavy traffic stops at a police checkpost to pay a toll, and four km later the road crosses the rim of the valley. In clear weather there are views (from east to west) of Ganesh Himal, Himal Chuli, and the twin peaks of Manaslu Himal. You also look down over incredible terracing rising from the Trisuli River and Mahesh Kola.

The road from the rim of the valley to Naubise is in extremely poor condition. It snakes down the hill in a series of switch-backs and is further enlivened by Tata trucks overtaking on blind corners. At Naubise, the Tribhuvan Highway joins the road after its spectacular journey from Hetauda (see the Terai chapter for details of that route).

NAUBISE TO MUGLING

From Naubise, the road follows the small Mahesh Khola to the point where it joins the Trisuli River just past Baireni (52 km from Kathmandu). It then continues along the Trisuli Valley through the small town of Gajuritar.

Around Malekhu the gorge is still attrac-tively forested. Just before Malekhu, a new bridge over the river leads to Trisuli Bazaar, superseding the old winding one track road that leaves the valley at Kakani.

Just after Malekhu there are a number of small restaurants, which are good places to break the journey and which also cater to intrepid rafters. The *Hill Top Restaurant* has a great view over the beach where most rafting trips start, and has good, reasonably priced food and clean toilets. The *Blue Heaven Restaurant* is virtually on the beach, which is about 70 km from Kathmandu and four km before Benighat.

At Benighat, the large Buri Gandaki River flows into the Trisuli from the north, giving the rafters the volume of water required for plenty of excitement. The road continues to follow the westward-flowing Trisuli to Mugling, where it meets the equally large eastward-flowing Marsyangdi.

The road from Naubise to Mugling was upgraded in the early 90s, and is, without doubt, the best bit of road in the country – beautifully engineered, smoothly surfaced – and as dangerous as hell. It seems ironic that accidents have increased since the road has been improved from the cratered, axle-busting slalom course that challenged drivers in the late 80s. The truth is that it's so good that every driver worth his dal bhat

goes as fast as his Tata will carry him. In absolute terms this is not very fast, but it is nonetheless about 30 km/h faster than is safe.

MUGLING

Mugling is at the junction between the most important road from the plains (from Nar-ayanghat) and the Kathmandu-Pokhara (Prithvi) Highway, so it is a popular stop for buses and trucks. It's 110 km from Kathmandu and 96 km from Pokhara, and it lies at an elevation of just 208m, making it the lowest town between Kathmandu and Pokhara.

The town is also at the junction of the eastward-flowing Trisuli and the westward-flowing Marsyangdi rivers, which together form the Narayani, a major tributary of the Ganges. This is the finishing point for most of the serious white-water rafting trips on the Trisuli, and the launching place for the more sedate trips down the Narayani to Nar-ayanghat and the Royal Chitwan National Park.

Mugling is not an attractive place. Poverty-stricken Magars from the surrounding hills scavenge a living alongside poverty-stricken refugees from the plains. The town is notorious for prostitution, although this will not be obvious to westerners stopping over for dal bhat during the day. The girls are sold by Magar families and the clientele are the long-distance truck drivers.

Places to Stay & Eat

There are literally dozens of restaurants that serve good dal bhat for around Rs 25. Most are owned by Thakalis, and there is little to distinguish one restaurant from another.

Mugling would not be a pleasant place to spend a night. There are dozens of hotels, but few are interested in having a westerner stay, since their main business is prostitution. One that does accommodate the occasional stranded backpacker is the *Hotel Laligurans & Lodge*, at the western end of town, near the suspension bridge over the river and the intersection with the Narayanghat road. The hotel has the advantage of being set back from the road, but it's very basic and not very clean. Singles/doubles are Rs 60/75.

For those who are able to afford it, there is

POKHARA

an attractive, slightly incongruous motel on the Pokhara side of town just over the bridge. The *Motel du Mugling* (☎ 01-225242; fax 225236) is operated by Hotel de l'Annapurna (see the Kathmandu, Patan & Bhaktapur chapter) and is comfortable, and expensive. Singles/doubles are $30/40 plus 10% tax; meals are $8.

MUGLING TO ABU KHAIRENI

Leaving Mugling, a long suspension bridge crosses the Narayani River just below the junction of the Trisuli and Marsyangdi rivers. Two km further on you reach the **Marsyangdi Hydroelectric Powerhouse**, which generates more than a quarter of the country's electricity. Water is diverted to the building you see beside the road from a dam 12 km away. The road deteriorates after Mugling, and there are some very rough, very dusty sections until you get past Dumre.

Eight km from Mugling you reach Abu Khaireni, another roadside bazaar town, which is at the intersection of the road to Gorkha, and is the starting point for the climb to **Manakamana**, one of the most popular temples in Nepal.

It is believed that the goddess Bhagwati will grant wishes in exchange for prayer and animal sacrifices, and she is particularly popular with newlyweds seeking sons. The hereditary role of temple priest is filled by a Magar (not a Brahman as is usually the case with Hindu temples), suggesting that the goddess is a survivor from the pre-Hindu, shamanistic religion of the Magars.

To get to the temple, turn right off the highway on the road to Gorkha; continue for a km until you see the Manakamana Hotel on the right; turn right and cross the river on a suspension bridge; and then climb for three or four hours!

GORKHA

The ninth Shah king, King Prithvi Narayan Shah, was born in the family's palace that perches over Gorkha. Prithvi Narayan was crowned King of Gorkha in 1743, and proved to be an extraordinary man.

At the time he came to power, Nepal was broken up into numerous small principalities, but by the time he died he had created a unified state that was sufficiently strong to successfully resist the colonial forces that engulfed virtually every other country in Asia.

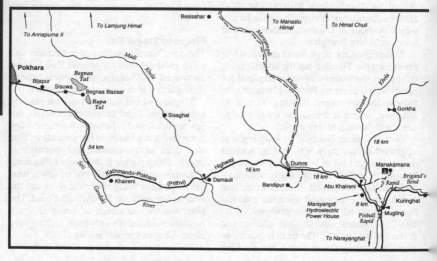

Although he was a great fighter, he was also an accomplished tactician and administrator. His reputation for religious and cultural tolerance, and for the justice and effectiveness of his administration, was a significant element in his success. He was able to maintain the commitment of his subjects through a process that continued for nearly 30 years – the Kathmandu Valley was not completely conquered until the early 1670s – and he succeeded in convincing a number of states to accept his rule without resorting to direct violence. He had the guile to exploit existing rivalries between states, and where necessary utilised expedient alliances, notably with Palpa (see the Tansen section in the Terai chapter).

Gorkha was the name given to the fearsome soldiers (mostly Bahuns, Thakuris, Chhetris, Magars and Gurungs) under his command. The term Gurkha was later applied to all Nepali soldiers, irrespective of where they were recruited and what group they belonged to. Many have served, and still serve, in the British and Indian armies.

Gorkha, 18 km north of the Kathmandu-Pokhara (Prithvi) Highway, is accessible by a good sealed road that intersects with the highway at Abu Khaireni, eight km west of Mugling. The countryside is spectacular and Gorkha itself is well worth visiting.

Gorkha Durbar

Gorkha Durbar, a fort, palace and temple complex, is the centrepoint and highlight of a visit to Gorkha. Some of the building is believed to date from the reign of King Ram Shah (1606-36), but successive generations have made alterations and additions, often utilising Newari craftspeople. The complex is a triumph of Nepali architecture – perched like an eagle's nest high above the town in a perfect defensive position – with superb views of plunging valleys and the soaring Himalaya. You can easily imagine an ambitious prince looking out over this dramatic landscape and dreaming of ruling all he could see – and more.

To get to Gorkha Durbar, walk north from the bus station until you come to several small temples (to Vishnu, Krishna and Ganesh) surrounding a tank. Head to your right until you come to a square, to the right of which is **Tallo Durbar**, a large, square

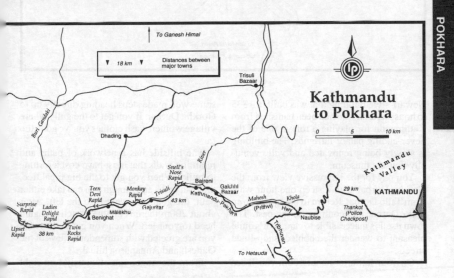

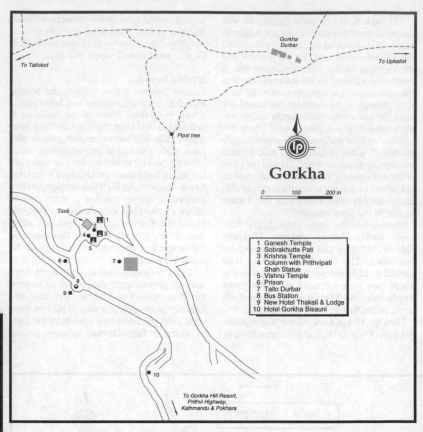

Gorkha

0   100   200 m

1 Ganesh Temple
2 Sobrakhutte Pati
3 Krishna Temple
4 Column with Prithvipati
   Shah Statue
5 Vishnu Temple
6 Prison
7 Tallo Durbar
8 Bus Station
9 New Hotel Thakali & Lodge
10 Hotel Gorkha Bisauni

To Tallokot

To Upkallot

Gorkha
Durbar

Pipal tree

Tank

To Gorkha Hill Resort,
Prithvi Highway,
Kathmandu & Pokhara

Newari-style building that was built in 1835
to house a Rana who had been banished from
Kathmandu for playing a role in one of the
never-ending palace intrigues. The building
is slowly being renovated and will eventually house a museum.

You pay for the impressive view from the
Gorkha Durbar with a steep one hour walk
from Tallo Durbar. Return to the square from
Tallo Durbar and continue to the east. The
town itself is inaccessible to cars, so it's quite
pleasant to wander the cobbled, shop-lined
streets.

On your left after about 100m you'll see
some well made steps heading directly up to
Gorkha Durbar. If you get to the gully where
village women wash clothes you've gone too
far.

The hillside has a network of paths and
retaining walls that must have cost a fortune
to build. When you get to the big pipal tree,
the path forks and though you can take either
path, the gentlest ascent is to the left. After
about 200m there is another junction; again
head to your left. When you get to the ridge
you are greeted with stupendous views of the
Ganesh and Annapurna himal.

From the ridge, you obviously turn right

to the palace, but if you turn left you soon come to **Tallokot**, a small, old fort now used as a sacrificial site.

Photography is not permitted once you are inside the Gorkha Durbar complex, and this rule is strictly enforced by soldiers, so you may want to try to capture something on film from here. Officially you are not allowed to wear leather inside the complex, so wear sandshoes or a thick old pair of socks if you are going to do some serious exploration, although this rule is not strictly enforced.

If you enter from the west, the first building on your left is the Kalika Temple (note the 'Star of David' window), which has some superb woodcarving. Only a special caste of Brahman priests and the king can enter, but sacrifices are made outside.

The main palace, or Dhuni Pati, has latticed windows all around the top floor, but, unfortunately, you are not allowed to enter, so you can only imagine the breezy rooms that lie behind. This was Prithvi Narayan's birthplace and an eternal flame has been kept burning inside ever since his rule.

Next, go up a few steps. There is a priests' house on the left and two bells on the right. Between the latter are stairs descending to a cave where a reclusive saint named Gorkhanath once lived.

Beyond the priests' house is a four faced Shiva lingam. You can descend to servants' quarters and a temple on the next level, then down again to a crude but dramatic repainted carving of Hanuman and six carved stele.

From here it's another half-hour walk east to **Upkallot**, the highest point on the ridge, with the ruins of a fort, and a telecommunications tower. The views over the palace and across to the Himalaya are stupendous.

Places to Stay

There are some cheap, basic places to stay near the Gorkha bus station, but the best budget place to stay is down the hill at the entrance to town. The *Hotel Gorkha Bisauni* (☎ 064-20107) is quite a decent place and also has a reasonable restaurant. There are dorm beds for Rs 50, rooms for Rs 200,

doubles with private bath for Rs 300, a deluxe rooms for Rs 500.

The *Gorkha Lodging Centre* (☎ 064-20128) on the way to the Gorkha Bisauni has large, clean rooms at Rs 100 to Rs 150.

The up-market *Gorkha Hill Resort* (☎ 01-227929) has a superb site four km before town (800m down a dirt road to the east of the main road). The buildings have been thoughtfully designed and most rooms have spectacular views. Though not cheap, the resort is worth $30/40 for singles/doubles. Main meals are $4/8 for breakfast/lunch-dinner.

Getting There & Away

There are several buses a day to and from Pokhara for Rs 50, and six buses to and from Kathmandu for Rs 75. Buses from Gorkha all leave early in the morning. There are also direct buses from Gorkha to Birganj and to Sunauli.

If you are dropped off at Abu Khaireni, eight km from Mugling on the Kathmandu-Pokhara (Prithvi) Highway, there are local minibuses to Gorkha (Rs 10). It's an enjoyable drive on a good road, but there's a steep climb for cyclists.

DUMRE

Dumre, 18 km past Abu Khaireni, a new town which only came into existence after the construction of the road, is a typical, dirty roadside bazaar. Apart from being the turn-off to Besisahar, the starting point for the Annapurna Circuit Trek, it has nothing at all to recommend it. For Circuit trekkers it's the last place where there is a decent range of supplies at reasonable prices.

Places to Stay & Eat

Trekkers may have to spend the night at Dumre if they arrive late. Try the basic *Hotel Mustang*, opposite the roadside temple in the middle of town, which has singles/doubles for Rs 60/75; beware the steep 50m climb to the outside toilet, and keep a torch (flashlight) handy! Another reasonable alternative is the *Manang Guest House* just off the main road.

& Away

... e is about five hours from
... d 2½ hours from Pokhara.
... ave from the Kathmandu bus
terminal, ... Rs 50 and could take longer;
from Pokhara it costs Rs 35. The tourist
buses that travel between Pokhara and
Kathmandu cost around Rs 150.

Many people start their trek by catching
shared jeeps or trucks to Besisahar. Expect
to pay around Rs 250, although porters pay
Rs 150. The road is very rough and the
journey can take up to five hours, although
three hours is more common.

BANDIPUR

Overlooking Dumre from its hilltop position, Bandipur is a beautiful Newari town
just south of the Kathmandu-Pokhara
(Prithvi) Highway. Before the construction
of the road, Bandipur was a major Newari
trading centre, and its bazaars still hint of
those days. Stone-paved roads pass between
temples and multi-storeyed houses, and
along the way there are excellent views of
the Annapurnas and Machhapuchhare. It

takes about two hours to walk up to Bandipur
from Dumre, and 45 minutes to drive.

DAMAULI

From Dumre it's just 16 km to the district
headquarters of Damauli which has a bustling bazaar. The main road in the town leads
to the panchayat building, while a path to the
left drops down to the junction of the Madi
Khola and Seti Gandaki rivers. If you walk
upstream about 100m you will find a beach
which is good for swimming.

DAMAULI TO POKHARA

Soon after Damauli the road crosses the Madi
Khola, via a large bridge, and follows the Seti
Gandaki River for the remaining 54 km to
Pokhara. The next town is Khaireni, where a
German-assisted agricultural project is based.

After Khaireni, the road passes the turn-
off to Rupa Tal and Begnas Tal, which are
the second and third largest lakes of the
Pokhara Valley. Sisuwa, only 12 km from
Pokhara, is the last place before you arrive at
the Pokhara bus station, which is immediately north of the airport and some distance
south of the busy bazaar area of the town.

The Terai

When people think of Nepal they think of soaring snow-clad mountains, not hot subtropical plains. Despite this, nearly half the country's population lives on a narrow strip of flat and fertile land that lies wedged between the Indian border and the mountains. This is known as the Terai (sometimes spelt Tarai).

With the Kathmandu Valley and the world's highest mountains a few hours away by bus, it is not surprising that the Terai is often just a transit zone for those travelling overland to and from India. Nonetheless, although there is nothing quite as startling as 8000m mountains, the region has a beauty of its own and some fascinating possibilities for travellers. The most well known are the magnificent Royal Chitwan National Park, famous for its elephant safaris and wildlife; Lumbini, the birthplace of Buddha; and Janakpur, the birthplace of Sita (Rama's wife, from the *Ramayana).*

Nobody could forget a dawn ride on an elephant through forests where you might come across tigers, rhinos, crocodiles and peacocks. Nor could anyone forget the neat mud-walled huts and brilliant saris amidst the vivid green rice paddies that stretch the length of the Terai, nor the strange waterlogged world of the Sapt Kosi's flood plain, with its birds, thatched villages, hyacinths and lilies.

Large sections of the Terai are still forested, and the land is cut by numerous rivers, often grey and turbulent with snow-melt and silt. These rivers burst from the hills onto the plains, a mere 100m above sea level yet over 1000 km from the Bay of Bengal. In most parts of the Terai western visitors are rare and in the farmland outside the towns there is little to disturb the ancient routines of ploughing, planting and harvesting.

While many hill people have settled the region (every ethnic group in Nepal is represented) there are also indigenous peoples and large groups that are culturally a part of the

HIGHLIGHTS

- Going on an elephant safari and viewing the wildlife, which includes the royal Bengal tiger and the Gangetic dolphin, at the magnificent Royal Chitwan National Park
- Visiting peaceful Lumbini, the birthplace of Siddartha Gautama, known as Buddha, the founder of Buddhism.
- Soaking up the special beauty of the waterlogged Sapt Kosi flood plain, dotted with thatched villages, rice paddies and water lilies, and partly protected in the Koshi Tappu Wildlife Reserve
- Enjoying the good-humoured and courteous hospitality of the varied ethnic groups and the indigenous people of the Gangetic plain

great Indian civilisations of the Gangetic plain. Despite this extraordinary diversity, the people of the Terai remain distinctively Nepali – unhurried, good-humoured, courteous and friendly.

Unfortunately, most of the border towns are new and unattractive, with Dickensian-looking industries on their outskirts, streets choked with buses and trucks, and little in the way of history or culture. The exceptions are the pilgrim centres of ancient Janakpur, with its sadhus and temples, and Lumbini, which remains more significant for what it was than what it is.

Chitwan should not be missed, and in the cool season (November to February) it is definitely worth travelling during the day and seeing the country, even if you have to suffer a crowded bus and stay in a grubby border town overnight. The western area of the Terai (west of Sunauli/Bhairawa) is one of the least visited, least developed and most interesting parts of the country. The completion of the Mahendra Highway, which will run the entire length of the Terai from Mahendranagar to Kakarbhitta, will link the

THE TERAI

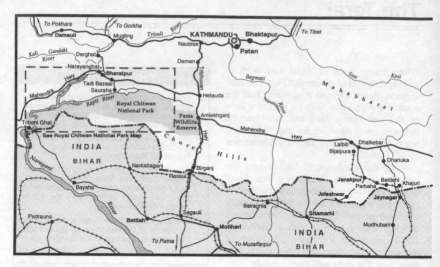

region with the rest of Nepal and with India, so rapid change is likely.

HISTORY

Over the centuries, parts of the Terai have been under the sway of both Nepali and Indian empires. Some regions were inhabited by sophisticated agricultural and urban communities as early as 800 BCE, but the empires have come and gone, and at times the countryside has been completely reclaimed by forest. The stories of decline and fall are largely unknown, but disease and war certainly played a role – some areas were most recently depopulated as a result of the Muslim invasions of the 14th century, and malaria was a major problem until the 1960s.

Without doubt the Terai's most famous son is Siddhartha Gautama – Buddha – who was born in 563 BCE at Lumbini. Siddhartha was the son of Suddhodana who ruled a small state from Kapilavastu. The ruins near Taulihawa, west of Lumbini, are believed to be his capital. Archaeologists have identified 13 successive levels of human habitation at the site. (See the Taulihawa section later in this chapter.)

The Terai's most famous daughter is Sita,

who is believed to have been born where present-day Janakpur stands. The daughter of Janak, the king of Mithila (also known as Videha), Sita is famous for her faithful marriage to Rama, the hero of the Hindu epic the *Ramayana*, which was first written in the 1st or 2nd century BCE. The kingdom of Mithila lives on in the rich culture and language of Nepal's eastern Terai and India's northern Bihar region.

By 321 BCE the Mauryan empire based at Patna, India was on the rise, swallowing the small principalities around it. Under the great Ashoka, the empire controlled more of the subcontinent than any subsequent ruler until the British. Ashoka was one of Buddhism's greatest followers and missionaries, so it was perhaps inevitable that he would visit nearby Lumbini, then a thriving religious centre. In 245 BCE he erected a stone pillar at Lumbini that can still be seen today. Some believe he travelled as far as Kathmandu.

The next great empire to rise in the region was the Gupta empire, again originally based in Patna, which flourished between 300 and 600 CE. The empire extended its influence to Kathmandu and beyond. In the early 13th

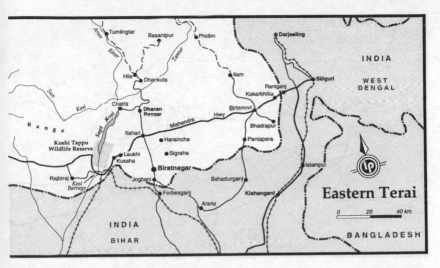

century invading Mughals occupied large parts of northern India, driving many Hindu refugees towards Nepal and the Kathmandu Valley. It is believed that one of these groups founded the Malla dynasty, which by the 15th century under King Yaksha Malla had extended its power from Kathmandu south to the Ganges River.

The next (and current) Kathmandu-based dynasty, the Shah, won power in 1768 and continued to expand Nepali borders until the kingdom was twice the size it is now – extending south into the Gangetic plain and east and west along the Himalaya. Eventually the Shahs and their famous Gurkha soldiers ran up against the British East India Company. In 1816, after two years of relatively inconclusive war, the Nepalis were forced to sign a treaty that considerably reduced their territory. Some land (including the city of Nepalganj) was actually returned to Nepal as a reward for its support for the British during the 1857 Indian Mutiny (or War of Independence as it is known in India today).

Most of the Terai was heavily forested until the 1960s, although limited areas were settled, and indigenous Tharu groups were widely dispersed through the region. However, the drainage and spraying programmes begun in 1954 markedly reduced the incidence of malaria and this allowed mass migration both south from the hills and north from India. Fertile soils and easy accessibility led to rapid development. The Terai is now the most important region for agricultural and industrial production in Nepal, and the fastest growing.

GEOGRAPHY

The Nepali Terai lies at the northern rim of the great Gangetic plain, ranges from 60m to 300m above sea level and never exceeds more than 40 km in width. The Gangetic plain runs table-flat from deep in India to the foothills of the Himalaya, the Chure Hills (known as the Siwalik Hills in India), which abruptly jump 1000m.

Several flat, wide 'valleys' known as the Inner Terai lie behind the first range of hills. These include the valley along the Narayani River (including part of Royal Chitwan National Park) and the Rapti River (east of Nepalganj).

The border with India, being a political

THE TERAI

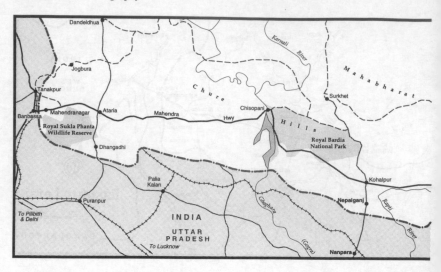

creation, does not conform to any particular geographic barrier. To further blur the demarcation, the inhabitants on both sides come and go as they please.

The Terai accounts for only 17% of Nepal's total area, but it is, in effect, the country's granary. In general, the soils are highly fertile and this, in addition to abundant water resources, permits the intensive cultivation of a wide variety of crops.

Unfortunately, outside the national parks the native forests are rapidly disappearing and suitable land is heavily exploited. Crop yields are already declining in some areas. The consequences of rapid population increase, deforestation and overworking the land are likely to be disastrous.

During the monsoon, parts of the Terai are subject to serious flooding. The relationship between deforestation in the hills and increased siltation and flooding on the plains is controversial, but there is no doubt that

Flora

The Terai is subtropical, and the flora reflects this. Rapid development has led to large-scale deforestation but fortunately, a surprising amount of forest remains.

Substantial areas are still cloaked in sal *(Shorea robusta)* forests. These forests characteristically grow on well drained soils and form relatively homogeneous communities. Sal is a magnificent, highly valued hardwood. It grows straight and true (averaging 30 metres when mature), and has long been used by builders and woodcarvers. The longevity of the buildings and the carvings in the Kathmandu Valley is due to the strength and durability of this wood.

On swampier ground there are scrubby forests of khair *(Acacia catechu)* and shisham *(Dalbergia sissoo)*. Simal trees *(Bombax ceiba)* stand out above the others. They are notable for their spring display of large red flowers and when they are old they develop huge buttresses at their base.

There are also grasslands that form a diverse and complex community of over 50 species. Elephant grasses (the saccharum family) can grow up to eight metres high, but there are also shorter species like khar that are vital for thatching. ■

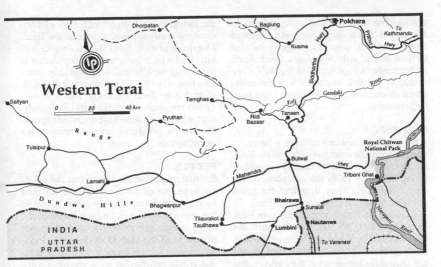

Western Terai

population growth in the hills and industrial development in the Kathmandu Valley are beginning to have a serious impact on downstream water quality. This is most critical in the dry season when many streams become mere trickles or dry up completely, and water flows are much reduced on even the major rivers.

CLIMATE

The Terai has a humid, subtropical climate with well over 1500 mm of rainfall in most

Fauna

The fauna of the Terai is striking although, as always, shy. From the road, the most obvious species are the handsome black-faced, grey langur monkeys *(bandar)* and the common, brownish-red rhesus monkeys. You may also catch a glimpse of some of the many species of deer – including the spotted (chital), barking *(mirga)*, sambar *(jarayo)*, hog *(laghuna)* and swamp deer. The blue cow *(nilgai)*, Asia's largest antelope, is also quite common, but you won't see this unless you make an effort.

The largest mammal is the Asian elephant, although it is likely there are now only a few individuals surviving in the wild at Royal Bardia National Park and Sukla Phanta Wildlife Reserve. Not far behind in scale and impressiveness is the great Indian one-horned rhinoceros, which can be seen at Chitwan.

There are a number of carnivores, the most magnificent being the royal Bengal tiger *(bagh)* that, thanks to the Terai's national parks, seems to have escaped extinction. There are also leopards *(chituwa)*, wild dogs, jackals, civets, various species of mongoose and cats.

You might also find sloth bears *(bhalu)*, wild boars, porcupines, hares, bats, squirrels and snakes *(sarpa)* – some of which are poisonous (cobra, krait and viper).

The rivers and lakes are home to small numbers of mugger and gharial crocodiles, and the extraordinary Gangetic dolphin.

The Terai is also a bird-watcher's delight with more than 400 migrant and local species recorded. There are cormorants, herons, egrets, storks, cranes, ibis, ducks, kites, goshawks, hawks, eagles, osprey, falcons, kestrel, quail curlews, sandpipers, snipe, gulls, terns, pigeons, parakeets, cuckoos, owls, kingfishers, woodpeckers, swallows, orioles, drongos, babblers, flycatchers, warblers...

The invertebrates range from butterflies to mosquitoes! ■

THE TERAI

places. The most pleasant time to visit is November to February when you can expect daytime temperatures to average in the mid to high 20°Cs, with cool nights. From April to September temperatures in the 40°Cs are common and this combines with the additional discomfort of the monsoon from June to September.

ECONOMY
Agriculture, as elsewhere in Nepal, is the major contributor to the economy, although the Terai is also home to most of the country's manufacturing industries (with the exception of the carpet industry). More than half the gross domestic product is produced in the Terai.

Many of the Terai's advantages come back to a single fact: it's flat! Development has been assisted by the relative ease with which roads and services can be established. Roads are crucial for industry, but they also enable health and education services, as well as fertilisers and improved seeds to be delivered more efficiently.

Cash crops like sugar cane, jute, tobacco and tea are grown alongside staples like rice, wheat and maize. Land-holdings are much larger than in the hills, but the average size is still under two hectares – hardly a Texan cattle ranch – and they are shrinking as the population grows. Many families work on a share-cropping basis for large landowners and *zamindars* (moneylenders) who take at least 50% of the crop and charge crippling rates of interest. Surplus food is sold to markets in the Kathmandu Valley, although a considerable amount is also given directly to less-fortunate relatives in the hills.

Mechanised transport, proximity to Indian raw materials and the Indian market, and the availability of hydroelectric power has allowed the development of some industry. This is largely concentrated between Birganj and Hetauda, and around Biratnagar. Amongst other things there are jute mills, a sugar refinery, tanneries and leather factories, biscuit and cigarette factories, and drug manufacturers.

POPULATION
The population has increased rapidly since the 1950s. In 1991, 46.6% of the population, or over 8.6 million people, lived in the Terai. Due to migration from the mountains and hills plus a high birth rate, the population is increasing rapidly and will probably overtake that of the hills. Unfortunately, it is now clear that the Terai will not be able to absorb excess population from the hills indefinitely, yet the hill population has continued to grow. Population pressures are mounting at an alarming rate.

PEOPLE
Internal migration has meant that the indigenous people of the Terai have been joined by representatives of every ethnic group in the country. However, and not surprisingly, many people are closely related to Indian groups in Bihar and Uttar Pradesh: Indo-Aryan subsistence farmers with dark skin, and Hindu beliefs that are sometimes combined with forms of animism. Although the common language throughout Nepal is usually Nepali, in the Terai, people are just as likely to speak Maithili, Bhojpuri or Hindi.

Maithili
The most widely spoken language of the Terai (excluding Nepali) is Maithili, a language and culture shared with people on the Bihar side of the border. It is spoken by around two million Nepalis, especially around Janakpur and Biratnagar. Maithili is the language of old Mithila and has its own script, Tirhuta, and a celebrated literature. Most of its speakers are farmers and orthodox Hindus.

Bhojpuri & Abadhi
The next most common language, Bhojpuri, is also used on both sides of the border and is spoken by around 1.5 million people in Nepal, especially around Birganj, though it mingles with Maithili.

Abadhi is another Indian-based language, spoken by around 250,000 Nepalis especially around Bhairawa and Nepalganj.

Tharu
One of the most visible groups in the Terai is

the Tharu, a race who are believed to be the earliest inhabitants of the Terai (and to be immune to malaria!). About 700, 000 Tharu speakers inhabit the length of the Terai, including the Inner Terai around Chitwan, although they primarily live in the west. There are caste-like distinctions between different Tharu groups or tribes. Most have Mongoloid physical features, and their animist religion is increasingly influenced by Hinduism.

Nobody is sure where they came from, although some believe they are the descendants of the Rajputs (from Rajasthan) who sent their women and children away to escape Mughal invaders in the 16th century. The women later married into local tribes. Another belief is that they are descended from the royal Sakya clan, Buddha's family, although they cannot be described as Buddhist.

Customarily the women were heavily tattooed, although these days this is unusual and tattoos are rarely seen on young women. Some groups wear simple white saris, others colourful calf-length dresses and a short blouse or bodice that exposes their belly. Tharu houses have mud-rendered walls and thatched roofs; they are high, dark and cool, with few if any windows. Reliefs of domestic animals are often moulded on the mud walls.

Apart from farming, the Tharu are enthusiastic hunting and fishing people. In particular, groups of young women and children will often be seen heading off on fishing expeditions. Their beliefs are largely animistic, although increasingly influenced by Hinduism, and they live a life that is cleverly adapted to their environment.

Many Tharu are heavily exploited by newly arrived hill people or zamindars. Large numbers have fallen into debt and have as a result entered into a form of bonded labour (known as the *kamaiya* system), little different to slavery.

Other Peoples
There are quite a number of smaller ethnic groups, none exceeding 40,000 people. They include the Danuwar, Darai, Djanghar, Koche, Majhi, Rajbansi, Satar and Tajpuri.

INFORMATION
There are tourist information centres at the borders at Kakarbhitta (☎ 023-20208), Birganj (☎ 051-22083), Bhairawa (☎ 071-20304) and Janakpur (☎ 041-20755).

Most services, including post, telephone and electricity are more widely and efficiently available in the Terai than in the rest of the country.

Malaria is the main worry. Make sure you take preventative medication. If you're coming from westernised Kathmandu you may have been lulled into a false sense of security. Don't drink water or use ice unless you know it has been boiled or properly treated. Skip the dairy products (with the exception of curd) and salads, and peel the fruit. Wash your hands before eating. (See the Health section in the Facts for the Visitor chapter for more details.)

GETTING THERE & AWAY
The Terai is easily accessible from West Bengal, Bihar and Uttar Pradesh in India and from Kathmandu and Pokhara. Bus and plane services are frequent and usually cheap. The long-distance express buses are even reasonably comfortable. The Indian metre-gauge railway system runs close to the border at several points, but most people use the buses because they are much quicker.

Air
Royal Nepal Airlines, Everest Air and Necon Air all fly to a number of towns in the Terai from Kathmandu. Royal Nepal services include Bharatpur ($50, daily), Biratnagar ($77, daily), Janakpur ($55, daily), Bhairawa ($72, twice a week) and Nepalganj ($99, four times a week). See the Getting There & Away sections in each town for more details.

Land
Roads enter the Terai at numerous border crossings in the south. Most travellers going to or from Nepal cross the border at Nautanwa (India) to Sunauli/Bhairawa (Nepal), but other

crossings used regularly include: Raxaul Bazaar (India) to Birganj (Nepal); and in the extreme east of the country, from Siliguri (India, near Darjeeling) to Kakarbhitta (Nepal). See the Getting There & Away chapter for travel on these routes.

GETTING AROUND
Bus

Although airlines service all the major cities, but buses are the way most normal mortals travel. This can be a serious penance, for although the price is not high when measured in rupees, it can be in terms of comfort and sanity! The express buses (often running at night only) are usually OK, although wherever possible you should check with a local as to which are the best companies.

Unfortunately, most day buses are of the stopping-all-stations variety and they can be horrifically crowded. Bodies occupy or cling to every possible centimetre. Under these circumstances, the most comfortable place to be is the roof, although you will need to protect yourself from the elements. There is one exception to this – the distinctive blue, government-run Sajha Yatayat buses. These run to timetables, are not overcrowded, are generally day buses and do not have a roof-rack.

The problem is that if you don't travel by day, you miss the views and if you do travel by day you run the risk of missing the views (because you are jammed inside a bus) and suffering extreme discomfort.

Whether you travel by day or night, you will get plenty of excitement. Combine high speeds with poorly maintained vehicles, suicidal overtaking manoeuvres, animals, Tata trucks, children, rickshaws, unmarked roadworks and the potential is obvious – and usually graphically illustrated by wrecked trucks and buses alongside the road. Although buses can't plummet over cliffs on the Terai, they can wind up to impressive speeds... (See the Getting Around chapter for more details on bus travel.)

Car

If you are travelling in a group, or if you have the necessary funds, it is worth considering hiring a car and driver in Kathmandu to explore the Terai. This is certainly not cheap at around $50 per day, plus petrol, for a Toyota Corolla (which would seat three passengers), but it has obvious advantages.

Bicycle

An even better alternative is to ride a bike, preferably a mountain bike that is sufficiently sturdy to deal with rough roads. Cycling conditions are ideal: motorised traffic is relatively sparse on the Mahendra Highway, there are villages at regular intervals, the climate during winter is mild and dry, and the countryside is beautiful and mostly flat.

Getting to the Terai from Kathmandu you either have to tackle the daunting Tribhuvan Highway via Daman (2322m!), or the section of the Kathmandu-Pokhara (Prithvi) Highway between Kathmandu and Mugling, which is very busy and dangerous. Consider catching buses over these sections.

See the Mountain Biking chapter for more details.

Royal Chitwan National Park

From the 19th century on, the Chitwan Valley was a centre for the hunting trips that British and Nepali aristocrats found so entertaining. King George V and his son the Prince of Wales, later Edward VIII, never made it to Kathmandu, but they did find time to slaughter wildlife in the Chitwan forests. In 11 fun-packed days during one safari in 1911 they killed 39 tigers and 18 rhinos.

Yet occasional hunting forays into the park did not seriously jeopardise the Terai's wildlife. In fact, the region's status as a hunting reserve probably helped protect it. However, after the success of the malaria eradication programme that began in 1954, the survival of tigers and rhinos was soon threatened.

Until the late 1950s, the only settlements in the Chitwan Valley were scattered Tharu villages inhabited by people whose apparent immunity to malaria was rumoured to be the result of their heavy drinking! After malaria was controlled by liberal applications of DDT, land-hungry people from the hills were quick to see the potential wealth of the region and the jungle was rapidly transformed into farmland.

As their habitat disappeared so did the tigers and rhinos. By 1973 the rhino population of Chitwan was estimated to have fallen to 100 and there were only 20 tigers left. (Compare those numbers with the British royals' epic hunting trip 60 years earlier!) Fortunately, this disastrous slide was halted when a sanctuary was established in 1964, although this was at the expense of 22,000 people who were forcibly removed from within its boundaries. The national park was proclaimed in 1973 and since that time the animal population has rebounded. The Chitwan now contains an estimated 400-plus rhinos and 80 tigers, quite apart from 50 other species of mammals and over 400 different types of bird.

Today the park offers one of the finest wildlife experiences in Asia, although it cannot be compared to the great game reserves of Africa. The wildlife is not as varied or great in number and the high grass and often dense forest mean the animals are much more difficult to find and observe. You have to be extremely lucky to see one of the park's elusive tigers or leopards. On the other hand, an elephant safari is an unforgettable experience, and you are almost certain to see rhinos, various species of deer, monkeys and numerous birds.

As with many other national parks throughout the world the park authorities have to tread a careful line between keeping the local people content and protecting the animals of the park. An often heavy-handed army presence, which involves over 1000 men, has kept poaching and woodcutting to a minimum. This no doubt contributes to local resentment, but the two most significant problems are that the park ties up

potential farming land and timber resources, and that surrounding crops are frequently damaged by the park's animals.

The animals do not respect the park's boundaries. Rhinos wander out in November to wreak havoc on rice crops, and then again in February and March when they attack mustard, lentils and wheat. Deer, monkeys and wild pigs also cause a great deal of damage. The little lookout towers (machan) you see in many fields outside the park are used by watchers who spend their nights in the fields waiting to scare off encroaching animals. Fortunately, tiger and crocodile attacks are rare, but they have caused fatalities.

On the positive side, in February each year neighbouring villagers are allowed into the park to harvest a number of grass species. Grass has numerous traditional uses, including roof thatching, and provides a valuable cash crop. Working for the park lodges also provides local employment though the many budget lodges in Sauraha, outside the park, arguably generate more money for the local economy. In contrast to the expensive lodges inside the park, where much of the money goes to owners in Kathmandu or overseas, many of the budget Sauraha lodges funnel money straight into the pockets of local families (although canny Kathmandu entrepreneurs are rapidly taking over).

The park is easily accessible from Kathmandu or Pokhara and is actually en route for those heading to/from the Indian border at Birganj and points east, and only a short detour if coming to/from western Nepal or the border at Sunauli. There is something for every budget: at one extreme you can spend $250 a night to stay at the famous Tiger Tops Lodge, while at the other extreme a simple double room in one of the many small lodges in Sauraha, right on the edge of the park in a prime game-viewing area, costs less than $2 a night.

Numerous travel agents in western countries, as well as in Pokhara and Kathmandu, offer package tours to the park. This is the best approach if you plan to stay in at one of the expensive lodges inside the park as you can book directly at the lodges' Kathmandu head offices and the package deals usually work out to be better value than the nightly rack rate.

However, packages are both unnecessary and relatively expensive if you plan to stay in the budget lodges at Sauraha. The booking agent obviously has to make money on the deal (which adds to the cost), and although you save a little effort, you pay for this by committing yourself to a particular lodge (which you may or may not like) and to a limited time frame.

Many people find the two night, three day packages too short, because by the time you

subtract travelling time (between six and seven hours by bus from Kathmandu or Pokhara) you only have one full day to explore. For most, a visit of two full days is sufficient, although the peaceful atmosphere, good-value accommodation in Sauraha, and the range of potential activities can easily seduce you into staying longer.

GEOGRAPHY

Along most of the Terai the Gangetic plain runs to the foot of the Chure Hills (which then merge with the higher Mahabharat Range), but here the Someshwar Hills form

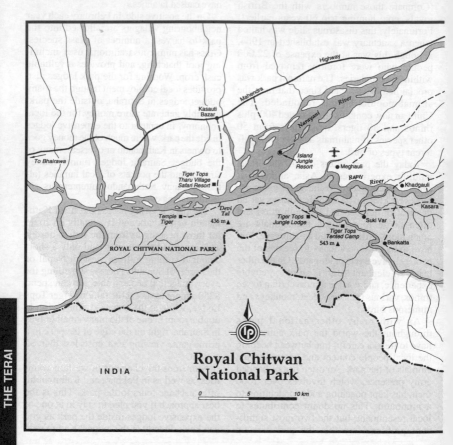

the Chitwan Valley, also described as the Inner Terai, which lies between the two.

To the north the park comprises a narrow strip of flood plain along the Narayani and Rapti rivers, a part of the Chitwan Valley and the most visited section of the park. South of this the bulk of the park encompasses the Someshwar Hills, which reach a maximum height of 738m, and are largely inaccessible to visitors. In the east the national park is adjoined by the Parsa Wildlife Reserve, which is not developed for visitors, but provides important additional territory for wildlife.

The park includes a number of small lakes or *tal*. The most interesting, particularly for viewing water birds, are Devi Tal near Tiger Tops, Lami Tal near Kasara, and Bis Hajaar Tal (literally '20,000 lakes') north-west of Sauraha.

The park, plus the adjoining Parsa Wildlife Reserve, covers 1431 sq km.

FLORA & FAUNA
Flora
The park has three basic vegetation types – open grasslands; riverine vegetation; and hardwood forests that are dominated by sal

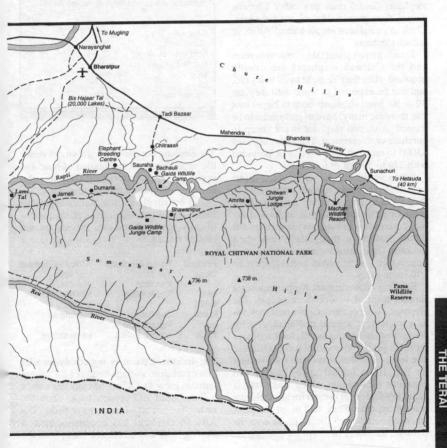

trees. The forests also have *shisham*, kapok, *palash* (or flame-of-the-forest), pipal, strangler fig and the scarlet-flowered *kusum* trees.

Fauna

Chitwan has over 50 different species of mammals; bird-watchers can search for 400 different bird types; and in 1987-88 butterfly spotters identified 67 different types of butterflies at the Machan Resort. Some of the most interesting creatures to be seen in Chitwan include elephants, rhinos and tigers.

Elephants Although you're likely to see more elephants *(hathi)* than any other Chitwan animal, there are no wild elephants in the park. Chitwan's elephants are all trained Asian, or Indian, elephants.

Training an elephant takes about two years and the Chitwan elephants are usually acquired when they're eight to 20 years old, and can be expected to work until they are 40 or 50. Even elephants born in Nepal (not that there are many) have to go to India to be trained. A trained elephant is not cheap to purchase or to maintain. Typically they cost $3000 to buy and then have to be provided with 270 to 300 kg of food a day.

When you're out on an elephant safari you'll see how even that isn't enough; they're constantly pulling up clumps of grass or other tasty vegetation, and shaking it around to dislodge any insects or dirt before stuffing it thoughtfully into their mouths. Their drinking capacity is just as impressive – an elephant needs more than 200 litres a day.

Keeping each elephant happy requires a support team of two or three people. The elephant's rider or master, commonly known as a mahout, is a *pahit* in Nepali. A pahit comes from India with the elephant and stays for three years while a local pahit is trained. The local pahit then stays with the elephant for life. He is backed up by one or two assistants *(patchouas)* whose main task is gathering the fodder to cater for an elephant's healthy appetite. They also assist the pahit when he saddles up the elephant with its howdah, the riding platform for passengers.

Notice the different ways elephants are ridden. At some lodges the howdah will be a square railed-in platform carrying one passenger at each corner, while at Sauraha the elephants often carry the pahit and two passengers, all three sitting astride the elephant's back.

Elephant Commands

If you have aspirations of becoming a pahit you'll first have to learn some elephant commands, although each pahit will have his own particular words and ways of saying them:

sit	*baith*
lie down	*sut*
stand up	*maile*
hold your trunk out for me to climb up	*utha*
stop	*rhaa*
go	*agat*
shower me	*chhop*

The elephant has one of nature's most versatile appendages, a combination of nose and upper lip. The trunk has 100,000 muscles and can hold over nine litres of water.

It is not simply ear size that distinguishes Indian (Asian) and African elephants; scientifically speaking, the two species are not closely related.

Feature	Asian Elephant	African Elephant
toes	five front	four front
	four rear	three rear
ears	fold forward	fold back
tails		bristly
trunk	one finger	two fingers
ear	India shaped	
trunk	white patches	white stripes

The Indian elephant is noticeably smaller (males reach an average height of 2.75m and females grow to 2.45m), has smaller ears, a bulbous head and convex back. Only the males, but not all of them, have tusks. The African elephant has enormous ears, a sloping head and a concave back; both the male and female have tusks. The Indian elephant has four nails on each hind foot where the African has only three.

Another major difference, as far as humans are concerned, is the domestication of these huge creatures. Indian elephants are easily trained, African elephants are not; though some people say that any elephant can be trained, and it is simply that in Africa training elephants has not been widely attempted.

Elephants have a gestation period of 22 months and the mother is always assisted by another female in looking after the young calf. The calf is fed for three years and there is usually about seven years between pregnancies, although the elephants are in musth once a year. In the wild, the elephants live in a basically matriarchal society; the bulls do not travel with the herd. Elephants have four teeth and grow six sets during their life. Once the sixth set is worn out the elephant dies of starvation.

The numerous rivers in the parks have some fine swimming holes and if you're staying at one of the park lodges don't pass up the opportunity to lend a hand at elephant bath time. On a hot day in the Terai there's no better way of cooling off than to sit on an elephant's back in a river and shout *chhop*. If your accent is right you'll be rewarded with a cold shower!

Rhinoceros While elephants are the creatures you see most often in Chitwan, it's the rhinoceros *(gaida)* you spend most time looking for, and with most hope of success. There are two types of rhino in Africa and three in Asia. The great Indian one-horned rhino, found in Chitwan, is larger than the African black rhino although smaller than the African white. A fully grown Indian rhino can reach 180 cm at the shoulder and weigh more than two tonnes.

Rhinos are generally solitary creatures although several may occupy the same area. Their diet is chiefly grass and they have very poor eyesight although their senses of smell and hearing are good. It's their poor sight which leads to the rhino's reputation for bad temper. As they cannot see very well, rhinoceroses are prone to assume almost any shape might be dangerous, so they charge it just in case.

Fortunately for the Indian rhino, its horn is not as large as the African variety and therefore not so valuable to poachers. Nevertheless, there are many superstitions about rhinos and almost every part of the creature is of value – the urine is considered a charm against disease and ghosts, a rhino-skin bracelet wards off evil spirits, rhino blood cures menstrual problems, and the horn is used for medicinal purposes and is famed as a sexual stimulant. Its value for Arab dagger handles has led to the disastrous decline in rhino numbers in Africa. Along the riverbanks in Chitwan a rhino would mark its territories by dropping excreta in mounds. Since they walked backwards to approach these mounds a waiting poacher had easy prey.

Tiger Chitwan's tigers are probably the most elusive of the park's wildlife. Without artificial assistance, such as staking a young buffalo calf out as live bait, you would be very lucky to see a tiger *(bagh)* in Chitwan. Though their numbers have increased considerably since the park was opened, tigers are solitary creatures and they mainly hunt by night.

Tigers require an enormous amount of space. A male commands a territory of about 60 sq km, and a female about 16 or 17 sq km. Both sexes occupy an exclusive territory although a male's territory may overlap with several females. Chitwan is simply not big enough to support the 50 breeding adults which is felt to be the minimum number to prevent interbreeding. This is part of the reason the adjoining Parsa Wildlife Reserve was proclaimed.

Other Mammals Chitwan is also known for more than 50 other mammals. Leopards *(chituwa)* are as elusive as tigers and the night prowling sloth bears *(bhalu)* are also rarely seen.

Chitwan has four types of deer and you will often catch a fleeting glimpse of them as they dash through the undergrowth. There's the tiny barking deer *(mirga)*, the attractive spotted deer *(chital)*, the hog deer *(laghuna)* and the big sambar deer *(jarayo)*. Gaur, the world's largest wild cattle, are also found in the park.

Langur monkeys *(bandar)* are a common sight, chattering noisily in the tree tops or scattering vegetation down below. The spotted deer often follow the langurs around, taking advantage of their profligate feeding habits. The smaller macaque monkeys are the monkeys commonly found at temples in Nepal and all over the subcontinent. Freshwater or Gangetic dolphins are found in some river stretches in the park, but they are rarely seen.

Reptiles Chitwan has snakes *(sarpa)* of course, including some impressive pythons, plus turtles and two types of crocodiles. The marsh muggers are found in marshes, lakes and occasionally in rivers while the rarer gharial crocodile is exclusively found in rivers. The gharial, which grows to seven metres in length and is a harmless fish eater, was in danger of extinction and is still very rare. The Gharial Breeding Centre near Kasara, the park headquarters, has had considerable success, hatching eggs and raising the youngsters to a reasonable size before releasing them into Terai rivers.

WHEN TO GO

Many of the park lodges are closed during the May to August monsoon months when visibility is poor, the ground muddy and the flooding rivers make large parts of the park inaccessible. In September the lodges start to reopen, although at first the rivers are too high for 4WDs and transfers to the lodges have to be made by elephant.

The best time to visit Chitwan is from October to February when the average daily temperature is 25°C. There are still cold, misty mornings, however, so a warm jacket is recommended. The Terai can be extremely hot and sticky, and even in October the humidity leaves everything feeling permanently damp.

From mid-January to the end of February the local villagers are allowed into the park to cut grass, which is an important part of the local economy. The grasslands are then burnt. While the villagers are crashing about, game is understandably scarce, but February through May is a prime time for game viewing, thanks to the fact that the grass cover has been removed. Sporadic thunderstorms begin in April and the weather becomes unpleasantly hot.

WHAT TO BRING

Park visitors should come prepared for every eventuality. At times the Terai can be stiflingly hot so cool clothes are essential. However, the sun can be fierce and there's not much shade when you're sitting on an elephant's back, so long sleeves, a shady hat and a good sunscreen are necessary. At the other extreme, winter months can be surprisingly chilly, particularly if you're out on foot or on elephant back at dawn. So, from November to February you should come prepared for the cold with sweaters and a jacket. Good walking shoes (that you don't mind getting wet) are essential at any time of year and you'll want a swimsuit for the rivers.

Neutral colours are best to ensure you blend into the background and are less likely to alert the wildlife. Reds, yellows and whites are particularly conspicuous.

Insect repellent is another Terai necessity. Malaria may have been wiped out, but there are still plenty of mosquitoes and a wide variety of other voracious and crafty insects. Even people who are normally immune to insect attack may discover later that while they were propping up the bar in the evening a full-scale attack was being mounted on their ankles.

In addition to camera gear, preferably with a telephoto lens, binoculars are invaluable.

Warning

Come prepared for Nepal's famous *jukha* (leeches). These operate in force during the monsoon and will still be waiting for unwary jungle walkers during the first month or two of the dry season. See the Health section of the Facts for the Visitor chapter for tips on how to deal with these pests.

We have also received a letter from someone who contracted typhus fever after being bitten by a tick. Check with your guide whether they are a problem, and inspect exposed skin after walking.

INFORMATION

The park entry fee is Rs 650 and is valid for two days. If you're staying at a lodge in the park this will usually be included in your overall charge, but if you stay outside the park in Sauraha you have to pay the fee yourself. This can be arranged by most Sauraha guest houses, or you can easily get it yourself from the ranger's office next to the park visitor centre, where you also book rides on government-owned elephants.

The ticket office and recently revamped visitor centre in Sauraha are open from 6 to 11 am and 1 to 6 pm daily. The visitor centre has an interesting small museum with exhibits about the park, its creation, the problems it faces and its wildlife. The park headquarters is further west at Kasara where there is a small museum of skulls and a gharial crocodile breeding project.

There's no bank in Sauraha and the black market is surprisingly subdued, so you are best off changing money elsewhere. There is a bank at Tadi Bazaar, a few hundred metres east of the Sauraha turn-off.

See the Books section in the Facts for the Visitor chapter for books on wildlife and the park.

THINGS TO SEE & DO
Elephant Rides

The greatest thrill at Chitwan is the traditional elephant safari in search of wildlife – seeing a rhino from atop an elephant is an experience not to be missed. You won't want to spend your entire visit aboard an elephant, however. It is not a comfortable mode of travel and your first ride is likely to leave you with aches in muscles you didn't know you had, not to mention an interesting selection of bruises!

The lodges inside the park all have their own elephants and safaris are a standard activity; two, three or sometimes four passengers ride on a wooden-railed howdah.

At Sauraha, government-owned elephants are available for one to 1½-hour excursions into the park costing Rs 650. Howdahs are not used and two or three passengers sit astride the elephants' back. At peak times the number of visitors exceeds the supply of elephants so it's wise to book your elephant ahead of time; the lodges will generally offer to do this for you. It's easy to make a booking yourself at the ranger's office near the visitor centre, although there can sometimes be a queue. Elephant safaris usually start in the early morning or late afternoon, prime game-viewing times; the government elephants leave at 8 am and 4 pm.

Several Sauraha lodges have elephants of their own. The going rate for a two hour safari varies from Rs 400 to Rs 550, but they are restricted to the Tikoli Forest, a buffer zone a few km to the west of the village and the elephant-breeding centre. This wildlife reserve is supposed to provide animals with a corridor they can use when moving between the park and the Chure Hills. While there are still plenty of trees, the zone is heavily utilised by local villagers grazing animals and collecting fodder and firewood, so it is by no means a wilderness. Some people have seen rhinos and leopards here, and the operators (naturally) claim that game-watching here is as good as in the park. This is extremely unlikely, however, given the proximity of villages and the presence of so many people. If you only have time and money for one ride you are much better off going into the park proper.

When booking a package tour in Kathmandu, or an elephant ride through a lodge, make sure you check whether your ride will take you inside or outside the park. People have been charged Rs 650 for a ride on one of the private elephants and have been misled into thinking that the buffer zone is actually part of the park proper. Ask to see your park entry ticket if you are being taken inside the park.

Jungle Walks

Visitors are allowed to enter the park on foot, but in order to get the most out of the experience, and for reasons of safety, it is best to go with a guide. Most lodges (including some in Sauraha) have their own naturalists, but there are also a number of independent guides. These young locals may not have much formal training, but they're often very knowledgeable about the park's wildlife and where to find it.

Walking is the ideal way to see the park's prolific butterflies and birds, and to see the flora close up. Walks are sometimes nothing more than a pleasant stroll through the jungle, but they can be exhilarating if you meet a rhino. Meeting a rhino when you're on foot is much scarier than seeing one from the lofty safety of an elephant's back. Caution is justified – tourists have been fatally injured by rhinos, and tigers and sloth bears can also be dangerous. Guides should brief you on safety procedures at the beginning of the walk.

Jungle walks from Sauraha usually cost around Rs 60 per person for two hours, Rs 150 for half a day, and Rs 250 for a full day. Short walks will generally cover grassland and riverine forest; you need a day to get into the jungle. Walks can also be combined with canoe trips (see the following section). Some lodges and guides organise longer overnight treks into remote parts of the park.

Canoeing

A canoe trip along the Rapti or Narayani rivers is the most restful way of seeing the wildlife, particularly water birds, and with a bit of luck you may also see mugger and gharial crocodiles. With a great deal of luck you might catch a glimpse of a freshwater Gangetic dolphin, although they are as rare a sight as tigers.

Canoe trips from Sauraha cost around Rs 100 per person, but trips are normally combined with a walk. The standard programme is a one hour float downriver, followed by a three hour guided walk back to the village (costing around Rs 300 in total).

Jeep Safaris

Animals are surprisingly unconcerned by vehicles, so a jeep safari can be more productive than you might expect. It also gives you a chance to get beyond the immediate Sauraha area. Most jeep rides take three or four hours and include a visit to the park headquarters at Kasara, about 20 km west of Sauraha, and the nearby Gharial Breeding Centre. The cost is around Rs 650. Bear in mind that jeeps may not be able to get across the river into the park until the water levels drop sufficiently (maybe from January to April).

Terai Culture

Staying in Sauraha gives you an excellent opportunity to explore the surrounding countryside, either on foot or bicycle. Originally, the area was dominated by Tharu, but over the last decade increasing numbers of hill people have bought up the land. Many villages are now a multicultural mixture. They're full of life (and hordes of children) and give a vivid insight into the rigours and pleasures of subsistence farming. The nearest Tharu village is **Bachauli**, east of Sauraha towards the Gaida Wildlife Camp.

Some lodges arrange visits to nearby villages and a number organise displays of traditional Tharu dances. The stick dance, with a great circle of men whacking their sticks together, is quite a sight. In Sauraha it's usually easy enough to find a lodge where there will be a performance; normally outside visitors are charged around Rs 50.

Wildlife Breeding

There are two important breeding projects associated with the national park: the elephant breeding camp four km west of Sauraha is worth visiting, as is the Gharial Breeding Centre near Kasara.

Cycling

Unfortunately, bicycles are not allowed into the park proper – apparently nothing infuriates a rhino more than a bike – but the surrounding countryside is ideal for touring. You can hire standard Indian-made single-speed bicycles in Tadi Bazaar and Sauraha

THE TERAI
Top: Janakpur, legendary birthplace of the goddess Sita
Bottom: Elephant patrol though the undergrowth, Royal Chitwan National Park

RICHARD EVERIST

RICHARD EVERIST

RICHARD I'ANSON

THE TERAI
Top Left: Bringing in the sheaves near Lalbiti.
Top Right: Typical Terai house with shady verandahs
Bottom: Upclose and friendly rhinoceros, Royal Chitwan National Park

for around Rs 60 per day, and these are adequate for negotiating the dusty tracks as long as you are not too ambitious about the distance you want to cover.

Just wandering along the tracks east and west of Sauraha is good fun, but if you like to have a specific destination, consider a trip to Bis Hajaar Tal (20,000 lakes) about 1½ hours north-west of Sauraha. The lake is famous for its prolific bird life. To get there, ride to Tadi, turn left (west) onto the Mahendra Highway at Tadi and continue for about three km until you reach a signposted bridge over the Khageri Khola. Cross the bridge and take the dirt road on the left (south). After another small bridge the road forks; take the right fork and continue for about five km. The lake is on the right.

PLACES TO STAY & EAT

Basically you can stay inside the park, or at Sauraha, and the division between cheap and expensive places to stay is almost equally straightforward – most of the expensive places are inside, and the cheap ones are at Sauraha.

For those who can afford it, the lodges inside the park offer considerable luxury, well organised game-watching activities, and an all-encompassing safari atmosphere. Although they can be pretty basic, the Sauraha lodges often have an interesting clientele, are scattered around an attractive, partly traditional village, and the full range of game-watching activities can be easily organised. When it comes to seeing the wildlife there's little difference between the two options. You've got just as much chance of seeing a rhino whether your room costs $2 or $200 a night.

Inside the Park

Most visitors to the park lodges arrive on package tours from Kathmandu, often as part of a larger tour of Nepal or the region. Advance bookings are necessary. Most of the lodges have attractive individual cottages dotted around a central dining room and bar area. Some have 'tented camps' with luxurious, semi-permanent tents – usually you won't have a private bathroom, but you certainly won't be uncomfortable.

The lodges generally quote either an all-inclusive daily charge, which covers park entry fees, activities (including rides on their privately owned elephants) and all meals; or a two or three day package that includes transport from Kathmandu. The only additional expenses will be for drinks and tips. Costs quoted here are per person on a double occupancy basis. There's usually a big price jump for single occupancy.

Tiger Tops (☎ 01-420322; fax 414075) PO Box 242, Durbar Marg, Kathmandu, is the best known and easily the most expensive of the lodges. This pioneer Chitwan jungle lodge is operated under the umbrella of Tiger Mountain, a very professional organisation, and enjoys a deservedly high reputation, particularly for its excellent guides and environmentally conscious approach. Whether you think it is worth the money probably depends on how much money you have. Although the accommodation is comfortable and the food good, those expecting to be pandered to with extravagant five star luxury can be disappointed. Tiger Tops has chosen neither to expand, nor to compromise the safari experience with unnecessary technological and consumerist trappings.

There are actually three Tiger Tops operations in the park. The well known *Jungle Lodge* ($270 a night including tax), is the original tree-top hotel. The buildings are on stilts and are constructed from local materials. Rooms are comfortable, the water is solar-heated, but there is no electricity. The *Tented Camp* ($162 a night) is three km east of the lodge in the beautiful Surung Valley. There are 12 safari tents with twin beds and modern toilet and shower amenities.

The *Tharu Village Safari Resort* ($162 a night) is the newest addition, and is built in traditional Tharu style: the long houses are constructed from timber, grass reeds and mud, and decorated with wall paintings. The rooms are attractive and comfortable; each has a queen-size and single bed, and a private bathroom, and there's a swimming pool. The village is actually just outside the park on the northern bank of the Narayani River.

The Jungle Lodge and Tented Camp are closed from October to May. Tharu Village Safari Resort is open all year round.

Temple Tiger (☎ 01-221585; fax 220178), PO Box 3968, Kantipath, Kathmandu, is at the western end of the park, not far from Tiger Tops. Accommodation consists of comfortable elevated individual cabins built largely from local materials, and each with a private viewing area over the grasslands. Minimal forest clearance has taken place here, so the atmosphere is really one of a jungle camp. The daily rate is $150, plus the park entry fee.

The *Island Jungle Resort* (☎ 01-225615; fax 223814), PO Box 2154, Durbar Marg, Kathmandu, is also at the western end of the park on a large island in the middle of the Narayani River. The site is superb, one of the best in the park, but the resort can be crowded and noisy with package-tour groups from India. Accommodation consists of safari tents and cottages which, although comfortable, are not particularly attractive. Costs are around $110 a day, although packages can be considerably cheaper, and very

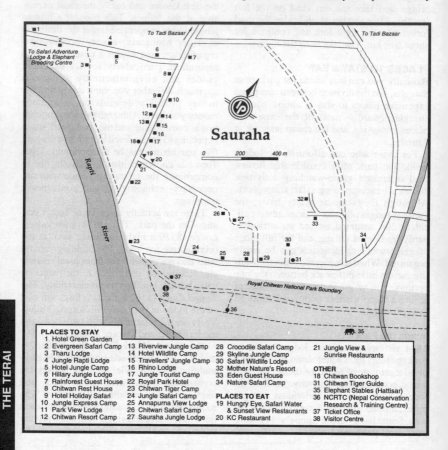

Sauraha

To Tadi Bazaar
To Tadi Bazaar
To Safari Adventure Lodge & Elephant Breeding Centre
Rapti River
Royal Chitwan National Park Boundary

0   200   400 m

PLACES TO STAY
1 Hotel Green Garden
2 Evergreen Safari Camp
3 Tharu Lodge
4 Jungle Rapti Lodge
5 Hotel Jungle Camp
6 Hillary Jungle Lodge
7 Rainforest Guest House
8 Chitwan Rest House
9 Hotel Holiday Safari
10 Jungle Express Camp
11 Park View Lodge
12 Chitwan Resort Camp

13 Riverview Jungle Camp
14 Hotel Wildlife Camp
15 Travellers' Jungle Camp
16 Rhino Lodge
17 Jungle Tourist Camp
22 Royal Park Hotel
23 Chitwan Tiger Camp
24 Jungle Safari Camp
25 Annapurna View Lodge
26 Chitwan Safari Camp
27 Sauraha Jungle Lodge

28 Crocodile Safari Camp
29 Skyline Jungle Camp
30 Safari Wildlife Lodge
32 Mother Nature's Resort
33 Eden Guest House
34 Nature Safari Camp

PLACES TO EAT
19 Hungry Eye, Safari Water
    & Sunset View Restaurants
20 KC Restaurant

21 Jungle View &
    Sunrise Restaurants

OTHER
18 Chitwan Bookshop
31 Chitwan Tiger Guide
35 Elephant Stables (Hattisar)
36 NCRTC (Nepal Conservation
    Research & Training Centre)
37 Ticket Office
38 Visitor Centre

THE TERAI

good value. Children aged three to 10 are charged 50%.

Further east is *Gaida Wildlife Camp* (☎ 01-220186), PO Box 2056, Durbar Marg, Kathmandu, which is not far from Sauraha in the only section of park north of the Narayani River. The *Gaida Wildlife Jungle Camp* is eight km south at the base of the Someshwar Hills. The main camp has comfortable thatched huts ($110), and the jungle camp has safari tents ($80). The wildlife is not particularly prolific immediately around the main camp, but is meant to be excellent around the jungle camp, which is open October to May.

At the eastern end of the park the *Chitwan Jungle Lodge* (☎ 01-228918; fax 228349), PO Box 1281, Durbar Marg, Kathmandu, has rooms constructed in traditional Tharu style with mud walls and thatched roofs. There's no electricity but otherwise the rustic lodge has all mod cons including a restaurant, private bathrooms, and a very pleasant open-air bar. The forest is relatively undisturbed in this part of the park and a river with a terrific swimming (and elephant-bathing) hole runs close by. A package is $250 for a stay of two nights and includes land transport from Kathmandu. If you want to get there by raft then the cost increases to $300.

Finally, at the eastern end of the park, close to the boundary of the adjoining Parsa Wildlife Reserve, is *Machan Wildlife Resort* (☎ 01-225001; fax 220475), PO Box 78, Durbar Marg, Kathmandu. This is a particularly attractive resort, but the wildlife is said to be scarcer at this end of the park. Machan compensates by offering excellent facilities including an attractive swimming pool and a video library of wildlife films. The accommodation is in well designed timber-frame bungalows with private bathrooms, and is decorated with superb Mithila murals. A two night stay costs $275 travelling overland from Kathmandu, $315 including a rafting trip. Additional nights are $100.

Sauraha

Sauraha is just outside the park on the northern bank of the Rapti River, which forms the park's boundary. It lies six km south of Tadi Bazaar (on the Mahendra Highway), where buses deliver you to a pack of waiting touts.

Sauraha is a simple, quiet little village, accessible only by jeep or bicycle. It's the sort of place nobody would usually visit – so it provides a good opportunity to observe rural life. There are verdant rice fields, neat mud-walled houses, barns and a village well in the 'centre' of town. Ox carts rumble by and there's a constant background scene of ducks, chickens and children.

Progress is, however, making its inexorable mark and although it is still a very pleasant place to spend a few days, it is showing signs that it could degenerate into a Terai Thamel. Electricity recently arrived and there are already a couple of two storey monstrosities. Unfortunately, as elsewhere, there appears to be a complete absence of planning and no control over new developments.

The welcome given by the Tadi Bazaar touts is the worst part of a visit to the Sauraha – with few exceptions they're slick, pushy and obnoxious. Treat all their claims with scepticism and definitely do not pay them for any tickets or tours until you have shopped around.

Normally, jeeps from Tadi to Sauraha cost Rs 30, so the touts' first gambit is to offer you a cheap, or even free, ride to a lodge. In theory this places you under no obligation, but in practice it's not easy to avoid staying. You are much better off to pay the Rs 30 (hardly a king's ransom) and make it absolutely clear that you intend to check a few different places before you commit yourself.

There are so many lodges and competition is so intense that prices are ridiculously low. Many lodges have therefore come to depend on 'invisible' add-on charges (commissions or service charges for organising bus tickets and game-watching activities) to make a profit. While there is nothing wrong with a charge for services rendered, they can get completely out of hand in Sauraha. Prices are sometimes inflated by ridiculous amounts – particularly since in almost all cases it's easy

THE TERAI

and straightforward to organise tickets and activities yourself.

With literally dozens of places, it is impossible to mention them all here. There's a certain lack of originality when it comes to naming these places; it seems they almost all have a three word name taken from a list of about half a dozen words – jungle, safari, Chitwan, tiger, camp, wildlife and river all feature prominently. Although most places have a telephone number, in the smaller places this is often just a nearby private STD phone office.

The most important variable is the quality of the staff and your fellow travellers, both of which change, so ask other travellers for recommendations and check places for yourself. The main north-south road is busier and more developed than the roads that run east and west.

Eating activity is centred around the main intersection in the village. There's a handful of small restaurants here, and a couple have shaded upstairs terraces with excellent views over the river, especially at sunset. The food is generally standard travellers' fare, and the quality is average. Restaurants here include the *Jungle View*, *Sunrise*, *Sunset View*, *Tiger*, *Hungry Eye* and *KC*.

Most accommodation places also do food, and most people seem to eat breakfast at their lodge, preferring to venture out at lunchtime and in the evening.

Bottom End The budget lodges at Sauraha are all very much out of the same mould: clean and simple mud and thatch cottages which sleep two and cost around Rs 50/100 for singles/doubles. Most have a small verandah, and those with a nice garden can be very pleasant places to stay. The mud-wall architecture keeps things surprisingly cool, and the rooms have insect screens on the windows and/or mosquito nets on the beds. Toilet and bathroom facilities are shared; hot water is unlikely, but this is not a major problem given the climate.

The *Chitwan Safari Camp* (☎ 056-20760) has a pleasant garden and a quiet, but central

position. It's old-fashioned and simple, and although it is a fraction more expensive than some of the other budget places (Rs 120/150 for singles/doubles) you really can't quibble at the price. In the same vein and close by is the *Sauraha Jungle Lodge*, which is also a recommended old-style place with standard prices.

The *Annapurna View Lodge* (☎ 056-29363) is another classic budget place with a nice atmosphere. Cottages cost Rs 50/100, or with bath it's Rs 150/300. There's also a small camping area at Rs 60 per person. Next door, the *Crocodile Safari Camp* is busy and friendly with standard rooms for Rs 50/100 and double rooms with private bath for Rs 300. The restaurant is good, but the garden is only ordinary.

Also in this area is the *Skyline Jungle Camp* (☎ 056-60172), a new place with standard brick cottages at Rs 50/100, and doubles with bath for Rs 300. The rooms have a verandah with a shady creeper on it.

The *Nature Safari Camp* is a modern concrete construction lacking shade, but the rooms and bathroom facilities are good. Standard rooms are Rs 50/100, and there are also a couple with agreeable outlooks and private bathrooms for the bargain rate of Rs 150/250.

The *Rainforest Guest House*, at the northern end of town, is a quiet and shady budget place with cottages for Rs 50/100, or Rs 400 with attached bath – it's recommended.

The *Travellers' Jungle Camp* (☎ 056-29363) is a friendly place with mud and thatch cottages at Rs 50/60, or doubles with attached bath at Rs 200/400. This place gets good reports from travellers.

The *Chitwan Resort Camp* (☎ 01-227711) has clean and decent rooms with private bath for Rs 300. The restaurant is particularly good.

The *Hotel Wildlife Camp* (☎ 056-29363) has a range of rooms starting at Rs 100 for a basic room with shared bath. Rooms with private bath are Rs 300.

Mid-Range An increasing number of lodges are moving up-market, or at the very least

THE TERAI

adding some brick cottages with private bathrooms and more-or-less guaranteed hot water. These new constructions are generally ugly additions to the scene, but someone must want them.

There are also a number of mid-range places dependent on the package trade which are happy to take on individuals if there are vacancies. Some are pretty good value with slightly more comfortable rooms and private bath from around $7/10 a single/double. Many of these places, eg the Rhino Lodge, Chitwan Tiger Camp, Jungle Express Camp amongst others, have offices in Kathmandu and Pokhara.

The standard tour offered is three days and two nights, including transport, food, accommodation, entry fees, jungle walks, a canoe trip, an elephant ride, a performance of Tharu folk dancing and a tour of a Tharu village. Typically, the packages cost around $85 if you travel to the park by bus, or around $140 if you travel by private car – it is possible to spend considerably less by yourself. They also have combined rafting/ Chitwan trips. These are competitively priced and can be as low as $150 for two nights and three days rafting on the Trisuli followed by two nights at the Chitwan.

The *Rhino Lodge* (☎ 056-60161), a reputable mid-range package-oriented place, has a range of rooms starting at Rs 300 and going up to Rs 600. The food is pretty ordinary, but the lodge is well geared for safari activities.

Riverview Jungle Camp (☎ 056-60164) is a decent place, and although central, is not in any way spoilt. It's worth a look, with much larger than usual double cottages for Rs 150, or more substantial brick cottages at Rs 600 with private bath.

The *Jungle Express Camp* is aimed at the package trade and has good facilities, though it's a bit overpriced for individuals at Rs 500.

The *Chitwan Tiger Camp* (☎ 056-29369) has an excellent position overlooking the river. There is a bamboo machan (platform) on stilts with the best views in Sauraha, although it could be a bit exciting in a high wind. Although this place has electric lights, hot water is solar heated or heated by back boilers in the kitchen. Singles/doubles cost $15/25 to $20/30 depending on the season, and discounts are possible. Some of the rooms have views over the river.

A new addition to the scene is the *Royal Park Hotel* (☎ 056-29361), with an excellent location close to the river. The substantial, spacious cottages all have attached bath and hot water, and beautiful slate floors. They also have wheelchair access. The cost is $15, or $20 including breakfast. There's also an area set aside for campers, and this costs $2 per person. The bar here is in a great spot with excellent river views.

Top-End At the top end, Sauraha has some very comfortable 'resorts' charging around $20/30; in all but position and price they are equivalent to the luxury lodges inside the park.

Safari Adventure Lodge (☎ 01-223763; fax 226912) is an up-market camp to the west of Sauraha in the Badreni area. All-inclusive prices (transport, accommodation, food and activities) start at $216 for three nights.

GETTING THERE & AWAY
Air
RNAC has daily flights to Meghauli, near the Tiger Tops, Temple Tiger and Island Jungle Resort lodges, for $72 each way. There are also daily flights to Bharatpur (Narayanghat) for $50 each way. The flights only take about half an hour.

Bus
Travellers intending to stay at Sauraha, the budget accommodation centre for Chitwan, first have to get to Tadi Bazaar (sometimes spelt Tandi Bazaar), on the Mahendra Highway, about 15 km east of Narayanghat.

Ordinary Sajha Yatayat buses to Tadi cost Rs 60 from Kathmandu or Pokhara. Alternatively, tourist buses cost from Rs 120 and the trip typically takes six or seven hours. From September to April there are also minibuses, which take around five hours and cost Rs 200. Any travel agent in Kathmandu or Pokhara can make a booking. In Sauraha, lodges will book tickets (but beware of in-

THE TERAI

flated prices) or you can book in Tadi at booking stalls near the main intersection.

To Sunauli on the Indian border, buses take about five hours and cost Rs 90; to Birganj buses take about three hours and cost Rs 45. Minibuses run from Tadi to Narayanghat, take 30 minutes and cost Rs 5.

There are a number of possible methods of covering the six km from Tadi to Sauraha. You can walk in a couple of hours – which is pleasant and interesting if it's not too warm. You can take an ox cart (Rs 15), which is only marginally more comfortable and certainly no quicker than walking, although if you're not in a hurry it's an interesting ride. If your baggage allows, you could rent a bicycle (Rs 50 per day); there are a couple of rental shops near the junction. The easiest and quickest method, however, is by jeep (Rs 30); jeeps and touts meet all incoming buses.

On the way, you have to cross a small river at the village of Chitrasali (also known as Gauthali). If the river is high and you're cycling or walking, you'll have to cross in one of the dugout canoes that shuttle back and forth (Rs 5).

Car

Visitors to the park lodges usually get there by car from Kathmandu or Pokhara and this is usually arranged by the lodge operators. A car typically costs around $70 and the 160 to 180 km trip (depending where you're going) takes four to five hours.

If you are coming or going from Kathmandu, you should try to convince your driver to take you one way via the Tribhuvan Highway passing through Daman and Hetauda. This route will cost extra as the narrow, winding road will add at least an hour to your travel time. The road itself, an engineering feat courtesy of the Indian government, is sealed the whole way and is in fair condition. The views along the way are stupendous. From Daman (80 winding km from Kathmandu) you can see the Himalaya stretching almost 180° from Dhaulagiri to Everest, weather permitting.

The cars usually drop you at the turn-offs from the main road, from where your lodge

vehicle will pick you up for the final trip into the park and across the river. This short trip is usually made by 4WD, although in the first month or two after the monsoon ends, September and October, the river may still be too high for vehicles and the transfer may be made by elephant. It's quite a surprise to arrive at the Chitwan Jungle Lodge turn-off, for example, and find an elephant waiting for the final seven km amble to the lodge!

Raft

Numerous Kathmandu rafting operators offer trips down the Trisuli River to Chitwan. Most park lodges will organise a rafting trip in conjunction with your stay in the park.

The rafting trips start from Mugling, where the road to Narayanghat and Chitwan turns off from the Kathmandu-Pokhara (Prithvi) Highway, or from further up the Trisuli. It takes two or three days to raft down to Chitwan. Don't expect white-water thrills; this section of the river is more a gentle drift, although there are some fine views and the sandy beaches along the riverside offer great camping spots.

Prices range from around $30 to $75 per day for rafting only, while rafting/Chitwan trips (four nights, five days) can be as low as $140. Shop around and establish details before you hand over your money: where does the rafting trip begin? What size are the groups? What activities are included at Chitwan? What transport is there from the river to your accommodation at Chitwan? See the Rafting & Kayaking chapter for more information.

The Terai from East to West

There are a number of choices that travellers can make travelling to and from India and Kathmandu, so it is not possible to present the information in this chapter in an order that will suit everyone. Places are described from east to west, from Kakarbhitta to Mahendranagar.

The main east-west link is the Mahendra Highway, which varies in quality from good to abominable. From Janakpur in the east to the Karnali River at the western end of Bardia National Park in the west the road is in pretty good condition. Further east or further west it rapidly deteriorates into a horrible mess of potholes, dust or mud (depending on the season) and treacherous creek crossings. The last 45 km of the section out to the far west are without doubt the worst on the Terai.

A number of attractive hill towns are accessible from the Mahendra Highway and for the sake of convenience they have been included in this chapter. They are Ilam (accessible from Birtamod); Hile, Dharan Bazaar and Dhankuta (accessible from Itahari); Daman, which is between Hetauda and Naubise; and Tansen, which is between Bhairawa and Pokhara.

KAKARBHITTA

The sole reason for the existence of Kakarbhitta is its proximity to India. This is the border post for road traffic going to or from Siliguri and Darjeeling. In fact, it's not much more than a glorified bus stop and it's difficult to imagine that anyone would want to stay longer than to make a bus connection.

The surrounding countryside is attractive, however, and you can tell you're not far from Darjeeling when you see the tea plantations on the outskirts of town.

Orientation & Information

There's a tourist office (☎ 023-20208) just inside Nepal, past customs on the northern side of the road (on the right if you're coming from India). The Nepal Rastra Bank isn't signposted, but it's the unmistakable pink monstrosity on the left (south) side of the road.

The border is open to tourists from 7 am to 7 pm. There are two banks on the Nepali side, but only the Nepal Rastra Bank changes money; it's also open from 7 am to 7 pm every day.

As you continue away from the border the main bus parking area is a dusty (or muddy, as the case may be) quadrangle on your right, followed by the bazaar and village.

Places to Stay & Eat

There are plenty of cheap but basic places to stay around the bazaar, but most are dreadful flophouses. If you want to give yourself an even chance of getting a decent night's sleep there are a few places scattered around in slightly quieter locales.

The *Shere Punjab Hotel* just past the tourist office has grubby cells for Rs 50/100, but has a decent Indian restaurant.

There are several places in the village behind the bazaar, a two minute walk from the bus station. The best is the *Upsara Lodge*, which is basic but clean and reasonably cheerful; singles/doubles are Rs 50/100. The *ABC Christian Lodge* is used for conferences and worship by local Christians. However, if you're a Christian and the lodge isn't full, you may be able to stay. Clean and comfortable doubles cost Rs 100.

Getting There & Away

There are plenty of land connections to destinations both in Nepal and India. Many people buy through tickets between Kathmandu and Darjeeling, but this is relatively expensive and unnecessary. With a through ticket you travel the Kakarbhitta to Kathmandu section at night and miss the sights.

Many travellers are ripped off buying through tickets between India and Nepal – bookings fail to materialise or are for lower quality services than were paid for. Admittedly, these problems are not nearly as common on this route as they are on some others. See the Getting There & Away chapter for more information.

To/From India It's a 10 minute walk from Kakarbhitta to the Indian border post of Raniganj; rickshaws cost about Rs 5 (Indian Rs 3). From Raniganj you take a minibus 36 km to Siliguri; this takes around one hour and costs around Indian Rs 5. From Siliguri you take a bus 78 km to Darjeeling; buses

THE TERAI

leave between 6 am and 6 pm, take around 3½ hours (make sure you catch an express) and cost Indian Rs 40. Depending on how quickly you made connections the total trip would not take more than six hours. It's possible to speed the process by an hour or two by catching a taxi from Raniganj to Siliguri (Indian Rs 30), or from Siliguri to Darjeeling (Indian Rs 100). The overnight buses from Kathmandu all arrive in Kakarbhitta before 10 am; they leave Kakarbhitta for Kathmandu between 3 and 5 pm.

To/From Pokhara or Kathmandu There is plenty of competition for your business if you plan to buy a bus ticket, so it's worth shopping around. The prices won't vary, but the departure times and the quality of the buses can.

Night buses for Kathmandu and Pokhara generally leave between 3 and 5 pm, take 17 or 18 hours, and cost Rs 255. Not only would this be an epic and unpleasant experience, but you'd miss the views. If time and weather allow, consider catching a day bus to Janakpur and stopping over there; they leave between 6.30 and 9 am, take up to eight gruelling hours and cost Rs 90. The road is particularly interesting between Itahari and Janakpur; it runs across the flood plain of the massive Sapt Kosi. See the Getting Around chapter for more details.

There is one day bus (leaving 8.30 am) for Birganj that takes 14½ hours and costs Rs 142.

Buses for Kakarbhitta leave from the Kathmandu Bus Terminal at 4 and 5 pm. Book a day in advance.

ILAM

Ilam is an attractive small town at the centre of Nepal's tea industry; the climate of the surrounding hills is similar to Darjeeling's. Few westerners visit, but there is some basic accommodation available, and there are good walks, and tea plantations to see.

The road from the Terai is very steep and the views are spectacular. The road itself is gradually being improved with a view to it being sealed. It already extends to Phidim

and is being pushed further into the hills. Buses leave from Birtamod on the Mahendra Highway 13 km west of Kakarbhitta. They depart from 7 am to 1 pm, take seven hours and cost Rs 75. Buses to Phidim cost Rs 175.

BIRATNAGAR

The observation that Biratnagar is the second largest city in Nepal, and an industrial centre, actually makes it sound worse than it is. It's an energetic, bustling place with the crowds and shops you would expect of a city with several hundred thousand inhabitants. However, there's just nothing much to attract the visitor unless you are particularly interested in Nepal's somewhat shaky industrial development, or the strongest, most politicised unions in the country. The border is not open to tourists.

The countryside and surrounding villages are interesting, but difficult to explore without private transport. One possibility is to continue north along Main Rd (with the Hotel Namaskar and Nepal Bank Ltd) – this veers left when you leave town; continue westwards until you reach a T-intersection; turn right (north) along a dirt road that parallels the sealed road and continue through Sigraha and Haraincha until you reach the Mahendra Highway to the west of Itahari.

Jute used to be grown in large quantities, and can still be seen, but the industry has been in decline for years. There are numerous groups of people in the region, but the most distinctive are the local Tharus and Danuwars. The Danuwars are very similar in culture and appearance to the Tharus, but the women wear a distinctive embroidered sari.

Places to Stay & Eat

There's quite a range of places at varying prices. Bear in mind, however, that anywhere on Main Rd or near the bus station will be pretty noisy.

The *Dhankuta Lodge*, opposite the bus station, is clean and reasonable with singles/ doubles at Rs 60/90, or Rs 80/110 with bathroom. *Padma Hotel & Lodge* is basic, but clean, and has rooms with/without bath for Rs 90/60.

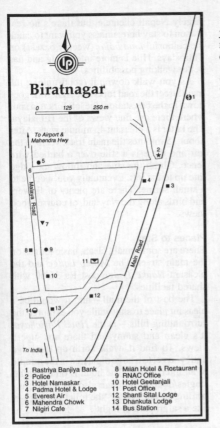

Biratnagar

0   125   250 m

To Airport &
Mahendra Hwy

Malaya Road

Main Road

To India

1 Rastriya Banjiya Bank
2 Police
3 Hotel Namaskar
4 Padma Hotel & Lodge
5 Everest Air
6 Mahendra Chowk
7 Nilgiri Cafe
8 Milan Hotel & Restaurant
9 RNAC Office
10 Hotel Geetanjali
11 Post Office
12 Shanti Sital Lodge
13 Dhankuta Lodge
14 Bus Station

Up the scale somewhat is the *Hotel Namaskar* (☎ 021-21199) on Main Rd, a 15 minute walk from the bus station, which has a range of rooms from Rs 180 to 500. At the top price you get air-con and a private sitting room, but the cheaper rooms are clean and quite adequate. There's a good, reasonably priced restaurant frequented by the local notables.

A little less formal, but still comfortable, the *Hotel Geetanjali* is also across from the bus station on Main Rd. Set in a pleasant garden, the hotel charges Rs 205/150 for doubles with/without bath. There's no restaurant, but decent Indian food is available.

The most recent offering is *Hotel Himalayan Kingdom* (☎ 021-27172; fax 24141), a modern place near Mahendra Chowk, with comfortable rooms at Rs 350/575.

Getting There & Away

There are daily RNAC (☎ 021-25576) flights, three times daily Necon Air (☎ 021-25987) flights, and twice daily Nepal Airways (☎ 021-25324) flights to Kathmandu for $77.

There are plenty of buses to Kathmandu, Kakarbhitta and Janakpur. Night buses to Kathmandu leave at 4.30 pm (17 hours, Rs 225). There are day buses to Kakarbhitta (Rs 45), Janakpur (Rs 70), Rajbiraj (Rs 40) and Dharan Bazaar (Rs 20).

ITAHARI

Itahari is an undistinguished town at the intersection of the Mahendra Highway and the Biratnagar to Dhankuta road. There is an interesting market held along the dusty lanes south-east of the main intersection.

There's one passable hotel in Itahari, which also has a decent restaurant. The *Jaya Nepal Hotel* has singles/doubles with shared bath for Rs 50/80.

Getting There & Away

All the long-distance, east-west buses stop in Itahari. There are also plenty of local buses which go to Biratnagar (one hour, Rs 10) and Dharan (30 minutes, Rs 7). One bus a day leaves at 6 am for Dhankuta (five hours, Rs 40). It's best to make an advance reservation if you want to get a seat on a Kathmandu bus; they leave from 3 to 5.30 pm and cost Rs 205.

DHARAN BAZAAR

Dharan lies right at the foot of the Chure Hills, but the transformation from the Terai is dramatic. It's a bustling bazaar town catering to the hill people of eastern Nepal. It has grown rapidly despite suffering a major earthquake in 1988.

There are no sights of note, but if you're heading into the mountains this will be your best chance for final purchases. A small number of trekkers bound for Hile and Basantpur come through town, and **Chatara**,

THE TERAI

the finishing point for raft trips on the Sun Kosi, is only 15 km to the west. Baraha Chhetra, five km north of Chatara, is the site for an annual religious festival in late October/early November.

Places to Stay & Eat

There are two possibilities, but they'll only look good if you've been trekking for at least two weeks! Coming from Itahari, turn right at the statue of the king. The *Hotel Gurans & Bamboo Lodge* is labyrinthine, gloomy and not terribly clean. Singles/doubles with private bath are Rs 100/120. The *Hotel Evergreen* is a notch above in cleanliness and price, but nothing to write home about. Singles/doubles are Rs 120/180. Both hotels have reasonable restaurants.

Getting There & Away

Dharan Bazaar is 50 km from the attractive hill town of Dhankuta. Hile, the starting point for a number of treks in eastern Nepal, is 12 km past Dhankuta. The spectacular road is sealed as far as Hile, but continues on to Basantpur, and is being pushed even further. Buses to Dhankuta take three hours and cost Rs 40; buses to Basantpur (via Hile) leave from 5 am to 2 pm, take five hours and cost Rs 82. There's also a direct link with Kakarbhitta, departing daily at 3 pm (Rs 215).

There's also one direct night bus daily in each direction to/from Kathmandu. The trip takes 12 hours, costs Rs 225 and departs at 3.30 pm from Kathmandu.

DHANKUTA

Although Dhankuta is only 50 km by excellent road from the Terai, it seems more like a million miles. The largest, flattest spot in the nearby vicinity is the bus station – it soon becomes hard to remember that expanses of water-logged plains exist.

The town is strung along a ridge that basically runs north-south; the bus station is below the ridge. The sad remnants of the forest that once covered the hill are at the northern end of town. There is a collection of small, but decent, lodges which cater to a

largely Nepali clientele, but there's no real reason to stay here, unless you want to catch the colourful *haat bajar* (weekly bazaar) on Thursdays. Hile is more interesting and has better walking possibilities.

As you walk downhill (south) along the main street the road forks: the right fork goes down to the bus station; the left fork to a spur where there are fine views of the Himalaya. The latter is a pleasant 45 minute walk. After about 15 minutes the main track veers to the left and there is a stile over a barbed wire fence. Climb the stile and follow the ridge line up to the left. Eventually you'll come to a small shrine. There are plenty of flowers and birds along the way and, of course, good views.

Places to Stay

There are some small, clean, basic lodges on the main street. The *Najulo Lodge* and the pleasant *Nauke Lodge* cost Rs 35/60 with shared facilities.

The best of them all – and it would be a pleasant place to stay while you explored the surrounding hills – is the *Hotel Parichaya*. It's clean and sunny and there are superb views. To find it, walk north up the ridge until you get to a large pipal tree in the middle of an intersection. The hotel is on the right; singles/doubles here are also Rs 35/60. According to one reader 'the toilet out back is like a safari park at night'.

Getting There & Away

Plenty of buses travel the spectacular road from Dhankuta to Dharan Bazaar (three hours, Rs 40). From Dhankuta the sealed road continues to Hile, then continues unsealed to Basantpur. Buses for Basantpur depart from 7.30 am to 2.30 pm, take three hours and cost Rs 52. The road is being pushed further into the hills, but there are no buses beyond Basantpur.

HILE

Hile, a bustling bazaar town, is the starting point for Arun Valley treks (possible for individuals) and for treks to Makalu (groups only). Kanchenjunga trekkers (also groups only) usually start at Basantpur. Hile would be a good base for day walks in the region.

Nepal's ethnic map is always complicated, but at Hile it's about as complicated as it gets, with Tibetans, Bahuns, Chhetris, Magars, Tamangs, Rais, Limbus and Indians.

There are fantastic views of the Himalaya, especially of the Makalu massif, from the ridge above the town. Walk along the Basantpur road past the army base and a few hundred metres past the army checkpost (there's a boom across the road) you can cut up to the left onto a grassy ridge.

Places to Stay & Eat

There are several decent, but basic trekkers' lodges, with not much to separate them. The *Hotel Gajur* has a recommended restaurant, and the *Dama Hotel* is run by a friendly family. Singles/doubles in both hotels go for Rs 35/60.

Getting There & Away

As well as local buses to Dhankuta and Dharan, there is a daily night bus to Kathmandu, leaving at around 3 pm. The trip takes 15 hours and costs Rs 253.

KOSHI TAPPU WILDLIFE RESERVE

The Koshi Tappu Wildlife Reserve protects a section of the Sapt Kosi's flood plain that lies behind the Kosi Barrage. The Sapt Kosi is one of the Ganges' largest tributaries, and the Kosi Barrage is designed to minimise destructive annual floods. Most of the reserve is surrounded by eight metre high embankments that control the spread of the river and funnel it towards the barrage.

The main highway skirts the reserve and crosses the river at the barrage. It's a beautiful, fascinating water world. Small thatched villages perch on what little high ground there is and wherever you look there are water birds, and ponds full of flowering plants, all overwhelmed by fields of rice stretching to the horizon.

Behind the embankments the river continuously changes course, and regularly floods during the monsoon, although only to shallow depths. The vegetation is mainly tall grass *(phanta)*, with some scrub and riverine forest. Local villagers are allowed to collect grass for thatching every January.

The reserve is home to the last surviving population of wild water buffalo *(arna)*, various deer, blue cow *(nilgai)*, gharial crocodiles and Gangetic dolphins. It is also either a permanent or temporary home to 280 different species of water birds (migratory and otherwise). These include 20 species of ducks, ibises, storks, egrets, cranes and herons. The migratory species, including the sarus crane from Siberia and the ruddy shelduck from Tibet, take up residence from November to February.

The reserve occasionally hosts birdwatchers between November and February, but very few people visit and the arrival of a tourist out of the blue gives everyone quite a shock. There's one deluxe safari camp, but there's no other accommodation, although there is an area where you could camp, and the helpful staff are happy to give visitors the use of a kitchen. The reserve has two elephants, which can be ridden for Rs 650 for one hour. Canoes can also be arranged.

Orientation & Information

The reserve headquarters is at Kusaha, where all visitors must pay a Rs 650 entrance fee. Kusaha is a three km walk from the highway, just outside the eastern embankment, on the eastern side of the barrage.

The turn-off to the reserve (unsignposted) is about 11 km north-east of the Kosi Barrage, and about two km before the village of Laukhi. Coming from Itahari, it's about 46 km to Laukhi and a further two km to the turn-off.

If you do plan a visit, and especially if you want to stay, ring ahead to get the latest information on access and the availability of facilities. Contact Kusaha through the neighbouring army camp (☎ 025-20881), or the Department of National Parks & Wildlife Conservation (☎ 01-220912), Babar Mahal, Kathmandu.

Places to Stay

The only formal accommodation is the *Koshi*

Tappu Wildlife Camp, which is in the north-eastern corner of the reserve, 24 km north of the barrage near the tiny fishing village of Prakashpur and accessible from Laukhi on the Mahendra Highway. Accommodation is in tented rooms, each with en suite bathroom, and there is a separate dining area. Most guests come on a package from Kathmandu, which usually includes Chitwan, and are quite expensive. Food and board rates are $125 per person, including guided game drives and walks. Bookings can be made through PO Box 536, Kamaladi, Kathmandu (☎ 01-226130; fax 224237).

RAJBIRAJ

Rajbiraj is a dusty uninteresting little town, but it lies on the edge of the Sapt Kosi flood plain, so the countryside and wickerwork villages to the east are fascinating. Rajbiraj is to the south of the main highway, but if you have private transport it's definitely worth the detour. You'd have to be pretty keen to build it into your itinerary if you are using local buses, but it could be done.

There's only one place to stay, the *Sinha Lodge*, on the main road. It's very, very basic and singles/doubles are Rs 40/60.

Getting There & Away

There is a daily Sajha Yatayat day bus in each direction between Rajbiraj and Kathmandu. The trip takes 12 hours and costs Rs 150. Private night buses are more expensive.

Ramayana

The *Ramayana*, or romance of Rama, is amongst the best loved and most influential stories in Hindu literature. Handsome Rama embodies chivalry and virtue, and his wife, the beautiful Sita, exemplifies devotion and chastity. Together with Rama's ally, the faithful monkey-god Hanuman, they are heroes and exemplars of immense popularity and like all great mythical archetypes they have somehow found an enduring place in the human psyche.

It's likely the legend has at least a basis in fact, and was first retold around village hearths. The *Ramayana* was first permanently recorded in Sanskrit, possibly as long as 2400 years ago by a sage and poet, Valmiki. Since then it has become a part of people's lives and imaginations throughout the subcontinent and, in various forms, as far as Bali, where to this day it features in puppetry and dance.

Rama was a reincarnation of Vishnu, born at the request of the gods to do battle with the ghastly demon king Ravana the King of Lanka (possibly Sri Lanka). He was reincarnated at Ayodhya (350 km west of Janakpur) as the eldest son of a wealthy king. Handsome, virtuous and strong, he grew up the idol of the people and especially of one of his half-brothers, Lakshman.

In the kingdom of Mithila, good King Janak discovered baby Sita, the reincarnation of Lakshmi, lying in a furrow of a ploughed field. She too grew up to be wise and beautiful and so many men wanted to marry her that Janak set a test – a successful suitor had to bend the divine bow of Shiva. Rama, of course, drew the bow and he and Sita looked into each other's eyes and knew divine love.

Rama and his three half-brothers were married in a single ceremony – the brothers to neighbouring princesses – and there was much feasting, flowers falling from heaven, gorgeous processions across the plains and so on. But this is where things took a turn for the worse.

After returning to Ayodhya, Rama and Sita were forced to leave the palace because of the intrigues of the detestable hunchback Manthara. While they wandered in exile, Rama and Lakshman were distracted by a golden deer, and Sita was kidnapped and carried off to Lanka by the demon king. Imprisoned, Sita was forced to defend herself from the disgusting advances of Ravana.

Meanwhile, Rama and Lakshman formed an alliance with a monkey kingdom. In particular they were served by the indomitable monkey god Hanuman. With Hanuman's loyal assistance Sita was finally rescued and the demon king, Ravana, destroyed.

Unfortunately, life didn't improve much for Sita who was forced to undergo an ordeal by fire to prove her chastity. Although Rama, now king of Ayodhya, believed her innocence, his people didn't and Sita was forced to go into exile again. Sita gave birth to Rama's twin sons and the family was later reunited, but Sita decided she had had enough of this mortal coil and was swallowed up by the earth.

There are many versions of the story recorded in many art forms and many different languages, including English. Trying to imagine the power and subtlety of the complete story by reading this condensation is a bit like trying to imagine a tree by looking at a match. ■

Local buses from Janakpur and Biratnagar are frequent and cost Rs 40.

The road starts to fall apart east of Rajbiraj and there are some very slow sections before the Kosi Barrage.

JANAKPUR

Janakpur is an interesting, attractive city of temples, pools, sadhus, rickshaws and rainbow-coloured saris. It's a tourist town, but the tourists are devout Indian pilgrims, not western backpackers.

Janakpur's religious significance is due to its role in the famous Hindu epic, the *Ramayana*. It is the legendary birthplace of Sita, an incarnation of Lakshmi, and the place of her marriage to Rama, who is one of Vishnu's most popular incarnations. At times, especially during festivals when strangely resonant vignettes from the *Ramayana* are played out in the streets, it can feel as if the ancient myth has come to life.

Janakpur is situated in what was once the kingdom of Mithila, a region now divided between Nepal and India. The Maithili language, which also has its own unique script, is spoken by approximately two million Nepalis; only Nepali is spoken by a greater number of people.

Janakpur is at least the third city to be built on this site, and most buildings are less than a century old. The city that was mythologised in the *Ramayana* existed around 700 BCE, but it apparently sank back into the forest, perhaps destroyed by disease. Simaraungarh grew up in its place, but it was destroyed by Muslims in the 14th century, and once again the region was reforested.

Theologically, Janakpur is paired with Ayodhya, near Faizabad in Uttar Pradesh, where Rama is believed to have been born. In December 1992 Hindu zealots provoked widespread bloodshed across the subcontinent by destroying a Muslim mosque in Ayodhya that they claimed was built over a shrine marking Rama's birthplace. Fortunately, none of this fanatical intolerance is apparent in Janakpur.

Modern Janakpur is a Terai city that works: it's green and clean and the narrow lanes are interspersed with temples, pilgrim hostels *(kutis)* and both large and small sacred ponds *(sagar* and *kunda)*. Legend says the ponds were created by King Janak for the use of the gods who came to the wedding of Rama and Sita. They take the place of a river for ritual bathing and are also used by the local dhobi caste who are clothes washers. Thanks to a successful development project, many are also stocked with the fish that provide an important supplement to the local diet.

The city authorities have managed to keep most traffic out of the centre of town, which makes it pleasant to wander around. Sometimes the city feels like a big village, but when you stand in the broad square before the Janaki Mandir, it can also have a definite grandeur. If, at dusk or dawn, you take a slow rickshaw ride to one of the many temples or ponds on the outskirts of town you'll discover a peaceful beauty.

If you do have the time and the inclination to experience something of the Terai, Janakpur should be at the top of your list. It's possible to visit on the way to/from Kakarbhitta. However, although the only railway in Nepal connects Janakpur to the Indian town of Jaynagar, tourists are not allowed to cross the border (see the Around Janakpur section).

Orientation & Information

Janakpur is a hopeless tangle of mostly narrow streets, so the best way to get your bearings is from the telecommunications tower and the large, elevated concrete water tank. The town itself lies to the east of the main road that runs through to Jaleshwar at the border.

The Janaki Mandir is just to the south of the water tank, and the bus station is to the south-west of the temple near the telecommunications tower. The railway station is about a 20 minute walk to the north-east of the large concrete water tank.

There is a helpful tourist office (☎ 041-20755) at Bhanu Chowk, not far from the railway station. Consider ringing to check the dates for major festivals. The office is

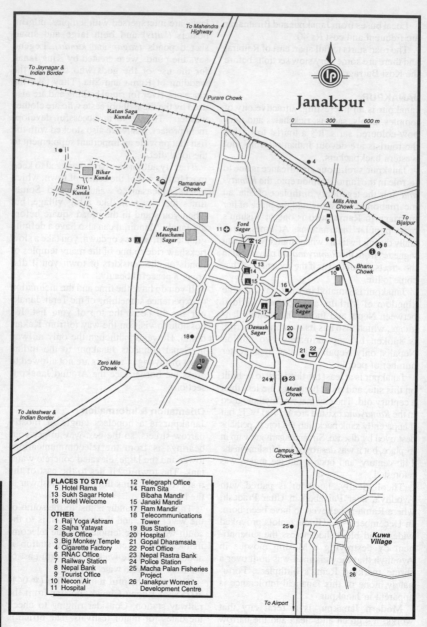

Janakpur

To Mahendra Highway

To Jaynagar & Indian Border

Purare Chowk

Ratan Saga Kunda

Bihar Kunda

Sita Kunda

Ramanand Chowk

Kopal Mauchami Sagar

Ford Sagar

Mills Area Chowk

To Bijalpur

Bhanu Chowk

Ram Sita Bibaha Mandir

Ganga Sagar

Danush Sagar

Zero Mile Chowk

To Jaleshwar & Indian Border

Murali Chowk

Campus Chowk

Kuwa Village

To Airport

0   300   600 m

PLACES TO STAY	
5	Hotel Rama
13	Sukh Sagar Hotel
16	Hotel Welcome

OTHER	
1	Raj Yoga Ashram
2	Sajha Yatayat Bus Office
3	Big Monkey Temple
4	Cigarette Factory
6	RNAC Office
7	Railway Station
8	Nepal Bank
9	Tourist Office
10	Necon Air
11	Hospital
12	Telegraph Office
14	Ram Sita Bibaha Mandir
15	Janaki Mandir
17	Ram Mandir
18	Telecommunications Tower
19	Bus Station
20	Hospital
21	Gopal Dharamsala
22	Post Office
23	Nepal Rastra Bank
24	Police Station
25	Macha Palan Fisheries Project
26	Janakpur Women's Development Centre

open from 10 am to 5 pm, Monday to Friday, but closes an hour earlier from November to January.

Janaki Mandir

The temple to Sita (who is also known as Janaki) is believed to be built over the spot where her father, King Janak, found her lying in the furrow of a ploughed field. It's impressively large yet, surprisingly, you come across it from the winding Janakpur streets almost without warning.

Although it has no great architectural or historical merit – it was built in 1912 and might be described as baroque Mughal – it is nonetheless a fascinating place. There are instances of fine work, especially in some of the carved stone screens, and in the beautiful silver doors to the inner sanctum.

The inner sanctum is opened from 5 to 7 am and 6 to 8 pm, to reveal a flower bedecked statue of Sita that was apparently miraculously found in the Saryu River near Ayodhya. She is accompanied by Rama and his three half-brothers, Lakshman, Bharat and Satrughna.

During the day, there are few people in the temple – some priests, sadhus and, if you're lucky, perhaps some musicians playing in the cloisters – but it comes alive in the evenings when Sita is displayed.

Ram Sita Bibaha Mandir

Virtually next door to the Janaki Mandir, but built with the traditional Nepali pagoda roof, this rather bizarre temple is built over the spot where Rama and Sita were married. There's a bit of a scam at the gate – you pay to take in a camera, or to have it looked after. Entry is Rs 5. The temple itself has glass walls so you can peer in at the kitsch life-sized models of Sita and Rama, his half-brothers and sisters-in-law.

Ram Mandir & Danush Sagar

Located in the city's oldest quarter, to the south-east of the Janaki Mandir, Ram Mandir is another Nepali-style temple that is the centrepoint for the Rama Navami celebrations. Immediately to its east is the Dhanush Sagar, which is considered to be one of the holiest ponds and is popular with pilgrims.

Other Temples & Ponds

There are numerous temples and ponds scattered around the outskirts of town. It is worth hiring a cycle rickshaw to see them, although you could track them down on foot if you were energetic. They're reached by brick-paved roads that meander into the paddy fields. If you hire a rickshaw, allow a couple of hours and expect to pay around Rs 50.

Start at the bizarre temple that is widely known as the **Big Monkey Temple**. Hanuman, the monkey god, is worshipped in the form of a rhesus monkey kept in a depressing cage. Despite this, it could well be monkey heaven since the attendants and pilgrims press food on their mascot. The constant supply of delicacies no longer arouses much interest or excitement, but temptation (or boredom) triumphs and the monkey keeps munching on. It is so enormously overweight it can hardly move.

Two of the most interesting and attractive ponds can be reached by following the brick-paved roads to the west. They are **Bihar Kunda** and **Ratan Saga Kunda**. The countryside is lush and tropical with coconut palms and huge trees framing the temples and ponds that are scattered across the fertile plains.

Janakpur Women's Development Centre

The Janakpur Women's Art Project (☎ 041-21080) was started to promote traditional Mithila painting skills and to empower the local women who live in a highly restrictive patriarchal society (see the aside on Mithila Painting).

The centre, on the southern outskirts of Janakpur, incorporates aspects of traditional architecture and the beautiful site is on the edge of an interesting village, a short rickshaw ride and walk from the centre of town. It is possible for visitors to see the women working at ceramics, painting, tapestry, silk-screen printing and sewing, and to purchase some of their striking creations at extremely reasonable prices; paintings start at Rs 200, ceramics at Rs 175. A visit is a must, and the centre is open Sunday to Thursday from 10 am to 5 pm, to 4 pm on Friday.

Take a rickshaw from town to Macha Palan, a large fisheries project with a red and white sign in Nepali. The rickshaw should cost around Rs 10. Coming from town, a brick road on the left forms a T-intersection just before the project. Follow it east to Kuwa village. Turn right at Kuwa village and continue until you reach a large, but unprepossessing temple. Turn left immediately before the temple and right immediately after it. Continue to the south; the road bends to the left, past a tank on the right. The centre is the only building in this vicinity, and it is enclosed behind a high, red-brick fence. The

Mithila Painting

Mithila culture is essentially a culture of the Gangetic plain, and Hindu caste structure is strictly upheld. Most people are subsistence farmers, but land-holdings are usually very small, and many families live on the edge of starvation. Many are in the grip of moneylenders, or *zamindars*.

Zamindars, usually from the Brahman (priest) or Kayastha (warrior, also Kshatriya) castes, occupy an almost feudal role as major landowners and through their traditional role as moneylenders. Their tenant farmers and debtors are effectively serfs trapped in a system of bonded labour.

Most Mithila people live in small villages, usually with no more than around 100 households. House walls are made from bamboo or thatch plastered with a mixture of cow dung and mud. The roofs are thatched, sometimes tiled. Most houses have a fenced courtyard which is also sealed with mud and cow dung.

Mithila women are raised with the expectation that they will be workers in their husband's home, and are frequently married as children. After puberty they are veiled so that they cannot be seen by males outside their family. As a part of their cultural and religious tradition, the women paint striking murals on the external walls of their homes. Inside, pottery storage containers and internal pillars also carry designs.

Different castes and different regions have developed distinctive styles and symbols, which are passed down from mother to daughter. Traditionally, painting and decoration is not undertaken purely to create an aesthetic result, nor is it purely cathartic or expressive. Painting largely springs from cultural and religious motives. The act of painting, as a part of some ritual, can be more important than the finished result itself, and completed paintings can act as charms, prayers and meditation aids.

Paintings often derive from Hindu mythology and can use complex symbols (sometimes with a

route sounds complicated, but ask directions if in doubt and you shouldn't have a problem. It's about a 10 minute walk from Macha Palan to the centre.

Special Events

On the fifth day of the waxing moon in late November or early December, thousands of pilgrims arrive to celebrate a re-enactment of Sita's marriage to Rama (Vivaha Panchami). This is also the occasion for an important fair and market that lasts a week. Rama's birthday (Rama Navami) in late March or early April is also accompanied by a huge procession.

Most Hindu festivals are major events in Janakpur. Deepavali is an interesting time to be in town, when the Mithila women repaint

---

distinct mandala-like quality), simple apparently abstract figures (including hand stencils, peacocks, pregnant elephants and fish), or can take on a narrative quality (representing religious stories). High castes, including the Kayastha, have developed extremely elaborate, abstract forms. Lower-caste paintings are often simpler and more realistic, but they have an energetic expressionistic style, and retain a strong sense of formal design.

Mithila paintings from Madubani in Bihar, India, have been discovered by the international art world. The most well known are the elaborate Kayastha wedding paintings that are presented to the groom as part of the build-up to an arranged marriage. Until fairly recently, little interest was taken in the art produced on Nepal's side of the border.

This changed with the foundation of the Janakpur Women's Art Project in 1989 which had the dual aim of promoting traditional Mithila painting skills and empowering the women painters. The project is housed in the Janakpur Women's Development Centre and it's possible to visit the centre to see the women working, and to buy what they produce. (See the entry under Janakpur.)

The project includes women of diverse castes and backgrounds and the art that is created reflects this variety: wedding paintings, pregnant elephants, gods, and abstract tattoo designs are just some of the subjects. Increasingly the paintings are changing to include scenes from the women's lives, including childbirth and marriage. In addition to paintings (acrylic on daphne paper) the women are also producing ceramics (plates and figures), papier-mâché, patchwork tapestry, silk-screen prints and woven wall hangings.

In Kathmandu, the project's goods are sold at Sana Hastakala, Mahaguthi, and a number of other reputable craft shops. See the Things to Buy sections in the Kathmandu, Patan & Bhaktapur chapter for more information. It's also possible to see examples of the women's work at the Kantipath branch of the Nepal Grindlays Bank, and at the United Nations building in Pulchowk. ■

the murals on their houses. On the day before Holi, Parikrama involves a ritual walk around the town's ring road. Holi itself can get very boisterous and wild; women should take care.

Places to Stay & Eat

Janakpur is desperately in need of a couple of decent hotels.

Despite the fact that it is somewhat run-down, the *Hotel Welcome* (☎ 041-20646; fax 20922) on Station Rd is not a bad option. The rooms are tolerably grubby, although some of the deluxe ones have the most sickening decor. On the plus side, the staff are friendly and helpful and the restaurant is good. Singles/doubles with private bath are Rs 200/250, for something a bit more comfortable (although it is relative), it's Rs 400/500. Ask to see several rooms before you pick one, check the plumbing, the mosquito nets and the cleanliness of the sheets, and avoid the front rooms which can be noisy. Checkout is 24 hours after check-in.

The *Sukh Sagar Hotel* (☎ 041-20488), very close to the Janaki Mandir, has large rooms which are passably clean, and reasonable value at Rs 120/220 with attached bath.

The best on offer is the somewhat gloomy, but recently redecorated, *Hotel Rama* (☎ 041-20059), in the northern part of town by Mills Area Chowk. The rooms are a good size, and range in price from very basic at Rs 75/110 with common bath to Rs 200/350 with fan and attached bath, Rs 250/300 with air-cooler and Rs 800/1000 with air-con.

Getting There & Away

RNAC (☎ 041-20185) has three flights a week to Kathmandu for $77, and Necon Air (☎ 041-20688) has five flights weekly.

Private buses for Kathmandu leave from the main bus station between 5 and 7 pm. There are half a dozen express buses to/from Kathmandu that cost Rs 130 and take about 12 hours. The government-operated Sajha Yatayat buses leave from a stop to the west of town on the main highway at Ramanand Chowk; they have day buses to Kathmandu leaving at 6.30 and 7 am, costing Rs 125 and

taking around nine hours. There are departures at the same time from the Kathmandu Bus Terminal.

Private buses leave Janakpur for Kakarbhitta every half hour from 4.30 to 10 am, and cost Rs 90; the journey takes nine hours. There are also day and night buses for Narayanghat for Rs 96, regular day buses for Birganj (five hours, Rs 50) and Biratnagar (six hours, Rs 70) and a night bus to Pokhara (15 hours, Rs 230).

AROUND JANAKPUR

The fields and villages around Janakpur form a lush and magical mosaic. It's worth exploring on foot or bicycle, or by rickshaw or train. Unfortunately, there are no formal bicycle-hire places, but if you ask around something may turn up. Western visitors are rare, so tread gently, and always ask before taking photos.

It doesn't really matter which direction you choose to go. Jaleshwar on the Nepali side of the border is a completely uninspiring town, but there are some interesting villages on the way. Other possibilities include the road that runs south to the airport, which turns to dirt and continues through a number of attractive villages, the road that runs north of the cigarette factory, and the road that runs west of Purare Chowk. **Dhanusa**, 15 km to the north, marks the spot where Rama allegedly drew Shiva's magic bow.

Janakpur is the terminus for two railway lines, one of which runs east to **Jaynagar** over the Indian border, and the other which runs north-west to Bijalpur, although only the former route carries passenger traffic these days. They're narrow-gauge trains and very slow, so they offer an interesting if somewhat crowded method of seeing the countryside.

To Jaynagar there are three daily services in each direction, so it is easy to put together a day trip. It's about 29 km (four hours!) to Jaynagar, but tourists are not allowed to cross the border into India, so you have to get off in one of the villages along the way. Trains leave both Janakpur and Jaynagar at 6 and 11 am and 3 pm. Tickets are Rs 24 in 1st class and Rs 9 in 2nd class.

The first stop after Janakpur is **Parbaha** (eight km, Rs 6.50/2 in 1st/2nd class), and there are interesting villages on either side of the tracks – you could walk back to town. Another interesting stop is **Baidehi**, about an hour (12 km, Rs 10/4) from Janakpur, where you could alight and catch the Janakpur-bound train that comes through an hour later. Alternatively, you could continue all the way to **Khajuri** (21 km, Rs 17.50/6.50), about eight km from Jaynagar on the Nepali side of the border and catch the afternoon Janakpur train.

BIRGANJ

Birganj is one of the main border crossings between Nepal and India, and one of Nepal's most important industrial cities. This is an unfortunate combination. It has been one of the most unattractive places on the planet for some time, but it is not resting on its laurels. It is growing rapidly and the pollution and squalor are getting worse.

Birganj seems to stretch northwards for miles, strung along the impossibly congested main road, although mercifully the heavy traffic bypasses the city centre on a recently constructed ring road. There are a large number of depressingly run-down factories, as the 'corridor' between Birganj and Hetauda is probably the most important centre for industrial development in Nepal. Amongst tanneries and other unattractive places there are a sugar factory and an agricultural implements factory.

There are immigrants from around Nepal and many from India; bear in mind that the only reason they come to Birganj is that the alternative of remaining in their place of birth is worse. The local language is Bhojpuri, which is spoken on both sides of the border.

Birganj is probably the most important entry point for Indian imports, but most travellers (especially those coming from Varanasi) enter through Sunauli to the west. Birganj remains the most convenient entry point, however, for those coming from Patna or Calcutta.

Fortunately, there are plenty of day and night buses to and from Kathmandu and Pokhara and points south (in India) so there should be no necessity to stay more than a night – hopefully not even that.

Orientation & Information

Birganj and Raxaul Bazaar (on the Indian side of the border) virtually run together, although it's a 30 minute rickshaw ride from one bus station to the other.

The Birganj bus station (the best or worse part of town, depending on whether you're coming or going) is on the ring road, about 500m east of the clocktower.

The various official offices on either side of the border are all open between 7 am and 7 pm, as is the bank on the Nepali side.

Things to See

If you do find yourself with a couple of hours to kill in Birganj you could hire a rickshaw for an hour or two (at around Rs 30 an hour) and have a bit of a wander. The town has a certain gruesome fascination and there are a

Birganj

0   250   500 m

To Hotel Samjhana (1 km) & Kathmandu

To Bus Station (500m)

Tank

Main Road

To Customs & Immigration (3 km) & Indian Border (4 km)

1 Clocktower
2 Maystan Temple
3 Gita Temple
4 Bal Mandir
5 Nepal Rastra Bank
6 Government Offices
7 Hotel Prakash
8 Hotel Kailas
9 Hotel Diyalo & Nepal Restaurant
10 Prakash Lodge
11 Hotel Cottage Fulwari

Bureaucratic Blackmail in Birganj – Warning
In the past, the Nepali immigration officers at Birganj have been known to run a particularly infuriating scam. They insist they can only accept the $25 visa fee in cash dollars. Although the bank or moneychangers at the border would happily change foreign currency and give an official Foreign Exchange Encashment Receipt, the immigration officials will under no circumstances accept rupees, or any other currency. This is definitely not official policy, but they have the magic stamp and so there's little you can do but be prepared. The best insurance is a visa already in your passport. ∎

---

couple of modern temples and muddy ponds. The most interesting is the **Bal Mandir**, a modern Buddhist temple about a km west from the main road.

Places to Stay & Eat
The places to stay are in the centre of town, clustered around what was the old bus station. The really cheap places are a pretty dismal lot, and can't seriously be recommended. If you're broke and stuck, try the *Prakash Lodge*, a dirt-cheap place which is both dirty and cheap.

The *Hotel Kailas* (☎ 051-22384) has a range of decent rooms and a good tandoori restaurant. Rooms with shared bath start at Rs 100/120, rise to Rs 200/270 with private bath and to Rs 700/850 with air-con.

Almost next door is the *Hotel Diyalo* (☎ 051-22370), a well run hotel with immaculate rooms that are reasonably priced for what you get. It also has a good restaurant. Singles/doubles with bath range from Rs 400/450 to Rs 600/650 with air-cooler and Rs 1100/1200 with air-con.

Further along the same road is the *Hotel Cottage Fulwari*, with a range of OK rooms at Rs 300/400 with air-cooling and Rs 1000/1200 with air-con.

The *Hotel Samjhana* (☎ 051-22122) is quite a distance from the bus station, but it has parking and decent food. This is the Birganj Ritz. A room in their new wing, with all mod cons including air-con cost Rs 1200/1600. The old section of the hotel is not particularly appealing, and rooms cost Rs 500/600. There is some room for bargaining if things are quiet.

Getting There & Away
To/From India It's a 30 minute, Rs 12 rickshaw between the Birganj bus station and the border, and another 30 minutes and Indian Rs 15 between the border and the Raxaul Bazaar bus station. Expect to pay Rs 50 for the five hour journey to Patna from Raxaul Bazaar.

To/From Nepal There are plenty of day and night buses to and from Kathmandu. The Sajha Yatayat buses, with an office at the new bus station, are recommended. They have night departures at 7 and 8 pm (Rs 113), and morning departures at 6.30, 7.30 and 8 am (Rs 90). From the Kathmandu Bus Terminal, Sajha Yatayat buses leave at 7, 7.30 and 7.45 am, and at 7 and 7.15 pm; the journey takes about seven hours.

Anything between 20 and 40 private buses leave Birganj each evening between 7 and 9 pm, arriving in Kathmandu around 5 am and costing Rs 112. A dozen or so day buses leave between 6 and 8 am and cost Rs 125.

There are also private buses for Pokhara (10 hours; 6.30 am to 2.30 pm, Rs 90; 7 and 8 pm, Rs 106), Kakarbhitta (16 hours, day Rs 142, night Rs 162) and Tadi (for Chitwan) for Rs 45.

Despite the fact that the Tribhuvan Highway from Hetauda to Naubise looks like the best route to Kathmandu, all buses travel west to Narayanghat before they climb into the hills. It is possible to catch a bus from Hetauda (Rs 20 from Birganj) to Kathmandu that traverses the Tribhuvan Highway – it's slow, but there are superb views. See the

Hetauda section later in this chapter, and the Getting Around chapter.

Getting Around

Rickshaws cost around Rs 30 per hour, and this will be the charge if you get one to take you all the way through to Raxaul Bazaar (recommended).

HETAUDA

Hetauda is the starting point for a cableway that carries cement from the Terai to Kathmandu. It's quite an amazing construction, similar in concept to a ski lift. The current cableway dates from 1958 and can carry 25 tonnes per hour; it takes 15 hours for goods to travel the distance. Unless you want to catch a bus over the superb Tribhuvan Highway, there's no need to stop. Normally, buses turn west to Narayanghat.

Places to Stay & Eat

The *Neelam Lodge* (☎ 057-20900), on the Daman road near the main chowk in the centre of town and beside a big pipal tree, has clean singles/doubles for Rs 100/140 with attached bath (cold water) – food value.

The *Hotel Seema* (☎ 057-20191), about 200m the other side of the chowk, is a relatively new place with decent rooms at Rs 80/160 with common bath, Rs 200/300 with attached bath and Rs 1200 for a deluxe aircon double room.

The *Motel Avocado* (☎ 057-20429; fax 292611), on the way out of town on the Tribhuvan Highway to Daman, has accommodation in a quiet, pleasant garden (with avocado trees). 'Luxury' rooms are in an old Nissen hut and are spacious, comfortable and rather idiosyncratic. They come with fans and air-con (don't expect too much of the air-con) and are a bit expensive at Rs 900/1200 for singles/doubles. There are some cheaper rooms – a lot smaller and a bit shabbier – for Rs 250/350.

Getting There & Away

One Sajha Yatayat bus a day runs over the magnificent Tribhuvan Highway via Daman. There are spectacular views and this route is well worth considering. The bus station in Hetauda is to the south-east of the main intersection and the Daman to Kathmandu bus leaves at 7 am. From the Kathmandu Bus Terminal the Sajha bus also leaves at 7 am (eight hours, Rs 60).

A number of private buses go to Kathmandu and Pokhara via Narayanghat and Tadi Bazaar. Buses to Tadi take around three hours and cost Rs 55. There are numerous buses to Birganj for Rs 20.

DAMAN

Daman is 2322m above sea level, midway between Kathmandu and Hetauda. Its claim to fame is that it has, arguably, *the* most spectacular outlook on the Himalaya – there are unimpeded views of the entire range from Dhaulagiri to Mt Everest. If you have the opportunity it should not be missed.

There is a viewing tower with a telescope (Rs 20 entry), which is part of a very uninspiring and cramped tented camp, a basic lodge/restaurant and not much else. On the Hetauda side of Daman there is a magnificent rhododendron forest – which would be particularly worth seeing in spring – then great views over the Terai to India.

Place to Stay

The *Daman Mountain Resort* consists of a number of permanent tents clustered around the viewing tower. The cost to stay here is a ridiculous Rs 740 for a double! Much more sensible, but far more basic, is the nearby *Hotel Sherpa*, a friendly local hotel with double rooms at Rs 200. You can also get food here, as long as you don't want anything more complicated than dal bhat.

Getting There & Away

Daman is about three hours by car from Kathmandu and four hours from Hetauda. Unless you're on your way to/from Birganj hiring a car and making a day trip from Kathmandu is the ideal way to get to Daman, but it won't be cheap. Think in terms of $60. If you have a group and it's clear weather, it would be worth it. Alternatively, this is one of the most spectacular (and most gruelling) mountain-bike routes in the world. See the Mountain Biking chapter for details.

From Daman there's one northbound (Kathmandu) and one southbound (Hetauda) Sajha Yatayat bus a day. Buses leave Kathmandu and Hetauda at 7 am (Rs 30).

TADI BAZAAR

In the Chitwan Valley between Hetauda and Narayanghat, the small town of Tadi Bazaar (sometimes spelt Tandi Bazaar) is nothing more than a junction town for Sauraha, the budget accommodation centre for Royal Chitwan National Park. For more details see the earlier section on the park.

Getting There & Away

See the Getting There & Away entry in the Royal Chitwan National Park section for details on transport to/from Tadi Bazaar and the nearby village of Sauraha.

NARAYANGHAT & BHARATPUR

Narayanghat is a fast-growing town on the banks of the large Narayani River, just downstream from the junction of the Kali Gandaki and Trisuli rivers. It has developed because it lies at the intersection (Pul Chowk) of the Mahendra Highway, which runs the length of the Terai, and the main road into the hills to Kathmandu and Pokhara. It is the administrative and trading centre for the district. Bharatpur is contiguous with Narayanghat, and has an airport.

Although on the map the most direct route from eastern Nepal to Kathmandu is the road from Hetauda to Naubise, almost all traffic takes the better road from Narayanghat to Mugling. The Tribhuvan Highway (or Tribhuvan Rajpath) from Hetauda to Naubise is a magnificent drive, but its endless narrow corners mean it is not appropriate for trucks and buses.

Narayanghat will, for most people, simply be a chai stop en route to Kathmandu, Chitwan or India, and apart from the river there's not much of interest in the town. However, it's not a bad spot to stop if you are exploring the Terai, and there's an interesting excursion to Devghat, a holy site north-west of town at the confluence of the Kali Gandaki and Trisuli rivers.

Places to Stay & Eat

If due to bad luck or bad management you are forced to stay the night, there are a few choices. Right by the main intersection, very handy for buses, is the *Regal Rest House* (☎ 056-20755). Rooms with common bath are Rs 125/150, while with attached bath and hot water it's Rs 200/300. Don't even contemplate staying here unless you can get a room at the back, as the road is very busy here with buses coming and going at all hours of the day and night. The rest house has a decent restaurant.

A much more pleasant option, but also somewhat inconvenient, is the *Gainda Cottages* (☎ 056-20590) on the western bank of the Narayani (across the bridge and first right). It's not exactly luxurious, and mosquito repellent is a good idea, but the welcome is warm, the rooms are clean, and there's a courtyard garden area. Rooms are perhaps somewhat overpriced at Rs 100/200 with common bath. Simple food is available.

There are some cheaper places around the northern bus station. The *Hotel River View* (☎ 056-21151) is a quiet, basic place which does indeed have a river view, although only from the upper floors. The rooms are a bit on the small side, but are good value at Rs 150 for a double with attached bath and mosquito nets.

Other than these places there are a couple of up-market choices in Bharatpur, and these are handy for the airport. *Hotel Narayani Safari* (☎ 056-20130, 20634) is primarily used as a base for trips to Chitwan. It is well run and has air-con, a swimming pool, tennis court and an excellent restaurant. Singles/doubles cost $35/45.

The *Hotel Chitwan Keyman* (☎ 056-20200) is a modern place with a quiet rear garden, and very comfortable rooms with air-con and TV for $34/40, although this is probably negotiable to a fairly large degree.

Getting There & Away

RNAC (☎ 056-20326) has three flights a week from Kathmandu to Bharatpur for $50.

As Narayanghat is such a major crossroad there are buses coming and going at all hours. Buses from Narayanghat to Pokhara leave from the bus park at the northern end of town on the road to Mugling. Buses to/from most Terai destinations and Kathmandu stop at the main T-intersection just to the east of the bridge. The Sajha Yatayat booking office is tucked away in the group of stalls next to the Gulf petrol station.

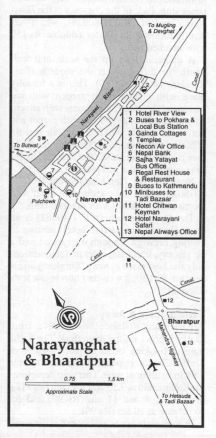

Narayanghat & Bharatpur

1 Hotel River View
2 Buses to Pokhara & Local Bus Station
3 Gainda Cottages
4 Temples
5 Necon Air Office
6 Nepal Bank
7 Sajha Yatayat Bus Office
8 Regal Rest House & Restaurant
9 Buses to Kathmandu
10 Minibuses for Tadi Bazaar
11 Hotel Chitwan Keyman
12 Hotel Narayani Safari
13 Nepal Airways Office

0   0.75   1.5 km
Approximate Scale

Private buses can be booked at the two red booths outside the Regal Rest House.

From Kathmandu the fare is Rs 65 to Narayanghat, and you can catch just about any bus heading for the Terai. One of the most convenient is the 9 am Sajha bus for Tadi.

From Narayanghat, there are Sajha buses (most en route from Kathmandu) for Janakpur (Rs 80/100 day/night), Nepalganj (Rs 128/162), Bhairawa (Rs 50/60), Tansen (Palpa) (Rs 58/72) and Birganj (Rs 50/60).

Private buses from Narayanghat run to Kakarbhitta (14 hours, 5 pm, Rs 199), Biratnagar (11 hours, 7.30 pm, Rs 167), Janakpur (eight hours, 9 pm, Rs 96), Mahendranagar (17 hours, 4.30 pm, Rs 231), Nepalganj (10 hours, 7.30 am and 7 to 9 pm, Rs 128/162 day/night), Pokhara (several daytime departures, five hours, Rs 48) and Kathmandu (hourly from 7 am to 1 pm, many at night, Rs 55/65).

Minibuses for Tadi Bazaar (Chitwan) leave from the side of the Mahendra Highway just before the second intersection east of the main T-intersection; they cost Rs 7 and take 30 minutes.

AROUND NARAYANGHAT

Devghat (also known as Deoghat and Harihara Chhetra) is an ancient holy site that was first mentioned in the Skanda Purana. It's a suitably beautiful spot, with forest-clad hills, a large sandy beach, and a number of shady shrines and temples overlooking the swirling waters where the Kali Gandaki and Trisuli meet. The confluence of rivers, particularly when they are major tributaries of the Ganges, is always regarded as religiously significant by Hindus, as it is believed a third spiritual river also joins.

Many elderly high-caste Hindus come here to quietly live out their last days, and finally to be cremated on the river banks, thus gaining religious merit and hopefully avoiding a stay in hell while they wait for reincarnation. In fact, all sorts of religious rites, including marriages, are performed at Devghat and they often involve large family

THE TERAI

groups. The atmosphere is peaceful and tranquil, not at all gloomy.

Devghat is one of the main sites for the festival of Magh Sankranti, and pilgrims come from around Nepal and India to immerse themselves in the river (see the later Ridi Bazaar section). This festival takes place on the first day of the Nepali month of Magh, in mid-January, and celebrates the gradually lengthening days and the onset of warmer weather.

Western visitors (untouchables) are rare, and should bear in mind that caste-related ideas of ritual pollution may mean that some of the orthodox pilgrims and inhabitants could be offended by any contact. Do not enter homes or temples without invitation and do not touch anything that could be holy (which means almost everything!). There is nowhere to stay, and not even a chai stall, so bring drinks and food.

Getting There & Away

There are frequent minibuses to/from Narayanghat. By road, you head north from town on the Mugling road for three km, turn left on a signposted dirt road just before a police checkpost and continue for two km, then take the right fork and continue for another three km. It is possible to walk along the eastern bank of the river, although the track here is a bit overgrown and it's easiest to pick up and follow it from the Devghat end.

BUTWAL

Lying at the very foot of the Chure Hills, Butwal is at first appearances an unattractive, dirty town. The approach from Tansen, to the north, is dramatic: one moment you're in a narrow mountain gorge, the next you are surrounded by people, dust, rickshaws and Hindi film posters.

If you find yourself stranded for a night, or have a couple of hours to kill waiting for a bus, it's well worth a wander through the old part of town on the west bank of the Tinau River. Historically, Butwal lay at the start of a trade route to Tibet and so has a good deal more history than most Terai towns. While there are no significant old buildings, the narrow, traffic-free streets of the old part of town are a million miles from new Butwal – kids play cricket in the street, women sit chatting in doorways and there is a general unhurried air. Walk across the main vehicle bridge, then head north through the old streets towards the hills, then cut back across the river on one of the two suspension foot/bicycle bridges.

Places to Stay & Eat

There are plenty of cheap hotels at Traffic Chowk on the main road in the centre of town, and this is also where the long-distance buses stop. Pick of the cheapies is the *Hotel New Gandaki* (☎ 071-40928), which has scruffy rooms at Rs 100 for a double, Rs 150 with attached bath.

A quantum leap up the scale and well worth the difference is the modern *Hotel Kandara* (☎ 071-40380). This is a friendly place with a nice small garden with car parking at the rear. Clean rooms with attached bath are Rs 200/350, or with carpet and hot water it's Rs 350/650, and air-con Rs 1050 for a double. Avoid the front rooms as they cop the street noise. The attached *Fedee Restaurant* is not a bad place to eat.

Nearby is the *Hotel Siddhartha* (☎ 071-40380), a clean and comfortable hotel with rooms at Rs 300/400 with attached bath.

The *Hotel Sindoor* (☎ 071-40381) is an up-market and expensive hotel catering to visiting bigwigs. Though overpriced and a bit gloomy, it's clean, quiet and unquestionably the best place in town. Singles/doubles here are $20/30; it wouldn't hurt to ask for a discount.

Getting There & Away

All the long-distance buses leave from Traffic Chowk on the main drag. The Sajha Yatayat booking office is just down from Traffic Chowk, opposite the modern temple built in traditional style. There are departures for Kathmandu at 7.15 and 7.45 pm (Rs 112), or at 7.30, 8 and 11 am (Rs 90) and for Nepalganj at 10 am (Rs 90).

Private night buses are booked at the small

shop with the red sign (Nepali writing) next to the Fedee Restaurant at Traffic Chowk. The booking office for day buses is between the Samrat and Siddhartha hotels, and also has a red sign in Nepali.

There are departures for Pokhara (via Mugling, 3 and 7 pm, Rs 99; via Tansen, eight hours, 5.50 am and noon, Rs 88), Nepalganj (10 am, 8 pm, Rs 114), Janakpur (5 pm, Rs 147), Narayanghat (throughout the day, Rs 46), Mahendranagar (7.15 am, Rs 180), Birganj (6 am, Rs 88), Gorkha (7.40 am, Rs 70) and Kathmandu (7 am and 5.30 to 9.30 pm, Rs 88/109).

There are also regular departures for Sunauli/Bhairawa (22 km).

SUNAULI & BHAIRAWA

Sunauli (pronounced 'soo-*nor*-li') is a small, grubby collection of offices and hotels right on the Indian border. Bhairawa is a somewhat more substantial, dusty, bustling town nearly four km inside Nepal; officially Bhairawa's name is Siddharthanagar, but this is rarely used.

There are three points in favour of visiting this part of the world. Firstly, Sunauli is by far the most popular and convenient border crossing between Nepal and northern and western India (including Varanasi, Agra and Delhi). Secondly, Bhairawa is the closest town to Lumbini, the birthplace of Buddha. And thirdly, although Sunauli and Bhairawa are hot and featureless, they're still relaxed and pleasant by comparison to Birganj, the next major crossing point to the east.

There is some small-scale industry, a couple of banks and government offices and plenty of shops. Most pre-arranged bookings to/from India involve a night's stop in Sunauli, and most individual travellers do the same.

Orientation & Information

Both the Nepali and Indian customs and immigration offices are open 24 hours, but between the hours of about 7 pm and 5 am you'll have to wake them up, something they are quite accustomed to. You are free to walk across the border between the Indian and Nepali sides without going through any formalities, although attempting this with a backpack on would be asking for trouble.

Indian rupees are accepted readily in Sunauli and Bhairawa, and also in major places such as Kathmandu and Pokhara. The exchange rate is set at Indian Rs 1 = Nepali Rs 1.60. Changing money is simple as there are a couple of official private moneychangers on the Nepali side (open long hours), as well as a branch of the Nepal Rastra Bank (open from 7.30 am to 6 pm daily). Outside these hours there are black-market operators who offer fairly poor rates. The bank on the

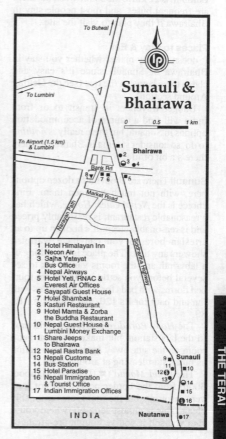

1 Hotel Himalayan Inn
2 Necon Air
3 Sajha Yatayat Bus Office
4 Nepal Airways
5 Hotel Yeti, RNAC & Everest Air Offices
6 Sayapati Guest House
7 Hotel Shambala
8 Kasturi Restaurant
9 Hotel Mamta & Zorba the Buddha Restaurant
10 Nepal Guest House & Lumbini Money Exchange
11 Share Jeeps to Bhairawa
12 Nepal Rastra Bank
13 Nepali Customs
14 Bus Station
15 Hotel Paradise
16 Nepali Immigration & Tourist Office
17 Indian Immigration Offices

To Butwal
To Lumbini
To Airport (1.5 km) & Lumbini
Bhairawa
Bank Rd
Market Road
Narayan Path
Siddhartha Highway
Sunauli
INDIA
Nautanwa

Sunauli & Bhairawa
0   0.5   1 km

Indian side of the border doesn't open until 10 am – after the buses have left – and is busy as hell. Nepali rupees are not easy to use in India, so get rid of them here if you are heading south.

There is a tourist office (☎ 071-20304) at the border. The Department of Tourism's *Visitors' Guide* (free) is worth picking up, but don't expect much more.

Bhairawa is a 20 minute rickshaw ride to the north. Most shops and businesses in Bhairawa are strung along Narayan Path or Bank Rd. The Siddhartha Highway runs along the eastern edge of town to the border. Lumbini is 22 km to the south-west, but there are frequent buses, and most people stay in Bhairawa if they plan to visit the site.

Places to Stay & Eat

It doesn't really matter whether you stay in Bhairawa or Sunauli since it's easy and cheap to go between the two (see the Getting Around section).

Budget travellers in transit to or from India will find a couple of accommodation options in Sunauli, but there really is *nothing* to do, so consider staying in Bhairawa where there's a bit of life.

Sunauli There are about half a dozen options here, with not much between them. First choice is the *Nepal Guest House*, which has a reasonable restaurant, is reasonably priced and is reasonably clean. It's hooked up to an artesian bore so you can have warmish showers any time. The place is something of a labyrinth and the rooms vary – ask to see several before you settle in. There are four-bed dorms with beds for Rs 20, doubles with fan and bath for Rs 120, and singles for Rs 80.

The *Hotel Paradise* is OK and right next to the bus station, but make sure you get a room on the side away from the bus station as buses start leaving at around 4 am.

The *Hotel Mamta* (☎ 071-20312), about 300m from the border post, does not look very inspiring, but the rooms are reasonably clean. This is almost certainly where you'll find yourself if you've bought pre-arranged

tickets through an agent. A single bed in a six-bed dorm costs Rs 25 and a double with common bath is Rs 125, and with attached bath Rs 225.

Apart from the restaurants attached to hotels, there are only a couple of small restaurants.

Bhairawa The best budget option is the *Sayapati Guest House*, which is close to the Sajha Yatayat bus stop on Bank Rd. It's a cheap and basic place to stay, with double rooms at Rs 250 with attached bath.

Further along the same road is the busy *Hotel Shambala*, which is marginally better, and costs Rs 300 for a double with attached bath.

The highest quality hotel in the area is the *Hotel Yeti* (☎ 071-20551; fax 20719) on the corner of Bank Rd and Siddhartha Highway. This is where the tour groups occasionally pass through stay. It's clean, there's a decent restaurant and, for what it delivers, the prices are reasonable – $15/20 for a single/double, or $25/30 with air-con. The only problem is the hotel overlooks a main intersection (where the buses stop) so it can be a bit noisy.

The *Hotel Himalayan Inn* (☎ 071-20347) is a bit out of town to the north on the Siddhartha Highway. Although it has been left behind by the Hotel Yeti and is struggling a bit, it's still just OK. There is off-road parking. The restaurant is cavernous, and empty, and the food distinctly average. Singles/doubles with bath are $15/18, but discounting brings this back to something more reasonable.

The *Kasturi Restaurant*, near the corner of Bank Rd and Narayan Path, is a pleasant high-ceilinged place with uniformed waiters and excellent vegetarian Indian food. Dishes like pulau and korma cost around Rs 30.

Getting There & Away

There are plenty of bus connections to destinations in both Nepal and India. Whether you have booked a 'through' ticket or not, everyone changes buses at the border and most people spend the night in Sunauli. There are no 'tourist' buses.

To/From India You catch buses to Indian cities from the Indian side of the border. There are direct buses to Varanasi for Indian Rs 81 to Rs 100, depending on the degree of luxury, and the journey takes about nine hours.

There are also buses to Gorakhpur where you can connect with the Indian broad-gauge railway (three hours, Indian Rs 25). From Gorakhpur, buses leave every half hour from 5 am to 7 pm; you'll need to catch a bus from Gorakhpur by 3 pm if you want to be sure of catching a night bus to Kathmandu the same day. See the Getting There & Away chapter for more information.

To/From Nepal RNAC (☎ 071-20175) operates four flights a week between Kathmandu and Bhairawa for $72. Nepal Airways (☎ 071-20536) has twice daily flights, as does Necon Air (☎ 071-20498). The Bhairawa airport is midway between Bhairawa and Butwal.

Travelling north, most buses leave from Sunauli, stopping in Bhairawa, but buses can be booked and boarded at either place. In Sunauli there's a bus booking office at the bus stand, and buses can only be booked on the day of departure. This office opens at 3 am. In Bhairawa the bus companies' offices are around the intersection of Bank Rd and the Siddhartha Highway. The Sajha Yatayat booking office is opposite the Yeti Hotel and these buses are recommended, although they only operate to Kathmandu (5.30 and 8 am, 6.30 and 7.30 pm, Rs 95/180 by day/night).

There are several private night buses to Pokhara and Kathmandu, and day buses for Pokhara. To travel by day from Sunauli to Kathmandu, take a Pokhara bus as far as Mugling and change there.

Buses for Pokhara (nine hours, Rs 80/111 by day/night) travel via Narayanghat and the trip is particularly beautiful (for great views of Machhapuchhare if you're heading north, get a seat on the left-hand side). A number of buses leave Sunauli between 4 and 10 am, and at 6.45 and 8 pm.

For Kathmandu there are only night buses from Sunauli, and there are at least seven buses each evening between 4.30 and 8 pm (Rs 180).

From Kathmandu, Sajha buses leave at 6.45 and 7.15 am, and 7 and 7.15 pm. Private buses leave half-hourly from 6 to 9 am, and from 5 to 8 pm.

If you want to go to Royal Chitwan National Park from Sunauli, there are buses for Birganj (seven hours, Rs 90) that leave at 5.30 and 7.30 am. Get off at Tadi Bazaar if you're heading to Sauraha (four hours, Rs 50). There are plenty of local buses to Butwal for Rs 10.

For transport to Lumbini see the Lumbini Getting There & Away section.

Getting Around
The only time you'll need transport will be to go between Sunauli and Bhairawa – four, hot, flat km. A rickshaw costs around Rs 15 and takes 20 minutes, a share jeep Rs 4.

LUMBINI
Lumbini is believed to be the birthplace of Siddhartha Gautama – the founder of Buddhism, known as Buddha, or the enlightened one. This is confirmed by the existence of an inscribed pillar erected 318 years after the event by the great Buddhist emperor Ashoka, and the presence of a number of ancient ruins.

Fittingly, Lumbini is an example of how ephemeral the results of human effort are. There's not much to see and it requires a serious effort of the imagination to conjure up the ghosts of the past. Lumbini is not a Bethlehem or Mecca – there is no city, no impressive architecture, no pilgrim-jammed car park, no heavily armed soldiers, no hustlers, not even a postcard stand.

In the end, it is the absence of all these things, and the peacefulness of Lumbini that make a visit worthwhile. In some ways, Tilaurakot (see that section later in this chapter), the site of Kapilavastu, the fortress-palace where Buddha was raised as a prince of the royal family, is more evocative.

It's curious that the Buddha should have

been born and raised on a fertile tropical plain, a place of such contrast to the deserts of the Middle East where so many religions originated; strange that he should have been born a wealthy prince; and almost bizarre that this privileged life and rich countryside should have inspired a belief that suffering is synonymous with existence.

Allow yourself an hour or two to wander around and soak in the atmosphere. The important sights don't take long to cover – the Maya Devi Temple, the Ashokan Pillar, the Sacred Pond and the Tibetan and Theravada *viharas* (monasteries). Then find a shady spot where you can watch the parrots squabbling in the branches of the massive *bo* trees.

There are grandiose plans for the development of Lumbini, with the aim of creating a place of pilgrimage, and a tourist attraction. It will be interesting to see whether this can be achieved by government decree. A plan by Japanese architect Kenzo Tange was adopted in 1978, involving canals, gardens, a library and museum, monastic zones, a pilgrim lodge and a hotel. There has been some slow progress. The major earthworks are complete, there are a couple of buildings quite a distance from the site proper, which are forlornly empty, and a luxury hotel, which is actually operating.

History

The great Indian emperor Ashoka visited Lumbini in 245 BCE, and left a number of his famous inscribed pillars in the region. In 403 CE the region was visited by Fa Hsien a Chinese pilgrim who described a ruined Kapilavastu and a deserted countryside.

In 636 Hsuan Tang, another pilgrim, described 1000 derelict monasteries and Ashoka's pillar at Lumbini, shattered by lightning and lying on the ground. Derelict it may have been, but the site was still known in 1312 CE when Ripu Malla visited, possi-

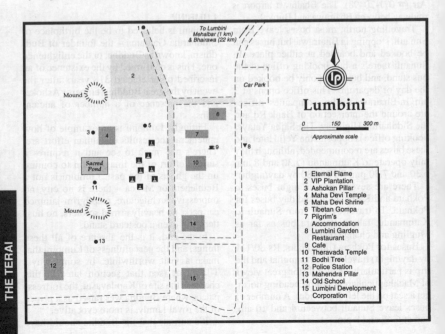

Lumbini

0   150   300 m

Approximate scale

1 Eternal Flame
2 VIP Plantation
3 Ashokan Pillar
4 Maha Devi Temple
5 Maha Devi Shrine
6 Tibetan Gompa
7 Pilgrim's Accommodation
8 Lumbini Garden Restaurant
9 Cafe
10 Theravada Temple
11 Bodhi Tree
12 Police Station
13 Mahendra Pillar
14 Old School
15 Lumbini Development Corporation

To Lumbini Mehalbar (1 km) & Bhairawa (22 km)

Car Park

Mound

Sacred Pond

Mound

THE TERAI

bly leaving the nativity statue which is still worshipped in the Maya Devi Temple.

Mughal invaders arrived in the region at the end of the 15th century, and in common with their zealous actions elsewhere on the subcontinent, it is likely that the remaining 'pagan' monuments at Kapilavastu and Lumbini were destroyed. The whole region returned to wilderness and the sites were lost to the jungle, until the governor of Palpa (Tansen), Khadga Shumsher Rana, who had a keen interest in archaeology, began the excavation of a pillar – which turned out to be Ashoka's Lumbini pillar – in late 1896.

Today, no trace of the Lumbini forest remains, but the pond where Maya Devi is believed to have bathed can still be seen, although in much restored form. The brick foundations of stupas and viharas dating from the 2nd century BCE can be seen around the pond. The Maya Devi Temple is built on ancient foundations, and these are now the site of an archaeological dig.

After the discovery of Lumbini, the ruins near Tilaurakot were identified as Kapilavastu. There has been some archaeological work, which has revealed the remains of moated city walls, impressive gates and the foundations for a palace complex.

Most of the surrounding countryside is now dominated by extremely poor Muslim peasant farmers. There are no Buddhists.

Ashokan Pillar

Emperor Ashoka is one of the greatest figures in Indian history. Throughout his massive empire he left pillars and rock-carved edicts, which to this day delineate the

---

Siddhartha Gautama

Two and a half thousand years ago the region at the foot of the Himalaya was broken up into a number of small republics and principalities which were vassal states to larger empires based on the Gangetic plain. Siddhartha Gautama was the son of Suddhodana (of the Sakya clan) who ruled the republic of Kapilavastu, and Maya Devi (of the Koliya clan) the daughter of the ruler of the neighbouring state of Dewadaha. The ruins of Kapilavastu lie at Tilaurakot, 27 km west of Lumbini, but Dewadaha has not been conclusively identified.

It is believed that Maya Devi was 10 months pregnant when she decided to visit her parents' house in Dewadaha. On the way from Kapilavastu, her entourage had to pass through the grove of Lumbini, which was a famous beauty spot with a pond surrounded by sal trees. On the day she reached Lumbini, in May 563 BCE the sal trees were in full bloom, so Maya Devi stopped to enjoy the scene and to bathe in the pond. Leaving the water, she suddenly felt labour pains. She raised her right hand and caught hold of the drooping branch of a pipal tree, and the baby was born.

Maya Devi returned to Kapilavastu where her son Siddhartha was given a sheltered, privileged upbringing. At the age of 29, while wandering in the town outside the palace walls, he came across an old man, a sick man, a corpse and a hermit. This confrontation with suffering and death impelled Siddhartha to renounce his luxurious life and to leave Kapilavastu.

He spent the next five years seeking to understand the nature of existence. Mostly he wandered as an itinerant ascetic – no doubt much like the Hindu sadhus of today – but he found that extreme self-denial did not provide him with any answers. Finally, after 49 days meditating under a bodhi tree at Bodhgaya he attained enlightenment. From Bodhgaya he travelled to Sarnath, near Varanasi, where he preached his first sermon.

The Buddha spent the next 46 years teaching his 'middle way'. Suffering, he taught, is a natural part of life, but suffering is caused by attachment, desire and delusion, and if these negative forces are controlled (by following the noble 'eightfold path'), it is possible to reach nirvana.

Although some people believe Buddha visited the Kathmandu Valley, there is no firm evidence for this. Most of his preaching was undertaken in northern India and across the Gangetic plain. He died at the age of 80 at Kushinagar, near Gorakhpur, about 100 km south-east of Lumbini.

Despite his disavowal of divinity, the main sites associated with Buddha's life (Lumbini, Kapilavastu, Bodhgaya, Sarnath and Kushinagar) soon became centres for pilgrimage, and monasteries and temples sprang up. There are only sparse records of Lumbini's and Kapilavastu's histories, however. ■

extent of his power. They can be seen in Delhi, Gujarat, Orissa, Uttar Pradesh, Madhya Pradesh – and Nepal.

The pillar at Lumbini commemorates Ashoka's pilgrimage to the birthplace of Buddha. It is six metres high, although half of it is underground, and it is inscribed with the following:

King Ashoka, the beloved of Gods, in the 20th year of the coronation, made a royal visit. A stone railing and a stone pillar were erected in honour of Buddha who was born here. Because Buddha was born here the village of Lumbini was freed from paying tax.

Maya Devi Temple

Until recently the Maya Devi Temple, parts of which were believed to be over 2000 years old, stood on the spot where the Buddha is though to have been born. A huge pipal tree, which was gradually tearing the temple apart, was believed by some to have been the tree that Maya Devi held while giving birth to Siddhartha.

In 1993 the tree was ripped out and the temple demolished to make archaeological excavations possible. At the time of writing these were still going on and the site was surrounded by an ugly yellow plastic screen. In 1995 archaeologists claim to have found a commemorative stone atop a platform of seven layers of bricks five metres below the old temple floor and dating from the era of Ashoka. Buddhist literature says Ashoka placed a stone on top of bricks at the birthplace of Prince Siddhartha, who was later called Lord Buddha. Ancient writings say Buddha was born while his mother Maya Devi, the queen of nearby Kapilvastu kingdom, was travelling towards her parents' home in Rangram, located in Nepal's Nawalparasi district. Passing through Lumbini, she went into labour, bathed in a sacred pond and walked 25 paces to deliver the child. The recently discovered stone is said to be the correct distance from the nearby pool.

When the temple was demolished the revered centrepiece of the temple, a stone carving showing the birth of Buddha, was moved to an ugly brick structure close by which looks like a public toilet block. Possibly dating from the Malla dynasty (about 14th century CE) the sculpture was the centre of a fertility rite, and it has almost been reduced to formlessness by the wear of constant puja. One can still make out Maya Devi, with her right hand raised to hold the pipal tree branch, as she gives birth. There is also a modern marble interpretation, along with a number of small sculptures left by devotees.

A major Hindu festival is held on the full moon of the Nepali month of Baisakh (April-May), when thousands of local Hindus come to worship Maya Devi as Rupa Devi, the mother goddess of Lumbini, and to celebrate Buddha as the ninth incarnation of Vishnu. The Buddhist celebration of Buddha's birthday, or Buddha Jayanti, is celebrated around the same time, but is lower key. During winter, when it's not too hot, Buddhist pilgrims from the Kathmandu Valley often come to worship on Purnima (the night of the full moon) and Astemi (the eighth night after the full moon).

Other Attractions

The square pool beside the temple is believed to be the spot where Maya Devi bathed before giving birth to Buddha; needless to say, it has been heavily restored. The foundations for a number of stupas and viharas dating from the 2nd century BCE to the 9th century CE lie in the vicinity.

There are also two modern temples although, unfortunately, neither are particularly interesting or well maintained – both are slated for demolition under the Lumbini Development Plan. One was built by the Nepali government in 1956, and the other was built in traditional Tibetan style in 1968.

The two large mounds on either side of the site are not impressive stupas, as you might suspect, but simply the spoils from modern archaeological digs.

Places to Stay & Eat

Most people simply make a day trip from Bhairawa, but there are a couple of places to stay and eat.

The *Lumbini Village Lodge* is a simple place in Lumbini Mehalbar, the small market

THE TERAI

town about one km east of the main site. The village is an undistinguished little place, but there is a lively market on Mondays, and the rest of the time it is simply a peaceful corner of the Terai. For what you get the prices are a bit steep; gloomy cell-like singles/doubles are Rs 150/250. There is reasonable food at around Rs 30 for dal bhat.

There's very, *very* basic accommodation in the *dharamsala* (pilgrims' rest house) between the two temples at the main site. Literally, all you get is a roof over your head and a bed (no mattress), and the toilets are vile. If you've got food and camping equipment and you do stay, pay a donation.

The best bet is the *Sri Lanka Pilgrims Rest House*, about three km north of the site, beyond the sacred flame and just off the dirt road to Tilaurakot. This clean and modern place has spacious dorms with beds at $5, but you can usually have a room to yourself. It would be handy to have a bicycle if you want to travel back and forth to the site.

At the top of the scale is the *Lumbini Hokke Hotel* (☎ 071-20236), close to the Sri Lanka Pilgrims Rest House. It has been built with Japanese pilgrims in mind, and most of the rooms have been furnished in traditional Japanese style with tatami floors, paper partitions and Japanese furniture. There are also a number of European-style rooms. All rooms are air-conditioned, and all have attached bathrooms. Considering the luxury, prices are not unreasonable, with singles/doubles at $84/120. Meals are expensive – lunch is $15 for non-guests. Mountain bikes are available for guests to use, but most people visit with their own transport, or as part of a tour.

Just by the main car park is the new *Lumbini Garden Restaurant*, which, judging by its appearance, is not part of the Lumbini Development Plan – it's a modern red-brick eyesore. The prices are relatively high, but it's the only decent place to eat and the food is OK.

Getting There & Away

There are regular minibuses that make the 22 km journey from Bhairawa to Lumbini for Rs 12, but they are agonisingly slow (1½ hours) and drop you off at Lumbini Mehal-bar on the main road a km from the main site. The roof is the place to be. The last bus back passes the turn-off at about 5 pm (check this time). They leave Bhairawa near the main intersection, across the road from the Hotel Yeti.

If you are in a group or have the funds it would be immensely preferable to hire an auto-rickshaw (from Rs 150 to Rs 250) or a taxi-jeep (from Rs 300 to Rs 500). These prices include two hours waiting time, which should be sufficient for most people.

The best method of transport for budget travellers would be bicycle, but there are no formal rental places in Bhairawa. If you ask around (start at your hotel, then try bicycle repair shops), you might turn something up.

TAULIHAWA & TILAURAKOT

Tilaurakot is nothing more than a tiny hamlet three km north of Taulihawa, which is a bustling Terai centre. Tilaurakot was once, however, the capital of the republic of Kapilavastu, where Buddha spent the first 29 years of his life.

Taulihawa is a vibrant town with the usual multicultural mix of peoples found in Terai cities. There is a temple complex known as **Tauleshwar**, now used by Shaivites, in the centre of town.

Although even less visited than Lumbini, Tilaurakot is in many ways the more atmospheric of the two spots. There is a small group of farming households outside the ruins of the city walls, which along with their moat, can be clearly discerned. The whole complex is shaded by large trees and has the peaceful atmosphere of a park.

The scattered foundations that can be seen within the walls give only the most minimal indication that there was once a palace, but archaeologists have found 13 successive layers of human habitation, dating back to the 8th century BCE. Today the only sign of life is a small run-down shrine to a Hindu goddess, Somaya Mai.

The scene outside the walls could be unchanged from that which Siddhartha him-

THE TERAI

self might have seen. Timeless patterns of subsistence farming unfold along the banks of the Banganga River, and on the north side of the river there is an expanse of untouched sal forest. It is not hard to imagine Siddhartha walking out through the imposing gateway of the palace and as he wandered, seeing an old man, a sick man, a corpse and a hermit...

About 400m from the ruins, a small museum (closed on Tuesday and Saturday) displays some of the artefacts that were found at the site – including coins and pottery.

Places to Stay & Eat

There are plenty of food stalls in Taulihawa. *Lumbini Hotel*, on the road to Tilaurakot, is very basic but acceptably clean, and singles/doubles cost Rs 50/80. There are no facilities at Tilaurakot.

Getting There & Away

A reasonable (though badly corrugated) dirt road links Taulihawa with Lumbini, 27 km to the east. The road passes the Lumbini Hokke Hotel, and a number of Muslim villages. Slow and crowded local buses link Taulihawa with Bhairawa, but once again a bicycle is the best method of transport.

Tilaurakot is three km north of Taulihawa. At the end of the bitumen the museum is on the left and the ruins are 400m away down a dirt track on the right. In winter it is possible to cross a ford over the Banganga River, and to continue 14 km due north along a dirt road through the Sagar Forest, finally joining the Mahendra Highway about 35 km west of Butwal and 80 km east of Lumihi (also spelt Lamahi).

TANSEN (PALPA)

Tansen is just off the Siddhartha Highway, between Pokhara and Sunauli/Bhairawa. Historically, it has enjoyed a strategic position on the trade and pilgrim route between the hills and the plains.

Prior to the unification of Nepal under the Shahs, Tansen was the capital of the Palpa kingdom, which was ruled by the Sen dynasty. Prithvi Narayan Shah, the Gorkha king who founded modern Nepal, was the product of an arranged marriage between the Shah and Sen families.

For many years Palpa fought in alliance with Gorkha, and together the two states defeated the independent kingdoms of western Nepal. Finally in 1806, the last king of Palpa, Prithivipal Sen, was lured to Kathmandu and beheaded. Palpa was annexed, but Tansen remained the administrative centre for the region. A number of its subsequent governors were high-ranking members of the ruling Shah and, later, Rana families who were exiled from Kathmandu for plotting against the king of the day.

Tansen is still the administrative centre for a large region, but it sees few visitors, and as it is increasingly sidelined by the development on the Terai and at Pokhara, it is gently falling apart.

The town sprawls over a steep ridge and quite a few of the main streets are too steep for cars, which helps to keep some of the less pleasant aspects of the 20th century at bay. In the older sections of the town, attractive Newari buildings line cobbled streets that are reminiscent of parts of Kathmandu.

Most of the surrounding countryside is dominated by Magars, but there are also Bahuns and Chhetris. Newars form the majority in Tansen itself. They migrated from the Kathmandu Valley to take advantage of the new opportunities for trade between the hills and India that opened up in the 19th century – traditional crafts and agricultural surpluses were traded for the products of the British industrial revolution (especially cotton fabrics) that were flooding into India from Britain. Tansen is still famous for metalware, and for *dhaka*, the woven material that is made into *topis* (Nepali hats).

There are great views over the bowl-shaped **Madi Valley** from the town itself and a spectacular view of the Himalaya from the nearby hill, Srinagar Danda. There are some interesting walks in the surrounding countryside, including a two hour trek to the banks of the Kali Gandaki River and the vast, deserted Ranighat Palace. Tansen is a pleasant place to break the journey from Pokhara (110 km, five hours!) to Bhairawa (55 km, two hours).

GREG ELMS

RICHARD EVERIST

TONY WHEELER

THE TERAI
Top: Precarious punt, Royal Chitwan National Park
Centre: Village tank choked with vegetation, Sapt Kosi flood plain
Bottom: Fording a stream, elephant-style, Royal Chitwan National Park

HUGH FINLAY

RICHARD I'ANSON

RICHARD EVERIST

ROYAL CHITWAN NATIONAL PARK, THE TERAI

Top: Saddled up (howdahed up?) and ready for an encounter with a tiger. You wish!
Bottom Left: Elephants' refreshment stop
Bottom Right: Sunset on the Narayani River

Amar Narayan Temple

The Amar Narayan is a classic three tiered pagoda-style temple, considered to be one of the most beautiful outside the Kathmandu Valley. There is some fine woodwork, with erotic figures on the roof struts, and beautifully carved doors. The temple was built in 1806 CE by Amar Singh Thapa, the general who annexed Tansen to Nepal. Sadhus often stay in the rest houses around the temple on their way to Muktinath, north-west of Pokhara on the popular Annapurna Circuit. There's a large bat colony in the surrounding trees, and several tanks where local women do their washing.

Tansen Durbar

The palace of the provincial governor was built in the heavy-handed Rana style in 1927 and is now home to the local bureaucrats. The imposing, though dilapidated, entrance gate on the eastern side of the compound is called Baggi Dhoka, or Mul Dhoka. It is meant to be the biggest and tallest gate in Nepal, and its dimensions allowed the governor to make a suitably impressive entrance on an elephant.

A public square called Sitalpati lies just outside the gate; it's named after the building in the centre, which was, before renovation, an unusual octagonal shape.

Bhagwati Temple

The Bhagwati Temple, near the durbar, is a rather garish construction that was unsympathetically renovated after an earthquake in 1935, and again in 1974. It was built originally in 1815 to commemorate the Nepali victory over the British at Butwal. There are some smaller temples in the vicinity, dedicated to Shiva, Ganesh and Saraswati.

Places to Stay

There are some hotels around the bus station with singles/doubles for around Rs 60/80, but they're all pretty awful.

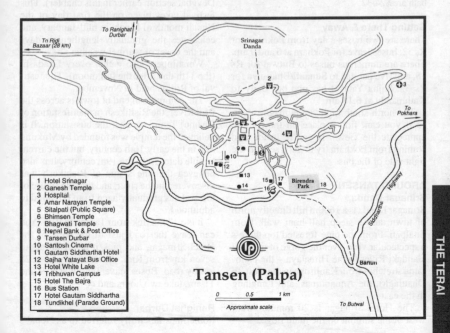

1 Hotel Srinagar
2 Ganesh Temple
3 Hospital
4 Amar Narayan Temple
5 Sitalpati (Public Square)
6 Bhimsen Temple
7 Bhagwati Temple
8 Nepal Bank & Post Office
9 Tansen Durbar
10 Santosh Cinema
11 Gautam Siddhartha Hotel
12 Sajha Yatayat Bus Office
13 Hotel White Lake
14 Tribhuvan Campus
15 Hotel The Bajra
16 Bus Station
17 Hotel Gautam Siddhartha
18 Tundikhel (Parade Ground)

To Ranighat Durbar
Tn Ridi Bazaar (28 km)
Srinagar Danda
To Pokhara
Birendra Park
Siddharthe Highway
Bartun
To Butwal

Tansen (Palpa)

0   0.5   1 km
Approximate scale

Just a short walk up the hill there's a much better option. The *Hotel The Bajra* (☎ 075-20443) is relatively new and still quite clean – so far. Rooms with common bath are Rs 50/100, or with attached bath and hot water they're Rs 150/250.

Further up the hill still are a couple more choices. The *Hotel White Lake* (☎ 075-20503) has some excellent views away to the south, and the rooms are well appointed and good value at Rs 300/500.

Close by is the much cheaper *Hotel Gautam Siddartha* (075-20280), which is basic, but clean, decent and quiet. Rooms with twin beds are Rs 120.

The most luxurious option is about two km away on the ridge above town. The *Hotel Srinagar* (☎ 075-20045; fax 20467) is rather isolated, but it's comfortable and the views are sensational. It would be worth ringing in advance because the hotel deals mainly with groups and isn't all that used to people arriving unannounced. Singles/doubles with private bath are $24/32.

Getting There & Away
There are two buses a day from Pokhara for Rs 52; buses leave for Pokhara at 6 and 9 am. There are numerous buses to Butwal for Rs 18, and five per day to Sunauli/Bhairawa for Rs 32. Sajha Yatayat has one bus daily to Kathmandu at 6.15 am.

The north-south highway is magnificent, so if you can, find a place on the roof to appreciate the views. If you're inside and coming from Pokhara try to get a seat on the right side of the bus.

AROUND TANSEN
Srinagar Danda
Srinagar Danda is a 1600m hill directly north of town, and a steep half-hour walk from Sitalpati. From the pine-forested top there's a spectacular view over the gorge of the Kali Gandaki River to the Himalaya – the panorama stretches from Kanjiroba in the west, to Dhaulagiri, the Annapurnas, and Langtang in the east.

The Hotel Srinagar is 20 minutes walk west of the summit on the main ridge.

Ridi Bazaar
Ridi is a holy town, mainly populated by Newars, at the confluence of the Kali Gandaki and Ridi rivers. The confluence of tributaries to the Ganges is always regarded as holy, and Ridi has been further sanctified by the presence of *saligrams*, black ammonite fossils that have a spiral shape and are regarded as emblems of Vishnu. Saligrams are found in a number of places along the Kali Gandaki, most notably north of Jomsom around Muktinath.

Although Ridi's religious popularity has declined, cremations are still relatively frequent, and pilgrims come for ritual bathing, marriage ceremonies and other rites and rituals. Pilgrims believe that if they fast and worship for three days, and then take a ritual bath in the Kali Gandaki, all their sins will be forgiven.

The most important festival is Magh Sankranti, when many pilgrims come here to immerse themselves in the river (see the Devghat section earlier in this chapter). This festival takes place on the first day of the Nepali month of Magh, in mid-January, and celebrates the gradually lengthening days and the onset of warmer weather.

Worshippers also gather every Ekadashi (the 11th day after the full moon). The festival of Ridi is held in November.

The commercial end of town is across the Ridi River; the Rishikesh (a manifestation of Vishnu) Temple is near the bus station. It is believed the temple was founded by Mukund Sen in the early 16th century, but the current temple dates from the 19th century. It is also believed that the statue of Rishikesh was discovered in the river, and that the figure of the god has gradually aged from boyhood to adulthood.

It is a 13 km trek from Tansen to Ridi. You can leave the road just to the west of the Hotel Srinagar, and pick it up again about seven km from Ridi. Alternatively, it is 28 km by road. Buses leave Tansen at 6, 9 and 11 am, take two hours and cost Rs 39.

Ranighat Durbar
Sometimes fancifully referred to as Nepal's

Taj Mahal, Ranighat Durbar was built by Khadga Shamsher Rana in 1896. Khadga was exiled to Tansen and made governor for plotting to become prime minister. While he was in exile, he consoled himself by building a spectacular palace, supposedly in memory of his wife, Tej Kumari.

The palace is now a huge, white baroque ruin dramatically perched on a rocky crag above the Kali Gandaki River. It was used for 25 years as a luxurious dharamsala by aristocrats who ostensibly came to bathe in the Kali Gandaki, and no doubt to party and plot with Khadga. Khadga was an ambitious man and in 1921 he made another abortive attempt to seize power. As a result he was exiled further away – this time in India. On his departure the building was stripped of its valuable furnishings, and has been gradually collapsing ever since.

The trail to Ranighat begins a short distance to the east of the Hotel Srinagar, at the edge of the pine forest. It's an attractive seven km hike down to the river and takes about two hours each way.

NEPALGANJ

The most important town in western Nepal, Nepalganj at times feels more Indian than Nepali. It's a border town that owes as much to trade (read smuggling) as it does to its position as a major administrative centre. It has more of an air of permanence than some other border towns and planners have had the good sense to run the highway to the west of the main town. Despite that it's a distinctly unattractive place, with few redeeming features.

Nepalganj is a densely crowded city, and every possible ethnic group in Nepal is represented. There is an unusually large Muslim community, many of whom settled here to escape the violence of the 1857 Indian Mutiny. The Muslim men are distinctive, with their long beards and skull caps, as are the women, some of whom dress in black and are completely veiled. The colourful throngs in the streets, however, include Shaivite sadhus, Tharu women (with tight bodices, bare midriffs and bright skirts), turbanned

Sikhs, Bajis (Abadhi speakers from India), Bahuns, Chhetris, Newars, Magars, Gurungs, Thakuris and even Tibetans (who look a bit hot in their traditional gear).

A steady trickle of travellers come through Nepalganj on their way to Royal Bardia National Park (see later in this chapter), or to Jumla. It can also be a useful back-door entry into Nepal from central Uttar Pradesh; Lucknow is about four hours away.

Orientation & Information

The airport is six km north of Birendra Chowk (with the statue), east of the main

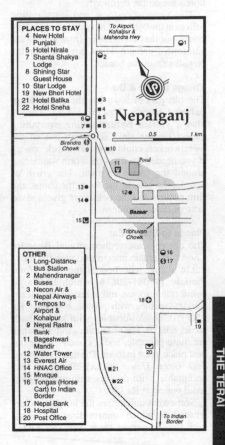

PLACES TO STAY
4 New Hotel Punjabi
5 Hotel Nirala
7 Shanta Shakya Lodge
8 Shining Star Guest House
10 Star Lodge
19 New Bhori Hotel
21 Hotel Batika
22 Hotel Sneha

Nepalganj

Birendra Chowk

OTHER
1 Long-Distance Bus Station
2 Mahendranagar Buses
3 Necon Air & Nepal Airways
6 Tempos to Airport & Kohalpur
9 Nepal Rastra Bank
11 Bageshwari Mandir
12 Water Tower
13 Everest Air
14 HNAC Office
15 Mosque
16 Tongas (Horse Cart) to Indian Border
17 Nepal Bank
18 Hospital
20 Post Office

THE TERAI

road. The long-distance bus station is also north of town. One km north of Birendra Chowk there's an accumulation of local buses (including buses for Mahendranagar) around a T-intersection. Turn right and continue for another km and you come to the long-distance bus station (for Kathmandu and points east). Book your return ticket before you go into town to save yourself a trip.

The town is about six km north of the border. The old, vaguely interesting part of town lies to the east of the main road around Tribhuvan Chowk, although virtually all the hotels are on the highway.

The various customs and immigration offices at the border all have different closing hours, but they are all open from 8 to 11 am and from 1 to 5 pm. There is no bank on the Nepali side of the border.

Things to See & Do
The old part of town has the garish **Bageshwari Mandir**, honouring Kali. There's also a vibrant **bazaar** selling everything except kitchen sinks (although one of the metalworkers could probably knock one up if you needed it). It is well worth wandering around the centre of town. The crush of people, the smells, the food, the shops, the film posters and the rickshaws give a vivid taste of the subcontinent.

Places to Stay & Eat
The cheapies are centred around Birendra Chowk, the main intersection with the inevitable statue. The best is the *New Hotel Punjabi* (☎ 081-20818) which has large comfortable rooms and is acceptably clean. Singles/doubles with private bath cost Rs 250/350; singles/doubles with shared bath are Rs 80/120. The restaurant's Indian dishes are quite passable, and it's undoubtedly the best place to eat in town. The nearby *Shining Star Guest House* (☎ 081-20664) is also acceptable, with doubles with private bath (cold water) at Rs 150.

Somewhat quieter are the hotels on Garwhari Tole, which connect Birendra Chowk with the old part of town. The *Star Lodge*

(☎ 081-22257) has singles/doubles at Rs 75/110 with common bath, and with attached bath at Rs 110/170.

Moving up the scale a bit is the *New Bheri Hotel* (☎ 081-20213), which offers the best value in town. The hotel is near the hospital in a quiet part of town, and has a pleasant garden. Room prices are $8/10 with attached bath and $16/20 with air-con, but with discounts you may have to pay only half that. It's a good place.

There are two reasonable top-end hotels, both south of town on the way to the Indian border on the highway. They're set back from the road so noise and parking aren't problems.

The *Hotel Sneha* (☎ 081-20119) has a range of large, clean rooms, and helpful staff. A new wing of high-standard rooms has been built around a courtyard behind the original hotel. Standard singles/doubles are $18/24, and deluxe rooms with air-con are $30/36, plus 12% tax. There's a restaurant here, although the food is pretty uninspiring.

Virtually next door, the *Hotel Batika* (☎ 081-21360) is owned by Nepal Airways and is used primarily to accommodate their air crews. There are, however, a number of comfortable rooms available for the public, but these are outrageously overpriced at $45/50. Forget it.

Getting There & Away
Air This is Royal Nepal Airlines' western headquarters (☎ 081-20239) and there's a modern airport, now somewhat run-down. Unfortunately, this doesn't mean that you are any more certain to arrive or depart on the promised hour or day than you are anywhere else in Nepal. There are RNAC flights to Jumla (daily, $44) and Kathmandu (daily, $99). Necon Air (☎ 081-20307) flies to Kathmandu (five times weekly, $99) and Mahendranagar (daily, $60). Nepal Airways (☎ 081-20646) has flights three times a week to both Kathmandu ($99) and Pokhara ($67).

Bus As usual, the Sajha Yatayat buses are the best option. There are two departures daily for Kathmandu; one leaves early morning, another early evening. They take about 16 hours and cost Rs 178. There are only night buses to Pokhara; they leave from 4.15 to 5.30 pm and cost Rs 190. You can get to Narayanghat for Rs 128 with both day and night departures.

Buses for Mahendranagar leave at 7 am (nine to 12 hours, Rs 160). It's advisable to book at least one day in advance, although you can be lucky.

Sajha Yatayat buses leave the Kathmandu Bus Terminal at 6 am and 4 pm.

Getting Around
There are shared tempos from Birendra Chowk to the airport for Rs 5, or you can take one 'reserve' for Rs 50. A cycle-rickshaw costs around Rs 30 but takes up to half an hour. To the Indian border by cycle-rickshaw also costs around Rs 30.

ROYAL BARDIA NATIONAL PARK
The Royal Bardia National Park is the largest untouched wilderness area in the Terai. It's bordered to the north by the crest of the Chure Hills and to the west by the large Geruwa River, a branch of the mighty Karnali, one of the major tributaries of the Ganges.

You stand a better chance of seeing a tiger here than anywhere else in Nepal (including Chitwan). It's a stunning place that seems a very long way from the 20th century – watching the sun rise over the forest from the back of an elephant is like having a box seat at the dawn of time.

Most of the 968 sq km park is covered with open sal forest, with the balance a mixture of grassland, savannah and riverine forest. The grassed areas (*phanta*) are excellent for game-viewing. Most people will visit in the hope of seeing a Royal Bengal tiger, but there are also leopards, jungle cats, mongoose, sloth bears, blue cow (nilgai), langur and rhesus monkeys, and sambar, spotted hog and barking deer. The Asian one-horned rhinoceros was reintroduced from Chitwan in 1986, and though breeding successfully the numbers are still small. There are at least two wild male elephants, and one is thought to be the largest in Asia.

The Geruwa River rushes through a gap in the hills at Chisopani, grey with silt and snow-melt. It's home to the famous mahseer game fish, gharial and mugger crocodiles, and the strange Gangetic dolphin.

More than 30 different mammals and 250 species of birds have been recorded in the park. Birds include numerous species of heron, stork, geese, duck and parakeet as well as endangered birds like the Bengal florican and sarus crane.

In some ways Bardia is like Chitwan; the major difference is the degree of isolation and the limited number of visitors. The main disadvantage of Bardia is that it takes a day of travelling to get to or from Kathmandu, although it also takes a minimum of five hours to get to Chitwan. This means you need a minimum of four days: day one – Kathmandu to Bardia; days two and three – exploring the park, the river and the surrounding villages; day four – Bardia to Kathmandu.

Orientation & Information
The park headquarters are at Thakurdwara, about 20 km south-west along a bumpy dirt road from Anbassa on the Mahendra Highway. Anbassa is about half a km from the Motipur checkpoint, where the highway actually enters the park, and this in turn is eight km from Chisopani. Virtually all tourist activity is centred around the western spur of the park which takes in the forest and grasslands around the Geruwa River; the large eastern portion of the park is untouched.

Entry is the usual Rs 650, and you can get a fishing permit for Rs 300 per rod. The national park also offers elephants at Rs 650 per person per hour from the park headquarters at Thakurdwara. The only trouble here is that you need at least 30 minutes by elephant to reach the 'core' area of the park for the best game viewing. It's also possible to enter the park on foot, although you need to take an experienced guide, something your lodge can arrange.

Also at the park HQ is a small holding area for marsh muggers and gharial which have been bred in captivity and are due for release into the river.

Places to Stay

In recent years a few basic Chitwan-style 'jungle cottages' have sprung up around Thakurdwara. There's no electricity and accommodation is very basic, but this is the perfect spot to hole up for a few days and allow yourself to be lulled by the relaxing pace and atmosphere of Terai village life.

One of the best places is *Forest Hideaway Cottages* (☎ 01-417685 in Kathmandu), a short walk along the northern park boundary from the park HQ and run by a Scottish-Nepali couple. It's a comfortable little place with cottages at Rs 300/350 with breakfast. Basic but perfectly adequate meals are available.

Right opposite the park entrance are the *Bardia Jungle Cottages* (☎ 084-29562), with cottages at Rs 300, or Rs 400 with bath. Meals are also available here.

There are a couple of even more basic places, including the *Hotel Elephant Camp* and the *Bardia Wildlife Paradise*.

Somewhat more sophisticated is *Rhino Express*, three km from Thakurdwara.

At the top of the range is the *Tiger Tops Karnali Lodge*, run by Tiger Mountain (☎ 01-420322; fax 414075), PO Box 242, Durbar Marg, Kathmandu, the same company that runs the Tiger Tops Lodge in Chitwan. The lodge is built right on the park boundary and is built out of local materials in Tharu village style – simply outstanding. The staff is knowledgeable and helpful, without being intrusive. It's a place where you can abdicate all responsibility, relax and just enjoy.

It also has the only accommodation inside the park, the *Karnali Tented Camp*, which has a superb location overlooking the Geruwa River, not far from Chisopani in the north-west corner of the park. A camp it might be, rough it is not. The beds are comfortable, the food is good and the water is hot. Again activities revolve around the elephants, but another highlight is a float down the river – a bird-watcher's delight.

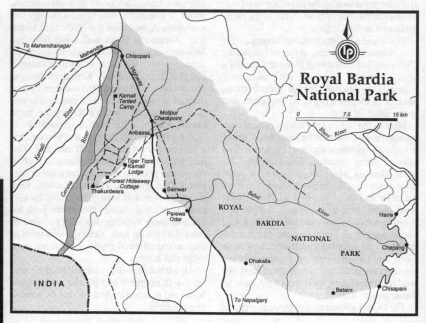

Royal Bardia National Park

Although they aren't cheap, at $165 a night including all meals and activities (elephant rides, guided walks), they do offer an extraordinary experience. Those that have been to both Chitwan and Karnali almost unanimously vote Karnali superior. The lodge and camp both close from the middle of May to the end of September during the monsoon.

Getting There & Away

The main highway is in excellent condition and the drive from Nepalganj takes less than 2½ hours, although local buses manage to take much longer. It's an interesting drive past thriving villages. For Thakurdwara, there are direct buses from Nepalganj at 11 am and noon, taking three to four hours and costing Rs 44. Departures from Thakurdwara are at 9 and 11 am.

If you are staying at the Tiger Tops Karnali Lodge or Tented Camp, they can arrange jeep transfers from Nepalganj for $10.

ROYAL SUKLA PHANTA WILDLIFE RESERVE

Sukla Phanta is smaller and more isolated than Bardia, yet similar in some respects. In the extreme south-west of the country, it covers 355 sq km of riverine flood plain, which includes open grass plains (phanta), forest (primarily sal), a lake and the Bahini River.

It is home to tigers, leopards, various species of deer (including an important colony of swamp deer), gharial and mugger crocodiles, otters and a wide variety of bird life.

The large swamp deer are found in large herds – often of as many as 1000 animals – and it's not unusual to see three or more herds on even a short game drive in the southern part of the park in the *sukla phanta*, literally white grass plains, found in this area. Although the deer are found in large numbers, Indian poachers are a real problem, and although army guards are stationed in this part of the park, they have to patrol by bicycle, which limits their capacity to be effective.

This is probably one of the least visited reserves in Nepal, but if you are travelling between Nepal and India it is not too difficult to make a diversion, especially if you can afford to stay at the tented camp.

Information

The ranger's office is three km past the airport (accessible by rickshaw from Mahendranagar). Entry is Rs 650, and it is possible to organise elephant rides for Rs 650.

Places to Stay

Silent Safari (☎ 099-21230; fax 22220, PO Box 1, Mahendranagar) is currently the only company operating in the park. It is run by an ex-army colonel, the very personable Hikmat Bisht, a keen naturalist who has spent many years in and around the park and now divides his time between the camp (even when there are no guests) and his house in Mahendranagar. Visitors who come here are generally keen birders who don't mind roughing it a bit. Accommodation is in comfortable safari tents, and the price ($150 per person) includes meals, game drives and walks, and visits to local Tharu villages can also be arranged. The camp is open from October to June, and advance bookings are essential.

Getting There & Away

Silent Safari picks guests up from the airport at Mahendranagar or Dhangadhi ($10).

MAHENDRANAGAR

Mahendranagar is an uninspired village that owes its existence to the nearby border crossing. There's absolutely nothing to see, and the locals are quite unused to dealing with tourists. A few words of Nepali are very useful. The surrounding countryside is inhabited by traditional Tharu communities, although here, as elsewhere, there is an increasing number of hill people.

Orientation

The town is laid out to the south of the main highway with the bus park actually on the highway, about a 10 minute walk from the centre of the village. The main landmark is the King Mahendra Square with streets one to five leading off from one side.

Mahendranagar is about five km from the Mahakali River, which forms the Nepal-Indian border. The border is open 24 hours for pedestrians, but for vehicles the barrage across the river on the Indian side is only open from 7 to 8 am, noon to 2 pm and again from 4 to 6 pm. It's a little-used border and the crossing is straightforward and quite fast.

Places to Stay & Eat

There are a few cheap hotels on the main street. The *Hotel New Anand* (☎ 099-21693) is the best of them; it's friendly and has double rooms for Rs 250 with attached bath and hot water delivered by the bucket. Food is also available.

Just around the corner from the New Anand is the cheaper *Green Lodge* (☎ 099-21950). Rooms here are a bit rough, but would do in a pinch, and cost Rs 125 for a double with attached bath.

Mahendranagar's Hilton is the *Hotel Sweet Dream* (☎ 099-22313), on the highway about a five minute walk east of the bus station. The rooms in this recently built hotel are large and have carpets. The cost is Rs 350 for a double with attached bath, and this is pretty good value. There's also a restaurant here.

Getting There & Away

Air There is an RNAC (☎ 099-21196) flight every Tuesday from Kathmandu ($160), via Dhangadhi, and this returns to Nepalganj ($77). Necon Air (☎ 099-21000) operates daily flights to Nepalganj ($60), or you can fly all the way to Kathmandu ($150).

Bus The road from the border to Nepalganj is a mess. The first 40 km, to Ataria, where there is a turn-off to Dhangadhi, is diabolical, with an old single lane of bitumen now so pot-holed that it's worse than no bitumen at all. From Ataria to Chisopani the road is good bitumen, although there are still quite a number of creeks which have to be forded.

Until the bridges are completed (don't hold your breath, although the Indians may be starting work on these soon), the road is a slow, dry-weather-only proposition. The last few km to Chisopani along the banks of the Karnali River are the worst on the entire highway.

There is a daily direct bus from Kathmandu to Mahendranagar at 12.30 pm. The trip takes a gruelling 18 hours and costs Rs 290. From Mahendranagar the daily departure is at 2 pm. There are also buses from Mahendranagar to Dhangadhi and Nepalganj.

To/From India Buses leave Mahendranagar roughly every half hour for the border. It's a one km walk (or rickshaw ride) between the Nepali and Indian posts, and then a further km to the Indian town of Banbassa.

Banbassa is on the Indian metre-gauge rail system, and there are also buses to Almora and Delhi. There are at least three direct buses a day to Delhi (noon, 2.30 and 5 pm); they take around 11 hours and cost Indian Rs 65.

DHANGADHI

Dhangadhi is rarely visited by westerners, but it is possible to cross the border here and to hook up with the Indian metre-gauge railway for places like Lucknow. The locals are friendly, but there's really nothing to see. The border crossing here is quite busy, as it is a major entry point for goods coming by truck.

Places to Stay

There are a few basic places to stay; the *Hotel Taruan* has been recommended, but don't expect too much.

Getting There & Away

RNAC (☎ 091-21205) has flights to Nepalganj (four weekly), Mahendranagar (weekly) and Kathmandu (twice weekly).

There are daily bus connections with Nepalganj and Kathmandu.

The Himalaya & Mountaineering

The word Himalaya is Sanskrit for 'abode of snows' and Nepal's stretch of the Himalaya includes eight peaks over 8000m, including the highest of them all, mighty Mt Everest (8848m). Known to the Tibetans as Chomolongma and to the Nepalis as Sagarmatha, the world's highest place was the overpowering attraction which drew in Nepal's first modern tourists – the mountaineers.

During the 1950s and 60s most of the important Nepali peaks were conquered, but just because it is no longer possible to be the first to set foot on top has certainly not diminished the attraction of Himalayan mountaineering. Climbing these giants today is often an adventurous sporting activity, whereas 30 years ago it required huge and well sponsored expeditions.

There are 14 peaks over 8000m in the world, and of the 10 highest no less than eight are in Nepal, although some of the peaks actually straddle borders – Everest is in Nepal and China for example, Kanchenjunga (8598m) is in Nepal and India. The heights of the 14 highest peaks, followed by the highest peaks in South America, North America, Africa, Russia, Antarctica, Europe, Australia and the United Kingdom can be seen in the Mountain Heights diagram.

Nepal's magnificent mountains can be enjoyed in three distinctly different fashions. The easiest way is to simply look at them. This can be done by flying past them – either on regular flights or the daily tourist-season mountain flights. Or you can admire them from the various popular mountain viewpoints such as Nagarkot or Dhulikhel near Kathmandu or Sarangkot above Pokhara. Getting to these viewpoints is covered in the appropriate chapters.

If simply looking at the mountains isn't enough you can get right in amongst them by trekking. Trekking is not mountain climbing: apart from high passes on certain treks and the approach to the Everest Base Camp you are unlikely to go above 3500m. Trekking, however, does provide breathtaking views. Full details on trekking are given in the Trekking chapter.

Finally, there is real mountain climbing and while getting to the top of an 8000m peak is strictly for the professionals, there are plenty of 'trekking peaks' which small-scale amateur expeditions can readily attempt. This is not to say that mountaineering in Nepal can be easy – climbing mountains this high always involves an element of risk – but getting to the top of a worthwhile Himalayan peak doesn't necessarily require millionaire status or big commercial backers.

Mountain Flights

Every morning during the clear dry-season months, Royal Nepal Airlines' and Everest Air's mountain flights offer panoramic dawn views of the Himalaya. Passengers on the Everest Air flight are all guaranteed a window seat, and the hour-long flight from Kathmandu costs $99. If the weather is clear, the views are stunning. ■

MOUNTAINEERING

Mountaineering became a fashionable pursuit in Europe during the second half of the 1800s and, having knocked off the great Alpine peaks, the much greater heights of the Himalaya were an obvious new challenge. An English gentleman named WW Graham made a mountaineering visit to Nepal in 1883 and reached the top of a 6000m peak. He was followed by another Englishman, Tom Longstaff, who climbed 7215m Trisuli in 1907. For the next 20 years this remained the highest summit reached anywhere in the world. An Italian attempt on K2 in Pakistan two years later was the first of the huge Himalayan expeditions with hundreds of porters.

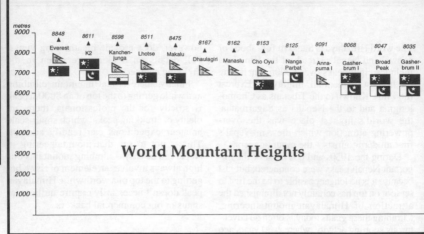

World Mountain Heights

First Attempts on Everest

During the 1920s and 30s, reaching the top of Mt Everest came to be seen as the major goal, but apart from the difficulties inherent in reaching such heights there were also political constraints. Nepal continued to be a totally secluded country and attempts on Everest were all made from the Tibetan side of the range.

British assaults were made in 1921, 1922 and 1924. The 1922 expedition used oxygen to reach 8326m, while the 1924 expedition fell just 300m short of the top, reaching 8572m without the use of oxygen. Apart from numerous climbers and support staff, the 1924 expedition utilised no less than 350 porters; such huge expeditions set a pattern which was to continue until recent years.

One of the enduring mysteries of mountaineering history has its origins in 1925 when the British climbers Mallory and Irvine disappeared within sight of the top. Did they reach it? We will never know. However, Mallory did leave behind the famous explanation of why mountaineers do what they do – he said he was climbing Everest 'because it's there'. Further expeditions followed through the 20s and 30s but no real progress

was made, although the 8000m level was breached on a number of occasions. Maurice Wilson added his name to the Everest legends, and the Everest death roll, when he died during a bizarre solo attempt on the mountain in 1934.

Post WWII Attempts

The west's new-found affluence after its recovery from WWII, together with more modern equipment, vastly improved oxygen apparatus, new mountaineering skills and the reopening of Nepal, led to a golden age of Himalayan mountaineering.

There hadn't been any Himalayan mountaineering in the 1940s, and through the 30s only two significant summits had been reached – Kamet at 7761m in 1931 and Nanda Devi at 7822m in 1936. Interestingly, the Kamet summit group included HW Tilman and the Nanda Devi group included Eric Shipton, whose descriptions of their trekking and mountaineering experiences helped to spark the current interest in trekking. Shipton was said to have planned his lightweight expeditions on the back of an envelope.

The prewar failures were abruptly reversed

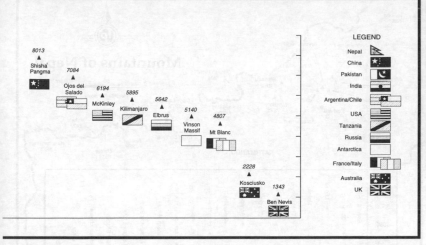

LEGEND

Nepal	
China	
Pakistan	
India	
Argentina/Chile	
USA	
Tanzania	
Russia	
Antarctica	
France/Italy	
Australia	
UK	

in the 50s, beginning with Maurice Herzog's valiant French expedition on Annapurna in 1950. His team's horrific storm-plagued struggle turned an already extremely difficult climb into an epic of human endurance – but for the first time mountaineers had reached the top of an 8000m peak. After descending the mountain they then had a month-long struggle through the monsoon with the expedition doctor having to perform amputations of frostbitten fingers and toes as they went.

Herzog's book *Annapurna* (Jonathan Cape, London, 1952) remains a classic of mountaineering literature. It's indicative of how things have changed in Nepal that Herzog had trouble even finding his way to the mountain! Today thousands of trekkers pass by the Annapurnas every year and, where Herzog once had to search desperately for supplies for his hungry climbers, there are now comfortable lodges offering bed and breakfast to trekking parties.

Conquest of Everest

Everest was also getting its share of attention, and in 1951 a climber who would soon become very famous took part in an exploratory expedition to the mountain – he was

New Zealander Edmund Hillary. Another name, soon to be equally famous, appeared on the list of climbers on the Swiss Everest expedition of 1952 when Sherpa climber Norgay Tensing reached 7500m. The conquest of Everest finally took place in 1953 when the British team led by John Hunt put those two climbers, Tensing and Hillary, on top of the world's highest peak.

Repeat performances came much easier than the first time and the second success came in 1956 when a Swiss party reached the summit. In 1960 it was the People's Republic of China which managed the feat, this time from the Tibetan side. A huge US expedition with the climbers backed up by nearly 1000 porters got to the top in 1963, and in 1965 it was the turn of an Indian expedition. Another huge party, this time from Japan, was on top in 1970 and one utterly fearless climber ensured his place in the Everest history books by making an extremely rapid descent on skis! Further attempts included the massive Italian expedition which reached the summit in 1973 and the victorious Japanese women's party which celebrated International Women's Year by putting a woman climber on top.

The success of the 1953 British expedition

THE HIMALAYA & MOUNTAINEERING

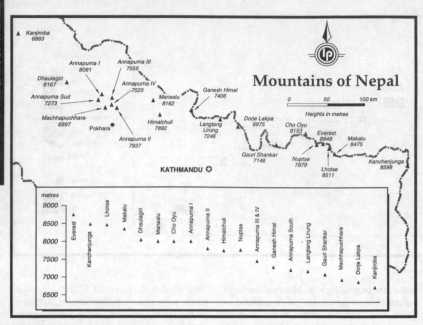

Mountains of Nepal

Heights in metres

0　50　100 km

Kanjiroba 6883

Annapurna I 8091

Annapurna III 7555

Dhaulagiri 8167

Annapurna IV 7525

Annapurna Sud 7273

Manaslu 8162

Ganesh Himal 7406

Machhapuchhare 6997

Pokhara

Himalchuli 7892

Langtang Lirung 7246

Dorje Lakpa 6975

Cho Oyu 8153

Everest 8848

Makalu 8475

Annapurna II 7937

Gauri Shankar 7146

Nuptse 7879

Lhotse 8511

Kanchenjunga 8598

KATHMANDU

metres

9000 — Everest, Kanchenjunga, Lhotse, Makalu

8500 — Dhaulagiri, Manaslu, Cho Oyu, Annapurna I

8000 — Annapurna II, Himalchuli, Nuptse, Annapurna III & IV

7500 — Ganesh Himal, Annapurna South, Langtang Lirung, Gauri Shankar

7000 — Machhapuchhare, Dorje Lakpa

6500 — Kanjiroba

to Everest had begun a trend for larger and larger expeditions. Proponents of this form of 'siege' mountaineering believed that this was the only way to conquer the great Himalayan peaks. A series of camps would be established higher and higher up the mountain with constant 'carries' of supplies eventually resulting in climbers reaching the top. This theory of Himalayan climbing reached its ultimate expression with the 73 Italian Everest expedition when 64 climbers were backed up by 100 sherpas and nearly 2000 porters! Helicopters ferried supplies and, hardly surprisingly, this massive effort put nine people on the summit in two parties.

The few climbers who did reach the summit from these expeditions required a huge pyramid of supporters below them. The effect on the country could be devastating as forests fell to provide firewood for the expeditions and vast amounts of mountaineering equipment and garbage were left behind. The Everest Base Camp has been aptly titled the 'world's highest garbage dump'. Lightweight expeditions had been successful, but Helmut Bhul's solo climb to the summit of Nanga Parbat in Pakistan and his lightweight expedition to the top of Broad Peak were looked upon more as aberrations requiring superhuman effort than as pointers towards a different way of doing things.

New-Style Mountaineering

Inevitably, a reaction set in and, while the checklist of important summits was methodically knocked over by huge and expensive expeditions, young climbers were perfecting a wholly different style of climbing on the peaks of Europe and North America. Getting to the top was no longer the sole aim, you had to reach the top with style.

The 'easy' ridge routes to the top were ignored while climbers scaled the most difficult faces, combining athletic skills and high-tech equipment. British mountaineer Chris Bonnington was the chief protagonist for this style of climbing and his brilliant conquest of the southern face of Annapurna in 1970, followed by an expertly organised race up the hitherto unthinkable south-western face of Everest in 1975, were supreme examples of this trend.

Lightweight Expeditions

Attempting the difficult faces and routes was one trend, but lightweight expeditions were another. In 1978 the Austrian expedition to Everest put Reinhold Messner and Peter Habler on top without the use of oxygen. Once this 'impossible' feat had been achieved other climbers also found they could reach the top without oxygen and, freed from the necessity of carting heavy oxygen cylinders up the mountains, much smaller parties could attempt the big mountains. Only two years later Reinhold Messner made a solo ascent of Everest, climbing the north face on the Tibetan side in the fastest ascent ever made.

In early 1990 Tim McCartney-Snape, an Australian, went several steps further. He walked and climbed from sea level, at the Bay of Bengal, to the top of Mt Everest, alone and without oxygen.

Mountaineering Today

Himalayan mountaineering today not only provides a great deal of free publicity for tourism to Nepal, it's also a very useful source of income for the government. If you want to attempt a Himalayan peak there's a fee to be paid to the government even before you get your climbing permit, and the higher and more famous the mountain the higher the fee that must be paid. Everest is currently $50,000 and is usually 'booked out' for years ahead. Annually, 600 to 900 climbers come to Nepal to try their luck, but there are still many sizeable peaks which have not been successfully climbed, and some which haven't even been attempted.

Today mountaineering is a sport pure and simple – there's no noise made about its scientific value. In fact the successes and failures of the various expeditions are regularly reported on the sports pages of the *Rising Nepal*. Of course it's also a decidedly dangerous sport: over 200 climbers have reached the top of Everest (some of them three, four and even five times), but about 100 climbers have died in the attempt. Some other mountains in Nepal have an even worse record: almost as many climbers have lost their lives climbing Annapurna as have managed to reach the top.

Permits To climb any of the mountain peaks that are open to expeditions, a mountaineering team should obtain permission from the Ministry of Tourism's Mountaineering Section (☎ 01-211286), Tripureshwar, Kathmandu. Every team must be represented by a licensed trekking agency in Nepal.

TREKKING PEAKS

There are many smaller mountains in Nepal called 'trekking peaks' (ranging from 5587m to 6654m) which keen trekkers can climb. Most Everest Base Camp trekkers make the ascent of Kala Pattar for the view of Everest and at 5545m this would be a substantial peak anywhere else in the world. In his book *Many People Come, Looking, Looking* (The Mountaineers, Seattle, 1980) Galen Rowell tells of a little jaunt up a 6500m peak as a pre-lunch side trip while crossing the Thorong La Pass on the Annapurna Circuit Trek.

The trekking peaks are:

Peak	Height
Chulu East	6584m
Chulu West	6419m
Hiunchuli	6441m
Imja Tse	6183m
Kangja Chuli	5844m
Khongma Tse (or Mehra)	5849m
Kusum Kanguru	6367m
Kwangde	6011m
Lubuje	6119m
Mardi Himal	5587m
Mera Peak	6654m
Paldor Peak	5896m
Parchemuche	6187m
Pisang	6091m
Pokalde	5806m
Ramdung	5925m
Singu Chuli (or Fluted Peak)	6501m
Tharpu Chuli (or Tent Peak)	5663m

THE HIMALAYA & MOUNTAINEERING

By Himalayan standards these are minor peaks, but some of them provide challenging snow and ice climbing. To climb trekking peaks, a permit is required from the Nepal Mountaineering Association, Kamaladi, PO Box 1435, Kathmandu.

Fees (or royalties, as they are often referred to) depend on the altitude of the peak, starting at $1000 for peaks below 6501m and rising $500 for every 500m increment to $3000 for peaks from 7501 to 8000m.

Climbing gear can be bought or rented in Kathmandu, and while tents, stoves, sleeping bags and down gear should pose no problems, socks, shoes, clothing and freeze-dried food are likely to be harder to find.

Bill O'Connor's book *The Trekking Peaks of Nepal* (Crowood Press, 1989) gives a detailed description of climbing each of the peaks plus the trek to the mountain. Equipment, applications, procedures, weather, health and other matters are also comprehensively covered.

Trekking

There are countless long treks in Nepal, many of which still see only a handful of western walkers each year. Many of the previously off-limits areas have been opened up, but only for trekkers in organised groups: upper Mustang, upper Dolpo, Manaslu, Humla and the Kanchenjunga Base Camp in the north-east of the country.

The six popular longer treks, described in detail in this chapter, are the Everest Base Camp Trek, Helambu, Langtang and Jomsom treks, the Annapurna Circuit and the Annapurna Sanctuary Trek.

For the people in the hills of Nepal, walking has always been the main method of getting from A to B. There were no roads into the hill country from the Terai and India until the Tribhuvan Highway to Kathmandu was constructed in the 1950s. Pokhara was not connected to the outside world by road until the 1970s. Even today the vast majority of villages can only be reached on foot, although every year the roads penetrate further into Nepal's endless ranges of hills.

The Nepali people, making their way from village to village on the well worn trails, were only joined by western visitors when Himalayan mountaineering came into vogue. It was the accounts of those pioneering mountaineers, who had to make their way to the base of the great peaks on foot, which inspired the first trekkers. The word 'trekking' was first applied to Nepali hiking trips in the 1960s and the enormous popularity of trekking today has developed since that time.

Trekking in Nepal means a walking trip following trails, many of which have been used for communication and trade for centuries. Trekking is not mountaineering. Some of the popular trekking trails are used by mountaineering expeditions on their approach marches, but most are used by Nepalis for everyday travel and trade. A trekking trip can be any length you choose – there are popular short treks around the

Kathmandu and Pokhara valleys which only take a day to complete, there are short treks of two or three days, or there are longer treks lasting from a week to a month. You could even string a series of popular treks together and walk for months on end.

Three major factors account for the enormous popularity of trekking – the scenery, the people, and the flora and fauna.

SCENERY

There is no question that Nepal offers some of the most spectacular and beautiful scenery in the world. Of course, it's the mountains that are best known, and the exploits of mountain photographers have made Everest, Machhapuchhare, Ama Dablam and other mountains instantly recognisable to keen walkers all over the world. Nepal has a near monopoly on the world's highest peaks – eight of the 10 highest are found in Nepal and a number of the popular trekking routes offer you wonderful views or even visits to the base camps used by mountaineering expeditions. Mountain flights may give you superb views, but there is absolutely nothing like waking up on a crystal-clear Himalayan day

Trekking & Cultural Awareness

Trekkers should respect Nepali culture and traditions. Dress modestly – women should not wear short or revealing clothes (loose pants or a calf-length dress are ideal) and men should not go shirtless. Don't put down what you may see as shortcomings in the Nepali lifestyle; remember that life in western countries has many problems and drawbacks as well. Every visitor's maxim should be: Nepal is here to change you, not for you to change it.

Before bargaining, try to establish a fair price by talking to guides and other travellers. Paying too much feeds inflation, while paying too little denies the locals a reasonable return for their efforts and investments. Not everything is subject to bargaining: respect standard food, bed and entry charges and follow the going rate for services.

Bargaining should never be treated as a matter of life and death importance – it's usually regarded as an integral part of a transaction and is, ideally, an enjoyable social exchange. Nepalis do not ever appreciate aggressive behaviour. A good deal is when both parties are happy. Try to remember that Rs 5 might make quite a difference to the seller, but in hard currency it amounts to less than $0.10.

Regrettably, some nationalities have established such a reputation for unpleasant, mean-minded bargaining that they are no longer welcome in many lodges or restaurants. Israelis will find that previous hard-core shoestring 'travellers' have created a negative impression that may well take a long time to erase.

Don't encourage begging children; tell them *Na raamro*, 'not good', and remember that hand-outs can create dependence and other negative side effects. (See Begging in the Facts about the Country chapter.) ∎

and seeing an 8000m peak towering over you, seemingly just an arm's length away.

The mountains may be the most obvious scenic attraction, but trekkers soon find there are plenty of other treats for the eye. The hill country is often breathtakingly beautiful with pretty little villages, attractive houses, neat fields and interesting temples. As you climb higher the subtropical lowlands give way to meadows, stretches of forest, swift-flowing rivers and deep canyons, before you reach the cold and often barren regions at the foot of the great peaks. The views change with the seasons, whether it is the cycle of planting and harvesting or the brilliant displays of wild flowers in spring and autumn.

PEOPLE

Nepal is a country of contrasts and this extends to the people as well as the landscape. Trekking in Nepal is not like hiking through the often uninhabited countryside of a North American, Australian or European national park. People are constantly passing by on the trails, and along many routes there are regularly spaced villages to pause in. The villages and their people can be as interesting as the scenery, as you meet people from many of Nepal's wide diversity of ethnic groups. The outgoing nature, general friendliness and good humour of the Nepalis is often commented on by trekkers. Colourful festivals can make trekking at certain times of year even more enjoyable.

Of course, your trekking companions can be another important part of the trekking experience. A long trek can be a great opportunity to enjoy yourself with good friends. Despite stories you may have heard about the Himalaya being overrun with hordes of trekkers the reality is very different. Certainly there may be many trekkers on the most popular routes, particularly the Jomsom Trek, but compared to the crowds visiting national parks in western countries the numbers are often minuscule. The trails of Nepal are a long way from being overcrowded.

About Trekking

Although Nepal offers plenty of opportunity for short treks lasting a day or less, most treks last considerably longer. From Pokhara or around the Kathmandu Valley you can make a variety of two, three or four day walks, but Nepal's most popular treks take at least a week. For the very popular Everest Base Camp and Annapurna Circuit treks you have to allow three weeks. Don't take on one of these classic long treks too lightly: the end of the first week is not the ideal time to discover you're not keen on walking.

INFORMATION

Two organisations offer free, up-to-date information on trekking conditions, health risks and how to minimise your impact on the environment; both are in Kathmandu, on Tridevi Marg near the immigration office.

The Kathmandu Environment Education Project (KEEP) is in the Potala Tourist Home (☎ 01-410303). It's open from 10 am to 5 pm except Saturdays and holidays and has a library and sells iodine bottles, biodegradable soap and other environmentally friendly trekking equipment; they also have an excellent notice board.

The Himalayan Rescue Association (HRA) Trekkers' Information Centre is upstairs in the Hotel Tilicho (☎ 01-418755), Kathmandu. It has information about altitude sickness and useful notebooks with up-to-date information from other trekkers. Both of these offices are excellent places to advertise for trekking companions.

For those who want trekking information, particularly related to independent trekking, probably the best source of impartial information in Kathmandu are the slide shows held regularly in the Kathmandu Guest House by Chris Beall, a British freelance photographer, writer, trek leader and long-time resident of Nepal. The slide shows give an introduction to Nepal and its various trekking regions. There's a question-and-answer session afterwards where you can get up-to-date information on trail conditions, and forthright advice as to what trails and style of trekking would most suit your budget, fitness and interests. This is something it can be difficult to get out of a trekking agency which simply wants to hook a customer.

These information sessions have been known to continue until midnight! The

Environmental Information

On the positive side, trekking plays a vital role in the economy of mountain areas. Without the influx of cash, many more people would be forced to abandon the villages for the cities, which are already suffering the negative results of rapid population increase. A number of impressive organisations are attempting to deal with the problems, including the Annapurna Conservation Area Project (ACAP), which has done a great deal to encourage sustainable development in the Annapurna region.

For more information on minimising your impact, visit the trekkers' information centres run by the Kathmandu Environmental Education Project (KEEP) and Himalayan Rescue Association (HRA). Most Thamel bookshops also stock *Trekking Gently in the Himalaya* by Wendy Brewer Lama (Rs 30), a small booklet that has essential tips for trekkers.

Information centre addresses are:

Annapurna Conservation Area Project (ACAP),
    King Mahendra Trust for Nature Conservation, PO Box 3712, Jawlakhel, Patan
    (☎ 01-526571; fax 526570)
Himalayan Rescue Association (HRA)
    PO Box 4944, Thamel, Kathmandu
    (☎ 01-418755)
Kathmandu Environmental Education Project
    (KEEP)
    PO Box 9178, Thamel, Kathmandu
    (☎ 01-410303; fax 411533)
Makalu-Barun National Park & Conservation
    Area Project
    PO Box 2785, Kathmandu
    (☎ 01-419224; fax 410073)
Sagarmatha Pollution Control Committee
    c/o WWW Nepal Programmes, PO Box 7660, Kathmandu (☎ 01-410137)

shows cost Rs 250 (including tea/coffee and biscuits), and if they are on you'll see posters up at various locations in Thamel, most notably the Kathmandu Guest House.

WHEN TO GO

Put very simply, the best time to trek is from October to May (the dry season) and the worst time is from June to September (the monsoon). This generalisation does not allow for the peculiarities of individual treks,

TREKKING

however. Some people even claim that the undeniable difficulties of trekking during the monsoon are outweighed by the virtual absence of western trekkers.

The first two months of the dry season, October and November, are probably the ideal period for trekking in Nepal. The air, freshly washed by the monsoon rains, is crystal clear, the mountain scenery is superb and the weather is still comfortably warm. At low altitudes in October it can actually be quite balmy, and trekkers may find they complete a whole trek in T-shirt weather.

December, January and February are still good months for trekking, but the cold can be bitter at high altitudes. Getting up to the Everest Base Camp can be a real endurance test and the Thorung La pass on the Annapurna Circuit is usually blocked by snow.

March and April offer better weather but the price is hazy visibility on long-distance views. By this time of year, the weather has been dry for a long time and dust is starting to hang in the air. The poorer quality of the Himalayan views is compensated for by the superb wild flowers, particularly Nepal's wonderful rhododendrons.

By May it starts to get very hot, dusty and humid, and the monsoon is definitely just around the corner. From June to September the trails can be dangerously slippery due to the monsoon rains, and raging rivers often wash away bridges and stretches of trail. Nepal's famous *jukha* (leeches) are an unpleasant feature of the wet season, but with care, trekking can still be possible and there are certainly fewer trekkers on the trail.

TRAIL CONDITIONS

Most trekkers want to get away from roads as quickly as possible, and although roads reach further into the hill country every year, it is still possible to leave them quickly behind. Nepali trails are often steep and taxing. The old adage that the shortest path between two points is a straight line appears to have been firmly drummed into the Nepalis, irrespective of any mountains which may get in the way! In compensation, the trails are often very well maintained.

Busy trails up steep slopes are often flagged with stones every step of the way.

Walking the trails of Nepal often entails a great deal of altitude gain and loss, and it is as well to remember that even the base of the great mountains of the Himalaya can be very high. Most treks which go through populated areas stick to between 1000m and 3000m, although the Everest Base Camp Trek and the Annapurna Circuit Trek both reach over 5000m. On high treks like these it is wise to ensure adequate acclimatisation, and the old maxim of 'walking high, sleeping low' is good advice: if possible, your night halt should be at a lower level than the highest point reached in the day.

A typical day's walk lasts from five to seven hours and involves a number of ascents and descents. It's rare to spend much time at the same level. On an organised camping trek the day is run to a remarkably tight schedule. A typical pattern would be: up at 6 am, start walking at 7 am, stop for lunch at 10 am, start after lunch at noon, stop walking at 3 pm. Nepalis rise early, eat very little for breakfast, eat a large lunch in the late morning and a second meal before dark, then retire early – you are best off following a similar schedule. Although a little rudimentary knowledge of Nepali will help to make your trek easier and more interesting, finding your way is rarely difficult on the major trekking routes and English is becoming more widely spoken.

HEALTH

See the Health section in the Facts for the Visitor chapter for more information on trekking health. Acute mountain sickness (AMS) or altitude sickness is the major concern on high-altitude treks, but for the majority of trekkers health problems are likely to be minor ones, such as stomach upsets and blisters. While paranoia is not required, common sense precautions are.

Basic rules for healthy trekking include taking care that water is always safe to drink. The best method is to treat water with iodine, as this is safe and does not require the use of firewood or kerosene. Diarrhoea is one of the

Garbage & Waste

While trekkers certainly contribute to the problems of firewood use and the appearance of rubbish along the trails, they are certainly not the only culprits. As modern nonbiodegradable packaging becomes increasingly common in Nepal, garbage is starting to appear even along village trails untravelled by western trekkers.

You can do several things that will reduce the amount of rubbish and pollution in the hills. One important contribution you can make is to reduce the volume of waste plastic in village rubbish heaps by not drinking bottled mineral water; carry a water bottle and treat the water with iodine. The empty plastic bottles are becoming a major problem – the Annapurna Conservation Area Project (ACAP) estimated that in 1995 alone 200,000 of these were dumped in the Annapurna region!

Independent trekkers should always carry their garbage out or dispose of it properly. You can burn it, but you should remember that the fireplace in a Nepali home is a sacred institution and throwing rubbish into it would be a great insult.

Toilet paper is a particularly unpleasant sight along trails: if you must use it, carry it out in a plastic bag until you can burn it. Better yet, carry a small plastic trowel to bury the shit (well away from any streams) and a small plastic water container so that – like the vast majority of people in the world – you can clean yourself with water instead.

Those travelling with organised groups should ensure that toilet tents are properly organised, and that rubbish is carried out.

Check on the company's policies before you sign up. ∎

comparatively minor problems which can ruin a trek so take care in what you eat and make sure your medical kit has a medication such as Lomotil or Imodium and also an antibiotic like norflocaxin.

The food on an organised trekking expedition is unlikely to cause any problems, but village-inn trekkers are at risk.

At high altitudes the burning power of the sun is much stronger, so make sure you have a pair of good sunglasses, and a maximum-protection sunscreen for your skin. If there is any likelihood that you'll be walking over snow, sunglasses are insufficient – you need mountaineering glasses with side pieces or, at the very least, you should rig up pieces of cardboard on the frames of your glasses to cut the glare, and don't forget about any porters you may have.

Blisters can take the fun out of trekking so make sure your shoes and socks are comfortable and come prepared with Band-aids and moleskins just in case they aren't. Many people suffer from knee and ankle strains, particularly if they are carrying their own pack. If you have a predisposition for these injuries, carry elastic supports or bandages.

Make sure you are in good health before

departing as there is very little medical attention along the trails and rescue helicopters are not only expensive but *must* be cleared for payment in advance! Your embassy can do this if you have registered with it (see the Safety section below). See the individual treks in this chapter for more information on possible medical assistance. In general, Himalayan hospitals can offer only very limited facilities and expertise.

The HRA can offer valuable advice on trekking medical matters and has an excellent pamphlet on acute mountain sickness. It is in the Hotel Tilicho, on Tridevi Marg, not far from Kathmandu's immigration office.

SAFETY

In the mid-70s it was possible to claim that Nepal was totally immune from theft, assaults and other assorted vices of contemporary western 'civilisation'. Unfortunately, that claim can no longer be made and in a number of places in Nepal it would not be wise to trek alone, and a sharp eye should be kept on your possessions.

If you're intending to trek independently and don't have a partner it's usually relatively easy to find one. Notice boards around

Kathmandu or Pokhara often have signs up from people looking for partners. In Kathmandu, the KEEP Information Centre and the Kathmandu Guest House have particularly good boards.

Usually, the further you get from roads and population centres the fewer problems there will be, but several basic rules should be followed. Don't trek alone, don't make ostentatious displays of valuable possessions and don't leave lodge doors unlocked or valuables unattended. If you hire porters make sure they are reputable by hiring them through a lodge or trekking agency or by getting good first-hand recommendations about a person. A porter or guide found at a street corner can easily disappear along the trail with all your gear – even if they are carrying a slew of letters from past clients certifying to their honesty.

Walking at high altitudes on rough trails can be dangerous. Watch your footing on slippery trails, and never underestimate the capacity of the weather to change extremely rapidly for the worse – at any time of the year. If you are crossing high passes where snow is a possibility, never walk with less than three people, carry a supply of emergency rations, have a map and compass (and know how to use them) and have sufficient equipment to deal with cold, wet blizzard conditions.

All embassies and consulates strongly recommend that their citizens register with them before they head off into the boon-docks. They have standard forms that record your name, rough itinerary, insurance details and next of kin, and can obviously speed up a search, or a medical evacuation. These are usually kept at the embassies' reception desks and take two minutes to complete. You can avoid a trip to the embassy by filling in a registration form at either the KEEP or the HRA Trekkers' Information Centre. They forward the forms on to the appropriate embassies on a regular basis.

ACCOMMODATION & FOOD

Organised treks camp each night and all you have to do is eat and crawl into your tent. Even erecting the tent is handled by the trekking crew who put it up for you at the site selected by your *sirdar* or group leader.

Independent trekkers usually stay in the small lodges, guest houses or village inns which have appeared along almost all the main trails. At first this sort of accommodation was simply a matter of local tea houses letting you unroll your sleeping bag on the floor. Today, along some of the most popular trails the lodges are quite luxurious and offer private rooms, extensive menus and even showers. It's possible to make quite long treks relying entirely on local food and accommodation. Nevertheless, it's still a good idea to carry a sleeping bag as lodges sometimes run out of bedding at peak season, and their bedding can contain unwanted sleeping companions.

On a typical organised trek your only con-

Trekking, Firewood & Forest Depletion

The depletion of forest is a severe problem throughout the Himalaya, and is a particular problem in Nepal. Trekkers can definitely do their part to aid Himalayan conservation. You can minimise the use of firewood by staying in lodges that use kerosene or fuel-efficient wood stoves and solar-heated hot water. Avoid using large open fires for warmth – wear additional clothing instead. Keep showers to a minimum, and spurn showers altogether if wood is burnt to produce the hot water.

Consolidate cooking time (and wood consumption) by ordering the same items at the same time as other trekkers. Dal bhat is usually readily available for large numbers of people, does not require special lengthy cooking time and is nutritious and inexpensive. Remember that local meals are prepared between 10 and 11 am, so eating then will usually not require an additional fire. Treat your drinking water with iodine, rather than boiling it.

Those travelling with organised groups should ensure that kerosene is always used for cooking. ■

cern with food is sitting down to eat it. The porters carry all the food along with them, and there will be a cook with well drilled assistants who can turn out meals of often stunning complexity. Baking a cake on a kerosene stove is just one of the tricks trekking cooks like to perform to display their virtuosity.

Independent trekkers will find numerous places to eat along the most popular trails, although it's often wise to carry some emergency food supplies such as cheese, dried fruit or chocolate bars. Food may vary from rice and dal bhat at simple tea houses to surprisingly good meals on the more popular trails.

KEEP and other environmentally concerned organisations point out that dal bhat is nutritious, easily prepared, available everywhere and requires a minimum of fuel for preparation. In most places they will give you a second helping of dal bhat for free. You lessen your impact and usually eat better if you try to adapt to the local diet. On the Everest and Annapurna treks it's unlikely that you will walk more than half an hour without coming across some sort of establishment that can offer tea, soft drinks, beer and often a full meal.

The standard of cuisine on the Jomsom Trek is so westernised that it has been dubbed 'the apple pie trail' as that dish features on so many village-inn menus. It's surprising how many places even have cold beer available as well; before you complain about the price contemplate the fact that somebody had to carry that bottle of beer all the way there and will probably have to carry the empty bottle back again!

If you're going right off the beaten track and exploring remote areas like Makalu (8475m) and Kanchenjunga (8598m) in the east or Jumla and Dolpo in the west, you need to be self-sufficient. In these relatively untouched areas there is probably very little surplus food for sale and the practice of catering to western trekkers has not yet developed. Tea houses are rare and when they occur are rudimentary, and sanitation conditions leave a lot to be desired.

Preparations in Nepal

PERMITS
Travel in Nepal is still highly restricted and your visa only allows you to visit the areas around the Kathmandu and Pokhara valleys, Royal Chitwan National Park and the routes covered by drivable roads. If you intend to strike out more than a day's walk from the main roads, you must first apply for a trekking permit.

If you are trekking with an organised group this will be arranged for you. If you're doing it yourself it is possible to obtain the permit the same day, although you must make your application as early as possible in the morning. Be prepared for a distinctly tiring battle with bureaucracy.

Trekking permits are issued in Kathmandu and Pokhara, and can only be extended in those cities.

Trekking permits can be obtained from Kathmandu's immigration office. It's open from 10 am to 1 pm Sunday to Thursday and 10 am to noon on Fridays for applications, although you have to go back later to retrieve your passport. It's wise to start the process early as it can be time-consuming.

There are regular trekking permit inspection points along most trails and you won't get far out of Kathmandu or Pokhara before being stopped and turned back if you don't have one. Trekking fees vary depending on the area you intend to explore. If you plan to trek in two different areas, two trekking permits are needed. Trekking permits and application forms are colour coded depending on the region in which you plan to trek; be sure to get the right form when you start the process. Two passport photos are required with each application and fees, though quoted in US dollars, are payable only in rupees.

Finally, if you plan to trek through a national park, wildlife reserve or conservation area – this will be necessary in the case of almost all treks – you will need to pay a park entrance fee. You can buy an entrance ticket in advance at the National Parks office in the basement of the Sanchaya Kosh Bhawan Shopping Centre across the road from the immigration office in Kathmandu, or you can just pay the fee when you arrive at the park entrance station. Currently, there is a Rs 650 entry fee for national parks and the Annapurna Conservation Area.

An additional fee is levied for video cameras that are taken into the national parks. This is currently an outrageous Rs 5000. The only alternative is to leave the camera at the entrance, and to collect it on your return. If you trek into the Seopuri Reserve at the north side of the Kathmandu Valley you must pay an additional Rs 250.

Area	Fee
Annapurna, Everest, Langtang, Gorkha, Jumla (& others)	$5 per week for first four weeks, $10 per week after that.
Kanchenjunga* & Lower Dolpo*	$10 per week for first four weeks, $20 per week after that
Upper Mustang* # & Upper Dolpo* #	$700 for up to 10 days, groups only
Manaslu* #	$75 per week low season, $90 high season
Humla*	$90 for seven days then $15 per day

* Treks to these regions must be fully equipped treks arranged by a trekking agency.

A government liaison officer must accompany treks to this region.

MONEY
Except in Khumbu and on the Jomsom Trek, changing foreign money is likely to be very difficult if not impossible. Bring enough money for the whole walk and carry it in small denominations (nothing larger than Rs 100 notes).

EQUIPMENT
It's always best to have your own equipment since you will be familiar with it and know for certain that it works. If there is some equipment which you do not have, however, you can buy or rent it from one of Nepal's many trekking shops. Much of the equipment available is of excellent quality and the rental charges are generally not excessive, but large deposits are often required (usually equal to a generous valuation of the equipment itself). Never leave your passport as a deposit.

In 1996 and depending on quality, rental rates per day were as follows:

Item	Rate
mattress	Rs 6 to Rs 10
sleeping bag	Rs 20 to Rs 40
down jacket	Rs 15 to Rs 40
pack	Rs 15 to Rs 30
tent	Rs 50 to Rs 150

Kathmandu is still the centre for trekking equipment and there are many outlets around Thamel. Pokhara also has some trekking-equipment places, as do popular destinations like Namche Bazaar. The equipment available in Nepal used to be mainly expedition leftovers, but there is also a great deal of new equipment obviously brought into the country purely for resale purposes.

Some trekking gear, including sleeping bags, down jackets, duffel bags, rucksacks, camera cases, ponchos and wind jackets, is manufactured in Kathmandu and sold in Thamel trekking shops at very reasonable prices. Much of this locally produced gear is decorated with well known brand names such as North Face, Karimor, Lowe Pro and Gore-Tex, but don't be deceived into thinking you're getting top quality merchandise at a bargain price. Even so, most items are well made and stand up well to the rigours of trekking.

Approximate retail prices for new Nepali-made gear with fake brand names are as follows:

Item	Cost
sleeping bag	Rs 5500
down jacket	Rs 5000
rain/wind jacket	Rs 1300
pile jacket	Rs 1200 to Rs 1500
day pack	Rs 1000 to Rs 2500
expedition pack	Rs 3500
duffel bag	Rs 350 to Rs 450

Clothing

The clothing you require depends on where and when you trek. If you're going up to the Everest Base Camp in the middle of winter you must be prepared for very cold weather with down gear, mittens and the like. On the other hand, if you do a short, low-altitude trek early or late in the season the weather is likely to be fine for T-shirts and perhaps a sweater, or better yet a pile jacket, to pull on in the evenings. If you don't have your own sleeping bag or down jacket, these can be rented in Kathmandu; however, they may not be particularly clean.

Apart from ensuring you have adequate clothing to keep warm, the important considerations are that your feet are comfortable and that you can keep dry if it rains or snows. Uncomfortable shoes or blistered feet are the worst possible trekking discomfort. Make sure your shoes fit well and are comfortable for long periods. Running shoes are adequate for low-altitude (below 3000m), warm-weather treks where you won't encounter snow, though they lack ankle support. The minimum otherwise is lightweight trekking boots, and these can be bought new (imported) in Kathmandu at Rs 1800 to Rs 2500.

Books & Maps

Books and maps are readily available in Kathmandu and Pokhara bookshops.

See Lonely Planet's *Trekking in the Nepal Himalaya* by Stan Armington for the complete story on trekking. It has considerable advice on equipment selection, an excellent medical section oriented towards trekking and the mountains, and comprehensive route descriptions not only of the popular treks covered more briefly in this book, but also of a number of interesting but less heavily used routes.

The Schneider Maps, named after their cartographer, are the best available trekking maps. They cover the entire Everest trek, Langtang and Annapurna, but they are expensive at Rs 1000 each. The locally produced Mandala series has the colour maps *Helambu & Langtang*, *Round Annapurna*, *Khumbu* and others priced at Rs 60 to Rs 140. For less popular routes, you'll have to rely on the older dyeline maps at Rs 70 each.

All the trekking maps, including the Schneider maps, suffer from a number of problems. For a start the trails change faster than the maps: you may well find a new trail in use or a route change necessitated by an avalanche or flood. Equally disorienting is the fact that Nepali villages are often hard to pinpoint (they sprawl over hills and down valleys) and often have very different names depending on which map you look at or whom you ask. Treat any map with scepticism.

Other Gear

In winter or at high altitudes a high-quality sleeping bag will be necessary. However, if you are going on an organised trek check exactly what equipment is supplied: it's a waste of time bringing your own sleeping bag if the company supplies one. If you need to hire one, it may be grubby; check for fleas or worse.

Rain is rare during most of the trekking season, though disturbances in the Bay of Bengal can cause massive rainstorms during the autumn, and there are sure to be a few rainy days in the spring season. You should be prepared for it by carrying waterproof gear, or at least an umbrella. The rainy season just before and after the monsoon also brings leeches and it's nice to have some salt or matches to deal with them.

Take a torch (flashlight) for those inevitable calls of nature on moonless nights.

Cigarettes and matches are popular small gifts to have with you on treks if you are travelling with porters, but beware of encouraging children begging for 'one rupee' or a 'school pen' – see the earlier aside on Trekking & Cultural Awareness.

TREKKING

INDEPENDENT TREKKING

At one extreme, independent trekking can mean simply trekking from lodge to lodge along the main trails with one or more friends. All you need is your trekking permit and your walking gear and off you go. The popular trekking trails all have accommodation along their entire length. People have even walked the complete Annapurna Circuit without a sleeping bag, although this is asking for trouble and is definitely not recommended.

For most moderately fit people, guides and porters are not necessary on the Annapurna or Mt Everest treks. A good guide/porter will enhance your experience, but a bad one will just make life more complicated.

There are many factors that influence how much you spend on an independent trek. In most places, dormitory accommodation costs around Rs 15, and a simple meal of rice and dal around Rs 30 – note that as you get further from the road on the Annapurna Circuit and in the Everest region, prices can be more than twice as high. After a long day hiking, however, most people will weaken when confronted by a cold beer, an apple pie or a hot shower and these will dramatically add to your costs. Around $8 per day in the Annapurnas and $10 in the Everest region is about right, and this includes the occasional luxury items you might treat yourself to.

According to some studies, competition on the Annapurna Circuit is so intense, and the need for money so desperate, that lodges have been known to provide food and accommodation at below cost. In almost all lodges prices are fixed and are more than reasonable. Remember this – and the real value of the rupee – if you start to get carried away with bargaining.

Guides & Porters

If you can't (or don't want to) carry a decent-sized pack, if you have children or elderly people in your party, or if you plan to walk in regions where you have to carry in food and tents, help should be considered. It's fairly easy to find guides and porters, but it is hard to be certain of their honesty and ability.

Unless you have first-hand recommendations, you're best to hire someone through a guest house or agency. Arranging expeditions where guides, porters, tents and food are required can be time-consuming and can quickly become extremely complicated. In such cases you're definitely best off putting this in the hands of a professional.

There is a distinct difference between a guide and a porter. A guide should speak English, know the terrain and the trails, and supervise porters, but will probably not be interested in carrying a load or doing menial tasks like cooking and putting up tents. Porters are generally hired for load-carrying, although an increasing number speak some English and know the trails well enough to act as guides.

If halfway through a trek you decide you do need some help (illness, problems with high altitude or ordinary old blisters might contribute) it will generally be possible to find someone. Most lodges can arrange a porter, particularly in large villages or near a hill-country airstrip where there are often porters who have just been paid off from a trekking party and are looking for another load to carry. Large organised trekking parties carry most of their own food, and as the food is used up fewer porters are needed and the extra porters are paid off along the route – so you can find experienced porters in the most unlikely places.

Whether you're making the arrangements yourself or dealing with an agency, make sure you clearly establish where you will go, how long you will take, how much you are going to pay and what you will be obliged to supply along the way. Traditionally, you pay for a guide's food and porters pay for their own food out of their wages. With a guide, you are better off agreeing on a daily rate for food rather than paying as you go. Arrangements where you pay for the guide or porter's accommodation and food can end up being surprisingly expensive. The amount of food a hungry Nepali porter can go through, when you're footing the bill, can be simply stunning.

You may also be responsible for outfitting

guides and porters to cope with cold and snow. If you are going above the snow line you must make absolutely certain that porters have goggles, shoes, shelter and appropriate clothing. There are still regular horror stories about ill-equipped porters tackling the Thorung La (the pass between Manang and Muktinath on the Annapurna Circuit). Frostbite, snow blindness and death have resulted.

Independent Trekking with Children

In 1994 Linda and I decided to have a family holiday in Nepal. We had both travelled and trekked extensively in Nepal – without kids – and thought it would be a good place to return to with our two children – Ella aged six and Vera 2½. It turned out to be an excellent choice, although there were moments when we doubted our sanity in carting two kids halfway across the world, exposing them to all manner of bugs, not to mention the pollution of Kathmandu, just so we could see some mountains with snow on them. At times Ella was inclined to agree: 'What's so special about them, Dad?', was her response at one stage, after having the snow-capped mountains pointed out to her by excited parents for the fifth time in as many minutes on the spectacular plane ride between Kathmandu and Pokhara.

One of the main goals of our trip was to do a week-long trek in the mountains. Many people we spoke to thought it was perhaps a bit of an ambitious thing to undertake with two small children, but this just made us more determined to give it a go – we could always turn back if it didn't work out. Our base point was to be Pokhara, seven bumpy and dusty but cheap hours by bus, or one easy, spectacular and not-too-expensive hour by plane (we opted for the latter) from Kathmandu.

As we were travelling on a fairly tight budget, we couldn't afford an organised trek where everything is taken care of for you. Instead we organised it all ourselves.

We approached many of the trekking agencies in Pokhara, and finally settled on one which we felt had its act together sufficiently to arrange for porters and transport to the trail head. Our plan was that we would have three porters – two to carry rucksacks, and a third to carry Vera most of the time, and Ella when she got tired of walking.

As it turned out, Ella walked virtually the whole way, which was a great effort, and Vera was carried in a *doko* (a large, conical, cane basket) on a porter's back. She felt safe being up off the ground, and was emboldened enough to pull faces at trekkers and locals as we passed along the trail. Her mode of travel certainly made her a curiosity to locals and foreigners alike. To wedge her in safely we sat her first in her backpack, placed this in the basket, and then filled the gaps with sleeping bags and items of warm clothing we shed as the day wore on.

The porters were great with the kids, and although we felt a bit like a travelling show at times, it was worth hiring enough porters to free us of any major load. At $5 per porter per day, it was money well spent.

Overall the trek went very well, but we realised early on that we had overestimated how far we would be able to walk in one day. Once we slowed down and basically let Ella set the pace, things were fine. The walking itself was not too strenuous, largely because of our slow pace, but we did get up to 3500m, and even at this altitude the children's breathing was being affected. In six days we were able to comfortably walk from Birethanti to Ghorepani/Deorali on the Jomsom Trek, cut across to Ghandruk on the Annapurna Circuit and return to Birethanti.

Staying in the tea houses along the way was a highlight for the kids. On arrival they would disappear into the candle-lit, smoky interiors of the kitchen, and usually emerge beaming some time later, brandishing a boiled potato or some other morsel kindly given by the hard-working women of the house.

The major problem we faced on the trek was a bout of giardia which Vera contracted, and this led to our second biggest problem: what to do with all the soiled disposable nappies. They're a bugger of a thing to get rid of at the best of times; in small villages in the mountains they are a disaster. The only really sound solution is to use cloth nappies. On a practical level this is very difficult (although not impossible), so with the disposables you need to roll the used ones up very tightly, store them in a strong plastic bag and carry them out to a place where you can dispose of them properly. This is not as offensive as it sounds!

Empty, plastic mineral-water bottles are another problem in the mountains, and it's recommended that you buy iodine tablets to purify your water. Some powdered flavouring helps to disguise the awful taste, but our two children steadfastly refused anything other than plain bottled water.

Hugh Finlay

If you make arrangements with one of the small trekking agencies in Kathmandu expect to pay $12 per day for a guide, $8 per day for a porter. If you find a porter yourself or through a guest house, the costs will be lower – say $5 per day. Local agencies are listed in the following section.

ORGANISED TREKKING

Organised treks can also vary greatly in standards and costs. At one extreme there are the big international adventure travel companies that market trips in western countries. You book your trek through them and everything is organised and arranged before you leave home. Your cost will probably include flights to and from Nepal, accommodation in Kathmandu before and after the trek, tours and other activities as well as the trek itself. A fully organised trek will provide tents, sleeping bags, food, porters and an experienced English-speaking sirdar (group leader), Sherpa guides and usually a western trek leader. All you need to carry is your day-pack and camera.

Companies organising trekking trips in Nepal include well known names like Mountain Travel or Wilderness Travel in the USA, World Expeditions or Peregrine Adventures in Australia, and Explore Worldwide in the UK. Although the trek leaders may be experienced western walkers from the international company the actual organisation in Nepal will probably be by a locally based trekking company.

Local Trekking Agencies

It's quite possible to arrange a fully organised trip when you get to Nepal (and save a lot of money), but if you have a large group it's best to make the arrangements well in advance. Many trekking companies in Nepal can put together a fully equipped trek if you give them a few days notice. With the best of these companies a trek may cost upwards of $60 or $70 a day and you'll trek in real comfort with tables, chairs, dining tents, toilet tents and other luxuries which seem quite incompatible with walking in the wilds! Some of the large Nepal-based trekking agencies that have been recommended include:

Organised Trekking with Children

Taking children trekking in Nepal can be surprisingly enjoyable. Both of our children's treks were of the organised variety.

Tackling a long, high-altitude trek like the Annapurna Circuit with small children might be asking too much. With our children we planned on shorter treks (we didn't want them getting fed up) which avoided very high altitudes. We also opted for organised treks to make it easier for both sides – we didn't have to worry about finding food and shelter and the kids were likely to eat better.

Our first trek with children was the short Annapurna Skyline Trek (see the Pokhara chapter) when our daughter Tashi was eight and our son Kieran was six. Back home, like most kids, they seemed to think getting from the car to the video recorder a long walk, but in fact they walked the whole way and still had energy for frantic games with the porters and local village kids after we set up camp each night.

Our enthusiasm must have been catching because three years later we found ourselves back in Nepal, this time with seven friends and neighbours and six children (two aged six, two aged eight, one 10 year old and one 11 year old). This time we opted for the Helambu Trek as it is reasonably short, doesn't go too high and is not too heavily trekked. Malla Treks in Kathmandu, who organised the trek for us, made it even more interesting by sending along a bunch of Nepali children, who also happened to be on school vacation. Our resulting 'international trek' was a great learning experience, and once again our kids turned out to be hardier than we'd expected. On one day only, when a misunderstanding with the porters resulted in us having to climb a 3500m pass late in the day, did the two six year olds require a little carrying. Apart from that, the whole noisy mob walked the entire eight days. We're already planning our next children's trek.

Tony Wheeler

Anta Dablam Trekking
  PO Box 3035, Lazimpat
  (☎ 01-415372; fax 416029)
Himalayan Adventures
  Maharajganj (☎ 01-411866; fax 410858)
International Trekkers
  PO Box 1273, Chabel
  (☎ 01-413397; fax 418561)
Malla Treks
  PO Box 5227, Lainchaur (☎ 01-410089; fax
  423143; e-mail: trekinfo@mallatrk.mos.com.np)
Thamserku Trekking
  Kamal Pokhari (☎ 01-416544; fax 412323)
  PO Box 3124, Naxal (☎ 01-411562; fax 227042)
Tiger Mountain (the same organisation as Tiger Tops)
  PO Box 170, Lazimpat (☎ 01-414508; fax 414075;
  e-mail: tiger@mtn.mos.com.np)

There are more than 300 trekking agencies in Nepal, from the big ones tied up with international adventure travel companies, to small agencies specialising in independent trekkers. These small agencies will often be able to fix you up with individual porters or guides. A group trek organised through a smaller agency might cost $30 to $50 a day. Group treks staying at village inns along the route can be cheaper still (around $25 a day including a guide and food).

Recommended agencies in this category include:

Asian Trekking
  Thamel (☎ 01-415506; fax 411878)
Greenhill Tours (agent for US Above
  the Clouds Trekking)
  Thamel (☎ 01-414803; fax 411933)
Himalayan Hilltreks & River Tours
  PO Box 1066, Dhobi Ghat (☎ 01-520609; fax 411277;
  e-mail: brian@hilltrek.mos.com.np)
Lamjung Treks & Expeditions
  Deo Building, Kopundol
  (☎ 01-522964; fax 226820)
Lucky Trekking Service
  PO Box 6632, Thahiti Tole
  (☎ 01-214769; fax 223690)
Mandala Trekking
  PO Box 4573, Kantipath
  (☎ 01-228600; fax 227600)
Nepal Tashi Taki Trekking
  Jyatha, Thamel (☎ 01-417121)

Everest Base Camp Trek

Everybody knows of Mt Everest, and that's the simple reason why the Everest Base Camp Trek is so popular. The trek takes

The Yeti

Like Big Foot in North America, the Loch Ness monster in Scotland or even the elusive bunyip in Australia, the yeti or abominable snowman is much hunted but little seen. The yeti is a shy humanoid creature which lives high in the most remote regions of the Himalaya. There are countless yeti legends told by the Sherpas and other hill peoples. They tell of its legendary strength, its ability to carry off yaks and even abduct people.

Nobody has ever managed to get a clear photograph of the yeti: footprints in the snow are generally the only indication that a yeti has been by, although hastily gnawed yak bones also add to the yeti legend.

Of course, there are plenty of scientific explanations for yetis. The footprints may have been a human print or some other natural footprint which has appeared to grow larger as the snow melts. Rigorous studies have been made of the yeti scalps found in various monasteries, in particular the one at the Khumjung monastery, and they have all turned out to be fakes. Keep your camera loaded though, a good photo of a yeti (even a small yeti) will probably be worth a fortune. ■

about three weeks and reaches a maximum height of 5545m at Kala Pattar, a small peak offering fine views of Mt Everest. Although the final part of the trek is through essentially uninhabited areas, these days small lodges operate during the trekking season so it's quite suitable for independent trekkers.

The trek has a number of stunning attractions, but it also has some distinct drawbacks which might well deter potential trekkers, were it not for the undeniable plus of being able to say you've been to the base of the highest mountain in the world.

The attractions include spectacular scenery and the outgoing Sherpa people of the Solu Khumbu, the region where Mt Everest and its attendant lesser peaks are located. The drawbacks include the long, hard slog to get there and the acclimatisation problems caused by the region's considerable altitude.

It's not until you get right into the Solu Khumbu region that the Everest trek really gets interesting. The first part of the trek is not only a hard slog, but is also pretty sparse in the breathtaking views department. The hard slog comes about because the trek doesn't follow valleys, like the Annapurna treks – instead the Everest trek cuts across the valleys. So for day after day it's a tiring process of dropping down one side of a steep valley and climbing up again on the other. By the time you reach the base camp your ascents will total almost 9000m, the full height of Everest from sea level!

The Everest trek starts in the Nepali-speaking Hindu lowlands and ends in the Tibetan-Buddhist highlands where the Sherpas are renowned for their enterprise, hard work, civic responsibility and devotion to the practice of Buddhism. In their often inhospitable land, the potato, a relatively recent introduction, is the main crop, but these days trekking and mountaineering are the backbone of the Sherpa economy. More than half the population in the region is now involved with tourism and Namche Bazaar looks more like an alpine resort than a Sherpa village.

Most Everest trekkers opt to fly one way to avoid having to repeat all those ups and downs. This introduces its own problems as flights to Lukla are notorious for cancellations, waiting lists and short-tempered trekkers. The situation has improved with the introduction of huge Russian MI-17 helicopters that carry 20 or more passengers, but flying in these is definitely a third world experience. If you have the time, walk in from Jiri and fly out from Shyangboche or Lukla. If you want to make a shorter trip you can fly in to Lukla, trek to Everest and then fly out, taking 15 days to trek to Kala Pattar or you can just visit Thami, Namche Bazaar and Tengpoche in a week or so.

The Everest trek may not be quite as good as the Pokhara area for village-inn treks, but these days plenty of accommodation is available during the trekking season even in the normally uninhabited areas around the high peaks.

MEDICAL SERVICES

There are small hospitals in Jiri, Phaplu and Khunde, while the HRA has a medical facility in Pheriche.

EVEREST BASE CAMP TREK
Day 1: Kathmandu via Lamosangu to Jiri

The Everest trek has been getting steadily shorter over the years. The members of the 1953 British expedition which put Hillary and Tensing on the top started their walk to Everest at Bhaktapur in the Kathmandu Valley. Today you can take the Kodari road to Lamosangu, 78 km from Kathmandu, and turn off there to Jiri, a further 110 km. Buses to Jiri leave from Kathmandu Bus Terminal on the ring road at 5.30, 6.30 and 10.30 am, cost Rs 98 and take around 10 hours (keep a close eye on your luggage).

Jiri at 1860m is a relatively new town which has expanded since the road was completed. It has a weekly market on Saturdays and there are many hotels in the town centre near the bus stop and also on the ridge near the market site. The bus stops at the far end of town so you walk back to find somewhere to stay. The *Sagarmatha Lodge & Restaurant* is pretty good with doubles for Rs 30.

TREKKING

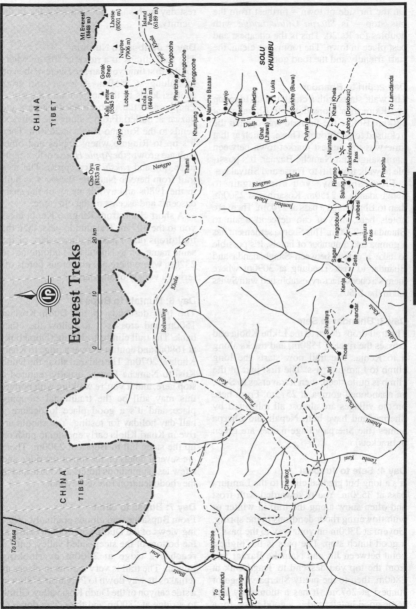

On the far side of town – furthest from the bus stop – is *Sherpa Guide Lodge* with doubles for Rs 20. This is the cheapest and best place in town. The rooms are clean, the staff friendly and the food good.

Day 2: Jiri to Bhandar
The walk starts with a climb to the ridge top at 2400m then drops down to Shivalaya at 1800m. Before the Jiri road was opened the trek used to go through Those, which at that time was the busiest market town between Lamosangu and Namche Bazaar. It's possible to walk from Jiri to Those and Shivalaya.

From Shivalaya you climb again to Sangbadanda at 2150m, Kosaribas at 2500m, then to Bhanjyang, a pass at 2705m. There are hotels here, or you can descend again to Bhandar at 2200m. This Sherpa settlement has a gompa and a number of hotels. It's possible to take a detour between Sangbadanda and Bhandar to visit Thodung at 3090m where there's a cheese factory, established with Swiss aid in the 1950s.

Day 3: Bhandar to Sete
The trail drops down to the Likhu Khola and crosses the river at 1580m, and tracks along it to Kenja. The trail now starts the long climb to Lamjura pass. The first part of the climb is quite steep, then it traverses to Sete, an abandoned gompa at 2575m. From here on the villages are almost all inhabited by Sherpas and have both Nepali and Sherpa names (the Sherpa village names are given in brackets).

Day 4: Sete to Junbesi
It's a long but gradual climb to the Lamjura pass at 3530m. You're rewarded with frost and often snow along the trail in winter or with flowering rhododendrons in the spring. Goyem at 3300m on your way to the pass is a good lunch stop. The pass is the highest point between Jiri and Namche Bazaar and from the top you descend to Tragdobuk at 2860m, then to the pretty Sherpa village of Junbesi at 2675m. It has a monastery and some good hotels, and is a good place for a rest day with some interesting walks in the vicinity.

Day 5: Junbesi to Nuntala
The trail climbs to a ridge at 3080m where for the first time you can see Everest, then on to Salung at 2650m. A lower trail from Junbesi leads to the hospital and airstrip at Phaplu and the district headquarters and bazaar at Salleri. From Salung the trail descends to the Ringmo Khola at 2650m. Then it's up to Ringmo where apples and other fruit are grown; the *Apple House* offers apple juice, pie and *rakshi* (rice spirit). The new trail from here to Namche Bazaar was built in the 1980s and avoids many of the steep descents and ascents of the old route.

A short climb from Ringmo Khola takes you to the 3071m Trakshindo pass, then the trail drops down past the monastery of the same name, on to Nuntala (Manidingma) at 2320m where there are numerous hotels offering a variety of standards.

Day 6: Nuntala to Bupsa
The trail descends to the Dudh Kosi at 1500m and crosses it to follow the other bank. The trail climbs to Jubing (Dorakbuk) at 1680m and continues over a ridge to Khari Khola at 2070m. The old trail along the Dudh Kosi to Namche Bazaar usually required a stop here, and if you're walking with porters this may still be the traditional stopping place, and it's a good place to declare a half-day holiday for resting. You should arrive in Khari Khola early enough to push on up the steep hill to Bupsa at 2300m. There are several hotels on the top of the ridge and a few less sumptuous hotels at Kharte and in the rhododendron forests beyond.

Day 7: Bupsa to Ghat
From Bupsa the trail climbs gradually, offering views of the Dudh Kosi 1000m below at the bottom of the steep-sided valley, until it reaches a ridge at 2900m overlooking Puiyan. The trail is very narrow in places as it makes its way down to Puiyan at 2730m in a side canyon of the Dudh Kosi valley. Climb to a ridge at 2800m and then drop down to

Surkhe (Buwa) at 2293m. Shortly beyond Surkhe is the turn-off to Lukla with its airstrip.

The trail continues to climb through Mushe and Chaunrikarka at 2680m to Chablung, then contours along the side of the Dudh Kosi valley before descending to Ghat (Lhawa) at 2550m. This is a longish day; there are plenty of hotels in Chaunrikarka and Chablung if you don't feel like pushing on.

Day 8: Ghat to Namche Bazaar
Climb past Ghat's gompa and large collection of *manis* (stones carved with a particular Buddhist chant), then trek along the river to Phakding at 2650m, a collection of about 20 hotels that provide the first night stop for people who have flown in to Lukla.

The trail crosses the river on a long swaying bridge, then treks along the river to Benkar at 2700m. It recrosses the river and climbs to Chomoa, with the curious *Hatago Lodge*, created by an eccentric Japanese gentleman. It's a short climb up to Monjo, where there are a number of good places to stay. Show your trek permit and entrance ticket at the Sagarmatha National Park entrance station, then drop down to cross the Dudh Kosi. On the other side it's a short distance to Jorsale at 2850m, then the trail crosses back to the east side of the river before climbing to the high suspension bridge over the Dudh Kosi. It's a steady climb from here to Namche Bazaar at 3440m.

Day 9: Namche Bazaar
This is the main centre in the Solu Khumbu region and a day should be spent here acclimatising. Remember that the victims of altitude sickness are often the fittest and healthiest people who foolishly overextend themselves. It's important to do a strenuous day walk to a higher altitude as part of your acclimatisation, coming back down to Namche to sleep. For this purpose the day walk to Thame (to the west) is worthwhile.

Namche Bazaar has shops, restaurants, a bakery, hotels with hot showers, pool hall, a national park office, a police checkpost (your trekking permit will be inspected here), a moneychanger and even a bank. Namche Bazaar and the surrounding villages have an ample supply of hydroelectricity, which is used for lighting and cooking as well as video parlours. The *Cafe Danfe*, *Khumbu Lodge*, *Tawa Lodge* and *Trekkers Inn* offer food as good as any restaurant in Kathmandu. There is a colourful market each Saturday.

Pay a visit to the Sagarmatha Pollution Control Committee office to find out about the conservation efforts that are being made in the region, and also visit the national park visitor centre on the ridge above town.

Day 10: Namche Bazaar to Tengpoche
The slightly longer route from Namche Bazaar to Tengpoche via Khumjung and Khunde is more interesting than the direct route. It starts by climbing up to the Shyangboche airstrip at 3720m. Above the airstrip is the Everest View Hotel, a Japanese scheme to build a deluxe hotel with great views of the highest mountains on earth. The idea fell flat on its face, since flying straight up to nearly 4000m is not good for people's health, especially for the elderly folk who were generally the ones who could afford it.

From the hotel or the airstrip you continue to Khumjung and then rejoin the direct trail to Tengpoche. The trail descends to the Dudh Kosi at 3250m where there is a small tea house and a series of picturesque waterdriven prayer wheels. A steep ascent brings you to Tengpoche at 3870m. The famous monastery, a photographer's favourite with its background of Ama Dablam, Everest and other peaks, was burnt down in 1989. It has been rebuilt as a large, impressive structure. There's a camping area, a number of places to stay, and during the November-December full moon the colourful Mani Rimdu festival is held here with much singing and dancing.

Day 11: Tengpoche to Pheriche
Beyond Tengpoche the altitude really starts to tell. The trail drops down to Devuche, crosses the Imja Khola and climbs past superb mani stones to Pangboche at 3860m.

The monastery here is worth visiting and the village is a good place for a lunch stop.

The trail then climbs to Pheriche at 4240m where there is a trekkers' aid post and possible medical assistance. Pheriche has a number of hotels and restaurants which usually feature exotic dishes left over from international mountaineering expeditions.

Day 12: Pheriche

Another acclimatisation day should be spent at Pheriche. As at Namche, a solid day walk to a higher altitude is better than just resting; Dingboche and Chukhung are possible destinations. You could also make a day trip to Nangkartshang Gompa or up past Dingboche. Either walk offers good views.

Day 13: Pheriche to Lobuje

The trail climbs to Phalang Karpo at 4340m then Duglha at 4620m before reaching Lobuje at 4930m. The lodge accommodation here is all dormitory-style and the altitude, the cold and the crowding combine to ensure less-than-restful nights.

Day 14: Day Hike to Gorak Shep & Kala Pattar

The trail continues to climb to Gorak Shep at 5160m. You reach in time to continue to Kala Pattar (black rock). At 5545m this small peak offers the best view you'll get of Everest without climbing it. An early start is advised so you can get up Kala Pattar before the clouds roll in.

If you want to actually get to the base camp then it's about six hours round trip from Lobuje, and there's no view. So, if you only have the energy for one side trip, then make it Kala Pattar.

Although there is usually accommodation at Gorak Shep it's nothing to write home about, so it's a better plan to return to Lobuje for the night. The altitude hits nearly everybody; getting back down to Lobuje, or even better to Pheriche, makes a real difference.

Day 15: Lobuje to Dingboche

Staying the night at Dingboche instead of Pheriche makes an interesting alternative.

It's a 'summer village' at 4360m with many good hotels.

Days 16, 17 & 18: Dingboche to Lukla

The next three days retrace your steps down to Lukla via Tengpoche and Namche Bazaar. There are helicopter flights out of Shyangboche, the airstrip above Namche Bazaar, so you could opt for a quick exit from the trek. Flights cost $120 and operate throughout the day. If you continue to Lukla, the flight – either by plane or by helicopter – costs $83. Many groups and individual trekkers fly out from Shyangboche, so there's less pressure on Lukla and it's fairly easy to get a seat out of Lukla these days. Unless you are on a tight schedule, there's probably no need to make advance reservations since there are three helicopter companies and one airline that operate flights here.

Lukla has several places to stay including the relatively expensive *Trekkers Cabin* and *Sagarmatha Hotel*, and life revolves around watching flights come and go.

Day 19: Lukla to Kathmandu

If the gods are with you, your flight comes in and your reservation hasn't been cancelled. Then, after it took you so many days to get here by road and foot, your aircraft only takes 35 minutes to fly you back.

VARIATIONS & SIDE TRIPS

See the Other Treks section later in this chapter for information on the long trek south from the Solu Khumbu region to Dhankuta, an interesting alternative to going straight back to Kathmandu. Alternatives to hanging around in Lukla waiting for flights or walking all the way back to Jiri are also possible but not very satisfactory. Going down to Phaplu, two or three days south of Lukla, is unlikely to get you out any faster. It's a four or five day walk down to Lamidanda from where there are several flights a week to Biratnagar and Kathmandu.

Experienced trekkers could take the little-frequented Barabise to Shivalaya route in, avoiding the Jiri road completely. It's an interesting six day round trip from Namche

MOUNTAIN TREKKING

Top: At the top of the world: Mt Everest from Kala Pattar
Centre: (left to right) Porter and his load, Annapurna Circuit; A climbing Sherpa near the top, Solu Khumbu; A yak, workhorse of the higher altitudes.
Bottom: Towards Nuptse, near Mt Everest.

STAN ARMINGTON

SIMON ROWE

JEFF WILLIAMS

JEFF WILLIAMS

PAUL STEEL

RICHARD EVERIST

JAMES LYON

TONY WHEELER

DAVID ALLARDICE

Top Left: Suspension bridge across the Tamba Kosi, near Sun Kosi
Top Right: Marpha, Jomson trek
Bottom Left: Mountain bike, Ichangu Narayan
Bottom Right: White-water rafting

Saligrams

The black fossils of marine animals known as saligrams are found at several points along the Kali Gandaki, most notably in the area north of Jomsom around Muktinath, but also at Ridi Bazaar and Devghat. These ammonite fossils date back to the Jurassic period over 100 million years ago and provide dramatic evidence that the mighty Himalaya was indeed once under water.

Saligrams are considered holy emblems. They are sometimes believed to represent Vishnu, and are often held during worship and when making a vow. In Pokhara, the image of the goddess Durga (Parvati) in her Binde Basini Bhagwati form is a saligram.

You will see many on sale in Pokhara or along the Jomsom trail. Think twice before buying them: firstly, it is actually illegal to collect them, because the government is concerned about potential damage to Nepal's fossil record, secondly, they're overpriced, and thirdly, adding rocks to your backpack is never a good idea! ∎

TREKKING

Bazaar to Gokyo and back. This trek ends at another Kala Pattar with fine, but different, views of Everest. You can even combine both Kala Pattars by crossing the 5420m Cho La pass, but you had better bring your ice axe and crampons and know how to use them.

A shorter side trip from Namche Bazaar is to Thami, the gateway to Tesi Lapcha and the Rolwaling Himal. You can do a round trip to Thami in a day, although it's better to stay overnight in order to catch the morning views.

Helambu & Langtang Treks

Although they are not as well known and popular as the Everest Base Camp or the Annapurna Circuit treks, these two treks offer a number of distinct advantages. They are north of the Kathmandu Valley, so both are easily accessible from Kathmandu. Indeed you can leave your hotel in Kathmandu and set foot on the Helambu trail within an hour.

The Helambu Trek only takes a week so it is ideal for people who do not have the time for one of the longer treks. Since it stays at relatively low altitudes it does not require fancy cold-weather equipment and clothing. It can start from and finish in the Kathmandu Valley, and although it does not offer superb mountain scenery it is culturally interesting. The maximum height reached is only 2800m and there is plenty of accommodation along the route, although it's still a good idea to carry a sleeping bag.

The Langtang Trek, on the other hand, gives you the opportunity to get right in amongst the Himalayan peaks and to walk through remote areas. The trek lasts 10 to 12 days if you walk in and out, but can be varied by flying out or by crossing a high pass either via the Gosainkund Lakes or across the 5000m Ganja La pass down to the Helambu region. There are fine views and interesting villages, and although there are some relatively uninhabited stretches, accommodation is available. The maximum height reached is 3800m.

MEDICAL SERVICES

The only medical facility on the Helambu

and Langtang treks is the Dhunche dispensary.

HELAMBU TREK

The Helambu Trek only takes seven days, starts from Sundarijal at the eastern end of the Kathmandu Valley and does not climb above 3500m. It makes a loop through the Sherpa-populated Helambu region to the north-east of Kathmandu and only the first day's walk is repeated on the return trip. The trek's main drawback is that it does not offer fine Himalayan views, like some other treks, but it can be trekked on a village-inn basis as there are guest houses and lodges in many of the villages along the trail.

The Sherpa people of the Helambu region are friendly and hospitable, just like their better known kinfolk of the Solu Khumbu region. In other ways, however, they are quite different from the Sherpas from around Mt Everest. The Sherpa women of Helambu are renowned for their beauty and during the Rana period many of them worked for aristocratic families in Kathmandu.

As in Solu Khumbu, the potato is a vitally important crop and not only forms a large part of the local diet, but is also exported to the Nepali lowland in exchange for rice and other lowland produce.

Day 1: Kathmandu via Sundarijal to Pati Bhanjyang

There's no direct bus to Sundarijal, 15 km from Kathmandu, but you can get to the start of the trail by taxi, or get a bus to Jorpati, just beyond Bodhnath, and catch a Sundarijal bus at the road junction. At Sundarijal you must pay a Rs 250 entrance fee to the Seopuri Water Resources & Wildlife Conservation Project, the organisation that administers the area.

From Sundarijal the trail starts off up concrete steps beside the pipeline which brings drinking water down to the valley. Eventually the trail leaves the pipeline from near the dam and reaches Mulkharkha, sprawling up the ridge around 1895m, 600m above Sundarijal. There are superb views back over the valley and some convenient tea houses for rest and refreshment.

The trail continues to climb, but less steeply, through Chisopani and then drops down to Pati Bhanjyang at 1770m. Chisopani is rather like a grubby little truck stop without the trucks but the mountain views in the morning can be very fine. Take care of your possessions here, it's still rather close to the Kathmandu Valley. There are lodges at Chisopani and at Pati Bhanjyang which also has a police checkpost where your trekking permit may be inspected.

Day 2: Pati Bhanjyang to Khutumsang

The trail rises and falls through Chipling at 2170m then over a 2470m pass and down past a large chorten to the village of Gul Bhanjyang. From here the trail climbs again to reach a 2620m pass before descending along a rocky route to Khutumsang at 2470m. The Rs 650 entry fee to the Langtang National Park is collected at the office here, although it's better to get it in Kathmandu before starting out. There are lodges at Gul Bhanjyang and Khutumsang or there's the *Dragon Lodge* beside a pleasant meadow about 45 minutes before Khutumsang.

Day 3: Khutumsang to Malemchigaon

The trail follows a ridge line with views of the Langtang and Gosainkund peaks through sparsely populated forests to Magen Goth with an army checkpost before finally reaching the Tharepati pass at 3490m. The trail to Gosainkund branches off north-west from here. Tharepati has several lodges including the nicely situated *Himaliya Lodge* on the Khutumsang side.

From the pass the trail turns east and descends rapidly down a ravine to the pretty Sherpa village of Malemchigaon at 2530m. There are a number of lodges in the village and a very brightly painted gompa.

Day 4: Malemchigaon to Tarke Gyang

From Malemchigaon the trail continues to drop, crossing the Malemchi Khola by a bridge at 1890m and then making the long climb up the other side of the valley to Tarke

Helambu & Langtang Treks

0   5   10 km

TREKKING

Gyang at 2743m. This is the largest village in Helambu and the prosperous Sherpas who live here specialise, amongst other things, in turning out 'instant antiques' for gullible trekkers. There are some lodges including the pleasant *Mount View Hotel* on the Malemchigaon side of the village. Tarke Gyang makes a good place for a rest day or you can take a side trip up to the peak overlooking the village. This is the end of the route down from the Ganja La pass.

Day 5: Tarke Gyang to Kiul

From Tarke Gyang there is a pleasant alternative route, described after the final day of this trek description. On the loop trek the wide and well used trail descends through rhododendron forests and past Buddhist chortens and mani walls to Kakani at 2070m and Thimbu at 1580m. There is a plan to build a huge water supply project here that will divert water from the Indrawati River through a long tunnel all the way to Kathmandu. By the time you reach Kiul at 1280m you have left the Sherpa highlands and entered the warmer lowland areas where rice is grown. Kiul is at a lower altitude than Kathmandu.

Day 6: Kiul to Pati Bhanjyang

The trail descends along a river, crossing it on the second suspension bridge at just 1190m then joining a wide trail at Mahenkal and following it to Talamarang at 940m. Here the trail leaves the road and climbs steeply to Batache and then Thakani, on the ridge top, at 1890m. From here the trail follows the ridge to Pati Bhanjyang where the Helambu circuit is completed.

Day 7: Pati Bhanjyang via Sundarijal to Kathmandu

The final day retraces the first day's walk.

Alternative Routes from Tarke Gyang

An alternative route can be followed from Tarke Gyang through Sermathang and then along a long ridge through Kakani and Dubhachaur to join the road at Malemchi Pul bazaar, south of Talamarang. This route is very pleasant as far as Malemchi and attracts relatively few trekkers. There are numerous lodges at Sermathang and Malemchi, but the choice is limited elsewhere.

From Malemchi the final stretch is along a dusty roadway which brings you out on the Kathmandu to Kodari road at Panchkhal, from where you will have to take a bus 55 km back to Kathmandu via Dhulikhel. You can usually get a ride on a bus or truck down the road from Malemchi and this route does avoid having to duplicate the final stretch from Pati Bhanjyang through Sundarijal.

Another Helambu alternative is to start and finish from Panchkhal on the main road, completing the shorter loop through Malemchi, Talamarang, Kiul, Tarke Gyang, Sermathang and Malemchi. It's also possible to walk on from Bahunpati to Sankhu or Nagarkot, completing a loop which starts and finishes in the Kathmandu Valley but does not retrace your steps at any point.

The alternative routes are as follows:

Day 5: Tarke Gyang to Sermathang

The easy trail descends gently through a beautiful forest to Sermathang, the centre of an important apple-growing area. Sermathang is more spread out than the closely spaced houses of Tarke Gyang and there are fine views of the Malemchi Khola Valley to the south. Trekking permits are checked at Sermathang and if you do the trek in the reverse direction this is where you must pay the Rs 650 entry fee to the Langtang National Park.

Day 6: Sermathang via Malemchi to Kathmandu

From Sermathang the trail continues to descend to Kakani and Dubhachaur then steeply down to Malemchi where it meets the road. You should be able to get a bus from here to Banepa where you change to a bus to Kathmandu.

LANGTANG TREK

Langtang Lirung (7246m) is visible to the north of Kathmandu on clear days. The Langtang Trek takes up to two weeks and leads to the foot of glaciers high in the Langtang Valley. The trail passes through Tibetan and Tamang villages and offers fine views of the Ganesh Himal. Though the trek passes through comparatively lightly populated and undeveloped areas, it's possible to stay at village inns along the route. Ascending from just 541m at Trisuli Bazaar to 3800m at Kyanjin Gompa, the trail passes through an ever-changing climate and offers trekkers an exceptional diversity of scenery and culture.

Day 1: Kathmandu via Trisuli to Dhunche

It's 72 km from Kathmandu to Trisuli Bazaar – about four hours by car or six by bus. The road is paved but very winding and offers some fine mountain views. Rani Pauwa is the only large village along the route. From here the 50 km road to Dhunche is steep, winding and rather hairy, passing through Betrawati and Thare. There are two buses per day from Kathmandu to Dhunche, and the 12 hour trip costs Rs 90.

Dhunche is a pretty village at 1950m and here you will have your trekking permit checked and must pay the entrance fee to the Langtang National Park, although it's preferable to buy a permit in Kathmandu before starting your trek. The road continues from here, winding its way over a mountain pass to the village of Somdang, at the foot of Ganesh Himal.

Day 2: Dhunche to Syabru

Soon after Dhunche the trail leaves the road and follows the Trisuli Khola, crossing it and climbing steeply and then leaving the Gosainkund trail and following a ridge to Bharku at 1860m. Most of the Trisuli River's water comes from the Bhote Kosi River, from Tibet. (Bhote Kosi means 'river from Tibet'.) From Bharku you climb to 2300m and enter the Langtang Valley with views of Himalayan peaks to the west, north and east. The trail descends rapidly to Syabru at 2130m where there are lots of good hotels.

There is an alternative route to Langtang by continuing the drive past Dhunche to Syabrubesi and then trekking up the Langtang Valley through Syapargaon, joining the primary route near Chongong.

Day 3: Syabru to Chongong

The trail descends through forest to the Langtang Khola at 1890m then follows the river upstream, crossing from the southern to northern bank to reach Chongong at 2380m. Some maps show this as Lama Hotel, the name of one of the places to stay here.

Day 4: Chongong to Langtang Village

The trail continues to follow the Langtang Khola, climbing steeply, at times very steeply, to Ghora Tabela at 3000m where there are fine views of Langtang Lirung. Although there is no permanent settlement here, there is a good lodge, and your trekking permit and national park entry permit will be checked again here.

From Ghora Tabela the trail climbs more gradually to Langtang village at 3500m. The national park headquarters is here and Langtang and the villages around are in Tibetan style with stone walls around the fields and herds of yaks.

Day 5: Langtang Village to Kyanjin Gompa

Passing through small villages it only takes the morning to climb to Kyanjin Gompa at 3800m where there is a monastery, a lodge and a cheese factory. There are a number of interesting walks from the gompa and if you are intending to continue over the Ganja La pass to Helambu you should spend some time here acclimatising. From the gompa climb up to 4300m on the glacial moraine to the north for the superb views of Langtang Lirung. Day walks can also be made to Yala or further up the valley for more spectacular views.

Alternative Routes from Kyanjin Gompa

There are several alternative routes back to Kathmandu. There are very occasional helicopter flights from the nearby STOL airstrip, but these are usually sightseeing trips and it's unlikely that you could get a seat on one. You

TREKKING

can simply retrace your route back down the valley to Dhunche or, if the season and weather permits, attempt the high route via the Gosainkund Lakes to Helambu. If you have a tent, stove and food, you could tackle the Ganja La pass.

Across the Ganja La Walking from the Kyanjin Gompa at the end of the Langtang route south to Tarke Gyang in Helambu involves crossing the 5106m Ganja La pass. The pass is usually blocked by snow from December to March and at any time a bad weather change can make crossing the pass decidedly dangerous. The walk takes four days and between Kyanjin and Tarke Gyang there is no permanent settlement. The final climb to the pass on both sides is steep and exposed. During most of the year there is no water for two days south of the pass, so you must be prepared for all these complications.

This is one of the more difficult passes in Nepal and should not be attempted without local advice, adequate acclimatisation, good equipment and some experience.

Gosainkund Lakes The trek via the Gosainkund Lakes is another way of crossing between Langtang and Helambu. Again, adequate preparation is necessary, but there are tea houses along the route, so finding food and accommodation is not a problem in the trekking season. There is often snow on the Gosainkund trail, so the route becomes impassable during much of the winter.

It takes four days to walk from Dhunche, at the start of the Langtang Trek, to Tharepati in Helambu, although this entails a big altitude gain (nearly 2500m) in a short time. It's better perhaps to gain altitude gradually by going into the Langtang Valley first, and visiting the lakes on the return to Kathmandu. The trek can also be made either from Helambu or by turning off the Langtang route from Syabru, and it's an excellent choice as a return route from the Langtang Trek.

Gosainkund is the site for a great pilgrimage in August each year – this is the height of the monsoon, not a pleasant time for trek-

king. The large rock in the centre of the lake is said to be the remains of a Shiva shrine and it is also claimed that a channel carries water from the lake directly to the tank at the Kumbeshwar Temple in Patan, 60 km to the south.

Day 1 takes you from Dhunche at 1950m to the Sing Gompa at 3350m. The route from Syabru to the gompa can be confusing. The second day's walk climbs steeply with fine mountain views then drops down to Saraswatikund at 4100m, the first of the Gosainkund Lakes. The second lake is Bhairabkund, the third is Gosainkund itself at 4380m. There are seasonal lodges at Gosainkund, and also stone shelters used by pilgrims during the festival at the August full moon. During the season, hotels operate along the route from Sing Gompa to the lakes.

From the lake the trail climbs still higher to the four lakes near the Lauribina pass at 4610m, then drops down to Gopte at 3430m where there are also seasonal lodges.

It was in the Gopte area that an Australian trekker got lost in 1991 and was not found for 43 days. It should be pointed out that he ended up in this predicament by straying from the major – and even minor – trails, and disregarded basically all the safety rules. Nearby is the place where a Thai International Airbus became lost in 1992 and crashed into a mountain.

The final day's walk descends to a stream and then climbs to Tharepati at 3490m. From Tharepati you can either take the direct route south to Pati Bhanjyang and Kathmandu or head west to Tarke Gyang and Helambu.

Jomsom, Annapurna Circuit & Other Pokhara Treks

Pokhara is the starting or finishing point for some of the best trekking in Nepal and the long Annapurna Circuit Trek is the most popular trek in the country.

The reasons for the area's popularity are numerous. Firstly, you can start your trek from Pokhara itself: no long, uncomfortable bus rides or problematic flights are required to get to the starting point. Secondly, you are in the mountains immediately: the Annapurna Range, the centre for these treks, is very close to Pokhara.

The treks in this part of the country offer a great deal of cultural and geographic diversity. For most of Nepal's length, the Himalaya form the border between Nepal and China. The Annapurna mountains are different, in that the border is well to the north so the Jomsom and Annapurna Circuit treks both go north of the Himalayan watershed, into the high-altitude, dry, desert area which is characteristic of the Tibetan Plateau. Finally, these treks are the best in Nepal for independent trekkers and a network of lodges and guest houses can be found all along the main trails. The Annapurna Circuit has even been dubbed 'the apple pie trail'.

The entire region is administered by the Annapurna Conservation Area Project (ACAP) which is working to conserve the natural and cultural resources of the area.

The Pokhara area also offers a number of one day treks or short three or four day treks. These are covered in the Around Pokhara section of the Pokhara chapter. There are three popular longer treks from Pokhara, all of which follow the same route at some point.

The Jomsom Trek, from Pokhara up the Kali Gandaki Valley, is the most popular in Nepal with superb scenery, interesting people and the best trailside accommodation in the country. It takes about a week to reach Muktinath, the end point of the trek. Walking back takes another week or you can fly back to Pokhara from Jomsom. Muktinath, the high point of the trek, is at 3700m.

The Annapurna Circuit takes a full three weeks completely encircling the Annapurna Range – for scenery and cultural diversity this is the best trek in Nepal. It crosses to the north of the main Himalayan range, on to the Tibetan Plateau, and crosses a 5400m pass. The last seven days of the walk from Muktinath to Pokhara are the same as the Jomsom Trek, but in reverse.

Finally, the Annapurna Sanctuary Trek starts from Pokhara and takes you through the centre of the Annapurna Range to the Machhapuchhare and Annapurna base camps. This trek takes about six days and reaches a maximum height of 3000m at the Annapurna Base Camp. Numerous lodges line the route.

MEDICAL SERVICES

Around the Annapurna Circuit the only facilities are the small hospitals at Jomsom, Besisahar and Baglung. There are two small government dispensaries and an HRA post on the Manang side of the Thorung La pass.

JOMSOM TREK

The Jomsom Trek is essentially the final third of the Annapurna Circuit. It follows the Kali Gandaki Valley between the soaring peaks of Annapurna and Dhaulagiri and finally emerges to the north of the main Himalayan range, on the dry, desert-like Tibetan Plateau. The final destination is the holy temple of Muktinath, a further day's walk beyond Jomsom. The return to Pokhara can either be made by retracing your steps down the Kali Gandaki Valley or by flying from Jomsom to Pokhara or Kathmandu.

Day 1: Pokhara to Tikedungha

Like many other treks in Nepal this one is getting shorter as roads gradually extend further into the mountains. Eventually it will probably be possible to drive all the way to Jomsom. A road has been pushed through the hills from Pokhara to Baglung. Buses leave for Baglung from the bus station in Bag Bazaar at the northern end of Pokhara.

Take the bus up the ridge to Naudanda and then down into the Modi Khola Valley and get off at Nayapul (new bridge). It's then a short walk up the Modi Khola to the large village of Birethanti at 1065m, where you can really see how civilised this trek is. Birethanti has a bakery, bank and even sidewalk cafes! A trail to Ghandruk turns off here. Birethanti has excellent hotels but you may want to continue further to shorten the next day's long climb. Sticking to the northern side of the Bhurungdi Khola, the trail climbs to Hille and nearby Tikedungha at 1525m. Both Tikedungha and Hille have places to stay.

It's still possible to walk to Birethanti of course. You can reach Naudanda by walking through Sarangkot (see the Pokhara chapter for details) and along the ridge to Kaski, which has the ruins of a small palace, and on to Naudanda. There are fine views of the whole Annapurna Range and back over Pokhara and Phewa Tal from this large village. Naudanda has a choice of hotels and a trekking permit checkpost, so for day trek-

kers without a permit this is the end of the line. From Naudanda, follow the road for a bit, then turn off past Lumle to Chandrakot and drop to Birethanti.

You can also avoid the long climb over the Ghorapani hill by taking the bus on to Maldhunga, seven km before Baglung. From here it's a two day walk up the Kali Gandaki to Tatopani.

Day 2: Tikedungha to Ghorapani
From Tikedungha the trail climbs very steeply to Ulleri, a large Magar village at 2070m. It continues to ascend, but more gently,

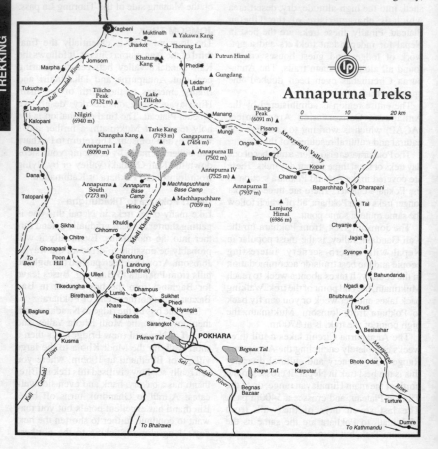

TREKKING

through fine forests of oak and rhododendron to Bahunthanti at 2250m, and then to Nayathanti at 2460m. Another hour brings you to Ghorapani at 2775m.

Only a short walk beyond Ghorapani is the Deorali pass *(deorali* actually means 'pass') with spectacular views. An hour's climb from here will take you to Poon (or Pun) Hill, one of the best Himalayan viewpoints in Nepal. There are hotels at Ghorapani and at Deorali. *Ghora* means 'horse' and *pani* means 'water' and indeed long caravans of pack horses are regularly seen all along the Jomsom Trek. A trail also runs from Ghorapani/Deorali to Ghandruk. This part of the trek is plagued by leeches during the monsoon and there may be snow on the trail in the winter.

Day 3: Ghorapani to Tatopani

The trail descends steeply to Chitre at 2390m where there are more lodges offering accommodation. From here the hills are extensively terraced as the trail drops down through Sikha, a large village with shops and hotels at 1980m, and then descends gently to Ghara at 1705m. A further steep descent of 500m takes you to the Ghar Khola where the trail crosses the river on a suspension bridge and then climbs up above the Kali Gandaki River before crossing that too.

Turning north the trail soon reaches Tatopani at 1180m. It's a busy population centre where you will find some of the best food along the whole trail, and you can even get a cold beer to go with it. *Tato* means 'hot' and *pani* is 'water', a name earned courtesy of the hot springs by the river. Tatopani is a popular destination for a shorter trek out of Pokhara.

Day 4: Tatopani to Kalopani

The trail follows the Kali Gandaki Valley all the rest of the way to Jomsom. The river cuts a channel between the peaks of Annapurna I and Dhaulagiri, thus qualifying the Kali Gandaki Valley for the title of the world's deepest gorge. The two 8000m mountaintops are only 38 km apart and the river flows between them at a height of less than 2200m.

The Kali Gandaki Valley is also the home for the Thakalis, a group noted for their trading and business expertise, particularly in running hotels and lodges not only here in their homeland but also in Pokhara and elsewhere in Nepal. Thakali women are very liberated and many of the lodges are run by women, whose menfolk have been taken elsewhere by business.

From Tatopani the trail climbs gradually to Dana at 1400m. This is where the difficult track branches off to Maurice Herzog's base camp, used for his historic ascent of Annapurna in 1950.

The trail continues to climb to Rukse Chhara and at one stage takes a precarious route through a very steep and narrow section of the gorge. Another suspension bridge crosses the river at 1935m and the trail then goes through Ghasa at 2000m, the first Thakali village.

A steep climb through forest takes you to the Lete Khola, then to the village of Lete at 2470m with a superb view of the western flank of Dhaulagiri and finally to Kalopani at 2560m. Kalopani has great mountain views and some comfortable lodges to view them from.

Day 5: Kalopani to Jomsom

For a distance from Kalopani there are trails on both sides of the river to choose from. Larjung on the west bank at 2560m has interesting alleyways and tunnels between the houses, an attempt to avoid the fierce winds that often whistle down the Kali Gandaki Valley. Khobang is the next village, with a gompa above it, and the mountain views on this stretch are the best to be seen.

Tukuche at 2590m is one of the most important Thakali villages, once a meeting place for traders from Tibet. Despite the growth of tourism in this area Tukuche is still a quieter, smaller place than it was during the era of trade with Tibet.

From here the landscape changes as you enter the drier and more desert-like country north of the Himalayan watershed. It also gets windier: gentle breezes from the north in the early morning shift to a gale from the

TREKKING

south as the morning wears on. Marpha, at 2665m, virtually huddles behind a ridge to keep out of the wind! The village also has some of the most luxurious accommodation to be found along the trail and is a good alternative to staying in Jomsom. A government established project between Tukuche and Marpha grows fruit and vegetables for the whole region.

At 2713m, Jomsom is the major centre in the region and has a hospital and the inevitable trekking-permit checkpoint. If you're heading in the opposite direction on the Annapurna Circuit you must get your permit stamped here as it will be checked further south. This is the last Thakali village – those further north are inhabited by people of Tibetan descent. Jomsom has regular flights to Kathmandu ($110) and Pokhara ($50), but the Kathmandu to Jomsom flights can be problematic since in winter Kathmandu is often closed by fog in the early morning while the wind stops flights into or out of Jomsom later in the morning. Pokhara to Jomsom flights are less likely to be affected.

Day 6: Jomsom to Muktinath

If you have time, it's worth making the side trip to the mediaeval-looking village of Kagbeni at 2810m. This very Tibetan influenced settlement is as close as you can get to Lo Monthang, the capital of the legendary kingdom of Mustang further to the north, without paying a $700 permit fee. From here the trail climbs steeply to rejoin the regular trail before Khingar is reached at 3200m. The trail climbs through a desert landscape then past meadows and streams to the interesting village of Jharkot at 3500m. A further climb brings you to Ranipauwa, the accommodation area of Muktinath, at 3710m.

Muktinath is a pilgrimage centre for Buddhists and Hindus. You'll see Tibetan traders as well as sadhus from the far south of India. The shrines in a grove of trees include a Buddhist gompa and the Vishnu temple of Jiwala Mayi. An old temple nearby shelters a spring and natural gas jets which provide Muktinath's famous eternal flame. It's the earth-water-fire combination that accounts for Muktinath's great religious significance.

From Muktinath you can retrace your steps to Pokhara, or simply to Jomsom and hope to catch a flight from there. It is possible to continue beyond Muktinath and cross the Thorung La pass to walk the rest of the Annapurna Circuit but this long walk is better made in the opposite direction.

ANNAPURNA CIRCUIT

Since it opened to foreign trekkers in 1977, the three week Annapurna Circuit has become the most popular trek in Nepal. It passes through country inhabited by a wide diversity of peoples, offers spectacular mountain scenery and goes to the north of the main Himalayan range on to the high and dry Tibetan Plateau. To many independent trekkers it also offers the considerable advantage of having accommodation available each night.

The circuit is usually walked in a counterclockwise direction because of the difficulties of crossing the Thorung La pass. Travelling clockwise the longer ascent and shorter descent from west to east is too much for many people to manage in one day. The Thorung La pass at 5416m is often closed by snow from mid-December to mid-March and bad weather can move in at any time. Trekkers should be prepared to turn back due to the weather or if they suffer from altitude sickness. If you take porters over this pass you must make sure they are adequately equipped for severe cold and snow.

Most people start the circuit from Dumre, on the Kathmandu to Pokhara road. There are jeeps and buses that ply the miserably rough road north from Dumre as far as Besisahar. Some treks now walk the circuit starting directly from Pokhara by walking from Begnas Bazaar, by Begnas Tal and Rupa Tal, through Karputar to Besisahar. Although this route avoids some tedious road travel it does cross country where you will have to camp since village inns are not (yet) available. Another variation at the beginning of the trek is to start from Gorkha and walk across to intersect the route up from

Dumre, again avoiding that tedious initial stretch of road.

After you cross the Thorung La pass from Manang to Muktinath the final seven days of the circuit trek are the same as the Jomsom Trek from Pokhara, but in reverse.

Day 1: Kathmandu via Dumre to Besisahar

It's a long and somewhat tedious drive from Kathmandu to the turn-off at Dumre. Starting from Pokhara is much easier since Dumre is 137 km from Kathmandu but only 70 km from Pokhara and, more importantly, the first stretch out of Kathmandu is in very bad condition. From Dumre, at 440m, buses and 4WDs run regularly to Besisahar at 790m. Just after the monsoon the road is a sea of mud, so you might get only as far as Bhote Odar, which is about three hours walk from Besisahar.

Day 2: Besisahar to Bahundanda

The trail drops, then climbs to Khudi at 790m. This is the first Gurung village that you reach (many of Nepal's Gurkha soldiers are Gurungs). From Khudi the trail offers fine views of Himalchuli and Peak 29 (Ngadi Chuli) as it climbs to Bhulbhule at 825m; it then goes to Ngadi before reaching Lampata at 1135m and nearby Bahundanda at 1310m. Both Lampata and Bahundanda have hotels although Lampata probably offers a better choice.

Day 3: Bahundanda to Chyanje

From Bahundanda the trail drops steeply to Syange at 1070m. The trail crosses the Marsyangdi River on a suspension bridge and then follows the river to the stone village of Jagat before climbing through forest to Chyanje at 1400m.

Day 4: Chyanje to Bagarchhap

The rocky trail follows the Marsyangdi River steadily uphill to Tal at 1675m, the first village in the Manang district. The trail crosses a wide, flat valley then climbs a stone stairway to 1860m before dropping down to another stairway. The trail continues up and down to Dharapani at 1890m, which is marked by a stone entrance chorten typical of the Tibetan influenced villages from here northwards. Bagarchhap at 2160m has flat-roofed stone houses of typical Tibetan design although the village is still in the transition zone before the dry highlands. A spectacular mudslide roared through the centre of this village in late 1995 and wiped out a lodge and several houses.

Day 5: Bagarchhap to Chame

The trail, often rough and rocky, climbs to Tyanja at 2360m and then continues through forest, but near the river, to Kopar at 2590m. Chame at 2685m is the headquarters of the Manang district and its buildings include many hotels and a bank. There are fine views of Annapurna II as you approach Chame and two small hot springs by the town.

Day 6: Chame to Pisang

The trail runs through deep forest in a steep and narrow valley, crosses a river on a long bridge at 2910m and then another bridge at 3040m. Views include the first sight of the soaring Paungda Danda rock face. The trail continues to climb to Pisang which sprawls between 3200m and 3300m and has many hotels.

Day 7: Pisang to Manang

The walk is now through the drier upper part of the Manang district, cut off from the full effect of the monsoon by the Annapurna Range. The people of this area herd yaks and raise crops for part of the year, but they also continue to enjoy special trading rights gained way back in 1784. Today they exploit these rights with shopping trips to Singapore and Hong Kong where they buy electronic goods and other modern equipment to resell in Nepal. Not surprisingly they are shrewd traders and hard bargainers.

From Pisang there are alternate trails north and south of the Marsyangdi River which meet up again at Mungji. The southern route by Ongre, with its airstrip, at 3325m involves less climbing than the northern route via Ghyaru, though there are better views on the trail that follows the northern bank of the river. The trail continues from Mungji past the picturesque but partially hidden village of Bryaga at 3475m to nearby Manang at 3535m where there are a number of hotels and a HRA post.

Day 8: Manang

It's important to spend a day acclimatising in Manang before pushing on to the Thorung La pass. There are some fine day walks and magnificent views around the village, and it's best to gain altitude during the day, returning back down to Manang to sleep. The Manangbhot people's legendary trading skills are seen at their keenest here – buy with caution!

Day 9: Manang to Ledar

From Manang it's an ascent of nearly 2000m to the Thorung La pass. The trail climbs steadily through Tengi, leaving the Marsyangdi Valley and continuing along the Jarsang Khola Valley. The vegetation becomes steadily more sparse as you reach Ledar (or Lathar) at 4250m.

Day 10: Ledar to Phedi

Finally, you descend to cross the river at 4310m and then climb up to Phedi at 4420m. There are hotels here and the range of accommodation is being expanded. At the height of the season as many as 200 trekkers a day may cross over the Thorung La pass and beds can be in short supply. Some trekkers find they are suffering from altitude sickness symptoms at Phedi.

If you find yourself in a similar condition you must retreat downhill; even the descent to Ledar can make a difference.

Day 11: Phedi to Muktinath

Phedi means 'foot of the hill' and that's where it is, at the foot of the 5416m Thorung La pass. The trail climbs steeply but is regularly used and easy to follow. The altitude and snow can be problems: when the pass is snow-covered it is often impossible to cross. It takes about four hours to climb up to the pass, marked by chortens and prayer flags.

The effort is worthwhile as the view from the top is magnificent. From the pass you have a tough 1600m descent to Muktinath.

Days 12-17: Muktinath to Pokhara

The remaining seven days of the trek simply follow the Pokhara, Jomsom, Muktinath route but in the opposite direction. Completing the Annapurna Circuit in 17 days allows for only one rest and acclimatisation day at Manang. It's very easy to slot a few additional days into the schedule.

ANNAPURNA SANCTUARY TREK

The walk up to the Annapurna Base Camp is a classic walk right into the heart of the mountains. The walk ends at a point where you are virtually surrounded by soaring Himalayan peaks. At one time this trek was a real expedition into an uninhabited wilderness area, but now there are a string of lodges that operate during the trekking season. The return trip takes 10 to 14 days and the walk to the base camp can be tacked on as a side trip from the Jomsom or Annapurna Circuit treks.

There are several routes to the sanctuary, all meeting at Chomrong. The diversion from the Jomsom and Annapurna Circuit treks is made from Ghorapani to Ghandruk.

The route to the Annapurna Sanctuary is occasionally blocked by avalanches. Check with the ACAP offices in Ghandruk or Khuldighar or at Lakeside in Pokhara for a report on current trail conditions, and do not proceed into the sanctuary if there is heavy rain or snow.

Day 1: Pokhara to Dhampus

The walk from Pokhara leaves the Jomsom and Annapurna Circuit routes at Phedi – you can take a bus or taxi to Phedi. From Phedi the trail climbs to Dhampus which stretches for several km from 1580m to 1700m and has a number of widely spaced hotels. Theft is a real problem in Dhampus, so take care.

Day 2: Dhampus to Ghandruk

The trail climbs to Pothana, descends steeply through a forest to Bichok, finally emerging in the Modi Khola Valley. It continues to drop to Tolka and then the Gurung village of Landruk at 1650m. The trail continues to descend to a suspension bridge at 1370m, then climbs steeply to join the trail from Birethanti and finally follows a long, long stone stairway to Ghandruk. There are many hotels in this large and confusing village; the biggest are near the top. From here Machhapuchhare really does begin to appear to have a fish tail. The ACAP visitor centre here offers advice and has displays and video shows describing the region; it also has a telephone for emergency use.

Day 3: Ghandruk to Chhomrong

The trail climbs to a pass at 2220m, then descends steeply to the Khumnu Khola at 1770m before climbing up again to Khumnu (or Kimrong). The trail continues to climb higher before dropping down to Chhomrong at 1950m, the last permanent settlement in the valley. There are a number of places to stay and to stock up on supplies.

Day 4: Chhomrong to Bamboo Lodge

The trail drops down to the Chhomrong Khola, then climbs to Khuldighar at 2380m where there is an ACAP checkpost and information centre. Continue on to Bamboo Lodge, a collection of five hotels. This stretch of trail has many leeches early and late in the trekking season.

Day 5: Bamboo Lodge to Hinko & Deurali

The trail climbs through bamboo, then rhododendron forests to Dovan, Himalayan Hotel and on to Hinko at 3020m. There is accommodation in Deurali, on the ridge above Hinko. This is the stretch of trail that is most subject to avalanches.

Day 6: Hinko to Annapurna Base Camp

The trail climbs on past the Machhapuchhare Base Camp (which isn't really a base camp since climbing the mountain is not permitted) to the Annapurna Base Camp. This area is called the Annapurna Sanctuary since it is totally surrounded by mountains. You can

stay at Machhapuchhare Base Camp or trek two hours on to Annapurna Base Camp where the mountain views are even more spectacular.

Back to Pokhara

On the return trip you can retrace your steps, or divert from Ghandruk to Ghorapani to visit Poon Hill and follow the Annapurna Circuit or Jomsom route back to Pokhara.

The Ghorapani to Ghandruk walk is becoming increasingly popular as a way of linking the Annapurna Sanctuary Trek with treks up the Kali Gandaki Valley. It's also used for shorter loop walks out of Pokhara (see the Around Pokhara section of the Pokhara chapter for details of these walks).

Other Treks

The Everest Base Camp Trek in the east, the Langtang and Helambu treks to the north of Kathmandu and the three Pokhara area treks in central Nepal are used by the vast majority of all trekkers. Yet there are other alternatives taking you to areas still relatively unvisited.

KANCHENJUNGA BASE CAMP

The trekking route up to the Kanchenjunga Base Camp in the extreme north-eastern corner of the country has recently been opened to trekkers, but you have to go with a recognised agency. The starting point can be Ilam or Basantpur by road, or Tumlingtar or Taplejung by air.

MAKALU BASE CAMP

It's a long but fine trek from Hile or Tumlingtar up the Arun River to the Makalu Base Camp in eastern Nepal. The area is protected by the recently established Makalu-Barun National Park and its associated conservation area.

SOLU KHUMBU TO HILE

As an alternative to flying back to Kathmandu from Lukla, or walking back to Jiri, the Everest Base Camp Trek can be extended by walking for 11 days east and then south to Hile. From Hile you can travel by road through Dhankuta and Dharan to Biratnagar from where there are buses and flights to Kathmandu.

DOLPO

Trekking to the Dolpo region has only been permitted since mid-1989. The region lies to the west of the Kali Gandaki Valley. A special permit is needed, and you must be well equipped and self-sufficient. From Pokhara it's a tough 14 day trek to Phoksumdo Lake and beyond.

RARA LAKE

The eight day round trip trek from Jumla to the Rara Lake and back still gets less than 50 trekkers a year. Trekking here requires real planning since flights are difficult to get on, porters are hard to find and little food is available.

MUSTANG

Mustang has lured trekkers for many years, but was closed for a time both because of a guerrilla war that was waged along the border with Tibet, and because of the ecological sensitivity of the region. The area is part of the Tibetan Plateau, and is high, dry and beautiful. It lies to the north-west of the Kali Gandaki, beyond Kagbeni, which is as far west as you can go on the Jomsom Trek. It is only possible to enter with an organised group, and permits are a steep $700 for 10 days.

Mountain Biking

This chapter was written by John Prosser, a keen cyclist who has explored many Nepali biking routes. In 1992 he started Equator Mountain Bikes, which operates cycling tours around Nepal.

With its strong wheels, knobbly tyres, wide selection of gears and overall strength, the mountain bike is an ideal machine for exploring Nepal. These attributes make it possible to escape paved roads, and to ride tracks and trails to remote, rarely visited areas of the country. Most importantly, they allow independent travel – you can stop whenever you like – and they liberate you from crowded buses.

Nepal's tremendously diverse terrain and its many tracks and trails create an ideal venue for mountain biking. Nepal offers challenging mountain roads that climb thousands of metres to reach spectacular viewpoints and reward with exhilarating descents. The Terai has flat, smooth roads, and mountain biking is an excellent way of getting to the Royal Chitwan National Park. For the adventurous there are large areas of the country, particularly in the west and the Terai, still to be explored by mountain bike.

The Kathmandu Valley has a vast network of tracks, trails and back roads, some of which are the most rugged in the country. Mountain biking is the perfect means of transport to visit the valley's wealth of temples, stupas and mediaeval towns. Where a mountain bike really comes into its own, however, is when you get off the beaten track and discover idyllic Newari villages that have preserved their traditional, rural lifestyle. To ride a network of trails alongside paddy fields to areas rarely visited by tourists allows you to experience the tranquillity of rural Nepal.

Many trails are narrow walkways and are not shown on maps, so you need a good sense of direction when venturing out without a guide. It is important to know the name of

the next village you wish to reach so locals can point you in the right direction. The most detailed Kathmandu Valley map is commonly referred to as the 'German map' (also Schneider and Nelles Verlag), and is widely available in Kathmandu.

TRAIL CONDITIONS

Traffic travels on the left-hand side with smaller vehicles giving way to larger ones. Bikes are at the bottom of the list, and definitely come off second best if they mess with Tata trucks! Nepali roads carry a vast array of vehicles: auto-rickshaws, tempos, buses, motorbikes, cars, trucks, tractors... Once you've throw in a few holy cows, wheelbarrows, dogs, people, chickens and rickshaws all moving at different speeds under a barrage of blowing horns, you have a typical Nepali street scene!

The centre of Kathmandu, unfortunately, is becoming a very unpleasant place to ride due to pollution and heavy traffic – if you are sensitive to traffic fumes, consider bringing some sort of mask.

Extreme care should be taken near villages as young children play on the trails and roads (I've even come across toddlers sitting right in the middle of a main highway!). All animals should be approached with caution

– chickens and buffaloes are particularly unpredictable.

A few intrepid mountain bikers have taken bikes into trekking areas hoping to find great riding. What they discovered is that these areas are not suitable for mountain biking. The tracks and trails through Nepal's hills and mountains usually have considerable sections of stone steps that are impossible to ride. In addition, there are always trekkers, porters and local people clogging up the trails. Bikers just add one more problem to these heavy-traffic areas.

Riders who have taken bikes to such places as the Everest Base Camp or around the Annapurnas have found that they carry their bikes for between 70% and 90% of the time! If you do insist on carrying something on your trek, try a bath tub. (I don't think anyone has done so yet, and the tub is potentially useful.)

Local buses are useful if you wish to avoid some of the routes that carry heavy traffic. You can place your bike on the roof for an additional charge, which varies between Rs 20 and Rs 60, depending on the length of the journey and the bus company.

The bus driver will normally provide rope and the luggage boy will assist you. It is important to make sure the bike is held securely to cope with the rough roads and that it is lying as flat as possible to prevent it catching low wires or tree branches. Unless you travel with foam padding it is hard to avoid the frame receiving a few scratches.

It is not possible to carry bikes on domestic flights.

EQUIPMENT

If you plan to do more than use roads it is a good idea to bring your own bike. At present the only bikes you can hire in Nepal are of low quality and are not suitable for the rigours of trail riding. In addition, rental shops do not supply pannier bags, luggage racks, or tools for on-road repairs. See the Kathmandu and Pokhara Getting Around sections for information on bike hire.

Your bike can be carried as part of your baggage allowance on international flights. You are required to deflate the tyres and turn the handle bars parallel with the frame. Nepali customs will sign the bike into your passport to make sure you take it with you when you leave the country.

If you bring your bike it is essential to bring tools and spare parts, as these are not available in Nepal. Unfortunately, carrying a complete tool kit and spares for everything that might fail is impractical, so it is quite likely you will have to improvise. Specialised tools, such as bottom-bracket wrenches, will not be available, but it might be possible to use a hammer and screw driver, or even to get tools made locally. If you put a hole in your tyre beyond repair, a local tyre will enable you to complete the journey.

Fortunately, what local bike repair shops lack in spare parts and knowledge of the latest fads, they make up in their ability to improvise. Their standard of skill is usually high.

ORGANISED BIKE TOURS

There are a small number of companies offering guided trips on mountain bikes. They provide high-quality bikes, local and western guides, pannier bags and helmets. There is normally a minimum of four clients per trip. Vehicle support is available for longer tours at extra cost.

Himalayan Mountain Bikes or HMB (☎ 01-417036; fax 416870) has an office in the compound next to the Kathmandu Guest House. HMB offers a range of tours from day trips (around $30), to overnight trips (around $80), to longer, fully supported tours of Nepal at around $45 a day.

Touring Routes

THE SCAR ROAD

The Scar Rd is considered to be the Kathmandu Valley's classic off-road adventure. It's a 70 km round trip.

Leaving Kathmandu, head towards Balaju only two km north of Thamel, and onto the Trisuli road. At this point you start to climb out of the valley towards Kakani, 23 km away at an altitude of 2073m. The road twists and turns at an even gradient past the Nagarjun forest reserve, which provides the road with a leaf canopy.

Once you're through the initial pass and out of the valley, the road continues in a north-westerly direction and offers a view of terraced fields on your left. On reaching the summit of the ridge turn right instead of continuing down to Trisuli Bazaar. From this point magnificent views of Ganesh Himal give the required inspiration to complete the remaining four km of steep, narrow blacktop to the *Tara Gaon Kakani Hotel* at the crown, for a well deserved rest.

It is possible to spend the night at the hotel to take advantage of sunrise and sunset. See the Kakani section of the Around the Kathmandu Valley chapter for details.

After admiring the view from the hotel's garden terrace, descend for just 30m and take the first left onto a jeep track. This track takes you in an easterly direction towards Shivapuri. The track ends abruptly, after a few km, at a metal gate. After passing through the gate, you are faced with a 10 minute walk up to an army checkpost with the Scar Rd clearly visible in front of you. Once you pass through the checkpost, you are at the day's high point – approximately 2200m.

Taking the right-hand side track you start to descend dramatically along an extremely steep, rutted single trail. The trail is literally cut into the side of the hill, with sharp drops on the right which challenge a rider's skill and nerve. As you hurtle along, take time to admire the sprawling Kathmandu Valley below.

The trail widens and, after one long climb before the saddle, is relatively flat through the protected Shivapuri watershed area. This beautiful mountain biking section lasts for nearly 25 km before the trail descends into the valley down a seven km spiral. The track joins a paved road, to the relief of jarred wrists and buttocks, at Budhanilkantha, where you can buy refreshments. The road descends gently for the remaining eight km back to Kathmandu.

DHULIKHEL

This two or three day circular tour takes you through a classic cross-section of valley sights. The first day to Dhulikhel is 32 km; the second day is 58 km. Dhulikhel is an interesting hilltop town at 1500m.

From Thamel, head out of town in the direction of Pashupatinath and once onto the Ring Rd proceed towards Tribhuvan airport. Shortly after the descent past the airport, branch left and climb up to join the beginning of the Arniko Highway (which runs through to the Tibetan border).

The Arniko Highway was built by the Chinese and carries an enormous amount of traffic, including Chinese-donated electric trolley buses. It is a far nicer ride along the old road via the village of Thimi, which is famous for its handicrafts. Take the first left off the main highway and onto the narrow road that heads back towards the airport before continuing on to complete the 16 km to the mediaeval town of Bhaktapur.

Mountain bikes are a great way to explore Bhaktapur's narrow streets. After time in this magical city, continue east. Facing Bhaktapur's 30m high Nyatapola Temple, take the exit from the square on your right-hand side. This narrow street twists and turns on its way out of the city. After leaving the brick-paved streets, join a tarmac road and continue straight on.

The tarmac road ends and continues in the form of a compacted track towards the rural village of Nala. This route is an excellent alternative to the Arniko Highway and takes you through a beautiful corner of the valley. The track climbs gradually, and becomes progressively steeper near the top. A gentle three km downhill gradient brings you to rural Nala with its pretty temples.

Turn right upon joining the tarmac road and continue for a couple of km to Banepa. Turn left and continue along the paved road for a further five km to Dhulikhel, which is visible on your right-hand side as you approach, thus completing the first day. See the Around the Kathmandu Valley chapter for more information on Dhulikhel.

Namobuddha is a popular day trek starting

and finishing in Dhulikhel and offers superb trail riding with spectacular views of the Himalaya. From Dhulikhel's main square, which has a small pond, head along a paved road in the direction of the Kali temple set on a hillside above the town. The paved road ends and starts to climb the hill in the form of a rough jeep track. The track twists its way up a testing three km to reach the temple, which is a spectacular viewpoint. From the temple you can see the track snake its way across the terraced landscape.

Continue along the track, which provides exhilarating downhill runs before it starts a five km climb towards Namobuddha. After completing the climb, descend for a short while until you reach a T-junction. Turn right and Namobuddha will appear shortly after on the left, so completing a 12 km journey from Dhulikhel. Refreshments are available in the small shops near the stupa, which provides an interesting place to rest before continuing to Panauti.

Leaving Namobuddha you continue down the track, which takes you through a series of turns – a great mountain bike descent. The track finally drops to the bottom of the valley and travels in undulating fashion to complete a 14 km ride to the historic city of Panauti. This ancient Newari town has some of the oldest temples in Nepal – cross the footbridge if you want to explore further. See the Around the Kathmandu Valley chapter for information about Panauti.

Leaving Panauti you join a paved road that runs flat along the valley to Banepa. From this point you can return to Kathmandu, which is 26 km via the Arniko Highway, or complete a 33 km circuit by returning to Dhulikhel.

KODARI & TIBETAN BORDER

It is possible to continue 82 km along the Arniko Highway from Dhulikhel to the Friendship Bridge at Kodari (1500m) that marks the Tibetan border. This is a four day return trip from Dhulikhel.

From Dhulikhel you immediately begin a descent into the Panchkhal Valley, with majestic views of the Himalaya adding to a

thrilling ride – you descend almost 900m. A couple of short climbs interrupt the descent as you cycle to Dolalghat, a popular starting point for Sun Kosi River rafting trips.

After 20 km you cross the bridge over the Indrawati River and climb out of the Panchkhal Valley to join the Bhote Kosi River which you follow for the rest of the journey. The road is a mixture of surfaced and unsurfaced, due mainly to landslide damage. Traffic can be quite heavy along this section as it is also the road to Jiri, a popular starting point for the Everest Base Camp Trek. The road climbs at a gentle gradient as it follows the river.

A couple of km past the turn-off to Jiri is Lamosangu, 23 km from Dolalghat. Lamosangu provides a far more pleasant place to spend the night than Barabise thanks to the fact that fewer buses stop. See the Arniko Highway section in the Around the Kathmandu Valley chapter for information on accommodation.

The next day's ride continues past Barabise where the road changes into a compacted track with a top layer of dust. This dust cover is transformed into choking clouds when buses pass, or mud in wet weather. Care should be taken during heavy rain as this section of the road is particularly vulnerable to landslides. The valley's sides begin to steepen and it gradually changes into a beautiful gorge with spectacular waterfalls. The track climbs practically the entire 34 km to Tatopani to complete the second day. Again, see the Arniko Highway section for information on accommodation.

Tatopani is five km from the border post of Kodari. This section, as it climbs towards the Friendship Bridge, is probably the most beautiful section of the ride. It is now possible to cycle beyond the bridge and climb a rough track to the Chinese customs checkpost (11 km) just outside Khasa, which is visible from the bridge. It should be possible to return as far as Lamosangu the same day, taking advantage of a mainly downhill ride.

The ride back to Dhulikhel is 43 km and includes the long climb out of Dolalghat which you should allow time for. Depending on how you feel after the climb, you can stay in Dhulikhel or complete the trip by returning to Kathmandu.

THE RAJPATH

The Tribhuvan Highway (or Rajpath as it is popularly known) was the first highway to connect Kathmandu with the rest of the world. The road switchbacks 150 spectacular km from Kathmandu to Hetauda. Most traffic from the Terai and India uses the highway between Narayanghat and Mugling which, although longer, is actually quicker. The Rajpath has a great mixture of light traffic and magnificent scenery, culminating at Daman with an incomparable Himalayan view. It's a classic ride.

The ride begins on the Kathmandu-Pokhara (Prithvi) Highway, which gives the only access to the valley. After leaving the valley, the highway descends to Naubise, at the bottom of the Mahesh Khola Valley, 27 km from Kathmandu, where the Rajpath intersects with the Kathmandu-Pokhara (Prithvi) Highway. Take the Rajpath, which forks to the left, and start a 35 km climb to Tistung at a height of 2030m. You climb through terraced fields, carved into steep hillsides. On reaching the pass you descend for seven km into the beautiful Palung Valley before the final steep nine km climb to Daman, at a height of 2322m.

This day's ride, almost all climbing, will take between six and nine hours in the saddle. It is possible to stay in Daman, which will give you the thrill of waking up to the broadest Himalayan panorama Nepal has to offer. On a clear morning you can see from Dhaulagiri to Everest, a view worth the peddle. The following day the road climbs a further three km to the top of the pass, at 2488m. At this point, you can savour the prospect of an exhilarating 2300m descent in 60 km!

As you descend towards the Indian plains you will notice a contrast with the side you climbed – the south side is lush and semitropical. The road eventually flattens out when you reach a series of electricity transformers. The rest of the journey is a gently undulating route alongside a river – a further 10 km

brings you to Hetauda. See the Hetauda section in the Terai chapter for details on accommodation. After a night's rest you can continue along the Rajpath towards India or turn right at the statue of the king in the centre of town and head towards Royal Chitwan National Park.

HETAUDA TO NARAYANGHAT

Hetauda is just to the east of Royal Chitwan National Park, which has a wide selection of accommodation, both in the park and in the town of Sauraha, as well as a great range of activities. See Royal Chitwan National Park section in the Terai chapter for more details. You are prohibited from riding inside the park, but are allowed to ride directly to your resort.

As you cycle along the flat, smooth road towards Narayanghat enjoying the lush subtropical scenery, watch for resort signposts on your left-hand side. Machan Jungle Resort's turn-off is 40 km from Hetauda, and the resort can be reached after a further four km of beautiful trail riding with three river crossings. Alternatively, a further 23 km from the Machan turn-off brings you to the Chitwan Jungle Resort turn-off. A further 14 km brings you to Tadi Bazaar and the turn-off for Sauraha, reached by an interesting six km jeep track.

Narayanghat, 20 km from Sauraha on the banks of the Narayani River, gives a choice of further routes. From here you can return to Kathmandu or Pokhara via Mugling, though the section from Narayanghat to Mugling is probably best avoided by catching a bus. If you're heading to Pokhara it's also a good idea to miss the busy highway between Mugling and Pokhara by catching a bus in Mugling.

POKHARA

Pokhara is famous for its beauty, and the spectacular views of the Annapurnas and Manaslu Himal. The surrounding area provides excellent opportunities for trail riding around lakes and rivers and towards the mountains. The area is less populated than the Kathmandu Valley, so although there are fewer trails, villages and temples to explore, the rides are more tranquil.

Sarangkot

The ride to Sarangkot provides an excellent, challenging day trip.

Leave early and ride along Lakeside (towards the mountains) to the intersection with the Manswara road (which returns to the bazaar area). Continue straight on (north) and after two km the road becomes a track which heads to Sarangkot. This turns into a single track which closely hugs the edge of Phewa Tal. Continue until you join the trail heading up an extremely steep spiral to Sarangkot. From this point it is far easier to continue straight ahead, riding narrow trails before descending to the valley of the winding Harpan Khola.

You will need to make a number of river crossings (impassable during monsoon) before rejoining the trail, which travels along narrow rice paddy fields – a good test of nerve and balance. The trail soon begins to climb to Kaski, towards the hill immediately in front of you. This section will take approximately one hour, and you will need to carry your bike on the steeper section near the crown of the hill. Once you have reached the top, you join a trail which connects Naudanda with Sarangkot, at approximately 1590m. The trail is narrow and rocky so you'll need to carry your bike for about 20% of the time.

The view from this ridge is spectacularly beautiful. Dhaulagiri, Manaslu, the Annapurnas and Machhapuchhare create a classic Himalayan panorama, especially on a cool, clear morning. To the south you can look down over Pokhara and Phewa Tal.

Naudanda

From Sarangkot point you have the choice of continuing left or right. Heading left towards Naudanda the trail continues along the spine of the ridge before joining the surfaced Pokhara-Baglung Highway which connects Pokhara with Lumle (a popular starting point for trekking in the Annapurnas). Naudanda is 32 km from Pokhara, above a twisting six km descent into the Madi Khola Valley. The highway has an excellent asphalt surface and descends gently as it follows the river, allowing an enjoyable coast almost all the way back to Pokhara.

An alternative is to turn right and head along the ridge for eight km to Sarangkot. After stopping to admire the view and have refreshments head steeply down stone steps, carrying the bike for half an hour, until you reach a jeep track. The track descends quickly in an exhilarating spiral pattern for eight km until it connects with the Pokhara-Baglung Highway, only four km north of Lakeside.

Rafting & Kayaking

The bulk of this chapter was written and researched by David Allardice, the operations manager for Ultimate Descents, a company which organises rafting and kayaking journeys in Nepal. The Information section was written by Ravi Fry.

About Rafting

Nepal is earning the reputation of being one of the best places in the world for rafting and kayaking. Its mountain scenery has drawn trekkers and climbers for many years; these same mountains shape an incredible variety of white-water challenges for paddlers. A series of the world's most outstanding river journeys is found here, ranging from steep, adrenalin-charged mountain streams to classic, big-volume wilderness expeditions.

The combination of spectacular rivers, mountain scenery and a rich cultural heritage makes Nepal an obvious river runner's destination. No other country has such a choice of trips on wild rivers with warm water, a subtropical climate (with no bugs!) and huge, white-sand beaches that are ideal for camping.

RIVER GRADING SYSTEM

Rivers are graded for difficulty on an international scale from class 1 to 6, with class 1 defined as easy-moving water with few obstacles, and class 6 being considered nearly impossible to negotiate and a hazard to life – something best attempted after your lover leaves you...

Anyone who's in reasonable physical shape and isn't afraid of water can safely go rafting on rivers with gradings from class 1 to 3. For more difficult and exciting class 4 rivers, people should be active, confident in water and preferably have some rafting experience. class 5 is a very large step up from class 4; long continuous sections of powerful

white water, strenuous paddling, steep constricted channels, powerful waves and the possibility of overturning a raft. Swimming in a class 5 rapid poses a significant risk.

Rafting in Nepal has an image of extremely difficult white water, which is well justified at times of high-water flow (during the monsoon), but at most flows there are many class 3 to 4 rivers. There are also many easier class 1 and 2 rivers where you can float along admiring the scenery and running a few small rapids.

WHEN TO GO

The best times for rafting are September to early December, and March to early June. From early September to early October, and May to June, the rivers can be extremely high with monsoon run-off. Any expeditions attempted at this time require a very experienced rafting company with an intimate knowledge of the river, and strong teams, as high flows are potentially the most dangerous times to be on a river. From mid-October onwards the weather is settled and this is one of the most popular times to raft. In December many of the rivers become too cold to enjoy unless you have wetsuits, and the days are short with the start of winter. A time to perhaps consider shorter trips? The summer season from March to early June has lower water flows to begin with, which generally means the rapids aren't as powerful. The rivers rise again in May with pre-monsoon storms and

389

some snow-melt, then it's high-water time again.

From June to August the monsoon rains arrive and the rivers carry 10 times their low-water flows, and can flood with 60 to 80 times as much. High flows can obviously make rivers much more difficult. Few rivers should be attempted at flood levels.

There is a definite relationship between volume and gradient and difficulty. River levels can fluctuate dramatically at any time, although as a general rule weather patterns in Nepal are quite stable.

TYPES OF RAFTING TRIPS

For many people a rafting trip in Nepal will be their first white-water experience. There are many different kinds of trips, and it is important to select a river that suits your interests and ability. The style of trip, difficulty of the river and length of time you have are all factors that will shape your decision.

Any raft can be paddled, or rigged with an oar frame and rowed. With an oar frame the guide normally sits in the middle and rows, while the other passengers enjoy the scenery – and hold on through the rapids. With a paddle raft the guide normally sits at the back calling instructions and steering, while the crew provides the power. Most active people prefer the teamwork of paddle rafting. With a strong team a paddle raft can probably run harder rapids than an oar raft, and the sense of achievement cannot be compared.

Rafting trips vary from quite luxurious trips where you are rowed down the river and staff do everything for you (pitch camp, cook and so on), to trips where you participate in the running of the expedition – pitching tents, loading the rafts and helping with the cooking. The quality of the rafting equipment is another variable, and can make a huge difference to the comfort and safety of participants.

Shaping the Future of River Running

With no regulating body, it's up to you to help shape the sport and future of Nepal's rivers. Your comments, feedback and attitude can have a very positive effect on what happens here. A few guidelines...

Rural Nepal is still very conservative so make sure you adhere to a minimum dress code and respect local customs; the people will, in turn, have more respect for you. This is especially important if you visit a temple or village.

Show respect for the environment and make sure that your group and company does the same. Camp sites should be kept scrupulously clean. Burn all burnable waste. Bury organic waste below the high-water mark, or dispose of it in the river – it feeds the fish. Well constructed toilet pits should be away from the camp and below the high-water level; everyone should use them. Toilet paper should be burnt. Leave only footprints.

Use only as much driftwood as you need, and do not use wood that would otherwise be used by villagers. Your trip should not place an additional burden on an already taxed environment, so if there is no driftwood available you should use an alternative fuel like gas or kerosene. See also the Trekking, Firewood & Forest Depletion and Garbage & Waste asides in the Trekking chapter.

Rural villagers are normally honest, but it's worthwhile making sure that you know where your valuables are at all times. Don't leave gear lying around the camp site – put it inside your tent. Don't take any valuables that you don't need on the river; store them in Kathmandu or Pokhara instead. Many of the operators will store them for you. As a general rule, local people don't leave their belongings lying around and there is a reason for it.

If you feel that any part of your trip varied considerably from what you were sold, or was unsafe and not run with respect for the environment and cultures, then do something about it. Support companies that practise these values and that run safe trips, then other companies will have to follow their example to stay in business.

If you have any suggestions or complaints, write to the Nepal Association of Rafting Agents (NARA; ☏ 01-221197), PO Box 2585, Kathmandu, or to the Nepal River Conservation Trust (NRCT; ☏ 01-271894), PO Box 6720, Kathmandu. ■

SAFETY

Safety is the most important part of any river trip. Unfortunately, at the moment there are no minimum safety conditions enforced by any official body in Nepal. This makes it very important to choose a professional rafting company. Not all rafting companies are created equal.

If a group has recently returned from a trip, speak to its members. This will give you reliable information about the quality of equipment, the guides, the food and the transportation. Question the company about how they get to and from the river, how many hours are spent paddling or rowing, where the camps are set up (near villages?), what food is available (rafting stimulates a very healthy appetite), who does the cooking and work around the camp, what cooking fuel is used (wood?), what happens to rubbish, what hygiene precautions are taken, and what activities there are at night. Many companies have a photo file or video in their office. Having a look at these will give an impression of their equipment and safety and how they operate trips. Ask a lot of questions.

The following check list is based on the experience of many international guides and should help in the process of selecting a company.

Raft Numbers

There should be a minimum of two rafts per trip. If anyone does fall out of a raft (known as a 'swimmer' in the trade) the second raft can help with the rescue. In higher water three rafts are safer than two. Many experts also agree that one or two safety kayakers can replace the second raft, though the kayakers need to be white-water professionals with the training, skill and experience not only to run the most difficult rapids on the river, but also to be able to perform rescues in these rapids. Good safety kayakers are invaluable on steeper rivers where they can often get to a swimmer in places no other craft could manage a rescue.

Check how many people have booked and paid for a trip, and the maximum number that will be taken. Obviously if the trip is leaving in two days and you are the only person booked, you are not going to have enough people to run a safe trip.

Safety Kayakers

Having good kayakers along will not only add to the safety of the trip, but on the easier river sections, they will often teach people to kayak. For more adventurous people, some of the inflatable kayaks and catamarans that are now turning up in Nepal are an excellent way to get the feel of controlling your own craft. These are a lot of fun, but it's important if you have these craft on a trip that the guides have the experience to know which rapids are safe to run. If you are interested in kayaking, a few companies have kayaks and kayaking gear for hire and also run instruction programmes.

Raft Guides

The person leading the trip must be a qualified, trained guide with a minimum of 50 days rafting experience. They should also have done at least five previous trips on the river they are guiding on. All raft guides should have done the river before.

If possible, speak with the guide who will lead the trip. This will give you a chance to form an impression of the people you will be spending time with and the type of trip they run. Ask them about their previous experience. Overseas experience or training allows the guides to keep up with the latest advances and safety training. Kayaking experience adds additional depth to a guide's skills.

All guides should have a current first-aid certificate and should also be trained in cardio-pulmonary resuscitation (CPR).

Equipment

Quality equipment is important, both for safety and comfort. The relatively new self-bailing rafts are essential for more difficult trips. Good life jackets and helmets are mandatory on any white-water trip. Modern plastic and alloy paddles are preferable to locally made wooden ones. New roll-top dry bags will keep your gear dry even if the raft flips, and waterproof camera containers will allow you to take photos all the way down the river. The companies should also supply tents. Ask how old the equipment is.

Ask what first-aid gear, supplies, spare parts and repair equipment are carried. On a river it's important that the guides are capable of dealing with any situation that occurs – especially if it is a long wilderness expedition. Many a trip has gone astray due to lack of preparation, not having the right equipment, or insufficient training to deal with the variety of situations which can arise.

On the River

At the river your guide should give you a comprehensive safety talk and paddle training before you launch off downstream. The more you know the safer it is. If you don't get a good safety talk it is probably good cause for concern.

- Always wear your life jacket in rapids. Wear your helmet whenever your guide tells you, and make sure that both the helmet and jacket are properly adjusted and fitted.
- Keep your feet and arms inside the raft. If the raft hits a rock or wall and you are in the way, the best you'll escape with is a laceration.
- If you do swim in a rapid, get into the 'white-water swimming position' – on your back, with your feet downstream and up where you can see them. Hold

on to your paddle as this will make you more visible. Relax and breathe when you aren't going through waves. Turn over and swim at the end of the rapid when the water becomes calmer. Self-rescue is the best rescue.

Information

Anyone who is seriously interested in rafting and kayaking, and especially anyone contemplating a private expedition, should get hold of *White Water Nepal*, an excellent guidebook by Peter Knowles & David Allardice. It should be possible to get copies of the book in Kathmandu. It has incredibly detailed information on river trips, with 60 maps, river profiles and hydrographs, plus advice on equipment and health – in short, all the information a prospective river runner could want.

INDEPENDENT RAFTING & KAYAKING

Anyone who plans to raft or kayak privately should also contact local rafting companies for up-to-date information. Himalayan rivers are dynamic, and rivers and their rapids change every monsoon.

Getting your Gear to Nepal

Most airlines will carry short kayaks on the same basis as surfboards or bicycles – there's no excess baggage charge as long as you are within the weight limits. If you are a group, negotiate a deal at the time of booking. If there are only one or two of you, try just turning up – put all your bulky light gear in the kayak, heavy items in your carry-on luggage and smile sweetly! (If you phone them in advance they have to quote the rule book and start talking of sending your gear as air cargo.)

Permits

Rafters and kayakers are required to have rafting permits, which are obtained from the Ministry of Tourism, Tripureshwar (near the football stadium), in Kathmandu, and cost $5. There's a list of rivers where rafting is

---

Nepal River Conservation Trust (NRCT)

The Nepal River Conservation Trust (NRCT) is a non-government organisation formed by Nepali river guides who feel an increased sense of responsibility to preserve the country's wild rivers. The NRCT runs biannual river trips on classic rivers that have the added bonus of incorporating conservation and educational opportunities. All profits go to the NRCT. In conjunction with specialists in various fields, the NRCT funds projects according to the needs of the river and riverside communities. For more information, write to Megh Ale (Founder & President), Nepal River Conservation Trust, PO Box 6720, Kathmandu (☎ 01-271894). ∎

permitted (including all the rivers in the following section), but this is constantly being expanded, so it's best to check the situation when you arrive.

ORGANISED RAFTING & KAYAKING

If you go on an organised rafting trip the necessary permits will be arranged for you. All specialised equipment is normally supplied. Usually you will only need light cotton clothing, with a slightly warmer change for nights. A swim-suit, sun hat, sunscreen and light tennis shoes or sandals that will stay on your feet are all necessary, but can also be bought in Kathmandu. For overnight trips a sleeping bag is necessary, but this can easily be hired. Temperatures on some rivers vary, so contact the company you are booking with – they will recommend what to bring.

There are about 90 companies in Kathmandu claiming to be rafting operators. A few are well established, older companies with good reputations, and the rest are newer companies, often formed by guides breaking away and starting their own operations, and sometimes people with very little experience of rivers. Although these new companies can be enthusiastic and good, they can be shoe-string operations that may not have adequate resources in terms of equipment and staff.

Most of the small agencies simply sell trips on commission, often with no real idea about the details of what they are selling and really only interested in getting bums on seats. To further confuse the situation, there are also sometimes complicated subcontracting arrangements between companies. It is immensely preferable to deal directly with the company you will be rafting with.

If your time is limited you may choose to book a trip before you leave home. However, all the operators accept bookings in Kathmandu, which gives you the opportunity to meet the people you will be rafting with before you make a commitment. Trips depart on a regular basis (at least one long trip a week during the season), and the best companies will refer you to a friendly competitor if they don't have any suitable dates.

Trips range in price from $15 to $70 a day,

and generally you get what you pay for. At $15 you don't get much at all. It is better to pay a bit more and have a good, safe trip, than to save $100 and have a lousy, dangerous trip. Bear in mind that trips in Nepal are generally less than half the cost of similar trips in the USA, so in relative terms all the prices are extremely reasonable. If you plan to do a more difficult trip it's particularly important to choose a company that has the experience, skills and equipment to run a safe and exciting expedition.

With the constant change in companies it's difficult to make individual recommendations; the fact that a company is not recommended here does not necessarily mean it will not deliver an excellent trip. Nonetheless, the following companies have been recommended for their professionalism. Their prices range from $40 to $70 a day.

Equator Expeditions
Tukche Peak Guest House compound, Thamel, Kathmandu; also in Pokhara. This is a smaller company with experienced staff, and specialises in long participatory rafting and kayaking trips. (☎ 01-416596; fax 411933)

Himalayan Encounters
Kathmandu Guest House compound, Thamel, Kathmandu. This company is associated with Encounter Overland, and has earned a solid reputation through many Trisuli and Sun Kosi trips. (☎ 01-417426; fax 417133)

Himalayan River Exploration
Hattisar, Kathmandu. This company is part of the Tiger Mountain organisation (one of Nepal's original companies) and is an up-market operation, running a lot of catered trips with rowing rigs. (☎ 01-420322; fax 414075)

Himalayan Wonders
Namche Bazaar building, Thamel. This new company is at the budget end of rafting. (☎ 01-215331; fax 229304)

Raging River Runner
Jyatha, Thamel. Another recommended budget company. (☎ 01-214712; fax 229983)

Ultimate Descents
Entrance to Northfield Cafe Compound, Thamel. This company has been operating for nine years. It specialises in participatory rafting and kayaking trips. (☎ 01-229389; fax 411933; e-mail: rivers@ultimate.wlink.com.np)

RAFTING & KAYAKING

Selecting a River

Before you decide what river you'll do, you need to decide what it is you want out of the river trip. There are trips available from two to 12 days on different rivers, all offering dramatically different experiences.

Firstly, don't believe that just because it's a river it's going to be wet 'n' wild. Some rivers, such as the Sun Kosi, which are incredible, full-on, white-water trips in September and October are basically flat and uneventful in the low water of early spring. On the flip side of that, early spring can be a superb time to raft rivers such as the Marsyangdi or Bhote Kosi, which would be suicidal during high flows. The Karnali is probably the only river which offers continually challenging white water at all flows, though in the high-water months of September and May it's a significantly more committing endeavour.

There is much more to rivers than just white water, but the climate in Nepal being what it is, many companies will promote whichever river they're running at the time as the pinnacle of white-water excitement. Not all companies run all rivers, especially the more technical and demanding rivers, and some companies shouldn't be running any rivers at all, but such is life. Buyer beware.

Longer trips such as the Sun Kosi (in the autumn) and the Karnali have the advantages of offering some real heart-thumping white water with the incredible journeying aspect of a long river trip. With more time on the river things are more relaxed, relationships progress at a more natural pace and memories become firmly entrenched for a lifetime. Long after the white water has blurred into one long, white-knuckled thrill ride, the memories of a moonrise over the river and the friends you inevitably make will remain. After spending the better part of their adult lives on different rivers, most hard-core river people can still distinctly remember the long expeditions they've been on; it's a much more involving and enveloping experience than a short two or three day trip. River trips are much more than gravity-powered roller-coaster rides: they're journeys traversed on very special highways. For many people they become a way of life.

If a long trip is simply impossible due to financial or time constraints, don't undervalue the shorter ones. Anyone who has ever taken a paddle-raft or kayak down the Bhote Kosi (at any flow) would be hard pressed to find anything better to do with two days in Nepal. There are also medium-length options which are perfect for people who want to experience river journeying but have limited time.

The following section describes the main commercially rafted rivers in Nepal. It is by no means a complete list, and private boaters who have the experience and equipment to run their own expeditions would be best advised to consult the aforementioned guidebook, *White Water Nepal*.

THE KARNALI

The Karnali is a gem, combining a lowland trek with some of the prettiest canyons and jungle scenery available in Nepal. Most experienced river people who have boated the Karnali find it to be one of the best all-round river trips they've ever done. In high water, the Karnali is a serious commitment, combining *huge*, though fairly straightforward rapids with a seriously remote location. At low water the Karnali is still a fantastic trip. The rapids become smaller, but the steeper gradient and constricted channel of the Karnali keep it interesting.

Being the longest and largest river in Nepal, the Karnali drains a huge and well developed catchment. Spring snow-melts can drive the river up dramatically in a matter of hours, and as the river rises the difficulty increases exponentially. The river flows through some steep and constricted canyons where the rapids are close together, giving little opportunity to correct for potential mistakes. Pick your company carefully.

The trip starts with a long, but interesting

bus ride over to the far west of Nepal, an area only recently opened to tourism. If you're allergic to bus rides, it's possible to fly to Nepalganj and cut the bus transport down to about five hours on the way over, and two hours on the way back. From the frontier town of Surkhet there is a lovely two day trek through lowland sal forests to the village of Sauli. From Sauli it's 180 km to the next road access at Chisopani, on the northern border of the Royal Bardia National Park.

The river section takes about seven days, giving plenty of time to explore some of the side canyons and waterfalls which come into the river valley Better-run trips also include a layover day, where the expedition stays at the same camp site for two nights. The combination of long bus rides and trekking puts some people off, but anyone who has ever done the trip invariably raves about it.

Finish with a visit to Royal Bardia National Park for an unbeatable combination.

SUN KOSI

This is the longest river trip offered in Nepal, winding 270 km through the beautiful Mahabharat Range from the 'put in' at Dolalghat

to the 'take out' at Chatara, far down on the Gangetic plain. It's quite an experience to begin a river trip just three hours out of Kathmandu, barely 60 km from the Tibetan border, and end the trip looking down the hot, dusty gun barrel of the north Indian plain just nine or 10 days later. Because it's one of the easiest trips to organise logistically, it's also one of the least expensive for the days you spend on a river.

The Sun Kosi starts off fairly relaxed, with class 2 and small class 3 rapids to warm up with during the first couple of days. Savvy guides will take this opportunity to get the teams working together with Swiss precision, as on the third day the rapids become more powerful and frequent, with high-water trippers finding themselves astonished at just how big a wave in a river can get. While the lower sections of large-volume rivers are usually rather flat, the Sun Kosi reserves some of its biggest and best rapids for the last days. At the right flow it's an incredible combination of white water, scenery, villages and truly quiet and introspective evenings along what many people consider to be one of the world's 10 classic river journeys.

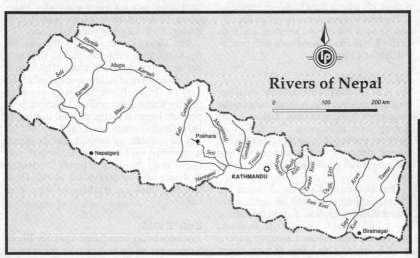

RAFTING & KAYAKING

TRISULI RIVER

Just out of Kathmandu, the Trisuli River is where the bulk of the commercial trips operate due to the easy access. Without a doubt this is the cheapest trip available in Nepal – if you sign onto a $20 a day raft trip, this is where you'll end up, and it's no wonder. What makes the Trisuli so cheap is also what makes it one of the least desirable rafting trips in the country. The easy access is provided by the Kathmandu-Pokhara (Prithvi) Highway, which runs right alongside the river. During most flows the rapids are straightforward and spread well apart. The large number of companies operating on the river drives the prices down, but also detracts considerably from the experience of the trip. Beaches are often heavily used and abused, with garbage, toilet paper and fire pits well in evidence. This, combined with the noise and pollution of the highway, makes the Trisuli a less than ideal rafting experience.

It's not all bad news though. During the monsoon months the Trisuli changes character completely as huge run-offs make the river swell and shear. There are fewer companies running during this time, and the garbage and excrement of the past season is well on it's way to Bangladesh as topsoil.

The best white water is found on the section between Baireni and Mugling, and trips on the Trisuli can be combined with trips to Pokhara or Chitwan.

KALI GANDAKI

The Kali Gandaki is an excellent medium-length river trip, recently made easy by the completion of the road from Pokhara to the starting point at Nayapul. The Kali is an excellent alternative to the Trisuli as there is no road alongside, and the scenery, villages and temples all combine to make it a great trip.

The rapids on the Kali Gandaki (class 3 to 4 depending on the flows) are much more technical and continuous than on the Trisuli, and in high water it's no place to be unless you are an accomplished kayaker experienced in avoiding big holes. At medium and lower flows, it's a fun and challenging river with rapids keeping you busy all but one day. Being one of Nepal's holiest rivers, every river junction on the Kali Gandaki is dotted with cremation sites and burial mounds. If you've been wondering what's under that pile of rocks, we recommend against investigating.

At Ranighat, on the lower section of river, lies a wonderful derelict palace which is slowly being taken over by the surrounding jungle. It's a fantastic place to stop and have a look around.

The most commonly rafted section is from Nayapul to Ramdhighat, a distance of about 100 km, which will take five days to complete. You can take out at Ramdhighat on the Siddhartha Highway between Pokhara and Sunauli, or you could continue on to the confluence with the Trisuli at Devghat. This adds another 130 km and three or four more days. The lower section doesn't have much white water, but it is seldom rafted and offers a very isolated area with lots of wildlife.

SETI RIVER

The Seti is an excellent two day trip in an isolated area, with beautiful jungle and plenty of easy rapids. Beware of companies who market this as a hot white-water trip. While it's a beautiful river valley well worth rafting, it's not a white-water bonanza.

The logical starting point is Damauli on the Kathmandu-Pokhara (Prithvi) Highway between Mugling and Pokhara. This would give you 32 km of rafting to the confluence with the Trisuli River. This is an excellent trip for learner/intermediate kayakers. It is possible to raft a higher section, starting at Dule Gouda, which would add another 30 km, but considering the quality of the rapids it probably isn't worth it. Beware if you decide to try the upper section of the river as it disappears underground above Dule Gouda! I think this is what they refer to as class 6...

BHOTE KOSI

Just three hours from Kathmandu, the Bhote Kosi is one of the best two day raft trips to be found anywhere in the world. It is one of the most recently opened rivers in Nepal, and represents the forefront of river rafting.

The Bhote Kosi is the steepest river rafted in Nepal – technical and totally committing. With a gradient of 24m per 1.61 km, it's a full eight times as steep as the Sun Kosi, which it feeds further downstream. The rapids are steep and continuous class 4, with a lot of continuous class 3 in between.

The usual run is from approximately Km 95 (above Barabise) to the dam at Lamosangu. The river has been kayaked above this point, but a raft trip here would not be recreational. At high flows several of the rapids become solid class 5, and consequences for mistakes on the entire river will become serious.

Rafting or kayaking this river are two of the most fun things you can do right out of Kathmandu and a great way to get an adrenalin fix during the low-water months. However, they should only be attempted with a company which has a lot of experience on the Bhote Kosi, and is using the best safety equipment and guides.

UPPER SUN KOSI

Not to be confused with the Bhote Kosi which finishes at Lamosangu, the upper Sun Kosi is a fun 20 km stretch of easy class 2 water and beautiful scenery. From Khadichour to Dolighat the river is crystal blue, with brilliant beaches to picnic on. A great place for a short family trip.

MARSYANGDI RIVER

Only recently opened to commercial rafting, the Marsyangdi is one of the best whitewater runs in the world. For people looking for a six to seven day trip with lots of demanding white water and great mountain scenery, the Marsyangdi is hard to beat.

The trip starts with a class 5 bus ride from Dumre to Beshisahar, which is a good opportunity to steel your nerves and awaken your fight-or-flight responses. If you make it to Beshisahar intact, you're in for a beautiful trek up to the village of Ngadi, with great views of the Manaslu and the Annapurnas ahead of you the whole time. The scenery is fantastic.

From Ngadi downstream to the end of the trip at Bimalnagar, it's pretty much solid white water. Rapids are steep, technical and consecutive, making the Marsyangdi a serious undertaking. Like the Bhote Kosi, successful navigation of the Marsyangdi is dependent on companies having previous experience on the river and using the best guides and equipment. Rafts must be self-bailing, and should be running with a minimum of weight and gear on board. Professional safety kayakers should be considered a standard safety measure on this river.

OTHER RIVERS

The **Bheri River**, which is in the west, is a great float trip with incredible jungle scenery and lots of wildlife. This is one of the best fishing rivers and can be combined with a visit to the Royal Bardia National Park. The **Arun River** from Tumlingtar in the far east makes an excellent three day wilderness trip, although the logistics of getting to the starting point are pretty complicated.

There is a plethora of rivers which could be rafted and kayaked in Nepal, but government permission is another matter. Things change quickly and capriciously in this part of the world, and the best advice is to check local information sources (several of them) to see what's running. One that we hope will open soon is the **Tamur River**, which drains all the mountains in the far east of Nepal. Well worth waiting for.

RAFTING & KAYAKING

Glossary

Beware of the different methods of transliterating Nepali and the other languages spoken in Nepal. There are many and varied ways of spelling Nepali words. In particular the letter 'b' and letter 'v' are often interchanged. The god Bhairab becomes Bhairav or the thunderbolt symbol changes from *vajra* to *bajra*.

Adi Buddha – the original self-generated Buddha of Tantric Buddhism who created the Dhyani Buddhas.

Aditya – ancient Vedic sun god.

Agni – ancient Vedic god of the hearth and fire. He rides a chariot drawn by parrots and his four arms hold flames, a ball of fire, a trident and a rosary.

Agnipura – Buddhist symbol for fire.

Aksobhya – the Dhyani Buddha of the east; his vehicle is an elephant and he is often seen with one hand touching the ground in the gesture known as subduing Mara.

Amitabha – the Dhyani Buddha of the west; his animal is the peacock.

Amoghasiddhi – the Dhyani Buddha of the north, his consort is Green Tara and in Nepali stupas he sits under a seven hooded snake canopy.

Ananda – the Buddha's chief disciple.

Ananta – the cosmic serpent upon which Vishnu reclines.

Annapurna – the goddess of abundance and an incarnation of Mahadevi.

arak – a fermented drink made from potatoes or grain.

Ashoka – Indian Buddhist emperor who spread Buddhism throughout the subcontinent.

Ashta Matrikas – the eight mother goddesses.

asla – river trout.

Asuras – demons ruled by Rawana, king of Lanka in the *Ramayana*. The name can be a suffix, as in Mahishasura.

Avalokitesvara – as Gautama Buddha is the Buddha of our era, so is Avalokitesvara the Bodhisattva of our era. In Nepal he has become a Hindu/Buddhist god of mercy whose incarnation is Machhendranath or Manjushri.

avatar – an incarnation of a deity living on earth.

bahal – a Buddhist monastery, usually two storeys high and built around a courtyard. There are a great number of bahals in the towns of the Kathmandu Valley, but few continue to function as monasteries. Many are used as schools.

bahil – a simpler version of a bahal.

bakba – Tibetan clay mask.

bajra – *see* vajra.

Balarama – Krishna's brother.

Balkumari – one of Bhairab's consorts.

Banrhas – Buddhist hereditary priesthood.

bazaar – market area; a market town is called a bazaar or bazâr.

bell – *see* ghanta.

bel tree – it is a Newari custom to 'marry' young girls to a bel tree so that they can never be widowed.

betel – mildly intoxicating concoction of areca nut and lime which is wrapped in betel leaf and chewed. The red splashes you see on the ground throughout south Asia are spat out by betel chewers. Regular betel chewing leads to dark-red stained teeth.

Bhadrakali – a Tantric goddess who is also a consort of Bhairab.

Bhagavadgita – Krishna's lessons to Arjuna, part of the *Mahabharata*.

Bhairab – the 'terrific' or fearsome Tantric form of Shiva in Nepal. Bhairab has 64 manifestations.

bhati – term for a tea house in Nepal.

Bhimsen – a deity noted for his strength and bravery.

Bhote – high-altitude desert valleys north of the Himalaya bordering Tibet. In Nepal Tibetans are known as Bhotes.

Bhot – Nepali for Tibet.

Bodhisattva – a near-Buddha who renounces the opportunity to attain nirvana in order to aid humankind.

bodhi tree – or bo tree, a pipal tree under which the Buddha was sitting when he attained enlightenment.

Bon – the animist religion of Tibet prior to Buddhism.

Brahman – the highest Hindu caste, said to originate from Brahma's head. Priests are drawn from this caste although Brahmans may have many other occupations.

chaitya – small stupa which usually contains a mantra rather than a Buddhist relic.

chakra – Vishnu's disc-like weapon, one of the four symbols he holds.

chang – Tibetan rice beer.

chapati – unleavened Indian bread.

Chaturmukha – Shiva lingam with four images of the god's face.

chautara – stone platforms around trees which serve as shady places for porters to rest.

Chenrezig – Tibetan name for Avalokitesvara.

Chhetris – the second caste of Nepali Hindus and the prince and warrior caste to which the Ranas and the Shah kings belonged. Chhetris are said to originate from Brahma's arms.

chirag – ceremonial oil lamp.

Chitrakar – special caste of Newari painters.

Chomolongma – the Tibetan name for Mt Everest; literally 'Mother Goddess of the World'.
chortens – Tibetan Buddhist stupas.
chowk – a courtyard or marketplace such as Indra Chowk, the old market area of Kathmandu.
chuba – long woollen Sherpa coat.
chura – beaten rice.
curd – yoghurt.

dal – lentil soup; the main source of protein in the Nepali diet.
Dalai Lama – incarnation of a Bodhisattva who is the spiritual leader of Tibetan Buddhists.
Damais – a caste of tailors who perform music at weddings.
danda – hill.
Dattatraya – deity who is thought of as an incarnation of Vishnu, Shiva's teacher, or the Buddha's cousin.
deval – Nepali word for temple.
Devanagari – Sanskrit Nepali script.
Devi – the short form of Mahadevi, the shakti to Shiva.
dhaki – handwoven cotton cloth.
dhami – priest claiming occult powers, a sorcerer.
dharma – Buddhist teachings.
dharamsala – rest house for pilgrims.
dhoka – door or gate.
dhwaja – metal ribbon streaming out from the roof of a temple and acting as a pathway for the gods.
dhyana – meditation.
Dhyani Buddhas – the original Adi Buddha created five Dhyani Buddhas who in turn create the universe of each human era. Amitabha is the Dhyani Buddha of our era.
dighur – Thakali cooperative economic system in which the members pool their money to support one person's plans.
doko – basket carried by porters.
doonga – boat.
dorje – Tibetan word for bajra or vajra.
durbar – palace.
Durga – fearsome manifestation of Parvati, Shiva's consort.
Dwarapala – door guardian figure.
dyochhen – a form of temple enshrining Tantric deities.
dzopkyo – male cross between a yak and a cow; also zopkiok.
dzum – female offspring of a yak and a cow; also zhum.
dzu-tch – large yeti that eats cattle.

ek – Nepali number one, a symbol of the unity of all life.
Ekamukha – Shiva lingam with one image of the god's face.

freaks – 1960s term from the overland era for the young westerners who wandered the East and could be found congregating in Bali, Kabul, Goa and Kathmandu.

gada – club-like weapon of Vishnu.
gaines – beggar musicians.
gajur – bell-shaped top to a bahal.
ganas – Shiva's 'companions'.
Ganesh – Shiva and Parvati's son, instantly recognisable by his elephant head.
Ganga – goddess of the River Ganges.
ganja – hashish.
Garuda – the man-bird vehicle of Vishnu.
Gautama Buddha – the Buddha of our era.
Gelugpa – reformed school of Tibetan Buddhism, headed by the Dalai Lama.
ghanta – Tantric bell which is the female equivalent of the dorje.
ghat – steps beside a river. A 'burning ghat' is used for cremations.
ghee – clarified butter.
gompa – Tibetan Buddhist monastery.
gopis – cowherd girls. (Krishna had a lot of fun with his gopis.)
Gorakhnath – 11th century yogi now said to be an incarnation of Shiva.
gurkha – Nepali mercenaries who have long formed a part of the British army. The name comes from the region of Gorkha.
Gurkhali – British army name for the Nepali language.
gurr – traditional Sherpa potato dish.
Gurungs – western hill people, predominantly from around Gorkha and Pokhara.
Guthi – Newari community group offering mutual support to its members.

Hanuman – monkey god.
Harisiddhi – a fearsome Tantric goddess.
harmika – eyes on a stupa which face the four cardinal directions, or the 13 steps of a stupa steeple, symbolising the 13 stages to enlightenment.
hashish – dried marijuana plant resin.
hiti – water conduit or tank with waterspouts.
hookah – water pipe for smoking.

impeyan pheasant – Nepal's national bird.
incarnation – a particular life form; in the case of mortals, determined by karma. Vishnu has 10 different incarnations.
Indra – king of the Vedic gods, god of rain.

Jagannath – Krishna as 'Lord of the World'.
Jambhala – god of wealth; look for his money bag and his attendant mongoose.
Jamuna – goddess of the River Jamuna.
janai – sacred thread which high-caste Hindu men

wear looped over their left shoulder and replace once each year; also Munja.

jatra – festival, as in Indra Jatra.

Jaya Varahi – Vishnu's consort when the god takes on his boar incarnation.

jhankri – sorcerer.

Jogini – mystical goddesses, counterparts to the 64 manifestations of Bhairab.

jukha – Nepali word for leech.

Kala – *see* Mara.

kalakuta – the poison which Shiva swallowed when he was in the form of Nilakantha.

kalasa – a pot, or a pot-shaped top to a temple.

Kali – most terrifying manifestation of Parvati.

Kalki – Vishnu's 10th, and as yet unseen, incarnation when he will come riding a white horse and wielding a sword to destroy the world.

Kalpa – a day in the age of Brahma.

Kam Dev – Shiva's 'companion'.

Karkotak – chief naga of the Kathmandu Valley.

karma – Buddhist and Hindu law of cause and effect which continues from one life to another.

Kartikkaya – god of war and son of Shiva, his animal is the cock or peacock and he carries a variety of weapons. Also known as Skanda or Kumar.

kata – the Tibetan prayer shawl which should be presented to an important Buddhist personage when introduced.

Kaukala – a form of Shiva in his fearsome aspect; he carries a trident with the skeleton of Vishnu's gate-keeper impaled upon it: a result of banning Shiva from Vishnu's palace!

Khas – Hindu hill people.

khola – stream or tributary.

khukuri – traditional curved knife of the Gurkhas.

kinkinimali – temple wind bells.

kosi – river.

Krishna – the fun-loving eighth incarnation of Vishnu.

Kshatriyas – Indian equivalent of the Chhetri caste.

Kshepu – snake-eating figure often seen on toranas.

Kubera – *see* Jambhala.

kundalini – female energy principle.

Kumar – *see* Kartikkaya.

Kumari – the living goddess, a peaceful incarnation of Kali.

kunda – water tank fed by springs.

la – mountain pass.

Lakshmi – goddess of prosperity and Vishnu's consort.

laliguras – Nepali word for rhododendron, the national flower.

lama – Tibetan Buddhist monk or priest.

lingam – phallic symbol of Shiva's creative powers.

Locana – consort of the Dhyani Buddha, Aksobhya.

Lokesvara – Lord of the World, an aspect of Avalokitesvara but often mingled with the Hindu gods in Nepal. He appears as Nilakantha, an aspect of Shiva, and as Natesvara, much like Natraj, the dancing Shiva whose cosmic dance created the world.

Machhendranath – patron god of the Kathmandu Valley and an incarnation of Avalokitesvara or Lokesvara.

Mahabharata – one of the major Hindu epics.

Mahadeva (Mahadeo) – another name for Shiva; *maha* translates as 'great', *deva* as 'god'.

Mahadevi – Great Goddess, sometimes known simply as Devi, the shakti to Shiva.

Mahakala – protector of the mandala and a Tantric equivalent of Shiva; literally 'great black one'.

maharishi – great teacher.

Mahayana – form of Buddhism (the 'greater vehicle') prevalent in East Asia, Tibet and Nepal.

Mahayuga – each day of Brahma (see Kalpa) is divided into 1000 Mahayugas or Great Ages.

Mahishasura – buffalo demon killed by Durga.

mahseer – game fish of the Terai rivers.

Maitreya – a Buddha who will come in a future era.

Makara – mythical water monster, often appears as a waterspout on buildings.

Mali – Newari gardener caste.

Malla – royal dynasty of the Kathmandu Valley responsible for most of the important temples and palaces of the valley towns.

mandala – geometrical and astrological representation of the world.

mandap – roofless Tantric shrine.

mandir – Nepali word for temple.

Manjushri – god who cut open the Chobar Gorge so that the Kathmandu Lake could become the Kathmandu Valley.

mani – stone carved with the Tibetan Buddhist chant *om mani padme hum*.

mantra – prayer formula or chant.

Mara – Buddhist god of death, has three eyes and holds the Wheel of Life.

math – Hindu priest's house.

mela – a country fair.

mithuna – Sanskrit term usually referring to a depiction of gods engaged in intercourse in erotic art; *yab-yum* in Tibetan.

moksha – spiritual release, Hindu equivalent of nirvana.

mudra – symbolic hand gesture of the gods.

Munja – *see* Janai.

naga – serpent deity. The eight nagas have control over water, and are often seen above house entrances to keep evil spirits away.

nagini – female naga.

Nagpura – Buddhist symbol for water.

nak – female yak.

namaste – Nepali greeting.

Nandi – the bull, vehicle of Shiva.
Narayan – Vishnu as the sleeping figure on the cosmic ocean. From his navel Brahma appears, and creates the universe. Narayan is Vishnu's most important appearance in Nepal but it is simply another name for Vishnu, not another incarnation.
Narsingha (Narsimha) – man-lion incarnation of Vishnu.
Newars – people of the Kathmandu Valley.
Nilakantha – blue-throated form of Shiva, a result of swallowing poison that would have destroyed the world.
nirvana – final escape from the cycles of existence.
Nriteshwar – god of dance.
Nyingmapa – school of Tibetan Buddhism founded by Padmasambhava.

om mani padme hum – sacred Buddhist mantra which translates as 'hail to the jewel in the lotus'.
oriflammes – prayer flags; the wind carries off the prayers written on them.

padma – lotus flower.
Padmapani – literally 'lotus in hand'; a manifestation of Avalokitesvara as he appears in many Nepali viharas, holding a tall lotus stalk.
Padmasambhava – Bodhisattva who founded Tibetan Buddhism. Also known as Guru Rinpoche.
pagoda – multi-storeyed Nepali temple. This style was later exported from Nepal to China and Japan.
panchayat – the non-party parliament of Nepal until 1990.
Panduravasini – consort of the Dhyani Buddha Amitabha.
Parvati – Shiva's consort.
pashmina – goat's wool blanket or shawl.
Pashupati – Shiva as Lord of the Animals.
patakas – *see* dhwaja.
path (pati) – small raised platform to shelter pilgrims.
patuka – waistcoat to carry things.
pith – open shrine for a Tantric goddess.
pokhari – large water tank.
prajna – female counterparts of male Buddhist deities.
Prajnaparamita – consort of the Dhyani Buddhas Vairocana and Aksobhya.
prasad – food offering.
prayer flags – each carries a sacred mantra which is 'said' when the flag flutters.
prayer wheels – cylindrical wheel inscribed with a Buddhist prayer or mantra which is 'said' when the wheel spins. There are even water-driven prayer wheels.
Prithvi – Vedic earth goddess.
puja (pooja) – religious offering or prayer.
Puranas – Hindu holy books of around 400 BCE

which heralded the shift from the Vedic gods to the Hindu trinity of Brahma, Vishnu and Shiva.
puri – town.

Radha – Krishna's wife.
rajpath – road or highway, literally 'king's road'.
rakshi – rice spirit.
Rama – Vishnu's seventh incarnation, and hero of the *Ramayana*.
Ramayana – Hindu epic which recounts the adventures of Rama, Sita, Hanuman and the demon king Rawana.
Rana – hereditary prime ministers who ruled Nepal from 1841 to 1951.
rath – the temple chariot in which the idol is conveyed in processions.
Ratnasambhava – Dhyani Buddha of the south.
Rawana (Ravana) – the demon king of Lanka in the *Ramayana*.
rikhi doro – golden thread worn around the waist by Shiva devotees.
rimpoche – honorific title which literally means 'precious one', often bestowed on Buddhist abbots.
Rudra – Vedic god of lightning, an early version of Shiva.

sadhus – wandering Hindu holy men, generally Shaivites who have given up everything to follow the trail to religious salvation. Many sadhus come from India to visit Pashupatinath, the great Shiva temple of Nepal.
Sagarmatha – Nepali name for Mt Everest.
Sakya – school of Tibetan Buddhism.
Sakyamuni – another name for Gautama Buddha.
sal – tree of the lower Himalayan foothills.
saligrams – black ammonite fossils of Jurassic period sea creatures, proof that the Himalaya was once under water.
sankha – conch shell symbol of Vishnu.
sanyasin – religious ascetic who has cut all ties with normal society.
saranghi – small violin played by the Gaines.
Saraswati – goddess of learning and the creative arts, and consort of Brahma. She can often be identified by the flute-like instrument which she plays called a *vina*.
satal – pilgrim's house.
Shaivites – followers of Shiva who cover their faces in ashes, paint three horizontal lines on their forehead and carry a begging bowl and Shiva's symbolic trident.
Shakti – dynamic female element in male-female relationships; a goddess.
Shantipura – Buddhist symbol for the sky.
Sherpas – literally 'people from the east', the Sherpas are Buddhist hill people famed for their stalwart work with mountaineering expeditions. With a small 's' sherpa means trek leader.

Sherpanis – female Sherpas.
Sheshnag – some believe that this snake, not Ananta, is the one which Vishnu reclines on.
shikhara – Indian-style temple with a tall corncob-like spire.
Shitala Mai – ogress who became a protector of children.
Shiva – most powerful Hindu god, the creator and destroyer.
Shivaratri – birthday of Shiva.
Simhanada – a form of Avalokitesvara who rides a lion.
sindur – red dust and mustard oil mixture used for offerings.
sirdar – leader/organiser of a trekking party.
Sita – Rama's wife in the *Ramayana*.
Skanda – *see* Kartikkaya.
Solu Khumbu – Everest region of eastern Nepal where the majority of the Sherpas live.
sonam – the karma acquired through successive incarnations.
STOL – short-take-off-and-landing aircraft used on mountain airstrips.
stupa – hemispherical Buddhist religious structure that houses relics; always walk around stupas clockwise.
Sudras – the lowest Nepali caste, said to originate from Brahma's feet.
sundhara – fountain with golden spout.
Surya – *see* Aditya.
suttee (sati) – practice of throwing widows on their husband's funeral pyre.

tabla – hand drum.
tahr – wild mountain goat.
Taleju Bhawani – Nepali goddess, an aspect of Mahadevi and the family deity of the Malla kings of the Kathmandu Valley. There are Taleju temples in the old royal palaces of Kathmandu, Patan and Bhaktapur.
Tantric Buddhism – form of Buddhism which evolved in Tibet during the 10th to 15th centuries.
Tara – as White Tara she is the consort of the Dhyani Buddha Vairocana, as Green Tara she is associated with Amoghasiddhi. Either way she is a very popular figure in the Buddhist pantheon and may also be adopted by the Hindus as Shiva's wife in her peaceful mood.
tempos – small Indian three wheeled transports commonly used in Kathmandu (similar to the Thai *samlor*).
Terai – flat land south of the Himalaya in Nepal.
Thakalis – people of the Kali Gandaki Valley who specialise in running hotels.
thangka – rectangular Tibetan painting on cotton, usually of mandalas or Tantric deities.
third eye – symbolic eye on Buddha figures, used to indicate the Buddha's clairvoyant powers.
thukba – thick Tibetan soup.

tika – red sandalwood paste spot marked on the forehead, particularly for religious occasions.
tole – street or quarter of a town, sometimes used to refer to a square such as Kel Tole in Kathmandu or Tachupal Tole in Bhaktapur.
topi – traditional Nepali cap.
torana – portico above temple doors which can indicate the god to whom the temple is dedicated.
Tribhuvan – king who ended the Rana period and Nepal's long seclusion in 1951.
trisul – trident weapon symbol of Shiva.
tsampa – barley-flour porridge of the Sherpas.
Tulku – Tibetan Buddhist reincarnation of a great lama.
tulsi – sacred basil plant.
tunal – carved temple strut.

Uma – one of the peaceful incarnations of Shiva's consort Parvati.
Uma Maheshwar – Shiva and Parvati in a pose where Shiva sits cross-legged and Parvati sits on his thigh and leans against him.
Upanishads – ancient Vedic scripts, the last part of the Vedas.
urna – the bump on the forehead of a Buddha or Bodhisattva.
Usha – Vedic goddess of the dawn.

vahana – a god's animal mount or vehicle.
Vairocana – the central Dhyani Buddha and the 'embodiment of perfection'.
Vaishnavites – followers of Vishnu.
Vaisya – caste of merchants and farmers, said to originate from Brahma's thighs.
vajra – the 'thunderbolt' symbol of Buddhist power in Nepal; (*dorje* in Tibetan).
Vajra Jogini – a Tantric goddess, shakti to a Bhairab.
Vajrapani – literally 'thunderbolt in hand', a manifestation of Avalokitesvara holding a thunderbolt.
Vajrayana – literally 'vehicle of the thunderbolts'; extension of Mahayana that includes Tantric Buddhism.
Vamana – *see* Vikrantha.
Varahi – Vishnu's boar incarnation.
Varuna – ancient Vedic god of wisdom and morality.
Vasudhara – wife of Jambhala the god of wealth; she rides a chariot drawn by a pig.
Vasupura – Buddhist symbol for the earth.
Vayupura – Buddhist symbol for the air.
Vedas – ancient spiritual texts, the orthodox Hindu scriptures.
Vedic gods – ancient Hindu gods of the Vedas.
vehicle – the animal which a Hindu god is associated with. Shiva's vehicle is a bull, Ganesh's is a mouse while Vishnu's is the man-bird Garuda.
vihara – Buddhist religious buildings and pilgrim accommodation.
Vikrantha – Vishnu's fifth incarnation when he

appeared as a dwarf, then grew so large that he could cross the universe in three strides.

Vishnu – the preserver, one of the three main Hindu gods.

Vishnu Chaturmurti – four faced Vishnu with faces of a lion, boar, human and demon.

Wheel of Life held by Mara, the god of death. The wheel's concentric circles show a stage of existence, those who are chained to the cycles of existence, the forces which keep the wheel turning or the desires which keep humankind chained to the cycle.

yab-yum – Tantric erotica.

yak – main beast of burden and form of cattle above 3000m.

yakshas – attendant deities.

Yama – Vedic god of death, son of Aditya or Surya; his messenger is the crow.

yeti – the abominable snowman.

yi-dam – protective deities of the Buddhas; they have a fierce form in contrast to the peacefulness of the Buddhas.

yoni – female sexual symbol, equivalent of a lingam.

Yuga – each Mahayuga is divided into four Yugas.

zamindar – absentee landlord and/or moneylender.

zhum – *see* dzum.

zopkiok – *see* dzopkyo.

Index

Index 407

THANKS

Thanks to all those travellers who took the trouble to write to us about their experiences in Nepal. Writers (apologies if we've misspelt your name) to whom thanks must go include:

Tali Adini, Prof Dan Adler, Petra Ahrens, Stephen Anich, Steve Anyon-Smith, Doug Armstrong, Barry Arthur

Krishna Prasad Baral, Natalie Barlow, Stefan Bartling, Susan Bartolacci JN Bastow, Isabelle Bermyn, Carina & Ramesh Bhattarai, OW Biddington, CLA Bijman, Margaret Bishop, G Boix & R Borras, Marielle Bourgeois, David Boyall, Frank Boys, Inge Bracke, Mark Briffa, Lucy Bryant, Cath Bulling, Mat Burbury, Sara Burke

Xavier Cabre i Playa, Lyn Caron, Amy Carr, Ian Carter & Grace Onions, Giovanna Caruso, Juliet Chamberlain, Robert Chen & Ellen Wild, Darryl Cherney, Rajendra Kumar Chitrakar, Colin Cho, Lisa Choegyal, Donna Clarke, Mark Clifford & S Kaur, J Collier & R Coulter, Barbara Colquitt, Rosemary Cooper, Jane Costello, Mr & Mrs FJ Crellin, Onn Crouvi, S Currie

Wim De Becker, David De Wit, S Deane & V Noonan, Pierene Dodi, Beverley Dow, Paula Downey & Dave Sheaffer, Stuart Dwyer

Amander Ellis, Naomi Engleman, Neil & Ruth Evans, Sue Evans

Tom Fallon, Mark Feitelberg & J Correiro, Anthony Fewenstein, Vickie Ficklin, Sara Fielder, Carl Flint, Kent Fortner, Rechelle Fowler, Chris Fox, Tyler Freed

Anna & Tomasz Galka, Ken Gallant, Ian Gardner, Jason Garman, Darren Gidding, Glen & Tori Gilbert, Elfi Gilissen, Narayan Giri, Sunita Godbole, Mrs P Godfrey, Sotiris Goulias, David Edward Graham, Paul Greening, Tom Grimm, Kerry & Jennifer Grimson, Jon Grocott, Laurent Guyonvarch

Jan Haas, Thorsten Hackl, Deborah Hammond, Robert Hanke, Graham Hardie, Chris Harper, Jennifer Harris, Chris Hayward, Ken Healy, Joyce Hee, Nyle Hendrizkson, Eleanor Henly, Robert Herrup, John Hickman, Patrick Holden, Catherine Holman, Jayne Hoskins, Dr Colin Howard, Fay Howard, Tracey Hudson, Emma Hughes, Harriet Hughes, Sally Humphrey, Leslie Hunter-Duvar

Paul Jacobs, Frank Janmaat, June Jones, Sara Jones, M Josui & P Shimazaki, Zoe Juniper

Melanie Kehaya, Greg Kennedy, George Kerr, Jonathan Knight, Tania Knight, Patricia Knox, Moses Koh, Jennifer Koivunera, Ivan Kolker, Lt Col Nilesh Kovgaokau, Marcia J Kramer, JA Kraushoer, Tom Krienheder, Birgitt Krohn, Marja-Leena Kultanen, Oliver Kunz

Rosalind Lahow, Michel Laikens, Catherine & Olivier Lair, Laurie Laird, Delia Lakich, Gerard Langendoen, Chad Leech, Hanan Leib, DA Lentz, Mike Linnett, UW Lippelt, Andrew Little, Amber Lloyd, David Lobley, Danny Lomas, Erik Loosveldt, C Lovelock

Joan Mackie, Sarah Manning, Andrew Manzardo, Francine Marshall, Markus Massisimo, Lesley May, Cathy & Myles Mayne, Jill McCallum, Sylvia McDonald, Shiela McFarlane, Laura Lyne McMurchie, Heather McNeice, Ian McRae, Karl Meyer, Natasha Mileusnic, David Millent, Charlie Moore, Linda Moore, Mr Mohan K Mulapati, Geraldine Murray

Barbara O'Brien, Kevin O'Farrell, Paul O'Reilly, Yasu Ohyagi, John Michael Oliver

John Paterson, William Paul, David Pindar, Chor Ping, Christine Platt, Horst & Marg Pohl, John Polush, Susan Preston-Martin, Belinda Price, Emma Pritchett

Kelly Rae, Susan Rainsford, A Ramos & C Suan, BK Rana, Eric James Rayner, Matt Redman, Sonja Reinke, Howard Reushaw, Andrew & Carol Rigby, Pinhas Rodan, Heikki Ronka, Elana Roseth, Dominique Ryan

Erik Schaap, Martin Schichtel, Carole Scriha, Ian Seels, Sadie Sesso, Dr S Alakha Shakti, K Shah, Jim Shaw, Philip Shirrefs, Victoria Short & D Harrison, Shekhar Shrestha, Carolyn Shurey, Mr & Mrs F Sims, Daphne Smith, Philippe Sohie, Aktar Somalya, Lisa Spratling, Robert J Steele, Peter Stewart, Alan Swarbrick

Jenny Thatcher-Eldredge, Isabelle Theytaz, Belinda Thomas, Ruth Thomas, Niels Thomsen, AR Thorp, Pat Tillman, Bianca Trenner & Manfred Mauler, Monica Tse

Coren Jenny Valk, Michel Van Dam, J Van Hal, Hanne & Kuun Vanessen, Renuka Vasudevan, Mostafa Vaziri, Agnes Videau, Livio Visintini, ME Volkoff

Leith Wallace, John Wealend, Sharleen West, Annette Willems, AP Wilson, Alexander Winter

Craig Yog

LONELY PLANET JOURNEYS

JOURNEYS is a unique collection of travellers' tales – published by the company that understands travel better than anyone else. It is a series for anyone who has ever experienced – or dreamed of – the magical moment when they encountered a strange culture or saw a place for the first time. They are tales to read while you're planning a trip, while you're on the road or while you're in an armchair, in front of a fire.

JOURNEYS books will catch the spirit of a place, illuminate a culture, recount a crazy adventure, or introduce a fascinating way of life. They will always entertain, and always enrich the experience of travel.

SHOPPING FOR BUDDHAS
Jeff Greenwald

'Here in this distant, exotic land, we were compelled to raise the art of shopping to an experience that was, on the one hand, almost Zen – and, on the other hand, tinged with desperation like shopping at Macy's or Bloomingdale's during a one-day-only White Sale.'

Shopping for Buddhas is Jeff Greenwald's story of his obsessive search for the perfect Buddha statue. In the backstreets of Kathmandu, he discovers more than he bargained for . . . and his souvenir-hunting turns into an ironic metaphor for the clash between spiritual riches and material greed. Politics, religion and serious shopping collide in this witty account of an enlightening visit to Nepal.

Jeff Greenwald is also the author of *The Size of the World* and *Mister Raja's Neighborhood*. Jeff's work has appeared in a range of newspapers and magazines, he writes a monthly column for *HotWired* and is the editor of GNN's *Big World* room on the Internet. He lives in Berkeley, California.

'Perfect for stuffing in every jet-age mystic's backpack. A sassy personal account . . . of [Greenwald's] search for the meaning of life'
– San Francisco Chronicle

Other Journeys titles:

FULL CIRCLE: A South American Journey
Luis Sepúlveda (translated by Chris Andrews)

THE GATES OF DAMASCUS
Lieve Joris (translated by Sam Garrett)

ISLANDS IN THE CLOUDS:
Travels in the Highlands of New Guinea
Isabella Tree

LOST JAPAN
Alex Kerr

SEAN & DAVID'S LONG DRIVE
Sean Condon

LONELY PLANET TRAVEL ATLASES

Lonely Planet has long been famous for the number and quality of its guidebook maps. Now we've gone one step further and in conjunction with Steinhart Katzir Publishers produced a handy companion series: Lonely Planet travel atlases – maps of a country produced in book form.

Unlike other maps, which look good but lead travellers astray, our travel atlases have been researched on the road by Lonely Planet's experienced team of writers. All details are carefully checked to ensure the atlas corresponds with the equivalent Lonely Planet guidebook.

The handy atlas format means no holes, wrinkles, torn sections or constant folding and unfolding. These atlases can survive long periods on the road, unlike cumbersome fold-out maps. The comprehensive index ensures easy reference.

- full-colour throughout
- maps researched and checked by Lonely Planet authors
- place names correspond with Lonely Planet guidebooks
  – no confusing spelling differences
- legend and travelling information in English, French, German, Japanese and Spanish
- size: 230 x 160 mm

Available now:
Chile; Egypt; India & Bangladesh; Israel & the Palestinian Territories; Jordan, Syria & Lebanon; Laos; Thailand; Vietnam; Zimbabwe, Botswana & Namibia

---

LONELY PLANET TV SERIES & VIDEOS

Lonely Planet travel guides have been brought to life on television screens around the world. Like our guides, the programmes are based on the joy of independent travel, and look honestly at some of the most exciting, picturesque and frustrating places in the world. Each show is presented by one of three travellers from Australia, England or the USA and combines an innovative mixture of video, Super-8 film, atmospheric soundscapes and original music.

Videos of each episode – containing additional footage not shown on television – are available from good book and video shops, but the availability of individual videos varies with regional screening schedules.

Video destinations include: Alaska; Australia (Southeast); Brazil; Ecuador & the Galápagos Islands; Indonesia; Israel & the Sinai Desert; Japan; La Ruta Maya (Yucatán, Guatemala & Belize); Morocco; North India (Varanasi to the Himalaya); Pacific Islands; Vietnam; Zimbabwe, Botswana & Namibia.

Coming soon: The Arctic (Norway & Finland); Baja California; Chile & Easter Island; China (Southeast); Costa Rica; East Africa (Tanzania & Zanzibar); Great Barrier Reef (Australia); Jamaica; Papua New Guinea; the Rockies (USA); Syria & Jordan; Turkey.

The Lonely Planet TV series is produced by:
Pilot Productions
Duke of Sussex Studios
44 Uxbridge St
London W8 7TG UK

Lonely Planet videos are distributed by:
IVN Communications Inc
2246 Camino Ramon
California 94583, USA

107 Power Road, Chiswick
London W4 5PL UK

Music from the TV series is available on CD & cassette.
For ordering information contact your nearest Lonely Planet office.

PLANET TALK

Lonely Planet's FREE quarterly newsletter

We love hearing from you and think you'd like to hear from us.

*When...*is the right time to see reindeer in Finland?
*Where...*can you hear the best palm-wine music in Ghana?
*How...*do you get from Asunción to Areguá by steam train?
*What...*is the best way to see India?

For the answer to these and many other questions read PLANET TALK.

Every issue is packed with up-to-date travel news and advice including:

* a letter from Lonely Planet co-founders Tony and Maureen Wheeler
* go behind the scenes on the road with a Lonely Planet author
* feature article on an important and topical travel issue
* a selection of recent letters from travellers
* details on forthcoming Lonely Planet promotions
* complete list of Lonely Planet products

To join our mailing list contact any Lonely Planet office.

Also available: Lonely Planet T-shirts. 100% heavyweight cotton.

LONELY PLANET ONLINE

Get the latest travel information before you leave or while you're on the road

Whether you've just begun planning your next trip, or you're chasing down specific info on currency regulations or visa requirements, check out the Lonely Planet World Wide Web site for up-to-the-minute travel information.

As well as travel profiles of your favourite destinations (including interactive maps and full-colour photos), you'll find current reports from our army of researchers and other travellers, updates on health and visas, travel advisories, and the ecological and political issues you need to be aware of as you travel.

There's an online travellers' forum (the Thorn Tree) where you can share your experiences of life on the road, meet travel companions and ask other travellers for their recommendations and advice. We also have plenty of links to other Web sites useful to independent travellers.

With tens of thousands of visitors a month, the Lonely Planet Web site is one of the most popular on the Internet and has won a number of awards including GNN's Best of the Net travel award.

http://www.lonelyplanet.com

LONELY PLANET PRODUCTS

Lonely Planet is known worldwide for publishing practical, reliable and no-nonsense travel information in our guides and on our web site. The Lonely Planet list covers just about every accessible part of the world. Currently there are eight series: *travel guides*, *shoestring guides*, *walking guides*, *city guides*, *phrasebooks*, *audio packs*, *travel atlases* and *Journeys* – a unique collection of travellers' tales.

EUROPE

Austria • Baltic States & Kaliningrad • Baltic States phrasebook • Britain • Central Europe on a shoestring • Central Europe phrasebook • Czech & Slovak Republics • Denmark • Dublin city guide • Eastern Europe on a shoestring • Eastern Europe phrasebook • Finland • France • Greece • Greek phrasebook • Hungary • Iceland, Greenland & the Faroe Islands • Ireland • Italy • Mediterranean Europe on a shoestring • Mediterranean Europe phrasebook • Paris city guide • Poland • Prague city guide • Russia, Ukraine & Belarus • Russian phrasebook • Scandinavian & Baltic Europe on a shoestring • Scandinavian Europe phrasebook • Slovenia • St Petersburg city guide • Switzerland • Trekking in Greece • Trekking in Spain • Ukrainian phrasebook • Vienna city guide • Walking in Switzerland • Western Europe on a shoestring • Western Europe phrasebook

NORTH AMERICA

Alaska • Backpacking in Alaska • Baja California• California & Nevada • Canada • Hawaii • Honolulu city guide • Los Angeles city guide • Mexico • Miami city guide • New England • Pacific Northwest USA • Rocky Mountain States • San Francisco city guide • Southwest USA • USA phrasebook

CENTRAL AMERICA & THE CARIBBEAN

Central America on a shoestring • Costa Rica • Eastern Caribbean • Guatemala, Belize & Yucatán: La Ruta Maya • Jamaica

SOUTH AMERICA

Argentina, Uruguay & Paraguay • Bolivia • Brazil • Brazilian phrasebook • Buenos Aires city guide • Chile & Easter Island • Chile travel atlas• Colombia • Ecuador & the Galápagos Islands • Latin American Spanish phrasebook • Peru • Quechua phrasebook • Rio de Janeiro city guide • South America on a shoestring • Trekking in the Patagonian Andes • Venezuela

Travel Literature: Full Circle: A South American Journey

ANTARCTICA

Antarctica

ISLANDS OF THE INDIAN OCEAN

Madagascar & Comoros • Maldives & Islands of the East Indian Ocean • Mauritius, Réunion & Seychelles

AFRICA

Arabic (Moroccan) phrasebook • Africa on a shoestring • Cape Town city guide • Central Africa • East Africa • Egypt• Egypt travel atlas• Ethiopian (Amharic) phrasebook • Kenya • Morocco • North Africa • South Africa, Lesotho & Swaziland • Swahili phrasebook • Trekking in East Africa • West Africa • Zimbabwe, Botswana & Namibia • Zimbabwe, Botswana & Namibia travel atlas

MAIL ORDER

Lonely Planet products are distributed worldwide. They are also available by mail order from Lonely Planet, so if you have difficulty finding a title please write to us. North American and South American residents should write to Embarcadero West, 155 Filbert St, Suite 251, Oakland CA 94607, USA; European and African residents should write to 10 Barley Mow Passage, Chiswick, London W4 4PH; and residents of other countries to PO Box 617, Hawthorn, Victoria 3122, Australia.

NORTH-EAST ASIA

Beijing city guide • Cantonese phrasebook • China • Hong Kong, Macau & Canton • Hong Kong city guide • Japan • Japanese phrasebook • Japanese audio pack • Korea • Korean phrasebook • Mandarin phrasebook • Mongolia • Mongolian phrasebook • North-East Asia on a shoestring • Seoul city guide • Taiwan • Tibet • Tibet phrasebook • Tokyo city guide

Travel Literature: Lost Japan

MIDDLE EAST & CENTRAL ASIA

Arab Gulf States • Arabic (Egyptian) phrasebook • Central Asia • Iran• Israel & the Palestinian Territories• Israel & the Palestinian Territories travel atlas • Jordan & Syria • Jordan, Syria & Lebanon travel atlas • Middle East • Turkey • Turkish phrasebook • Trekking in Turkey • Yemen

Travel Literature: The Gates of Damascus

ALSO AVAILABLE:

Travel with Children • Traveller's Tales

INDIAN SUBCONTINENT

Bangladesh• Bengali phrasebook• Delhi city guide • Hindi/Urdu phrasebook • India • India & Bangladesh travel atlas • Indian Himalaya • Karakoram Highway • Nepal • Nepali phrasebook • Pakistan • Sri Lanka • Sri Lanka phrasebook • Trekking in the Indian Himalaya • Trekking in the Karakoram & Hindukush • Trekking in the Nepal Himalaya

Travel Literature: Shopping for Buddhas

SOUTH-EAST ASIA

Bali & Lombok • Bangkok city guide • Burmese phrasebook • Cambodia • Ho Chi Minh city guide • Indonesia • Indonesian phrasebook • Indonesian audio pack • Jakarta city guide • Java • Laos • Lao phrasebook • Laos travel atlas • Malay phrasebook • Malaysia, Singapore & Brunei • Myanmar (Burma) • Philippines • Pilipino phrasebook • Singapore city guide • South-East Asia on a shoestring • Thailand • Thailand travel atlas • Thai phrasebook • Thai audio pack • Thai Hill Tribes phrasebook • Vietnam • Vietnamese phrasebook • Vietnam travel atlas

AUSTRALIA & THE PACIFIC

Australia • Australian phrasebook • Bushwalking in Australia• Bushwalking in Papua New Guinea • Fiji • Fijian phrasebook • Islands of Australia's Great Barrier Reef • Melbourne city guide • Micronesia • New Caledonia • New South Wales & the ACT • New Zealand • Northern Territory • Outback Australia • Papua New Guinea • Papua New Guinea phrasebook • Queensland • Rarotonga & the Cook Islands • Samoa • Solomon Islands • South Australia • Sydney city guide • Tahiti & French Polynesia • Tasmania • Tonga • Tramping in New Zealand • Vanuatu • Victoria • Western Australia

Travel Literature: Islands in the Clouds • Sean & David's Long Drive

THE LONELY PLANET STORY

Lonely Planet published its first book in 1973 in response to the numerous 'How did you do it?' questions Maureen and Tony Wheeler were asked after driving, bussing, hitching, sailing and railing their way from England to Australia.

Written at a kitchen table and hand collated, trimmed and stapled, *Across Asia on the Cheap* became an instant local bestseller, inspiring thoughts of another book.

Eighteen months in South-East Asia resulted in their second guide, *South-East Asia on a shoestring*, which they put together in a backstreet Chinese hotel in Singapore in 1975. The 'yellow bible', as it quickly became known to backpackers around the world, soon became *the* guide to the region. It has sold well over half a million copies and is now in its 8th edition, still retaining its familiar yellow cover.

Today there are over 180 titles, including travel guides, walking guides, language kits & phrasebooks, travel atlases and travel literature. The company is one of the largest travel publishers in the world. Although Lonely Planet initially specialised in guides to Asia, we now cover most regions of the world, including the Pacific, North America, South America, Africa, the Middle East and Europe.

The emphasis continues to be on travel for independent travellers. Tony and Maureen still travel for several months of each year and play an active part in the writing, updating and quality control of Lonely Planet's guides.

They have been joined by over 70 authors and 170 staff at our offices in Melbourne (Australia), Oakland (USA), London (UK) and Paris (France). Travellers themselves also make a valuable contribution to the guides through the feedback we receive in thousands of letters each year.

The people at Lonely Planet strongly believe that travellers can make a positive contribution to the countries they visit, both through their appreciation of the countries' culture, wildlife and natural features, and through the money they spend. In addition, the company makes a direct contribution to the countries and regions it covers. Since 1986 a percentage of the income from each book has been donated to ventures such as famine relief in Africa; aid projects in India; agricultural projects in Central America; Greenpeace's efforts to halt French nuclear testing in the Pacific; and Amnesty International.

'I hope we send the people out with the right attitude about travel. You realise when you travel that there are so many different perspectives about the world, so we hope these books will make people more interested in what they see. These are guidebooks, but you can't really guide people. All you can do is point them in the right direction.'
– Tony Wheeler

lonely planet

LONELY PLANET PUBLICATIONS

Australia
PO Box 617, Hawthorn 3122, Victoria
tel: (03) 9819 1877 fax: (03) 9819 6459
e-mail: talk2us@lonelyplanet.com.au

USA
Embarcadero West, 155 Filbert St, Suite 251,
Oakland, CA 94607
tel: (510) 893 8555 TOLL FREE: 800 275-8555
fax: (510) 893 8563
e-mail: info@lonelyplanet.com

UK
10 Barley Mow Passage, Chiswick,
London W4 4PH
tel: (0181) 742 3161 fax: (0181) 742 2772
e-mail: 100413.3551@compuserve.com

France:
71 bis rue du Cardinal Lemoine, 75005 Paris
tel: 1 44 32 06 20 fax: 1 46 34 72 55
e-mail: 100560.415@compuserve.com

World Wide Web: http://www.lonelyplanet.com